The Waite Group's

MICROSOFT QUICKBASIC™ PRIMER PLUS

The Waite Group's

MICROSOFT QUICKBASIC™ PRIMER PLUS

Stephen Prata with Harry Henderson

PUBLISHED BY
Microsoft Press
A Division of Microsoft Corporation
One Microsoft Way
Redmond, Washington 98052-6399

Library of Congress Cataloging-in-Publication Data

Prata, Stephen.
The Waite group's Microsoft QuickBASIC primer plus / Stephen Prata with Harry Henderson.
p. cm.
Includes index.
ISBN 1-55615-269-8
1. BASIC (Computer program language) 2. Microsoft QuickBASIC (Computer program) I. Henderson, Harry. II. Waite Group. III. Title
QA76.73.B3P73 1990
005.26'2--dc20 90-45498
CIP

Printed and bound in the United States of America.

1 2 3 4 5 6 7 8 9 MLML 4 3 2 1 0

Distributed to the book trade in Canada by General Publishing Company, Ltd.

Distributed to the book trade outside the United States and Canada by Penguin Books Ltd.

Penguin Books Ltd., Harmondsworth, Middlesex, England
Penguin Books Australia Ltd., Ringwood, Victoria, Australia
Penguin Books N.Z. Ltd., 182-190 Wairau Road, Auckland 10, New Zealand

British Cataloging-in-Publication Data available

As used in this book, DOS refers to the Microsoft MS-DOS operating system and the IBM version of the MS-DOS operating system, also known as PC-DOS.

For Microsoft Press:
Project Editors: Mary Renaud, Megan E. Sheppard
Technical Editors: Gerald Joyce, Mary DeJong
Acquisitions Editor: Dean Holmes

For The Waite Group:
Developmental Editor: Mitchell Waite
Content Editor: Mitchell Waite
Editorial Director: Scott Calamar
Editorial Assistant: Joel Fugazzotto

Dedication

To those charming and lovable pests—

er, pets—Kate, Talley, and Jessie

S. P.

Acknowledgments

We thank Scott Calamar and Joel Fugazzotto of The Waite Group

for the aid they extended,

and we thank Mitchell Waite for his editorial advice.

Special Offer

Companion Disk for
The Waite Group's
MICROSOFT QUICKBASIC™ PRIMER PLUS

Get a quick start on your QuickBASIC programming with the step-by-step examples and program listings in this book. Microsoft Press has created a timesaving Companion Disk for The Waite Group's MICROSOFT QUICKBASIC PRIMER PLUS that contains complete program listings—even if only part of the code is listed in the book. Plus, some small programs in other languages are included on disk in compiled form, ready to use. Now you don't have to spend hours typing in and debugging the more than 180 program listings from this book. This Companion Disk is guaranteed to save you time and effort!

The MICROSOFT QUICKBASIC PRIMER PLUS Companion Disk is organized into chapter directories. Within each chapter directory you'll find each of the program listings ready to load into QuickBASIC for immediate use. Get started right away. Order today!

Domestic Ordering Information:
To order, use the special reply card in the back of the book. If the card has already been used, please send $19.95, plus sales tax in the following states if applicable: AZ, CA, CO, CT, DC, FL, GA, ID, IL, IN, KY, ME, MD, MA, MI, MN, MO, NE, NV, NJ, NM, NY, NC, OH, SC, TN, TX, VA, and WA. Microsoft reserves the right to correct tax rates and/or collect the sales tax assessed by additional states as required by law, without notice. Please add $2.50 per disk set for domestic postage and handling charges. Mail your order to: **Microsoft Press, Attn: Companion Disk Offer, 21919 20th Ave SE, Box 3011, Bothell, WA 98041-3011.** Specify 5 1/4-inch or 3 1/2-inch format. Payment must be in U.S. funds. You may pay by check or money order (payable to Microsoft Press) or by American Express, VISA, or MasterCard; please include credit card number, expiration date, and cardholder signature. Allow 2–3 weeks for delivery.

Foreign Ordering Information (except within the U.K., see below):
Follow procedures for domestic ordering. Add $6.00 per disk set for foreign postage and handling.

U.K. Ordering Information:
Send your order in writing along with £17.95 (includes VAT) to: Microsoft Press, 27 Wrights Lane, London W8 5TZ. You may pay by check or money order (payable to Microsoft Press) or by American Express, VISA, MasterCard, or Diners Club; please include credit card number, expiration date, and cardholder signature. Specify 5 1/4-inch or 3 1/2-inch format.

Microsoft Press Companion Disk Guarantee:
If a disk is defective, a replacement disk will be sent. Please send the defective disk along with your packing slip (or copy) to: Microsoft Press, Consumer Sales, One Microsoft Way, Redmond, WA 98052-6399.

Send your questions or comments about the files on the disk to
The Waite Group, QB Primer Disk, c/o Microsoft Press,
One Microsoft Way, Redmond, WA 98052-6399

The Companion Disk for The Waite Group's
MICROSOFT QUICKBASIC PRIMER PLUS
is available only from Microsoft Press.

Contents

Introduction

BASIC has introduced more people to computer programming than has any other computer language. Over the years, this accessible and widely used language has also been significantly strengthened and improved. Today, for example, QuickBASIC offers powerful modern programming features in a well-designed environment.

New QuickBASIC control statements provide the readability and reliability of structured programming. User-defined types let you represent related data in a powerful yet simple manner. QuickBASIC's design emphasizes the modular approach, which is so important to producing programs that are easy to debug, modify, expand, and maintain. And QuickBASIC programs are fast—fast to compile, fast to run. But QuickBASIC is still faithful to its BASIC roots. It's easy to learn and easy to use. QuickBASIC's friendly demeanor clearly sets it above the competition.

Perhaps you are new to BASIC, or perhaps you are an old hand returning to see what the language is like today. In either case, welcome to this guide to programming in QuickBASIC on an IBM PC, PS/2, or compatible computer. In this book we attempt to cover a wide range of QuickBASIC capabilities. Because we assume no special or advanced background on your part, we explain the programming concepts we use as well as the language features. In doing so, we follow the usual guidelines of a Waite Group primer:

- Clarify concepts with short, concise programs
- Provide clear, helpful explanations
- Use drawings and charts to illustrate ideas
- Supply interesting examples and insights

This book takes you further into QuickBASIC than most introductions to the language. For instance, it offers extensive coverage of QuickBASIC's graphics tools. It also takes you through fundamental debug routines, and it even includes several mixed-language programs.

To sharpen your QuickBASIC skills, we've divided the book into six sections that help you progress from simple to advanced topics. Part I, "Surface," provides an overview of the QuickBASIC language and environment. Part II, "Rudiments," presents the most elementary and essential concepts of QuickBASIC. You'll learn how QuickBASIC deals with numeric and textual information, how it reads information from the keyboard and displays it on the screen, and how it allows you to work with simple files. You'll also learn about control statements that enable your programs to repeat actions and make decisions. You'll become familiar with using arrays to handle data and with writing your own custom functions. Part II emphasizes QuickBASIC's powerful modular features, which let you break programs into small, manageable, and efficient sections.

Part III, "Records," introduces more advanced programming topics, including creative use of user-defined types. You'll also look at sequential, random access, and binary files and at QuickBASIC's ability to store and retrieve various kinds of information with these files.

Part IV, "Multimedia," teaches you how to use QuickBASIC's impressive graphics and sound capabilities to liven up your programs and make them more professional. Part V, "Pokes, Peeks, Ins, and Outs," covers the hardware-related facets of QuickBASIC, including memory manipulation and the use of printers and modems.

Part VI, "Development," presents some of the advanced concepts of professional program development. You'll learn how to minimize errors in your programs (and how to handle errors that do occur), how to interface with the DOS environment, and how to use QuickBASIC in conjunction with other languages such as assembly language and Microsoft C.

Each chapter in this book begins by listing the QuickBASIC statements, functions, and other keywords that are discussed in detail within that chapter. Sample programs focus your attention on designing, constructing, modifying, and debugging programs. (All numbered program listings are available on a companion disk, which can be ordered from Microsoft Press; ordering information appears in the front of this book.) All chapters conclude with review questions that cover key points.

To begin using *The Waite Group's Microsoft QuickBASIC Primer Plus,* you'll need a copy of QuickBASIC 4.5 and a suitable computer—an IBM PC, PS/2, or compatible with at least 384 KB of memory and at least 720 KB capacity in disk drives. For best performance, you'll want 640 KB of memory and a hard drive. And a mouse is helpful, too.

We've tried to create a book that is both understandable to the novice and useful to the knowledgeable programmer. If you have questions or comments, please address your correspondence to

The Waite Group
100 Shoreline Highway, Building A, Suite 285
Mill Valley, California 94941

PART I

Surface

1

Overview of BASIC/QuickBASIC Structure and Rules

CLS
PRINT

A Brief BASIC Review

When Dartmouth professors John Kemeny and Thomas Kurtz developed BASIC (Beginner's All-purpose Symbolic Instruction Code) in 1963 and 1964, they sought to create a language that required little familiarity with mathematics or computers. Accordingly, they modeled much of BASIC after a popular—but more complex—language: English. In the seventies, Bill Gates and Paul Allen brought BASIC to the world of microcomputers. Indeed, the presence of BASIC on most of the early personal computers contributed to the immense popularity enjoyed today by both personal computers and the BASIC language.

BASIC is far and away the most widely used computer language on personal computers. Over the years it has evolved from an experimental educational language to a hobbyist's language to a professional programmer's language. And Microsoft Chairman of the Board Bill Gates promises that BASIC will play an even greater role in the future. For example, you can already use a BASIC-like language to customize Microsoft Word for Windows to meet your special needs.

Currently BASIC's most powerful incarnation, QuickBASIC retains all the advantages of BASIC: It's easy to learn, easy to use, and lets you perform useful tasks. In this book we'll show you how to put the power of QuickBASIC to work.

An Introduction to QuickBASIC

Although QuickBASIC is both a language and a work environment, we devote most of this book to its language features, explaining the various QuickBASIC statements and demonstrating how to use them. If you've been using an earlier version of BASIC, you'll be impressed with the new features QuickBASIC offers (Figure 1-1).

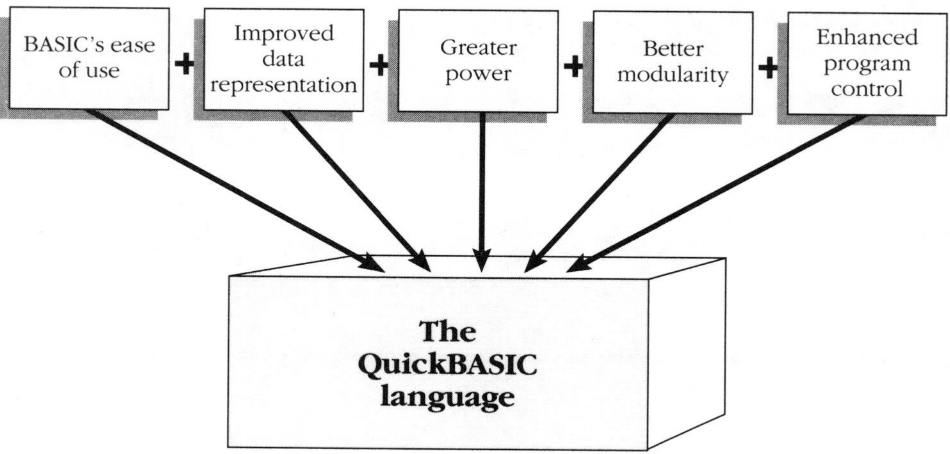

Figure 1-1.
QuickBASIC improves on the BASIC language.

The work environment has changed for the better, too. And, if you're accustomed to earlier versions of BASIC, note that QuickBASIC is a compiler, not an interpreter like BASICA and GW-BASIC (Figure 1-2).

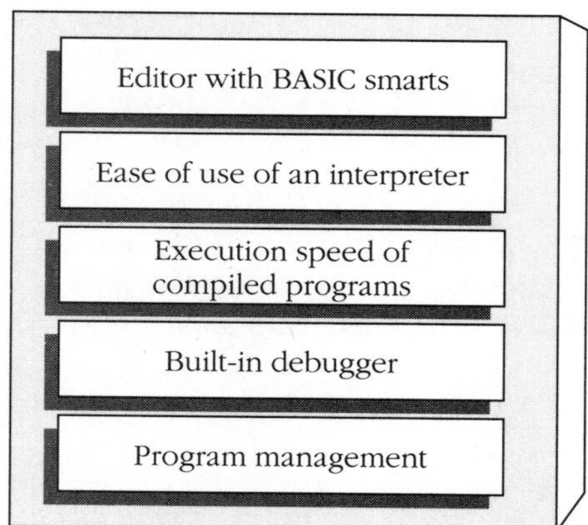

Figure 1-2.
QuickBASIC is an integrated environment.

Compilers and Interpreters

At some point, a program written in a high-level language such as QuickBASIC must be translated into *machine language,* the language native to the computer's *central processing unit* (CPU). Computer scientists have developed two types of programs to perform these translations: *compilers* and *interpreters.* Although QuickBASIC is a compiler, it incorporates some interpreter features. Let's take a quick look at compilers, interpreters, and QuickBASIC.

The Traditional Compiler Strategy

Traditional compilers offer the least user-friendly approach to program translation. To create a working program with a compiler, you would typically perform the following steps:

1. Use a text-editing program to write a program in a high-level language such as FORTRAN.
2. Save your program, quit the editor, and submit the program to the compiler, which creates a file containing the machine-code equivalent of your original code.
3. Repeat steps 1 and 2 to correct any errors caught by the compiler.
4. Submit the compiler output to another program called a *linker.* (Some systems do this step for you.) The linker adds other code as necessary and creates the final, executable form of the program. Under DOS, the executable program is identified by the presence of an EXE extension—that is, the end of the filename is a period and the letters *EXE.* For example, the filename WOW.EXE has an EXE extension.
5. Run the executable program. (In DOS, you simply type the name of the executable file.) Repeat steps 1 through 4 if you encounter any errors.

To run the program again, retype the program name and press Enter.

Note that you must write the complete program before you proceed to the translation stage; you don't receive immediate feedback. In addition, you must use several different programs to get the job done. And because the compiler doesn't communicate errors to the text editor, you must act as the intermediary.

The Interpreter Strategy

Compared with the compiler, the interpreter provides a more interactive environment for program development and translation: In BASIC, the text editor is integrated into the interpreter, and programs are translated line by line instead of as an entire block. As a result, you can start the interpreter and use its text editor to type a line like the following:

```
PRINT "Let's get down to BASIC."
```

As soon as you type the line and press the Enter key, the interpreter executes the machine-language instructions that cause the following to appear on screen:

```
Let's get down to BASIC.
```

If you make an error in typing the line, you find out immediately.

To create a program with an interpreter, you would follow these steps:

1. Start the interpreter program, and use its editor to write the program.
2. Correct errors that the interpreter catches.
3. Save the code in a file.

To run the program, start the interpreter (if it's not already running), load the saved program, and then run it.

Compiler/Interpreter Trade-offs

In general, an interpreter provides a better means for developing programs, but the compiler results in a better final product:

- You can write a working program quickly by using an interpreter, but a compiled program runs much more rapidly—perhaps 10 to 100 times faster, depending on what the program does.
- An interpreted program can be run only from within the interpreter, but the compiler can create a stand-alone program.

In-Memory Compilation

One annoying aspect of compiling is that you must sit idly by while the compilation process takes place. QuickBASIC uses modern software technology to increase the compilation speed. Specifically, it uses a method called *in-memory compilation,* in which all work is done in memory without using files. The advantage is great speed. The disadvantage is that the method doesn't create a permanent executable file. But QuickBASIC also supplies a slower, more traditional compiling process that creates a stand-alone executable program—a file you can run even if QuickBASIC is not running.

The QuickBASIC Strategy

QuickBASIC borrows from both the compiler and the interpreter strategies. Like an interpreter, it provides an integrated environment. Like a compiler, it produces a fast-running program. Let's examine the steps you use to create a QuickBASIC program:

1. Start QuickBASIC and use the built-in text editor to write a program. Because the editor is specifically designed for BASIC, it knows enough BASIC to catch some errors as you type them. Because the compiler is integrated with the editor, it can compile lines, at least in part, as you enter them. You can save your code in a file, updating it easily as you make changes.
2. After the program is complete, use the built-in compiler to finish compiling the program. At this time, the compiler might catch additional errors. If it does so, it will identify them and their location in your program.
3. Run the compiled program from QuickBASIC. If the program doesn't behave the way you expect, use the built-in debugger to help you find errors as the program runs.

To run the program again, you can start QuickBASIC, load your original code, and then compile and run the program. Or you can request that QuickBASIC create a stand-alone executable file in the manner of traditional compilers.

Using QuickBASIC

Now that you have an idea of how QuickBASIC programming works, let's look at the details of using QuickBASIC. We'll assume you've used the SETUP program that comes with QuickBASIC to install the QuickBASIC files in a hard-disk directory called QB45. (You can use QuickBASIC without a hard drive, but you'll sacrifice speed and convenience.)

After you've installed QuickBASIC, we recommend that you work through the Getting Started section of *Learning to Use Microsoft QuickBASIC,* the manual that comes with QuickBASIC. It teaches you how to enter and edit text, how to use a menu, and how to use the essential features of QuickBASIC.

Hardware Requirements

QuickBASIC requires a minimum of 384 KB (kilobytes) of available memory; Microsoft recommends 640 KB for best performance. Also, QuickBASIC requires at least 720 KB of disk-drive capacity. That requirement can be met by two 360-KB 5¼-inch floppy-disk drives, by a 1.2-MB 5¼-inch floppy-disk drive, by a 720-KB or 1.44-MB 3½-inch floppy-disk drive, or by a hard-disk drive. Microsoft recommends a hard-disk drive for best performance.

Starting QuickBASIC

To start QuickBASIC, go to the QB45 directory and enter the following command:

```
QB
```

QuickBASIC displays a screen like that shown in Figure 1-3. The screen has several parts, of which we'll use three:

- The *menu bar* at the top of the screen lets you tell QuickBASIC what to do (open a file, run a program, and so on).
- The large work area at the center of the screen (labeled "Untitled") is the *View window*. You write your programs within this window. After you create a program and save it in a file, the filename replaces Untitled.
- The small window at the bottom of the screen (labeled "Immediate") is the *Immediate window*. You use this window to try out QuickBASIC statements and obtain immediate feedback.

To move from the View window to the Immediate window, press the F6 key. Or, if you have a mouse, move the mouse pointer to the window you want and then click the mouse button.

To resize the window you're in (called the *active window*), use Alt-plus sign (+) to increase the size or Alt-hyphen (-) to decrease the size. (You can use the plus sign and the hyphen either from the numeric keypad or from the number row on your keyboard.) Or position the mouse pointer on the line dividing the two windows, hold down the mouse button, and drag the boundary up or down.

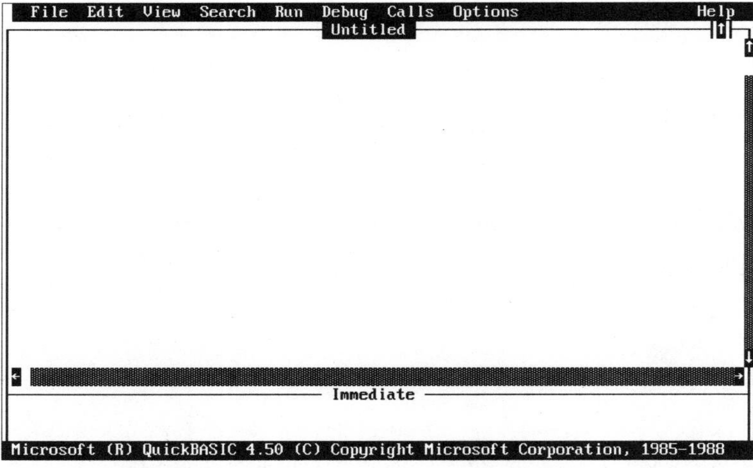

Figure 1-3.
The QuickBASIC screen.

Although you are likely to do most of your programming in the View window, you'll find that the Immediate window offers instant gratification: It lets you see what a particular QuickBASIC statement does before you type it in the View window. For example, try the BASIC statement we used earlier:

```
PRINT "Let's get down to BASIC."
```

When you press the Enter key, the display changes to the usual DOS screen, and the following words appear:

```
Let's get down to BASIC.
```

In addition, these instructions appear at the bottom of the screen:

```
Press any key to continue
```

Follow this advice, and you'll return to the QuickBASIC display.

A QuickBASIC Program

Let's use the View window to illustrate both the QuickBASIC language and the QuickBASIC environment. Position the cursor in the View window and type the following lines exactly as they appear below. (We have deliberately included errors.) Press the Enter key as you finish each line.

```
cls
print        "Let's get down to BASIC."
pirnt "We'll begin by using the View window."
print "Say, this is easy.
```

Note that QuickBASIC makes some changes when you press the Enter key. The final result should look like this:

```
CLS
PRINT "Let's get down to BASIC."
pirnt "We'll begin by using the View window."
PRINT "Say, this is easy."
```

First, QuickBASIC converted *cls* to CLS and *print* to PRINT. The CLS statement (clear screen) and the PRINT statement (print to the screen) are QuickBASIC *keywords*—commands that are part of the QuickBASIC language. The QuickBASIC editor automatically capitalizes keywords. You can use this feature to your benefit when typing your programs: Simply avoid using all caps when typing keywords. Then, if QuickBASIC fails to convert the word to uppercase, you'll know that you've probably mistyped something. (And that's exactly what happened with *pirnt* in our example. Now go back and fix the error.)

Second, QuickBASIC removed the extra spaces following the first PRINT statement. The QuickBASIC editor has its own firm ideas about spacing, which result in program listings having a uniform appearance.

Third, QuickBASIC caught and corrected an error. In the final PRINT statement, we omitted the closing double quotation mark. QuickBASIC was quick to add it.

Saving the File

Before going further, save the file. (Did you change *pirnt* to *PRINT*?)

1. Drop down the File menu, and select Save As.
2. Choose a name (such as PROG1), and press Enter.

QuickBASIC adds a BAS extension to the name you selected and saves the file as PROG1.BAS.

Running the Program

Next run the program. Select Start from the Run menu, or press Shift-F5. You'll see the following display:

```
Let's get down to BASIC.
We'll begin by using the View window.
Say, this is easy.
```

Once again, pressing any key returns you to the QuickBASIC screen.

> **The Save As Formats**
>
> The QuickBASIC Save As dialog box offers you two choices for the format used to save the file: The default—the QuickBASIC format—produces a small file that can be read or saved rapidly. The Text format produces a larger file that can be read with other text editors and with the DOS TYPE command.

When All Is Not Well

Let's see what happens when the program is not quite right. Select Save As from the File menu, and save the previous example under a new name. Then add a line to the file so that it reads as follows:

```
CLS
PRINT "Let's get down to BASIC."
PRINT "We'll begin by using the View window."
PRINT "Say, this is easy."
pirnt "Goodbye, for now."
```

This time, try running the program with PRINT mistyped as *pirnt*. A dialog box appears informing you that QuickBASIC has detected a *syntax error*, and the word *pirnt* is highlighted. A syntax error indicates that you've misused the BASIC language. (For example, in English, the would-be sentence "I to the market" has a syntax error because it lacks a verb.) Although you could press Enter to eliminate the box, use the Tab and Enter keys or the mouse to select the Help option in the box. QuickBASIC will then favor you with some advice on the topic:

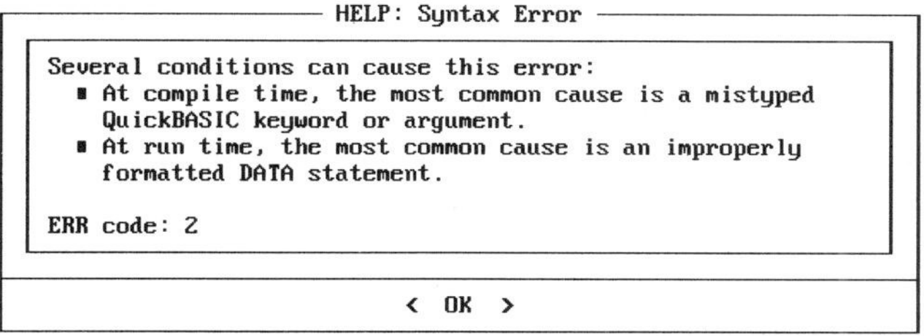

Help got it right: You mistyped a keyword. So correct the error and try to run the program again. You can save the corrected file now by using Save from the File menu. (This choice appears on the menu if you've selected Full Menus from the Option menu.) Otherwise, when you start a new file or quit QuickBASIC, you'll be asked if you want to save the file.

> **NOTE:** *A* compile-time error *is an error that occurs while the program is being compiled, and a* runtime error *is an error that occurs while a program is running.*

Creating a Stand-alone Program

When you saved the two preceding programs, you saved a copy of the QuickBASIC statements. We call these statements the *source code*. The compiled version (the *executable code*) was kept in your computer's memory. When you compiled the second program, its executable code replaced the code for the first program in memory. So, at this point, you don't have a permanent copy of the executable program. Instead, to run the first program again after you've closed the file, you must reopen and recompile the program. With QuickBASIC, this doesn't take much time. Still, you might want a permanent copy of the executable program that you can run without first running the QuickBASIC program. If so, QuickBASIC is at your service.

Let's work through an example. With QuickBASIC running, select Open Program from the File menu, and open the first program. We'll assume it's in a file named PROG1.BAS.

After the program is on screen, drop down the Run menu, and select Make EXE File. This puts a dialog box on screen. The dialog box suggests a name for the executable file by replacing the BAS extension with an EXE extension. In our case, it suggests PROG1.EXE. We'll stick with that. The dialog box also lets you choose between two forms of executable files:

```
Make EXE File
EXE File Name: [PROG1.EXE                              ]

  [ ] Produce Debug Code          Produce:
                                  (•) EXE Requiring BRUN45.EXE
                                  ( ) Stand-Alone EXE File

 < Make EXE >  < Make EXE and Exit >  < Cancel >  < Help >
```

The default (EXE Requiring BRUN45.EXE) produces an executable file that's not quite independent. Instead, it uses some common QuickBASIC code that is kept in the BRUN45.EXE file. This file, which comes with QuickBASIC, is called a *runtime module* because it is used when the QuickBASIC program runs. When you run the program, you need the BRUN45.EXE file as well. The second choice (Stand-Alone EXE File) puts all the code into your executable file.

Each method has advantages and disadvantages. The BRUN45 approach produces a smaller file that doesn't hold all the code. The non-BRUN45 approach produces a larger, completely independent file.

You might use the first approach, for instance, if you've produced 10 executable QuickBASIC programs for your own use. All 10 of these programs can use the same BRUN45.EXE file, saving a lot of space. But if you're sending a program to a friend who might not have BRUN45.EXE, you'll want to use the second approach. We'll try each approach and see what happens.

Using the Runtime Module

Begin by accepting the BRUN45.EXE option and selecting the Make EXE button. The DOS screen appears and displays text of the following form:

```
BC C:\QB45\PROG1.BAS/T/C:512;
Microsoft (R) QuickBASIC Compiler Version 4.50
(C) Copyright Microsoft Corporation 1982-1988.
All rights reserved.
Simultaneously published in the U.S. and Canada.

43869 Bytes Available
43522 Bytes Free

    0 Warning Error(s)
    0 Severe  Error(s)
LINK @~QBLNK.TMP

Microsoft (R) Overlay Linker  Version 3.69
Copyright (C) Microsoft Corp 1983-1988.  All rights reserved.

Object Modules [.OBJ]: /EX PROG1
Run File [PROG1.EXE]: C:\QB45\PROG1.EXE
List File [NUL.MAP]:
Libraries [.LIB]: C:\QB45\BRUN45.LIB
```

All this information simply describes the steps QuickBASIC takes to compile and link your program. When QuickBASIC completes these steps, the QuickBASIC screen reappears. If you exit to DOS, you can run the program by entering *PROG1*, provided the BRUN45.LIB file is present. The result looks like this:

```
C>PROG1
```

[Screen clears]

```
Let's get down to BASIC.
We'll begin by using the View window.
Say, this is easy.
C>
```

What QuickBASIC Did

The text displayed temporarily during compilation represents the work done to create the executable file. QuickBASIC is following the traditional compile-and-link approach we outlined earlier, and it's giving us a step-by-step description. It uses the BC.EXE compiler and the LINK.EXE linker that come with QuickBASIC. The BC (BASIC compiler) program is a command-line compiler, which means it runs from the usual DOS command line. QuickBASIC temporarily suspends its environment and runs this compiler for you (Step 2 in our compiler discussion). BC creates an intermediate file of code with the OBJ extension.

Next QuickBASIC runs the linker program LINK to create the final executable program (Step 4 in our compiler discussion). Note that it uses the BRUN45.LIB library; this file also comes with QuickBASIC. The @~QBLNK.TMP file that LINK uses is a temporary file containing information for LINK; QuickBASIC creates this file for LINK and then erases it when it is no longer needed. When dust and stray bits clear, you're left with PROG1.EXE, the BRUN45-assisted stand-alone program.

Making a Stand-alone Version

Now let's make the completely independent stand-alone version:

1. Drop down the Run menu, and select the Make EXE File option. (To distinguish this from the previous example, enter PROG1SA.EXE for the name.)
2. Select the Stand-Alone option.
3. Select the Make EXE button.

Again, QuickBASIC runs the BC and LINK programs:

```
BC C:\QB45\PROG1.BAS/O/T/C:512;
Microsoft (R) QuickBASIC Compiler Version 4.50
(C) Copyright Microsoft Corporation 1982-1988.
All rights reserved.
Simultaneously published in the U.S. and Canada.

43837 Bytes Available
43490 Bytes Free

    0 Warning Error(s)
    0 Severe  Error(s)
LINK @~QBLNK.TMP
```

```
Microsoft (R) Overlay Linker  Version 3.69
Copyright (C) Microsoft Corp 1983-1988. All rights reserved.

Object Modules [.OBJ]: /EX PROG1
Run File [PROG1.EXE]: C:\QB45\PROG1SA.EXE
List File [NUL.MAP]:
Libraries [.LIB]: C:\QB45\BCOM45.LIB
```

This looks much like the previous compilation, but two important differences result in a completely stand-alone program:

- BC uses the /O option.
- LINK uses the BCOM45.LIB library instead of the BRUN45.LIB library.

Again, QuickBASIC takes care of choosing the correct options and libraries for you. You can, if you want, run BC and LINK from DOS without QuickBASIC's help, but then you must make the correct command-line choices yourself.

Let's look at the sizes of the files for our examples. Here's an edited DOS listing:

```
BRUN45   EXE    77440  09-28-88   1:43a
PROG1    EXE     3320  10-24-90   7:47p
PROG1SA  EXE    13182  10-24-90   7:52p
```

The non-BRUN45 version (PROG1SA.EXE) is quite a bit larger than PROG1.EXE. However, because it uses only a small portion of the available BASIC resources, PROG1SA.EXE is much smaller than BRUN45.EXE. For one program, using the non-BRUN45 approach requires less total space. But for a large number of programs, using the BRUN45 approach requires less total space.

QuickBASIC vs. Earlier Versions of BASIC

If you're an old hand at BASIC, you might be wondering what happened to line numbers. In earlier versions of BASIC, the interpreter translated unnumbered lines immediately. But if you used line numbers, the interpreter didn't start translating until you asked it to. Also, you could use the line numbers to specify the order in which statements should be executed.

QuickBASIC still accepts line numbers. For instance, try running the following BASICA program. If a number is used as a label, QuickBASIC uses it the same way BASICA does. Otherwise, it simply ignores the line numbers.

```
10 CLS
20 PRINT "I'm a logical"
30 PRINT "kind of machine."
```

Running this program clears the screen and displays the following:

```
I'm a logical
kind of machine.
```

Note that QuickBASIC doesn't reorder lines numerically. For example, consider the following program:

```
10 CLS
40 PRINT "I conquered."
20 PRINT "I came."
30 PRINT "I saw."
```

If you run the program under QuickBASIC, you get this output:

```
I conquered.
I came.
I saw.
```

The lines are printed in the same order in which they appear in the program. However, if you run the program under, say, BASICA, you get this output:

```
I came.
I saw.
I conquered.
```

BASICA executes the statements in numeric order, and QuickBASIC executes the statements in the order in which they appear. Furthermore, if you list the program in the BASICA environment, it rearranges the text lines into numeric order.

Programs written in BASICA can run under QuickBASIC with little or no alteration. Appendix D outlines the differences.

Are We There Yet?

You now know how to write a simple program using QuickBASIC. You know how to run the program from the QuickBASIC environment and how to create two kinds of executable files. What's left to learn? Only a few minor details: using variables, looping, branching, working with strings, creating modules, adding sound and graphics, using functions, working with arrays, using files.... The remaining chapters of this book will help you learn these skills and put QuickBASIC's power to use.

Review Questions

At the end of each chapter we'll pose a few questions that might prove useful in testing your knowledge or clarifying specific points. You'll find the answers in Appendix G.

1. How does the QuickBASIC compiler resemble a BASIC interpreter?
2. What can the QuickBASIC compiler do that an interpreter can't do?
3. Write a QuickBASIC program that clears the screen and prints your name.
4. How do you run a QuickBASIC program from within the QuickBASIC environment?
5. How do you create and run a stand-alone BASIC program?

PART II

Rudiments

2

Variables and Simple Data Types

!	**-**	**DEFLNG**	**INTEGER**
#	**/**	**DEFSNG**	**LET**
$	****	**DEFSTR**	**LONG**
%	**^**	**DIM**	**MOD**
&	**CONST**	**DOUBLE**	**REM**
*****	**DEFDBL**	**END**	**SINGLE**
+	**DEFINT**	**INPUT**	**STRING**

We live in the Information Age, and the computer is the quintessential wheeler-dealer in the information market. QuickBASIC lets you work with two fundamental kinds of information: numbers and text. In this chapter you'll examine the way QuickBASIC deals with both numeric and textual information. You'll learn about variables, constants, and data types. Also, you'll take an introductory look at the INPUT statement.

Numbers: Literals, Variables, and Constants

We'll start with numbers, the staple of many a computer diet. In QuickBASIC, you can represent numbers literally—that is, you can use 2, 3.14, 101, and the like in your programs. A number written this way is called a *literal*. You can also represent numbers symbolically by letting, say, *x* represent the number 2. In QuickBASIC, a *variable* is a symbol whose value you can alter, and a *constant* is a symbol whose value, once set, you can't alter. Let's take a closer look at these topics.

Numeric Literals

The simplest way to introduce literal numbers to a program is to use the PRINT statement to print a number. Because a PRINT statement uses only one line, you can use the Immediate window to enter the example. The result will appear on the output screen. Let's look at some examples. For simplicity, we'll show the PRINT statement on one line and the resulting screen output on the following line. So type the first line below and press the Enter key:

```
PRINT 1990
 1990
```

Here *1990* is a numeric literal, and as you would expect, the PRINT statement prints that value.

Like other computer languages, QuickBASIC is a bit picky about how numbers can be written. Let's make a naive attempt to print the number 1,990:

```
PRINT 1,990
 1             990
```

QuickBASIC doesn't recognize commas as part of a number. Instead of reading *1,990* as a single number, the PRINT statement interprets it as a list of two numbers. It then prints the value as two separate numbers: *1* and *900*.

The number 1990 is an example of an *integer,* or whole number. QuickBASIC also recognizes numbers with fractional parts:

```
PRINT 1.44
 1.44
PRINT .25
 .25
```

These are called *decimal fractions,* or *real numbers*. QuickBASIC supports two kinds of decimal fractions, two kinds of integers, and several ways of writing each. As we discuss different types of variables, we'll also discuss the different ways of expressing numeric literals.

Numeric Variables

The cornerstone of programming is using symbols to represent values and then manipulating the symbols. Let's look at how QuickBASIC uses variables to represent numbers symbolically. For example, suppose you want *Salary* to represent your monthly salary of $20,000. (Hypothetical examples might as well be pleasant.) You can use QuickBASIC's assignment statement to create a variable called *Salary* and to assign it the value 20000. (QuickBASIC deals with pure numbers, so we omit the dollar sign and the comma.) Try the following in the Immediate window:

```
LET Salary = 20000
PRINT Salary
 20000
```

The first line, *LET Salary = 20000*, is the assignment statement. If this is the first mention of the variable, the assignment statement allocates storage in the computer's memory and labels that location *Salary*. The statement places the number 20000 there (Figure 2-1). When you enter *PRINT Salary*, the computer goes to the location labeled *Salary*, looks up the value stored there (20000), and displays it (Figure 2-2).

```
LET Salary = 20000
```

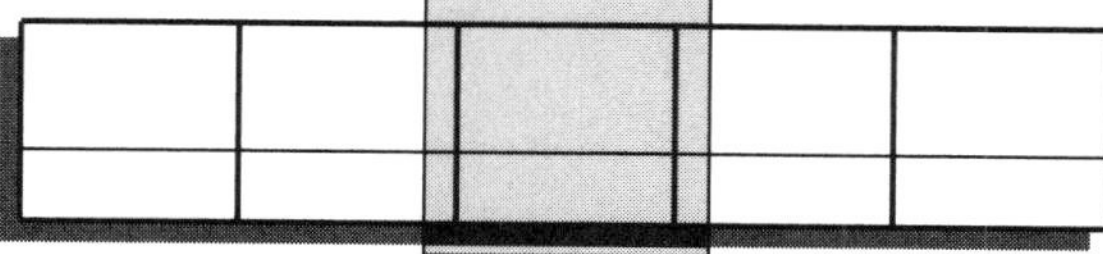

1. Allocate storage for the variable

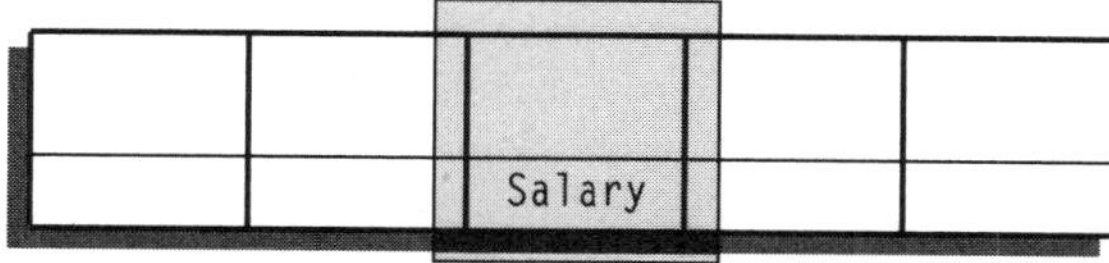

2. Label the storage

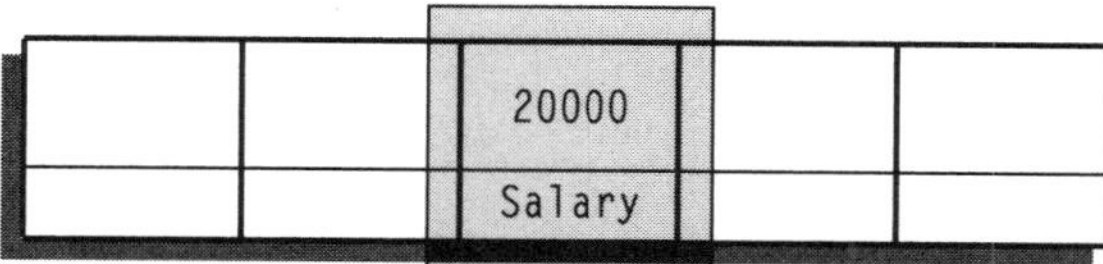

3. Assign a value to the variable

Figure 2-1.
Creating a variable.

QuickBASIC Syntax

As we introduce QuickBASIC statements, we'll summarize their *syntax*—that is, their manner of use. For example, the assignment statement has the following syntax:

```
[LET] variablename = value
```

This statement assigns *value* to a variable called *variablename*. In syntax statements, we use italics to indicate expressions for which you substitute your own values. For instance, in Figure 2-1 we substituted *Salary* for *variablename* and *20000* for *value*. Elements such as LET and the equal sign are typed literally. Elements within brackets, such as LET in this example, are optional.

```
PRINT Salary
```

62	289	20000	8	5134
Age	Days	Salary	Cars	Pages

1. Locate the variable

62	289	20000	8	5134
Age	Days	Salary	Cars	Pages

2. Obtain the variable's value

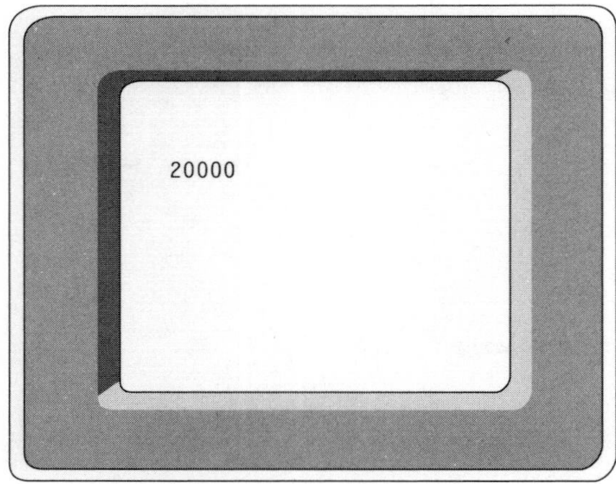

3. Use the value (in this case, display it)

Figure 2-2.
Using a variable.

You can read the preceding example as "Let the variable *Salary* be assigned the value 20000." Note that the word LET is optional. If you leave it out, QuickBASIC still knows what you mean. Let's illustrate that by giving you a well-deserved raise:

```
Salary = 22000
PRINT Salary
 22000
```

This example also illustrates why we call *Salary* a variable—we can vary, or change, its value.

Variables are one of the most useful, necessary, and powerful components of a computer language, and we'll use them throughout this book.

What's in a Name?

In the early days of the BASIC language, you had limited choices for naming variables: You could use a single letter or a letter followed by a single digit. Thus, you were restricted to names such as *U*, *B1*, and *K9*. This was adequate at the time, but choosing descriptive names was difficult. And as programs grew larger, you had to take care not to use the same name twice. QuickBASIC allows you much more flexibility. Here are the rules for selecting a QuickBASIC variable name:

- You can use as many as 40 characters in a variable name.
- The first character in a name must be a letter (but not the letters *FN*, which have a special meaning to QuickBASIC).
- For the other characters, you can use letters, digits, and periods. For instance, *Nerd*, *chocolate.mousse*, and *CATCH22* are valid names.
- QuickBASIC doesn't distinguish between uppercase and lowercase variable names. Thus, *joy*, *Joy*, and *JOY* all represent the same name.
- The final character in a name can be one of these special characters: % & ! # $. (These special characters can appear only at the end of a name—not within a name.) These characters identify the data type for the variable.
- You can't use any of QuickBASIC's built-in names, such as PRINT or LET. Such names are *reserved words*, or *keywords*. You'll find a complete list of keywords in Appendix A. (Incidentally, if you receive a puzzling error message the first time you use a variable, check to see if you've used a reserved word by mistake. For example, trying to use *Print* as a variable name can produce an error message because PRINT is one of the reserved words. However, you can use a reserved word as part of a name, as in *REPRINT.NUM5*.)

The following table lists some valid variable names along with similar names that don't work (and the reasons why):

Valid	*Invalid*	*Why Invalid*
X	*10*	Doesn't start with a letter
HumptyDumpty	*Humpty Dumpty*	Contains a space
CHOICE1	*1CHOICE*	Starts with a digit
Lettuce	*Let*	A reserved word
Fun.Spring	*FnSpring*	Begins with *FN*
Hello!	*Hello!You*	! not last character

Throughout this book, we'll capitalize only the first letter of variable names (or the first letter of each word in a single variable name such as *SalaryScale*). That will help distinguish them from reserved words, which the QuickBASIC editor places in all uppercase.

Numeric Constants

You can also represent constant values symbolically by using the CONST keyword. This keyword doesn't work in the Immediate window, so you'll need to enter the following example in the View window and then use Shift-F5 or choose Start from the Run menu to run the program:

```
CONST pi = 3.14159
PRINT pi
END
```

The reserved word END marks the end of the program. It isn't needed in a program this simple because QuickBASIC will quit executing the program when it runs out of program lines. But some programs do need END, so you should get in the habit of using it. The resulting output looks like this:

```
 3.14159
```

So far *pi* works much as *Salary* did. But now modify the program so that it looks like this:

```
CONST pi = 3.14159
PRINT pi
pi = 4.2
PRINT pi
END
```

When you try to run this program, an error message appears: *Duplicate definition*. Because CONST makes *pi* a constant, you can't change its value. When QuickBASIC finds the line *pi = 4.2*, it decides you couldn't be foolish enough to try to change a constant. Instead, it decides you were foolish enough to try to create a new variable using a name you had used earlier (*pi*). So it warns you that you have two definitions for the same name and aborts the program.

Why use a constant? Symbolic names have several advantages.

First, a symbolic name is more mnemonic than a number. For example, if you were looking through a program to find a tax rate—say, 0.28—you could find it more easily if the value were associated with a constant named *taxrate*. Second, using a symbolic name simplifies any updates to a program. If the tax rate rises to 0.32, simply change the tax rate definition once—in the CONST statement—rather than changing 0.28 to 0.32 in 10 places in your program. Using a variable also offers both of these advantages, but by using a constant you additionally prevent a program from changing a value accidentally.

The rules that apply to variable names also apply to constant names. Throughout this book, we'll begin constant names with a lowercase character to make them easy to distinguish from variables and from reserved words.

Simple Numeric Data Types

QuickBASIC offers a choice of four distinct internal representations, or *types,* for numbers. These types are called *integer, long integer, single precision,* and *double precision.* With such a wide range to choose from, you can always select the best type for a given situation. After we introduce the types, we'll examine how each type is best used.

The integer and long integer types store whole numbers, and the single-precision and double-precision types store decimals (fractional numbers). The QuickBASIC reserved words for describing these types are INTEGER, LONG, SINGLE, and DOUBLE. The long integer, as its name suggests, is an integer that occupies more bytes than a regular integer. Thus a long integer variable can hold a larger number than an integer variable can hold. The single-precision and double-precision types are similar to each other, with the double-precision variety capable of storing more digits. Let's take a quick look at the two families.

The Integer Family

An integer is a whole number—that is, a number without a fractional part. For instance, 7, 0, and –22 are integers, whereas 2.05 and 0.9999 are not.

QuickBASIC uses 2 bytes to store regular integers, whose values range from –32768 through 32767. Long integers—which range in value from –2147483648 through 2147483647—require 4 bytes. Because long integers generally require a longer processing time than regular integers, it's better to use regular integers unless you need the extra size.

Bits, Bytes, and Words

The fundamental unit of computer memory is the *bit.* A bit is always set either to 1 or to 0.

Computer memory is organized into larger units called *bytes.* Each byte consists of 8 bits. A byte can be set to 256 different combinations of 1 and 0, meaning that a byte can represent any number in the range –128 through 127.

The original IBM PCs and ATs use processors (the 8088 and the 80286) that can handle chunks of data 16 bits (2 bytes) in size. We say that 2 bytes is the *natural size* for these processors, and we call the natural size a *word.* The integer type corresponds to a word. With some effort, these machines can also handle units 32 bits in size—what we call a *double word.* The long integer type corresponds to a double word.

You might find long integers especially helpful in dealing with dollars. Because using decimal fractions can lead to rounding errors, you should convert dollars to cents and use an integer type. The regular integer type restricts you to 32,677 cents, or $326.77. But the long integer type lets you work with up to 2,147,483,647 cents, or $21,474,836.47—an adequate sum for most household budgets.

Creating Integer Variables

Suppose you decide to create a variable for storing an integer type or a long integer type. How do you tell QuickBASIC which you want? The answer is in the name. One way to indicate type is to use a *type suffix*. Variables whose names end with the percent character (%) are integer variables; those whose names end with the ampersand character (&) are long integer variables.

Try the following in the Immediate window:

```
MyNumber% = 30
PRINT MyNumber%
 30
MyNumber% = 18.7
PRINT MyNumber%
 19
```

This example creates a variable (*MyNumber%*) of the integer type. You can assign the value 30 to *MyNumber%* with no difficulty. But when you try to assign the value 18.7 to *MyNumber%*, the value is rounded to 19, the nearest integer. As you can see, the % suffix indeed limits *MyNumber%* to holding integers.

Now try the following:

```
MyNumber% = 50000
```

The *Overflow* error message appears, indicating that 50000 is too large to fit in the *MyNumber%* variable; it "overflows" the would-be container.

But 50000 should fit into a long integer type. Let's try it:

```
MyBigNumber& = 50000
PRINT MyBigNumber&
 50000
```

Note that the % and & suffixes really are part of the name. Look what happens if you use the Immediate window to try to print the value of *MyBigNumber&* but omit the & suffix:

```
PRINT MyBigNumber
 0
```

Without the suffix, *MyBigNumber* appears to be a new variable, distinct from *MyBigNumber&*. And because you didn't assign a value to this new variable, QuickBASIC gives it a value of 0 by default.

Rounding

When assigning a decimal fraction value to an integer or long integer type, QuickBASIC rounds the value to the nearest whole number. If the fractional part is exactly 0.5, QuickBASIC rounds to the nearest even whole number—that is, 18.5 rounds to 18, as does 17.5. QuickBASIC uses this method of rounding for statistical accuracy. If you have a large number of varied values ending in 0.5, this method rounds about half of the values up and half down. This makes the sum of the rounded values about the same as the sum of the original values, which wouldn't be true if every half-integer value were rounded up.

Writing Integers

Integers are written without decimal points. You can use a mathematical sign to indicate whether a number is positive or negative, but only minus signs are printed:

```
PRINT -500
-500
PRINT +625
 625
```

Decimal Fractions (Real Numbers)

Programs often deal with numbers with fractional parts, such as 3.14159. We call such numbers decimal fractions or real numbers. QuickBASIC uses the single-precision and double-precision types to represent them. As you might expect, QuickBASIC uses special suffixes to indicate real variables, too. The ! suffix indicates a single-precision value in QuickBASIC, and the # suffix indicates a double-precision value. Names without special suffixes (such as *Salary* and the other examples earlier in this chapter) are single precision by default. (Assigning an integer to a single-precision variable, as we did in one of our examples, causes the value to be converted to the single-precision form.)

Using Other Number Bases

You can also express integers in *octal* (base 8) and in *hexadecimal* (base 16) notation. Because both 8 and 16 are powers of 2, octal and hexadecimal notation are closely related to the *binary* (base 2) system that computers use internally. Some QuickBASIC graphics commands, for example, use hexadecimal numbers to represent patterns. An &, &O, or &o prefix indicates octal, and an &H or &h prefix indicates hexadecimal. For instance, &O20 is octal 20 (decimal 16), and &H20 is hexadecimal 20 (decimal 32). See Appendix B for details on these number bases.

A single-precision value uses 4 bytes of memory and provides 7-digit precision. A double-precision value, in contrast, uses 8 bytes of memory and provides 15-digit precision. Double precision also allows a greater range of powers of 10.

Single-Precision and Double-Precision Literals

We've already used one form of single-precision literal:

```
PRINT 14.92
 14.92
```

The decimal point makes this a real number. Because the value contains only four digits, QuickBASIC stores it as a single-precision value. Suppose you use more digits:

```
PRINT 189332.29013
 189332.29013
```

This number has too many digits to be considered a single-precision value, so QuickBASIC stores it as a double-precision value. Both of these values are written in *fixed-point notation,* which means that the decimal point is fixed between the integer and the fractional parts of the number.

Exponential notation: For single-precision values, you can also use exponential (scientific) notation, known as *E notation:*

```
PRINT 1.23E6
```

The number to the right of the *E* represents a power of 10, which is then multiplied by the value to the left:

Thus, *1.23E6* represents the following value:

$$1.23 \times 10^6$$

The number 10 to the 6th power is simply 1 followed by six zeros, so this becomes

$$1.23 \times 1000000$$

or

$$1230000$$

These are called *floating-point* values because you can move the decimal point by changing the exponent. For instance, 1.23E6 has the same value as 12.3E5.

You can use either a lowercase e or an uppercase E with this notation, and you can use a positive or a negative sign for the power. So both 8.28e22 and 1.98E+30 are valid QuickBASIC numbers. And because the part to the left of the E doesn't need a decimal point, 2e8 is fine, too.

Floating-point numbers can be much larger than integers. The largest integer in E notation, for example, is about 3.4E38.

Using a negative sign for the power amounts to dividing by a power of 10 instead of multiplying:

```
PRINT 8.4E-5
 .000084
```

Here *8.4E-5* represents

84×10^{-5}

which is equivalent to

$8.4 \div 100000$

or

0.000084

Another way of looking at this is that *E–5* means "move the decimal point five places to the left" whereas *E+5* means "move the decimal point five places to the right."

Using E notation instead of ordinary decimal notation doesn't affect how the computer stores a number—that is, 123456.7 and 1.234567E5 are simply two ways of writing the same number. The two numbers would be stored identically in the computer. Also, when PRINT prints a number, it uses the size of the number to determine which form it will use. For example, PRINT displays 1.23E6 as *1230000* but switches to E notation for larger exponents, in order to save space:

```
PRINT 1.23e7
 1.23E+07
```

In the next chapter you'll see how to have PRINT follow your orders in choosing the display format.

Figure 2-3 summarizes the properties of the different numeric types. (Note that the maximum and minimum values for single-precision and double-precision numbers indicate the range of exponent values—that is, these values indicate the range of a number's possible proximity to zero.)

Type	***Suffix****	***Maximum***	***Minimum***
Integer	%	32767	−32768
Long integer	&	2147483647	−2147483648
Single-precision (7-digit)	!	±3.402823E+38	±1.401298E−45
Double-precision (15-digit)**	#	±1.7976931D+308	±4.9406565D−324

*By default, QuickBASIC variable names that lack type suffixes are single precision.
**Double-precision values have been rounded to 8 digits.

Figure 2-3.
Properties of numeric types.

D Notation

QuickBASIC also offers D notation, which works much like E notation:

```
PRINT 5.50D5
 550000
```

By using D instead of E, you cause the computer to store the number using double precision instead of single precision. The greater space allows a D notation number to be as large as (roughly) 1.79D308.

Precision

What does 7-digit precision really mean? Let's return to the Immediate window:

```
Donk! = 0.000123456789
PRINT Donk!
 1.234568E-04
```

After the value is assigned to the single-precision variable *Donk!*, the value is rounded to the first 7 digits. Note that leading zeros are not included in the count.

Now let's try a double-precision type:

```
Rent# = 987654321.123456789
PRINT Rent#
 987654321.1234568
```

Here QuickBASIC displays 16 digits. But because you can't count on the accuracy of the final digit (the 8, in this case), QuickBASIC claims only 15-digit precision.

Exceeding the Bounds of Propriety

As you've seen, QuickBASIC rounds decimal fraction values to the proper number of digits. But what if the number is too large? For example, a single-precision value can't exceed 3.402823E+38 (Figure 2-3). Let's go to the Immediate window:

```
Donk! = 1.2E40
```

Once again the *Overflow* error message appears. If a real number contains too many digits for the specified type, the extra digits are cut. But if the number is too large, you receive an *Overflow* message.

Now let's see what happens if the number is too small for the type:

```
Donk! = 1.2E-50
PRINT Donk!
 0
```

This time no error message appears. Instead, QuickBASIC replaces the too-small value with 0.

Real "Integers"

Sometimes you might assign an integer value to a real variable, as in the following example:

```
DinnerCost! = 12
PRINT DinnerCost!
 12
```

Is *DinnerCost!* single precision, as indicated by the ! suffix, or integer, as suggested by the value 12?

The answer is that *DinnerCost!* is single precision. True, *DinnerCost!* holds the value 12, but it stores the value as a decimal fraction whose fractional part happens to be .000000.

Constants and Types

QuickBASIC constants accept the same type suffixes as QuickBASIC variables do. For example, try compiling and running the following program:

```
CONST price% = 24.67
PRINT price%
END
```

The output is this:

```
 25
```

Values assigned to integer constants are rounded to the nearest whole number, as they are for integer variables.

You can even apply the type suffixes to literals. For example, *2%* is the value 2 stored as an integer, and *2!* is 2 stored in a floating-point format. Sometimes, depending on the context, the QuickBASIC editor will add a suffix to a number you enter. For instance, if you enter *32.0*, the editor will substitute *32!*.

Choosing a Type

You've now seen that QuickBASIC lets you choose from four numeric types. In order of decreasing simplicity, they are integer, long integer, single precision, and double precision. Which should you select?

In general, the simpler the type, the less space it takes in computer memory and the faster the computer can process it. So select the simplest type that suffices:

- If you need only integers, use one of the integer types.
- If you don't need large integers, use integer instead of long integer.
- If you need real values, use single precision unless you need the greater precision or range of double precision.

Simple Arithmetic

Now that you have the various numeric types at your disposal, you can do arithmetic. QuickBASIC uses several arithmetic operators to perform calculations: addition, subtraction, multiplication, two forms of division, finding a modulus, and exponentiation. Let's use the Immediate window to look at these operations.

Addition and Subtraction

QuickBASIC uses the plus sign (+) to indicate addition:

```
PRINT 3 + 8
 11
```

Note that the PRINT statement evaluates *3 + 8* and prints the result rather than simply printing *3 + 8* literally.

As you might expect, the minus sign (–) indicates subtraction:

```
PRINT 28 - 6
 22
```

You also can use the minus sign to change the sign of a value:

```
A = -2.5
B = -A
PRINT B
 2.5
```

Multiplication and Division

For multiplication, QuickBASIC uses an asterisk (*):

```
PRINT 5 * 7
 35
```

You have two choices for division. The slash (/) is used for ordinary division, the kind you learned in grade school:

```
PRINT 11 / 3
 3.666667
```

Unless at least one of the numbers involved is double precision, ordinary division is calculated as a single-precision operation. If you use a double-precision value, as in the following example, the result is double precision:

```
PRINT 11# / 3
 3.666666666666667
```

The second form of division is called *integer division* because the result is truncated to an integer—that is, the fractional part is discarded. This form uses the backslash operator (\):

```
PRINT 11 \ 3
 3
```

Note the difference between truncation and rounding. Rounding converts a number to the nearest integer, whereas truncation drops the fractional part of the number. Rounding 3.666667 produces 4, but truncating it produces 3.

The integer division operator converts real numbers to integers before dividing:

```
PRINT 3.51 \ 1.49
 4
```

In the example above, 3.51 rounds to 4, 1.49 rounds to 1, and the resulting expression (4 \ 1) evaluates to 4.

Finding a Modulus

The MOD operator is related to integer division. It gives the remainder resulting when one integer is divided by another.

```
PRINT 11 MOD 3
 2
```

Here, for example, 3 goes into 11 three times with a remainder of 2.

This operator is handy if, say, you want to convert 138 inches to feet and inches. The expression *138 \ 12* returns 11, the number of feet, and the expression *138 MOD 12* returns 6, the number of inches.

Exponentiation

Finally, ^ is the exponentiation operator:

```
PRINT 2 ^ 8
 256
```

Here *2 ^ 8* represents 2 to the 8th power—that is, the result of multiplying eight 2's together.

Here's another example of exponentiation: The brightness of an object is proportional to the 4th power of the temperature. Some stars are five times hotter than the sun. How much brighter would the sun be if it got as hot as one of those stars (while keeping the same size)? The brightness ratio would be 5 to the 4th power. Let's have QuickBASIC calculate the value:

```
PRINT 5 ^ 4
 625
```

That's a change you'd notice!

By using a fractional power, you can obtain roots. The modern musical scale is divided into 12 notes spaced so that the ratio of frequencies of two adjacent notes is the 12th root of 2. Exactly how big is that ratio? QuickBASIC speaks:

```
PRINT 2 ^ (1 / 12)
 1.059463
```

A Timely Program

Because integer division and the MOD operator are the least familiar arithmetic operations, let's look at an example that uses them. The following program asks you to enter a number of minutes and then converts that value to hours and minutes. For example, it converts 93 minutes to 1 hour and 33 minutes. One new feature is our use of QuickBASIC's INPUT statement to obtain user input from the keyboard; we'll describe it in a moment. Here's the program:

```
CONST minPerHour% = 60
INPUT Minutes%
Hours% = Minutes% \ minPerHour%
MinutesLeft% = Minutes% MOD minPerHour%
PRINT Hours%, MinutesLeft%
END
```

When we compile and run this program, we obtain results such as the following:

```
? 88
 1             28
```

First we use a constant to represent the number of minutes per hour. If the world, in some metric madness, should ever decide to use 100 minutes to the hour, we would simply need to redefine *minPerHour%* as 100.

Next we use the INPUT statement. When the program runs, this statement displays a question mark on the screen to prompt you to enter data. (When it encounters an INPUT statement, a QuickBASIC program pauses and waits until you enter data from the keyboard.) After you type a number and press the Enter key to enter your response, the INPUT statement assigns it to the variable *Minutes%*. (We'll show you a lot more about INPUT later in this chapter and in the next one.)

Then we use integer division to obtain the number of hours and the MOD operator to obtain the number of minutes. Here, for example, 60 goes into 88 once with a remainder of 28, so our answer is 1 hour and 28 minutes.

Finally we print the results. By using a comma in the PRINT statement, we give PRINT a list of values to print, so we can use one statement to print both the hours and the minutes.

Note that we used the integer type throughout because we didn't need fractions or huge numbers.

Rules of Operator Precedence

When an expression has more than one arithmetic operator, QuickBASIC needs a method to establish which operation is performed first. Consider this expression:

```
10 + 20 * 5
```

If you do the addition first, this expression becomes *30 * 5*, or 150. But if you do the multiplication first, the expression becomes *10 + 100*, or 110. QuickBASIC does it the second way. We say that multiplication has a *higher precedence* than addition, meaning that multiplication is done first. Figure 2-4 shows QuickBASIC's ranking of arithmetic operators, from high to low.

Operation	***Operator***
Exponentiation	^
Negation	–
Multiplication and division	* /
Integer division	\
Modulo arithmetic	MOD
Addition and subtraction	+ –

Figure 2-4.
Arithmetic operator precedence.

You can use parentheses to enforce an alternative order of operations, as the following sample from the Immediate window shows:

```
PRINT 2 ^ 3 * 5
 40
PRINT 2 ^ (3 * 5)
 32768
```

In the first statement, the ^ operator has higher precedence than the * operator. So 2 is first raised to the 3rd power, yielding 8. Then 8 is multiplied by 5, resulting in 40. In the second statement, QuickBASIC begins by multiplying 3 by 5 to get 15. Next, 2 is raised to the 15th power, yielding 32768.

If two operators have the same precedence, the leftmost operation is done first:

```
PRINT 3 / 4 * 5
 3.75
```

First, 3 divided by 4 evaluates to 0.75; next, 0.75 times 5 yields 3.75.

Normally the left-to-right rule for operators having the same precedence is not important for addition and subtraction. For example, the following equation results in 100 whether you do the addition or the subtraction first:

```
50 + 80 – 30
```

The left-to-right rule can be important if you are near the size limits for a type, however. For instance, this statement works smoothly:

```
PRINT 30000% - 8000% + 4000%
 26000
```

But the following equation results in an *Overflow* message:

```
PRINT 30000% + 4000% - 8000%
```

In this case, the first operation adds the integers 30000% and 4000%. The result is 34000, which is greater than the limit of 32767 for the integer type. With the first approach, subtraction comes first, so no overflow occurs.

Text and Strings

About the same time you learned to add and subtract numbers in grade school, you learned to read and write text. QuickBASIC can deal with text, too. It uses a data type called a *string* to represent text. A string is simply a sequence of characters treated as a single unit. In many ways, QuickBASIC treats strings like numbers, so you might find this description of string basics familiar.

Like numbers, strings can be literals, variables, or constants. QuickBASIC, in fact, has two varieties of string variables. In this chapter we'll discuss the traditional form found in previous versions of BASIC—the variable-length string. We'll take up the newer fixed-length string in the chapter on user-defined types (Chapter 10).

String Literals

Suppose you want to print the word *Hello.* You can try using PRINT:

```
PRINT Hello
 0
```

That doesn't work. As shown earlier, when QuickBASIC sees *PRINT Hello,* it assumes *Hello* is the name of a variable. Because you haven't assigned a value to *Hello,* QuickBASIC assigns it the default numeric value of 0.

To print the word *Hello*, you need to supply a *string literal.* You accomplish that by placing the word within double quotation marks:

```
PRINT "Hello"
Hello
```

The quotation marks are not part of the string. They are *delimiters*—that is, they mark the limits of the string for QuickBASIC.

You can use any characters except double quotation marks in the string, including spaces and punctuation marks:

```
PRINT "Precisely how much fun are you having?"
Precisely how much fun are you having?
```

QuickBASIC lets you place as many as 32,767 characters in a string. Few users find this unduly restrictive.

String Variable Types and Constants

QuickBASIC uses the $ suffix to indicate the string data type. Here, for instance, we create a string variable called *Message$*, assign it a value, and print it:

```
Message$ = "Don't forget the $ suffix for string variables."
PRINT Message$
Don't forget the $ suffix for string variables.
```

By using the keyword CONST, you can create string constants. Also, you can read strings from the keyboard by using the INPUT statement. Using a string variable with INPUT tells QuickBASIC to expect a string to be entered, as illustrated in the following program:

```
CLS
CONST message$ = "Here is the string you entered:"
PRINT "Please enter a string:"
INPUT Response$
PRINT message$
PRINT Response$
END
```

The CLS statement clears the screen. Here is a sample run:

```
Please enter a string:
? Bach's Air on the G String
Here is the string you entered:
Bach's Air on the G String
```

Amplified INPUT

The INPUT statement lets you combine prompting for an answer with reading the response. In the preceding program, we let INPUT use the default prompt, a question mark. But you can also use INPUT in the following way:

```
INPUT stringliteral, variablename
```

When used in this fashion, INPUT prompts with the specified string literal instead of a question mark. We'll employ this method to give one of our earlier examples a friendlier user interface. Also, we'll use strings to clarify the output. The resulting program follows.

```
CLS
CONST minPerHour% = 60
INPUT "Please enter the number of minutes: ", Minutes%
Hours% = Minutes% \ minPerHour%
MinutesLeft% = Minutes% MOD minPerHour%
PRINT Minutes%; "minutes ="; Hours%; "hours and"; MinutesLeft%; "minutes"
END
```

Here is a sample run:

```
Please enter the number of minutes: 179
 179 minutes = 2 hours and 59 minutes
```

The prompt string is much more effective than the default question mark for telling the user what to do.

In this program we used PRINT to mix strings and numeric output. If you use semicolons to separate a list of items, as we did here, PRINT displays each item in the list. Chapter 3 describes PRINT formatting in detail.

More About Creating Variables

So far we have followed the classic BASIC technique for creating a variable: Simply use it. The first time you use a variable in a program, QuickBASIC creates storage and assigns the variable's name as a label for that storage. If you don't provide a value for a numeric variable, QuickBASIC sets its value to 0. The default value for a string variable is the *null string*, which contains no characters. To specify the data type for a variable, you use a %, &, !, #, or $ suffix to indicate an integer type, a long integer type, a single-precision type, a double-precision type, or a string type, respectively.

But QuickBASIC does offer some alternatives for creating and typing variables, as described in the following sections.

Creating Name Defaults

By default, a variable name without a type suffix refers to a single-precision variable. For instance, the following statement creates a single-precision variable called *Flips*:

```
Flips = 200
```

Even though we wrote *200* as an integer, it's converted to floating-point form when assigned to *Flips*.

QuickBASIC lets you override that default by specifying that all names beginning with a certain range of letters will be of a particular type. The DEFINT, DEFLNG, DEFSNG, DEFDBL, and DEFSTR statements create defaults for the integer, long integer, single-precision, double-precision, and string types. For instance, the following statement makes variables beginning with the letter J integer type:

```
DEFINT J
```

Remember that BASIC doesn't distinguish between uppercase and lowercase, so this statement would make *jingle*, *Jungle*, and *JANGLE* all integer type.

You use a hyphen to indicate a range. Thus

```
DEFDBL Q-S
```

makes variables beginning with the letters Q through S double-precision type.

The usual type suffixes override these defaults, so a variable called *Quick&* is long integer type, even though it begins with a Q. Also, if two DEF defaults overlap, the last one applies. Suppose you use these statements:

```
DEFINT A-M
DEFSTR L-T
```

In that case, *King* is an integer variable, but *Mouse* is a string variable.

Many programmers believe that creating multiple name defaults can lead to confusion, especially in large programs. If you use a type suffix, you leave no doubt about the type of a variable. However, one name default is widely used:

```
DEFINT A-Z
```

Because integer calculations are faster than floating-point calculations and are not subject to rounding errors, it's reasonable to make integer type the default. If you do need other types, you can always use the standard suffixes.

Using DIM to Create Simple Variables

Many languages require that you list a program's variables near the beginning of the program before the variables are used. This practice has the advantage of documenting in one place the variables used by the program. QuickBASIC lets you do something similar with the DIM statement. Originally, DIM was used to create a special data type called an *array*. It still is used for that, as we'll discuss in Chapter 6. But DIM also lets you specify a type explicitly, without using one of the type suffixes. The following program shows how this works:

```
CLS
DIM Rows AS INTEGER
PRINT Rows
Rows = 23.394
PRINT Rows
END
```

Here is the output from the compiled program:

```
0
23
```

As the output reflects, the DIM statement creates a variable called *Rows* and assigns it the value 0. The AS INTEGER part makes *Rows* an integer type and causes 23.394 to be rounded to 23.

We used the following form of the DIM statement:

```
DIM variablename AS typename
```

The type name can be INTEGER, LONG, SINGLE, DOUBLE, or STRING. (It can also be a user-defined type, which we'll explain in later chapters.)

Design and Debugging Tips

One of the advantages of QuickBASIC's naming scheme is that it lets you create descriptive names for variables. For example, if a variable represents income, you can name the variable *Income* rather than *I*. The more complex a program is, the more important descriptive names are. They make programs easier to read, understand, and debug. If you see, say, *I/2* in a program, you might not be alarmed. But *Income/2*, especially if it's your income, should get your attention.

Comments

If necessary, you can add comments to further document the meaning of a variable:

```
DIM Mpg89 AS SINGLE      ' Average mpg for car fleet (1989)
DIM Mpg90 AS SINGLE      ' Average mpg for car fleet (1990)
```

In QuickBASIC, a single quotation mark denotes the beginning of a comment, which extends to the end of the line. QuickBASIC ignores comments when compiling a program; they are there solely to help the reader understand the program.

You can also use the keyword REM instead of a quotation mark to indicate a comment. REM can share a line with another statement, but only if REM is preceded by a colon:

```
Age% = 30          ' Jill's estimate
REM Jack thinks suspect might be older than 30
Height% = 71       :REM That's in inches
```

We strongly recommend that you use comments to document your programs.

The Case of the Mistaken Variable

As you have seen, QuickBASIC lets you create variables on the fly. This can sometimes cause problems. For example, if you misspell a variable, QuickBASIC creates a new variable with the misspelled name and a value of 0. Try the following in the Immediate window:

```
Ltrs = 1440
PRINT Lrts
 0
```

You are much more likely to notice that you've misspelled *Liters* as *Lirets* than to notice that you've misspelled *Ltrs* as *Lrts.* This is another argument for using descriptive names.

Type suffixes can also cause problems, as the following program shows:

```
CLS
INPUT "Enter the number of miles traveled: ", Miles!
INPUT "Enter the gallons of gas used: ", Gallons!
Mpg! = Miles% / Gallons!
PRINT "Miles per gallon ="; Mpg!
END
```

Here is the output:

```
Enter the number of miles traveled: 429
Enter the gallons of gas used: 13.9
Miles per gallon = 0
```

Suffixes are part of the variable name, making *Miles!* and *Miles%* two separate variables. Because we didn't assign *Miles%* a value, it is set to 0.

Review Questions

1. Identify the types of the following literals:

   a. 15
   b. "Sam and Janet"
   c. &H19
   d. 1.98E30
   e. 4.2D40
   f. 29392012

2. Identify the types of the following variables:

   a. *Tubs!*
   b. *Weight%*
   c. *Items&*
   d. *Cost*
   e. *Budget#*
   f. *Logo$*

3. Why does QuickBASIC have several numeric types instead of only one?

4. What would be a suitable type to represent each of the following?
   a. The number of floppy disks in your office
   b. The number of floppy disks stocked by a computer store chain
   c. The average number of floppy disks per household
   d. What you say when you find that your computer can no longer read data from your most important floppy disk
   e. Position and velocity data to be used to calculate a satellite orbit
5. Evaluate the following expressions:
   a. 10 + 6 / 4
   b. 10 + 6 \ 4
   c. (10 + 6) / 4
   d. 200 – 72 / 6 * 2
   e. 10 ^ 6 / 2
   f. 1.23E5 + 3.1E4
   g. 8.812E21 + 1%
6. Write a program that asks the user to enter a number and then prints the result of raising that number to the 3rd power.

3

Input and Output

CLOSE	**LINE INPUT #**	**PRINT**	**SPC**
INPUT	**LOCATE**	**PRINT #**	**TAB**
INPUT #	**OPEN**	**PRINT USING**	**WRITE**
LINE INPUT	**OUTPUT**	**PRINT # USING**	

As a programmer, you must be able to establish communication between a program and a user. You've already seen how helpful INPUT and PRINT are for this purpose. In this chapter we'll present additional properties of these QuickBASIC statements and introduce you to other input/output (I/O) statements, such as LINE INPUT, PRINT USING, and WRITE. We'll also introduce you to simple file input and output and even begin creating a modest database.

The INPUT Statement

As you've already seen, the INPUT statement reads values entered from the keyboard and assigns them to variables. It can also display a prompt string of your choosing. Let's look at an example to review how we've used INPUT so far:

```
CLS
INPUT Number!                      ' Use the default prompt
PRINT Number!
INPUT "Enter a word: ", Word$      ' Specify a custom prompt
PRINT Word$
END
```

As usual, we use the CLS statement to clear the screen and the END statement to mark the end of the program. Also, we capitalize the first letter of variables and use a QuickBASIC suffix to indicate the type. And we use the single quotation mark to introduce comments. Here is a sample run:

```
? 47
 47
Enter a word: porcupine
porcupine
```

When—as in the first line—you don't supply a prompt string, INPUT prints a question mark and a space. You then enter the response on the same line as this prompt. We entered *47*, and, as the PRINT statement reveals, this value was assigned to the *Number!* variable. Whenever you use the INPUT statement, you must provide at least one variable to hold the information entered.

For the second INPUT statement in the program, we provided an input string enclosed in double quotation marks. Note that our prompt string includes an intentional space after the colon. This leaves a space between the colon and the cursor on the screen. (Most users feel more comfortable having some room between the prompt and their input.) The prompt string must be a string literal; you cannot use a symbolic string, such as a string variable or a string constant. Also note that you should follow the quoted prompt with a comma. (If you use a semicolon instead of a comma, INPUT adds a question mark to the end of the prompt.)

Now that we've summarized our existing knowledge of the INPUT statement, let's look at the rest of the package. We'll follow the usual rules for describing syntax:

- Items in *italics* are placeholders for which you substitute your own values.
- Items in [brackets] are optional.
- Items in braces and separated by a broken pipe symbol { ¦ } indicate a choice. For instance, the following syntax line indicates that if you do use a prompt string, it must be followed by a semicolon or a comma:

  ```
  INPUT [;] ["promptstring"{;¦,}] variablelist
  ```

The INPUT statement reads values from the keyboard and assigns them to the variables in *variablelist*. INPUT examines the types of the variables to determine what sort of input to expect. A semicolon immediately after INPUT causes the cursor to remain on the same line after the user presses the Enter key. INPUT prints the string *promptstring* to prompt the user. A semicolon following *promptstring* causes a question mark to be appended to the prompt string, but a comma in the same position suppresses a question mark. If *promptstring* is omitted, INPUT prompts with a question mark.

The following program illustrates the two uses of the semicolon:

```
CLS
INPUT ; "First name: ", F$       ' Leave cursor on same line
INPUT " Last name: ", L$
INPUT "Age"; Age!                ' Append question mark to prompt string
PRINT "I'll keep that information in mind."
END
```

Here is a sample run:

```
First name: Tharg Last name: Whonkmammoth
Age? 23242
I'll keep that information in mind.
```

Following the first INPUT keyword with a semicolon keeps the cursor on the same line. Accordingly, the second input string follows the response to the first input request. The third INPUT statement uses a semicolon to separate the prompt string from the variable name and thus appends a question mark to the prompt string.

Input Matching

Let's see what happens when a user's entry doesn't match what INPUT expects. For instance, the first program in this chapter expects us to enter a number and then a string. Here's how it deals with mismatched input:

```
? huh

Redo from start
? 1 9   9  2
 1992
Enter a word: 2001
2001
```

First, puzzled by the ? prompt, we entered *huh*. (The vagueness of the ? prompt is a good reason to provide your own prompt.) QuickBASIC responded by moving down a line, telling us *Redo from start,* and showing us the prompt again. This response means that our input did not meet QuickBASIC's expectations, and QuickBASIC wants us to try again. The program expects a number because *Number!* is a single-precision numeric variable, but we entered a string.

Next, we tried again by entering some numbers. Here INPUT did something surprising. It ignored the spaces in our input and ran the digits together to form a single number: *1992*.

Finally, we tried to confuse the program again, this time by entering a number when it expected a string. But this mismatch did not trigger a *Redo* message. Because a string is any series of characters, including digits, *2001* is read as a string, not a number—that is, it is read as a *2* character followed by two *0* characters followed by a *1* character. You can see the difference in the output. The PRINT statement printed the number *1992* with a leading space, which serves as a placeholder; if a number is negative, the space is used for the minus sign. But the string *2001,* like other strings, is printed flush left. If this doesn't convince you that *Word$* is a string, not a number, go to the Immediate window and try the following:

```
PRINT Word$ + 4
```

A dialog box warns of a type mismatch. You can't add a number directly to a string, even if the string consists of digits.

But what happens if you don't enter anything? What if you simply press the Enter key? We'll run the program again:

? <Enter> ———————— No value entered

0 ———————————— Registers as 0

Enter a word: <Enter> ———— No text entered

———————————— Registers as a null string

The numeric variable was assigned the value 0, and the string variable was assigned the null string (a string containing no characters).

Reading More Than One Variable

So far we've used INPUT to read only one variable at a time. But you can also supply a list of variable names to INPUT, as illustrated in this program:

```
CLS
PRINT "This program calculates miles per gallon."
INPUT "Enter distance traveled and gallons used: ", Dist!, Gals!
PRINT "Now calculating your miles per gallon..."
Mpg! = Dist! / Gals!
PRINT Mpg!
END
```

Here is a sample run:

```
This program calculates miles per gallon.
Enter distance traveled and gallons used: 410 12.8

Redo from start
Enter distance traveled and gallons used: 410, 12.8
Now calculating your miles per gallon...
 32.03125
```

QuickBASIC requires that commas separate multiple input values to a single INPUT statement. As you saw before, INPUT ignores the spaces and interprets *410 12.8* as a single number, 41012.8. But because QuickBASIC expects two values, you get a *Redo* message. Remember to use the comma, and all goes well.

Now let's try a similar example with multiple strings instead of numbers. The following program prints the strings on separate lines so that you can see which string is assigned to each variable:

```
CLS
INPUT "Please enter three strings: ", S1$, S2$, S3$
PRINT S1$
PRINT S2$
PRINT S3$
END
```

Here is a sample run:

```
Please enter three strings: one cat, two dogs, three mice
one cat
two dogs
three mice
```

Again, you must use a comma to separate one input value from the next as you enter your response. What if you want to include a comma as part of an input string? Then you can enclose the entire string in double quotation marks:

```
Please enter three strings: "Or, say, try", the, port.
Or, say, try
the
port.
```

A string in quotation marks, such as *"Or, say, try"*, is called a *quoted string*, and one not in quotation marks, such as *three mice*, is called an *unquoted string*. Note that the quotation marks delimit the string but aren't assigned to the variable; they are not part of the string. A quoted string consists of all characters between the opening quotation mark and the next quotation mark, and an unquoted string starts with its first character and runs to the next comma or to the end of the line, whichever comes first.

Because a quoted string terminates at the second quotation mark, you can't embed a quotation mark within a quoted string. However, a quotation mark can be part of an unquoted string—that is, part of a string that doesn't begin with a quotation mark. The next run illustrates this point:

```
Please enter three strings: Ron "Rotgut" Gups, is, back
Ron "Rotgut" Gups
is
back
```

Although *Ron "Rotgut" Gups* contains double quotation marks, it is an unquoted string because its first character is not a double quotation mark.

NOTE: *The single quotation mark (') in an input string has no special meaning to the INPUT statement; it is treated like any other character.*

Input Editing

Until you press the Enter key (which sends your input to the program), you can edit any INPUT line by using the editing keys shown in Figure 3-1. You'll probably use the Backspace key and the arrow keys most frequently.

Key	Action
Right Arrow or Ctrl-\	Moves cursor right one character
Left Arrow or Ctrl-]	Moves cursor left one character
Ctrl-Right Arrow or Ctrl-F	Moves cursor right one word
Ctrl-Left Arrow or Ctrl-B	Moves cursor left one word
Home or Ctrl-K	Moves cursor to beginning of input line
End or Ctrl-N	Moves cursor to end of input line
Ins or Ctrl-R	Toggles insert mode on and off
Tab or Ctrl-I	Tabs right and inserts (insert mode on); tabs right and overwrites (insert mode off)
Del	Deletes character at cursor
Backspace or Ctrl-H	Deletes character to left of cursor; if cursor is at beginning of a line, deletes character under cursor
Ctrl-End or Ctrl-E	Deletes to end of line
Esc or Ctrl-U	Deletes entire line
Enter or Ctrl-M	Sends line to program
Ctrl-T	Toggles function-key label display at screen bottom
Ctrl-Break or Ctrl-C	Terminates input and stops program

Figure 3-1.
Input editing keystrokes.

The PRINT Statement

Now that you've seen how to feed information to a program, let's examine how you can use PRINT to display information. Listing 3-1 demonstrates those properties of PRINT we've used so far. (As noted in the Introduction, all numbered program listings in this book are available on a companion disk.)

```
CLS
CONST lots% = 4
Area! = 12.03
Cost! = 63450000
Name$ = "Gregor D'Amore"
PRINT lots%, Area!, Cost!, -200      ' Use comma separators
PRINT lots%; Area!; Cost!; -200      ' Use semicolons
PRINT Name$, "is gone."              ' Use commas
PRINT Name$; "is gone."              ' Use semicolons
PRINT Name$; " has"; lots%; "lots."
END
```

Listing 3-1.

Here is the output:

```
 4             12.03         6.345E+07     -200
4  12.03  6.345E+07 -200
Gregor D'Amore              is gone.
Gregor D'Amoreis gone.
Gregor D'Amore has 4 lots.
```

As you see, you can use PRINT to display literal values (*–200* and *"lots"*) as well as symbolic values (*lots%* and *Area!*). Note how using the semicolon between strings runs them together.

Unlike C or Pascal, QuickBASIC doesn't make you specify the format for each value. However, as we'll discuss, you do have the option of specifying the format if you want something other than the default display.

You can use more complex expressions with PRINT. For example, try the following in the Immediate window:

```
PRINT 20 * 9 / 5 + 32
 68
```

QuickBASIC first evaluates such expressions and then prints the value. To print the expression literally (without evaluation), place it within double quotation marks to make it a string.

You can also "add" strings. Try the following in the Immediate window:

```
PRINT "What you see is wh" + "at you get."
What you see is what you get.
```

Combining strings so that the first character of the second string immediately follows the last character of the first string is known as *string concatenation*.

Let's look at the PRINT syntax:

```
PRINT valuelist[{,¦;}]
```

valuelist consists of the values to be printed. They can be literals, constants, variables, or, more generally, expressions with a value. Let's examine these elements and the ways in which they can be displayed.

Output Spacing

PRINT is followed by a list of *arguments* (*valuelist* in the syntax line above). For instance, the arguments in the following statement are the variables *X!*, *Y!*, and *Z$*:

```
PRINT X!, Y!, Z$
```

To separate arguments, use either commas or semicolons, depending on how you want the values to appear when printed.

Using Commas as Separators

When you use commas to separate arguments, each argument is printed in a field 14 characters wide. If the argument exceeds the 14-character field, the field is increased to the smallest multiple of 14 that will hold the argument. By using a comma, you guarantee that at least one space will separate adjacent items. For instance, *Gregor D'Amore* in Listing 3-1 is exactly 14 characters (including the space). If the next string were to be placed in the next 14-character field, it would start immediately after the *e* in *D'Amore*, so QuickBASIC skips an entire field before displaying *is gone.*

With comma separators, strings and negative numbers start at the beginning of a field. Positive numbers are displayed with a leading space. The first and third lines of output from Listing 3-1 demonstrate these properties; also see Figure 3-2.

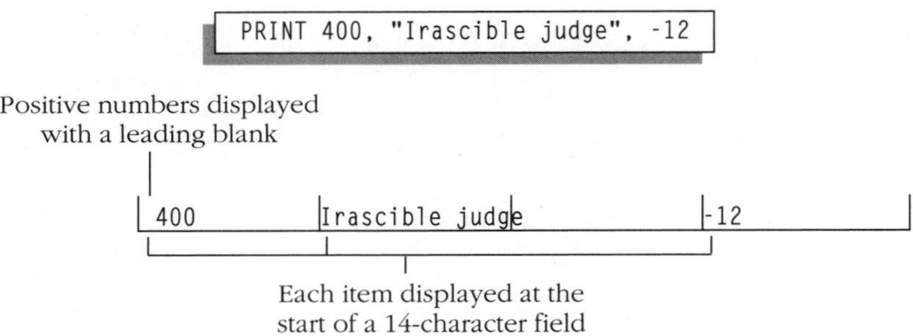

Figure 3-2.
PRINT spacing using commas.

Using Semicolons as Separators

When you use semicolons to separate strings, the strings run together, as the fourth line of output from Listing 3-1 shows. So if you want a space between the strings, you must include it as part of a string, as we did with *has.* Numbers, however, are always followed by a space, even when separated by a semicolon. Also, as with the comma separator, numbers are displayed with a leading space if positive and with a leading minus sign if negative (Figure 3-3).

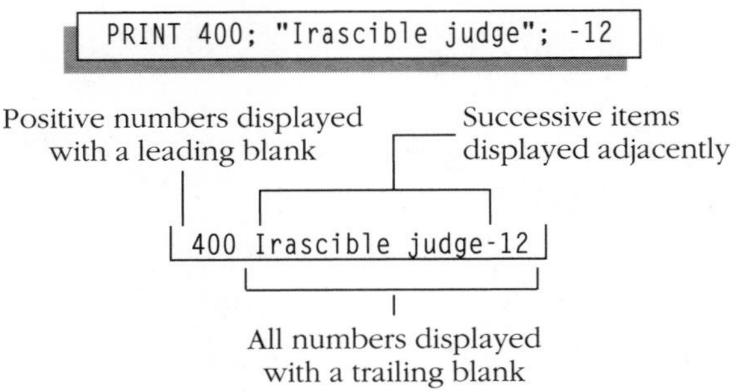

Figure 3-3.
PRINT spacing using semicolons.

If you separate arguments with a space or a tab, the QuickBASIC editor supplies semicolons for you. Suppose you type the following in the View window:

```
PRINT 10 20 30
```

After you press the Enter key or the Down Arrow key, the editor converts this statement to the following:

```
PRINT 10; 20; 30
```

However, suppose you enter this:

```
PRINT 10 40 -25
```

The editor converts it to the following:

```
PRINT 10; 40 - 25
```

In this case, QuickBASIC interprets the minus sign as indicating subtraction, not the sign of a negative number. So don't get lazy and let QuickBASIC do your punctuation. You're better off typing your own commas and semicolons.

> **NOTE:** *These changes take place only in the View window, not in the Immediate window.*

Number Format

Note that although Listing 3-1 assigns the value 63450000 to *Cost!*, the program prints it as *6.345E+07.* If PRINT can display a single-precision number using fixed-point notation in seven or fewer digits with no loss of accuracy, it does so, as with *12.03*. Otherwise, PRINT switches to E notation, as it did with *Cost!*.

Similarly, PRINT displays a double-precision number in fixed decimal form if it can do so with 16 or fewer digits. Otherwise, PRINT switches to D notation.

Starting New Lines

Normally, each PRINT statement displays information on a new line. However, if you terminate a PRINT statement with a semicolon or a comma, the output from the next PRINT statement will continue on the same line, as shown in the following program:

```
CLS
CostOfHairdo! = 34.99
CostOfShampoo! = 11.99
PRINT "Hairdo = $"; CostOfHairdo!,
PRINT "Shampoo = $"; CostOfShampoo!;
PRINT "Total = $"; CostOfHairdo! + CostOfShampoo!
END
```

The output looks like this:

```
Hairdo = $ 34.99            Shampoo = $ 11.99 Total = $ 46.98
```

The PRINT USING Statement

Although the PRINT statement provides decent-looking output and some flexibility, you might want to exercise greater control over the appearance of your output. That's where the PRINT USING statement comes in. It uses a string to describe the particular form, or *format,* to be used in displaying values. This string appears immediately before the list of values to be printed, as shown in the following syntax line:

```
PRINT USING formatstring; valuelist[{,|;}]
```

formatstring contains the printing instructions and can be a string literal or a string variable. QuickBASIC provides several special symbols that can be used in the string. Note that *formatstring* must be followed by a semicolon. *valuelist* is a list of arguments, as it is in the PRINT statement, but in this case commas and semicolons are interchangeable as separators because *formatstring* dictates the spacing.

The PRINT USING statement has an extensive set of formatting instructions that can go into *formatstring*. Because our needs are modest, we'll examine only a few of them. (Appendix E contains a complete list of the PRINT USING formatting instructions.)

Formatting Strings

PRINT USING has three string formatting characters that control the number of characters printed:

- ! prints only the first character of the string.
- \\ lets you specify a particular number of characters to be printed.
- & prints the entire string.

For example, enter the following in the Immediate window:

```
PRINT USING "!"; "Tough cookies"
T
```

With ! as the format string, only the first letter of *Tough cookies* is displayed.

The \\ combination specifies a field width for printing a string. You can include spaces between the backslashes; the field width equals 2 plus the number of spaces. Again, go to the Immediate window to see how this works:

```
PRINT USING "\  \"; "Tough cookies"
Toug
```

With a field width of 2 plus the two spaces between the backslashes, the first four characters of *Tough cookies* are displayed.

If you specify a field width greater than the length of the string, the entire string is printed, beginning at the left of the field.

The & character works like an ordinary PRINT statement:

```
PRINT USING "&"; "Tough cookies"
Tough cookies
```

At this point you might wonder about the purpose of the & formatter, because you could more easily use a regular PRINT statement. You can, however, use & to combine one or more format characters with regular text in the format string. The following program provides an example:

```
CLS
PRINT USING "See & run."; "Dick"
Dog$ = "Spot"
PRINT USING "See & run."; Dog$
END
```

Note that you can use either a string literal or a string variable in the variable list. Here is the output:

```
See Dick run.
See Spot run.
```

The regular characters in the format string are printed literally, but & is replaced with the corresponding string. You could get the same effect with the following:

```
PRINT "See "; "Dick"; " run."    ' Using semicolons
Dog$ = "Spot"
PRINT "See " + Dog$ + " run."    ' Using concatenation
```

But the PRINT USING form can be more compact and convenient.

Multiple Formats

If you use more than one format character in a format string, the first format applies to the first value displayed, the second format to the second value displayed, and so on, as shown in the following program (which also illustrates the use of a symbolic constant as the format):

```
CONST format$ = "!. &'s eyes are &."
INPUT "What's your first name?  ", First$
INPUT "What's your last name?  ", Last$
INPUT "What's your eye color?  ", Eyes$
PRINT USING format$; First$; Last$; Eyes$
END
```

Here is a sample run:

```
What's your first name? Zippy
What's your last name?  Zapparoni
What's your eye color?  blue
Z. Zapparoni's eyes are blue.
```

Here *!. &'s eyes are &.* is the format string. Again, all regular characters—the spaces, letters, and punctuation—are printed literally. But ! is replaced by the first letter of the first argument (the value of *First$*), and the two & characters are replaced by the next two arguments.

If the format string contains more arguments than format characters, PRINT USING cycles through the format characters again. For instance, try the following in the Immediate window:

```
PRINT USING "Name: &  Initial: !  "; "Bob"; "Ed"; "Jo"; "Ann"
Name: Bob  Initial: E  Name: Jo  Initial: A
```

QuickBASIC applies the format to *Bob* and *Ed* and then reapplies it to *Jo* and *Ann.*

Formatting Numbers

QuickBASIC provides 10 formatting characters for numbers. They are used in the same fashion as string formatting characters, as part of the format string. Let's look at a few simple examples. (Remember that Appendix E contains additional information for those of you who would like to know more.)

You can control the width of the field used to display an integer. The # symbol represents a digit position in the output field. For instance, the combination ##### specifies a field five digits wide. Here is an example using the Immediate window:

```
PRINT USING "#####"; 2, 3.8, 123, 989822
    2    4  123%989822
```

A few notes about the output:

- If the value displayed uses fewer digits than the number reserved by the # symbols, the display is right justified—that is, the number is printed at the right end of the five-digit field. As you can see, this happened with 2 and 123.
- Note that 3.8 is rounded to 4. If you use only # symbols in the format string, only integers are printed.
- The value 989822 is greater than the field width. In this case, QuickBASIC prints the entire number along with a % prefix to indicate that the printed number exceeds the specified field width.

Floating-Point Numbers

When you work with floating-point numbers, you might want to control how many decimal places are displayed. To do so, incorporate a decimal point into the format string. For instance, *###.##* specifies three digits to the left of the decimal point and two digits to the right. This format is useful for tidying the appearance of floating-point values when they are printed, as shown in the following example:

```
PRINT USING "###.##"; 2, .8, 81.93, 1.2386
  2.00  0.80 81.93  1.24
```

Each number is printed with two places following the decimal point. If the original number has more decimal places than requested, the displayed value is rounded to fit. Also note that if # appears to the left of the decimal point, QuickBASIC prints a leading zero when the value is less than 1.

To display a number that has commas, simply place a comma to the left of the period in the format string:

```
PRINT USING "######,.###"; 123456 / 1.2
102,879.996
```

Suppose you want to write a value of the form $23.45. The regular PRINT statement always places a space in front of the number, so the best it can do is *$ 23.45*. But with PRINT USING, the form *$$##.##* allows you to print a dollar sign to the immediate left of the number:

```
PRINT USING "Cost = $$##.##"; 23.45
Cost =  $23.45
```

Of course, you can combine more than one formatting symbol to create a format description. For example, *$$##,###.##* displays values using the dollar sign and commas. You can even have several formats in one format string, each applying to a different variable. And you can intermingle ordinary text. The following program presents a short example:

```
CLS
CONST rate! = 572.5
INPUT "What's your first name? ", First$
INPUT "What's your last name? ", Last$
INPUT "How many days did you work? ", Days!
Pay! = rate! * Days!
PRINT USING "Pay for &, &: $$##,###.##"; Last$; First$; Pay!
END
```

Here is a sample run:

```
What's your first name? Jack
What's your last name? Benimble
How many days did you work? 23.7
Pay for Benimble, Jack:  $13,568.25
```

Another Input Statement: LINE INPUT

You'll recall that the INPUT statement uses commas in the input line to separate items. Consider the following example from the Immediate window. (Note that you must respond to the first prompt before entering the PRINT statement.)

```
INPUT "Enter two makes of autos: ", Auto1$, Auto2$
Enter two makes of autos: Fiat, Saab
PRINT Auto1$, Auto2$
Fiat          Saab
```

Because INPUT interprets commas as separators, it can't read strings that contain commas unless the whole string is enclosed in double quotation marks. For instance, try the following in the Immediate window:

```
INPUT "What did she say? ", Said$
What did she say? Well, she didn't say much.

Redo from start
What did she say?
```

Here the INPUT statement expected one string, but the comma in the reply made the input look like two strings. Because the number of input items didn't match the number of variables, you got an error message.

Now try the same thing using LINE INPUT:

```
LINE INPUT "What did she say? ", Said$
What did she say? Well, she didn't say much.
PRINT Said$
Well, she didn't say much.
```

The entire line, including the comma, is read and assigned to *Said$*. Even quotation marks in the input line become part of the input string:

```
LINE INPUT "What did she say? ", Said$
What did she say? "I love the way you use QuickBASIC."
PRINT Said$
"I love the way you use QuickBASIC."
```

The LINE INPUT statement is useful for programs that read text input because it doesn't impose the restrictions that INPUT does.

Here is the syntax for the LINE INPUT statement:

```
LINE INPUT[;] ["promptstring";] stringvariable
```

The entire line of input is assigned to *stringvariable*.

Another Output Statement: WRITE

The WRITE statement is similar to PRINT, but WRITE separates output items with commas and puts double quotation marks around the strings it prints. The following program illustrates the differences:

```
CLS
Age% = 82
Name$ = "Piet Poirot"
Prize! = 735.42
PRINT Age%, Name$, Prize!
WRITE Age%, Name$, Prize!
END
```

Here is the output:

```
 82            Piet Poirot    735.42
82,"Piet Poirot",735.42
```

This is the syntax for the WRITE statement:

```
WRITE [valuelist]
```

valuelist is a comma-separated list of expressions. If *valuelist* is omitted, WRITE prints a blank line on the screen. Otherwise it prints all items in the list, separating them with commas. Strings are displayed enclosed in double quotation marks.

Screen Positioning

Conceptually, the standard screen is a matrix of 2000 character cells arranged in 25 rows of 80 columns each. So far, we've let output fall where it may on this matrix. But QuickBASIC provides the TAB and SPC functions and the LOCATE statement, which let you dictate the location of the screen cursor and output. These instructions are useful tools for organizing the appearance of the display.

The TAB Function

The TAB function is the simplest of the three instructions.

Here is the syntax for TAB:

```
TAB(column)
```

TAB moves the current print position to the column specified by *column*. Columns are numbered from left to right, with the leftmost column labeled 1.

- If the current print position is already beyond *column*, the print position is moved to the *column* position on the next line.
- If *column* is greater than the screen width, *column* MOD *screenwidth* is used. *screenwidth* can be 40 or 80, depending on the screen mode and screen width settings.

TAB can be used only with the PRINT and the LPRINT statements. For instance, *TAB(22)* means move to column 22. The TAB function is useful for aligning output, as illustrated in the following program:

```
CLS
Player1$ = "Amos Piggs"
Player2$ = "Etta Snoutly"
Player3$ = "Herb Swinelove"
PRINT TAB(3); "Player's Name"; TAB(22); "Rank"
PRINT TAB(3); Player1$; TAB(22); 1
PRINT TAB(3); Player2$; TAB(22); 2
PRINT TAB(3); Player3$; TAB(22); 3
END
```

Here is the output:

```
  Player's Name      Rank
  Amos Piggs          1
  Etta Snoutly        2
  Herb Swinelove      3
```

Note that the output starts in column 3 because of the *TAB(3)* function. The second column of data starts in column 22. Because integers are printed with a leading space, the visible part of the numbers actually starts in column 23.

The SPC Function

The SPC function is similar to the TAB function, but it performs a movement relative to the current cursor position rather than an absolute movement. For example, *TAB(22)* means move to column 22, whereas *SPC(22)* means move 22 spaces over from the current position.

Here is the syntax for SPC:

```
SPC(n)
```

SPC moves the print position *n* spaces to the right of the current print position.

Let's modify the preceding program by replacing TAB with SPC:

```
CLS
Player1$ = "Amos Piggs"
Player2$ = "Etta Snoutly"
Player3$ = "Herb Swinelove"
PRINT SPC(3); "Player's Name"; SPC(22); "Rank"
PRINT SPC(3); Player1$; SPC(22); 1
PRINT SPC(3); Player2$; SPC(22); 2
PRINT SPC(3); Player3$; SPC(22); 3
END
```

Now the output looks like this:

```
Player's Name                     Rank
Amos Piggs                      1
Etta Snoutly                      2
Herb Swinelove                      3
```

Note that *TAB(3)* causes the output to start in column 3, whereas *SPC(3)* skips three columns, causing output to start in column 4. Also, the second column begins 22 spaces to the right of the end of the first column of output. Because the items in the first column are of unequal length, the second column of data is no longer aligned.

The LOCATE Statement

Up to this point, we've printed our messages in what is sometimes called the *Teletype mode:* Each output line follows the preceding line. When output reaches the bottom of the screen, the old lines scroll off the top of the screen, much as paper advances in a Teletype machine. You can produce a better interface by using the LOCATE statement to position the screen cursor.

Here is the syntax for LOCATE:

```
LOCATE [row][, [column][, [visibility][, [start][, stop]]]]
```

row is the row, or line, in which the cursor appears; numbering starts with 1 at the top. If this argument is not specified, the row is unchanged. *column* is the column in which the cursor appears; numbering starts with 1 at the left. Similarly, if this argument is not specified, the column is unchanged.

If *visibility* has a value of 0, the cursor is turned off; a value of 1 turns the cursor on. *start* is the starting scan line and *stop* is the ending scan line for forming the cursor.

Listing 3-2 modifies one of our earlier programs to demonstrate how the LOCATE statement works.

```
CONST rate! = 572.5
CLS
LOCATE 1, 15
PRINT "The Super-Duper Payroll Program"
LOCATE 6, 15
INPUT "What's your first name?     >> ", First$
LOCATE 8, 15
INPUT "What's your last name?      >> ", Last$
LOCATE 10, 15
INPUT "How many days did you work?  >> ", Days!
Pay! = rate! * Days!
LOCATE 3, 15
PRINT USING "Pay for &, &: $$##,###.##"; Last$; First$; Pay!
END
```

Listing 3-2.

The CLS statement clears the screen. The command *LOCATE 6, 15* locates the cursor on line 6, column 15. Here's the output from a sample run:

```
The Super-Duper Payroll Program

Pay for Bond, Frodo:   $8,587.50

What's your first name?      >> Frodo

What's your last name?       >> Bond

How many days did you work?  >> 15
```

The LOCATE statement lets us position the output of the final PRINT USING statement above the output of the three preceding INPUT statements.

Controlling Cursor Appearance

The fourth and fifth arguments of the LOCATE statement dictate the appearance of the cursor.

To understand how these arguments work, you must visualize how the cursor is formed on screen. The various characters are formed from horizontal scan lines. The fourth argument gives the starting scan line that is used to form the cursor, and the fifth argument gives the ending scan line. The scan lines are numbered from top to bottom in the box in which the character is drawn. For example, the CGA display has eight lines numbered 0 through 7, so *LOCATE 5, 5, 1, 7, 7* produces a cursor of one scan line near the bottom of the character box, and *LOCATE 5, 5, 1, 0, 7* produces a full-height, box-shaped cursor. The following program gives you a look at three possibilities:

```
CLS
PRINT "Press Enter to see successive cursor forms."
LOCATE 5, 1, 1, 0, 0
INPUT "Cursor #1 >> ", Junk$
LOCATE , , , 0, 7
INPUT "Cursor #2 >> ", Junk$
LOCATE , , , 7, 7
INPUT "Cursor #3 >> ", Junk$
END
```

To go from one cursor to the next, simply press the Enter key. Doing so assigns a null string to the string variable *Junk$* and brings the next cursor into view.

This program also illustrates what happens if you omit values for arguments. The last two LOCATE statements omit the row, column, and visibility information but keep the commas so that QuickBASIC can tell that the remaining values are the fourth and fifth arguments. If a row or column argument is omitted, LOCATE uses the current value. In this case, the INPUT statement places the cursor at the end of the prompt string, and that is the position used by LOCATE. If any of the last three arguments are omitted, LOCATE uses the values from the preceding LOCATE statement. In our example, we set the visibility argument to 1, which was also used for the subsequent LOCATE statements.

If you set the second scan line smaller than the first (as in *LOCATE , , , 5, 1*), LOCATE produces a two-part cursor for some but not all video adapters.

File Input/Output

Eventually, the simple programs that read input from the keyboard and send output to the screen might not fulfill your needs. For example, you might want to save a program's output and use it again in another program. To do so, use *files,* which are blocks of information stored in permanent memory devices such as floppy disks and hard disks. You can both save information in files and read information from files into your program—a practice known as *file input/output* (or *file I/O*).

In its simplest form, file input/output is not much more involved than what we've done so far with INPUT and PRINT. The following basic examples (and those in the next few chapters) give you a framework that will help you understand the more advanced examples shown in Chapter 11.

Basic Concepts

On a PC, files are usually stored on floppy disks and on hard disks. Part of the computer's job is to keep track of these files. When you format a disk, the computer sets aside some of the disk's space for a table (the File Allocation Table, or FAT) describing the files the disk contains. When you use the DOS TYPE command, for example, the computer scans this table to learn where to place the drive heads to read the file. Dealing with files on the level of the operating system involves a lot of detailed, technical information. Fortunately, QuickBASIC provides us with a fairly simple interface.

Let's look at the QuickBASIC model for files. To use a file, you must first *open* it. When you open a file, you indicate how it is to be used—for reading, writing, appending, or whatever. You supply the name for the file, and QuickBASIC finds it on the hard disk or floppy disk. While a file is open, you can use special I/O statements for files. QuickBASIC takes care of activating and moving the drive heads and transferring information. When you've finished, you close the file, and QuickBASIC updates the FAT. In other words, QuickBASIC lets you deal with a conceptual picture of a file while it deals with the details. See Figure 3-4 for a sketch of this process.

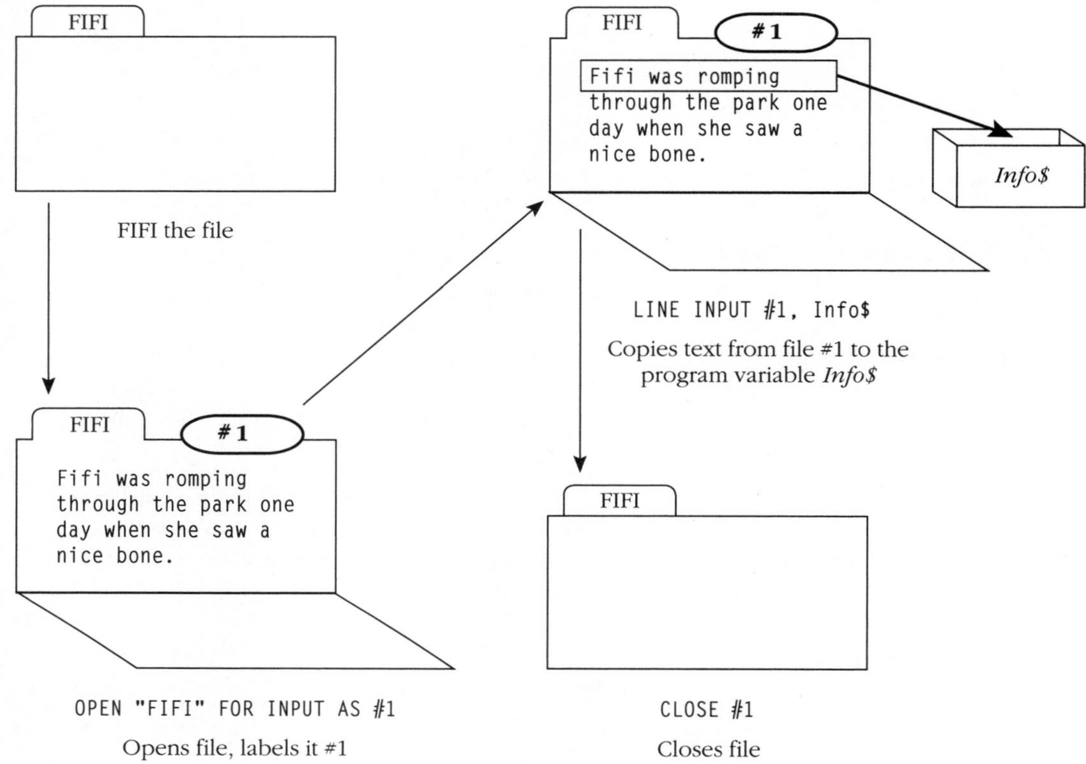

Figure 3-4.
QuickBASIC and files.

QuickBASIC uses the OPEN statement for opening files and the CLOSE statement for closing them. For reading a file, you can use INPUT # and LINE INPUT # statements, among others. And for writing to a file, you can use PRINT # or PRINT # USING. As you might guess from their names, these statements are similar to their keyboard and screen cousins.

A Simple Example

Listing 3-3 shows a program that reads two lines from the keyboard, stores them in a file, and shows you the contents of the file.

```
CONST format$ = "Name: &; Phone Number: &"
CLS
PRINT "This program stores names and phone numbers."

OPEN "PHONES" FOR OUTPUT AS #1          ' Open file for writing

LINE INPUT "Enter name: ", Name$        ' Get information
LINE INPUT "Enter phone number: "; Phone$  '  from keyboard and
PRINT #1, USING format$; Name$; Phone$  '  put info into file
LINE INPUT "Enter next name: ", Name$
LINE INPUT "Enter phone number: "; Phone$
PRINT #1, USING format$; Name$; Phone$

CLOSE #1                                ' Close file
OPEN "PHONES" FOR INPUT AS #1           '  and reopen it for reading

PRINT
PRINT "Here are the current contents of the PHONES file:"
LINE INPUT #1, Info$                    ' Take info from file and
PRINT Info$                             '  display it on screen
LINE INPUT #1, Info$
PRINT Info$

CLOSE #1
PRINT "Bye."
END
```

Listing 3-3.

Here is a sample run:

```
This program stores names and phone numbers.
Enter name: Petunia Pomfrit
Enter phone number: 555-3245
Enter next name: Chester Chips
Enter phone number: 555-9292

Here are the current contents of the PHONES file:
Name: Petunia Pomfrit; Phone Number: 555-3245
Name: Chester Chips; Phone Number: 555-9292
Bye.
```

Opening a file is one of the central concepts in this program:

```
OPEN "PHONES" FOR OUTPUT AS #1
```

Here is the simplified syntax for the OPEN statement:

```
OPEN filename FOR mode AS #filenum
```

filename is a string giving the filename. *mode* specifies how the file will be opened. INPUT mode is for reading a file, and OUTPUT mode is for writing to a file. A file must exist before it can be opened in INPUT mode. OUTPUT mode creates a file if *filename* doesn't exist. If *filename* exists, opening it in OUTPUT mode discards the original contents. *filenum* is an integer in the range 1 through 255 that QuickBASIC uses to identify the file.

In Listing 3-3, the string *PHONES* specifies the name of the file to be opened. The phrase *FOR OUTPUT* specifies the mode. In this case, we are opening the file to send output to it. *AS #1* establishes an identification number for the file, which subsequent statements use instead of the filename to identify the file.

The first time you run this program, it creates the file PHONES. If you run the program again, the program uses the file you created the first time. However, when you open a file in OUTPUT mode, the file is *truncated:* The contents are discarded, and the new output replaces the previous contents. Thus, whenever you use the program in Listing 3-3, the new information replaces the old information. (APPEND mode, described in the next chapter, lets you add new material to a file while leaving the current contents intact.)

The following statement writes the strings *Name$* and *Phone$* to the file:

```
PRINT #1, USING format$; Name$; Phone$
```

Here *#1* identifies the file to be written to. If we had opened the file using *AS #2,* we would have used *PRINT #2, USING*. Except for the additional term identifying which file to use, *PRINT #1, USING* works like the PRINT USING statement.

As you might expect, the following statement closes the file:

```
CLOSE #1
```

Next the program reopens the file to read input from it:

```
OPEN "PHONES" FOR INPUT AS #1
```

Because we closed the file earlier, we can reuse the number 1 as an identification number. However, we could have selected 2, 3, or any other number in the range 1 through 255.

The following statement works like an ordinary LINE INPUT statement, but the program reads a line from the file identified as file number 1 instead from the keyboard:

```
LINE INPUT #1, Info$
```

After the program reads the file contents, it displays them on the screen. However, if you leave QuickBASIC and return to DOS, you can use the DOS TYPE command to see that the PHONES file contains the information you wrote to it.

Obviously, our sample program is very limited—it writes and reads exactly two lines. Nonetheless, it is one step toward developing a database.

Review Questions

1. Describe the appearance of the screen after each of the following input statements:

   a. `INPUT Years!`

   b. `INPUT "Your age", Years!`

   c. `INPUT "Your age"; Years!`

2. What would the following program display? (You'll need to run the program to get some of the exact numeric values.)

```
CONST pi! = 3.14159
Radius! = 63700!
Mass# = 2E+30
Mass! = 2E+30
Planet$ = "Earth"
PRINT Mass#, Mass!, Mass&
PRINT Radius!, "The one and only", Planet$
PRINT "Circumference is", 2 * pi! * Radius!
PRINT Mass#; Mass!; Mass&
PRINT Radius!; "The one and only"; Planet$
PRINT "Circumference is"; 2 * pi! * Radius!
END
```

3. Suppose you have the following two input statements:

```
INPUT "Name? ", Name$
LINE INPUT "Name? ", Name$
```

   How would each statement respond to each of the following input lines?

   a. `Donkey Hotey`

   b. `Hotey, Donkey`

   c. `"Hotey, Donkey"`

4. What will the following program print?

```
S1$ = "Washington"
S2$ = "Iowa"
PRINT USING "&!"; S2$; S1$
PRINT USING "&!"; S2$; S1$; S2$
PRINT USING "& &"; S2$; S1$
PRINT USING "\ \ \   \"; S2$; S1$
END
```

5. What will the following program print?

```
N1 = 1234.567
N3 = 3
PRINT USING "####"; N3; -N1; N3
PRINT USING " ####"; N3; N1; N3
PRINT USING "#####.##"; N3; N1; N3
PRINT USING "$$####.##"; N3; N1; N3
END
```

6. What are the differences between PRINT and WRITE?

7. Provide three ways to print *Hello* starting in column 10.

8. What does the following statement accomplish?

```
OPEN "PAYROLL" FOR OUTPUT AS #2
```

9. How would you alter the statement in Review Question 8 to allow the program to read information in the file?

4

Control Flow and Decisions

AND	**EXIT DO**	**IMP**	**SELECT CASE**
APPEND	**EXIT FOR**	**INKEY$**	**STEP**
DO/LOOP	**FOR/NEXT**	**IS**	**WHILE/WEND**
EOF	**GOTO**	**NOT**	**XOR**
EQV	**IF/THEN/ELSE**	**OR**	

Now that you've learned to converse with a QuickBASIC program, it's time to give the program the means to produce something worth talking about. For this, you need the power and flexibility of *control statements,* which enable programs to repeat actions automatically and to make decisions. QuickBASIC provides you with several control statements, each with its own purpose:

- For repeated cycling through a set of instructions (*looping*), you have FOR, DO (in four variations), and WHILE.
- For enhanced looping, you can use the EXIT FOR and EXIT DO statements.
- For decision making, you have a choice of several variations of IF, along with SELECT CASE.

We'll look at all of these, as well as at the various relational and logical operators that many of these statements use to test the computational waters. We'll also learn about INKEY$ and EOF, two QuickBASIC functions commonly used with loops. And no discussion of QuickBASIC control statements would be complete without mention of the GOTO statement. Along the way, we will draw on some of our previous examples and extend the simple database we introduced in Chapter 3.

The FOR Statement

What's a loop, and why would you want one? Suppose you want to print an attractive character pattern, such as your name, 100 times. You can use 100 PRINT statements, of course. Or you can use one loop containing 1 PRINT statement. Properly directed, the loop will repeat the PRINT statement 100 times—that is, the loop goes through 100 *cycles*.

Loops are actually more versatile than this example might suggest: You can also alter what happens in each cycle. For example, you can use a loop to print mortgage payments for 20 different interest rates, changing the rate each cycle.

The FOR loop is probably the easiest loop to use. It lets you execute a statement or a block of statements a specified number of times. You need only identify the beginning and the end of the block of statements to be repeated and the number of repetitions you want.

Here is the syntax for the FOR statement:

```
FOR indexvariable = start TO stop [STEP stepsize]
    statementblock
NEXT [indexvariable]
```

The FOR line marks the start of the block, and the NEXT line marks the end of the block. *indexvariable* is a name of your choosing for a numeric variable. *start* and *stop* are numbers that represent the starting and stopping values for *indexvariable*. *stepsize* represents how much the value in *indexvariable* is increased in each cycle. (The default is 1.) Although using *indexvariable* after NEXT is optional, it makes the program more understandable, especially when you use loops within loops.

Let's look at an example.

Creating a FOR Loop

Suppose you want to print the numbers 1 through 7. You can use a FOR loop in which the value of the index variable varies from 1 through 7, as shown:

```
FOR I% = 1 TO 7       ' I% is a variable
    PRINT I%
NEXT I%               ' Set I% to next value
PRINT "Loop completed"
END
```

We named the loop variable *I%*. The first time through the loop, *I%* has the value 1. When the program reaches the *NEXT I%* line, it increases *I%* by 1 to the value 2, and then it goes to the beginning of the loop and repeats the sequence. When *I%* reaches 7, the loop executes one last time and quits. (Note that we indented the statement in the loop. QuickBASIC doesn't require this, but such indents make code much more readable.)

Here is the output:

```
1
2
3
4
5
6
7
Loop completed
```

Figure 4-1 presents another view of how a loop works. (It also includes an optional STEP feature that we'll discuss later.)

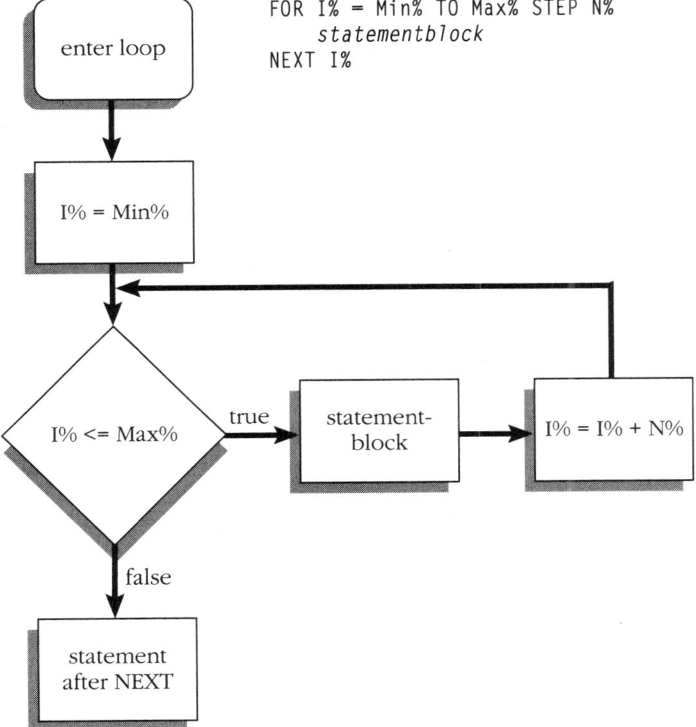

Figure 4-1.
FOR loop flowchart.

The index variable is simply another variable and can be used as such:

```
FOR I% = 2 TO 6
    PRINT I%; "squared is"; I% * I%
NEXT I%
PRINT "After loop, I% ="; I%
END
```

Here is the output:

```
 2 squared is 4
 3 squared is 9
 4 squared is 16
 5 squared is 25
 6 squared is 36
After loop, I% = 7
```

If you wondered what happens to a loop index variable after the loop terminates, this program answers your question. The last action in each loop cycle is the *NEXT I%* line. After using the value 6 for *I%*, the loop increases *I%* to the next value, 7. The loop never uses this value, which exceeds the limits set by the FOR statement. But the variable doesn't disappear—you can use it even after the loop is finished.

Flexing Your Loops

There's a bit more to be learned about the FOR loop. For instance, you can use variables and expressions as well as constants for the loop limits. Just be sure to set values for the variables before using them:

```
INPUT "Enter a starting value: ", Start%
INPUT "Enter number of rules: ", Count%
PRINT "Computer rules to remember:"
FOR I% = Start% TO Start% + Count% - 1
    PRINT "Rule Number"; I%
    PRINT "I will back up important files!"
NEXT I%
PRINT "Amen"
END
```

As the program illustrates, you can have more than one statement in a loop. Here is a sample run:

```
Enter a starting value: 5
Enter number of rules: 3
Computer rules to remember:
Rule Number 5
I will back up important files!
Rule Number 6
I will back up important files!
Rule Number 7
I will back up important files!
Amen
```

After the loop limits are set, they remain fixed. For example, if you change the value of *Count%* inside the loop, QuickBASIC won't reevaluate the upper limit for the loop index variable. It's possible to reset the value of the loop index variable inside the loop, however. This is not something you should do in most cases; rather, it's an error you should watch out for. If, for instance, you have a loop that never seems to quit, you might check to see if you've accidentally reset the loop index variable inside the loop, preventing it from reaching its final value.

Names Again

The "computer rules" program uses *Start%* as the lower limit of the loop. Although you might be tempted to use *Stop%* or *End%* as the upper limit, you can't. Both STOP and END are QuickBASIC keywords and thus can't be used as variable names, even with a numeric type suffix. *Stopp* and *Endd* are fine, however. Speaking of names, you can't use *Name%* as a variable name either, because NAME is also a keyword. Oddly enough, you can use keywords with the string suffix; *End$* and *Name$* are acceptable variable names.

Taking Another Step

Another feature of the FOR loop allows you to increase the loop index variable by a value other than 1. The FOR statement has an optional STEP clause that lets you specify how the loop index variable is to be changed in each loop cycle. In the following program, we add this feature to the squaring program shown earlier in the chapter so that it prints out the squares of even numbers only:

```
FOR I% = 2 TO 10 STEP 2
    PRINT I%; "squared is"; I% * I%
NEXT I%
PRINT "After loop, I% ="; I%
END
```

The loop increases the value of *I%* by 2 in each cycle. Here is the output:

```
 2 squared is 4
 4 squared is 16
 6 squared is 36
 8 squared is 64
 10 squared is 100
After loop, I% = 12
```

What happens if your step size makes you miss the stop value for the loop? For instance, suppose you set up a loop of the following type:

```
FOR I% = 1 TO 11 STEP 3
    PRINT I%
NEXT I%
PRINT "After loop ends, I% is"; I%
END
```

Let's look at the output:

```
 1
 4
 7
 10
After loop ends, I% is 13
```

The loop quits when *I%* exceeds the loop limit.

Counting Backward

Suppose you want a loop to count backward. A loop of this form won't work:

```
FOR Count% = 5 TO 0        ' Does not loop
    PRINT Count%
NEXT Count%
```

Although this code is perfectly valid, QuickBASIC will skip over the loop entirely. The stop value for this loop is 0. Because the loop index variable, which initially is 5, exceeds the stop value, the loop terminates without executing even once. To avoid this problem, use a negative value for the step size. This causes the loop to terminate only when the loop index variable is less than the stop value:

```
CLS
' Exam day in Indianapolis
FOR Index% = 5 TO 0 STEP -1
    PRINT Index%; "!..."
NEXT Index%
PRINT "Gentlepersons, start your minds."
END
```

Here is the output:

```
 5 !...
 4 !...
 3 !...
 2 !...
 1 !...
 0 !...
Gentlepersons, start your minds.
```

Loop Index Variables and Types

You might have noticed that we've used the integer type for loop index variables. Although QuickBASIC also allows you to use long integer, single-precision, and double-precision types, you should use the integer type when possible. It requires the least amount of memory, and, more important, integers can be processed much more rapidly and efficiently than the other types.

Despite being slower, the single-precision type is handy if you need a loop that takes fractional steps. Suppose you want to construct a table that converts multiples of tenths of miles to kilometers. You can use a single-precision index and a step size of 0.1, as shown in the following program:

```
CONST milesToKm = 1.609344
PRINT "Miles", "Kilometers"
FOR Miles! = .1 TO 1! STEP .1
    PRINT Miles!, milesToKm * Miles!
NEXT Miles!
END
```

We typed *1.0* for the upper limit, but the QuickBASIC editor converts 1.0 to 1!. Here is the output:

```
Miles          Kilometers
 .1             .1609344
 .2             .3218688
 .3             .4828032
 .4             .6437376
 .5             .804672
 .6             .9656065
 .7             1.126541
 .8000001       1.287475
 .9000001       1.44841
```

This program also illustrates the rounding problems commonly encountered with noninteger types. Because 0.1 isn't a power of 2 or a combination of powers of 2, it can't be represented exactly as a single-precision binary value. After adding 0.1 to the index a few times, we get a value that is slightly off. At the end of the ninth cycle, *Miles!* becomes 1.000001. This value is larger than the loop limit of 1.000000, causing the loop to terminate.

To solve this problem, choose a slightly larger upper limit, such as 1.01. You can also use the PRINT USING statement to print only three or four digits for each value. Another approach is to use an integer index and a little arithmetic:

```
CONST milesToKm = 1.609344
PRINT "Miles          Kilometers"
FOR Miles% = 1 TO 10
    PRINT Miles% / 10, milesToKm * Miles% / 10
NEXT Miles%
END
```

Here is the output for this version:

```
Miles          Kilometers
 .1             .1609344
 .2             .3218688
 .3             .4828032
 .4             .6437376
 .5             .804672
 .6             .9656064
 .7             1.126541
 .8             1.287475
 .9             1.44841
 1              1.609344
```

In short, single-precision indexes are a programming convenience, but they are slower and less predictable than integers. If a program is designed to be used heavily, you might want to convert to integer indexes.

Nested Loops

Loops can be used together in a form called a *nested* loop. One loop, called the *outer* loop, contains a second loop, called the *inner* loop. For each cycle of the outer loop, the inner loop executes a complete set of cycles. Let's look at an example:

```
CLS
FOR N% = 1 TO 3                         ' Outer loop starts
    PRINT "Outer loop: N% ="; N%
    FOR M% = 1 TO 4                     ' Inner loop starts
        PRINT "    Inner loop: M% ="; M%
    NEXT M%                             ' Inner loop ends
    PRINT
NEXT N%                                 ' Outer loop ends
END
```

Here is the output:

```
Outer loop: N% = 1
    Inner loop: M% = 1
    Inner loop: M% = 2
    Inner loop: M% = 3
    Inner loop: M% = 4

Outer loop: N% = 2
    Inner loop: M% = 1
    Inner loop: M% = 2
    Inner loop: M% = 3
    Inner loop: M% = 4

Outer loop: N% = 3
    Inner loop: M% = 1
    Inner loop: M% = 2
    Inner loop: M% = 3
    Inner loop: M% = 4
```

Each cycle of the outer loop begins by printing the current value for *N%*. Next the inner loop kicks in. It executes all its cycles, printing the value of *M%* each time. When the inner loop terminates, program control returns to the outer loop and to the final PRINT statement, which simply prints a blank line. That completes one cycle for the outer loop. Each single cycle of the outer loop includes a complete run of the inner loop.

You can have the two loops interact by letting the outer loop change the limits of the inner loop so that the inner loop changes with each cycle of the outer loop:

```
CLS
FOR N% = 1 TO 8
    FOR M% = 1 TO N%            'Make inner loop depend on outer
        PRINT "Hello! ";
    NEXT M%
    PRINT
NEXT N%
END
```

Here is the output:

```
Hello!
Hello! Hello!
Hello! Hello! Hello!
Hello! Hello! Hello! Hello!
Hello! Hello! Hello! Hello! Hello!
Hello! Hello! Hello! Hello! Hello! Hello!
Hello! Hello! Hello! Hello! Hello! Hello! Hello!
Hello! Hello! Hello! Hello! Hello! Hello! Hello! Hello!
```

The first time through the outer loop, the loop variable *N%* has the value 1, which gives the inner loop these limits:

```
FOR M% = 1 TO 1
```

As a result, *Hello!* is printed only once. The second time through the outer loop, *N%* has the value 2, and the inner loop prints *Hello!* twice on the same line. This continues until the inner loop prints *Hello!* eight times during the eighth cycle of the outer loop.

Decisions, Decisions: The IF Statement

When running a FOR loop, QuickBASIC must decide whether to run another loop cycle or quit. It does so by comparing the current value of the loop variable to the stop value. This decision making takes place behind the scenes, but QuickBASIC lets you make similar decisions explicitly in your programs.

The IF statement is QuickBASIC's decision maker. It comes in two forms: the one-line and the block.

The one-line form has the following syntax:

```
IF testcondition THEN statement
```

If *testcondition* is true, *statement* is executed. Otherwise, *statement* is skipped. Typically, *testcondition* is a relational expression; however, any expression that evaluates to 0 is false, and any nonzero expression is true.

The block form has the following syntax:

```
IF testcondition THEN
    statementblock
END IF
```

If *testcondition* is true, the statements in *statementblock* between THEN and END IF are executed. Otherwise, they are skipped.

Let's look at an example:

```
CLS
FOR Kids% = 1 TO 3
    PRINT "Kids% is"; Kids%
    IF Kids% = 2 THEN PRINT "Twins!"
    IF Kids% = 3 THEN
        PRINT "Triplets!"
    END IF
NEXT Kids%
END
```

Here is the output:

```
Kids% is 1
Kids% is 2
Twins!
Kids% is 3
Triplets!
```

The loop sets *Kids%* to three different values. The one-line IF statement prints *Twins!* only when *Kids%* has the value 2, and the block IF statement prints *Triplets!* only when *Kids%* has the value 3.

Figure 4-2 shows a flowchart for the simple block form of the IF statement.

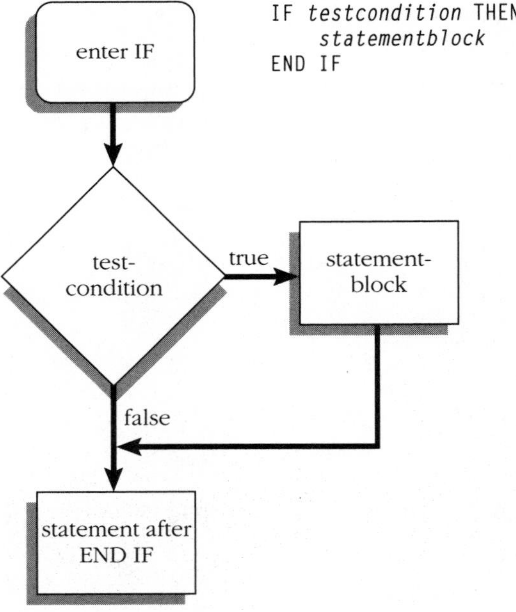

Figure 4-2.
IF/THEN flowchart.

Relational Expressions

In the previous example, the test condition *Kids% = 2* is a *relational expression*—an expression that compares quantities. This expression is true if *Kids%* has the value 2. Relational expressions are an important part of using IF statements.

Our example used the *relational equality operator* (=). An expression using this operator is true if the value to the left of the operator equals the value to the right. Note that QuickBASIC uses the equal sign for two operations: *relational equality* and *assignment*. Consider these statements:

```
X = 3
Name$ = "Poe"
```

Here the equal sign is used as the assignment operator, assigning values to *X* and *Name$*. Now consider these statements:

```
IF X = 3 THEN PRINT "You are wrong."
IF Name$ = "Poe" THEN PRINT "Nevermore."
```

Here the equal sign is used as the relational operator to compare values. QuickBASIC checks to see whether the conditions *X = 3* and *Name$ = "Poe"* are true or false. (QuickBASIC uses the context to tell which meaning of the equal sign is required.)

QuickBASIC has six relational operators, as shown in Figure 4-3. Any of them can be used as part of the test condition in an IF statement. They can be used to compare numbers or to compare strings.

Operator	***Test***	***Example***	***True If***
=	Equal to	X = 5	X equals 5
<>	Not equal to	X <> 5	X does not equal 5
<	Less than	X < 5	X is less than 5
>	Greater than	X > 5	X is greater than 5
<=	Less than or equal to	X <= 5	X is less than or equal to 5
>=	Greater than or equal to	X >= 5	X is greater than or equal to 5

Figure 4-3.
Relational operators.

Relational expressions are a special case of *Boolean expressions*—expressions that evaluate to true or false. They are named after the English mathematician George Boole, who developed a way to express logical relationships with mathematics. Every IF statement uses a Boolean expression to test its validity in order to determine whether or not to execute the subsequent statements. We'll take a closer look at Boolean expressions and at how QuickBASIC represents true and false later in this chapter.

Using ELSE

IF identifies statements to be executed only if a test condition is true. By using ELSE, you can identify statements to be executed only if the same test condition is false.

The full IF statement has two syntax forms. The first uses only one line:

```
IF testcondition THEN statement1 ELSE statement2
```

If *testcondition* is true, *statement1* is executed. Otherwise, *statement2* is executed. Typically, *testcondition* is a relational expression; however, any expression that evaluates to 0 is false, and any expression that evaluates to a nonzero value is true.

The block form has this syntax:

```
IF testcondition THEN
    statementblock1
ELSE
    statementblock2
END IF
```

If *testcondition* is true, the statements between THEN and ELSE are executed. Otherwise, those statements are skipped, and the statements between ELSE and END IF are executed.

Listing 4-1 provides an example of the one-line form. The program asks you to guess a number; it then uses IF to respond with *Right!* or *Wrong!*. It also uses an IF statement to decide whether to prompt you for a new response.

Integer and Noninteger Comparisons

Comparisons work better with integers than with single-precision or double-precision values. The integer 5 is exactly 5, for example, whereas a single-precision 5 might actually be represented as 4.999999. Calculations can also produce slight errors because of precision limitations. Here is an example:

```
A! = 1 / 3
IF 3 * A! = 1 THEN PRINT "equals 1" ELSE PRINT "isn't 1"
END
```

When you run this program, it prints *isn't 1*. If you print the value of *A!*, you'll find that it is 0.3333333. And although the expression $3 \times \frac{1}{3}$ evaluates to 1, the expression *3 × A!* evaluates to 0.9999999.

```
CLS
INPUT "I have a secret number. Guess it! ", Num%
FOR N% = 3 TO 19 STEP 4
    IF Num% = N% THEN PRINT "Right!" ELSE PRINT "Wrong!"
    IF N% < 19 THEN
        INPUT "I have a new secret number. Guess it! ", Num%
    END IF
NEXT N%
PRINT "I'm bored. Bye."
END
```

Listing 4-1.

Here is a sample run:

```
I have a secret number. Guess it! 7
Wrong!
I have a new secret number. Guess it! 7
Right!
I have a new secret number. Guess it! 4
Wrong!
I have a new secret number. Guess it! 10
Wrong!
I have a new secret number. Guess it! 19
Right!
I'm bored. Bye.
```

We used the one-line form of IF here, but it is often difficult to fit both alternatives on the same line on the screen. Thus, the block form is usually a better choice. For example, we could create a more informative response if we replaced the one-line IF/THEN/ELSE with this block:

```
IF Num% = N% THEN
    PRINT "You are absolutely correct!"
ELSE
    PRINT  "Wrong! It was"; N%
END IF
```

With the block form, all statements between THEN and ELSE are executed if the test expression is true, and all statements between ELSE and END IF are executed if the test expression is false (Figure 4-4).

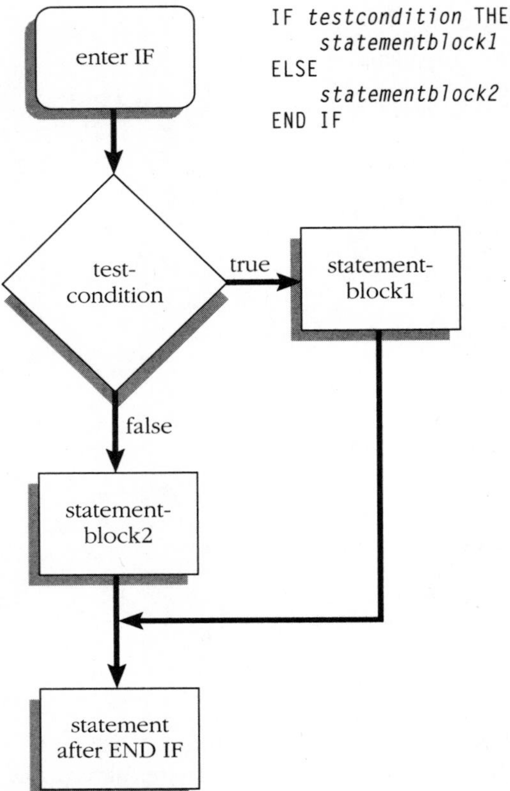

Figure 4-4.
IF/THEN/ELSE flowchart.

On to ELSEIF

The one-line form of IF limits you to two choices, but you can use ELSEIF with the block form to offer additional choices. For example, suppose Pattie Pocatello sells potatoes for 20 cents a pound for the first 200 pounds, 15 cents a pound for the next 300 pounds, and 10 cents a pound for any quantity greater than 500 pounds. She asks you to write a program to calculate the total charge for a potato purchase. The program must select from among three different methods of calculation, depending on the total amount of potatoes purchased. As Listing 4-2 shows, ELSEIF can be used to solve that problem.

```
CONST format$ = "#### pounds of potatoes will be $$###.##."
' The first 200 pounds cost $40. The first 500 pounds are $85.
CLS
PRINT "Welcome to Pattie's Potato Palace."
INPUT "How many pounds of potatoes do you want? ", Taters!

IF Taters! < 200 THEN
    Charge! = .2 * Taters!
ELSEIF Taters! < 500 THEN
    Charge! = 40! + .15 * (Taters! - 200)
ELSE
    Charge! = 85! + .1 * (Taters! - 500)
END IF

PRINT USING format$; Taters!; Charge!
PRINT "Please come again."
END
```

Listing 4-2.

Here is a sample run:

```
Welcome to Pattie's Potato Palace.
How many pounds of potatoes do you want? 400
 400 pounds of potatoes will be   $70.00.
Please come again.
```

The IF/THEN/ELSEIF/ELSE sequence used in this program presents an easy-to-read list of choices. Here's how it works: If *Taters!* is less than 200, the program calculates the charge using a rate of 0.20 and then skips to the first statement following the END IF line.

But if *Taters!* is not less than 200, the program goes to the ELSEIF test condition. If the ELSEIF test (*Taters!* less than 500) is true, then you (and the program) know that the purchase is in the range of 200 to 500 pounds. In that case, the program uses the second formula to calculate the charge.

If the second test also is false, *Taters!* is equal to or greater than 500, and the program uses the third formula to calculate the charge.

In our example, ELSE acts as a catchall. If none of the preceding tests are true, the statements following ELSE are executed. You can omit ELSE, however, to ensure that the total cost is calculated only if one of the tests is true.

The DO Statement

The DO loop combines elements of the FOR loop and the IF statement. Instead of cycling for a fixed number of times, as a FOR loop does, the DO loop uses a test condition to determine when to quit.

The DO loop has four variants:

- DO/LOOP UNTIL
- DO UNTIL/LOOP
- DO/LOOP WHILE
- DO WHILE/LOOP

DO/LOOP UNTIL

The DO/LOOP UNTIL statement has the following syntax:

```
DO
    statementblock
LOOP UNTIL testcondition
```

A program first executes *statementblock* and then evaluates *testcondition*. If *test-condition* is true, the loop terminates. Otherwise, the program repeats this cycle.

To ensure that the loop eventually terminates, your program must alter the test condition. Consider this example:

```
Counter% = 0
DO
    PRINT "Salutations, oxygen-breather!"
    Counter% = Counter% + 1
LOOP UNTIL Counter% = 3
END
```

Here is the output:

```
Salutations, oxygen-breather!
Salutations, oxygen-breather!
Salutations, oxygen-breather!
```

The variable *Counter%* is increased by 1 in each cycle, and the loop keeps cycling until *Counter%* reaches the value 3.

Let's use this loop to improve the guessing game shown in Listing 4-1 so that it lets you guess until you get the right answer. Also, by using an IF statement, we'll have the program in Listing 4-3 give hints.

```
Secret% = 22
CLS
INPUT "I have a secret number. Guess it! ", Num%
DO
    IF Num% < Secret% THEN
        INPUT "Too low--try again. ", Num%
    ELSEIF Num% > Secret% THEN
        INPUT "Too high--try again. ", Num%
    END IF
LOOP UNTIL Num% = Secret%
PRINT "You got it!"
END
```

Listing 4-3.

Here is a sample run:

```
I have a secret number. Guess it! 7
Too low--try again. 36
Too high--try again. 16
Too low--try again. 25
Too high--try again. 21
Too low--try again. 22
You got it!
```

DO/LOOP UNTIL is a *conditional* loop because it uses a test condition to determine when to stop. Specifically, it's called an *exit-condition* loop because testing occurs at the exit end of the loop, after the loop statements have been executed. An exit-condition loop always cycles at least once.

DO UNTIL/LOOP

The DO statement also has an *entry-condition* form, DO UNTIL/LOOP, in which the test is performed before the loop starts. If the initial test is false, the loop is not entered. To make an entry-condition loop, simply move the test to the DO line, as shown in Listing 4-4.

```
Top% = 1234
CLS
PRINT "I divide"; Top%; "by your input."
INPUT "Enter a number: ", Num%
DO UNTIL Num% = 0                ' Can't enter loop if Num% is 0
    PRINT Top%; "divided by"; Num%; "is"; Top% / Num%
    INPUT "Enter next number (0 to terminate): ", Num%
LOOP
PRINT "Bye."
END
```

Listing 4-4.

Here is a sample run:

```
I divide 1234 by your input.
Enter a number: 0
Bye.
```

The test condition is examined before the loop is entered. Because the first number entered is 0, the loop is not started. (QuickBASIC would produce a runtime error message if you tried to divide by 0.)

This example also illustrates a common construction for entry-condition loops, in which testing occurs immediately after each input. Generalized, the construction looks like this:

```
get first input
DO UNTIL test
    statementblock
    get next input
LOOP
```

Figures 4-5 and 4-6 show flowcharts for these conditional loops.

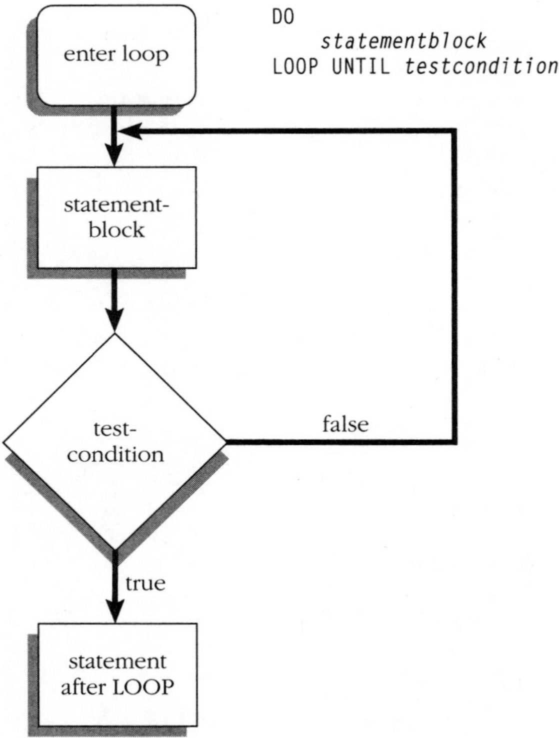

Figure 4-5.
DO/LOOP UNTIL flowchart.

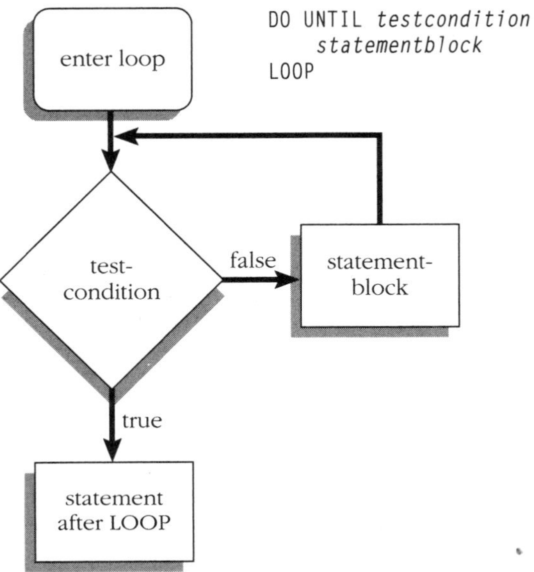

Figure 4-6.
DO UNTIL/LOOP flowchart.

WHILE with a DO Loop

For both the exit-condition and entry-condition DO loops, you can use the keyword WHILE instead of UNTIL. As the terms suggest, using WHILE causes a loop to continue as long as the test condition remains true, and using UNTIL causes a loop to continue as long as the test condition remains false. You can substitute one for the other merely by changing the test condition to the logical opposite. For instance, you can use the line

```
DO WHILE Num% <> 0
```

instead of this line:

```
DO UNTIL Num% = 0
```

The flowcharts for the WHILE forms are the same as the charts for the UNTIL forms except that the positions of the true and false branches are reversed.

Conditional Loops and INKEY$

The keyboard input statements we've used so far require that you press the Enter key to transmit your input to the program; that is, the program pauses until you enter something. INKEY$, however, is different.

INKEY$ is a *function*—a programming unit that produces a value and *returns* the value to a program. For instance, the hypothetical function name *GoFish%* can be used as follows:

```
X% = GoFish%
```

This statement *calls* the *GoFish%* function. The function then comes up with a value, which is returned to the program and assigned to the integer variable *X%*. Functions use the same name conventions as variables do; the name *GoFish%* means that this function returns an integer.

The INKEY$ function, as the $ suffix indicates, returns a string. If you press a key before the function is executed, INKEY$ returns the key as a string; for example, if you press the B key, INKEY$ returns the string *b*. But if no key has been pressed, INKEY$ returns the null string, and the program moves to the next statement. The INKEY$ function does not cause the program to pause. This feature is useful when you want the program to keep running until you press a key, as shown in Listing 4-5.

```
Count% = 1
CLS
PRINT "Press any key to terminate."
DO
    PRINT TAB(Count% MOD 50);
    PRINT "Lassie loves Spuds."
    Count% = Count% + 1
    Key$ = INKEY$
LOOP WHILE Key$ = ""
PRINT "Program terminated by the "; Key$; " key."
END
```

Listing 4-5.

Here is a sample run:

```
Press any key to terminate.
Lassie loves Spuds.
 Lassie loves Spuds.
  Lassie loves Spuds.
   Lassie loves Spuds.
    Lassie loves Spuds.
     Lassie loves Spuds.
Program terminated by the q key.
```

The loop kept cycling until we pressed the Q key. Note that INKEY$ does not *echo* the keystroke—that is, it does not show the keystroke on the screen. Non-echoing input functions such as INKEY$ send the keystroke to the program but don't show it on the screen.

Often a program simply needs to know whether any key has been pressed; the specific key is not important. In such cases, you can replace the final two lines of the loop with a single line:

```
LOOP WHILE INKEY$ = ""
```

Here you don't save the actual keystroke value. You can think of INKEY$ as being replaced by its return value.

The EXIT DO and EXIT FOR Statements

If you need to terminate a loop in the middle of a cycle, the EXIT DO and EXIT FOR statements are useful. As the names suggest, an EXIT DO statement terminates a DO loop, and an EXIT FOR statement terminates a FOR loop. Execution continues with the next statement following the loop. Listing 4-6 shows an example.

```
Format$ = "& & qualifies for our special offer."
CLS
PRINT "Enter a blank line to terminate this program."
LINE INPUT "Enter a first name: "; FirstName$
DO WHILE FirstName$ <> ""
    LINE INPUT "Enter a last name: "; LastName$
    IF LastName$ = "" THEN EXIT DO
    PRINT USING Format$; FirstName$; LastName$
    LINE INPUT "Enter a first name: "; FirstName$
LOOP
PRINT "Goodbye for now."
END
```

Listing 4-6.

If you respond to the first LINE INPUT prompt by pressing only the Enter key, the DO test terminates the loop. If you enter a first name but respond to the second prompt by pressing only the Enter key, the IF statement detects the empty string and uses the EXIT DO statement to terminate the loop. Here is a sample run:

```
Enter a blank line to terminate this program.
Enter a first name: Ted
Enter a last name: Bright
Ted Bright qualifies for our special offer.
Enter a first name: Jay
Enter a last name: <Enter>
Goodbye for now.
```

If you use EXIT DO within a nested loop, it terminates only the innermost loop containing the statement. To exit the outer loop, you need an additional EXIT DO statement. Similarly, as shown in the following example, you need two EXIT FOR statements to exit both the inner and the outer FOR loops.

```
FOR I% = 1 TO 10
    FOR J% = 1 TO 15
        :
        IF Things$ = "Weird" THEN EXIT FOR
        :
    NEXT J%
    IF Things$ = "Weird" THEN EXIT FOR
    :
NEXT I%
```

The WHILE Loop

The DO loop family is the newest addition to QuickBASIC's repertoire of loops. It extends the capabilities of another relatively recent newcomer, the WHILE loop. This loop is equivalent to the DO WHILE/LOOP statement.

Here is the WHILE syntax:

```
WHILE testcondition
    statementblock
WEND
```

The loop first examines the *testcondition* expression. If it is true (nonzero), the statements between WHILE and WEND are executed. Then *testcondition* is tested again, and, if it is still true, the statements are executed again. This continues until *testcondition* becomes false (0). At that point, execution passes to the statement following the loop.

We can rewrite Listing 4-4 to use WHILE, as shown here in Listing 4-7.

```
Top% = 1234
CLS
PRINT "I divide"; Top%; "by your input."
INPUT "Enter a number: ", Num%
WHILE Num% <> 0
    PRINT Top%; "divided by"; Num%; "is"; Top% / Num%
    INPUT "Enter next number (0 to terminate): ", Num%
WEND
PRINT "Bye."
END
```

Listing 4-7.

The WHILE line marks the beginning of the loop, and the WEND line marks the end. With a WHILE loop, the test condition must come first. You cannot use UNTIL instead of WHILE. Also, there is no EXIT statement for the WHILE loop. Because the DO loop does everything the WHILE loop can, plus a little more, we won't use WHILE in this book, although you might see this form elsewhere.

Boolean Expressions

Let's take a longer look at Boolean (true/false) expressions. You've already seen one form: the relational expression, in which two quantities are compared. QuickBASIC also has Boolean functions, which return a value of true or false when called. And the *logical operators* in QuickBASIC allow you to construct more elaborate tests that can, for example, evaluate two conditions simultaneously.

A Boolean Function: EOF

In Chapter 3 we developed a program that stored two lines of information in a file and then read the file. By using conditional loops, however, you can store and read any number of lines.

Consider reading input from the keyboard. You can use a DO loop to keep reading lines until you press a specific key, such as Enter, to terminate the loop:

```
LINE INPUT "Enter name: ", Name$                ' Get name
DO WHILE Name$ <> ""
    LINE INPUT "Enter phone number: "; Phone$ ' Get phone
    PRINT #1, USING Format$; Name$; Phone$    ' Save in file
    LINE INPUT "Enter next name: ", Name$     ' Next person
LOOP
```

The loop continues as long as you enter names in response to the name prompt. But if you press Enter without entering a name, LINE INPUT places a null string in *Name$*, and the loop ends. Because the program reads the first name before starting the loop, the loop is bypassed entirely if your first response is to press Enter.

You can also have a loop terminate when the program, reading from a file, reaches the end of the file. The QuickBASIC EOF (end-of-file) function returns a Boolean value of true if the program has reached the end of the file and false if it has not. To identify the file, use the file identification number from the OPEN statement. For example, if the file number is 1, you can do the following:

```
DO UNTIL EOF(1)
    LINE INPUT #1, Info$
    PRINT Info$
LOOP
```

This program fragment reads lines from a file and displays them on the screen until the end of the file is reached. The file number 1 used with EOF tells the EOF function which file to check.

Note that an entry-condition loop is used for file input. It is always important to check for the end of a file *before* reading the file. With an exit-condition loop, the program tries to read the file before checking for the end; if the file is empty, the program could crash trying to read nonexistent data. An entry-condition loop is used to read keyboard input for the same reason.

Listing 4-8 combines the keyboard-input loop with the file-reading loop. We'll use APPEND mode for the file, which causes the program to add lines to the existing contents of the file. (Using OUTPUT mode, you recall, overwrites the original contents—that is, the file is wiped clean before new data is added.)

```
CONST format$ = "Name: &; Phone Number: &"
CLS
OPEN "NAMES" FOR APPEND AS #1  ' Open file to add information
PRINT "This program stores names and phone numbers. To quit,"
PRINT "press Enter without entering a name."
LINE INPUT "Enter name: ", Name$
DO WHILE Name$ <> ""
    LINE INPUT "Enter phone number: "; Phone$
    IF Phone$ = "" THEN EXIT DO
    PRINT #1, USING format$; Name$; Phone$
    LINE INPUT "Enter next name: ", Name$
LOOP
CLOSE #1

OPEN "NAMES" FOR INPUT AS #1   ' Open file to show contents
PRINT "Here are the current contents of the NAMES file:"
DO UNTIL EOF(1)
    LINE INPUT #1, Info$
    PRINT Info$
LOOP
PRINT "Bye."
END
```

Listing 4-8.

Here are two sample runs. Because we began without a NAMES file, the program creates the file the first time we use it.

```
This program stores names and phone numbers. To quit, press Enter
without entering a name.
Enter name: Artemis Anchovy
Enter phone number: 999 412-1212
Enter next name: Felicia Nalgene
Enter phone number: 000 428-9999, Ext. 123
Enter next name: <Enter>
Here are the current contents of the NAMES file:
Name: Artemis Anchovy; Phone Number: 999 412-1212
Name: Felicia Nalgene; Phone Number: 000 428-9999, Ext. 123
Bye.

This program stores names and phone numbers. To quit, press Enter
without entering a name.
Enter name: George Diddlebean
Enter phone number: 999 100-0001
Enter next name: Rhonda Fonda-Honda
Enter phone number: 001 975-5121
Enter next name: <Enter>
```

```
Here are the current contents of the NAMES file:
Name: Artemis Anchovy; Phone Number: 999 412-1212
Name: Felicia Nalgene; Phone Number: 000 428-9999, Ext. 123
Name: George Diddlebean; Phone Number: 999 100-0001
Name: Rhonda Fonda-Honda; Phone Number: 001 975-5121
Bye.
```

Note that APPEND mode causes the program to keep a cumulative record of entries in the NAMES file. Also note that by using the EOF function we can read the file without knowing in advance how many lines it contains.

Logical Operators

It's often useful or necessary to test more than one condition at a time. QuickBASIC's logical operators let you combine simple Boolean expressions, such as relational expressions and Boolean operators, into more complex Boolean operations.

QuickBASIC has six logical operators: OR, AND, NOT, XOR, EQV, and IMP. The first three are the most commonly used. Figure 4-7 summarizes the properties of all six.

Subexpression Values				
X	True	True	False	False
Y	True	False	True	False
Logical Expressions				
X OR Y	True	True	True	False
X AND Y	True	False	False	False
NOT X	False	False	True	True
X XOR Y	False	True	True	False
X EQV Y	True	False	False	True
X IMP Y	True	False	True	True

Figure 4-7.
Values produced by logical operators.

The OR Operator

Consider a simple game in which the user is given four chances to guess a secret word. We want a loop that quits after four cycles or after a correct guess. The logical OR operator lets you check for both conditions. Listing 4-9 shows how it works and how relational operators can be used with strings as well as with numbers.

```
Secret$ = "Duck"
CLS
Wrong% = 0
INPUT "Guess the secret word and win cash! ", Word$
DO UNTIL (Word$ = Secret$) OR (Wrong% = 4)    ' Two tests
    Wrong% = Wrong% + 1
    IF Wrong% < 4 THEN
        INPUT "Wrong! Guess again! ", Word$
    ELSE
        PRINT "I'm sorry; you've run out of guesses."
    END IF
LOOP
IF Word$ = Secret$ THEN PRINT "That's correct!"
Prize% = 100 - Wrong% * 25
PRINT USING "$$### is your prize."; Prize%
END
```

Listing 4-9.

Here are two sample runs:

```
Guess the secret word and win cash! fig
Wrong! Guess again! thalassotherapy
Wrong! Guess again! to
Wrong! Guess again! xylophonist
I'm sorry, you've run out of guesses.
   $0 is your prize.

Guess the secret word and win cash! dog
Wrong! Guess again! cynanthropy
Wrong! Guess again! duck
Wrong! Guess again! Duck
That's correct!
  $25 is your prize.
```

The loop terminates after a correct guess or four incorrect guesses (whichever comes first), thanks to the OR operator in this line:

```
DO UNTIL (Word$ = Secret$) OR (Wrong% = 4)
```

Note that string comparisons take capitalization into account. That's why *duck* is rejected and *Duck* is accepted.

The OR operator combines two Boolean expressions into a single Boolean expression that is true if either of the original expressions is true (or if both happen to be true). Thus, the expression

```
(Word$ = Secret$) OR (Wrong% = 4)
```

is true if *Word$* equals *Secret$* or if *Wrong%* equals 4, as shown in Figure 4-8. (By the way, the first possibility shown in the figure—that both expressions are true—will never occur in this program because guesses are made only when *Wrong%* is less than 4.)

Word$ = Secret$	***Wrong% = 4***	***(Word$ = Secret$) OR (Wrong% = 4)***
True	True	True
True	False	True
False	True	True
False	False	False

Figure 4-8.
True/false values for an OR expression.

When the loop ends, this program needs to know the reason for the termination. The program uses an IF statement to check the value of *Word$*. If the loop terminated because the user guessed correctly, this statement prints an acknowledgment.

The AND Operator

The AND operator combines two Boolean expressions into a single expression that is true if and only if *both* of the original expressions are true (unlike the OR operator, whose combined expression is true if *either* of the original expressions is true). The AND operator narrows down possibilities—limiting a number to a certain range, for example. The following program fragment prints its message only if *Age%* is in the range 13 through 19:

```
IF (Age% > 12) AND (Age% < 20) THEN
    PRINT "So you're a teenager!"
END IF
```

Or suppose you want a loop to run as long as there are 20 or fewer entries and as long as each entry is less than 100:

```
Count% = 0
INPUT "First number: ", Num!
Count% = Count% + 1
DO WHILE (Count% < 20) AND (Num! < 100)
    ⋮
    Count% = Count% + 1
    INPUT "Next number: ", Num!
LOOP
```

Because the DO loop allows you to use WHILE or UNTIL, you can often use either OR or AND to state the same condition. We can replace the previous example with the following:

```
Count% = 0
INPUT "First number: ", Num!
Count% = Count% + 1
DO UNTIL (Count% >= 20) OR (Num! >= 100)
    ⋮
    Count% = Count% + 1
    INPUT "Next number: ", Num!
LOOP
```

In the new version, we replaced AND with OR and WHILE with UNTIL, and we reversed the sense of each comparison.

The NOT Operator

The NOT operator negates a Boolean expression, changing true to false and false to true. For instance,

```
IF NOT EOF(1) THEN statement
```

causes the program to execute *statement* if the end of the file has not been encountered.

The XOR Operator

The XOR (exclusive or) operator also combines two Boolean expressions into one. The result is true if one or the other expression is true but not if both are true. For example, the following program fragment prints its message if *TimeLapse%* exceeds 2 or if *IdNum%* is less than 12010 but not if both conditions are true:

```
IF (TimeLapse% > 2) XOR (IdNum% < 12010) THEN
    PRINT "You are eligible for a promotion."
END IF
```

The OR operator, in contrast, prints the message even if both expressions are true. As its name suggests, the exclusive XOR operator excludes more instances than the regular OR operator does.

The EQV and IMP Operators

The EQV (equivalence) operator combines two Boolean expressions into a single expression. The result is true if both expressions are true or if both are false. Otherwise, the result is false.

The IMP (implication) operator also combines two Boolean expressions into a single expression. The result is false only if the first expression is true and the second expression is false. Otherwise, the result is true.

The Value of Truth

Computers know about numbers, but what do they know about truth? QuickBASIC represents true and false numerically, as shown here:

```
PRINT "The value of TRUE is "; 2 + 2 = 4  ' A true expression
PRINT "The value of FALSE is "; 3 = 5     ' A false expression
END
```

Here is the output:

```
The value of TRUE is -1
The value of FALSE is  0
```

Because relational expressions have numeric values, you can use numbers instead of relational expressions as test conditions, as shown here:

```
FOR X% = -4 TO 4
    IF X% THEN
        PRINT X%; "is true."
    ELSE
        PRINT X%; "is false."
    END IF
NEXT X%
END
```

Here is the output:

```
-4 is true.
-3 is true.
-2 is true.
-1 is true.
 0 is false.
 1 is true.
 2 is true.
 3 is true.
 4 is true.
```

QuickBASIC treats 0 as false and all other numeric values as true. In most cases, you needn't be concerned with this numeric representation of true and false. You should know, however, that the six logical operators can be used with any integer values, not only with Boolean expressions. Indeed, programmers use the logical operators to manipulate individual bits in a value, which is sometimes necessary when controlling hardware devices. We'll look at this topic in later chapters.

Some programmers also use shortcuts based on the numeric equivalents of true and false. For instance, the statement

```
IF Num% <> 0 THEN statement
```

can be replaced with this statement:

```
IF Num% THEN statement
```

If *Num%* is 4, then the expression *Num% <> 0* is true and hence nonzero. But so is *Num%* itself. Similarly, if *Num%* is 0, then *Num%* and the expression *Num% <> 0* are both false and are both equal to 0.

Operator Precedence

QuickBASIC operator precedence is designed to minimize the need for parentheses in grouping expressions. For instance, the arithmetic operators have higher precedence than the relational operators. You can use a line such as

```
IF 2 * X > Y + 5 THEN PRINT "OK"
```

rather than the following:

```
IF (2 * X) > (Y + 5) THEN PRINT "OK"
```

Both statements carry out the arithmetic operations before comparing results. However, the latter is clearer, especially if you also program in languages having a different order of precedence.

Similarly, the relational operators have higher precedence than the logical operators. Thus, each relational expression is evaluated before the results are combined using AND. For example, this line

```
IF Answer$ = "Fillmore" AND Tries% < 4 THEN PRINT "Correct!"
```

means the following:

```
IF (Answer$ = "Fillmore") AND (Tries% < 4) THEN PRINT "Correct!"
```

Figure 4-9 summarizes the precedence of QuickBASIC operators, from high to low.

Operation	***Operator***
Exponentiation	^
Negation	–
Multiplication and division	* /
Integer division	\
Modulo arithmetic	MOD
Addition and subtraction	+ –
Relational operators	= <> > >= < <=
Logical negation	NOT
Logical and	AND
Logical or	OR
Logical exclusive or	XOR
Logical equivalence	EQV
Logical implication	IMP

Figure 4-9.
QuickBASIC operator precedence.

The SELECT CASE Statement

QuickBASIC has another flexible statement to control program flow: the SELECT CASE statement, which lets a program choose a course of action from a list of alternatives. You provide an expression to evaluate and a list of possible values, which act as labels. QuickBASIC then takes you to the label (value) that matches the original expression.

Here is the syntax for the SELECT CASE statement:

```
SELECT CASE testexpression
    CASE labelexpression1
        [statementblock1]
    [CASE labelexpression2
        [statementblock2]]
    ⋮
    [CASE ELSE
        [statementblockn]]
END SELECT
```

testexpression is any expression, including a simple variable, that evaluates to a number or a string. Control goes to the CASE *labelexpression* that matches *testexpression*, and the subsequent *statementblock* is executed. The CASE ELSE *statementblock* is executed if no CASE *labelexpression* matches *testexpression*.

labelexpression must be one of the following:

- A single value, such as `5` or `"Iowa"` or `X% + Y%`
- A comma-separated list of values, such as `"Q", "q"`
- A range, such as `10 TO 30`
- A relational operator followed by an expression; the keyword IS precedes the operator, as in `IS >= 31`

The program in Listing 4-10 illustrates the SELECT CASE statement.

```
CLS
PRINT "This is Auntie Zelda's Famous Advice Program."
DO
    PRINT "Enter the letter corresponding to your choice."
    PRINT "B. Business Advice            R. Romantic Advice"
    PRINT "T. Tennis Advice              G. General Advice"
    PRINT "Q. Quit"
    LINE INPUT Choice$
    SELECT CASE Choice$
        CASE "B"
            PRINT "Buy low, sell high."
        CASE "R"
            PRINT "Try a little tenderness."
        CASE "T"
            PRINT "Watch the ball."
        CASE "G"
            PRINT "Do unto others as you would have them ";
            PRINT "do unto you."
        CASE "Q", "q"
            PRINT "Bye!"
```

Listing 4-10. *(continued)*

Listing 4-10. *continued*

```
        CASE "a" TO "z"          'A range of choices
            PRINT "Please use uppercase letters."
        CASE ELSE                'If no other match is found
            PRINT "Please enter B, R, T, G, or Q."
    END SELECT
LOOP UNTIL Choice$ = "Q" OR Choice$ = "q"
END
```

Here is a sample run:

```
This is Auntie Zelda's Famous Advice Program.
Enter the letter corresponding to your choice.
B. Business Advice          R. Romantic Advice
T. Tennis Advice            G. General Advice
Q. Quit
3
Please enter B, R, T, G, or Q.
Enter the letter corresponding to your choice.
B. Business Advice          R. Romantic Advice
T. Tennis Advice            G. General Advice
Q. Quit
r
Please use uppercase letters.
Enter the letter corresponding to your choice.
B. Business Advice          R. Romantic Advice
T. Tennis Advice            G. General Advice
Q. Quit
R
Try a little tenderness.
Enter the letter corresponding to your choice.
B. Business Advice          R. Romantic Advice
T. Tennis Advice            G. General Advice
Q. Quit
Q
Bye!
```

The following line identifies *Choice$* (the string you type before pressing Enter) as the expression to be evaluated:

```
SELECT CASE Choice$
```

When you enter your response, QuickBASIC scans the list of CASE choices to find the one that matches *Choice$*. This line shows a label used to match *Choice$*:

```
CASE "R"
```

If *Choice$* contains the string *R*, the block of statements following the *CASE "R"* label is executed. A block extends from one CASE to the next or to the *END SELECT* line, whichever comes first.

This special label marks the block of statements to be executed if none of the other CASE labels matches *Choice$*:

```
CASE ELSE
```

You can omit *CASE ELSE*, but it is useful for catching unexpected or unwanted responses.

CASE Varieties

The simplest form of the CASE expression is a single value, as in the following:

```
CASE "R"
```

This value can be a string or a number, and it must be the same type as the SELECT CASE test expression. The value can be a literal, a constant, a variable, or any other expression that reduces to a string or a number. Literals are used most frequently.

When you want to use more than one value to label a block of statements, you can provide a list of values. For example, the following lets you quit by entering either an uppercase or a lowercase Q:

```
CASE "Q", "q"
```

If you want to specify a consecutive set of values, you can identify a range by using TO. For instance, the following label matches all lowercase letters:

```
CASE "a" TO "z"
```

If you are using numeric values, you can indicate numeric ranges:

```
CASE 100 TO 199
```

The range must be in ascending order. If you want to specify values from –10 to –20, use the following:

```
CASE -20 TO -10
```

Even though its magnitude is greater, –20 is less than –10 in value.

You can use relational operators too. Suppose you want to indicate all values less than or equal to 50:

```
CASE IS <= 50
```

You can define overlapping cases so that more than one case matches the SELECT CASE test expression; in fact, you can even use the same label twice. But in these situations, only the first matching case is executed. For instance, in Listing 4-10, a *q* response matches both of the following:

```
CASE "Q", "q"
    PRINT "Bye!"
CASE "a" TO "z"        'A range of choices
    PRINT "Please use uppercase letters."
```

But when *q* is entered, only the *PRINT "Bye!"* statement, the first of the two matching cases, is executed.

You can often use either a SELECT CASE statement or an extended IF statement for the same purpose. In general, SELECT CASE is more efficient than IF when you have more than three alternatives.

The GOTO Statement

In its early days, BASIC required you to number every line. It had a weak IF statement—only one line and no ELSE. It had a FOR loop but no conditional loops. For cases in which we would now use an IF statement or a DO loop, BASIC programmers used the GOTO statement.

The form of the GOTO statement is simple:

```
GOTO line
```

line originally was a line number, although today it can be a line number or a line label (a name used to identify a line). A line number needs no special punctuation; for a line label, use *line:* (with a colon) for the label itself, but use *line* (no colon) in the GOTO statement. You can use line labels and GOTO to create the equivalent of a DO/WHILE LOOP structure, as shown here:

```
CLS
INPUT "Enter the word FISH to end the loop: ", Word$
StartLoop:                          'Example of a line label
    IF Word$ = "FISH" THEN GOTO LoopEnd
    PRINT Word$; " is not FISH!"
    INPUT "Try again: ", Word$
    GOTO StartLoop                  'No colon after label here
LoopEnd:
PRINT "Congratulations. You now know how to type FISH."
END
```

The following example shows how to mimic an IF/THEN/ELSE statement using line numbers:

```
100 LINE INPUT "What's your first name? ", FirstName$
110 IF FirstName$ > "M" THEN GOTO 140
120 PRINT FirstName$; " placed in Group 1"
130 GOTO 150
140 PRINT FirstName$; " placed in Group 2"
150 PRINT "Bye"
160 END
```

A DO loop or an IF statement is easier to read than multiple GOTO statements. A DO WHILE/LOOP construction, for instance, is clearly a conditional, entry-condition loop. But GOTO can be part of a loop, part of a choice-making structure, or something else altogether. If, for example, you place an IF/THEN/ELSE emulation inside a loop and then begin nesting IF statements and loops, a program using GOTO can become very difficult to read.

But the problems with the GOTO statement go beyond program readability. You can in fact do too much with these statements. Many early BASIC users programmed on the fly, using GOTO to leap back and forth across program code. It was nearly impossible to follow this "spaghetti coding," and debugging and modifying code became frustrating and difficult. In reaction, computer scientists developed a much more disciplined style of programming, using only a few well-defined program structures. If you limit yourself to these structures, your programs will be more reliable, easier to debug, and easier to read.

Most of QuickBASIC's newer structures were added to facilitate this *structured programming*. Most modern programmers recommend using GOTO rarely if at all. Because this statement is essential to older BASIC programs, however, QuickBASIC supports it.

A Look at Debug

The QuickBASIC debugger, which is accessed through the Debug menu, is a useful tool for finding errors in your programs. Among its many talents, the debugger lets you run your program step by step while you monitor the values of variables.

The following program contains a simple error. Enter the program exactly as shown and run it. But be prepared to press Ctrl-Break.

```
CLS
I% = 0
DO WHILE I% < 5
    PRINT "Happy birthday to you!"
    I% = I + 1
LOOP
PRINT "And enjoy yourself!"
END
```

The intent is to execute the loop five times, but the output looks like this:

```
Happy birthday to you!
Happy birthday to you!
Happy birthday to you!
Happy birthday to you!
Happy birthday to you!
Happy birthday to you!
Happy birthday to you!
Happy birthday to you!
Happy birthday to you!
Happy birthday to you!
Happy birthday to you!
  ⋮
```

And so on. When you tire of the display, press Ctrl-Break. QuickBASIC will halt the program and return you to the editor.

Let's use Debug to monitor the value of *I%*, which controls the loop. Open the Debug menu and select Add Watch. A dialog box asks you to enter the expression to be added to the Watch window. Type *I%* and then press Enter to return to the editor. The Watch window will appear just below the menu bar. QuickBASIC is now set up to watch the value of *I%*.

Next restart the program by selecting Restart from the Run menu. The first program statement is highlighted, and *I%* in the Watch window is now followed by the value 0.

Now execute the program step by step by pressing the F8 key—each time you press the key, the program advances one step. QuickBASIC highlights each line just before it is executed. Continue until this line is highlighted:

```
I% = I + 1
```

The Watch window still reports that *I%* is 0. Press F8 to execute the statement, and move the highlight to the LOOP line. Now the Watch window shows that *I%* is 1.

If you press F4, you'll see that the first birthday greeting has been printed on the output screen. Press F4 again to return to the editor.

Continue pressing F8. The highlight returns to the DO statement, and the loop begins its second cycle. When you reach the LOOP line this time, *I%* is still 1. It didn't increase to 2, which indicates that the problem must be with this line:

```
I% = I + 1
```

Because we forgot to use the *%* suffix for the second *I*, QuickBASIC assumed that *I* was a new variable, which by default has the value 0. Thus our line doesn't increase *I%* by 1 in each loop; instead, it simply sets *I%* to 1 in each cycle. You can check this analysis by adding *I* to the Watch window, using the same method we used with *I%*. Or you can highlight the *I* variable and then select Add Watch from the Debug menu, which places the variable in the Watch window. If you do so, you'll see that the value of *I* is indeed 0.

The next step is to fix the code. Change *I* to *I%*, select Restart from the Run menu, and run the program again. Now it works correctly.

Review Questions

1. What does each of the following programs print?

a.
```
FOR I% = 1 TO 5
    PRINT I%;
NEXT I%
PRINT
PRINT I%
END
```

b.
```
FOR I% = 1 TO 5 STEP 2
    PRINT I%;
NEXT I%
PRINT
PRINT I%
END
```

c.
```
FOR I% = 1 TO 5 STEP 3
    PRINT I%;
NEXT I%
PRINT
PRINT I%
END
```

2. What does the following program print?

```
CLS
FOR N% = 4 TO 1 STEP -1
    FOR M% = 1 TO N%          ' Make inner loop depend on outer
        PRINT "Hello! ";
    NEXT M%
    PRINT
NEXT N%
END
```

3. What, if anything, is wrong with each of the following statements?

a. `IF X% = "House" PRINT "$200,000"`

b.
```
IF Funds < 100000 THEN
    PRINT "Insufficient funds."
    PRINT "See our loan officer."
```

4. Devise a loop that prints the following:

```
-3 -2 -1  1  2  3
```

5. Given the statements

```
LET X% = 5
LET Y% = 3
```

which of the following relational expressions are true?

a. `X% > Y%`

b. `X% >= 2 * Y% - 1`

c. `X% <> Y%`

d. `X% \ 2 + 1 > Y%`

6. Suppose *Age%* is a variable.

   a. Write a statement that prints *RAD* if *Age%* is less than 25 and that prints *VERY NICE* otherwise.

   b. Write a statement that prints *RAD* if *Age%* is less than 25, *GROOVY* if *Age%* is in the range 25 through 45, and *NEAT* otherwise.

7. a. What does the following program print?

```
N% = 1
DO UNTIL N% > 3
    PRINT "Loop #1 prints"; N%
    N% = N% + 1
LOOP
N% = 1
DO
    PRINT "Loop #2 prints"; N%
    N% = N% + 1
LOOP UNTIL N% > 3
END
```

   b. What does the program print if the two assignment statements that read

```
N% = 1
```

   are both changed to the following?

```
N% = 5
```

8. How do the WHILE forms and the UNTIL forms of the DO loop differ?

9. If 1 is established as a file identifier, which of the following loops are suitable for reading the file? Explain what is wrong with the faulty loops.

   a.
```
DO WHILE EOF(1)
    LINE INPUT #1, Stuff$
    PRINT Stuff$
LOOP
```

   b.
```
DO UNTIL EOF(1)
    LINE INPUT #1, Stuff$
    PRINT Stuff$
LOOP
```

   c.
```
DO WHILE NOT EOF(1)
    LINE INPUT #1 Stuff$
    PRINT Stuff$
LOOP
```

   d.
```
DO
    LINE INPUT #1, Stuff$
    PRINT Stuff$
LOOP UNTIL EOF(1)
```

10. Write code that prints *Hi!* for each of the following conditions:

    a. *Age* is greater than 40 and less than 60.

    b. *Age* is less than 40 or greater than 60.

    c. *Age* is not less than 70.

    d. *Height* is greater than 60 or *Weight* is greater than 150, but not both.

    e. *Age* is not equal to 35 and either *Weight* is greater than 200 or *Height* exceeds 72 (or both).

11. What is wrong with the syntax of the following program? What is wrong with the design?

```
CLS
PRINT "This is a program of sorts."
PRINT "Enter a number and see what happens."
DO
    INPUT Choice$
    SELECT CASE Choice$
        CASE 1
            PRINT "One partridge"
        CASE 2 - 4
            PRINT "Some birds"
        CASE 5, 6, 7
            PRINT "Five to seven swans"
        CASE 2 * 3
            PRINT "Two sets of triplets"
        ELSE
            PRINT Choice$; " is a reasonable response."
    END
LOOP UNTIL Choice$ = 10
END
```

5

Procedures and Subroutines

CALL	EXIT SUB	GOSUB/RETURN	VAL
DECLARE	FUNCTION	SUB	

BASIC began as the language anyone could use, accessible and straightforward. Although many people enjoyed its simplicity and ease of use, others eventually found it a bit lacking in power and unsuitable for larger tasks. In fact, BASIC seemed distinctly déclassé compared to some of the newer languages such as Pascal and C. Faced with this competition, BASIC might have faded away. Instead, Microsoft took on the challenge of combining the power of modern programming languages with BASIC's innate friendliness. Today QuickBASIC is a competitive, reliable, flexible language with a lot of punch.

Two changes converted BASIC into the contemporary and productive language we call QuickBASIC: the addition of modern control structures (described in Chapter 4) and the introduction of modular programming features. BASIC's first steps toward the modern era of modular programming were to add the independent programming units of *subroutines* and *user-defined functions* (forms you've probably encountered if you've worked with BASICA). More recently, QuickBASIC introduced programming structures called *procedures,* which come in two forms: the SUB procedure, also called a *subprogram,* which improves on the subroutine concept; and the FUNCTION procedure, an improvement over the previous user-defined function. Procedures let you break a program into small, manageable segments that are easy to understand, maintain, and debug. A procedure can be defined once and executed any number of times throughout a program.

In this chapter we'll examine subprograms and their predecessors, subroutines. We'll also take an initial look at one of QuickBASIC's functions. (Functions are described in more detail in Chapters 8 and 9.)

Modules, Module-Level Code, and Procedures

With QuickBASIC, you can spread a program over several files, or *modules,* each containing QuickBASIC code. The module in which the program starts is called the *main* module. For now, we'll use single-module programs—that is, those having only a main module.

A module itself has two parts: *module-level code* and the *procedures section,* which contains any subprograms and functions you've written for the program. Our previous examples have used only module-level code; in this chapter we'll add procedures. Subprogram procedure code is contained between SUB and END SUB statements. Similarly, FUNCTION and END FUNCTION statements mark the beginning and the end of function procedure code. Any code not contained in these statements is module-level code. See Figure 5-1.

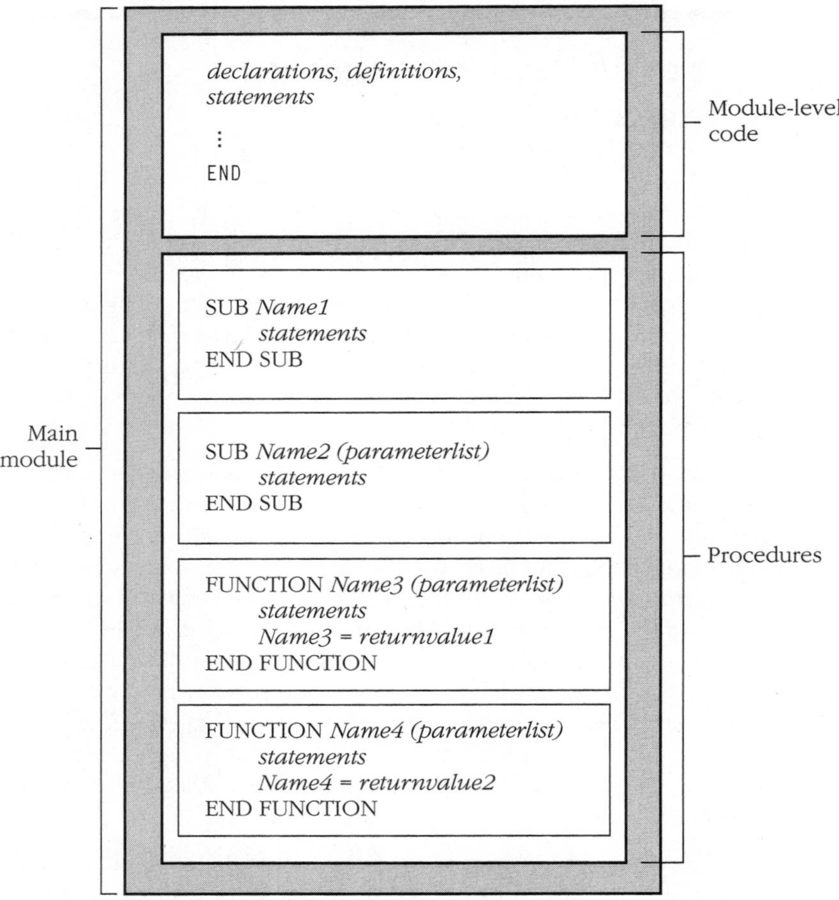

Figure 5-1.
A single-module program containing module-level code and procedures.

Single-module programs contain both module-level code and procedures in a single file. But the QuickBASIC editor emphasizes the difference between the two parts by using a separate View window for each one. When you create a subprogram, for instance, the editor opens a new window for it. Don't be disturbed; you can always return to the module-level code.

Modular Programming: An Overview

The key to modular programming is to first outline a program, concentrating on the overall organization. You then use procedures to implement the details. In other words, you conceptually divide a program into separate tasks and write a specific procedure for carrying out each task. To see how this works, let's write a program that calculates the average of the numbers we enter from the keyboard.

First we outline the tasks we want the program to accomplish:

- Tell the user what to do
- Read and add numbers, and calculate their average

Next we create subprograms—modular programming units that will be plugged into the larger program—to carry out these main tasks. At this point, we don't actually write the subprograms. Instead, we give them descriptive names and plan what they should do:

```
CLS
CALL Instruct          ' Execute the Instruct subprogram
CALL SumNumbers
END
```

Here CLS is a standard QuickBASIC statement, and *Instruct* and *SumNumbers* are subprograms we will write. The CLS statement means "clear the screen and proceed to the next line." The *CALL Instruct* statement means "instruct the user and proceed to the next line." The *CALL SumNumbers* statement means "calculate the result and proceed to the next line."

This program outlines the main tasks to be performed. But if we try to run the program at this stage, we get the message *Subprogram not defined.* It's not enough to simply name a subprogram—we must write the code for it.

The *Instruct* Subprogram

To create the first subprogram for our example, enter the following anywhere in the View window (typically on the line following the first call to the subprogram):

```
SUB Instruct
```

The keyword SUB triggers the QuickBASIC editor to open a new View window containing the following text:

```
SUB Instruct

END SUB
```

Now enter the subprogram between these two boundary lines:

```
SUB Instruct
    PRINT "Type in numbers, and this program will compute ";
    PRINT "their average."
END SUB
```

These are the instructions executed when the program reaches the *CALL Instruct* line. (The indent is a QuickBASIC readability convention.)

At this point, you can use the View menu or the F2 key to bring up a dialog box that lets you select which part of the program (the module-level code or the subprogram) you want to see in the editor. Although these two parts are displayed in different windows, they both belong to the same program and are contained within a single file. The QuickBASIC environment separates these parts to help develop a logical organization within the entire program. The Shift-F2 combination will cycle through your selection of module-level code and procedures. Try switching between the module-level code and the subprogram to become familiar with the process. You also have the option of selecting a split-screen mode, with the module-level code in one View window and the subprogram code in the other or with the same code in both windows.

When we save this program, the editor adds a QuickBASIC *declaration* to the top of the module-level code:

```
DECLARE SUB Instruct ()
```

The declaration comes at the beginning of the module-level code, before the SUB is used. This particular declaration tells QuickBASIC that when it encounters the *Instruct* identifier in the program, it should look for a subprogram of that name. (Like some BASIC functions such as EOF, subprograms can have arguments. In the example above, however, the empty parentheses indicate that the *Instruct* subprogram uses no arguments.)

The *SumNumbers* Subprogram

To complete this program, we must write the code for the other subprogram, *SumNumbers.* Enter the following in either the module-level code window or the subprogram window:

```
SUB SumNumbers
```

A new screen contains the following:

```
SUB SumNumbers

END SUB
```

NOTE: *Another way to set up the new subprogram is to select New SUB... from the Edit menu and then type the subprogram name in the dialog box.*

The second subprogram is more complex than the first because it must deliver what the first subprogram promises—it must calculate the average of the numbers we enter. Conceptually, part of this subprogram is simple. It will read numbers from the keyboard (keeping a running total of their sum and of the number of entries) and then divide the sum by the number of entries. You now know enough about the DO loop to make that part easy. The more difficult part is letting the program know when the user has finished entering numbers.

One option is to have the program quit after it accepts a specific number of values. Another option is to use a specific number or range of numbers to signal the end of input. For example, we can use negative numbers to terminate input. We'll take this approach for our first pass at *SumNumbers*. Listing 5-1 shows the complete module-level code and procedures for our program.

```
' Module-level code
DECLARE SUB SumNumbers ()
DECLARE SUB Instruct ()
CLS
CALL Instruct     ' Execute the Instruct subprogram
CALL SumNumbers   ' Then execute the SumNumbers subprogram
END
' Subprograms follow

' Instruct tells the user what to do
SUB Instruct
    PRINT "Type in numbers, and this program will compute ";
    PRINT "their average."
END SUB

' SumNumbers reads numeric input until a negative number
'  is entered. It keeps a running total of the values entered
'  and of the number of entries, and it reports the average of
'  the values entered.
SUB SumNumbers
    Total! = 0
    Count! = 0
    PRINT "Enter a negative number to terminate."
    INPUT "Enter first number >> ", Num!
    DO WHILE Num! >= 0
        Count! = Count! + 1        ' Number of entries
        Total! = Total! + Num!     ' Sum of entries
        INPUT "Enter next number >> ", Num!
    LOOP
    IF Count! > 0 THEN
        PRINT Count!; "values average to "; Total! / Count!
    ELSE
        PRINT "No values entered."
    END IF
END SUB
```

Listing 5-1.

The DO/WHILE loop counts the number of entries and calculates their sum. The loop continues as long as the last number entered is not negative. (We use an entry-condition loop in case the first number entered is negative.)

Calculating an average makes sense only if input has occurred. Therefore, the program uses IF/THEN/ELSE to check the value of *Count!* and to calculate an average only if entries exist. If no entries exist, *Count!* is 0, and the IF/THEN/ELSE statement does not calculate an average.

Here are two sample runs:

```
Type in numbers, and this program will compute their average.
Enter a negative number to terminate.
Enter first number >> 10
Enter next number >> 20
Enter next number >> 30
Enter next number >> -1
 3 values average to  20

Type in numbers, and this program will compute their average.
Enter a negative number to terminate.
Enter first number >> 2
Enter next number >> 4
Enter next number >> <Enter>
Enter next number >> -1
 3 values average to  2
```

The second sample run reveals a problem. If you enter an empty value by pressing the Enter key, INPUT assigns a value of 0 to *Num!*. Accordingly, the program reports three values entered, not two, and it calculates the average of those three.

VAL to the Rescue

If a modular program doesn't work correctly, you must first identify which procedure is at fault and then fix that procedure. Obviously, using one procedure per task helps to simplify debugging. In the program shown in Listing 5-1, the *SumNumbers* subprogram has two deficiencies: It can work only with nonnegative numbers, and it reads blank responses as 0. We can solve both problems by reading input as a string rather than as a number, which causes the program to read a blank response as a null (empty) string. We can use the following loop test:

```
DO WHILE Num$ <> ""
```

Now we can use the blank response to terminate input. This approach works well because we don't need to use negative numbers to terminate input, and a blank response isn't converted to 0. A new problem arises, however: We can't do arithmetic with strings. Fortunately, QuickBASIC provides the VAL function, which converts strings to numbers.

Recall that a function is a programming unit that returns a value to the program using the function. Many QuickBASIC functions also accept one or more arguments, which are enclosed in parentheses. The VAL function takes one argument—a string—and returns the numeric value that the string represents. For example, the following line assigns the numeric value 321 to the integer variable *Books%*:

```
Books% = VAL("321")
```

Here the string *321* is the argument, and the number 321 is the return value.

Our new plan, then, is to read input as a string, terminate input on the null string, and convert strings to numeric values for calculation. Listing 5-2 presents the new version of our program.

```
' Module-level code
DECLARE SUB SumNumbers ()
DECLARE SUB Instruct ()
CLS
CALL Instruct
CALL SumNumbers
END
' Subprograms follow

' Instruct tells the user what to do
SUB Instruct
    PRINT "Type in numbers, and this program will compute ";
    PRINT "their average."
    PRINT "Press Enter at the beginning of a line to terminate."
END SUB

' SumNumbers reads numeric input until a blank line
'  is entered. It keeps a running total of the values entered
'  and of the number of entries, and it reports the average of
'  the values entered.
SUB SumNumbers
    Total! = 0
    Count! = 0
    INPUT "Enter first number >> ", Num$  ' Read as string
    DO WHILE Num$ <> ""                   ' Halt on blank line
        Num! = VAL(Num$)                  ' Convert to number
        Count! = Count! + 1
        Total! = Total! + Num!
        INPUT "Enter next number >> ", Num$
    LOOP
    IF Count! > 0 THEN
        PRINT Count!; "values average to "; Total! / Count!
    ELSE
        PRINT "No values entered."
    END IF
END SUB
```

Listing 5-2.

Here is a sample run:

```
Type in numbers, and this program will compute their average.
Press Enter at the beginning of a line to terminate.
Enter first number >> 32
Enter next number >> -12
Enter next number >> 10
Enter next number >> <Enter>
 3 values average to  10
```

Local Variables

Microsoft greatly strengthened QuickBASIC by allowing the use of *local variables* in procedures. A local variable is unique to the procedure that contains it, even if the variable name duplicates a name used in module-level code or in another procedure. In the previous example, *SumNumbers* is therefore the only part of the program that knows about *Total!*, *Count!*, and *Num!*. *Global variables,* in contrast, are known to all parts of a program.

Local variables allow you to change a variable in one procedure without inadvertently changing another variable of the same name in the module-level code or in another procedure. Consequently, you don't need to invent an endless number of new variable names (*I%*, *Ind%*, *Index%*, *Index1%*, *SonOfIndex%*), and you don't need to check for duplication. Local variables are especially important in large programs with many procedures.

Listing 5-3 shows an example of a local variable in a subprogram.

```
DECLARE SUB Widget ()
CLS
X% = 47
PRINT "In the module-level code, X% starts out as"; X%
CALL Widget
PRINT "In the module-level code, X% ends up as"; X%
END

SUB Widget
    PRINT "In Widget, X% starts out as"; X%
    X% = 19
    PRINT "Then it is"; X%
END SUB
```

Listing 5-3.

Here is the output:

```
In the module-level code, X% starts out as 47
In Widget, X% starts out as 0
Then it is 19
In the module-level code, X% ends up as 47
```

The *X%* in *Widget* is independent of the *X%* in the module-level code. The two variables have the same name, but they are stored in separate locations (Figure 5-2). Note that, in *Widget*, *X%* starts out as 0, the default value for a variable without an assigned value. As you can see, using the same name for different variables doesn't confuse QuickBASIC. But because it can confuse someone reading your program, we don't recommend it.

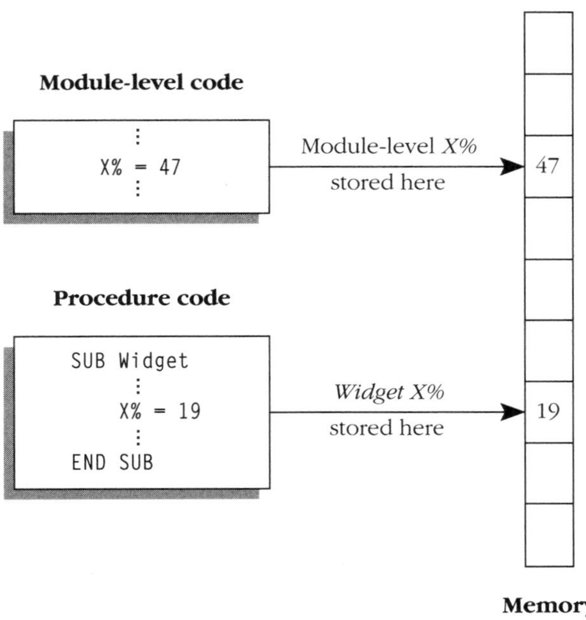

Figure 5-2.
Local variables.

A Debug View of Local Variables

You can use Debug to examine how QuickBASIC handles the two *X%* variables in Listing 5-3. First, while in the module level, place the original *X%* in the Watch window by selecting Add Watch from the Debug menu. If you do this before running the program, the Watch window will look like the following. (LIST-03.BAS is the filename we used.)

```
LIST-03.BAS X%:
```

Now use the F8 key to step through the program. As you execute the first assignment statement, the Watch window reports a value of 47. When the *CALL Widget* line is highlighted and you press F8, the View window switches to the *Widget* subprogram, and the Watch window reads as follows:

```
LIST-03.BAS X%: <Not watchable>
```

This message tells you that the *Widget* subprogram doesn't know about the *X%* in the module-level code.

While in *Widget*, add *X%* to the Watch window again. (You can add new variables to the Watch window while the program is running.) The window will look like this:

```
LIST-03.BAS X%: <Not watchable>
Widget X%:  0
```

Debug is now tracking both *X%* variables. Press F8 until the *Widget X%* shows the value 19. Continuing to press F8 eventually brings you back to the module-level code and the following Watch window:

```
LIST-03.BAS X%:  47
Widget X%: <Not watchable>
```

When the program returns to the module-level code, the original *X%* is recognized, and the *Widget X%* is no longer available.

Subprograms with Argument Lists

Subprograms, like some QuickBASIC functions, can use argument lists, which allow a subprogram to use values that originate in the module-level code. In other words, the calling program can use arguments to pass (or send) values to a subprogram.

Arguments and Parameters

To receive the values passed to it, a subprogram must contain a *parameter list* in its definition. *Parameters* are variables that take on the values passed to the subprogram.

The subprogram definition has this basic form:

```
SUB subprogramname [(parameterlist)]
    statementblock
END SUB
```

parameterlist is a comma-separated list of variables of any type. Each variable in the list can be a simple name, or it can take the form *name* AS *type*, as in *Brand AS STRING.*

Let's use a subprogram called *Cube* to see how argument passing works. We'll pass a number to the subprogram, and it will calculate and display the cube of that number:

```
DECLARE SUB Cube (Num!)              ' Added when program is saved
CLS
CALL Cube(5)                         ' 5 is an argument
END

SUB Cube (Num!)                      ' Num! is a parameter
    CubeNum! = Num! * Num! * Num!
    PRINT Num!; "cubed is"; CubeNum!
END SUB
```

Note that QuickBASIC adds a declaration for the subprogram when you save the program. The program produces the following output:

```
5 cubed is 125
```

The argument list for *Cube* consists of a single argument, the number 5. The subprogram *Cube* must be able to accept the argument that is sent. It does so by using a parameter that appears in parentheses after the subprogram name in the subprogram definition (the line beginning with SUB). The parameter for *Cube* is the variable *Num!*. The standard QuickBASIC suffixes indicate the variable type. The following statement informs QuickBASIC that the *Cube* subprogram expects to be passed one argument, which should be a single-precision value:

```
SUB Cube (Num!)
```

The subprogram call

```
CALL Cube(5)
```

passes the argument *5* to the subprogram, causing *Num!* to take the value 5. Thus, the value 5 is used wherever *Num!* occurs in the *Cube* subprogram. Similarly, if *10* is used as an argument, the parameter *Num!* has the value 10.

In short, arguments are values that appear in a statement calling a subprogram, and parameters are variables that appear in the definition of a subprogram. When a subprogram is called, the parameter takes the value of the argument (Figure 5-3). A parameter must be a variable because it must be able to assume whatever valid value is passed. Arguments, however, are less restricted in form.

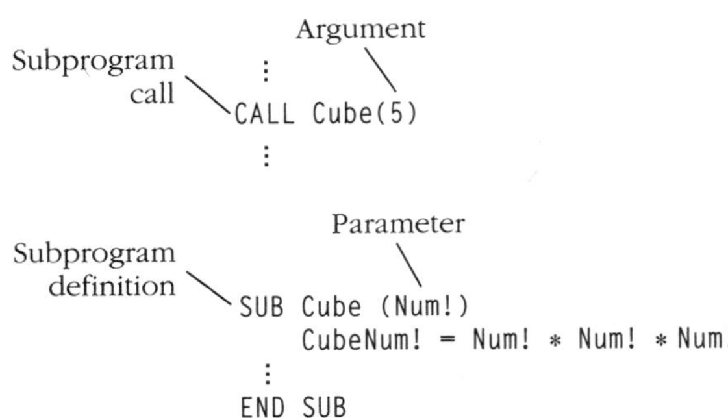

Figure 5-3.
The parameter Num! *takes the value of the argument* 5.

Varieties of Arguments

An argument must reduce to a value compatible with the type of the corresponding parameter in the subprogram. As shown in Listing 5-4, you can use literals, variables, constants, expressions, and functions as arguments if they are the right type.

```
DECLARE SUB Cube (Num!)
CLS
CALL Cube(5)                      ' Literal as an argument
X! = 4
CALL Cube(X!)                     ' Variable as an argument
CALL Cube(X! + 3)                 ' Expression as an argument
CALL Cube(VAL("1.1"))             ' Function as an argument
END

SUB Cube (Num!)                   ' Num! is a parameter
    CubeNum! = Num! * Num! * Num!
    PRINT Num!; "cubed is"; CubeNum!
END SUB
```

Listing 5-4.

Here is the output:

```
5 cubed is 125
4 cubed is 64
7 cubed is 343
1.1 cubed is 1.331
```

In one respect, QuickBASIC treats variables differently than it treats other forms of arguments. When you pass an argument such as *5* or *X! + 3* to *Cube*, the subprogram creates a new variable called *Num!* that is assigned a specific value of 5 or, say, 7 (if *X!* equals 4). But when you pass a variable such as *X!* by itself (not as part of an expression), *Cube* doesn't create a new variable. Instead, it uses the *X!* variable but calls it *Num!*—that is, *Num!* is an *alias* for the original *X!* variable. If the subprogram changes *Num!*, the *X!* in the original program is changed too. Listing 5-5 shows how this feature works.

```
DECLARE SUB CubePlus (Num!)
CLS
X! = 10
CALL CubePlus(X!)
PRINT X!
CALL CubePlus(X! + 2)
PRINT X!
END
```

Listing 5-5. *(continued)*

Listing 5-5. *continued*

```
SUB CubePlus (Num!)
    CubeNum! = Num! * Num! * Num!
    PRINT Num!; "cubed is"; CubeNum!
    Num! = Num! + 1        ' Change Num! and see what happens
END SUB
```

Here is the output:

```
10 cubed is 1000
11
13 cubed is 2197
11
```

When you first call *CubePlus* and pass *X!* as an argument, *Num!* becomes an alias for *X!*. When you increase *Num!* by 1, the value of *X!* also increases by 1 because these are simply two names for the same variable. When you call *CubePlus* again but pass *X! + 2* as an argument, increasing *Num!* has no effect on *X!* because *Num!* is now a new, separate variable. The former process is called *passing by reference,* and the latter is called *passing by value.*

Multiple Arguments

In a subprogram using several arguments and parameters, the argument list and the parameter list each consist of a set of variables separated by commas. The arguments must match the parameters in number and in type. Listing 5-6 presents a simple example of passing two arguments to a subprogram.

```
DECLARE SUB SumSquare (A!, B!)
CLS
INPUT "Enter two numbers: ", X!, Y!
CALL SumSquare(X!, Y!)    ' Pass two arguments
END

SUB SumSquare (A!, B!)    ' Two parameters
    PRINT "The sum of the squares of"; A!; "and"; B!;
    PRINT "is"; A! * A! + B! * B!
END SUB
```

Listing 5-6.

Here is the output:

```
Enter two numbers: 10,20
The sum of the squares of 10 and 20 is 500
```

Strings as Arguments

Suppose you want to print repeated character patterns—for example, a row of 64 asterisks and a row of several +--+ sequences. You could write a separate subprogram for each task:

```
SUB Asterisks64
    FOR Times% = 1 TO 64
        PRINT "*";
    NEXT Times%
END SUB

SUB RepeatPattern (N%)
    FOR Times% = 1 TO N%
        PRINT "+--+";
    NEXT Times%
END SUB
```

But it makes better sense to write one subprogram that does both jobs. You need to use two arguments: the string to be printed and the number of repetitions. You can use a string argument if you also use a string type parameter in the subprogram. The subprogram *RepeatString* in Listing 5-7 illustrates this approach.

```
DECLARE SUB RepeatString (S$, N%)
CLS
CALL RepeatString("*", 64)         ' First argument is a string
PRINT
CALL RepeatString("+--+", 16)
FOR Lines% = 1 TO 7
    PRINT TAB(4 * Lines%);
    CALL RepeatString("+--+", 16 - 2 * Lines%)
    PRINT
NEXT Lines%
FOR Lines% = 7 TO 0 STEP -1
    PRINT TAB(4 * Lines%);
    CALL RepeatString("+--+", 16 - 2 * Lines%)
    PRINT
NEXT Lines%
CALL RepeatString("*", 64)
END

SUB RepeatString (S$, N%)          ' First parameter is a string
REM This subprogram prints the string S$ N% times
    FOR Times% = 1 TO N%
        PRINT S$;
    NEXT Times%
END SUB
```

Listing 5-7.

This example also demonstrates the usefulness of subprograms: When a block of code is needed several times, enter it only once, as a subprogram, and then call the subprogram as necessary.

Here is the output:

```
****************************************************************
+--++--++--++--++--++--++--++--++--++--++--++--++--++--++--++--+
    +--++--++--++--++--++--++--++--++--++--++--++--++--++--+
        +--++--++--++--++--++--++--++--++--++--++--++--+
            +--++--++--++--++--++--++--++--++--++--+
                +--++--++--++--++--++--++--++--+
                    +--++--++--++--++--++--+
                        +--++--++--++--+
                            +--++--+
                            +--++--+
                        +--++--++--++--+
                    +--++--++--++--++--++--+
                +--++--++--++--++--++--++--++--+
            +--++--++--++--++--++--++--++--++--++--+
        +--++--++--++--++--++--++--++--++--++--++--++--+
    +--++--++--++--++--++--++--++--++--++--++--++--++--++--+
+--++--++--++--++--++--++--++--++--++--++--++--++--++--++--++--+
****************************************************************
```

Matching Arguments to Parameters

The number of arguments you provide when calling a subprogram must be the same as the number of parameters used in the subprogram definition. The type of each argument must also match the corresponding parameter. QuickBASIC checks these matches in a process called *type checking*. If you use the command-line compiler (BC), type checking cannot be turned on without the DECLARE SUB declaration. Recall that the QuickBASIC editor adds this statement when you first save the file.

When QuickBASIC adds the DECLARE SUB statement, it includes the parameter list:

```
DECLARE SUB Cube (Num!)
```

If the subprogram does not contain a parameter list, the DECLARE SUB statement uses empty parentheses:

```
DECLARE SUB Instruct ()
```

What happens when an argument doesn't match the corresponding parameter? Go back to the program in Listing 5-4, and replace

```
CALL Cube(5)
```

with the following statement:

```
CALL Cube("Five")
```

When you run the program, you get a *Type mismatch* message.

Next replace the call to *Cube* with this call:

```
CALL Cube(2, 4)
```

When you run the program this time, you receive the error message *Argument-count mismatch*. You provided two arguments, but the *Cube* definition uses only one parameter.

QuickBASIC can convert mismatched numeric types to fit—for instance, an integer argument is converted to a single-precision value if the corresponding parameter is single precision—unless the original value is too large to be accommodated by the parameter. For example, the call

```
CALL Cube(2.3D200)
```

produces an *Overflow* message when you run the program.

CALL: Optional or Required?

In QuickBASIC, the keyword CALL is not required in order to call a subprogram. Either of the following statements calls the *Instruct* subprogram:

```
CALL Instruct           ' You can use CALL,
Instruct                '  or you can omit it
```

If the subprogram uses arguments, omit the parentheses when omitting CALL:

```
CALL RepeatString("Kiss me ", 8)    ' Use parentheses
RepeatString "You fool! ", 5        ' Omit parentheses
```

However, if you use the command-line compiler, CALL is optional for a subprogram *only* if you've used DECLARE SUB to declare the subprogram.

Here are the two syntax choices for CALL:

```
CALL subprogramname[(argumentlist)]
subprogramname [argumentlist]
```

Note that when CALL is omitted, subprogram calls look like the built-in QuickBASIC statements such as PRINT. Indeed, you can think of subprograms as user-defined statements.

The EXIT SUB Statement

When a subprogram reaches the END SUB statement, the subprogram terminates, and the program flow returns to the line following the one that called the subprogram. You can exit the subprogram before reaching the END SUB statement by using EXIT SUB. EXIT SUB in a subprogram works the same way as EXIT FOR and EXIT DO work in loops.

In Listing 5-8, the subprogram from Listing 5-7 has been modified so that it won't print the strings if the total line length exceeds 64 characters. Note that CALL has been omitted.

```
DECLARE SUB RepeatString (S$, N%)
CLS
INPUT "Enter a string you want to print: ", Thing$
DO WHILE Thing$ <> ""
    INPUT "Enter the number of times to print it: ", Times%
    RepeatString Thing$, Times%  ' Look, Ma! No CALL!
    PRINT
    INPUT "Enter a string you want to print: ", Thing$
LOOP
PRINT "Bye"
END

SUB RepeatString (S$, N%)
REM This subprogram prints the string S$ N% times
REM If the total length exceeds 64, the subprogram exits
    IF LEN(S$) * N% > 64 THEN EXIT SUB
    FOR Times% = 1 TO N%
        PRINT S$;
    NEXT Times%
END SUB
```

Listing 5-8.

This example also uses the QuickBASIC function LEN, which takes a string as an argument and returns the number of characters in the string—*LEN("Fido")*, for instance, returns the value 4. (We'll come back to this function in Chapter 7.)

Here is a sample run:

```
Enter a string you want to print: "I say yes! "
Enter the number of times to print it: 5
I say yes! I say yes! I say yes! I say yes! I say yes!
Enter a string you want to print: "You say no! "
Enter the number of times to print it: 10

Enter a string you want to print: What?
Enter the number of times to print it: 6
What?What?What?What?What?What?
Enter a string you want to print: <Enter>
Bye
```

The string *You say no!* contains 12 characters (including a trailing space). Printing it 10 times requires more than 64 characters, so the subprogram executes the EXIT SUB statement and prints nothing.

We'll continue our discussion of procedures in Chapter 8, which examines some of the more complicated aspects of managing variables in a subprogram. Meanwhile, let's look at the subprogram's predecessor, the subroutine.

Subroutines

Subroutines are segments of code accessed by the GOSUB statement. A label identifies the start of a subroutine, and a RETURN statement marks the end. Like subprograms, subroutines let you encapsulate code that can then be executed as often as needed. But subroutines differ from subprograms in important respects:

- Subroutines do not accept arguments.
- Subroutines use global rather than local variables.
- Subroutines are part of module-level code, not procedure code.
- In multimodule programs, a subroutine is limited to the module containing it, whereas a subprogram can be used by all the modules.

Because subprograms are more powerful and more convenient than subroutines, you should use them in developing new programs. Older code, however, frequently includes subroutines.

Subroutines have the following syntax:

```
GOSUB {labelnumber1 ¦ labelname1}
    ⋮
{labelnumber1 ¦ labelname1:}
    statementblock
RETURN [{labelnumber2 ¦ labelname2}]
```

The GOSUB statement sends program control to the indicated line. Lines can be labeled with either numbers or names. If the label in the statement is the line number 300, control goes to line 300. If the label is the name *Sonic*, control goes to the line labeled *Sonic:*. (The colon is used in the line label but not in the GOSUB statement.) Statements following the label are executed until the program encounters a RETURN statement. Then program control passes to the line whose label is indicated in the RETURN statement. If no label is provided, program control returns to the statement following the original GOSUB statement.

The optional line label in the RETURN statement should be used carefully. A subroutine is much clearer if it simply returns to the statement following GOSUB.

A subroutine is part of module-level code. You can place it anywhere in a program, but we recommend putting it after an END, STOP, GOTO, or RETURN statement so that the subroutine isn't executed without being called.

Listing 5-9 shows a rewritten version of the program in Listing 5-7, using a subroutine instead of a subprogram.

```
CLS
S$ = "*"                              ' Set variables for
N% = 64                               '  subroutine
GOSUB RepeatString                    ' Go to the subroutine
PRINT
S$ = "+--+"
N% = 16
GOSUB RepeatString
FOR Lines% = 1 TO 7
    PRINT TAB(4 * Lines%);
    S$ = "+--+"
    N% = 16 - 2 * Lines%
    GOSUB RepeatString
    PRINT
NEXT Lines%
FOR Lines% = 7 TO 0 STEP -1
    PRINT TAB(4 * Lines%);
    S$ = "+--+"
    N% = 16 - 2 * Lines%
    GOSUB RepeatString
    PRINT
NEXT Lines%
S$ = "*"
N% = 64
GOSUB RepeatString
END

RepeatString:                         ' Subroutine label
' This subroutine prints the string S$ N% times
    FOR Times% = 1 TO N%
        PRINT S$;
    NEXT Times%
RETURN                                ' Don't use Times% elsewhere
```

Listing 5-9.

> **NOTE:** *Because a subroutine is part of module-level code, no SUB window is opened when the subroutine is created.*

This program produces the same output as the program in Listing 5-7. But because you cannot use arguments, it is difficult to communicate information to the subroutine. Each time you call the subroutine, you must first set the subroutine variables to the desired values. Also, the variables *S$*, *N%*, and *Times%* are used here in module-level code and thus cannot be used anywhere else in module-level code. For example, if you use *Times%* in another subroutine, its value there would change every time you run *RepeatString*.

Review Questions

1. What are the two parts of a QuickBASIC module? Describe each part.
2. What will the following program print?

```
DECLARE SUB Vapid ()
X% = 4
CALL Vapid
END

SUB Vapid
    FOR I% = 1 TO X%
        PRINT "Have a nice day!"
    NEXT I%
END SUB
```

3. Change the example used in Review Question 2 so that the value of *X%* in the module-level code will determine the number of times the *Vapid* message is printed.
4. Complete the following program:

```
CLS
REM The following subprogram prints a greeting
CALL Greetings
REM The following subroutine asks your first name and
REM  places your response in the variable NameF$
GOSUB FirstName
REM The following subprogram asks your last name and
REM  places your response in the variable NameL$
CALL LastName(NameL$)
REM The following subprogram prints your name in the
REM  form last name, first name
CALL ShowName(NameF$, NameL$)
END
```

5. How would you write the following lines if you did not want to use the keyword CALL?

```
CALL ShowMotto
CALL FineDay(X%)
CALL Retrofit(N%, M%)
```

6. List two advantages of using a subprogram instead of a subroutine.

7. Find the errors in the program in Listing 5-Q7 and correct them.

```
'THIS PROGRAM CONTAINS ERRORS
DECLARE SUB Explain
DECLARE SUB Multiply (N%)
CLS
Limit% = 5
CALL Explain()
CALL Multiply(Limit%)
END

SUB Explain
    PRINT "This program calculates the product of all"
    PRINT "the numbers you enter. It accepts numbers"
    PRINT "until you enter an empty line or reach"; Limit%
    PRINT "numbers, whichever comes first."
END SUB

SUB Multiply (N%)
    Count% = 0
    INPUT "Enter a number >> ", Num$
    DO UNTIL Num$ = "" OR Count = N%
        Product! = Product! * Num!
        IF Count% < N% THEN
            INPUT "Next value >> ", Num$
    LOOP
    PRINT "Product = "; Product!
END SUB
```

Listing 5-Q7.

8. Rewrite the following program to use a subprogram instead of a subroutine:

```
CLS
Times% = 2
Pignumber% = 3
GOSUB Pigs
Times% = 4
Pignumber% = 8
GOSUB Pigs
Times% = 3
Pignumber% = 5
GOSUB Pigs
END
Pigs:
    FOR I% = 1 TO Times%
        PRINT Pignumber%; "little piggies!"
    NEXT I%
RETURN
```

6

Arrays and Data

CLEAR	**ERASE**	**READ**	**$STATIC**
DATA	**FRE**	**REDIM**	**SWAP**
DIM	**LBOUND**	**RESTORE**	**UBOUND**
$DYNAMIC	**OPTION BASE**	**SHARED**	

Are you afflicted with unsightly data? Is your computer submerged in lists of all the naval vessels used in World War II? Has your niece strewn your box of index cards with addresses all around your study? If your answer to these or similar questions is yes, you probably have a lot of work to do. QuickBASIC can help, for it offers a variety of ways to represent and handle data.

In programming, you often need to represent a number of related data items: sales figures for each of 12 months, names of 30 admirers, or ID numbers of the 1500 members of the local Yodeling Club, for instance. Using a separate variable for each value would be awkward, even painful. But you don't need to. QuickBASIC provides the *array,* a special kind of variable capable of holding many individual values.

In this chapter we will investigate ways of creating and using arrays, including arrays with more than one dimension. We'll also see how loops and procedures work with arrays and discuss the differences between static and dynamic arrays.

An Introduction to Arrays

Thus far, we've used *simple variables,* each of which holds only one value. The *array variable,* in contrast, can hold several values. An array consists of separate units, called *elements,* each holding one value.

To keep track of the elements, QuickBASIC numbers them, beginning with 0 by default. These numbered labels are called *subscripts.* You can use a subscript to access a particular element. For instance, the notation *Alphonse(0)* identifies the element with the subscript 0 in an array named *Alphonse.* Similarly, *Alphonse(1)* identifies the element with the subscript 1 (Figure 6-1).

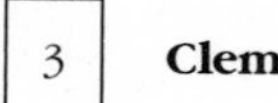

A simple variable holding one value

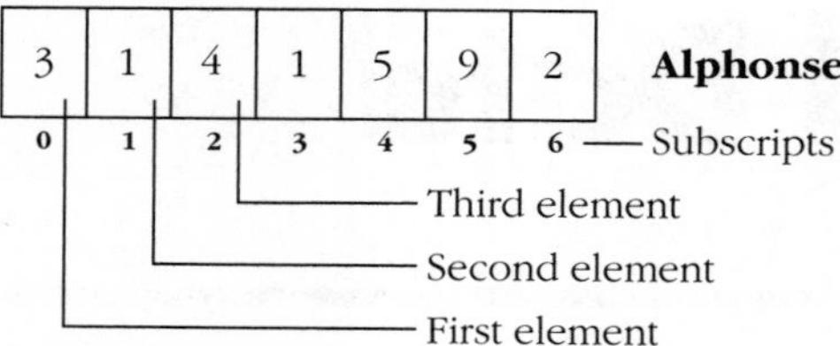

An array holding seven values

Figure 6-1.
A simple variable and an array.

Like simple variables, array variables have types. All the elements of a given array must be the same type—an integer array can hold only integers, a string array can hold only strings, and so on.

Creating Arrays

With QuickBASIC, you can create arrays in several ways. The least formal method is to use an array element in a program. Let's try that in Listing 6-1.

```
CLS
' Use some array elements
Debts!(0) = 20.5                ' Set element 0 to 20.5
Debts!(1) = 40.99
Debts!(2) = .25
' Print out some of the array elements
FOR Index% = 0 TO 2
    PRINT "Debt Number"; Index%; "is"; Debts!(Index%)
NEXT Index%
END
```

Listing 6-1.

Here is the output:

```
Debt Number 0 is 20.5
Debt Number 1 is 40.99
Debt Number 2 is .25
```

When you use the variable *Debts!(0)*, QuickBASIC creates the *Debts!* array. It contains three elements, which have subscripts 0 through 2. This example also illustrates the importance of the FOR loop in handling arrays. This loop is the natural tool for this task because the FOR loop index can represent the array index.

The array index should be an integer. (We used integers and an integer variable in our example.) If you use, for instance, single-precision values as subscripts, QuickBASIC converts them to integers.

This approach—simply using array elements to create the array—has limitations, as Listing 6-2 shows.

```
CLS
' Use some array elements
Debts!(0) = 20.5            ' Set element 0 to 20.5
Debts!(1) = 40.99
Debts!(2) = .25
' Print out some elements
FOR Index% = 0 TO 11
    PRINT "Debt Number"; Index%; "is"; Debts!(Index%)
NEXT Index%
END
```

Listing 6-2.

When you let the index go to 11, you get an error message: *Subscript out of range.* This message indicates that *Index%* exceeded its allowable values. If you use the F4 key to toggle back to the output screen, you see the following:

```
Debt Number 0 is 20.5
Debt Number 1 is 40.99
Debt Number 2 is .25
Debt Number 3 is 0
Debt Number 4 is 0
Debt Number 5 is 0
Debt Number 6 is 0
Debt Number 7 is 0
Debt Number 8 is 0
Debt Number 9 is 0
Debt Number 10 is 0
Debt Number 11 is
```

You've run out of elements, because the arrays created by the simple mechanism used here have subscripts only through 10. Array variables, like other QuickBASIC variables, are set to 0 when created unless you assign other values to them.

Another drawback to this method of creating arrays is that QuickBASIC always provides a full set of subscripts through 10, even if you need only a few elements. To better control the number of elements, you must use the DIM statement to establish the array dimensions.

Using the Short Form of the DIM Statement

QuickBASIC's DIM statement provides a more formal way to create an array and to dimension it—that is, to specify its size.

The simplest DIM syntax for creating arrays is the following:

```
DIM arrayname(upper)
```

The DIM statement should appear at the beginning of a program. *arrayname* is the name of the array, and *upper* is the upper limit for the subscript values. By default, the lower limit is 0. As it does for simple variables, the name indicates the array type. Thus, the following statement creates an array of strings for which the subscripts can vary from 0 through 100:

```
DIM Mantovani$(100)
```

Because the first subscript is 0, this statement dimensions the array *Mantovani$* to hold 101 strings.

Now let's choose an array size. We can calculate the first 16 powers of 2 and store them in an array, as shown in Listing 6-3.

```
DIM PowersOfTwo&(15)            ' Create an array with 16 elements
CLS                             '  each of which is type long integer
PowersOfTwo&(0) = 1             ' Set first element to 1
                                ' Multiply each element by 2 to
FOR I% = 1 TO 15                '  get next element
    PowersOfTwo&(I%) = 2 * PowersOfTwo&(I% - 1)
NEXT I%
PRINT "Here are some powers of 2"
FOR I% = 0 TO 15        '       ' Loop to print results
    PRINT "2 to the"; I%; "power is"; PowersOfTwo&(I%)
NEXT I%
END
```

Listing 6-3.

Here is the output:

```
Here are some powers of 2
2 to the 0 power is 1
2 to the 1 power is 2
2 to the 2 power is 4
2 to the 3 power is 8
2 to the 4 power is 16
2 to the 5 power is 32
2 to the 6 power is 64
2 to the 7 power is 128
2 to the 8 power is 256
2 to the 9 power is 512
2 to the 10 power is 1024
2 to the 11 power is 2048
```

```
2 to the 12 power is 4096
2 to the 13 power is 8192
2 to the 14 power is 16384
2 to the 15 power is 32768
```

Again, we use a FOR loop to manage the array. But now we can vary the number of subscripts. (By the way, we used an array of long integers because the final calculated value of 32768 is greater than the largest regular integer in QuickBASIC.)

Using the OPTION BASE Statement

If you find it disconcerting that the statement

```
DIM PowersOfTwo&(15)
```

uses the value 15 to create 16 elements, you can use the OPTION BASE statement to set the low end of the subscript range to 1 instead of 0. Then the number used in the DIM statement will match the number of elements.

The OPTION BASE statement has the following syntax:

```
OPTION BASE n
```

n represents the lower limit for the subscript; it must be either 0 or 1. You can use this statement only once in a module, and it must appear before any arrays are created. All arrays will then use the same OPTION BASE value.

Using the OPTION BASE statement to set the lower limit can be unwieldy. First, when you have an array created with the DIM statement, you must search for a separate OPTION BASE statement to see which lower limit (0 or 1) is being used. Second, all your arrays must use one option or the other; you can't vary the lower limits. Third, you have only two choices. Fourth, if you need subscripts in the range 273 through 373, for example, you must either waste the part of the array that has subscripts less than 273 or use an awkward notation like *I% – 273* for subscripts (which would let you set *I%* to the proper range but would allow the subscripts to vary from 0 through 100).

The latest versions of QuickBASIC, however, overcome these limitations by extending the DIM syntax.

Using the Full Form of the DIM Statement

The full DIM syntax lets you set both the lower and the upper limits for array subscripts. Thus, if you want to use an array to represent yearly rainfall in the 1980s, you can create a 10-element array with a subscript range of 1980 through 1989.

Here is the full syntax for the DIM statement:

```
DIM [SHARED] arrayname([lower TO] upper) [AS type]
```

If the optional SHARED attribute (discussed later in this chapter) is used, all the procedures in the module can use the array by name.

The DIM statement should appear at the beginning of a program or procedure. *lower* and *upper* values in the DIM statement define the subscript range. Array subscripts can be in the range –32768 through 32767. For example, the statement

```
DIM WineRating%(1972 TO 1987)
```

dimensions a 16-element array of integers with subscripts 1972 through 1987.

If the *lower* TO portion of the DIM statement is omitted (and the OPTION BASE statement is not used), the lower limit is taken to be 0. Thus, the statement

```
DIM Wits$(10)
```

creates an 11-element array with the subscript range 0 through 10.

The array type is indicated by the name or by the AS component of the statement. The following statements create an array (*Sales!*) of 12 single-precision values and an array (*ChemAnalysis*) of 10 double-precision values:

```
DIM Sales!(1 TO 12)
DIM ChemAnalysis(1 TO 10) AS DOUBLE
```

Even if you're used to the short form of the syntax, you'll probably find this full form useful. It lets you see the subscript limits at a glance, and it lets you choose values suitable to your programming needs. The syntax nicely parallels that of a FOR loop:

```
DIM Sales!(1 TO 12)
:
FOR Month% = 1 TO 12
    PRINT Sales!(Month%)
NEXT Month%
```

The loop limits match the DIM limits.

Listing 6-4 demonstrates the DIM syntax, using an array that holds strings.

```
CLS
DIM GrammyWinners$(1980 TO 1984)
GrammyWinners$(1980) = "Sailing"
GrammyWinners$(1981) = "Bette Davis Eyes"
GrammyWinners$(1982) = "Rosanna"
GrammyWinners$(1983) = "Beat It"
GrammyWinners$(1984) = "What's Love Got to Do with It?"
INPUT "Choose a year from 1980 to 1984: ", Year%
DO WHILE (Year% >= 1980) AND (Year% <= 1984)
    PRINT "The Grammy Best Record winner for"; Year%;
    PRINT "is "; GrammyWinners$(Year%)
    INPUT "Enter a year from 1980 to 1984 to continue: ", Year%
LOOP
PRINT "Bye"
END
```

Listing 6-4.

Here is a sample run:

```
Choose a year from 1980 to 1984: 1981
The Grammy Best Record winner for 1981 is Bette Davis Eyes
Enter a year from 1980 to 1984 to continue: 1983
The Grammy Best Record winner for 1983 is Beat It
Enter a year from 1980 to 1984 to continue: 1940
Bye
```

Using the years as array subscripts makes this program easier to write and to read.

Debugging Tip

It's possible to inadvertently create arrays that have not been dimensioned. Recall that if you use an array that has not been created with a DIM statement, QuickBASIC assigns it a subscript range of 0 through 10. If you get the message *Subscript out of range*, check to see that you haven't mistyped an array name somewhere. You might have done something like this:

```
DIM Sum%(1 TO 30)
⋮
FOR I% = 1 to 30
    ⋮
    PRINT Sum(I%)
NEXT I%
```

Because the % suffix is not used with *Sum* in the loop, QuickBASIC considers *Sum* a new array with a maximum subscript value of 10.

The READ and DATA Statements

Let's look at a new way to incorporate data into the program itself. We've done this in previous examples by initializing a constant or a variable to some value, as in the following:

```
CONST pi! = 3.141593
Limit% = 12
```

But what if you must initialize an array of data? For instance, you might want to store the number of days in each month. Doing so element by element would be tedious:

```
Days(1) = 31
Days(2) = 28
⋮
```

This is where READ and DATA come in handy. The DATA statement lets you identify as data a sequence of numbers or strings in the program, and the READ statement lets the program read that data. A READ statement resembles an INPUT statement, but it takes data from DATA statements rather than from the keyboard.

The DATA statement has the following syntax:

```
DATA valuelist
```

valuelist is a comma-separated list of values, which can be numeric or string literals. Strings do not need to be enclosed in quotation marks unless they contain commas, colons, leading spaces, or trailing spaces. The following is a sample DATA statement:

```
DATA 5, Idaho, "Polk, John", 3.14E7, 4444444
```

The READ statement has the following syntax:

```
READ variablelist
```

variablelist is a comma-separated list of variables.

Listing 6-5 shows a sample program that fills an array by using READ and DATA and then prints the contents of the array.

```
DIM Days%(1 TO 12)             ' Dimension array for the 12 months
' The DATA statement contains the number of days in each month
DATA 31,28,31,30,31,30,31,31,30,31,30,31
CLS

FOR Month% = 1 TO 12
    READ Days%(Month%)         ' Read from DATA statement
NEXT Month%

FOR Month% = 1 TO 12
    PRINT Days%(Month%);
NEXT Month%
PRINT
END
```

Listing 6-5.

Here is the output:

```
 31  28  31  30  31  30  31  31  30  31  30  31
```

The first time the READ statement is used, it reads the first item in the DATA list. Each subsequent use advances to another item until the READ loop has read the entire list.

DATA Details

You can place DATA statements anywhere in a program, although if you try to include them in a procedure, QuickBASIC will move them to module-level code. (The command-line compiler, however, will not move them.)

The positions of DATA statements relative to other parts of a program are not important, but their positions relative to one another are, because DATA statements are read in order of occurrence. In principle, you could scatter them throughout a program. In practice, it's a good idea to group them together, usually at the beginning or the end of the module-level code.

If the data won't fit on one line, use additional DATA statements. If more data exists than is read, the unread data is simply not used. If the program tries to read more data than is available, you get an *Out of data* error message. Listing 6-6 shows how to use more than one DATA statement.

```
DIM Days%(1 TO 12)              ' Integer type, 12-element array
DIM Months$(1 TO 12)            ' String type, 12-element array
DATA 31,28,31,30,31,30,31,31,30,31,30,31
DATA January, February, March, April, May, June, July
DATA August, September, October, November, December
CLS

FOR Month% = 1 TO 12
    READ Days%(Month%)          ' Read first 12 data items
NEXT Month%

FOR Month% = 1 TO 12
    READ Months$(Month%)        ' Read next 12 data items
NEXT Month%

FOR Month% = 1 TO 12
    PRINT Months$(Month%); " has"; Days%(Month%); "days."
NEXT Month%
END
```

Listing 6-6.

Here is the output:

```
January has 31 days.
February has 28 days.
March has 31 days.
April has 30 days.
May has 31 days.
June has 30 days.
July has 31 days.
August has 31 days.
September has 30 days.
October has 31 days.
November has 30 days.
December has 31 days.
```

The preceding program reads all the day values and then all the month names. You could also set it up to read the data in pairs—that is, you could design a loop such as the following:

```
FOR Month% = 1 TO 12
    READ Days%(Month%), Months$(Month%)
NEXT Month%
```

But you would need to store the data in the same order in which the program attempts to read it:

```
DATA 31, January, 28, February, 31, March, 30, April, 31, May
:
```

Going Back: The RESTORE Statement

The RESTORE statement allows a program to back up and reread information in DATA statements. For instance, some variables originally set to default values might change while the program runs, and you might want to reset them to the defaults. The RESTORE statement lets you do this.

Here is the syntax for RESTORE:

```
RESTORE [{linenumber ¦ linelabel}]
```

linenumber is a line number for a DATA statement, and *linelabel* is a name label for a DATA statement. If a line number or a line label is used, the next READ statement starts at that line. Otherwise, the next READ statement starts with the first DATA statement in the program.

To see how this works, we'll write a program (Listing 6-7) that initializes an array to certain values, changes them, and then restores the original values.

```
DATA red, yellow, green
DATA background, foreground, highlight
DIM Colors$(1 TO 3)         ' Dimension string type, three-element array
DIM Display$(1 TO 3)        ' Dimension string type, three-element array

FOR Part% = 1 TO 3          ' Read default colors
    READ Colors$(Part%)
NEXT Part%

FOR Part% = 1 TO 3          ' Read display types
    READ Display$(Part%)
NEXT Part%
```

Listing 6-7. *(continued)*

Listing 6-7. *continued*

```
CLS
PRINT "Here are the current screen settings:"
FOR Part% = 1 TO 3
    PRINT Display$(Part%); " is "; Colors$(Part%)
NEXT Part%
PRINT

Colors$(1) = "cyan"          ' Reset colors
Colors$(2) = "white"
Colors$(3) = "magenta"

PRINT "Here are the new screen settings:"
FOR Part% = 1 TO 3
    PRINT Display$(Part%); " is "; Colors$(Part%)
NEXT Part%
PRINT

RESTORE                      ' First data statement will be read
FOR Part% = 1 TO 3           ' Reread default values
    READ Colors$(Part%)
NEXT Part%

PRINT "Here are the restored screen settings:"
FOR Part% = 1 TO 3
    PRINT Display$(Part%); " is "; Colors$(Part%)
NEXT Part%
END
```

Here is a sample run:

```
Here are the current screen settings:
background is red
foreground is yellow
highlight is green

Here are the new screen settings:
background is cyan
foreground is white
highlight is magenta

Here are the restored screen settings:
background is red
foreground is yellow
highlight is green
```

Note that RESTORE does not itself restore the original values. It simply readies the program to allow the next READ statement to reread the original DATA statement. You can think of READ as moving a pointer through the list of DATA items and RESTORE as resetting the pointer to the beginning of the list (Figure 6-2).

```
DATA 31, 28, 31, 30, 31
     ↑ Pointer indicates next item to be read

READ Jan%, Feb%, Mar%

DATA 31, 28, 31, 30, 31
                 ↑
READ statement advances pointer

RESTORE

DATA 31, 28, 31, 30, 31
     ↑ RESTORE statement places pointer back at beginning
```

Figure 6-2.
The READ and RESTORE statements.

Two-Dimensional Arrays

Thus far, we've discussed *one-dimensional arrays,* which use one subscript at a time. A one-dimensional array is like a list of values. Sometimes, however, you must work with a table of values. For instance, you might want to represent a table of the words used for the four seasons in three languages:

English:	spring	summer	autumn	winter
Japanese:	haru	natsu	aki	fuyu
Italian:	primavera	estate	autunno	inverno

Instead of a single list, you have rows and columns of data. All words in the same row have something in common: their language. All words in the same column have something in common: their meaning. To identify a particular word, you need to know both its language and its meaning (its row and its column).

To represent such a two-dimensional arrangement of values, you can use a *two-dimensional array,* which has two subscripts. One subscript can represent the row, and one the column.

To create a two-dimensional array, use two subscript ranges, separated by a comma, in the DIM statement:

```
DIM Seasons$(1 TO 3, 1 TO 4)
```

To access a specific element of the array, indicate the two subscript values:

```
Seasons$(1, 2) = "summer"
```

If the first subscript represents the row and the second the column, the preceding example sets the element in row 1, column 2 to the string *summer.* (See Figure 6-3 for another example.) We use these methods in Listing 6-8 to set and print the values for a table.

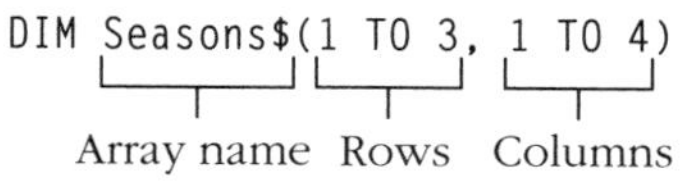

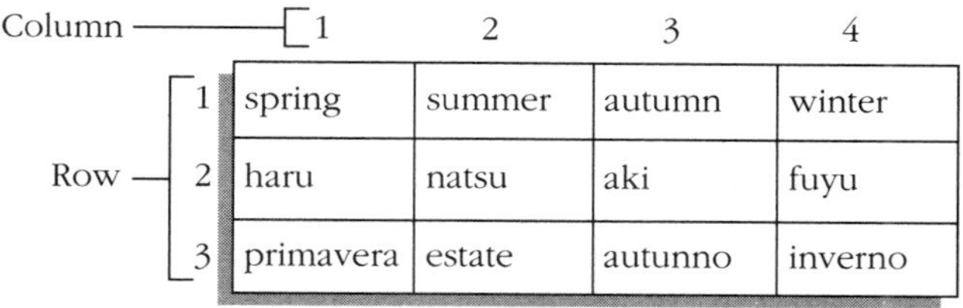

Seasons$(2, 3) is row 2, column 3: *aki*

Figure 6-3.
A two-dimensional array.

```
' English terms
DATA spring, summer, autumn, winter
' Japanese terms
DATA haru, natsu, aki, fuyu
' Italian terms
DATA primavera, estate, autunno, inverno
DIM Seasons$(1 TO 3, 1 TO 4)          ' Two-dimensional array

CLS
FOR Language% = 1 TO 3                ' Loop to place data into array
    FOR Season% = 1 TO 4              ' Nested loop
        READ Seasons$(Language%, Season%)
    NEXT Season%
NEXT Language%

FOR Language% = 1 TO 3                ' Loop to print data
    FOR Season% = 1 TO 4
        PRINT TAB(10 * Season%); Seasons$(Language%, Season%);
    NEXT Season%
    PRINT
    PRINT
NEXT Language%
END
```

Listing 6-8.

Here is the output:

```
spring    summer    autumn    winter

haru      natsu     aki       fuyu

primavera estate    autunno   inverno
```

NOTE: *We could have placed the data in one or two DATA statements instead of three, but it's clearer to reserve one statement for each row of data.*

Nested FOR loops are the natural tools for handling two-dimensional arrays. One loop controls the row subscript, and another loop controls the column subscript. Consider the first set of nested loops in Listing 6-8. The outer loop begins with *Language%* (the row subscript) set to 1. The inner loop then varies *Season%* (the column subscript) from 1 through 4, reading in the first four DATA items.

The main complication in using two-dimensional arrays is keeping track of which range of subscripts goes with each set of elements. For example, suppose we had used this set of nested loops:

```
FOR Language% = 1 TO 3
    FOR Season% = 1 TO 4
        READ Seasons$(Season%, Language%)
    NEXT Season%
NEXT Language%
```

We would have received the message *Subscript out of range*, because the reversed subscripts in the READ statement try to create an array with four rows and three columns rather than the previously dimensioned array of three rows and four columns.

Multidimensional Arrays

You can create three-dimensional arrays, four-dimensional arrays, and so on. In fact, QuickBASIC allows arrays with as many as 63 dimensions. Use as many subscript ranges in the DIM statement as necessary:

```
DIM ThreeD%(1 TO 8, 1 TO 8, 1 TO 8)    ' Three-dimensional array
```

Because multidimensional arrays can require a lot of computer memory, however, the limit of 63 dimensions is a theoretical one; the practical limit is much smaller. To determine the number of elements in a multidimensional array, multiply the number of elements in each dimension. For instance, the preceding *ThreeD%* array has eight elements in each dimension, so the total number of elements is $8 \times 8 \times 8$, or 512. The number of elements becomes prohibitive as you add more dimensions: A 32-dimension array with only two elements per dimension has 2^{32}—or more than 4 billion—elements.

Two-dimensional arrays are useful in a variety of situations. For instance, you could represent your household heating bill records with a two-dimensional array using the columns for months and the rows for years. Or you could represent text shown on the screen using an array with 80 columns and 25 rows to represent the screen's columns and rows.

Arrays and Procedures

Now that we've discussed the basics of creating and using arrays, let's turn to some programming techniques. Writing a procedure, or subprogram, is often the best way to perform an array-related task. Modular programming makes your programs easier to follow and to correct, and it can provide you with reusable programming tools.

The first hurdle in writing a subprogram that processes arrays is telling the subprogram which array to use. You can do this either by passing the array as an argument (generally the best method) or by sharing arrays between module-level code and a subprogram.

Passing Arrays as Arguments

It's easy to pass an array as an argument. Simply use the array name followed by empty parentheses, as in the following:

```
CALL FillArray(Lotto%())
```

Here *FillArray* is a subprogram, and *Lotto%* is an array. Similarly, when you define a procedure, use the array name followed by empty parentheses to indicate an array parameter:

```
SUB FillArray (Arr%())
```

The parameter array type in the procedure definition must match the argument array type in the procedure call. In the preceding example, *Arr%* serves as an alias for *Lotto%* or any other array used as an argument, demonstrating how to use a procedure to assign values to an array.

To illustrate the use of arrays and procedures, we'll simulate entering a lottery. One subprogram will ask the user to choose numbers. A second subprogram will display the choices. To remind you how to call subprograms, we'll use both methods: with CALL and without CALL. (Note that we enclose the argument in parentheses only when CALL is used.) Finally we'll simulate a typical result with a PRINT statement. The program is shown in Listing 6-9.

```
DECLARE SUB FillArray (Arr%())
DECLARE SUB ShowArray (Arr%())
DIM Lotto%(1 TO 6)
CLS
CALL FillArray(Lotto%())          ' Pass an array argument
ShowArray Lotto%()                ' Alternative calling form
PRINT "Alas, you lose."
END

SUB FillArray (Arr%())            ' Declare array parameter
    INPUT "Enter your first number: ", Arr%(1)
    FOR I% = 2 TO 6
        INPUT "Next number: ", Arr%(I%)
    NEXT I%
    PRINT "Here are your choices:"
END SUB

SUB ShowArray (A%())
    FOR I% = 1 TO 6
        PRINT A%(I%);
    NEXT I%
    PRINT
END SUB
```

Listing 6-9.

As usual, QuickBASIC provides the subprogram declarations when we save the program. Here is a sample run:

```
Enter your first number: 10
Next number: 12
Next number: 14
Next number: 16
Next number: 23
Next number: 29
Here are your choices:
 10  12  14  16  23  29
Alas, you lose.
```

The *FillArray* subprogram fills the *Arr%* array. But because a subprogram array parameter is an alias for the argument used in the procedure call, filling *Arr%* in fact fills the *Lotto%* array. Then the *ShowArray* subprogram prints the contents of the *Lotto%* array. This time, *A%* serves as an alias for *Lotto%*.

Using subprograms to process arrays makes the program structure clearer. It also makes it easier to concentrate on individual parts of the program. For example, the preceding program could limit your choices of lottery numbers to a specific range and could allow you to avoid selecting the same value twice. In other words, you can modify and refine the subprogram until it has all the features you want.

Generalizing Procedures

It's usually a good idea to generalize procedures so that you can reuse them in slightly different circumstances. The array procedures used in the lottery example work only for arrays with the subscript range 1 through 6. But you can alter them to work with arrays of various sizes.

Using Arguments to Specify Array Size

You can use additional arguments to indicate array size. For example, you can alter *ShowArray* as follows:

```
SUB ShowArray (Arr%(), Limit%)
    FOR I% = 1 TO Limit%
        PRINT Arr%(I%);
    NEXT I%
    PRINT
END SUB
```

Then, if you want to print an array of 12 elements, you can make this call:

```
CALL ShowArray(Items%(), 12)
```

By adding another argument, you can also make the lower limit selectable.

Using LBOUND and UBOUND to Specify Array Size

The most powerful way to generalize an array procedure is to use QuickBASIC's LBOUND and UBOUND functions, which return the lower limit and the upper limit for an array's subscripts. A subprogram can use these functions to determine the loop limits.

For simple arrays, the syntax is the following:

```
LBOUND(arrayname)
UBOUND(arrayname)
```

The LBOUND function returns the lower limit for the array's subscript range, and the UBOUND function returns the upper limit.

In Listing 6-10, we modify Listing 6-9 to use these functions. Note that the argument for LBOUND and UBOUND is *Arr%*, not *Arr%()*; only the array name is used.

```
DECLARE SUB FillArray (Arr%())
DECLARE SUB ShowArray (Arr%())
DIM Lotto%(1 TO 6)
CLS
CALL FillArray(Lotto%())       ' Subprogram to fill array
ShowArray Lotto%()             ' Subprogram to show array
PRINT "Alas, you lose."
END
```

Listing 6-10. *(continued)*

Listing 6-10. *continued*

```
SUB FillArray (Arr%())
    Begin% = LBOUND(Arr%)       ' Find lower limit
    INPUT "Enter your first number: ", Arr%(Begin%)
    FOR I% = Begin% + 1 TO UBOUND(Arr%)
        INPUT "Next number: ", Arr%(I%)
    NEXT I%
    PRINT "Here are your choices:"
END SUB

SUB ShowArray (A%())
    FOR I% = LBOUND(A%) TO UBOUND(A%)
        PRINT A%(I%);
    NEXT I%
    PRINT
END SUB
```

You can assign the value of LBOUND (or of UBOUND) to a variable, as we did with *Begin%*, or you can use the functions directly as loop limits.

But which method of specifying array size is best? Each has advantages. Using LBOUND and UBOUND is simpler (because you don't need to enter arguments) and more fool-proof (because you can't accidentally provide the wrong limits). Using arguments allows greater flexibility—you can process part of an array by using the appropriate arguments, for example. In the preceding program, you could display only the first half of the *Lotto%* array by passing 3 as the upper limit.

Using Shared Arrays in Subprograms

Instead of passing an array as an argument, you can use the SHARED option of the DIM statement to share an array between the module-level code and the subprograms. The SHARED option is technically called an *attribute* of the DIM statement because it changes how the statement works.

Recall that variables (other than parameters) defined inside a subprogram are local variables, independent of variables in the module-level code. The SHARED attribute makes an array declared in the module-level code directly available to subprograms (Figure 6-4). Typically, an array is shared when it contains a block of data that several parts of a program can use—constant data, for example, the kind you would include in a DATA statement. Thus the SHARED attribute and the READ statement are often used together.

To demonstrate the use of a shared array, let's put together a program in which the user enters the month and day, and the program calculates the day of the year—the 51st day, the 178th day, or whatever. The program should ignore leap years and accept months in numeric form only (1 means January, 2 means February, and so on).

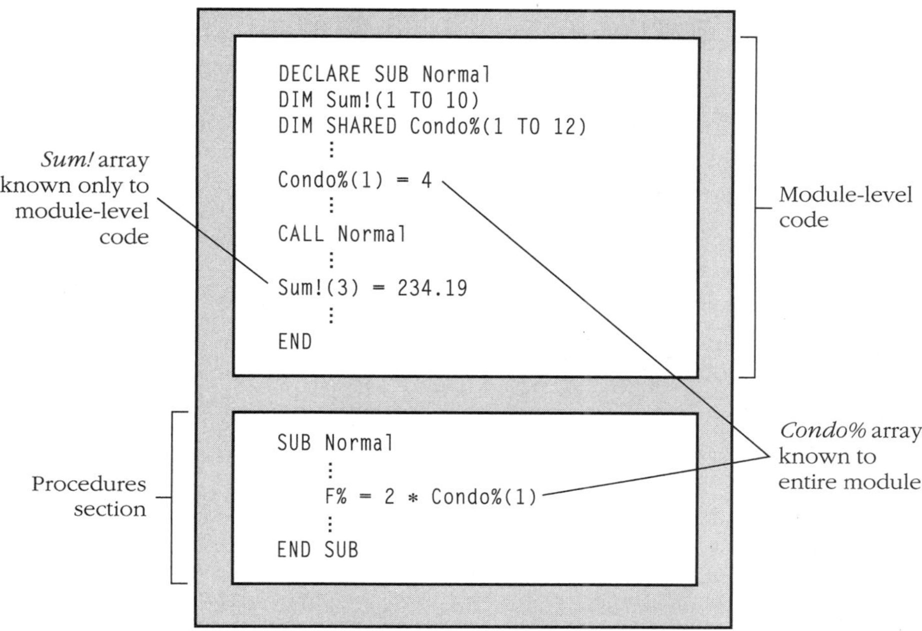

Figure 6-4.
Shared and nonshared arrays.

To calculate the day of the year for April 15, our program must add 15 to the total number of days in all the preceding months. We can use the *Days%* array we created in Listing 6-6, which indicates the number of days in each month. If we make *Days%* a shared array, we can use the array in a subprogram, as shown in Listing 6-11.

```
' This program displays the day of the year when you enter
'  the month and the day of the month
DECLARE SUB DayOfYear (Mn%, Dd%)
DIM SHARED Days%(1 TO 12)          ' Array shared with subprogram
DIM SHARED Months$(1 TO 12)        ' Array shared with subprogram
DATA 31,28,31,30,31,30,31,31,30,31,30,31
DATA January, February, March, April, May, June, July
DATA August, September, October, November, December

FOR Month% = 1 TO 12
    READ Days%(Month%)             ' Initialize array with days per month
NEXT Month%

FOR Month% = 1 TO 12
    READ Months$(Month%)           ' Initialize array with months' names
NEXT Month%
```

Listing 6-11. *(continued)*

Listing 6-11. *continued*

```
CLS
INPUT "Enter the month number (1-12): ", MonthNum%
DO WHILE MonthNum% >= 1 AND MonthNum% <= 12
    INPUT "Enter the day date (1-31): ", DayDate%
    DayOfYear MonthNum%, DayDate%  ' Call subprogram
    INPUT "Next month number (0 to quit):  ", MonthNum%
LOOP
PRINT "Bye!"
END

' This subprogram calculates the day of the year, given the
'  month number Mn% and the day of the month Dm%
SUB DayOfYear (Mn%, Dm%)
    Total% = Dm%
    FOR Month% = 1 TO Mn% - 1
        Total% = Total% + Days%(Month%)
    NEXT Month%
    PRINT Months$(Mn%); Dm%; "is day"; Total%
END SUB
```

Note that we use the *Days%* and *Months$* arrays in both the module-level code and the subprogram. The SHARED attribute in the DIM statements makes that possible.

Here is a sample run:

```
Enter the month number (1-12): 1
Enter the day date (1-31): 20
January 20 is day 20
Next month number (0 to quit):  12
Enter the day date (1-31): 31
December 31 is day 365
Next month number (0 to quit):  0
Bye!
```

In the *DayOf Year* subprogram, *Total%* is initially set to the day number. Then the upper limit for the loop of *Mn% – 1* causes the loop to calculate the number of days in the preceding months. Recall that a FOR loop is skipped if the upper limit is less than the lower limit. Thus, if the month is January, the loop is skipped.

When you use a shared array in a procedure, the array name is built into the procedure. This option is adequate when the procedure is intended to work with an array containing some standard data, as in our example. But if you are designing a more general-purpose procedure, such as one that adds up the elements of an array, you should use an array argument, which allows the procedure to work with any suitable array.

Using Procedures and Two-Dimensional Arrays

Amanda Firkin is keeping track of the yearly sales of her mystery novels. She asks you to write a program that will calculate total sales for each novel, total sales for each year, and a grand total. You can use a two-dimensional array to hold the raw data. Wanting to look like an experienced programmer, you naturally plan to use procedures to do the calculations. But how do you communicate two-dimensional arrays to a procedure? The easy solution to this problem is to use the SHARED attribute when creating the arrays. A better solution is to use arguments and parameters, which allow you to develop a procedure that can be used with other arrays too.

Passing two-dimensional arrays as arguments is no more difficult than passing a one-dimensional array. In fact, the method is exactly the same:

- For the argument, use the array name followed by empty parentheses.
- For the procedure parameter, use a name followed by empty parentheses. The procedure then uses this name as an alias for the argument array.

Listing 6-12 shows you how to use procedures with two-dimensional arrays. The *Sales!* array holds the sales figures for three book titles and for four years. For reference, the *Titles$* array holds the titles. The *YearTotals!* and *TitleTotals!* arrays hold the results.

```
DECLARE SUB AddAll (Label$, Values!())
DECLARE SUB FindTitleTotals (Money!(), Items!())
DECLARE SUB FindYearTotals (Money!(), Sums!())
' The Big Gat title and sales
DATA The Big Gat, 2345.12, 4500.29, 3211.71, 1203.33
' Murder, She Moaned title and sales
DATA "Murder, She Moaned", 3001.77, 3023.31, 3421.34, 4211.50
' Deathly Pale title and sales
DATA Deathly Pale, 0, 6000.00, 4083.43, 5021.31

DIM Titles$(1 TO 3)                         ' Array for book titles
DIM Sales!(1 TO 3, 1987 TO 1990)            ' Array for sales by book and year
DIM YearTotals!(1987 TO 1990)               ' Array for yearly sales total
DIM TitleTotals!(1 TO 3)                    ' Array for book sales total
CLS

' Read titles and sales
FOR Title% = 1 TO 3
    READ Titles$(Title%)
    FOR Year% = 1987 TO 1990
        READ Sales!(Title%, Year%)
    NEXT Year%
NEXT Title%
```

Listing 6-12. *(continued)*

```
FindYearTotals Sales!(), YearTotals!()      ' Pass arrays to subprogram
FOR Year% = 1987 TO 1990                    ' Print yearly totals
    PRINT "Sales for"; Year%;
    PRINT USING "= $$#####.##"; YearTotals!(Year%)
NEXT Year%
FindTitleTotals Sales!(), TitleTotals!()    ' Pass arrays to subprogram
FOR Title% = 1 TO 3                         ' Print book totals
    PRINT "Sales for "; Titles$(Title%);
    PRINT USING " = $$#####.##"; TitleTotals!(Title%)
NEXT Title%
AddAll "All titles", TitleTotals!()         ' Pass variable and array
AddAll "All years", YearTotals!()
END

' Find the sum of all elements of the array Values!
' Print result, labeling it with Label$
SUB AddAll (Label$, Values!())
    Sum! = 0                                ' Initialize total to 0
    FOR I% = LBOUND(Values!) TO UBOUND(Values!)
        Sum! = Sum! + Values!(I%)
    NEXT I%
    PRINT USING "& =$$#####.##"; Label$; Sum!
END SUB

' Total the sales by book
SUB FindTitleTotals (Money!(), Items!())
    FOR Item% = 1 TO 3                      ' Loop for each book
        Items!(Item%) = 0
        FOR Yr% = 1987 TO 1990              ' Nested loop for each year
            Items!(Item%) = Items!(Item%) + Money!(Item%, Yr%)
        NEXT Yr%
    NEXT Item%
END SUB

' Total the sales by year
SUB FindYearTotals (Money!(), Sums!())
    FOR Yr% = 1987 TO 1990
        Sums!(Yr%) = 0
        FOR Item% = 1 TO 3
            Sums!(Yr%) = Sums!(Yr%) + Money!(Item%, Yr%)
        NEXT Item%
    NEXT Yr%
END SUB
```

Here is the output:

```
Sales for 1987 =   $5346.89
Sales for 1988 =  $13523.60
Sales for 1989 =  $10716.48
Sales for 1990 =  $10436.14
```

```
Sales for The Big Gat =  $11260.45
Sales for Murder, She Moaned =  $13657.92
Sales for Deathly Pale =  $15104.74
All titles = $40023.11
All years = $40023.11
```

The title of each book is included in the same DATA statement as its sales, a technique that allows us to keep related data together. To get the data into the correct arrays, the program must first read a title and place it in one array and then read the corresponding sales figures and put them in a second array. The first FOR loop contains a READ statement to read a title and a nested FOR loop to read the sales for that book.

The *FindYearTotals* subprogram then calculates the total sales for each year, taking two arrays as arguments. The first array, *Sales!*, is the two-dimensional array holding the data. The second array, *YearTotals!*, receives the results. So one array carries information to the subprogram, and the second array carries information back. The code itself uses a nested loop:

```
SUB FindYearTotals (Money!(), Sums!())
    FOR Yr% = 1987 TO 1990
        Sums!(Yr%) = 0
        FOR Item% = 1 TO 3
            Sums!(Yr%) = Sums!(Yr%) + Money!(Item%, Yr%)
        NEXT Item%
    NEXT Yr%
END SUB
```

Remember that the array names in the subprogram parameter list are aliases for the arguments in the calling statement—*Money!* is really *Sales!*, and *Sums!* is really *YearTotals!*. The inner loop totals the sales for a particular year by title. The outer loop ensures that this operation is carried out for each year. The *FindTitleTotals* subprogram is constructed along the same lines, except that the inner loop totals the data by year rather than by title and the outer loop ensures that this calculation is performed for each title.

For the *AddAll* subprogram, we took a more general approach. Using LBOUND and UBOUND avoids tying the function to one particular range of subscripts:

```
' Find the sum of all elements of the array Values!
' Print result, labeling it with Label$
SUB AddAll (Label$, Values!())
    Sum! = 0
    FOR I% = LBOUND(Values!) TO UBOUND(Values!)
        Sum! = Sum! + Values!(I%)
    NEXT I%
    PRINT USING "& =$$#####.##"; Label$; Sum!
END SUB
```

To demonstrate the versatility of this subprogram, we use it with both *TitleTotals!* (with a subscript range of 1 through 3) and *YearTotals!* (with a subscript range of 1987 through 1990). Because both subprogram calls represent the sum for all titles and all years, the two return values are the same.

It might be useful to modify the other two procedures to make them as general as *AddAll*—after all, totaling the rows and totaling the columns of a two-dimensional array are common tasks. That raises the question of how to use LBOUND and UBOUND with two-dimensional arrays.

Extending LBOUND and UBOUND to Greater Dimensions

Recall that *LBOUND(Beasts$)* is the low end of the subscript range for *Beasts$* if *Beasts$* is a one-dimensional array. To use LBOUND with a two-dimensional array, you must use a second argument to tell the function which subscript you mean. For example, recall our *Sales!* array:

```
DIM Sales!(1 TO 3, 1987 TO 1990)
```

LBOUND(Sales!, 1) is the lower limit for the first subscript and therefore equals 1. *LBOUND(Sales!, 2)* is the lower limit for the second subscript, so it equals 1987.

Here is the full syntax for LBOUND and UBOUND:

```
LBOUND(arrayname[, dimension])
UBOUND(arrayname[, dimension])
```

LBOUND returns the smallest usable value for the *dimension* subscript for *arrayname*. UBOUND returns the largest usable value for the *dimension* subscript for *arrayname*.

If *dimension* is omitted, it's considered 1—for example, *LBOUND(Har!)* is the same as *LBOUND(Har!, 1)*, the lower limit for the first subscript.

Let's use these properties to replace *FindYearTotals* with a more general procedure, one that totals the rows of any two-dimensional array of single-precision values:

```
' Arr! is a two-dimensional array. This program adds the values
'  in each row of Arr!, placing the total in the corresponding
'  element of Sums!, i.e., Sums!(N%) = sum of row N% of Arr!
SUB SumRows (Arr!(), Sums!())
    FOR Col% = LBOUND(Arr!, 2) TO UBOUND(Arr!, 2)
        Sums!(Col%) = 0
        FOR Row% = LBOUND(Arr!, 1) TO UBOUND(Arr!, 1)
            Sums!(Col%) = Sums!(Col%) + Arr!(Row%, Col%)
        NEXT Row%
    NEXT Col%
END SUB
```

As an exercise, try converting the *FindTitleTotals* subprogram to a general column-totaling procedure.

Static and Dynamic Arrays

QuickBASIC allocates memory for arrays in two ways. One method allocates memory when the program is compiled, creating a *static array.* The other method allocates memory while the program is running, creating a *dynamic array.* The size of a static array is fixed when the program is compiled, whereas the size of a dynamic array is set when the program runs. Thus you must decide the size of a static array when you write the program, but you can delay choosing the size of a dynamic array until the program is running.

In general, static arrays are preferred because they can be processed more rapidly. Dynamic arrays, however, offer greater flexibility and control of memory. For example, you can erase a dynamic array to free memory for other tasks.

Specifying the Memory Mode

By default, QuickBASIC creates a static array if you dimension the array using literals (constant or numeric values); it creates a dynamic array if you dimension the array using variables or other expressions:

```
DIM Electric&(1 TO 10) ' Creates a static array
DIM Gas&(1 TO N%)      ' Creates a dynamic array (N% is a variable)
```

Recall that you can create an array without using DIM, simply by using an array element in your program. These *implicitly dimensioned arrays* are static.

The *metacommands* $STATIC and $DYNAMIC allow you to override the default behavior for arrays dimensioned using literals. Metacommands are commands that tell QuickBASIC how to compile programs. The $STATIC metacommand makes all arrays with literal subscript limits static; this is the regular default mode. The $DYNAMIC metacommand makes all arrays (except implicitly dimensioned arrays) dynamic. A metacommand on the module level affects only module-level code, however. To affect procedures, you must place a metacommand on the procedure level.

Metacommands, oddly enough, must appear in program comments. For instance, here are two valid examples:

```
REM $DYNAMIC

' $STATIC
```

Another way to create dynamic arrays is to use the REDIM statement (discussed later) instead of the DIM statement to dimension the array.

Managing Arrays: The ERASE Statement

The QuickBASIC ERASE statement helps you manage arrays. It clears a static array, setting each element to 0 (or to the null string in a string array). The same statement completely erases a dynamic array, however, removing it from memory.

The ERASE statement syntax is as follows:

```
ERASE arraynamelist
```

arraynamelist is a comma-separated list of array names. No parentheses are used.

Listing 6-13 illustrates the effect of ERASE on a static array.

```
DECLARE SUB ShowArray (Arr%())
DATA 1,2,4,8,16,32,64,128,256,512,1024
DIM TwoPowers%(0 TO 5)          ' Static array

FOR Power% = 0 TO 5
    READ TwoPowers%(Power%)     ' Place values into array
NEXT Power%
CLS
PRINT "Static array before ERASE:"
CALL ShowArray(TwoPowers%())
ERASE TwoPowers%                ' Reset all array elements to 0
PRINT "Static array after ERASE:"
CALL ShowArray(TwoPowers%())
END

SUB ShowArray (Arr%())
    FOR I% = LBOUND(Arr%) TO UBOUND(Arr%)
        PRINT Arr%(I%);
    NEXT I%
    PRINT
END SUB
```

Listing 6-13.

Here is the output:

```
Static array before ERASE:
 1  2  4  8  16  32
Static array after ERASE:
 0  0  0  0  0  0
```

If *TwoPowers%* had been a dynamic array, the program would have halted after the ERASE statement—there would no longer have been an array to print.

After a dynamic array has been erased, you can reuse the name to create a new array, as shown in Listing 6-14. Note that in this program we give the new dynamic array a different size. (You could also give it a different name.)

```
DECLARE SUB ShowArray (Arr%())
DATA 1,2,4,8,16,32,64,128,256,512,1024
' $DYNAMIC
DIM TwoPowers%(0 TO 5)          ' Dynamic array

FOR Power% = 0 TO 5
    READ TwoPowers%(Power%)     ' Place values into array
NEXT Power%
CLS
PRINT "Dynamic array before ERASE:"
CALL ShowArray(TwoPowers%())
ERASE TwoPowers%                ' Delete array

DIM TwoPowers%(0 TO 7)          ' Make new array
RESTORE                         ' Reset to read first data item
FOR Power% = 0 TO 7
    READ TwoPowers%(Power%)     ' Place values into new array
NEXT Power%

PRINT "New dynamic array after ERASE:"
CALL ShowArray(TwoPowers%())
END

REM $STATIC
SUB ShowArray (Arr%())
    FOR I% = LBOUND(Arr%) TO UBOUND(Arr%)
        PRINT Arr%(I%);
    NEXT I%
    PRINT
END SUB
```

Listing 6-14.

Here is the output:

```
Dynamic array before ERASE:
 1  2  4  8  16  32
New dynamic array after ERASE:
 1  2  4  8  16  32  64  128
```

The $DYNAMIC metacommand in Listing 6-14 applies only to module-level code. Note that because the *Arr%* array in the procedure is an alias for the *TwoPowers%* array in the module level, the *Arr%* array is a dynamic array. If you create a new array in the procedure, however, it will be static by default. If you want to use dynamic arrays in the procedures too, you can change the metacommand in the procedures from $STATIC to $DYNAMIC.

Getting a Clean Slate: The CLEAR Statement

Whereas the ERASE statement erases a specified array, the CLEAR statement clears all arrays and variables and resets them to 0 (or to the null string). In addition, it closes any open files in the program. Using CLEAR has the same effect as terminating a program and starting it up again, so don't use it casually.

The CLEAR statement also clears the *stack* and lets you resize it. The stack is a portion of memory set aside for passing argument information to procedures and functions. Unless you use a great many variables, you rarely need to resize the stack. But *procedure recursion,* in which a procedure calls itself repeatedly, can require a lot of stack space, because each recursive call generates a new, additional set of variables, which can require even more stack space. (Chapter 8 discusses recursion.) If you use CLEAR to resize the stack, you should do so at the beginning of a program before assigning values to variables and arrays. Because CLEAR also resets all variables and arrays to 0 (or to null strings), using it later in the program will undo earlier assignments.

Here is the syntax for CLEAR:

```
CLEAR [, , stack]
```

The CLEAR statement

- Closes all files and releases the file buffers
- Clears all variables declared in a COMMON statement (discussed in Chapter 8)
- Sets numeric variables and arrays to 0
- Sets all string variables and arrays to null
- Reinitializes the stack and (optionally) adds bytes to the stack size already required by QuickBASIC

The pair of commas preceding *stack* are relics of CLEAR's BASICA heritage.

Managing Arrays: The REDIM Statement

The REDIM statement allows you to resize dynamic arrays. It can't be used with static arrays. The REDIM statement has essentially the same effect as using ERASE and DIM in succession. The original contents of the array are lost, and you end up with a fresh array in which each element is set to 0 or to the null string.

The REDIM statement has basically the same syntax as DIM:

```
REDIM [SHARED] arrayname([lower TO] upper) [AS type]
```

arrayname is a dynamic array. REDIM changes its size, erasing its original contents. If *arrayname* doesn't exist, REDIM creates it as a dynamic array.

Despite its name, REDIM does not allow you to change the number of dimensions of an array—a one-dimensional array remains a one-dimensional array, for example. REDIM merely allows you to change the subscript ranges.

Listing 6-15 demonstrates how the REDIM statement works. Here *TwoPowers%* is a dynamic array, despite its literal subscript limits, because we first create it using REDIM instead of DIM.

```
DECLARE SUB ShowArray (Arr%())
DATA 1,2,4,8,16,32,64,128,256,512,1024
REDIM TwoPowers%(0 TO 10)           ' Dimension as an
                                    '  11-element dynamic array
FOR Power% = 0 TO 10
    READ TwoPowers%(Power%)
NEXT Power%
CLS
PRINT "Dynamic array before REDIM:"
CALL ShowArray(TwoPowers%())
REDIM TwoPowers%(0 TO 5)            ' Redimension with 6 elements
RESTORE
FOR Power% = 0 TO 5
    READ TwoPowers%(Power%)
NEXT Power%

PRINT "New dynamic array after REDIM:"
CALL ShowArray(TwoPowers%())
END

SUB ShowArray (Arr%())
    FOR I% = LBOUND(Arr%) TO UBOUND(Arr%)
        PRINT Arr%(I%);
    NEXT I%
    PRINT
END SUB
```

Listing 6-15.

Here is the output:

```
Dynamic array before REDIM:
 1  2  4  8  16  32  64  128  256  512  1024
New dynamic array after REDIM:
 1  2  4  8  16  32
```

Note that the number of elements has changed.

The FRE Function and Available Memory

Arrays can use a great deal of memory. If you are a careful programmer, you'll want to ensure that your computer has sufficient memory available before you create a large array. QuickBASIC's FRE function can help by informing you how many bytes of memory are available. Let's look at the three kinds of memory FRE can report.

For data storage, QuickBASIC organizes available memory into three areas: the stack, *heap space,* and *string space.* (String space is simply a more restricted form of heap space.) The terms *heap* and *stack* indicate how QuickBASIC manages the memory. The stack is an orderly system in which new items are added to memory sequentially. It is a last-in-first-out (LIFO) system—that is, when QuickBASIC frees memory in the stack, it first removes the item that was most recently added.

A heap is more disorderly, allowing blocks of memory to be freed in any order. If, for instance, you create dynamic arrays A, B, and C and then use ERASE to remove array B, you can wind up with an unused chunk of memory between the two remaining arrays. QuickBASIC is fairly sophisticated, however. When a block is deleted, it monitors the heap and moves memory blocks around in order to close up the holes. This *compacting* leaves the available space contiguous instead of fragmented.

Different kinds of data go into different areas of memory. The stack holds program addresses telling programs where to go when they complete procedures. It also holds the temporary variables that are created when you use expressions instead of variables as procedure arguments. Ordinary variables and strings go into string space. Dynamic arrays (other than strings) go into heap space. Static arrays go into string space if you are using a stand-alone EXE program and into heap space if you are working in the QuickBASIC environment.

Where does FRE fit in? It has the following syntax:

```
FRE(number)
FRE(string)
```

If *number* is –1, FRE returns the size in bytes of the largest available block of heap space. If *number* is –2, FRE returns the available stack space. If *number* is any other value, FRE returns the size of the next available block of string space. If FRE uses a string, FRE first compacts the string space and then returns the size of the largest available block of string space. (Because the current version of QuickBASIC compacts memory automatically, the last two options produce the same result. In earlier versions of BASIC, where the string space is not compacted automatically, the results of the two options can be different.)

Listing 6-16 demonstrates how FRE works. The program begins by reporting the amount of heap space and the amount of string space. Then it creates a string array and a dynamic integer array, reporting memory at various stages.

```
' Down memory lane
DATA 1,2,4,8,16,32,64,128,306,512,1024
DATA Show me the way, to San Francisco Bay
DATA There once was a hound, who swam the Puget Sound

CLS
PRINT TAB(30); "Heap Space"; TAB(42); "String Space"

' Display memory values before creating arrays
PRINT "Initially:"; TAB(30); FRE(-1); TAB(42); FRE(0)

' Create static string array, and then show memory values
DIM Words$(1 TO 4)
PRINT "After DIM string array:";
PRINT TAB(30); FRE(-1); TAB(42); FRE(0)

' Create dynamic integer array, and then show memory values
REDIM TwoPowers%(0 TO 10)
PRINT "After REDIM integer array:";
PRINT TAB(30); FRE(-1); TAB(42); FRE(0)

' Place data into arrays, and then show memory values
FOR Power% = 0 TO 10
    READ TwoPowers%(Power%)
NEXT Power%
FOR I% = 1 TO 4
    READ Words$(I%)
NEXT I%
PRINT "After arrays are read:";
PRINT TAB(30); FRE(-1); TAB(42); FRE(0)
END
```

Listing 6-16.

Here is a sample run:

```
                              Heap Space  String Space
Initially:                     206910      47214
After DIM string array:        206910      47214
After REDIM integer array:     206878      47214
After arrays are read:         206788      47124
```

Merely creating the string array does not affect the amount of available memory. At that point, the program doesn't know how large the strings will be. But after the program reads the strings into the array, FRE shows that the amount of string space has been reduced by 90 bytes. Creating the integer array immediately affects the heap space, however, because knowing the number of integers is enough to determine the array size.

Sorting Arrays

Eventually, you will need to sort data, a task usually accomplished with arrays. Suppose you want a program to sort scores entered from the keyboard. You'll need a general plan such as this one:

1. Read data from the keyboard into an array.
2. Display the data in its original order to verify the input.
3. Sort the array.
4. Display the sorted array.

This plan suggests that you'll need three procedures to accomplish the major tasks: reading the input, displaying the array, and sorting the array. The main program, on a first pass, might look like this:

```
CALL GetScores(Scores!())
PRINT "Here is the input list:"
CALL ShowScores(Scores!())
CALL SortScores(Scores!())
PRINT "Here is the sorted list:"
CALL ShowScores(Scores!())
```

The *Scores!* array must be large enough to hold all the data but not so large that it wastes a lot of space. A dynamic array is the obvious tool. Because the user will know—roughly—the number of scores to be entered, you can ask her or him to supply an upper limit for the array size. But because you don't want to require the user to count the scores exactly, you'll need to allow the user to terminate input before the limit is reached. These features make the program easier to use but harder to construct. First, you must allow two conditions to terminate the input loop. Second, because part of the array might be empty, you'll want to show and sort only the full part. Thus you'll need to change the basic design a bit:

```
INPUT "Maximum number of scores: ", Lim%
DIM Scores!(1 TO Lim%)
CALL GetScores(Scores!(), Size%)     ' Fill array, count input
PRINT "Here is the input list:"
CALL ShowScores(Scores!(), Size%)
CALL SortScores(Scores!(), Size%)
PRINT "Here is the sorted list:"
CALL ShowScores(Scores!(), Size%)
```

The *GetScores* subprogram will count the number of input items and assign the result to *Size%*, the new argument added to the argument lists. *Size%* is then passed as an argument to the subsequent subprograms so that they will know how much of the array to show and sort.

Reading the Data

Now you must write the procedures. You can base *GetScores* on a similar procedure from Listing 6-10:

```
' This subprogram places input in the array Arr!. Input quits
'  when the array is filled or when the user enters a blank line,
'  whichever comes first. The subprogram assigns the number of
'  entries to N%. The procedure assumes LBOUND is 1.
SUB GetScores (Arr!(), N%)
    N% = 0
    Max% = UBOUND(Arr!)
    INPUT "Enter first number: ", Num$
    DO WHILE Num$ <> "" AND N% < Max%
        Num! = VAL(Num$)
        N% = N% + 1
        Arr!(N%) = Num!
        IF N% < Max% THEN
            INPUT "Enter next number: ", Num$
        ELSE
            PRINT "Array is filled."
        END IF
    LOOP
END SUB
```

The input loop terminates if you enter a blank line or if *N%* reaches the maximum value of *Max%*. Input values are converted to numbers and placed in the array. The procedure assigns to the parameter *N%* the number of array elements filled. Because a parameter is simply an alias for a variable argument, changing *N%* is the same as changing *Size%*.

Showing the Data

Showing the array is simple:

```
SUB ShowScores (Arr!(), N%)
    FOR I% = LBOUND(Arr!) TO LBOUND(Arr!) + N% - 1
        PRINT Arr!(I%);
    NEXT I%
    PRINT
END SUB
```

You can spiff up this procedure later. For example, if you have too many scores to fit on one line, you can start a new line after every 20 scores.

Sorting the Data

Now you come to the heart of this program: sorting. Many sorting algorithms have been developed for computers, but you can use one of the simplest here—the *selection sort*.

Here is a plan in outline form (what programmers call *pseudocode*):

```
FOR N = First TO Next-to-last element,
  find largest remaining number and place it in element N
NEXT N
```

This pseudocode tells the computer to do the following:

First start with *N = 1*. Scan the entire array, find the largest number, and exchange it with the first element. Next set *N = 2*, and scan all but the first element of the array. Find the largest remaining number, and swap it with the second element. Continue this process until reaching the next-to-last element. Compare the two remaining elements, and place the larger in the next-to-last position, leaving the smallest element in the array in the final position.

A FOR loop could accomplish this task, but you must describe the "find and place" process—the process of selecting the largest remaining value—in more detail. One method allows you to compare the first and second elements of the remaining array. If the second is larger, swap the two values. Now compare the first element with the third. If the third is larger, swap those two. Each swap moves a larger element to the top of the list. Continue in this way until you have compared the first and the last elements. The largest number is now the first element of the remaining array. You have sorted the array for the first element, although the rest of the array is in a jumble. In outline:

```
FOR M = Second element TO Last element,
    compare Mth element with first element;
    if Mth is greater, swap values
NEXT M
```

You need another FOR loop, nested in the first one. The outer loop indicates which array element is to be filled, and the inner loop finds the value to put there. (See Figure 6-5 for another view of the sorting scheme.)

Now you can execute the entire plan in QuickBASIC code:

```
' This SUB sorts the array Arr! in decreasing order
SUB SortScores (Arr!(), N%)
    Low% = LBOUND(Arr!)
    High% = LBOUND(Arr!) + N% - 1
    FOR Top% = Low% TO High% - 1
        FOR Comp% = Top% TO High%
            IF Arr!(Comp%) > Arr!(Top%) THEN
                SWAP Arr!(Comp%), Arr!(Top%)
            END IF
        NEXT Comp%
    NEXT Top%
END SUB
```

The QuickBASIC SWAP statement is used here. This statement takes two variables (which can be array elements) as arguments and exchanges their values.

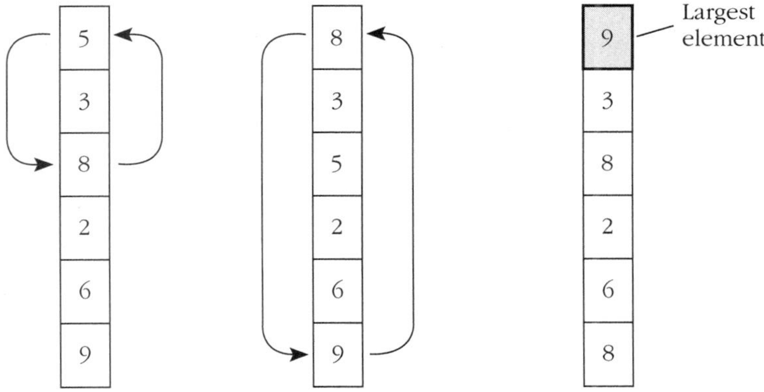

Compare each element with the first element, and swap if the first element is smaller. Repeat the process for all elements until the largest number is first.

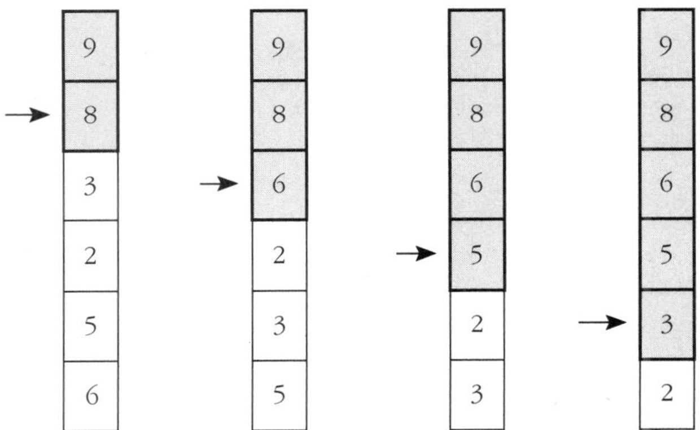

Compare the remaining elements to the element in the next position, and put the largest remaining value there.

Figure 6-5.
Sorting array values.

Here is the SWAP syntax:

```
SWAP variable1, variable2
```

The two variables must be of the same type—integer, long, single precision, double precision, string, or record (a user-defined type we'll cover in Chapter 10). The statement exchanges their values.

The Final Program

Putting all the pieces together gives you the final program shown in Listing 6-17.

```
' SORT.BAS--reads an array of numbers and sorts it
DECLARE SUB SortScores (Arr!(), N%)
DECLARE SUB ShowScores (Arr!(), N%)
DECLARE SUB GetScores (Arr!(), N%)
DECLARE SUB StatePurpose ()

CLS
CALL StatePurpose                       ' Provide user information
INPUT "Maximum number of scores: ", Lim%
DIM Scores!(1 TO Lim%)                  ' Dimension dynamic array
CALL GetScores(Scores!(), Size%)        ' Fill array, count input
PRINT "Here is the input list:"
CALL ShowScores(Scores!(), Size%)       ' Display scores before sorting
CALL SortScores(Scores!(), Size%)       ' Sort scores
PRINT "Here is the sorted list:"
CALL ShowScores(Scores!(), Size%)       ' Display scores after sorting
END

' This subprogram places input in the array Arr!. Input quits
'  when the array is filled or when the user enters a blank line,
'  whichever comes first. The subprogram assigns the number of
'  entries to N%. The procedure assumes LBOUND is 1.
SUB GetScores (Arr!(), N%)
    N% = 0
    Max% = UBOUND(Arr!)
    INPUT "Enter first number: ", Num$
    DO WHILE Num$ <> "" AND N% < Max%
        Num! = VAL(Num$)
        N% = N% + 1
        Arr!(N%) = Num!
        IF N% < Max% THEN
            INPUT "Enter next number: ", Num$
        ELSE
            PRINT "Array is filled."
        END IF
    LOOP
END SUB

SUB ShowScores (Arr!(), N%)
    FOR I% = LBOUND(Arr!) TO LBOUND(Arr!) + N% - 1
        PRINT Arr!(I%);
    NEXT I%
    PRINT
END SUB
```

Listing 6-17.

(continued)

Listing 6-17. *continued*

```
' This SUB sorts the array Arr! in decreasing order
SUB SortScores (Arr!(), N%)
    Low% = LBOUND(Arr!)
    High% = LBOUND(Arr!) + N% - 1
    FOR Top% = Low% TO High% - 1
        FOR Comp% = Top% TO High%
            IF Arr!(Comp%) > Arr!(Top%) THEN
                SWAP Arr!(Comp%), Arr!(Top%)
        END IF
        NEXT Comp%
    NEXT Top%
END SUB

SUB StatePurpose
    PRINT "Type in scores, and this program will display ";
    PRINT "them in the original and in sorted order."
    PRINT "Press Enter at the beginning of a line to terminate."
END SUB
```

Here is a sample run:

```
Type in scores, and this program will display
them in the original and in sorted order.
Press Enter at the beginning of a line to terminate.
Maximum number of scores: 4
Enter first number: 68
Enter next number: 84
Enter next number: 59
Enter next number: 90
Array is filled.
Here is the input list:
 68  84  59  90
Here is the sorted list:
 90  84  68  59
```

Back to Debug

Suppose you want to design a program that will calculate the first 20 factorials and store them in an array. (The factorial of an integer is the product of all the positive integers from 1 through the integer itself—for instance, 4 factorial is $1 \times 2 \times 3 \times 4$.) When you enter an integer, the program will report its factorial. Let's look at a possible program (Listing 6-18) and see what happens when you try to run it.

```
CLS
DIM Factorial#(1 TO 20)           ' Dimension 20-element static array
Factorial#(1) = 1                 ' Initialize at 1
FOR I% = 2 TO 20                  ' Calculate array values
    Factorial#(I%) = I% * Factorial#(I% - 1)
NEXT I%
PRINT "Enter an integer from 1 to 20 (0 to quit)";
PRINT " and see its factorial."
INPUT "Integer 1-20: ", N%
DO WHILE (N% > 0) AND (N% < 21)   ' Display selected array element
    PRINT N%; "factorial is"; Factorial#(N%)
LOOP
END
```

Listing 6-18.

Here is a sample run:

```
Enter an integer from 1 to 20 (0 to quit) and see its factorial.
Integer 1-20: 15
 15 factorial is 1307674368000
 15 factorial is 1307674368000
 15 factorial is 1307674368000
   ⋮
```

The program could run endlessly; you must press Ctrl-Break to stop it. Let's use the Debug menu to find the programming error. Start by selecting Reset from the Run menu, which gives you a clean slate. The problem seems to be in the output loop, so put *N%* in the Watch window. The Watch window can also handle expressions, so add the WHILE loop test expression. Use the mouse or the arrow keys to highlight the test:

```
(N% > 0) AND (N% < 21)
```

Then select Add Watch from the Debug menu to place the entire expression in the window. Keep in mind that QuickBASIC represents true with the value –1 and false with the value 0.

Creating Breakpoints

Next run the program up to the WHILE loop. You can use the F8 key to single-step through the program, but you'll have to traverse all 19 cycles of the FOR loop. Let's take a shortcut. Place the cursor on the line that reads as follows:

```
INPUT "Integer 1-20: ", N%
```

You can make this line a *breakpoint*—in other words, when you run the program in the regular fashion (selecting Start from the Run menu or pressing Shift-F5), it will halt when it reaches that line. To make the line a breakpoint, either press the F9 key or select Toggle Breakpoint from the Debug menu. QuickBASIC then highlights the line using the breakpoint color scheme (as determined by the Display dialog box in the Options menu).

You can set as many breakpoints as you want. Pressing Shift-F5 (or selecting Start from the Run menu) runs the program to the first breakpoint. Pressing F5 (without Shift) causes the program to continue to the next breakpoint. Because you have only one breakpoint here, pressing Shift-F5 takes you to the INPUT line. At this point, *N%* is 0 because you haven't entered a value. This value of *N%* also makes the test condition 0, or false:

```
LIST-18.BAS N%:  0
LIST-18.BAS (N% > 0) AND (N% < 21): 0
```

Press F8 to advance one step at a time. Action switches to the output window, and you are asked to enter an integer. Type *5* and then press Enter. The Watch window now shows that *N%* is 5 and the test condition is –1 (true):

```
LIST-18.BAS N%:  5
LIST-18.BAS (N% > 0) AND (N% < 21): -1
```

Continue pressing the single-step F8 key. When you reach the LOOP statement, you can use the F4 key to check the output window:

```
Enter an integer from 1 to 20 (0 to quit) and see its factorial.
Integer 1-20: 5
 5 factorial is 120
```

All is going well. Press F4 to return to the View window, and press F8 a few more times. The program keeps going through the loop. Checking the Watch window, you see that *N%* is still 5 (and the test statement is still true). Because you forgot to have the program read the next value for *N%*, the value stays the same. You can fix the program by changing the loop to read as follows:

```
DO WHILE (N% > 0) AND (N% < 21)
    PRINT N%; "factorial is"; Factorial#(N%)
    INPUT "Integer 1-20: ", N%
LOOP
```

Now when you press F8 to step through the program, you'll be prompted for a new value. If you enter 0, the program terminates as planned.

When the program works properly, remove the breakpoint. Position the cursor on the breakpoint line, and use the F9 key or the Toggle Breakpoint selection to turn off the breakpoint.

Executing to the Cursor Position

For a quicker, less formal way to run a program to a particular line, position the cursor on the line where you want the program to stop. Press the F7 key, and the program executes to that point. This is probably the easiest method if you want to stop a program at only one place. But if you want to stop it at several key places, the breakpoint approach is better.

Figure 6-6 summarizes the function keys we've used so far with Debug.

Key	***Action***
Shift-F5	Starts program execution from beginning
F5	Continues program execution from current statement
F7	Executes program to current cursor position
F8	Executes next program statement as a single step
F10	Single-steps, tracing around a procedure call
F9	Toggles the Debug menu Breakpoint command
F4	Toggles between View window and output window

Figure 6-6.
Debug function keys.

Watchpoints

Suppose you want to run the program until some particular condition occurs, but you don't know exactly when that will happen. For instance, suppose you want to find out when the factorials first exceed 2 billion in value, which will happen somewhere in the FOR loop. Putting a breakpoint in the loop isn't very helpful because it requires going through the loop cycle by cycle. But the QuickBASIC debugger has a useful feature called a *watchpoint.* A watchpoint is a conditional test; the program will run until the watchpoint becomes true. Let's try it.

First select Restart from the Run menu to start from the beginning. Next select Delete All Watch from the Debug menu. Add the expressions *I%* and *Factorial#(I%)* to the Watch window, which will allow you to watch the array values as they are set.

You could simply single-step through the loop, watching the values. Instead select Watchpoint from the Debug window, and enter the expression *Factorial#(I%) > 2000000000.* That expression now becomes a watchpoint, and it is also displayed in the Watch window. Now run the program (Shift-F5 or Start). The program runs until this watchpoint condition becomes true. The Watch window looks like this:

```
LIST-18.BAS I%:  13
LIST-18.BAS Factorial#(I%):  6227020800
LIST-18.BAS Factorial#(I%) > 2000000000: <TRUE>
```

As shown, 13 factorial is 6227020800. It is the first factorial larger than 2000000000.

Review Questions

1. How do you create an array of 20 elements? Can you create such an array in more than one way?
2. Is an element of an array different from an ordinary variable of the same type?
3. Write a program that sets the first element of a 20-element array to 0 and the second element to 1. Each subsequent element is set to the sum of the preceding two elements—that is, the next few values would be 0 + 1, or 1; 1 + 1, or 2; 1 + 2, or 3; 2 + 3, or 5; and so on. Print the results.
4. Suppose you have an array whose elements must be assigned a standard set of values, such as a set of part numbers. The program will use the same values each time it runs. What is the easiest way to set the array values?
5. How would you declare an array designed to hold monthly sales figures for five districts?
6. How do you tell a subprogram that it should accept an array as an argument?
7. Why is passing by reference convenient for array-processing procedures?
8. Write a subprogram that takes an array and a value as arguments and then multiplies each element in the array by that value. You should be able to use this subprogram to rescale arrays.
9. Describe an advantage and a disadvantage of using a shared array.
10. Write a procedure that totals the columns of a two-dimensional array.

7

String Toolbox

ASC	**LCASE$**	**OCT$**	**STRING$**
CHR$	**LEFT$**	**RIGHT$**	**UCASE$**
DEFSTR	**LEN**	**RTRIM$**	**VAL**
HEX$	**LTRIM$**	**SPACE$**	
INSTR	**MID$**	**STR$**	

Although we have used strings throughout earlier chapters, we've spent most of our time describing how to store and display them. In this chapter we'll describe how to *process* them, using QuickBASIC's diverse string-processing tools. You'll learn how to put strings together, take strings apart, search through strings, and use the computer's internal code for characters.

String Fundamentals

As you know from Chapter 2, a string is a series of characters strung together into a unit. A character can be a letter, a digit, a punctuation mark, a space character, or even a nonprinting character (which we'll discuss later). A string is essentially an array of characters, with the characters stored in adjacent elements (Figure 7-1).

String Variables

You can create string variables in several ways: with the $ suffix, the DEFSTR statement, or the DIM statement. Most often, you'll use the $ suffix to indicate a string variable and double quotation marks to indicate a string literal. This statement, for example, creates the string variable *Job$* and assigns it the string *Programmer*:

```
Job$ = "Programmer"
```

The double quotation marks are not part of the string; rather, they are delimiters, special markers that indicate the beginning and the end of the string. Without them, the program would read *Programmer* as the name of a variable.

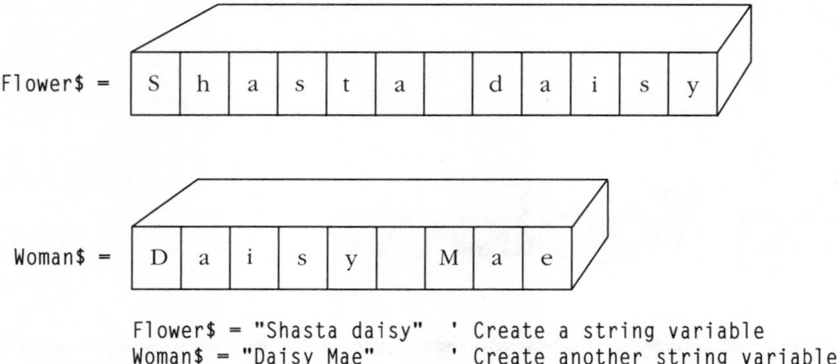
Flower$ =
S h a s t a d a i s y
Woman$ =
D a i s y M a e
Flower$ = "Shasta daisy"   ' Create a string variable
Woman$ = "Daisy Mae"   ' Create another string variable

Figure 7-1.
Strings store one character per element.

The double quotation marks around a string can be omitted in a program only in a DATA statement and then only if the string does not contain a comma:

```
DATA dumplings, hall monitor, "Twain, Mark", hoe
```

Because only literals can be used in a DATA statement, QuickBASIC knows that *dumplings* must be a string, not a variable.

You can use the DEFSTR statement to establish that variables beginning with certain letters are string variables, even without a $ suffix. For instance, the following line at the beginning of a program would indicate that any variable name starting with S and not ending with a QuickBASIC type suffix is a string variable:

```
DEFSTR S
```

Type suffixes override DEFSTR, however—*State*, for example, would be a string variable, but *Size%* would be an integer variable.

Here is the syntax for DEFSTR:

```
DEFSTR range1[, range2]...
```

range1 and *range2* are either single letters, such as an *S*, or a hyphenated range, such as *P–W*.

You can also use AS STRING in conjunction with DIM, REDIM, or SHARED (as well as with STATIC or COMMON, both discussed in Chapter 8) to create string variables without a $ suffix:

```
SHARED Clan AS STRING                  ' Shared string variable
DIM HomeState AS STRING                ' String variable
DIM GrandParents(1 TO 4) AS STRING     ' Array of strings
```

Any statement that offers an AS option lets you use AS STRING to create strings.

The Null String

If you create a string variable without assigning it a value, QuickBASIC sets it to the null string. The null string is a string of zero length—that is, no characters—and is represented as "". The null string is an important QuickBASIC concept; we've already used it a few times, and it will appear again throughout the book. Note that the null string is not the same as a space, which is represented as " " (a space between two double quotation marks).

Fixed-Length and Variable-Length Strings

So far, we've used only *variable-length* string variables. The string variable *HomeState*, for example, can be assigned strings of various lengths: *Ohio*, *California*, or *State of Total Confusion*. In principle, a string can hold as many as 32,767 characters.

QuickBASIC also supports *fixed-length* strings, which are set to specified, unalterable lengths. You can create a fixed-length string by following AS STRING with an asterisk and the string length:

```
DIM President AS STRING * 12
```

This statement creates a blank string called *President* in which you can store strings of as many as 12 characters (Figure 7-2).

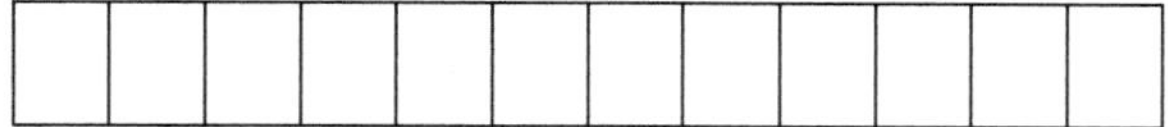

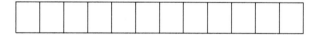

```
DIM President AS STRING * 12
```

Creates an empty fixed string with 12 elements

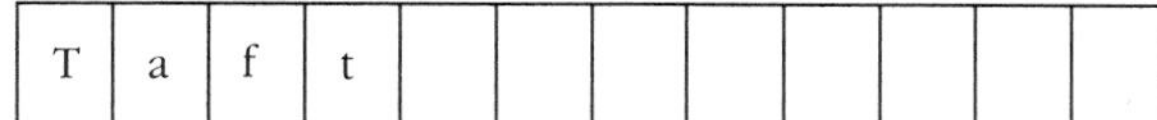


```
President = "Taft"
```

Stores "Taft" in the string

Figure 7-2.
A fixed-length string.

Listing 7-1 contrasts a variable-length string and a fixed-length string.

```
DIM Handle AS STRING * 5          ' Fixed-length string
DIM Moniker AS STRING             ' Variable-length string
CLS
PRINT "Fixed-length string"
Handle = "Susan"
PRINT Handle; "!"
Handle = "Sue"
PRINT Handle; "!"
Handle = "Susannah"
PRINT Handle; "!"
PRINT "Variable-length string"
Moniker = "Susan"
PRINT Moniker; "!"
Moniker = "Sue"
PRINT Moniker; "!"
Moniker = "Susannah"
PRINT Moniker; "!"
END
```

Listing 7-1.

Here is the output:

```
Fixed-length string
Susan!
Sue  !
Susan!
Variable-length string
Susan!
Sue!
Susannah!
```

If you assign a string smaller than the size limit to a fixed-length string variable, QuickBASIC fills the rest of the string with spaces, as the second output line shows. If you assign an oversize string to a fixed-length string, QuickBASIC truncates the extra characters. A variable-length string, however, shrinks or expands as necessary. (In this chapter we use variable-length strings exclusively.)

String Input/Output

Programs can read strings from the keyboard both with INPUT and with LINE INPUT. The INPUT statement uses a comma-separated list of variables, and the keyboard entries must also be separated by commas. When you type strings to be read by INPUT, double quotation marks are optional unless you include a comma in the string, as illustrated in the following program:

Debug and Expressions

To see fixed-length strings and variable-length strings in action, you can use Debug with Listing 7-1.

1. Select Restart from the Run menu to reset the program.
2. Add these expressions to the Watch window: *Handle, LEN(Handle), Moniker,* and *LEN(Moniker).* (Although *LEN(Handle)* and *LEN(Moniker)* are not part of the program, you can put these expressions in the Watch window for Debug to evaluate.)
3. Use F8 to step through the program.

LEN(Handle) remains at 5 throughout the program, whereas *LEN(Moniker)* changes from 0 to 5 to 3 to 8 as the contents of the string change.

```
CLS
INPUT "Enter three strings: ", S1$, S2$, S3$
PRINT S1$, S2$, S3$
END
```

Here is the output for two sample runs:

```
? Enter three strings: Hello, my heart, sing to me
Hello         my heart      sing to me

? Enter three strings: "Hello", "my heart, sing", to me
Hello         my heart, sing              to me
```

Notice that when double quotation marks are used, they do not become part of the string.

The LINE INPUT statement reads the entire input line, including any punctuation, and assigns it to the input string. Use quotation marks with this statement only if you want them to be part of the string. The following program provides an example:

```
CLS
LINE INPUT "Right? ", S$
PRINT S$
END
```

Here are the results of two sample runs:

```
Right? Yes, that's right.
Yes, that's right.

Right? "Yes, that's right."
"Yes, that's right."
```

The PRINT Statement and Strings

The PRINT statement prints string arguments in successive fields 14 characters wide if the arguments are separated by commas and adjacently if the arguments are separated by semicolons, as illustrated by this program:

```
CLS
PRINT "the", "rein"
PRINT "the"; "rein"
END
```

Here is the output:

```
the           rein
therein
```

The PRINT USING Statement and Strings

As you learned in Chapter 3, the PRINT USING statement uses a format string to specify how output should be printed. Recall that this statement provides three special notations for displaying strings:

- ! prints the first character of a string.
- \ \ prints 2 + *n* characters, where *n* is the number of spaces between the two backslashes.
- & prints an entire string.

Note that you must use backslashes for the third notation, not slashes. The following program demonstrates these properties:

```
CLS
INPUT "Please enter your first name: ", Firstname$
INPUT "Now enter your last name: ", Lastname$
PRINT USING "Well, !. &, your first"; Firstname$; Lastname$;
PRINT USING " name begins with \  \."; Firstname$
END
```

Here is the output:

```
Please enter your first name: Melissa
Now enter your last name: Marvelia
Well, M. Marvelia, your first name begins with Meli.
```

! in the first PRINT USING statement is replaced by the first letter of the string *Firstname$*, and & is replaced by the entire *Lastname$* string. In the second PRINT USING statement, \ \ is replaced by the first four characters of *Firstname$* because there are two spaces between the backslashes.

String Operations

Chapter 4 introduced the use of relational operators with strings. Two strings are the same—that is, they are equal—if they consist of the same characters in the same order. For instance, the following statement prints the word *Wright* if the variable *Response$* has the value *Orville*:

```
IF Response$ = "Orville" THEN PRINT "Wright"
```

Note that case is important: The string *orville* is different from *Orville*. (A *rose* is not a *Rose* is not a *ROSE*.) Also note that spaces are considered characters. In the following code, *A$* and *B$* differ because one has a trailing space and the other does not:

```
A$ = "tuna "
B$ = "tuna"
```

Two fixed-length strings of different lengths are therefore always unequal, as Listing 7-2 shows.

```
DIM S1 AS STRING * 5
DIM S2 AS STRING * 6
CLS
S2 = "Hog"
S1 = S2                 ' Things are not what they seem!
PRINT S1, S2
IF S1 = S2 THEN
    PRINT "Strings are the same"
ELSE
    PRINT "Strings are different"
END IF
END
```

Listing 7-2.

Here is the output:

```
Hog           Hog
Strings are different
```

Although you can't discern it from the first PRINT statement, *S1* has two trailing spaces after HOG, whereas *S2* has three. Thus the two strings are not equal.

The inequality operators (< >) test strings alphabetically, not by size. B is considered greater than A because it follows A in the alphabet. (The comparison is based on the ASCII code for the two characters. We'll discuss ASCII, which represents characters by numbers, later in this chapter.)

The + operator can also be used with strings. Each + operator joins, or concatenates, two strings into one; several + operators can be used in one statement to join several strings. Suppose you use this statement:

```
Title$ = "spinach" + "king"
```

The + operator appends the second string to the first, and *Title$* is assigned the string *spinachking*. If you want spaces, you must provide them. The following statement assigns the string *Miss Sugar Beet* to *Title$*:

```
Title$ = "Miss " + "Sugar Beet"
```

The + operator is typically used with string variables as well as with literals, as shown in Listing 7-3.

```
CLS
INPUT "Enter the name of an animal: ", Animal$
INPUT "Enter a color: ", Color$
INPUT "Enter an adjective: ", Adj$
INPUT "Enter a name: ", Name$
Phrase$ = "The " + Adj$ + " " + Animal$ + " ate poor "
Phrase$ = Phrase$ + Name$ + "'s " + Color$ + " hat."
PRINT Phrase$
END
```

Listing 7-3.

Here is a sample run:

```
Enter the name of an animal: wombat
Enter a color: pink
Enter an adjective: obsessed
Enter a name: Waldo
The obsessed wombat ate poor Waldo's pink hat.
```

Note that two lines are used to construct the final sentence. The screen could not display the sentence on a single PRINT line without scrolling portions of the statement off the screen. (QuickBASIC allows a line to be as long as 255 characters.) But by assigning the strings cumulatively to a variable, you can break the task into smaller chunks and make your program more readable on the screen.

A semicolon can serve the same purpose as the + operator in a PRINT statement. The following two statements produce the same output:

```
PRINT "Mis"; "spell"
PRINT "Mis" + "spell"
```

The first statement prints two strings, whereas the second combines two strings into one and then prints the one string.

Character Basics

Let's take a closer look at characters, the building blocks of strings. Computers actually work with numbers, not characters. When a computer stores a character or string of characters in memory, it must use a numeric code for each character. The most widely accepted code—and the one used in IBM PC and compatible computers—is the *American Standard Code for Information Interchange* (ASCII, for short). ASCII code uses the values 0 through 127 to represent a standard set of characters. The values 65 through 90 represent the capital letters A through Z, and the values 97 through 122 represent the lowercase letters a through z. Other values represent numerals, punctuation marks, and symbols. Additionally, the IBM PC and compatibles use the values 128 through 255 to represent a set of special characters and symbols, known as an *extended character set.* Appendix C contains the complete ASCII character set and the IBM extended character set.

QuickBASIC provides two functions that make working with ASCII easier: The CHR$ function returns the character corresponding to a particular ASCII code, and the ASC function returns the code for a given character.

Here is the syntax for the CHR$ and ASC functions:

```
CHR$(n)
ASC(string)
```

The CHR$ function returns the character that corresponds to the ASCII value *n*. (*n* is an integer in the range 0 through 255.) For example, *CHR$(65)* returns the character A because 65 is the ASCII code for A. The ASC function returns the ASCII code for the first character of *string*. *ASC("B")* returns 66, the ASCII code for B, for example.

Try using CHR$ to show the ASCII code for a few characters:

```
CLS
FOR I% = 55 TO 68
    PRINT I%; "is the ASCII code for "; CHR$(I%)
NEXT I%
END
```

Here is the output:

```
 55 is the ASCII code for 7
 56 is the ASCII code for 8
 57 is the ASCII code for 9
 58 is the ASCII code for :
 59 is the ASCII code for ;
 60 is the ASCII code for <
 61 is the ASCII code for =
 62 is the ASCII code for >
 63 is the ASCII code for ?
 64 is the ASCII code for @
 65 is the ASCII code for A
 66 is the ASCII code for B
 67 is the ASCII code for C
 68 is the ASCII code for D
```

Note that numerals, punctuation marks, and symbols are considered characters. Also note that the ASCII code for the 7 character, for instance, is not 7; it's 55.

CHR$ and Double Quotation Marks

The CHR$ function is handy for generating characters that you can't type directly, such as double quotation marks. Try the following in the Immediate window:

```
PRINT ""Come hither," said Lola."
```

You get this output:

```
 0  0          said Lola.
```

QuickBASIC interprets "" as a null string and prints nothing for that part. *Come hither* is read as two variables: *Come* and *hither*, each with the default value 0 because no values have been assigned to them. The phrase *" said Lola."* is interpreted as a string.

Obviously, you can't use double quotation marks within double quotation marks. But you can use CHR$ with 34, the ASCII code for the double quotation mark; *CHR$(34)* returns the double quotation mark. Let's try it in the Immediate window:

```
PRINT CHR$(34) + "Come hither," + CHR$(34) + " said Lola."
```

Here is the result:

```
"Come hither," said Lola.
```

Note that although you can't use CHR$ inside quotation marks, you can use the + operator to combine the results of the CHR$ function with other strings.

Control Characters

So far we've discussed the kinds of characters you see in novels and newspapers: alphabetic characters, numerals, and punctuation marks. Computers also use other characters, such as *control characters,* which are produced by pressing a key while the Ctrl key is held down. For example, you can terminate a QuickBASIC program by pressing Ctrl-C. Many control characters have special meanings in QuickBASIC output. Ctrl-G, for instance, causes the speaker to beep, and Ctrl-M (the carriage-return character) causes the cursor to move to the beginning of the next line. Control characters can also be used to control printers.

If you want to use control characters in a program, you can't simply type something like *PRINT "Ctrl-G"*. Instead, you must use the ASCII code for the control character, which in this case is 7. You can use Ctrl-G to catch a user's attention, as shown in the following example:

```
CLS
PRINT CHR$(7)
LINE INPUT "Enter your name: ", Name$
PRINT CHR$(7) + "Sorry, " + Name$ + ", ";
PRINT "you are denied access."
END
```

The program beeps to alert the user to enter a name and then beeps again to call attention to its response.

The Extended Character Set

Many computer systems offer extended character sets, which use values beyond those of the standard ASCII code. The IBM PC and compatibles, for example, use the values 128 through 255 to represent a variety of display characters, including the graphics patterns used in the scroll bars of the QuickBASIC environment. Appendix C lists these characters, and the following program displays the extended set on the screen:

```
CLS
FOR CODE% = 128 TO 255
    PRINT CODE%; "= "; CHR$(CODE%); ": ";
    IF CODE% MOD 8 = 7 THEN PRINT
NEXT CODE%
END
```

Although the standard ASCII character set is common to many computer systems and printers, the extended set is not standardized. Sending extended codes to a printer, for example, can produce characters different from IBM's screen display set—for instance, many printers use extended codes to represent italic characters rather than the special characters shown on the screen.

Working with Strings

Now that we've examined the components of strings, let's turn to the host of QuickBASIC functions (and a QuickBASIC statement) designed to work with strings. In addition to LEN, which we used in Chapter 5, other functions let you analyze a string by extracting parts from the beginning, the middle, or the end. Still others look for strings inside of strings, convert strings to uppercase or lowercase, replace part of one string with another string, trim extra blank spaces from strings, and create strings. Together, these functions constitute a powerful arsenal of support for text-related programming.

The LEN Function

The LEN function returns the number of characters in a string. LEN has a more general use, too, for it also returns the length (in bytes) of any type of variable. Because QuickBASIC uses 1 byte of memory for each character in a string, these two uses of LEN are not contradictory.

Here is the LEN syntax:

```
LEN(string)
LEN(variable)
```

The argument can be a variable of any type or a string expression (variable, literal, or combination such as *Name$ + "erino"*). The LEN function returns the number of characters in a string expression or the number of bytes needed to hold a variable, as shown in the following example:

```
CLS
INPUT "Enter a basic food group: ", Food$
PRINT Food$; " contains"; LEN(Food$); "letters."
PRINT "Type DOUBLE uses"; LEN(Doubvar#); "bytes."
END
```

Here is a sample run:

```
Enter a basic food group: chocolate
chocolate contains 9 letters.
Type DOUBLE uses 8 bytes.
```

NOTE: *If you use LEN with a fixed-length string, the function returns the full assigned length of the variable.*

The LEFT$ and RIGHT$ Functions

To understand these two functions, think of a string as a horizontal grouping of characters. The LEFT$ and RIGHT$ functions return the left and right sides of a string. Each function takes two arguments: the string and the number of characters to be returned. For example, *LEFT$("Sapience", 3)* returns the first three characters of the string, or *Sap*. Similarly, *RIGHT$("Intent", 4)* returns the last four characters, or *tent*.

Here is the syntax for the LEFT$ and RIGHT$ functions:

```
LEFT$(string, n)
RIGHT$(string, n)
```

string is a string expression, and *n* is an integer. LEFT$ returns the leftmost *n* characters of *string*, and RIGHT$ returns the rightmost *n* characters of *string*. If *n* equals or exceeds the length of the string, the entire string is returned.

You can use the return value like any other value—you can print it or assign it to a variable, for example. These string functions do not alter the original string. Rather, they create a new string that is a copy of part of the original string. Listing 7-4 demonstrates the use of LEFT$ and RIGHT$.

```
CLS
INPUT "Enter your first name: ", Name$
Limit% = LEN(Name$)
FOR N% = 1 TO Limit%
    PRINT RIGHT$(Name$, N%)
    Stretch$ = Stretch$ + LEFT$(Name$, N%)
    IF N% < Limit% THEN Stretch$ = Stretch$ + "-"
NEXT N%
PRINT Stretch$ + "!"
END
```

Listing 7-4.

Here is a sample run:

```
Enter your first name: Igor
r
or
gor
Igor
I-Ig-Igo-Igor!
```

Each loop cycle prints an additional letter of the user's name. The program uses the RIGHT$ function to first print the rightmost character in the string; each subsequent cycle adds one character to the left. LEN calculates how many loop cycles will be executed. LEFT$ is used to build the *Stretch$* string, adding first the *I*, then the *Ig*, and so on as *N%* increases.

The MID$ Function

The MID$ function lets you extract the middle of a string. It takes three arguments: the string, the position of the first character to be extracted, and the number of characters to be extracted. *MID$("therapy", 4, 3),* for example, returns *rap,* the three characters starting with the fourth character in *therapy.* If you omit the third argument, QuickBASIC assumes that you want everything from the starting position to the end of the string. Thus *MID$("crayon", 4)* returns the string *yon*.

Here is the syntax for the MID$ function:

```
MID$(string, start[, n])
```

MID$ returns a string of *n* characters beginning at position *start* in *string* (the string expression). If *n* is omitted, MID$ returns everything from position *start* to the end of the string expression. If *start* is greater than the length of the string, MID$ returns the null string.

The MID$ function is commonly used to examine individual characters in a string. In Listing 7-5, for example, we use MID$ to display a string backward. The FOR loop uses LEN to find the position of the last character and prints it first. Then, using a step of –1, the loop moves backward along the string, printing each character.

```
CLS
LINE INPUT "Enter some text: ", Text$
PRINT Text$
PRINT "backward is"
' Print one letter at a time, last letter first
FOR N% = LEN(Text$) TO 1 STEP -1
    PRINT MID$(Text$, N%, 1);
NEXT N%
PRINT
END
```

Listing 7-5.

Here is a sample run:

```
Enter some text: Able was I ere I saw Elba
Able was I ere I saw Elba
backward is
ablE was I ere I saw elbA
```

Listing 7-6 provides another example, using several string functions to break a phone number into its separate parts. These simple techniques could be used in a more ambitious program that analyzes a database.

```
CLS
PRINT "Enter a phone number. "
INPUT "Use 415-555-1100 format: ", Phone$
IF LEN(Phone$) <> 12 THEN
    PRINT "Sorry, wrong number format."
ELSE
    PRINT "Area Code = "; LEFT$(Phone$, 3)
    PRINT "Local prefix = "; MID$(Phone$, 5, 3)
    PRINT "Rest of number = "; RIGHT$(Phone$, 4)
END IF
END
```

Listing 7-6.

Here is a sample run:

```
Enter a phone number.
Use 415-555-1100 format: 800-468-3472
Area Code = 800
Local prefix = 468
Rest of number = 3472
```

The INSTR Function

The INSTR function searches one string for the presence of a second string. If it finds the second string, INSTR returns the starting position of that string. For instance, *INSTR("Potatoes", "toe")* returns the number 5—the string *toe* is found in the string *Potatoes* beginning at the fifth character. (The searched-for string needn't be a separate word in the first string.) If it cannot find the string, INSTR returns 0. *INSTR("our house", "smoking")* returns 0 because there is no *smoking* in *our house.*

Here is the syntax for the INSTR function:

```
INSTR([start, ]sourcestring, string)
```

INSTR searches *sourcestring* for the presence of *string.* If the optional argument *start* is used, the search begins at the character position specified by *start* (an integer in the range 1 through 32767). If *start* is omitted, the search begins at the first character of *sourcestring.* If *string* is found in *sourcestring,* the INSTR function returns the position in *sourcestring* at which the first occurrence of *string* begins. If *string* is not found, INSTR returns 0. It also returns 0 if *start* is greater than the length of *sourcestring* or if *sourcestring* is a null string. If *string* is a null string, INSTR returns *start* or, if *start* is not used, 1.

Listing 7-7 uses INSTR in a simple program.

```
CLS
LINE INPUT "Enter a string: "; Sample$
Position% = INSTR(Sample$, "rat")
IF Position% <> 0 THEN
    PRINT "Your string contains rat beginning at ";
    PRINT "character"; Position%
ELSE
    PRINT "Your input is rat-free."
END IF
END
```

Listing 7-7.

Here are two sample runs:

```
Enter a string: The irate fishmonger hurled a cod
Your string contains rat beginning at character 6

Enter a string: This crate has a rat in it
Your string contains rat beginning at character 7
```

Note that spaces count as characters and that if a string contains more than one *rat* string, INSTR reports only the first one.

If you want to test for the presence of a string but don't need its location, you can write code along the following lines:

```
IF INSTR(Sample$, "rat") THEN
    PRINT "Your string contains rat.";
ELSE
    PRINT "Your input is rat-free."
END IF
```

If *rat* is in *Sample$*, INSTR returns the location, which is a nonzero value, and hence true. If *rat* is not in *Sample$*, INSTR returns 0, or false.

The syntax allows a third argument to specify the starting point of a search—for instance, you might know that the information you want is located after the first 100 characters. Also, as Listing 7-8 shows, you can use INSTR to find additional occurrences of a string in a source string. Because INSTR returns the starting position of a string, you can simply begin a new search at the character following that position (Figure 7-3).

```
CLS
Count% = 0
LINE INPUT "Enter a string: "; Sample$
Position% = INSTR(Sample$, "rat")
DO WHILE Position% <> 0
    PRINT "Your string contains rat beginning at ";
    PRINT "character"; Position%
    Count% = Count% + 1
    Position% = INSTR(Position% + 1, Sample$, "rat")
LOOP
IF Count% >= 1 THEN
    PRINT "Your string contained"; Count%; "rat(s)."
ELSE
    PRINT "Your string is rat-free."
END IF
END
```

Listing 7-8.

Here is a sample run:

```
Enter a string: Drat, a rat's on the grate!
Your string contains rat beginning at character 2
Your string contains rat beginning at character 9
Your string contains rat beginning at character 23
Your string contained 3 rat(s).
```

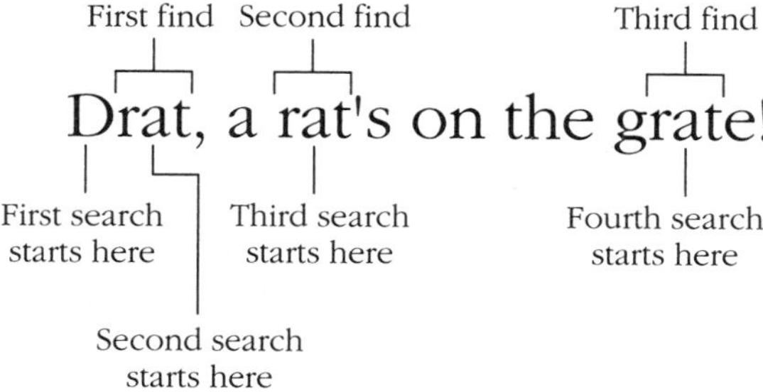

Figure 7-3.
Multiple strings in a string.

The UCASE$ and LCASE$ Functions

Because QuickBASIC distinguishes between uppercase and lowercase letters in a string, you can sometimes run into problems when comparing strings. Consider the following program:

```
CLS
PRINT "I'm thinking of a four-letter word for an aquatic"
INPUT "bird. What is it? ", Bird$
DO WHILE Bird$ <> "duck"
    INPUT "Wrong! Guess again: ", Bird$
LOOP
PRINT Bird$ + " is correct."
END
```

Here is a sample run:

```
I'm thinking of a four-letter word for an aquatic
bird. What is it? DUCK
Wrong! Guess again: Duck
Wrong! Guess again: duck
duck is correct.
```

The user not only must enter the right answer but also must use the correct case. The LCASE$ and UCASE$ functions make the user's task easier by converting responses to one case.

Here is the syntax for LCASE$ and UCASE$:

```
LCASE$(string)
UCASE$(string)
```

The LCASE$ function returns a copy of *string* with all the letters converted to lowercase, whereas UCASE$ returns a copy of *string* with all the letters converted to uppercase.

You can use LCASE$ to modify the preceding program so that *DUCK* isn't rejected:

```
CLS
PRINT "I'm thinking of a four-letter word for an aquatic"
INPUT "bird. What is it? ", Bird$
DO WHILE LCASE$(Bird$) <> "duck"
    INPUT "Wrong! Guess again: ", Bird$
LOOP
PRINT Bird$ + " is correct."
END
```

Here is a sample run:

```
I'm thinking of a four-letter word for an aquatic
bird. What is it? DUCK
DUCK is correct.
```

Now the program converts the response (*DUCK*) to the same case as the correct answer (*duck*). Note that LCASE$ leaves the original string unchanged, as shown when *Bird$* is printed at the end. To change the string, use the following:

```
Bird$ = LCASE$(Bird$)
```

The MID$ Statement

MID$ plays two roles in QuickBASIC. As you've seen, it's a function that returns part of a string. But it's also a statement that lets you replace part of a string with another string. The arguments used with the MID$ statement identify the part to be set.

Here is the syntax for the MID$ statement:

```
MID$(stringvariable, start[, n]) = stringexpression
```

The first *n* characters in *stringexpression* are assigned to *stringvariable*, starting at character position *start*. If *n* is omitted, all of *stringexpression* is used. However, because *stringvariable* is never extended beyond its original length, extra characters from *stringexpression* are dropped if necessary.

The following program shows how this statement works:

```
CLS
Sample$ = "The cat is at home!"
PRINT "Originally, Sample$ = "; Sample$
MID$(Sample$, 5) = "dog"
PRINT "Now Sample$ = "; Sample$
MID$(Sample$, 15) = "the University."
PRINT "Now Sample$ = "; Sample$
END
```

Here is the result:

```
Originally, Sample$ = The cat is at home!
Now Sample$ = The dog is at home!
Now Sample$ = The dog is at the U
```

The first use of the MID$ statement replaces *cat* with *dog*, and the second replaces *home!* with *the U.* The additional characters from *the University.* are dropped to prevent *Sample$* from extending beyond the original size.

The RTRIM$ and LTRIM$ Functions

You'll sometimes find unwanted spaces at the beginning or the end of a string—a user might add a leading space before entering a response to a LINE INPUT statement, for instance, or a fixed-length string might be padded with spaces at the end to reach the set length. Such extra spaces can complicate comparisons. Listing 7-2, for example, showed that *Hog* stored in a five-character string is not the same string as *Hog* stored in a six-character string.

The RTRIM$ function is useful in this situation, for it returns a string "trimmed" of trailing spaces—for instance, *RTRIM$("Hi ")* returns the string *Hi* with no spaces at the end. Listing 7-9 modifies our earlier program by applying RTRIM$ to the strings before comparing them.

```
DIM S1 AS STRING * 5
DIM S2 AS STRING * 6
CLS
S2 = "Hog"
S1 = S2                             ' Things are not what they seem!
PRINT S1, S2
IF RTRIM$(S1) = RTRIM$(S2) THEN     ' Compare trimmed strings
    PRINT "The trimmed strings are the same"
ELSE
    PRINT "The trimmed strings are different"
END IF
END
```

Listing 7-9.

Here is the output:

```
Hog           Hog
The trimmed strings are the same
```

Because RTRIM$ returns the strings without the trailing spaces, the two strings are now reported as identical.

Similarly, LTRIM$ returns a string trimmed of leading spaces. The program in Listing 7-10 reports the first word in a string by finding the first space in the string and printing the string up to that point. Because this approach works only if no spaces come before the first word, LTRIM$ comes in handy.

```
CLS
LINE INPUT "Enter a sentence: "; Sentence$
PRINT "You entered"
PRINT Sentence$
Sentence$ = LTRIM$(Sentence$)
FirstSpace% = INSTR(Sentence$, " ")
PRINT "The first word in "; Sentence$
IF FirstSpace% > 1 THEN
    PRINT "is "; LEFT$(Sentence$, FirstSpace% - 1)
ELSE
    PRINT "is "; Sentence$
END IF
END
```

Listing 7-10.

Here are two sample runs:

```
Enter a sentence: See Spot's nose.
You entered
See Spot's nose.
The first word in See Spot's nose.
is See

Enter a sentence:       See Spot's nose run!
You entered
      See Spot's nose run!
The first word in See Spot's nose run!
is See
```

The second input contains six leading spaces, which were initially assigned to the variable *Sentence$*. But the line

```
Sentence$ = LTRIM$(Sentence$)
```

reassigns *Sentence$* the return value of LTRIM$, which is *Sentence$* trimmed of its leading spaces.

The SPACE$ and STRING$ Functions

If you need to produce strings consisting of one repeated character—beginning a string with enough spaces to center it, for instance, or using a line of asterisks as a border—QuickBASIC's SPACE$ and STRING$ functions make your task simple.

Here is the syntax for SPACE$ and STRING$:

```
SPACE$(length)
STRING$(length, code)
STRING$(length, string)
```

The SPACE$ function returns a string consisting of *length* spaces. The STRING$ function returns a string of *length* identical characters. The second argument of the STRING$ function should be either an ASCII code for the character or a string. If it's a string, the first character of the string is used. For both functions, *length* should be an integer in the range 0 through 32767. *code* should be an integer in the range 0 through 255. Noninteger numbers are rounded to integers.

Try the following in the Immediate window:

```
PRINT SPACE$(10) + "HELLO"
          HELLO

PRINT STRING$(20, "+")
++++++++++++++++++++
```

The first command uses SPACE$ to create a string of 10 spaces, and the second command creates a string of 20 plus signs.

Listing 7-11 uses both of these functions to display a title page. The *PrintCentered* subprogram takes two arguments: a string and a line width. It subtracts the string length from the line width to find the number of available empty spaces. Dividing this number by 2 gives the number of spaces needed to center the string. The SPACE$ function then produces the required number of spaces.

```
DECLARE SUB PrintCentered (S$, Wide%)
CLS
Title$ = "Let Me Repeat That"
Author$ = "Dewey Looper"
PRINT STRING$(64, "*")          ' Top row of *
PRINT
CALL PrintCentered(Title$, 64)
PRINT
CALL PrintCentered("by", 64)
PRINT
CALL PrintCentered(Author$, 64)
PRINT
PRINT STRING$(64, "*")          ' Bottom row of *
END

SUB PrintCentered (S$, Wide%)
    L% = LEN(S$)                ' Get length of string
    IF L% >= Wide% THEN
        PRINT S$
    ELSE                        ' Add spaces to center string
        PRINT SPACE$((Wide% - L%) / 2) + S$
    END IF
END SUB
```

Listing 7-11.

Here is the output:

```
**************************************************************

                       Let Me Repeat That

                               by

                          Dewey Looper

**************************************************************
```

SPACE$ and SPC

Don't confuse the SPACE$ function with the SPC function. The SPACE$ function returns a string, whereas the SPC function positions the cursor in a PRINT statement. The following statements both result in output of 10 spaces followed by *Hello*:

```
PRINT SPACE$(10); "Hello"
PRINT SPC(10) "Hello"
```

Because SPACE$ returns a string, it can also be combined with other strings, as follows:

```
New$ = Part$ + SPACE$(5) + Id$
```

SPC, however, causes the cursor to jump over spaces and cannot be used in string concatenation.

Numbers and Strings

A number in a program can be either a numeric value or a string. For instance, the statement

```
Beans% = 14253
```

stores 14253 as a numeric value in the variable *Beans%*. Because the QuickBASIC integer type uses 2 bytes of memory, this statement stores 14253 as a binary number in a 2-byte memory unit. But the statement

```
Beans$ = "14253"
```

stores 14253 as a string—that is, 5 bytes of memory are used to hold the ASCII codes in binary form for the characters 1, 4, 2, 5, and 3 (Figure 7-4).

00110111	10101101

14253 stored as an integer in 2 bytes
(binary representation of the value 14253)

ASCII code for 1	ASCII code for 4	ASCII code for 2	ASCII code for 5	ASCII code for 3
00110001	00110100	00110010	00110101	00110011

14253 stored as a string in 5 bytes
(binary representation of ASCII codes)

Figure 7-4.
Numeric and string representations of a number.

Although arithmetic operations deal with numbers in numeric form, other operations work most effectively with numbers in string form. And some programs must be able to deal with numbers in both forms.

QuickBASIC makes some conversions automatically. Consider the following:

```
INPUT "Enter a number: ", Num%
Num% = 2 * Num%
PRINT "Doubled, that's"; Num%
```

When you enter the number 43, you first press the 4 key and then the 3 key, which sends the ASCII code for each digit to the program in sequence. Because *Num%* is an integer type, QuickBASIC converts this string of characters to the numeric equivalent and assigns the result to *Num%*. When the arithmetic is completed using this numeric value, QuickBASIC converts the number back to a string, whose characters can be displayed on the screen.

You can rely on QuickBASIC to make these conversions, but you can also control string-to-number and number-to-string conversions explicitly with the VAL and STR$ functions.

The VAL and STR$ Functions

As you saw in Chapter 5, it's sometimes convenient to read a number into a string variable and then explicitly convert the string to a number:

```
INPUT "Enter first number: ", Num$
DO WHILE Num$ <> ""
    Num! = VAL(Num$)
     ⋮
    INPUT "Enter next number: ", Num$
LOOP
```

This form allows you to terminate a loop by pressing the Enter key at the beginning of a line. It uses the VAL function, which converts a string to a number. QuickBASIC also offers the STR$ function, which converts a number to a string. *VAL("1054"),* for example, returns the number 1054, and *STR$(1990)* returns the string *1990* (including one leading space).

Here is the syntax for the VAL and STR$ functions:

```
VAL(string)
STR$(number)
```

The VAL function returns the numeric value of *string*. The STR$ function returns the string representation of *number*.

The STR$ function places a minus sign in front of negative numbers and a space in front of non-negative numbers. This can cause problems in comparing string representations of numbers. For example, the string *123* is not equal to the statement *STR$(123)*; *STR$(123)* produces a string that is four, not three, characters long because it includes a leading space.

The program in Listing 7-12 finds the sum of the digits in a number. (For instance, the sum of the digits in the number 214 is 2 + 1 + 4, or 7.)

```
CLS
INPUT "Enter an integer: ", Num&
PRINT Num&; "squared is"; Num& * Num&
Strnum$ = STR$(Num&)            ' Convert long integer to string
FOR Digit% = 1 TO LEN(Strnum$)
    Sum% = Sum% + VAL(MID$(Strnum$, Digit%, 1))
NEXT Digit%
PRINT "Sum of digits in"; Num&; "="; Sum%
END
```

Listing 7-12.

Here is a sample run:

```
Enter an integer: 1234
 1234 squared is 1522756
Sum of digits in 1234 = 10
```

VAL and ASC

Don't confuse the VAL function with the ASC function. VAL returns the numeric value of the entire set of characters in a string, whereas ASC returns the ASCII code for the first character of the string. For example, *VAL("500")* returns the number 500, but *ASC("500")* returns 53, the ASCII code for the character 5.

First the program uses STR$ to obtain the string equivalent of a number. Then it uses MID$ to extract the first character of the string and VAL to convert the character back to a numeric value that can be added to *Sum%*. A FOR loop is used to examine each digit in turn. The program also squares the input value, an illustration of handling the input as a numeric value.

The OCT$ and HEX$ Functions

A number can be written many ways: 32, for example, is 100000 in binary notation, 40 in octal (base 8) notation, and 20 in hexadecimal (base 16) notation. (See Appendix B for more details on number bases.) QuickBASIC uses the & prefix (&40) to indicate an octal number and the &H prefix (&H20) to indicate a hexadecimal number within a program. To display a number in octal or hexadecimal form, use the OCT$ or HEX$ function.

Here is the syntax for the OCT$ and HEX$ functions:

```
OCT$(n)
HEX$(n)
```

The OCT$ function returns a string that is the octal representation of the number *n*. The HEX$ function returns a string that is the hexadecimal representation of the number *n*. In general, *n* can be any numeric expression; noninteger values are rounded to integers before being converted.

For example, *OCT$(25)* returns the string *31*. Note that the string is simply the number itself without the QuickBASIC & prefix. The program in Listing 7-13 uses OCT$ and HEX$ to show the octal and hexadecimal equivalents for the numbers entered.

```
CLS
INPUT "Enter first integer to be converted: ", Num$
DO WHILE Num$ <> ""
    Num% = VAL(Num$)
    PRINT "Decimal ="; Num%;
    PRINT ": Octal = " + OCT$(Num%);
    PRINT " : Hexadecimal = " + HEX$(Num%)
    INPUT "Enter next number: ", Num$
LOOP
END
```

Listing 7-13.

We use the string variable *Num$* to store the number so that we can terminate input by pressing Enter at the beginning of a line. Here is a sample run:

```
Enter first integer to be converted: 32
Decimal = 32 : Octal = 40 : Hexadecimal = 20
Enter next number: 1990
Decimal = 1990 : Octal = 3706 : Hexadecimal = 7C6
Enter next number: <Enter>
```

Using the String Functions Together

Because the various string functions are designed to work together, let's look at two programs that integrate the use of these functions. We'll begin with a cipher program that replaces *a* with *z*, *z* with *a*, *b* with *y*, and so on, for a line of input; *cab* is converted to *xzy*, for instance. The method, or *algorithm,* for finding the replacement character will use ASCII codes. If the ASCII codes for *a*, *b*, and *c* were 0, 1, and 2, and so on, the method would be simple:

New code = 26 – old code

or

New code = code("z") – old code

This method converts 0 to 26 and 26 to 0, or *a* to *z* and *z* to *a*. But in fact the code for *a* is 97, not 0, which means that we must add an offset of 97 to the formula. This offset is the ASCII code for *a*, so we can write the formula this way:

New code = ASC("z") – old code + ASC("a")

or

New code = ASC("z") + ASC("a") – old code

For uppercase letters, we simply replace *a* with *A* and *z* with *Z*.

This method can be embedded in a loop that examines each character in the string. We can use the MID$ function to obtain the character and the MID$ statement to change its value. Suppose we want to convert the third character in the string *Text$*:

```
Ch$ = MID$(Text$, 3, 1)                      ' Get third character
Newcode% = ASC("Z") + ASC("A") - ASC(Ch$) ' Get new code
MID$(Text$, 3, 1) = CHR$(Newcode%)           ' Convert to character
```

In Listing 7-14 we condense this programming code and put it into a loop.

```
UCinvert% = ASC("A") + ASC("Z")                  ' Uppercase offset
LCinvert% = ASC("a") + ASC("z")                  ' Lowercase offset
CLS
LINE INPUT "Enter a line: "; Text$
PRINT Text$ + " becomes"
FOR Char% = 1 TO LEN(Text$)
    Ch$ = MID$(Text$, Char%, 1)                  ' Look at one character
    IF ((Ch$ >= "a") AND (Ch$ <= "z")) THEN      ' Lowercase conversion
        MID$(Text$, Char%, 1) = CHR$(LCinvert% - ASC(Ch$))
    ELSEIF ((Ch$ >= "A") AND (Ch$ <= "Z")) THEN  ' Uppercase conversion
        MID$(Text$, Char%, 1) = CHR$(UCinvert% - ASC(Ch$))
    END IF
NEXT Char%
PRINT Text$
END
```

Listing 7-14.

Here is a sample run:

```
Enter a line: I went to the Zoo.
I went to the Zoo. becomes
R dvmg gl gsv All.
```

Note that we alter only alphabetic characters, not spaces or punctuation.

Our second example is a program that counts the number of characters, digits, and vowels in a line of code. Again, we can use a loop and MID$ to examine each character in a string. The SELECT CASE statement can identify which characters are digits and which are vowels:

```
SELECT CASE MID$(Text$, Char%, 1)
    CASE "0" TO "9"
        DigitCount% = DigitCount% + 1
    CASE "a", "e", "i", "o", "u"
        VowelCount% = VowelCount% + 1
END SELECT
```

Although the vowels can also be capitalized, the program doesn't need to test for uppercase vowels if the input is first converted to lowercase.

Listing 7-15 presents the code for this program. Note that we put the entire text analysis section inside a loop so that we can analyze several lines of text. The loop is controlled by the response to a common computer prompt:

```
Continue? <y/n>
```

Some users might enter *y*, *Y*, or *yes*; others might enter a space before responding. Our program uses the LTRIM$, LEFT$, and LCASE$ functions to accommodate all these possibilities.

```
CLS
PRINT "This program will analyze text you enter."
LINE INPUT "Do you wish to continue? <y/n> "; Ans$
Ans$ = LTRIM$(Ans$)                ' Trim leading spaces
Ans$ = LEFT$(Ans$, 1)              ' Take first letter
Ans$ = LCASE$(Ans$)                ' Make lowercase
DO WHILE (Ans$ = "y")
    LINE INPUT "Enter a line: "; Text$
    Text$ = LCASE$(Text$)          ' Simplify for vowel count
    CharCount% = 0                 ' Initialize counts to 0
    DigitCount% = 0
    VowelCount% = 0
    FOR Char% = 1 TO LEN(Text$)    'Loop for each character in string
        CharCount% = CharCount% + 1
        SELECT CASE MID$(Text$, Char%, 1)
            CASE "0" TO "9"
                DigitCount% = DigitCount% + 1
```

Listing 7-15. *(continued)*

Listing 7-15. *continued*

```
            CASE "a", "e", "i", "o", "u"
                VowelCount% = VowelCount% + 1
        END SELECT
    NEXT Char%
    PRINT "That line contained"; CharCount%; "characters,";
    PRINT DigitCount%; "digits, and"; VowelCount%; "vowels"
    LINE INPUT "Continue? <y/n> ", Ans$
    Ans$ = LCASE$(LEFT$(LTRIM$(Ans$), 1)) ' Short form
LOOP
END
```

Here is a sample run:

```
This program will analyze text you enter.
Do you wish to continue? <y/n> Yes
Enter a line: I have 14 keys.
That line contained 15 characters, 2 digits, and 4 vowels
Continue? <y/n>     yup
Enter a line: That'll be $12,344, please.
That line contained 27 characters, 5 digits, and 5 vowels
Continue? <y/n> n
```

Review Questions

1. How is a string like an array?
2. How do you create a string variable called *Job*?
3. How do you create a fixed-length string of 12 characters? How does it differ from a variable-length string?
4. What does the program in Listing 7-Q4 print?

```
CLS
Sample$ = "The Resplendent Programmer"
PRINT Sample$
PRINT LEN(Sample$)
PRINT ASC(Sample$)
PRINT CHR$(ASC(Sample$))
PRINT LEFT$(Sample$, 7)
PRINT RIGHT$(Sample$, 7)
PRINT MID$(Sample$, 7)
PRINT LEFT$(Sample$, INSTR(Sample$, " "))
END
```

Listing 7-Q4.

5. Write a program that reads a line of input and prints it in uppercase letters.
6. Write a program that reads a line of input and prints it with the first word in uppercase letters. (Assume there are no leading spaces.)
7. Write a program that reads a line of input and prints it, replacing every occurrence of the string *rat* with the string *dog* (the common word-processing function search-and-replace).
8. Write a program that reads a line of text and replaces each *a* with *c*, each *b* with *d*, and so on, with *y* becoming *a*, and *z* becoming *b*—in other words, each letter is shifted two positions in the alphabet. The program should treat uppercase letters in the same fashion.

8

Functions and More Procedures

COMMON	**EXIT FUNCTION**	**SHARED**
DEF FN	**FUNCTION**	**STATIC**

In Chapter 5 you learned about one kind of procedure, the subprogram. Now we'll examine the second kind, the function procedure. You've already seen how useful QuickBASIC's built-in functions such as LEN, MID$, and ASC can be. Now you'll learn to write your own custom function procedures. After you're comfortable with that new skill, we'll discuss some of the more advanced aspects of procedures, such as local and shared variables, static variables, and recursive procedures. We'll also look at the DEF FN (user-defined) function and at multimodule programs.

Function Procedures

Function procedures share many properties with subprograms (Figure 8-1).

- Both are defined in the procedures section of a file rather than in the module-level code.
- Both use local variables by default, eliminating worries about duplicating variable names.
- Both use arguments to provide values for the parameter variables used by the procedure.

The primary difference between a function procedure and a subprogram is that a function procedure, like a built-in QuickBASIC function, returns a value. Suppose you write a function called *CubeFun!* that calculates the cube of a number. To assign the cube of 6 to a variable, you can do the following:

```
Result! = CubeFun!(6)
```

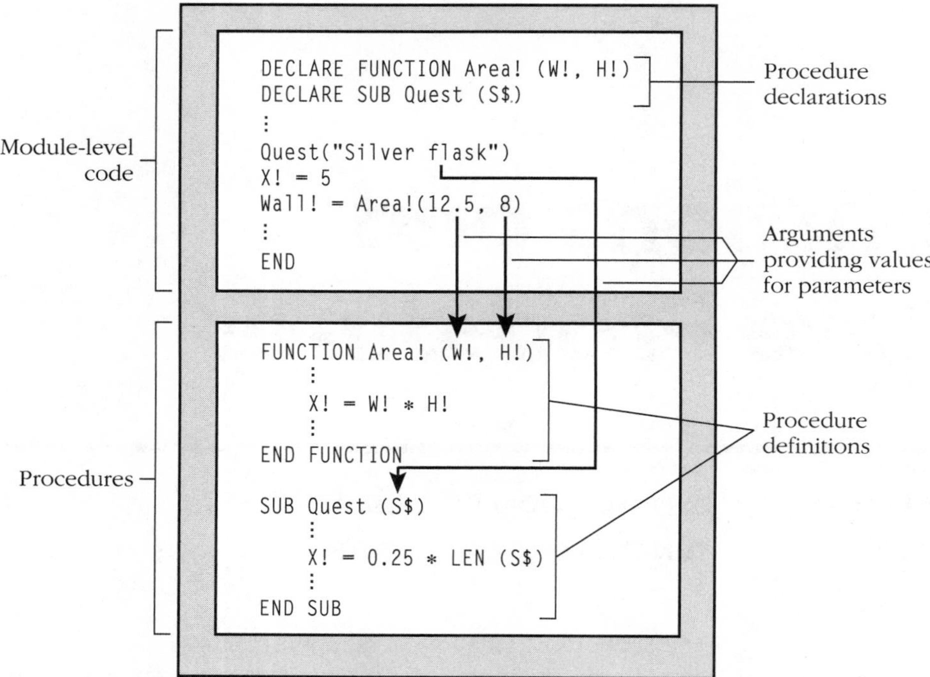
DECLARE FUNCTION Area! (W!, H!)
DECLARE SUB Quest (S$)
Quest("Silver flask")
X! = 5
Wall! = Area!(12.5, 8)
END
FUNCTION Area! (W!, H!)
X! = W! * H!
END FUNCTION
SUB Quest (S$)
X! = 0.25 * LEN (S$)
END SUB
Module-level code
Procedures
Procedure declarations
Arguments providing values for parameters
Procedure definitions
The X!'s in Area!, Quest, and the module-level code are three distinct, independent variables

Figure 8-1.
Properties of procedures.

This statement calls, or invokes, the *CubeFun!* function. The argument of *CubeFun!* is 6, and its return value is 216. You can conceptualize a function as a black box: You feed it a value or list of values, and it gives you back a new value. When a function appears in a statement, you can think of it as being replaced by its return value.

The function procedure call has the following form:

```
functionname[(argumentlist)]
```

functionname (containing as many as 40 characters) must reflect the type of the value returned by the function—ending in % if the function returns an integer, for example. *argumentlist* is a comma-separated list of values, which can be literals, constants, variables, functions, or expressions. The function return value can be assigned to a variable, used as part of an expression, or used as a value. If *argumentlist* is omitted, the parentheses are not used.

The function definition has the following form:

```
FUNCTION functionname [(parameterlist)]
    [statementblock1]
    functionname = returnvalue
    [statementblock2]
END FUNCTION
```

parameterlist is a comma-separated list of variable names, and *returnvalue* represents the value the function returns. Note that *returnvalue* is assigned to *functionname*. The dual role of *functionname* allows the function to identify which value to return.

Consider the following program, which demonstrates calling a function:

```
CLS
X! = 12
X3! = CubeFun!(X!)                  ' Calling the function
PRINT X!; "cubed is"; X3!
PRINT " 5 cubed is"; CubeFun!(2 + 3)
END
```

The *CubeFun!* function is used in two ways here. First, the following statement calls the function:

```
X3! = CubeFun!(X!)
```

CubeFun! calculates the cube of its argument and returns the result, which is assigned to *X3!*. Second, the final PRINT statement uses *CubeFun!* to provide a value for printing.

Defining a Function Procedure

Defining a function procedure is similar to defining a subprogram. Enter the following in the View window:

```
FUNCTION CubeFun! (N!)
```

QuickBASIC opens a new View window containing the following text:

```
FUNCTION CubeFun! (N!)

END FUNCTION
```

Alternatively, you can select New Function from the Edit menu. In either case, you next enter the code. When you save the file, QuickBASIC places a function declaration at the top of the module-level code. Listing 8-1 shows a sample program.

```
DECLARE FUNCTION CubeFun! (N!)      ' Added when program saved
CLS
X! = 12
X3! = CubeFun!(X!)                  ' Calling the function
PRINT X!; "cubed is"; X3!
PRINT " 5 cubed is"; CubeFun!(2 + 3)
END

FUNCTION CubeFun! (N!)              ' Function definition
    CubeFun! = N! * N! * N!         ' Return value
END FUNCTION
```

Listing 8-1.

Here is the output:

```
12 cubed is 1728
5 cubed is 125
```

The argument for the first function call is 12, which is assigned to the function parameter *N!*. The second call totals the expression *2 + 3* and assigns 5 to *N!*. The final result of the procedure is assigned to the function name to create a return value. The function is called *CubeFun!*, and the following line makes the expression *N!* × *N!* × *N!* the return value:

```
CubeFun! = N! * N! * N!
```

The ! suffix in *CubeFun!* indicates that this function's return value is single precision. (In this instance, the type suffix is used only for clarity; because single precision is the default type, you could omit the suffix.)

The DEF*type* Statements

The DEF*type* statements, which set default name types for variables (discussed in Chapter 2), can also be used with functions. Suppose the following lines appear at the beginning of your program:

```
DEFINT I-N
DEFSTR S
```

In that case, the *Ignatz* function would return an integer, and the *Snide* function would return a string. But, because a QuickBASIC type suffix overrides these defaults (as it does with variables), both *Sweet!* and *Nice!* would return single-precision values.

Using Variables in a Function Procedure

Statements such as the following suggest that the name of a function acts like a variable:

```
CubeFun! = N! * N! * N!
```

Because the function name can appear only on the left side of an assignment statement in a function definition, however, you must sometimes use an additional variable for intermediate stages of a function. Listing 8-2 presents a function that counts the lines in a text file. We assign the final count to the function name in the function definition. But we must use a separate variable to update the count in the loop.

```
DECLARE FUNCTION FileLineCount% (Name$)
CLS
PRINT "This program counts the lines in a text file."
INPUT "Enter the filename: ", FileName$
Lines% = FileLineCount%(FileName$)      ' Call the function
PRINT Lines%; "lines in "; FileName$
END

FUNCTION FileLineCount% (Name$)
' This function returns the number of lines in the
'  text file whose name is given by the string Name$
    Linecount% = 0
    OPEN Name$ FOR INPUT AS 111
    DO WHILE NOT EOF(111)               ' Loop counts lines
        LINE INPUT #111, Stuff$
        Linecount% = Linecount% + 1
    LOOP
    CLOSE 111
    FileLineCount% = Linecount%         ' Return value
END FUNCTION
```

Listing 8-2.

FileLineCount% takes a string argument and returns an integer, as the function heading indicates:

```
FUNCTION FileLineCount% (Name$)
```

The temporary variable *Linecount%* in the function keeps track of the lines. We can't use *FileLineCount%* to keep a running total because the function name cannot be used on the right side of an assignment statement. Thus the following statement is invalid:

```
FileLineCount% = FileLineCount% + 1  ' No can do
```

Exiting a Function

Listing 8-3 provides an example of what happens if you use a function name more than once in the function.

```
DECLARE FUNCTION Testing! (N!)
CLS
TestValue! = Testing!(3)
PRINT TestValue!
END

FUNCTION Testing! (N!)
    Testing! = N!
    PRINT "Now on line 2"
    Testing! = N! * 2
    PRINT "Now on line 4"
    Testing! = N! * 10
    PRINT "Now on line 6"
END FUNCTION
```

Listing 8-3.

Here is the output:

```
Now on line 2
Now on line 4
Now on line 6
 30
```

Regardless of where the assignment statements are located, the function executes to the END FUNCTION line before exiting. The function's return value is the value most recently assigned to the function name.

Debugging Tip

If you do not assign a value to the function name in the function definition, the function returns 0 if it is a numeric type and returns the null string if it is a string type. If a function procedure unexpectedly or consistently returns 0 or the null string, check to be sure you assigned a value to the function name and that you spelled the name correctly, including the suffix. For example, the following function always returns 0 because the value was assigned to the variable *Triple* instead of to the function *Triple%*—that is, the suffix was omitted.

```
FUNCTION Triple% (X%)
    Triple = 3 * X%      'Should be Triple%
END FUNCTION
```

You can also exit a function by using the EXIT FUNCTION statement, as shown in Listing 8-4. This listing presents a program in which the *SmallDiv&* function returns the smallest divisor other than 1 that goes evenly into a long integer.

```
DECLARE FUNCTION SmallDiv& (Num&)
CLS
INPUT "Enter a positive integer: ", Divideme&
DO WHILE Divideme& > 0
    PRINT "Smallest divisor of"; Divideme&;
    PRINT "is"; SmallDiv&(Divideme&)     ' Call the function
    INPUT "Next value (0 terminates): ", Divideme&
LOOP
END

FUNCTION SmallDiv& (Num&)
Divisor& = 2
DO WHILE Divisor& * Divisor& <= Num&
    IF Num& MOD Divisor& = 0 THEN        ' Check for divisor
        SmallDiv& = Divisor&
        EXIT FUNCTION                    ' Exit if conditional is true
    END IF
    Divisor& = Divisor& + 1
LOOP
SmallDiv& = Num&
END FUNCTION
```

Listing 8-4.

Here is a sample run:

```
Enter a positive integer: 35
Smallest divisor of 35 is 5
Next value (0 terminates): 123457
Smallest divisor of 123457 is 123457
Next value (0 terminates): 132457
Smallest divisor of 132457 is 13
Next value (0 terminates): 0
```

To save computation time, the program checks only for divisors smaller than or equal to the square root of the original number (by comparing the square of the divisor to the number). If a number is not divisible by anything equal to its square root or smaller, it's not divisible at all. If a divisor is found, the conditional statement assigns the divisor as the return value of the function and then executes the EXIT FUNCTION statement to return to the module level. If no divisor is found, the original number is assigned to the return value, and the procedure is completed.

Using Function Procedures and Arrays

You can pass an array as an argument to a function procedure, just as we passed arrays as arguments to subprograms in Chapter 6. When an array is used as an argument, the array name is followed by empty parentheses to identify the argument as an array. Similarly, in the function definition, empty parentheses identify the corresponding parameter as an array. As it is for subprograms, an array parameter is simply an alias for the array passed as an argument.

Let's look at an example. In Listing 8-5, we define a function that returns the average value of the elements of an array. For comparison, we've used a subprogram to print the array values. For both the *ShowArray* subprogram and the *Average!* function, the *Arr!()* parameter is an alias for the *RainFall!()* array; *Average!*, however, has a return value.

```
DECLARE SUB ShowArray (Arr!())
DECLARE FUNCTION Average! (Arr!())
DATA 30.3, 29.9, 18.1, 9.6, 8.2, 4.8
DATA 8.4, 9.2, 9.6, 14.9, 18.3, 24.7
DIM RainFall!(1 TO 12)
CLS
FOR I% = 1 TO 12                    ' Place data into array
    READ RainFall!(I%)
NEXT I%
Ave! = Average!(RainFall!())        ' Call function, passing array
PRINT "Here are the monthly rainfall values:"
CALL ShowArray(RainFall!())
PRINT "The average rainfall is"; Ave!
END

FUNCTION Average! (Arr!())          ' Parameter is an array
    FOR I% = LBOUND(Arr!) TO UBOUND(Arr!)
        Count% = Count% + 1
        Sum! = Sum! + Arr!(I%)
    NEXT I%
    Average! = Sum! / Count%        ' Assign return value
END FUNCTION

SUB ShowArray (Arr!())              ' Display array values
    FOR I% = LBOUND(Arr!) TO UBOUND(Arr!)
        PRINT Arr!(I%);
    NEXT I%
    PRINT
END SUB
```

Listing 8-5.

Here is the output:

```
Here are the monthly rainfall values:
 30.3  29.9  18.1  9.6  8.2  4.8  8.4  9.2  9.6  14.9  18.3  24.7
The average rainfall is 15.5
```

Note that in order to use the *Average!* function generally—not only for a 12-element array—we used LBOUND and UBOUND to determine the array limits.

Using Function Procedures and Strings

Writing functions for string variables is no different from writing functions for numeric variables. You can pass strings as arguments, and you can have functions return strings. If a function returns a string, the function name should end in $.

Listing 8-6 presents three examples. One function, *CountChar%*, counts how often a particular character appears in a string. It takes two string arguments and returns an integer. The second function, *FirstWord$*, returns the first word of a string. It takes one string argument and returns a string. The third function, *NotFirst$*, returns all but the first word of a string.

```
DECLARE FUNCTION CountChar% (S1$, Ch$)
DECLARE FUNCTION FirstWord$ (S$)
DECLARE FUNCTION NotFirst$ (S$)
CLS
PRINT "Enter a line of text:"
LINE INPUT "> "; Text$
LINE INPUT "Now enter a character: "; Char$
Char$ = LEFT$(Char$, 1)           ' Reduce response to one character
PRINT "The text contains"; CountChar%(Text$, Char$);
PRINT "instances of the "; Char$; " character."
PRINT "First word = "; FirstWord$(Text$)
PRINT "The rest of the text follows:"
PRINT NotFirst$(Text$)
PRINT "Second word = " + FirstWord$(NotFirst$(Text$))
END

FUNCTION CountChar% (S1$, Ch$)    ' Count character Ch$ in string S1$
    FOR Char% = 1 TO LEN(S1$)
        IF MID$(S1$, Char%, 1) = Ch$ THEN
            Count% = Count% + 1
        END IF
    NEXT Char%
    CountChar% = Count%           ' Return value is an integer
END FUNCTION
```

Listing 8-6. *(continued)*

Listing 8-6. *continued*

```
FUNCTION FirstWord$ (S$)          ' Get first word of string
    Temp$ = LTRIM$(S$)
    FirstSpace% = INSTR(Temp$, " ")
    IF FirstSpace% <> 0 THEN
        FirstWord$ = LEFT$(Temp$, FirstSpace% - 1)
    ELSE
        FirstWord$ = Temp$        ' Return value if no spaces
    END IF
END FUNCTION

FUNCTION NotFirst$ (S$)           ' Get string minus first word
    Temp$ = LTRIM$(S$)
    FirstSpace% = INSTR(Temp$, " ")
    IF FirstSpace% <> 0 THEN
        NotFirst$ = MID$(Temp$, FirstSpace%)
    ELSE
        NotFirst$ = ""            ' Return value if no space
    END IF
END FUNCTION
```

Here is a sample run:

```
Enter a line of text:
> It was a dark and stormy night.
Now enter a character: a
The text contains 4 instances of the a character.
First word = It
The rest of the text follows:
 was a dark and stormy night.
Second word = was
```

For *CountChar%*, we use the MID$ function inside a loop to examine each character in a string. Because *CountChar%* can appear only on the left side of an assignment operator in the function definition, we use a regular variable (*Count%*) in the loop and then assign the final value of *Count%* to *CountChar%*.

The *FirstWord$* and *NotFirst$* functions resemble each other. Both use LTRIM$ to skip leading spaces in the text and INSTR to find the first space in the remaining portion of the string. Then *FirstWord$* returns text up to the first space, and *NotFirst$* returns the rest of the text.

Note the final print statement:

```
PRINT "Second word = " + FirstWord$(NotFirst$(Text$))
```

This statement demonstrates that a function's return value can be used like any value of the same type. Because the *FirstWord$* function takes a string as an argument, it can accept the *NotFirst$* function return value, which is a string. Similarly, the + operator, which combines two strings, concatenates the strings *Second word =* and the return value of *FirstWord$* into a single string.

This example also illustrates how functions work with one another. Because the *NotFirst$* function returns everything but the first word of the text, applying *FirstWord$* to the *NotFirst$* return value string yields the second word of the text.

Listing 8-6 also used the line

```
Temp$ = LTRIM$(S$)
```

instead of the following:

```
S$ = LTRIM$(S$)
```

Either form would work. But because *S$* is an alias for *Text$* in the module-level code, changing *S$* also changes *Text$*. *Temp$*, however, is a local variable, and changing it has no effect on *Text$*. In most cases, you'll want to define the actions of a function by the arguments you give it and by the value it returns, without side effects such as the function changing the values of its arguments.

Procedures and Variables

QuickBASIC's method of handling variables in procedures (both functions and subprograms) has many interesting ramifications. Let's look at several aspects of variables that you need to understand in order to use procedures effectively.

Parameters: Passing by Value and Passing by Reference

You'll recall that variables defined inside a procedure are local variables, known only to the procedure. A variable defined as a procedure parameter, however, behaves a bit differently, as you saw in Chapter 5. Now let's take another look at how parameters behave.

Computer languages have developed two common ways of passing arguments to parameters: passing by value and passing by reference (Figure 8-2). When an argument is passed by value, the parameter is a newly minted variable that is assigned the value of the argument. For instance, if *X%* is an argument with the value 101 and *Num%* is the corresponding parameter in the called procedure, *X%* and *Num%* are two separate variables, and *Num%* is assigned the value 101.

Passing by reference passes the memory address of the variable, and that address is used for the corresponding parameter—that is, the argument and the parameter use the same address and thus are really the same variable. Thus, if *X%* is an argument passed by reference and *Num%* is a parameter, *X%* and *Num%* become alternative names for the same variable. Any changes made to *Num%* also change *X%*.

Passing by value allows greater flexibility because it lets you use any kind of argument that has a value: a variable, a constant, an expression, a function. Passing by reference, in contrast, restricts you to using only variables as arguments, because the parameter is simply another name for the argument variable.

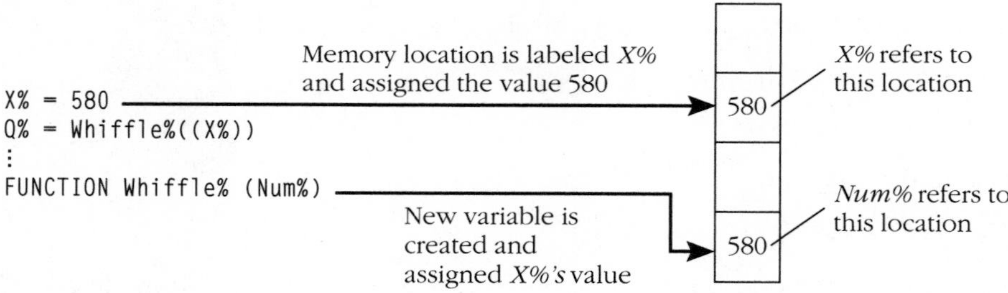

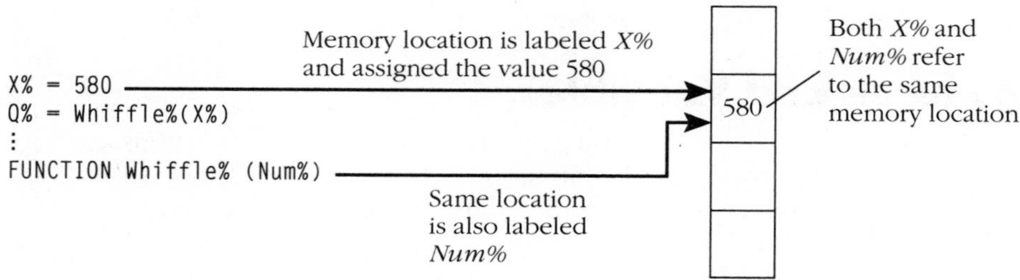

Figure 8-2.
Passing by value and passing by reference.

Passing by value also allows you to preserve data more easily because you work with a copy of the original data. If you somehow alter data in the copy, the original data is unaffected. But passing by reference requires you to work with the original data, and any changes in the parameters will therefore also affect the arguments.

Sometimes it might be desirable for a procedure to modify the original arguments—for example, you might want a procedure that requests keyboard input and conveys the results back to the calling level. The following statement could give values to *Name$* and *IDNum%*:

```
CALL GetInfo(Name$, IDNum%)
```

Passing by reference allows you to pass values in either direction, whereas passing by value lets you pass values only from the calling level to the subprogram.

QuickBASIC in fact can pass arguments only by reference. Passing arguments by value is simulated in QuickBASIC by first assigning the arguments to temporary variables and then passing these variables by reference. If you use an expression as an argument, QuickBASIC evaluates the argument, assigns its value to an invisible temporary variable, and passes the address of that variable. As far as the user is concerned, the result is passing by value.

Listing 8-7 illustrates QuickBASIC's ability to pass arguments by reference and also, in effect, "by value." It also demonstrates a trick for using a variable as an argument while preventing the procedure from changing the variable's value.

```
DECLARE SUB FeetToInch (Length%)
CLS
Feet1% = 10
Feet2% = 100
Feet3% = 1000
PRINT "Originally, Feet1% ="; Feet1%; "and Feet2% ="; Feet2%;
PRINT "and Feet3% ="; Feet3%
CALL FeetToInch(Feet1%)       ' Use variable to pass by reference
CALL FeetToInch(Feet2% * 3)   ' Use expression to pass by value
CALL FeetToInch((Feet3%))     ' Use variable as expression to pass by value
PRINT "Ultimately, Feet1% ="; Feet1%; "and Feet2% ="; Feet2%;
PRINT "and Feet3% ="; Feet3%
END

SUB FeetToInch (Length%)
    PRINT Length%; "feet equals";
    Length% = 12 * Length%
    PRINT Length%; "inches"
END SUB
```

Listing 8-7.

Here is the output:

```
Originally, Feet1% = 10 and Feet2% = 100 and Feet3% =  1000
 10 feet equals 120 inches
 300 feet equals 3600 inches
 1000 feet equals 12000 inches
Ultimately, Feet1% = 120 and Feet2% = 100 and Feet3% =  1000
```

The variable *Feet1%* is passed as an argument, making *Length%* in the subprogram an alias for *Feet1%*. Thus, multiplying *Length%* by 12 in *FeetToInch* also changes *Feet1%* from 10 to 120. The variable *Feet2%*, however, is passed as part of the expression *Feet2%* × *3*. In this case, *Length%* is a temporary variable assigned the value 300. When *Length%* is changed to 3600, *Feet2%* is unchanged. The trick we mentioned involves *Feet3%*. Instead of passing *Feet3%* as an argument, which would be passing a variable, we pass (*Feet3%*), which is considered an expression. Again, *Length%* is a temporary variable, and changing it does not change *Feet3%*. Other methods would be to use *1* × *Feet3%* or *Feet3%* + *0* as arguments. These, too, are expressions that have the same value as the variable *Feet3%*.

In short, if you want a subprogram to retain the values of an original argument, enclose that argument in parentheses.

Local and Shared Variables

If you define the variable *I%* in module-level code, it is known only to the module-level code, not to the function procedures or subprograms in the file. If you define *I%* in a function procedure, it is known only to that function, not to other functions, subprograms, or the module-level code. You can even use the same name for two variables, one in module-level code and the other in a function procedure. Using such local variables protects a program's integrity, letting you change the value of a variable in a procedure without creating unwanted changes elsewhere in the program. For instance, using *I%* as a loop counter in a function does not affect the value of the variable *I%* in the module-level code.

Although local variables are usually the best choice, QuickBASIC also allows global variables, whose visibility is not restricted to one part of a program. Global variables are useful, for example, if you have a large chunk of data, such as an array or record, that you want to share in a program. QuickBASIC in fact allows all the following varieties of variables:

- Variables local to a procedure or to the module-level code
- Variables shared between a particular procedure in a module and the module-level code
- Variables shared among the module-level code and all the procedures in the module
- Variables shared among all the module-level code sections of multimodule programs
- Variables shared among all module-level code sections and particular procedures in a multimodule program
- Variables shared among all module-level code sections and all procedures in a multimodule program

Because only the last category of variables is truly global, we'll refer to variables that are known to more than one part of a program as "shared variables." Let's look next at the kinds of shared variables used in single-module programs. (We'll discuss multimodule programs later in the chapter.)

Sharing Variables: The SHARED Statement

The method for sharing a variable between a particular procedure and module-level code is simple: At the beginning of the procedure, use the keyword SHARED followed by a list of the variables you want to share. In Listing 8-8, we make *X%* a shared variable.

```
DECLARE SUB Widget ()
CLS
X% = 47
PRINT "X% starts as"; X%
CALL Widget
PRINT "X% ends up as"; X%
END

SUB Widget
    SHARED X%                           ' Shared variable
    PRINT "In Widget, X% starts as"; X%
    X% = 19
    PRINT "Then it is"; X%
END SUB
```

Listing 8-8.

Here is the output:

```
X% starts as 47
In Widget, X% starts as 47
Then it is 19
X% ends up as 19
```

The variable *X%* in the *Widget* subprogram begins with the value it had in the module-level code. Changing *X%* in the subprogram changes *X%* in the module-level code—that is, both code sections use the same variable, *X%*.

To share two or more variables, separate them with commas:

```
SHARED X%, HousePlant$, Dose!
```

When you use SHARED with a list of variables, the variable types must be given in the same form as that used in the module-level code. Thus, if you use AS in the module-level code, you must also use AS in the SHARED statement:

```
DIM Count AS INTEGER
DIM Name AS STRING
  :
END

SUB Moron
    SHARED Count AS INTEGER, Name AS STRING
    :
END SUB
```

Here is the syntax for the SHARED statement:

```
SHARED variablelist
```

The variables in *variablelist* must be identified using the AS *type* syntax if AS *type* was used to define these variables in the module-level code.

Sharing Among Procedures

Although using the SHARED statement in a procedure causes the variables to be shared between the procedure and the module-level code, it does not cause the variables to be shared with other procedures. If you want two procedures to share a variable, you can use a SHARED statement in each procedure. The module-level code must also use the variable, because the statements in fact cause each procedure to share the variable with the module-level code.

Another option is to use the SHARED keyword in the module-level code, which causes the indicated variables to be shared among all parts of the module. You can't use SHARED as a stand-alone statement in the module-level code, however. Instead, you must use it as a modifier (an attribute) of a DIM, a REDIM, or a COMMON statement. For example, the following statement in the module-level code creates an array that can be used by all the procedures in the module:

```
DIM SHARED Months$(1 TO 12)
```

We used this method in Chapter 6 (Listing 6-11) to create a date array that was used in the module-level code and by subprograms.

Let's look at another example.

An Example of Sharing

The program in Listing 8-9 asks you for a year's worth of monthly energy costs and lets you choose one of two display modes. The program illustrates different levels of variable visibility by using several kinds of variables. The *Months$* array is created by using DIM with the SHARED attribute and is therefore available to all procedures. Month names are a good example of data you might want to share among the parts of a program.

The *Mode%* variable is shared between *ShowData* and the module-level code because it is declared with the SHARED statement in the *ShowData* procedure. The *Mode%* variable in the *GetMode%* function, however, is a separate, local variable because it is not declared using SHARED in that function. The several *Month%* variables used in the main module and in the *GetData* and *ShowData* subprograms are local variables, independent of one another. The *Arr!* parameters in *ShowData* and *GetData* are aliases for *GasBill!*, the array used as the argument for the two subprogram calls.

```
' This program reads monthly heating costs for a year and
'  gives you the choice of two display modes for the data.
'  It also illustrates local and shared variables.
DECLARE FUNCTION GetMode% ()
DECLARE SUB ShowData (Arr!())
DECLARE SUB GetData (S$, Arr!())
DATA January, February, March, April, May, June
DATA July, August, September, October, November, December
DIM SHARED Months$(1 TO 12)         ' Shared in whole module
DIM GasBill!(1 TO 12)
FOR Month% = 1 TO 12
    READ Months$(Month%)            ' Set array to month names
NEXT Month%
CLS
Prompt$ = "Enter heating costs for the year:"
CALL GetData(Prompt$, GasBill!())   ' Data input procedure
Mode% = GetMode%
CALL ShowData(GasBill!())           ' Data output procedure
END

' This subprogram reads a year's worth of monthly data from the
'  keyboard. The string S$ describes the desired input, and Arr!
'  is the alias for the array used to store the input.
SUB GetData (S$, Arr!())
    PRINT S$
    FOR Month% = 1 TO 12
        PRINT Months$(Month%);
        INPUT ""; Arr!(Month%)
    NEXT Month%
END SUB

' This function illustrates data validation by accepting
'  only the value 1 or 2 as valid input.
FUNCTION GetMode%
    DO
        INPUT "Enter display mode <1 or 2>: ", Mode%
    LOOP UNTIL Mode% = 1 OR Mode% = 2
    GetMode% = Mode%
END FUNCTION

' This subprogram provides a choice of two display modes
'  for displaying a year's worth of monthly data.
' Mode 1 uses the full names of the months.
' Mode 2 uses abbreviated month names.
SUB ShowData (Arr!())
    SHARED Mode%
    IF Mode% = 1 THEN Indent% = 11 ELSE Indent% = 5
    FOR Month% = 1 TO 12
        IF Mode% = 1 THEN           ' Full month names used
            Mon$ = Months$(Month%)
```

Listing 8-9. *(continued)*

Listing 8-9. *continued*

```
        ELSE                            ' Abbreviated month names used
            Mon$ = LEFT$(Months$(Month%), 3)
        END IF
        PRINT Mon$ + ":"; TAB(Indent%);
        PRINT USING "$$###.##"; Arr!(Month%)
    NEXT Month%
END SUB
```

Here are two sample runs:

```
Enter heating costs for the year:
January? 62.35
February? 54.93
March? 38.12
April? 25.53
May? 14.39
June? 6.89
July? 3.20
August? 2.39
September? 4.53
October? 12.34
November? 34.96
December? 48.29
Enter display mode <1 or 2>: 1
January:    $62.35
February:   $54.93
March:      $38.12
April:      $25.53
May:        $14.39
June:        $6.89
July:        $3.20
August:      $2.39
September:   $4.53
October:    $12.34
November:   $34.96
December:   $48.29

Enter heating costs for the year:
January? 33.31
February? 28.80
March? 18.25
April? 10.76
May? 5.44
June? 2.33
July? 0
August? 0
September? 3.45
October? 8.99
November? 25.52
December? 29.84
```

```
Enter display mode <1 or 2>: 2
Jan:  $33.31
Feb:  $28.80
Mar:  $18.25
Apr:  $10.76
May:   $5.44
Jun:   $2.33
Jul:   $0.00
Aug:   $0.00
Sep:   $3.45
Oct:   $8.99
Nov:  $25.52
Dec:  $29.84
```

The *Months$* array is a logical candidate to be a shared array because it consists of constant values used in several places. But it is better to pass *GasBill!* as an argument than to make it a shared array. Passing it as an argument lets you generalize the *GetData* and *ShowData* procedures, freeing them for use in other arrays and other programs. For example, you could easily expand this program to include water bill and telephone bill arrays and then use the procedures with these arrays too.

Note two other points about the program in Listing 8-9: First, instead of being shared, *Mode%* could have been passed as an argument. Arguments and shared variables offer two separate communication channels between module-level code and procedures. Second, the *GetMode%* function illustrates the important concept of data validation. Because the *ShowData* subprogram recognizes only two mode values, *GetMode%* is allowed to accept only valid values for the mode. If the value is invalid, a loop makes the user try again.

Static Variables

Besides being local by default, procedure variables are also *automatic* variables—that is, memory for them is allocated when the procedure is called and freed when the procedure terminates, which conserves memory. When memory is freed from a finished procedure, it is available to be reused for the variables of another procedure. This method does slow a program down, however, because the program must allocate and free memory each time it uses a procedure. In addition, for at least some applications, the value of an automatic variable is forgotten between calls to a procedure.

The alternative is to use *static* variables, which remain unchanged between procedure calls. Memory for a static variable is allocated once, when the program is compiled, and the variable persists as long as the program is running. You could use a static variable, for example, in a procedure that keeps a running total of its arguments. Each time you called the procedure, it would add the latest argument to the total, which it remembers from the preceding call by using a static variable. Because static variables retain their values between procedure calls, they can speed up a program. But they can also increase the program's memory requirements.

Shared variables also last for the duration of a program because they are really part of module-level code. But shared variables are shared between the module-level code and the procedures, whereas static variables are local, as shown in Figure 8-3.

Class	***Scope***	***Persistence***
Shared	Shared	While program runs
Automatic	Local	During procedure call
Static	Local	While program runs

Figure 8-3.
Shared, automatic, and static variables.

To create static variables in a procedure, use the STATIC keyword either in a STATIC statement or as an attribute of a SUB or a FUNCTION statement.

The STATIC Statement

The STATIC statement in a procedure identifies the variables that are to be static. This statement makes a variable both static and local, overriding any sharing specifications. You can also use STATIC in DEF FN functions (described later in this chapter). But you cannot use it in module-level code.

The STATIC statement has a simple syntax:

```
STATIC variablelist
```

variablelist is a comma-separated list of the variables you want to be static. Variables are listed by name. Optionally, you can use the AS *type* form:

```
STATIC FussBudget!, Noodge AS SINGLE
```

The STATIC statement can be used in subprogram procedures, function procedures, and DEF FN definitions.

The example in Listing 8-10 demonstrates that static variables retain their value between function calls, whereas automatic variables do not.

```
DECLARE SUB ShowStatic ()
CLS
PRINT TAB(13); "Attic% "; "Cellar%"
PRINT "First call:"
CALL ShowStatic
PRINT "Second call:"
CALL ShowStatic
PRINT "Third call:"
CALL ShowStatic
END
```

Listing 8-10. *(continued)*

Listing 8-10. *continued*

```
SUB ShowStatic
    STATIC Attic%                        ' Make Attic% static variable
    PRINT TAB(14); Attic%; TAB(21); Cellar%
    Attic% = Attic% + 10                 ' Static variable keeps value
    Cellar% = Cellar% + 10               ' Automatic variable does not
    PRINT TAB(14); Attic%; TAB(21); Cellar%
END SUB
```

Here is the output:

```
            Attic% Cellar%
First call:
             0      0
             10     10
Second call:
             10     0
             20     10
Third call:
             20     0
             30     10
```

At each call, the variable *Cellar%* begins with the value 0, the default value initially assigned to variables. The static variable *Attic%* also starts with the default value 0. Adding 10 to each variable increases the values to 10. Being static, *Attic%* remembers its value between calls, and on the second call it begins with the value 10. Adding 10 increases *Attic%* to 20, the value with which it begins on the next call. But *Cellar%*, being automatic, starts with the value 0 each time.

You can use Debug's Watch window to monitor the two variables. When you are in the main module, the Watch window says that the variables are not watchable, because both are local variables. But when you step through the procedure, you'll see the two variables. Furthermore, you'll see that *Attic%* retains its value between calls and that *Cellar%* is reset.

The STATIC Attribute

You can also use STATIC as an attribute of a SUB or a FUNCTION statement. In general, an attribute modifies how the statements work; in particular, the STATIC attribute, when applied to a procedure, makes internal variables in the procedure static by default. Unlike the STATIC statement, the STATIC attribute is overridden by SHARED statements. Suppose you have the following code:

```
SUB Dingo(Arf) STATIC
    SHARED Woof
    Bark = 200
    Yap = 20
    :
END SUB
```

Bark and *Yap* are static variables, local to *Dingo*. But *Woof* is shared with the module-level code. Note that the STATIC statement overrides SHARED, whereas SHARED overrides the STATIC attribute.

Here is the syntax for the STATIC attribute:

```
SUB name [parameterlist] [STATIC]
FUNCTION name [parameterlist] [STATIC]
```

In Listing 8-11, we've modified Listing 8-10 to use the STATIC attribute.

```
DECLARE SUB ShowStatic ()
CLS
PRINT TAB(13); "Attic% "; "Cellar%"
PRINT "First call:"
CALL ShowStatic
PRINT "Second call:"
CALL ShowStatic
PRINT "Third call:"
CALL ShowStatic
END

SUB ShowStatic STATIC                  ' STATIC attribute
    PRINT TAB(14); Attic%; TAB(21); Cellar%
    Attic% = Attic% + 10               ' Static variable by default
    Cellar% = Cellar% + 10             ' Static variable by default
    PRINT TAB(14); Attic%; TAB(21); Cellar%
END SUB
```

Listing 8-11.

Here is the output:

```
            Attic% Cellar%
First call:
              0      0
              10     10
Second call:
              10     10
              20     20
Third call:
              20     20
              30     30
```

Note that in this program both variables remember their values between calls.

Procedure Recursion

QuickBASIC allows a subprogram or a function procedure to be recursive—that is, the procedure can call itself, starting a new instance of the procedure that in turn can call itself, and so on. The subprogram *Coda*, for example, can contain a CALL statement that causes *Coda* to call itself. This feature of QuickBASIC is useful for solving certain programming problems; for instance, a very effective sorting algorithm called Quicksort uses recursion. Here, however, we'll simply concentrate on how recursion works.

When a procedure calls itself, it sets up a chain of calls that will go on indefinitely unless the program runs into a limit such as lack of memory or unless the procedure provides a way to terminate the sequence. Listing 8-12 presents a short example of how to set up, use, and terminate recursion.

```
DECLARE SUB CallSelf (N%)
CLS
CALL CallSelf(1)                        ' Call recursive procedure
PRINT "All done!"
END

SUB CallSelf (N%)
    PRINT "Level"; N%
    IF N% < 3 THEN                      ' If N% < 3, the procedure
        CALL CallSelf(N% + 1)           '  calls itself (recursion)
    END IF
    PRINT "LEVEL"; N%
END SUB
```

Listing 8-12.

The *CallSelf* procedure is recursive—it calls itself. Each call uses an argument larger by 1 than the argument it started with. The IF statement terminates recursive calls when the argument reaches a value of 3.

The module-level code starts the sequence with this call:

```
CALL CallSelf(1)
```

When *CallSelf* is invoked, it makes the following call:

```
CallSelf(2)
```

That in turn leads to the following call:

```
CallSelf(3)
```

At this point, the IF statement prevents the process from continuing indefinitely. Here is the output:

```
Level 1
Level 2
Level 3
LEVEL 3
LEVEL 2
LEVEL 1
All done!
```

The output demonstrates an interesting property of recursion. Statements that appear before the recursive call are executed in the same order in which the recursive calls are made, and statements that appear after the recursive call are executed in the opposite order of the calls. Thus, the PRINT statement preceding the IF statement uses *Level*, whereas the PRINT statement following IF uses *LEVEL*. Let's step through the program and see why.

Initially, we call *CallSelf* (level 1) with an argument of 1. The subprogram prints the *Level 1* message and then executes the IF statement. Because the test is true, *CallSelf* (level 2) is called with an argument of 2. The program cannot move on to print *LEVEL 1* until the second level of *CallSelf* is finished. (The statements in the IF block must be completed before a statement following the IF block is reached.) Similarly, the second level of *CallSelf* prints the *Level 2* message, but because the IF statement is still true, *CallSelf* (level 3) is called with an argument of 3.

CallSelf next prints the *Level 3* message. Now the IF test fails, and the subprogram moves on to print *LEVEL 3*. That terminates the third-level *CallSelf* invocation, so execution returns to the second level at the end of the IF block. It completes, printing *LEVEL 2* and returning execution to the end of the IF block in level 1. Level 1 completes, printing *LEVEL 1* and returning control to the module-level code.

Note that when the program reaches the last in a series of recursive calls, it doesn't jump back to the beginning. Instead, it backs up through the different levels of recursion one by one. When a procedure finishes, it always passes control back to the procedure or module-level code that called it (Figure 8-4).

Now that we've examined some of the more advanced features of subprograms and function procedures, let's look at a less sophisticated QuickBASIC feature.

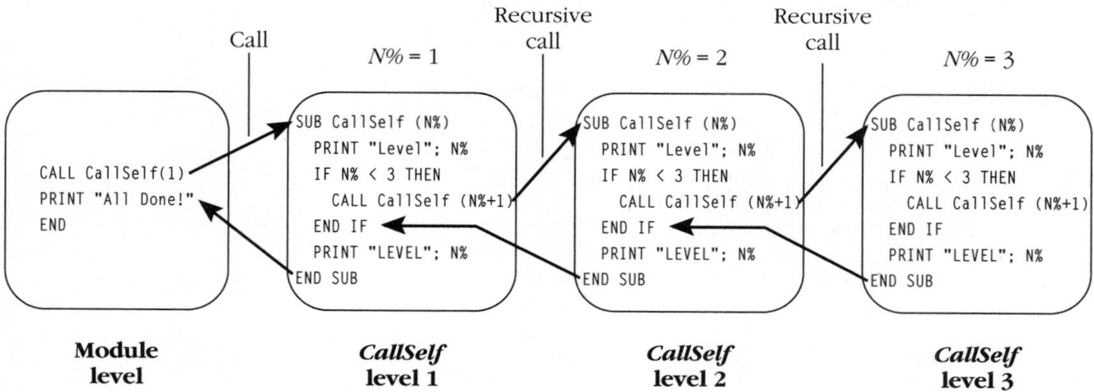

Figure 8-4.
Recursive procedure calls.

DEF FN Functions

Just as the GOSUB mechanism preceded the more powerful SUB mechanism, the DEF FN mechanism preceded the more powerful FUNCTION mechanism for creating functions. Although a DEF FN function is similar to a function defined by the FUNCTION procedure, it differs in several important ways:

- The name of a DEF FN function must begin with FN.
- DEF FN functions use shared variables by default (except variables in the parameter list, which are local), whereas functions defined by the FUNCTION procedure use local variables by default. (Both defaults can be overridden.)
- DEF FN functions pass arguments by value, whereas FUNCTION procedure functions pass them by reference.
- DEF FN functions are limited to the module that contains them, whereas FUNCTION procedure functions can be used by all modules of a multimodule program.
- A DEF FN function cannot call itself—that is, it cannot be recursive—whereas a FUNCTION procedure function can.
- The code for a DEF FN function must appear before the program calls the function; hence these functions are usually defined above the main code.

The DEF FN function comes in two forms: one-line and block.

The One-Line DEF FN Function

The one-line form is handy for very brief functions. The function name determines the function type—a function called *FNCompute%* returns an integer, whereas *FNCompute* returns a single-precision value. Because these are different types—and hence different functions—you could use both names in the same program.

Here is the one-line DEF FN syntax:

```
DEF FNname [(parameterlist)] = expression
```

parameterlist is a comma-separated list of variables. Each variable can use suffixes or the AS *type* notation to indicate type. *expression*, which generally uses the parameters, is evaluated to yield the function's return value. The return value type is determined by the function name type, not the expression type. If *expression* is omitted, the return value is 0 for numeric types and the null string for the string type. The parameters are local to the function, and function calls pass arguments by value. The following program illustrates the use of DEF FN functions:

```
DEF FNSumSq! (X!, Y AS SINGLE) = X! * X! + Y * Y
DEF FNSumSq% (X!, Y!) = X! * X! + Y! * Y!
CLS
PRINT FNSumSq!(3, 5), FNSumSq%(3, 5)
PRINT FNSumSq!(1.2, 1.5), FNSumSq%(1.2, 1.5)
END
```

Here is the output:

```
34          34
3.69        4
```

The two suffixes indicate two separate functions: One returns a single-precision value, and the other returns an integer. Both take single-precision arguments, as indicated by the ! suffix and the AS SINGLE notation. As shown in the second PRINT statement, even though *FNSumSq%* calculates a single-precision value, the return value is an integer (4), matching the type indicated by the name *FNSumSq%*.

The Block DEF FN Function

The block form of DEF FN is similar to the one-line form, but the block form allows you to use more than one line of statements to define the function.

Here is the block syntax:

```
DEF FNname [(parameterlist)]
    [STATIC variablelist]
    statements
    FNname = expression
    statements
END DEF
```

The block form gives you more room to develop the function code. Listing 8-13 shows a brief example.

```
DEF FNMax! (X!, Y!)                 ' Return maximum of X!, Y!
    IF (X! >= Y!) THEN
        FNMax = X!
    ELSE
        FNMax = Y!
    END IF
END DEF

CLS
INPUT "Enter two numbers in n, m form: >> ", Num1!, Num2!
PRINT "The larger number is"; FNMax!(Num1!, Num2!)
END
```

Listing 8-13.

Here is the output:

```
Enter two numbers in n, m form: >> 10, 15
The larger number is 15
```

QuickBASIC also has an EXIT DEF statement that can be used to exit a block DEF FN function. It works in much the same way as EXIT FUNCTION works in a function procedure.

A Multimodule Example

Now that you've examined the basic elements of procedures and modular design, let's use them to expand our earlier database example (Listing 3-3). Previously, we've written code to save names and phone numbers in a file, to show the file contents, and to count the lines in a file. We've also seen how to sort arrays and search for strings within a string. Now we'll combine all these elements into one program and create a simple menu from which you can select the action to be performed. Because several procedures will be included, we'll create a multimodule program that uses one file to hold the module-level code and a second file to hold the procedures (a standard approach). QuickBASIC makes it easy to join the two files into one program.

The first step is to design the overall structure of the program. We can build the program around a SELECT CASE structure, as shown in Listing 8-14.

```
' FILEMAIN.BAS
' Start with a general outline for the program
CONST msg$ = "The number of lines in the file ="
File$ = "NAMES.DAT"
CLS
Response$ = MenuSelection$      ' Variable set by function return value
DO WHILE Response$ <> "q" AND Response$ <> "Q"
    SELECT CASE Response$
        CASE "D", "d": CALL ShowFile(File$)
        CASE "A", "a": CALL AddToFile(File$)
        CASE "C", "c": PRINT msg$; FileLineCount%(File$)
                       PRINT
        CASE "S", "s": CALL SortFile(File$)
        CASE "F", "f": CALL FindString(File$)
        CASE ELSE: PRINT "I don't understand that response."
    END SELECT
    Response$ = MenuSelection$
LOOP
PRINT "Farewell"
END
```

Listing 8-14.

Listing 8-14 will form the core of the module-level code that goes into the first file, which we'll call FILEMAIN.BAS.

Note that the variable *File$* represents the file and that it is passed as an argument to the file-manipulation procedures. This lets us change the file used by changing only the one variable assignment. It also allows us to add a new menu item that lets the user select which file to use.

Developing the Procedures

The *MenuSelection$* function will show the menu choices and get the user response, as shown in the following program fragment:

```
FUNCTION MenuSelection$
    PRINT "Enter the letter of your choice:"
    PRINT "D) Display file contents   A) Add to file"
    PRINT "C) Count lines in file     S) Sort file"
    PRINT "F) Find a string           Q) Quit"
    LINE INPUT "> ", Ans$
    MenuSelection$ = LEFT$(Ans$, 1)
END FUNCTION
```

We'll put this in a second file called FILEPRCS.BAS. We cannot use LINE INPUT to assign a value directly to the function name *MenuSelection$*, because the function name can be used only in an assignment statement. Also, we use only the first letter of the response—that is, entering *Q* is the same as entering *Quit*.

Testing the Program Design and the Multimodule Approach

When developing a large modular program, it's a good idea to test the individual program parts. At this point, we can check the menu selection function and the SELECT CASE statement. The trick is to substitute simple *stub* procedures for procedures that are not yet written. For instance, we can add procedures to our second file (FILEPRCS.BAS) so that it looks like Listing 8-15.

```
' FILEPRCS.BAS
' This version contains the menu plus stub procedures
DECLARE FUNCTION MenuSelection$ ()
DECLARE FUNCTION FileLineCount% (Name$)

SUB AddToFile (File$)
    PRINT "AddToFile Subprogram reached."
END SUB

FUNCTION FileLineCount% (Name$)
    PRINT "FileLineCount% Function reached."
    FileLineCount% = 100
END FUNCTION

SUB FindString (File$)
    PRINT "FindString Subprogram reached."
END SUB
```

Listing 8-15. *(continued)*

Listing 8-15. *continued*

```
FUNCTION MenuSelection$
    PRINT "Enter the letter of your choice:"
    PRINT "D) Display file contents   A) Add to file"
    PRINT "C) Count lines in file     S) Sort file"
    PRINT "F) Find a string           Q) Quit"
    LINE INPUT "> ", Ans$
    MenuSelection$ = LEFT$(Ans$, 1)
END FUNCTION

SUB ShowFile (File$)
    PRINT "ShowFile Subprogram reached."
END SUB

SUB SortFile (File$)
    PRINT "SortFile Subprogram reached."
END SUB
```

These simple procedures act as placeholders, letting us check the menu and selection process. When we verify that it is working smoothly, we can replace the stub functions with the real ones.

Now let's run the two files as one program. Here is what we must do:

1. Open the FILEMAIN.BAS (Listing 8-14) file.
2. Select the Load File option from the File menu.
3. Select FILEPRCS.BAS (Listing 8-15) from the list of displayed files, and press the Enter key to load the file. QuickBASIC now knows and will remember that these two files (FILEMAIN.BAS and FILEPRCS.BAS) are part of one program. FILEMAIN.BAS does not yet contain the function and subprogram declarations, however.
4. Save the file. This puts the subprogram declarations at the top of the FILEMAIN.BAS file because the subprogram calls are in this module. The function declarations appear at the top of the FILEPRCS.BAS file, the module in which they are defined.
5. Select Subs from the View menu. Both files will be listed, with the procedures listed under the second file, as shown here:

```
FILEMAIN.BAS
FILEPRCS.BAS
  AddToFile
  FileLineCount
  FindString
  MenuSelection
  ShowFile
  SortFile
```

6. Choose FILEPRCS.BAS to edit in the active window, select the function declarations there, and copy them.
7. Open the View menu, choose FILEMAIN.BAS to edit in the active window, and paste the function declarations at the top of the program.

You have now created a multimodule program. The most difficult part is getting the proper function procedure declarations into the main module. Now you can test the program to see if the menu activates all the procedures as designed. The next step is to replace the stub procedures with the final versions.

Switching Between Modules

When you open one file and then use the Load command to load a second file, think of the two files as a single unit. Because of this joining, you should use the View menu, not the File menu, to switch between the files of a multimodule program.

Developing the Rest of the Procedures

The *ShowFile* subprogram will show the file contents, and *AddToFile* will append data to the file. We can adapt most of the code for the subprograms *ShowFile* and *AddToFile* from Listing 4-8, and we've already developed *FileLineCount%* in Listing 8-2. Sorting the file is more complicated. We'll use two subprograms. The first, *SortFile*, copies the file into an array, calls a sorting procedure, and copies the sorted array back to the file. The second, *SortArray*, does the actual sorting. (It's essentially the same subprogram as *SortScores* from Listing 6-17. This time, however, we have a function that tells us how many lines are in the data file, allowing us to create a dynamic array exactly the right size to hold the file contents. So we don't have to worry about sorting a partially filled array.)

To search for a string, we'll have *FindString* request a string from the user and then use the INSTR function to examine each line in the file for the string. Listing 8-16 shows the final product.

```
' FILEMAIN.BAS
' This program shows a database file and lets you add to it.
'  The module-level code is in the main module in file
'  FILEMAIN.BAS, and the procedures are in the procedure-level
'  part of a second module in file FILEPRCS.BAS.
' Use Load File from the File menu to add FILEPRCS.BAS to FILEMAIN.BAS.

DECLARE FUNCTION FileLineCount% (Name$)   ' Count lines in file
DECLARE FUNCTION MenuSelection$ ()        ' Show menu, return response
```

Listing 8-16. *(continued)*

Listing 8-16. *continued*

```
DECLARE SUB FindString (File$)          ' Find specific string in file
DECLARE SUB SortFile (File$)            ' Sort file contents
DECLARE SUB ShowFile (File$)            ' Display file contents
DECLARE SUB AddToFile (File$)           ' Append data to file
CONST msg$ = "The number of lines in the file ="
File$ = "NAMES.DAT"                     ' Data filename
CLS
Response$ = MenuSelection$
DO WHILE Response$ <> "q" AND Response$ <> "Q"
    SELECT CASE Response$               ' Menu response chooses procedure
        CASE "D", "d": CALL ShowFile(File$)
        CASE "A", "a": CALL AddToFile(File$)
        CASE "C", "c": PRINT msg; FileLineCount%(File$)
                       PRINT
        CASE "S", "s": CALL SortFile(File$)
        CASE "F", "f": CALL FindString(File$)
        CASE ELSE: PRINT "I don't understand that response."
    END SELECT
    Response$ = MenuSelection$
LOOP
PRINT "Farewell"
END


' FILEPRCS.BAS
' This file contains the functions and procedures for the program
DECLARE FUNCTION FileLineCount% (Name$)
DECLARE FUNCTION MenuSelection$ ()
DECLARE SUB SortArray (Arr$())      ' Called from SortFile; sort arrays
CONST format$ = "Name: &; Phone Number: &"

SUB AddToFile (File$)               ' Append data to file
    PRINT "Begin adding new names and phone numbers to the";
    PRINT "file. To quit, press Enter without entering a name."
    OPEN File$ FOR APPEND AS #1
    LINE INPUT "Enter name: ", Name$
    DO WHILE Name$ <> ""
        LINE INPUT "Enter phone number: "; Phone$
        IF Phone$ = "" THEN EXIT DO
        PRINT #1, USING format$; Name$; Phone$
        LINE INPUT "Enter next name: ", Name$
    LOOP
    CLOSE #1
    PRINT "The new information has been added."
    LINE INPUT "Press Enter to continue.", Stuff$
    PRINT
END SUB
```

(continued)

Listing 8-16. *continued*

```
FUNCTION FileLineCount% (Name$)
' This function returns the number of lines in the
'  text file whose name is given by the string Name$
    LineCount% = 0
    OPEN Name$ FOR INPUT AS 111
    DO WHILE NOT EOF(111)
        LINE INPUT #111, Stuff$
        LineCount% = LineCount% + 1
    LOOP
    CLOSE 111
    FileLineCount% = LineCount%
END FUNCTION

SUB FindString (File$)              ' Look for specified string
    LINE INPUT "Enter the string you want to find: ", Thing$
    IF Thing$ = "" THEN
        PRINT "No string specified"
        PRINT
        EXIT SUB
    END IF
    OPEN File$ FOR INPUT AS #1
    DO UNTIL EOF(1)
        LINE INPUT #1, Info$
        IF INSTR(Info$, Thing$) THEN
            PRINT Info$
        END IF
    LOOP
    CLOSE #1
    PRINT "End of search"
    PRINT
END SUB

FUNCTION MenuSelection$             ' Show menu, return response
    PRINT "Enter the letter of your choice:"
    PRINT "D) Display file contents   A) Add to file"
    PRINT "C) Count lines in file     S) Sort file"
    PRINT "F) Find a string           Q) Quit"
    LINE INPUT "> ", Ans$
    MenuSelection$ = LEFT$(Ans$, 1)
END FUNCTION

SUB ShowFile (File$)                ' Display file contents
    PRINT "Here are the file contents:"
    OPEN File$ FOR INPUT AS #1
    DO UNTIL EOF(1)
        LINE INPUT #1, Stuff$
        PRINT Stuff$
    LOOP
    CLOSE #1
```

(continued)

Listing 8-16. *continued*

```
    LINE INPUT "Press Enter to continue.", Stuff$
    PRINT
END SUB

SUB SortArray (Arr$())              ' Sort array
    Low% = LBOUND(Arr$)
    High% = UBOUND(Arr$)
    FOR Top% = Low% TO High% - 1
        FOR Comp% = Top% TO High%
            IF Arr$(Comp%) < Arr$(Top%) THEN
                SWAP Arr$(Comp%), Arr$(Top%)
        END IF
        NEXT Comp%
    NEXT Top%
END SUB

SUB SortFile (File$)                ' Sort file contents
    Lines% = FileLineCount%(File$)
    DIM Info$(1 TO Lines%)
    OPEN File$ FOR INPUT AS #1
    FOR I% = 1 TO Lines%
        LINE INPUT #1, Info$(I%)
    NEXT I%
    CLOSE #1
    CALL SortArray(Info$())         ' Call procedure to sort array
    OPEN File$ FOR OUTPUT AS #1
    FOR I% = 1 TO Lines%
        PRINT #1, Info$(I%)
    NEXT I%
    CLOSE #1
    PRINT "File has been sorted."
END SUB
```

> **NOTE:** *If you run the program before the file NAMES.DAT exists, you must run the Add option first. Trying to open a nonexistent file for reading is an error. (In later chapters we'll develop the tools to deal with that situation.)*

Here is a sample run:

```
Enter the letter of your choice:
D) Display file contents   A) Add to file
C) Count lines in file     S) Sort file
F) Find a string           Q) Quit
> A
Begin adding new names and phone numbers to the
file. To quit, press Enter without entering a name.
Enter name: Droll, Siegmund
Enter phone number: 555-1010
Enter next name: Bungee, Alice
Enter phone number: 100-0002
```

```
Enter next name: Pilaff, Rico
Enter phone number: 555-2020
Enter next name: <Enter>
The new information has been added.
Press Enter to continue. <Enter>

Enter the letter of your choice:
D) Display file contents    A) Add to file
C) Count lines in file      S) Sort file
F) Find a string            Q) Quit
> D
Here are the file contents:
Name: Droll, Siegmund; Phone Number: 555-1010
Name: Bungee, Alice; Phone Number: 100-0002
Name: Pilaff, Rico; Phone Number: 555-2020
Press Enter to continue. <Enter>

Enter the letter of your choice:
D) Display file contents    A) Add to file
C) Count lines in file      S) Sort file
F) Find a string            Q) Quit
> sort
File has been sorted.
Enter the letter of your choice:
D) Display file contents    A) Add to file
C) Count lines in file      S) Sort file
F) Find a string            Q) Quit
> d
Here are the file contents:
Name: Bungee, Alice; Phone Number: 100-0002
Name: Droll, Siegmund; Phone Number: 555-1010
Name: Pilaff, Rico; Phone Number: 555-2020
Press Enter to continue. <Enter>

Enter the letter of your choice:
D) Display file contents    A) Add to file
C) Count lines in file      S) Sort file
F) Find a string            Q) Quit
> F
Enter the string you want to find: 555
Name: Droll, Siegmund; Phone Number: 555-1010
Name: Pilaff, Rico; Phone Number: 555-2020
End of search

Enter the letter of your choice:
D) Display file contents    A) Add to file
C) Count lines in file      S) Sort file
F) Find a string            Q) Quit
> quit
Farewell
```

Attempting to write this entire program from the beginning using only module-level code would have been a formidable task, with many possibilities for error. But by using a modular approach and drawing on earlier work, we were able to construct a rather large program relatively easily.

Sharing Variables Across Modules

As you saw earlier, the SHARED statement allows you to share variables between module-level code and procedures. The COMMON statement lets you share variables among different modules. Suppose you want to access the two variables *Flick* and *Flack*, which appear in two separate modules. You could place the following statement in each module:

```
COMMON Flick, Flack
```

Here is the syntax for the COMMON statement:

```
COMMON [SHARED] [/blockname/] variablelist
```

The SHARED attribute makes the variables in *variablelist* available to all procedures in the module, as it does when it is used with the DIM statement or the REDIM statement. If you omit this attribute, the variables are available only to the module-level code. You can also use the SHARED statement in individual procedures to access variables in the COMMON block.

/blockname/ creates a named COMMON block with the name *blockname*. Omitting */blockname/* creates a *blank*, or unnamed, block. A module can contain no more than one blank block, but it can contain several named blocks. Using named blocks lets you share several groups of variables with multiple modules.

The variables in *variablelist* can be any QuickBASIC type, including arrays and user-defined types. Use parentheses to identify array names—that is, if *Dances%* is an array, use *Dances%()* in the list.

Let's look at a program that illustrates the mechanics of using COMMON. Listing 8-17 shows the main module, which defines a blank COMMON block and a named COMMON block called *Things*. Listing 8-18 shows the second module, which holds the subprograms used by the main module.

```
' The main module
DECLARE SUB Report ()
DECLARE SUB Study ()
COMMON Mice%, Men%                  ' A blank COMMON block
COMMON /Things/ Chips%, Anvils%     ' A named COMMON block

Mice% = 200
Men% = 5
Chips% = 25
CLS
```

Listing 8-17. *(continued)*

Listing 8-17. *continued*

```
CALL Report
CALL Study
PRINT "We need"; Anvils%;
PRINT "anvils for the musical entertainment."
END
```

```
' Module-level code in the second module
COMMON SHARED Mice%, Persons%       ' Available to module-level code and
                                    '  all procedures in this module.
                                    '  Persons% is equivalent to Men%.
COMMON /Things/ Chps%, Anvils%      ' Available to module-level code and
                                    '  any procedures using SHARED

SUB Report                          ' Procedure-level code
    SHARED Chps%
    PRINT "Expect"; Mice% + Persons%; "guests ";
    PRINT "We have"; Chps%; "bags of chips on site."
END SUB

SUB Study
    SHARED Anvils%
    Anvils% = Mice% / 10
END SUB
```

Listing 8-18.

Different names can be used for the same variable in the COMMON blocks of various modules, but the types of the names and the positions in the variable list must match; note that we used *Men%* in one module and *Persons%* in another. In this case, QuickBASIC checks to see that the second variables in the COMMON variable list are the same type and then treats the two names as aliases for the same variable.

In the second module, we used the SHARED attribute in the first COMMON statement, which makes the two variables available to all the procedures in that module. We also could have used SHARED in the main module if that module had contained procedures that required the values of the variables listed in the COMMON block.

The *Things* COMMON block in the second module doesn't use the SHARED attribute. But we can use the SHARED statement in individual procedures to access variables contained in the *Things* block. Thus, *Report* knows the value of *Chps%* (also known as *Chips%* in the main module), and *Study* knows the value of *Anvil%*.

Here is a sample run:

```
Expect 205 guests at the company picnic.
We have 25 bags of chips on site.
We need 20 anvils for the musical entertainment.
```

Although most of the programs in this book aren't explicitly shown as multimodule programs, you might want to practice modular techniques and use two or more files to store larger programs. In your own work, consider using separate modules for procedures that might be used in more than one program. Then, when you need them, simply use Load File to add them to a program.

Review Questions

1. List two features that subprograms and function procedures have in common. What is the main distinction between the two kinds of procedures?

2. Complete the following program:

```
REM The following subprogram prints a greeting
CALL Greetings
REM The FirstName$ function asks your first name and
REM  returns your response
NameF$ = FirstName$
PRINT "Vile "; NameF$;
INPUT ", enter your dollar value!: ", Dollars!
REM The DollarToGlox! function converts dollars to glox,
REM  with 1 dollar equal to 0.83 glox
Glox! = DollarToGlox!(Dollars!)
PRINT "That's"; Glox!; "glox in real money."
END
```

3. What's different about the way function procedures and DEF FN functions use arguments?

4. How do the SHARED statement and the SHARED attribute differ?

5. Describe the effect of making a procedure variable static.

6. Write a function that returns a single-character response from the user. It should reject input until the user enters a character found in a string passed to the function as an argument. Such a function could, for example, read a user's menu choice, accepting only valid selections.

7. Write a function that returns the sum of the elements of a single-precision array.

8. Use a static variable to write a function *Sum!* that returns the running total of all the arguments passed to it. The function should work in the short program that follows.

```
DECLARE FUNCTION Sum! (N!)
PRINT "Enter numbers one line at a time; press Enter "
PRINT "at the beginning of a line to quit."
LINE INPUT "Number: ", Num$
DO WHILE Num$ <> ""
    Num! = VAL(Num$)
    PRINT "Running total is"; Sum!(Num!)
    LINE INPUT "Next value: ", Num$
LOOP
PRINT "Thank you and goodbye."
END
```

9. Write a program using a recursive procedure that reads numbers from the keyboard until you enter 0. It should then print the numbers in the opposite order, beginning with 0.

10. How do you combine separate modules into one program?

9

Time and Math Operations

ABS	**COS**	**INT**	**SIN**
ATN	**CSNG**	**LOG**	**SQR**
CDBL	**DATE$**	**RANDOMIZE**	**TAN**
CINT	**EXP**	**RND**	**TIME$**
CLNG	**FIX**	**SGN**	**TIMER**

If you enjoy math, you'll be pleased with QuickBASIC's math capabilities. And if you don't enjoy math, you'll be pleased that QuickBASIC can help you overcome mathematical obstacles. The computer's ability to calculate rapidly and accurately is one of its great strengths. QuickBASIC supports this ability by providing many of the most common math functions, including square root, trigonometric, exponential, logarithmic, and random-number functions. In this chapter we'll show you how to put these functions to work. We'll also look at how you can access the system clock through the time-related functions. Because time waits for no one, we'll begin with that topic.

Time Is on Your Side

QuickBASIC's time-related functions and statements give you access to your system's internal clock. You can use the functions to get the current time, date, and elapsed time—which are useful, for example, in time and date stamping printouts or in calculations of how long it takes to run a program. And if your computer's clock is not correctly set, you can use the time-related statements to reset it.

The TIME$ and DATE$ Functions

QuickBASIC is always willing to give you the time of day—simply ask with the TIME$ function. And the DATE$ function gives you the date. These two easy-to-use functions have the following syntax:

```
TIME$
DATE$
```

Neither function takes arguments, and both return a string. The TIME$ function returns the time string in the form *hh:mm:ss*. QuickBASIC uses a 24-hour clock starting at midnight; leading zeros are used if needed. Thus 3:00 P.M. is *15:00:00*, and 3:00 A.M. is *03:00:00*. The DATE$ function returns the date string in the form *mm-dd-yyyy*. Months and days are represented by two-digit numbers; leading zeros are used if needed. April 1, 1991, for example, is *04-01-1991*.

The following program illustrates how the two functions can be used:

```
CLS
PRINT "The time is " + TIME$ + " and the date is " + DATE$
END
```

Here is a sample run:

```
The time is 09:55:04 and the date is 07-11-1991
```

Creating Other Date Formats

If you want the date to appear in the form *July 11, 1991*, you can use QuickBASIC's string functions to analyze DATE$'s return value and convert it to another form, as shown in Listing 9-1.

```
' This program prints the date in an alternative format
DECLARE FUNCTION WordDate$ ()
DATA January, February, March, April, May, June, July
DATA August, September, October, November, December
CLS
DIM SHARED Months$(1 TO 12)
FOR M% = 1 TO 12                    ' Set array to full month names
    READ Months$(M%)
NEXT M%
PRINT "The date is " + WordDate$
END

' This function converts month numbers to month names,
'  strips leading zeros from the day, and formats the date
'  in Month Daynumber, Year format
FUNCTION WordDate$
    Ndate$ = DATE$                  ' Get date in mm-dd-yy form
```

Listing 9-1. *(continued)*

Listing 9-1. *continued*

```
' Convert month number string to array element--"07" to Months$(7)
    Nmonth$ = Months$(VAL(LEFT$(Ndate$, 2)))
    Nday$ = MID$(Ndate$, 4, 2)
' Delete day number leading zero, if present--"04" to "4"
    IF LEFT$(Nday$, 1) = "0" THEN
        Nday$ = RIGHT$(Nday$, 1)
    END IF
    Nyear$ = RIGHT$(Ndate$, 4)
    WordDate$ = Nmonth$ + " " + Nday$ + ", " + Nyear$
END FUNCTION
```

Here is a sample run:

```
The date is July 11, 1991
```

The string array *Months$* holds the month names. Because the first two characters in the return value of DATE$ are the month number as a string, we can use LEFT$ to obtain these characters and VAL to convert them to numeric form. This number is used as the subscript in the *Month$* array to obtain the corresponding month name. Next we use MID$ and RIGHT$ to extract the day and the year from the string. Leading zeros are stripped from the day value, and the + operator is used to construct the final string.

The TIME$ and DATE$ Statements

The TIME$ and DATE$ functions have statement counterparts that let you set the time and date on your computer.

Here is the syntax for the TIME$ and DATE$ statements:

```
TIME$ = timestring
DATE$ = datestring
```

The TIME$ statement sets the system clock to the indicated time. *timestring* uses digits to represent hours, minutes, and seconds, based on a 24-hour clock. It can appear in the following forms:

timestring *Form*	***Example***	***Meaning***
hh	"13"	1:00 P.M.
hh:mm	"09:23"	9:23 A.M.
hh:mm:ss	"11:15:48"	11:15:48 A.M.

The DATE$ statement sets the system clock to the indicated date. *datestring* uses digits to represent the month, the day, and the year. It can appear in the following forms:

datestring Form	**Example**	**Meaning**
mm-dd-yy	"06-08-90"	June 8, 1990
mm-dd-yyyy	"07-11-1991"	July 11, 1991
mm/dd/yy	"10/12/92"	October 12, 1992
mm/dd/yyyy	"12/05/1990"	December 5, 1990

Your System Stopwatch: The TIMER Function

The TIMER function, which returns the number of seconds elapsed since midnight, provides a different way to use the system clock.

The TIMER function has the following syntax:

```
TIMER
```

The function takes no arguments and returns the seconds elapsed since midnight as a single-precision value.

Because the return value is single precision, it can represent fractions of a second. This makes the function handy for timing parts of a program, as Listing 9-2 shows.

```
' This program uses TIMER to time a loop
CLS
PRINT "This program times a loop."
INPUT "Enter the desired number of loop cycles: ", Loops&
Start! = TIMER
FOR I& = 1 TO Loops&
    Sum! = Sum! + 1! / (I& * I&)
NEXT I&
Finish! = TIMER
PRINT "Sum = "; Sum!
Elapsed! = Finish! - Start!
PRINT Loops&; "loop cycles took"; Elapsed!; "seconds."
LoopsPerSec& = Loops& / Elapsed!
PRINT "Loops per second = "; LoopsPerSec&
END
```

Listing 9-2.

Here is a sample run:

```
This program times a loop.
Enter the desired number of loop cycles: 10000
Sum =  1.644725
 10000 loop cycles took .7109375 seconds.
Loops per second = 14066
```

Don't be confused by the many decimal places shown in the time. Because the system clock "clicks" approximately 18 times a second, the time advances in increments of about 0.05 seconds.

If you put TIMER in the Watch window, you can see the TIMER value updated each time you press F8 to step through the program.

We'll examine another use for TIMER later in this chapter.

It's a Math, Math World

Let's turn to mathematical operations now. We'll divide them into four groups: number sign functions, number conversion functions, calculator functions, and random-number operations. The functions in the first two groups are important, though a bit dull; the functions and the statement in the last two groups are more interesting and varied in scope.

Number Sign Functions

The ABS function is concerned with the size of a number and ignores the number's positive or negative sign. The SGN function, in contrast, is concerned only with whether the number is positive, negative, or 0.

The ABS and SGN functions have the following syntax:

```
ABS(numericexpression)
SGN(numericexpression)
```

ABS returns the absolute value, or magnitude, of an expression. Thus *ABS(–5)* is 5, as is *ABS(5)*. SGN returns the sign of an expression—more precisely, it returns 1 for a positive value, 0 for a zero value, and –1 for a negative value. *SGN(–100)*, for example, returns –1.

When would you use these functions? You would typically use ABS when you're concerned with the size of a number and not its sign. For instance, you might want to examine data for unusually large fluctuations from an average. The program in Listing 9-3 calculates the average rainfall for several years and prints information about years in which rainfall varied from the average by more than 15 inches. Using the ABS function simplifies testing for those years in which rainfall deviates from the average. The SGN function is used to indicate whether a particular year is below or above the average. (The program should also remind you how to use functions with arrays.)

```
' Find the years with most abnormal rainfall
DECLARE FUNCTION Average! (Arr!())
DATA 28.2, 25.3, 24.5, 60.8, 5.8, 35.0, 31.6
DIM RainFall!(1977 TO 1983)                 ' Array holds yearly data
FOR Year% = 1977 TO 1983
    READ RainFall!(Year%)
NEXT Year%
CLS
AveRain! = Average!(RainFall!())
FOR Year% = 1977 TO 1983
    Diff! = RainFall!(Year%) - AveRain!
    IF SGN(Diff!) = 1 THEN                  ' If > average (positive)
        Kind$ = "inches above normal."
    ELSE                                    ' If <= average (0 or negative)
        Kind$ = "inches below normal."
    END IF
    IF ABS(Diff!) > 15 THEN                 ' Magnitude of difference
        PRINT "Abnormal rainfall in"; Year%; "was ";
        PRINT USING "##.# &"; ABS(Diff!); Kind$
    END IF
NEXT Year%
END

FUNCTION Average! (Arr!())                  ' Average of array values
    FOR I% = LBOUND(Arr!) TO UBOUND(Arr!)
        Sum! = Sum! + Arr!(I%)
    NEXT I%
    Average! = Sum! / (UBOUND(Arr!) - LBOUND(Arr!) + 1)
END FUNCTION
```

Listing 9-3.

Here is the output:

```
Abnormal rainfall in 1980 was 30.6 inches above normal.
Abnormal rainfall in 1981 was 24.3 inches below normal.
```

By using ABS and SGN, we made the output more readable, printing the differences as unsigned numbers and using the sign to control the word choice.

Number Conversion Functions

By now you know that QuickBASIC can change one numeric type to another. For example, when you assign a number of one type to a variable of another type, the number is converted to match the variable's type. QuickBASIC also provides several functions for converting types explicitly. Three of these functions convert numeric expressions to integers.

Here is the syntax for the conversion-to-integer functions, CINT, FIX, and INT:

```
CINT(numericexpression)
FIX(numericexpression)
INT(numericexpression)
```

numericexpression is any expression with a numeric value.

The CINT function returns the value of the expression rounded to the nearest integer—that is, 3.51 is rounded to 4, and 3.49 is rounded to 3. If the fractional part of the number is exactly 0.5, the number is rounded to the nearest even integer: 2.5 is rounded to 2, and 3.5 is rounded to 4.

The FIX function truncates the expression to an integer, discarding the fractional part. Thus *FIX(2.3)* is 2, as is *FIX(2.999)*. Negative numbers are truncated toward 0: both *FIX(-2.2)* and *FIX(-2.9)* are truncated to −2.

Like FIX, the INT function also truncates the expression to an integer. But INT always truncates downward. For example, both *INT(−2.2)* and *INT(−2.9)* return −3, a value less than −2.2 or −2.9. INT and FIX work identically for positive numbers.

The following program illustrates these properties:

```
DATA 3.8, 2.5, 1.5, 1.1, -1.1, -3.8
CLS
PRINT "DATA", "CINT", "FIX", "INT"
FOR I% = 1 TO 6
    READ Number!
    PRINT Number!,
    PRINT CINT(Number!), FIX(Number!), INT(Number!)
NEXT I%
END
```

Here is the output:

```
DATA          CINT          FIX           INT
 3.8           4             3             3
 2.5           2             2             2
 1.5           2             1             1
 1.1           1             1             1
-1.1          -1            -1            -2
-3.8          -4            -3            -4
```

Later in this chapter we'll discuss some practical applications for these functions.

Next let's take a brief look at those functions that convert numbers to the other numeric types: CLNG, CSNG, and CDBL.

Here is the syntax for the CLNG, CSNG, and CDBL functions:

```
CLNG(numericexpression)
CSNG(numericexpression)
CDBL(numericexpression)
```

The CLNG function rounds its argument to the nearest long integer. If the fractional part of the argument is exactly 0.5, CLNG rounds to the nearest even integer.

The CSNG function converts its argument to a single-precision value, and the CDBL function converts its argument to a double-precision value.

The following program demonstrates how these functions work:

```
CLS
X! = 83323.18
PRINT X!; "converts to"; CLNG(X!)
PRINT "3/7 in single precision is"; CSNG(3 / 7)
PRINT "3/7 in double precision is"; CDBL(3 / 7)
END
```

Here is the output:

```
 83323.18 converts to 83323
3/7 in single precision is .4285714
3/7 in double precision is .4285714285714285
```

Calculator Functions

Now let's look at a more interesting, powerful set of functions: QuickBASIC's calculator functions (listed in Figure 9-1). These functions are commonly found on scientific hand calculators.

Function	Argument	Returns
SQR	A non-negative number	Square root of the number
SIN	An angle in radians	Sine of the angle
COS	An angle in radians	Cosine of the angle
TAN	An angle in radians	Tangent of the angle
ATN	A number	Arctangent of the number
EXP	A number	Exponential of the number
LOG	A number	Natural logarithm of the number

Figure 9-1.
Calculator functions.

Rooting for Answers: The SQR Function

The SQR function returns the square root of a non-negative number—*SQR(49)* is 7, for example. If you try to take the square root of a negative number in QuickBASIC, you'll be told that you've made an illegal function call. (QuickBASIC does not use imaginary numbers, which are needed to find the square root of a negative number.)

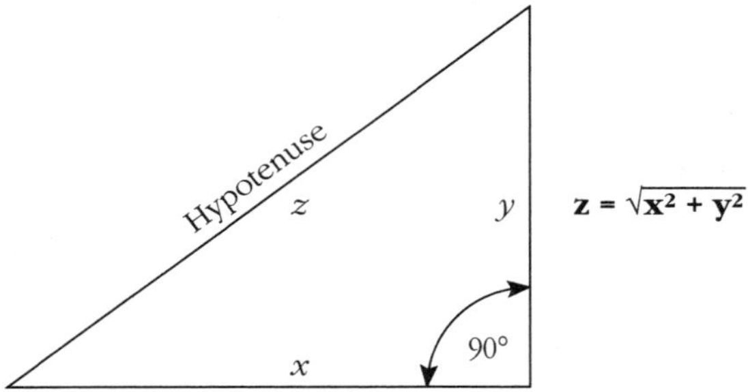

Figure 9-2.
The Pythagorean theorem.

A common use of the square root function is to find the length of the third side of a right triangle. More than 2000 years ago, Pythagoras demonstrated that the longest side of a right triangle (the hypotenuse) is equal in length to the square root of the sum of the squares of the other two sides (Figure 9-2). The following program uses SQR to find the hypotenuse of a right triangle:

```
DECLARE FUNCTION Hypotenuse! (Side1!, Side2!)
CLS
INPUT "Enter the two sides of a right triangle: ", S1!, S2!
PRINT "The third side is"; Hypotenuse!(S1!, S2!)
END

FUNCTION Hypotenuse! (Side1!, Side2!)
    Hypotenuse! = SQR(Side1! * Side1! + Side2! * Side2!)
END FUNCTION
```

Here is a sample run:

```
Enter the two sides of a right triangle: 50, 100
The third side is 111.8034
```

If, for example, you want to run a fence diagonally across a lot that measures 50 feet by 100 feet, you will need at least 111.8 feet of fencing.

Trigonometric Functions: SIN, COS, TAN, and ATN

The common trigonometric functions are defined in terms of ratios of the sides of a right triangle. If *A* is an angle in a right triangle (Figure 9-3), the following definitions result:

sine(A) = opposite/hypotenuse

cosine(A) = adjacent/hypotenuse

tangent(A) = opposite/adjacent

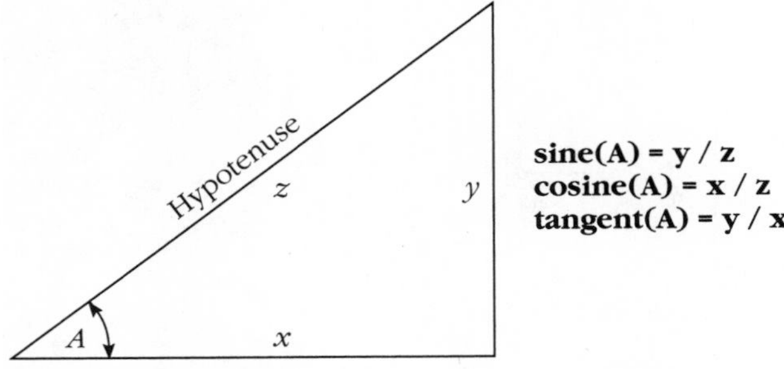

Figure 9-3.
Trigonometric functions.

Any two right triangles having the same angle *A* will have the same values for these ratios. QuickBASIC uses the SIN, COS, and TAN functions to represent these three definitions. In addition, the definition

arctangent(x) = angle whose tangent is x

is represented in QuickBASIC with the ATN function, the inverse of TAN. The TAN function tells you what ratio of sides corresponds to a given angle, and the ATN function tells you what angle corresponds to a given ratio of sides.

Here is the syntax for the trigonometric functions:

```
SIN(numericexpression)
COS(numericexpression)
TAN(numericexpression)
ATN(numericexpression)
```

For SIN, COS, and TAN, *numericexpression* is an angle measured in radians. These functions return the sine, the cosine, and the tangent of the angle. ATN returns the arctangent, in radians, of its argument. If *numericexpression* is double precision, these functions return double-precision values; otherwise, they return single-precision values.

Note that the trigonometric functions use radians rather than degrees for measuring angles. One radian equals approximately 57.29577951 degrees; 180 degrees corresponds to π radians.

Trigonometric functions have many uses. For example, the following formula lets you calculate the flight distance *d* for a projectile in the absence of air resistance:

$$d = v^2\sin(2A)/g$$

The maximum height *h* of flight is given by this equation:

$$h = v^2\sin^2(A)/2g$$

Here v is the launch velocity, A is the launch angle measured from the horizontal, and g is the acceleration of gravity (Figure 9-4). The velocity should be measured in units compatible with the units used for g—for instance, if you use a value of 32 feet per second squared for g, v should be measured in feet per second.

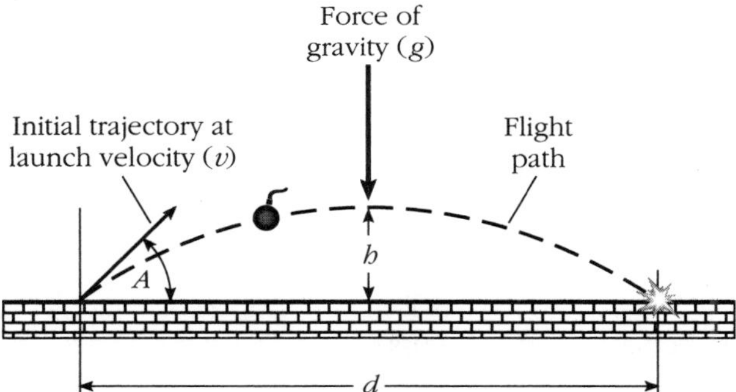

Figure 9-4.
Calculating projectile flight.

In Listing 9-4, we use these formulas to calculate distances and maximum height for several projectile paths.

```
DATA 10, 20, 30, 40, 45, 50, 60, 70, 80
CONST pi = 3.141592654#           ' pi needed for degrees -> radians
CONST g = 32.1                    ' Acceleration of gravity (ft/sec/sec)
DIM Angles!(1 TO 9)               ' Array holds angles to be used
FOR I% = 1 TO 9
    READ Angles!(I%)
NEXT I%
CLS
INPUT "Enter initial speed in ft/sec: ", V!
DO WHILE V! > 0
    PRINT "Initial speed ="; V!; "feet/sec"
    PRINT "Angle", "Range", "Height"
    PRINT "degrees", "feet", "feet"
    FOR I% = 1 TO 9
        Angle! = Angles!(I%) * pi / 180     ' Degrees to radians
        Range! = V! * V! * SIN(2 * Angle!) / g
        Height! = V! * V! * SIN(Angle!) * SIN(Angle!) / (2 * g)
        PRINT Angles!(I%), CINT(Range!), CINT(Height!)
    NEXT I%
    INPUT "Enter initial speed in ft/sec: ", V!
LOOP
END
```

Listing 9-4.

Here is a sample run:

```
Enter initial speed in ft/sec: 88
Initial speed = 88 feet/sec
Angle          Range          Height
degrees        feet           feet
 10             83               4
 20             155             14
 30             209             30
 40             238             50
 45             241             60
 50             238             71
 60             209             90
 70             155            107
 80             83             117
Enter initial speed in ft/sec: 0
```

For the next example, use the Immediate window. Suppose you take some measurements of your driveway and find that it rises 5 feet for every 20 horizontal feet (Figure 9-5). You can use trigonometric functions to find the slope of the driveway in degrees. Because the tangent of an angle is equal to the opposite divided by the adjacent sides, a rise of 5 feet per 20 horizontal feet is shown by the following:

TAN(A) = a/b = 5/20 = 0.25

To find the angle *A*, use the ATN function:

A = ATN(0.25)

Because this answer is in radians, you must multiply by 57.3 to find the angle. The following calculation tells you that the driveway has a 14-degree slope:

```
PRINT 57.3 * ATN(0.25)
 14.03728
```

The trigonometric functions also come in handy when you work with graphics, as we'll see in Chapter 12.

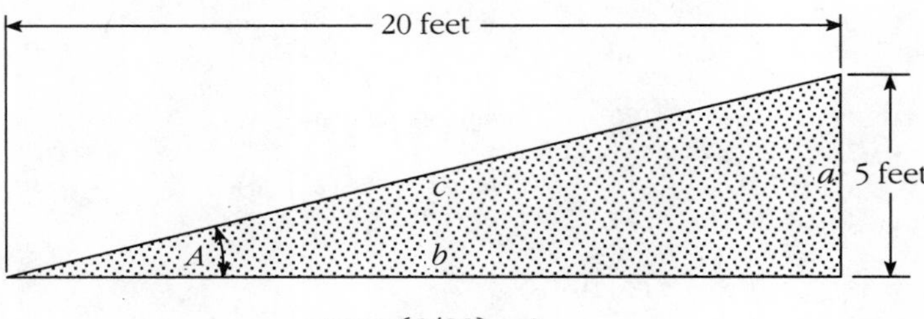

Figure 9-5.
Using trigonometric functions to calculate slope.

The EXP and LOG Functions

The exponential and logarithm functions are often used in science and engineering. EXP, the exponential function, is defined as follows:

$$\text{exponential}(x) = e^x$$

Here *e* is the base of natural logarithms, a mathematical constant approximately equal to 2.718281828. Many natural phenomena—population growth, for example—exhibit exponential growth.

The logarithm function is defined with respect to a particular base. The two most common bases for logarithms are 10 and *e*. In most notations, *log* indicates a base-10 logarithm and *ln* indicates a base-*e* logarithm. QuickBASIC, however, uses the term LOG to represent a base-*e* logarithm. The LOG function is the inverse of the EXP function:

$$\text{LOG } x = p \text{ implies } x = e^p$$

If *p* is the logarithm of a number *x* to base *b*, then *b* to the *p* power is *x*. Many measuring schemes, such as the decibel scale for sound, the Richter scale for earthquakes, and the magnitude system for stars, are based on logarithms.

Here is the syntax for the EXP and LOG functions:

```
EXP(numericexpression)
LOG(numericexpression)
```

The EXP function returns *e* to the power given by *numericexpression*. The LOG function returns the natural logarithm of *numericexpression*. EXP and LOG return single-precision values unless *numericexpression* is double precision, in which case they return double-precision values.

Let's look at some examples, beginning with EXP, of how these functions are used.

Quantities that grow exponentially are characterized by what is called a *doubling time*—if a population has a doubling time of 30 years, the population will double every 30 years. Such growth can be represented by the following equation:

$$pop = pop_0 e^{(t \ln(2)/td)}$$

Here *pop* represents the population at time *t*, pop_0 is the starting population, and *td* is the doubling time. The following program is built around this equation:

```
CLS
INPUT "Enter a starting population: ", Pop0!
INPUT "Enter a doubling time: ", TimeDbl!
INPUT "Enter the number of years per step: ", YearStep%
INPUT "Enter the number of steps: ", StepNum%
PRINT "Years", "Population"
FOR Year% = 0 TO (StepNum% - 1) * YearStep% STEP YearStep%
    PRINT Year%, Pop0! * EXP(Year% * LOG(2) / TimeDbl!)
NEXT Year%
END
```

Here is a sample run:

```
Enter a starting population: 240E+6
Enter a doubling time: 30
Enter the number of years per step: 10
Enter the number of steps: 16
Years         Population
 0              2.4E+08
 10             3.023811E+08
 20             3.809763E+08
 30             4.8E+08
 40             6.047621E+08
 50             7.619525E+08
 60             9.6E+08
 70             1.209524E+09
 80             1.523905E+09
 90             1.92E+09
 100            2.419048E+09
 110            3.04781E+09
 120            3.84E+09
 130            4.838097E+09
 140            6.09562E+09
 150            7.68E+09
```

Thus, a doubling time of 30 years results in increasing the population by a factor of 10 in approximately a century.

QuickBASIC's LOG function is base *e*, although base-10 logarithms are more common in everyday use. QuickBASIC doesn't offer a base-10 log function, but you can easily convert base-*e* logarithms to base 10 by dividing the LOG function by LOG 10. Listing 9-5, for example, prints yearly sales totals along with their base-10 logarithms.

```
DATA 100, 250, 625, 1560, 3910, 9770, 24400
DIM Sales!(1980 TO 1986)                    ' Store sales in array
FOR Year% = 1980 TO 1986
    READ Sales!(Year%)
NEXT Year%
CLS
PRINT "Year", "Sales", "Log10 Sales"
FOR Year% = 1980 TO 1986
    L10! = LOG(Sales!(Year%)) / LOG(10#)   ' Log 10 of sales
    L10Rnded! = CINT(100 * L10!) / 100     ' Round to two decimal places
    PRINT Year%, Sales!(Year%), L10Rnded!
NEXT Year%
END
```

Listing 9-5.

Here is the output:

```
Year          Sales          Log10 Sales
 1980          100            2
 1981          250            2.4
 1982          625            2.8
 1983          1560           3.19
 1984          3910           3.59
 1985          9770           3.99
 1986          24400          4.39
```

If you needed to chart these sales, you'd find it easier to fit the logarithms on a graph than to show the actual sales because the range of the logarithms is much smaller.

Note that we used the CINT function to round the logarithms to two decimal places. CINT rounds to the nearest integer, so we multiplied the value by 100, rounded it, and then divided by 100 again to get the result. This approach to rounding differs from that used with PRINT USING: Here we've rounded the numbers themselves, whereas PRINT USING simply rounds the output.

Incidentally, the exponentiation operator ^ and the EXP function are closely related. Note the following equivalence:

```
A ^ B = EXP (B * LOG(A))
```

Random-Number Operations

QuickBASIC can generate random numbers, a convenient feature if, for example, you want to simulate dice rolls or roulette spins or produce abstract patterns on the screen. The RND function generates random numbers, and the RANDOMIZE statement affects the sequence of the random numbers.

Here is the syntax for the RND function:

```
RND[(n)]
```

If *n* is greater than 0 or if the argument is omitted, the RND function returns a single-precision random number between 0 and 1. If *n* equals 0, RND returns the same number it returned on the previous call. If *n* is less than 0, RND always returns the same value for a given value of *n*—that is, *RND(–3)* consistently returns one particular value, and *RND(–2)* returns another particular value.

Because the RND function is commonly used without arguments, we'll examine that form. The following program generates six random numbers:

```
CLS
FOR I% = 1 TO 6
    PRINT RND
NEXT
END
```

Here is the output:

```
.7055475
.533424
.5795186
.2895625
.301948
.7747401
```

Changing the Range of Random Numbers

The RND function generates random numbers between 0 and 1. Suppose, however, that you want to simulate a dice roll, which requires integers in the range 1 through 6. Begin by multiplying RND by 6, which gives a single-precision value between 0 and 6. Use INT to truncate this value, producing an integer in the range 0 through 5. Then add 1 to get an integer in the range 1 through 6, as shown in this program:

```
CLS
FOR I% = 1 TO 20
    PRINT INT(6 * RND) + 1;  ' Integer from 1 through 6
NEXT
PRINT
END
```

Here is the output:

```
 5  4  4  2  2  5  1  5  5  5  1  3  6  5  3  6  6  1  6  3
```

In general, if you want to generate integers in the range *m* through *n*, use the following form:

```
INT((n - m + 1) * RND) + m
```

Seeding the Random-Number Generator

If you run the preceding program a second time, a problem becomes apparent, as shown in the following output:

```
 5  4  4  2  2  5  1  5  5  5  1  3  6  5  3  6  6  1  6  3
```

The second list of "random" numbers is exactly the same as the first list. The RND function actually generates *pseudorandom* numbers—numbers that are distributed among the possible values but that appear in the same sequence each time you run the program.

The RANDOMIZE statement helps you solve this problem. RND works by starting with a *seed* value to generate a sequence of numbers. Each time you run a program, RND starts with the same seed, leading to the same sequence of numbers. The RANDOMIZE statement, however, lets you choose a new seed, which leads to a different set of pseudorandom numbers.

Here is the syntax for the RANDOMIZE statement:

```
RANDOMIZE [seed]
```

The RANDOMIZE statement resets the random-number generator (RND) seed to *seed*. This value should be a number in the range –32768 through 32767. (Larger arguments are truncated to this range.) If you omit the argument, RANDOMIZE prompts you to enter one.

The following program demonstrates the use of the RANDOMIZE statement:

```
CLS
RANDOMIZE
FOR I% = 1 TO 20
    PRINT INT(6 * RND) + 1;   ' Integer from 1 through 6
NEXT
PRINT
END
```

Here are two sample runs:

```
Random-number seed (-32768 to 32767)? 20
 1  3  4  6  4  1  5  1  1  1  5  4  3  6  5  4  4  1  4  6

Random-number seed (-32768 to 32767)? 5
 1  3  6  2  6  2  6  2  2  1  3  6  3  1  2  1  4  5  5  6
```

Automated Seeding

To make the output of RND even less predictable, you need a way to set the seed to a different value each time you call RANDOMIZE. One approach is to use TIMER to provide the seed value. Because the time is always changing, the following statement produces a different seed value with each use:

```
RANDOMIZE TIMER
```

In Listing 9-6, we use this technique in a program that examines how often RND selects each value. The program calls RND 3000 times to generate 3000 values from 1 through 6. It uses an array to keep track of how often each value is picked—that is, *Occurs%(1)* counts how many times 1 is generated, and so on. (IF ELSE or SELECT CASE could also be used to keep track of the count, but it's simpler to use the array subscripts themselves.)

```
DIM Occur%(1 TO 6)
CLS
RANDOMIZE TIMER
FOR I% = 1 TO 3000                        ' 3000 throws of the dice
    Throw% = INT(6 * RND) + 1             ' A single throw
    Occur%(Throw%) = Occur%(Throw%) + 1   ' Totals throws by die value
NEXT I%
PRINT "Number of occurrences of die values:"
FOR Throw% = 1 TO 6
    PRINT Throw%; ":"; Occur%(Throw%)
NEXT Throw%
END
```

Listing 9-6.

Here are two sample runs:

```
Number of occurrences of die values:
 1 : 481
 2 : 484
 3 : 515
 4 : 500
 5 : 535
 6 : 485

Number of occurrences of die values:
 1 : 514
 2 : 502
 3 : 517
 4 : 480
 5 : 478
 6 : 509
```

Using RANDOMIZE TIMER causes RND to be seeded to a different value each time the program is run. (With only 65,356 possible values for the seed, you will occasionally get repeats.) Note that the random process produces fluctuations from exactly even distributions of choices; the larger the sample, the smaller the relative deviations. Here, for instance, are the results of modifying the program, first, to generate 3 million random values and, second, to generate 30 random values:

```
Number of occurrences of die values
 1 : 499564
 2 : 499082
 3 : 500967
 4 : 499997
 5 : 500265
 6 : 500125

Number of occurrences of die values:
 1 : 5
 2 : 4
 3 : 4
 4 : 9
 5 : 4
 6 : 4
```

In the large sample the maximum variation from the average value of 500000 is less than 0.2 percent, whereas in the small sample the maximum variation from 5 is 80 percent. These deviations from perfect regularity are what gamblers perceive as luck. In the program in Listing 9-6, for example, "luck" favored 5 in the first run and 3 in the second.

Review Questions

1. What is the difference between the TIME$ function and the TIME$ statement?

2. What's wrong with the following program?

```
FOR I% = 1 to 2000
    X# = X# + 1
NEXT I%
PRINT "Loop time ="; TIMER
END
```

3. Evaluate the following expressions:

   a. *CINT(2.9) + CINT(2.3)*

   b. *INT(2.9) + INT(2.3)*

   c. *INT(2.9 + 2.3)*

   d. *INT(2.3) + INT(-2.3)*

   e. *FIX(2.3) + FIX(-2.3)*

4. Sometimes you want fractional values to be rounded up instead of down or to the nearest integer—for example, if you need 5.23 cans of paint to paint your house, you must buy 6 cans. Write a function that rounds its argument up.

5. The radius of a circle having area A is the square root of A/π. Write a function that takes the area of a circle as an argument and returns the circle's radius.

6. If a triangle has two sides of length X and Y and if the angle between the two sides (the included angle) is A, the length of the third side is the square root of the following expression:

   $$X^2 + Y^2 - 2 \times X \times Y \times \cos(A)$$

   Write a function that takes the two sides and the included angle as arguments and returns the length of the third side.

7. Radioactive elements are characterized by a half-life during which half of the remaining radioactive atoms decay. This behavior is called exponential decay and can be represented by the following formula:

   $$\text{amount left} = \text{original amount} \times e^{(-t \times \ln(2)/th)}$$

   Here t is the time and th is the half-life. Write a function that takes a time and a half-life as arguments and returns the fraction of radioactive atoms remaining.

8. Write a program that simulates picking one card at random from a deck.

PART III

Records

10

Custom Data Structures

TYPE

Custom data structures take you beyond QuickBASIC's fundamental types. You can, of course, use a string variable to hold your name, an integer variable to hold your weight, a single-precision variable to hold your bank account. But what if you want to store all this information in a single variable? You can do this with the *user-defined type,* the newest addition to QuickBASIC's variety of types. The user-defined type is an example of a custom data structure—a structure that you can design to hold a specific combination of data. User-defined types make it simpler to represent, organize, and process related data. In this chapter you'll learn how to create and use new types.

User-defined Types: The TYPE Statement

QuickBASIC's TYPE statement is the tool for creating your own types. You can, for example, design a single user-defined type of variable to hold a person's name, job title, salary, and phone number. This single variable is called a *record variable* or a *data structure* (because it is structured to hold several items of data). The parts, or elements, can be any QuickBASIC type except arrays or variable-length strings.

Creating a Type Template

To create a user-defined type, you must provide a name for the type and names for the individual elements of the type. For example, let's design a type that holds information about a compact disc. We'll limit the information to the recording company, the title, the playing time, and the cost. We can use strings for the first two items and single-precision elements for the other two. As shown in the following definition, we can use the QuickBASIC keyword TYPE to create a template describing a structure that consists of two strings and two single-precision values.

```
TYPE CD
    Label AS STRING * 40
    Title AS STRING * 40
    Time AS SINGLE
    Cost AS SINGLE
END TYPE
```

The identifier CD is the name of the new type. *Label*, *Title*, *Time*, and *Cost* are names for the four components of this type. *Label* and *Title* are fixed-length string elements, and *Time* and *Cost* are single-precision elements (Figure 10-1).

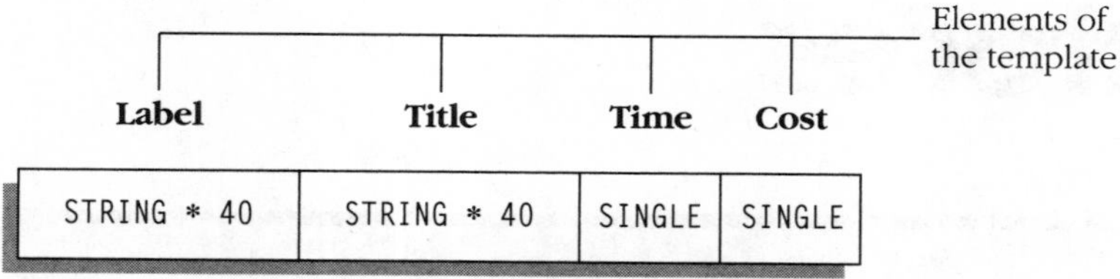

Figure 10-1.
The CD template: A user-defined type.

Creating and Using a Record Variable

The TYPE statement above makes the identifier CD a type name, like INTEGER or DOUBLE, rather than the name of a variable. As a type name, it can be used to declare a record variable that matches the CD description. For example, the following statement creates a variable called *MyCd* that follows the template laid down in the TYPE statement:

```
DIM MyCd AS CD
```

To access the individual elements of a CD type record variable, use the element names from the type definition. To construct a name, append a period and the element name to the variable name. For instance, *MyCd.Label* is the label element of the *MyCd* record variable. (This method of identifying record elements is also used in Pascal and C.) Note that *CD.Label* is not a valid name; CD is a custom type, not a variable. The expression *MyCd.Label*, however, can be used in the same ways a fixed-length string variable is used.

Periods in Names

Although QuickBASIC allows periods as part of variable names—*Free.Ice*, for instance—you should reserve the period for accessing, or identifying, individual record elements. That way you won't confuse the two uses. And you should not use a period as part of the name of a record or a record element—a name with a period will confuse both you and the QuickBASIC compiler.

The program in Listing 10-1 creates a CD type record variable and accesses its elements. Each element is used in the same manner as a variable of the same type. For example, because *MyCd.Time* and *MyCd.Cost* are both single precision, we can divide one by the other.

```
TYPE CD                         ' Create the record template
    Label AS STRING * 40        ' First element
    Title AS STRING * 40        ' Second element
    Time AS SINGLE              ' Third element
    Cost AS SINGLE              ' Fourth element
END TYPE
DIM MyCd AS CD                  ' Create a variable fitting the template
CLS
INPUT "CD label: ", MyCd.Label  ' Access Label element of MyCd
INPUT "CD title: ", MyCd.Title
INPUT "CD playing time in minutes: ", MyCd.Time
INPUT "CD cost: ", MyCd.Cost
PRINT "Title: " + MyCd.Title
PRINT "Label: " + MyCd.Label
PRINT "Minutes per dollar =";
PRINT USING "##.##"; MyCd.Time / MyCd.Cost
END
```

Listing 10-1.

Here is a sample run:

```
CD label: Exotica Digital
CD title: Barnswill's Banjo Concerto Number 56
CD playing time in minutes: 58
CD cost: 11.99
Title: Barnswill's Banjo Concerto Number 56
Label: Exotica Digital
Minutes per dollar = 4.84
```

Here is the TYPE statement syntax:

```
TYPE usertype
    elementname AS type
    elementname AS type
    :
END TYPE
```

Watching Elements

You can use the Watch window to examine record elements that are standard QuickBASIC types, such as *MyCd.Title*. But you cannot put the *MyCd* identifier itself in the Watch window. Debug does not watch the record as a whole; it simply looks at the record's individual components.

In the TYPE syntax, *usertype* is the user-selected name for the new type. *elementname* is a user-selected name for an element of the new type. Type names and element names must conform to the rules used for QuickBASIC variable names. *type* can be integer, long integer, single precision, double precision, fixed-length string, or another user type. Variable-length strings and arrays are not permitted as types in this context. Types can be declared only in module-level code, not in procedures, although they can be used anywhere in the module, including in procedures.

After a type has been defined, you can create a variable of that type with a DIM, REDIM, COMMON, STATIC, or SHARED statement. Thus you can control whether a record is global or local, static or dynamic, automatic or persistent.

Using Records Within Records

The TYPE syntax allows a record element to be another user-defined type, which can help you organize data hierarchically. To include one type within another, you must first define the included type. For example, the following defines two types:

```
TYPE NameType
    First AS STRING * 12
    Last AS STRING * 18
END TYPE

TYPE PhoneList
    Person AS NameType
    Phone AS STRING * 20
END TYPE
```

Because *NameType* is defined first, it can be used in the *PhoneList* definition. (Note that you cannot use *Name* as a label because NAME is a QuickBASIC keyword.)

Next create a *PhoneList* variable:

```
DIM Boss AS PhoneList
```

This statement makes *Boss* a *PhoneList* record variable and the element *Boss.Phone* a fixed-length string. Now consider *Boss.Person*. According to the *PhoneList* definition, *Boss.Person* is type *NameType*—that is, *Boss.Person* is a record element that contains other record elements, not a simple variable. To access its elements, use the period mechanism again. Thus *Boss.Person.First* is a fixed-length string, as is *Boss.Person.Last*. Listing 10-2 shows this nomenclature in action.

```
' Using a record in a record
TYPE NameType                               ' User-defined type
    First AS STRING * 12
    Last AS STRING * 18
END TYPE
```

Listing 10-2. *(continued)*

Listing 10-2. *continued*

```
TYPE PhoneList
    Person AS NameType              ' User-defined type as part of new type
    Phone AS STRING * 24
END TYPE

DIM Boss AS PhoneList
CLS
INPUT "First name: ", Boss.Person.First
INPUT "Last name: ", Boss.Person.Last
LINE INPUT "Phone Number: ", Boss.Phone
PRINT Boss.Person.Last + ", " + Boss.Person.First;
PRINT ": " + Boss.Phone
END
```

Here is a sample run:

```
First name: Mortimer
Last name: Snerd
Phone Number: 800-555-1212, Ext 23
Snerd             , Mortimer    : 800-555-1212, Ext 23
```

Why does the output contain so many spaces? Recall that fixed-length strings are padded with spaces to equal the full length of the string; these spaces appear when the string is printed. To eliminate the trailing spaces in a fixed-length string, use RTRIM$, as shown in Listing 10-3.

```
' Tidy up output of fixed-length strings with RTRIM$
TYPE NameType
    First AS STRING * 12
    Last AS STRING * 18
END TYPE

TYPE PhoneList
    Person AS NameType
    Phone AS STRING * 24
END TYPE

DIM Boss AS PhoneList
CLS
INPUT "First name: ", Boss.Person.First
INPUT "Last name: ", Boss.Person.Last
LINE INPUT "Phone Number: ", Boss.Phone
PRINT "Data Summary:"
PRINT RTRIM$(Boss.Person.Last) + ", ";
PRINT RTRIM$(Boss.Person.First) + ": " + RTRIM$(Boss.Phone)
END
```

Listing 10-3.

Here is a sample run using the revised program:

```
First name: Elmer
Last name: Fudd
Phone Number: 1-800-555-2121, Ext. 401
Data Summary:
Fudd, Elmer: 1-800-555-2121, Ext. 401
```

See Figure 10-2 for another view of a record within a record (nested records).

First	Last

1. Define the *NameType* template with record elements *First* and *Last*.

Person		Phone
First	Last	

2. Define the *PhoneList* template with record elements *Person* and *Phone*. The *NameType* template is used to define *Person*.

Boss		
Person		Phone
First	Last	
`Elmer`	`Fudd`	`1-800-555-2121, Ext. 401`

3. Use the *PhoneList* template to structure the record *Boss*. *Elmer* is stored in the record element identified as *Boss.Person.First*.

Figure 10-2.
Nested records.

Using Arrays of Records

Creating an array of records, which lets you tie a great deal of related information into a single unit, is one of the most useful applications of user-defined types. For example, you can use the template for the *PhoneList* type to create an array that holds information for several people. The DIM statement defines the array, this time with a user-defined type:

```
DIM OfficeMates(1 TO 30) AS PhoneList
```

This statement creates *OfficeMates*, an array of 30 *PhoneList* records, each holding a first name, a last name, and a phone number. *OfficeMates(1)* is the first element of the array. Thus *OfficeMates(1)* is a *PhoneList* record, and *OfficeMates(1).Phone* is the *Phone* element of the *OfficeMates(1)* record. In other words, the array element is the record, so the period and the element name are appended to the array element identifier, exactly as they would be appended to a variable record identifier.

In Listing 10-4, we use an array of records, called *Trip*, to keep track of gasoline purchases: date of purchase, miles traveled, gallons purchased, miles per gallon, and the cost of the purchase. For comparison, we also use a single record, *Town*. Note how we access the various elements of *Town* and the records in the array. Also note that the *Miles* and *Gallons* elements of each record are used to calculate the value for the *Mpg* element.

```
' Use an array of records to track gasoline purchases
' Data statement format is Date, Miles, Gallons, Cost
DATA 06/01/90, 302.2, 12.4, 13.55
DATA 06/03/90, 235.4, 8.7, 9.25
DATA 06/04/90, 378.1, 11.2, 13.75
DATA 06/04/90, 177.5, 6.5, 7.50
DATA 06/05/90, 421.9, 13.8, 14.85
DATA 06/07/90, 315.2, 10.1, 10.30
TYPE GasInfo                            ' Define type
    Date AS STRING * 20
    Miles AS SINGLE
    Gallons AS SINGLE
    Mpg AS SINGLE
    Cost AS SINGLE
END TYPE
DIM Town AS GasInfo                     ' Single record
DIM Trip(1 TO 5) AS GasInfo             ' Array of records
CLS
    ' Initialize one record and calculate mpg
READ Town.Date, Town.Miles, Town.Gallons, Town.Cost
Town.Mpg = Town.Miles / Town.Gallons
    ' Initialize array of records, calculate mpg
FOR Tank% = 1 TO 5
    READ Trip(Tank%).Date, Trip(Tank%).Miles
    READ Trip(Tank%).Gallons, Trip(Tank%).Cost
    Trip(Tank%).Mpg = Trip(Tank%).Miles / Trip(Tank%).Gallons
```

Listing 10-4. *(continued)*

Listing 10-4. *continued*

```
NEXT Tank%
PRINT "Date"; TAB(21); "Miles"; TAB(30); "MPG"
PRINT RTRIM$(Town.Date); TAB(21);    ' Print first record
PRINT USING "###.#"; Town.Miles;
PRINT TAB(30);
PRINT USING "##.#"; Town.Mpg
FOR Tank% = 1 TO 5                   ' Print remaining records from array
    PRINT RTRIM$(Trip(Tank%).Date); TAB(21);
    PRINT USING "###.#"; Trip(Tank%).Miles;
    PRINT TAB(30);
    PRINT USING "##.#"; Trip(Tank%).Mpg
NEXT Tank%
END
```

Here is the output:

```
Date                Miles    MPG
06/01/90            302.2    24.4
06/03/90            235.4    27.1
06/04/90            378.1    33.8
06/04/90            177.5    27.3
06/05/90            421.9    30.6
06/07/90            315.2    31.2
```

Because *Trip* is an array of records, *Trip(Tank%)* represents an individual record, as *Town* does. Thus *Trip(Tank%).Miles* is a record element representing the number of miles traveled. Like *Town.Miles*, it is a single-precision value. Listing 10-4 uses these means of identifying record elements to read data into the six records. The program does not read values for the *Mpg* element; instead, it calculates them using the following statement:

```
Trip(Tank%).Mpg = Trip(Tank%).Miles / Trip(Tank%).Gallons
```

Records and Procedures

You can use subprograms and function procedures to process records in several different ways:

- A procedure that works with arguments of a certain type can also work with record elements of the same type.
- Procedures can work with an entire record.
- Procedures can work with arrays of records.

We'll look at each approach in turn.

Record Elements as Procedure Arguments

We begin by using single-precision parameters to write a procedure that prints the cost per gallon for gasoline:

```
SUB GallonPrice (Dols!, Gals!)
    PRINT "Price Per Gallon is ";
    PRINT USING "$$#.##"; Dols! / Gals!
END SUB
```

Calling this function requires two arguments, each a single-precision value. All of the following calls are legitimate:

```
CALL GallonPrice(14.32, 13.50)
CALL GallonPrice(Cost!, Gallons!)
CALL GallonPrice(Town.Cost, Town.Gallons)
CALL GallonPrice(Trip(Tank%).Cost, Trip(Tank%).Gallons)
```

Each call passes two single-precision arguments.

Listing 10-5 demonstrates the use of *GallonPrice* with record elements as arguments. The program uses the same data set and the same user-defined type as the program in Listing 10-4.

```
' Use a procedure with record elements as arguments
DECLARE SUB GallonPrice (Dols!, Gals!)
DATA 06/01/90, 302.2, 12.4, 13.55
DATA 06/03/90, 235.4, 8.7, 9.25
DATA 06/04/90, 378.1, 11.2, 13.75
DATA 06/04/90, 177.5, 6.5, 7.50
DATA 06/05/90, 421.9, 13.8, 14.85
DATA 06/07/90, 315.2, 10.1, 10.30
TYPE GasInfo
    Date AS STRING * 20
    Miles AS SINGLE
    Gallons AS SINGLE
    Mpg AS SINGLE
    Cost AS SINGLE
END TYPE
DIM Town AS GasInfo                ' Single record
DIM Trip(1 TO 5) AS GasInfo        ' Array of records
CLS
READ Town.Date, Town.Miles, Town.Gallons, Town.Cost
FOR Tank% = 1 TO 5
    READ Trip(Tank%).Date, Trip(Tank%).Miles
    READ Trip(Tank%).Gallons, Trip(Tank%).Cost
NEXT Tank%
CALL GallonPrice(Town.Cost, Town.Gallons)
FOR Tank% = 1 TO 5
    CALL GallonPrice(Trip(Tank%).Cost, Trip(Tank%).Gallons)
NEXT Tank%
END
```

Listing 10-5. *(continued)*

Listing 10-5. *continued*

```
SUB GallonPrice (Dols!, Gals!)
    PRINT "Price Per Gallon is";
    PRINT USING "$$#.##"; Dols! / Gals!
END SUB
```

Here is the output:

```
Price Per Gallon is $1.09
Price Per Gallon is $1.06
Price Per Gallon is $1.23
Price Per Gallon is $1.15
Price Per Gallon is $1.08
Price Per Gallon is $1.02
```

A QuickBASIC record element, like a regular variable, is passed by reference—that is, changing the value of a parameter in a procedure also changes the value of a record element being used as an argument.

Records as Procedure Arguments

Now let's pass an entire record as an argument. We can rewrite Listing 10-4 so that a procedure calculates the value of the *Mpg* element from a *GasInfo* type record. We'll pass a single argument of type *GasInfo* and then let the procedure use the elements of the record.

We must first tell the procedure that its parameter is of type *GasInfo*, as shown here:

```
SUB DoMpg (Gi AS GasInfo)          ' Parameter is a record
    Gi.Mpg = Gi.Miles / Gi.Gallons
END SUB
```

This program fragment makes *Gi* a *GasInfo* type record, allowing us to use *Mpg* and other record element identifiers in the procedure. Now we can make procedure calls such as the following, in which an entire record serves as an argument:

```
CALL DoMpg(Town)
CALL DoMpg(Trip(Tank%))
```

Listing 10-6 uses this procedure.

```
' Use a record as a procedure argument
DECLARE SUB DoMpg (Gi AS ANY)
DATA 06/01/90, 302.2, 12.4, 13.55
DATA 06/03/90, 235.4, 8.7, 9.25
DATA 06/04/90, 378.1, 11.2, 13.75
DATA 06/04/90, 177.5, 6.5, 7.50
DATA 06/05/90, 421.9, 13.8, 14.85
DATA 06/07/90, 315.2, 10.1, 10.30
```

Listing 10-6. *(continued)*

Listing 10-6. *continued*

```
TYPE GasInfo
    Date AS STRING * 20
    Miles AS SINGLE
    Gallons AS SINGLE
    Mpg AS SINGLE
    Cost AS SINGLE
END TYPE
DIM Town AS GasInfo            ' Single record
DIM Trip(1 TO 5) AS GasInfo    ' Array of records
CLS
READ Town.Date, Town.Miles, Town.Gallons, Town.Cost
CALL DoMpg(Town)               ' Argument is a record
FOR Tank% = 1 TO 5
    READ Trip(Tank%).Date, Trip(Tank%).Miles
    READ Trip(Tank%).Gallons, Trip(Tank%).Cost
    CALL DoMpg(Trip(Tank%))    ' Argument is a record in an array
NEXT Tank%
PRINT "Date"; TAB(21); "Miles"; TAB(30); "MPG"
PRINT RTRIM$(Town.Date); TAB(21);
PRINT USING "###.#"; Town.Miles;
PRINT TAB(30);
PRINT USING "##.#"; Town.Mpg
FOR Tank% = 1 TO 5
    PRINT RTRIM$(Trip(Tank%).Date); TAB(21);
    PRINT USING "###.#"; Trip(Tank%).Miles;
    PRINT TAB(30);
    PRINT USING "##.#"; Trip(Tank%).Mpg
NEXT Tank%
END

SUB DoMpg (Gi AS GasInfo)      ' Parameter is a record
    Gi.Mpg = Gi.Miles / Gi.Gallons
END SUB
```

Here is the output:

```
Date                Miles    MPG
06/01/90            302.2    24.4
06/03/90            235.4    27.1
06/04/90            378.1    33.8
06/04/90            177.5    27.3
06/05/90            421.9    30.6
06/07/90            315.2    31.2
```

The following statement makes *Gi* in the procedure an alias for *Town*:

```
CALL DoMpg(Town)
```

This allows the procedure to use the values *Town.Miles* and *Town.Gallons* and to set the value of *Town.Mpg*. Similarly, when *Tank%* has the value 1, the following call uses the values of *Trip(1).Miles* and *Trip(1).Gallons* to set the value of *Trip(1).Mpg*:

```
CALL DoMpg(Trip(Tank%))
```

Arrays of Records as Procedure Arguments

We've passed both a record element and a complete record as arguments. Let's take one more step and pass an entire array of records as an argument. The two preceding examples used an array of records representing gasoline purchases for a trip. To calculate the average mileage for an entire trip, you must use data from all the records in the array, which can be accomplished by passing the whole array as an argument to a function. Again, the key is to declare the function parameter correctly:

```
' Calculate mpg for entire trip:
'  This function totals all the gallon elements and, separately,
'  all the distance elements of an array of records
FUNCTION Mpg! (Arr() AS GasInfo)
    FOR I% = LBOUND(Arr) TO UBOUND(Arr)
        Gallons! = Gallons! + Arr(I%).Gallons
        Miles! = Miles! + Arr(I%).Miles
    NEXT I%
    Mpg! = Miles! / Gallons!
END FUNCTION
```

Declaring the parameter as an array of *GasInfo* records allows us to use *Trip* as an argument. Listing 10-7 incorporates this function into a new program. QuickBASIC adds a function declaration to the top of the program when you save it. Instead of stating that the array is type *GasInfo*, however, QuickBASIC describes it as an array of ANY, a generic term indicating that the type is user defined and that type checking of the parameter has been turned off.

```
' Program calculates average mpg for entire trip
'  by passing an array of records as a function argument
DECLARE FUNCTION Mpg! (Arr() AS ANY)
DATA 06/03/90, 235.4, 8.7, 9.25
DATA 06/04/90, 378.1, 11.2, 13.75
DATA 06/04/90, 177.5, 6.5, 7.50
DATA 06/05/90, 421.9, 13.8, 14.85
DATA 06/07/90, 315.2, 10.1, 10.30
TYPE GasInfo
    Date AS STRING * 20
    Miles AS SINGLE
    Gallons AS SINGLE
    Mpg AS SINGLE
    Cost AS SINGLE
END TYPE
DIM Trip(1 TO 5) AS GasInfo                ' Array of records
CLS
FOR Tank% = 1 TO 5
    READ Trip(Tank%).Date, Trip(Tank%).Miles
    READ Trip(Tank%).Gallons, Trip(Tank%).Cost
NEXT Tank%
PRINT "Average mpg for entire trip = ";
```

Listing 10-7. *(continued)*

Listing 10-7. *continued*

```
PRINT USING "##.# mpg": Mpg!(Trip())     ' Use return value of function
END

' Function adds gallons and miles and then divides the total
'  number of miles by the total gallons
FUNCTION Mpg! (Arr() AS GasInfo)         ' Arr is an array of records
    FOR I% = LBOUND(Arr) TO UBOUND(Arr)
        Gallons! = Gallons! + Arr(I%).Gallons
        Miles! = Miles! + Arr(I%).Miles
    NEXT I%
    Mpg! = Miles! / Gallons!
END FUNCTION
```

Here is the output:

```
Average mpg for entire trip = 30.4 mpg
```

User-defined Types: Assignment

You can't read or write a user-defined type as a unit with READ, INPUT, or PRINT. The following statements, for example, don't work when *Town* is a record and *Trip* is an array of records:

```
INPUT "Enter all the data: ", Town    ' Doesn't work for records
PRINT Trip(3)                         ' Ditto
```

Instead, you must specify each individual record element for input and output operations, as we did in the preceding programs. But you can assign records as a unit—that is, if *Town* and *Work* are both variables of the same user-defined type, you can do the following:

```
Work = Town    ' Assign contents of one record to another
```

This assignment lets you avoid copying records element by element. You can't use a loop to access the elements of a record as you can with arrays, because the record elements are not numbered, whereas array elements are.

The SWAP statement also works with record variables and facilitates sorting records. Thus the following is a valid statement:

```
SWAP Work, Town    ' Exchange record contents
```

Listing 10-8 uses both record assignment and record swapping to copy an array of records and to sort the copy in order of increasing miles per gallon. Because we now print two arrays, we put the array-printing code into a subprogram.

```
' Sorting an array of records
DECLARE SUB ShowRecs (Arr() AS ANY)
DECLARE SUB SortMpg (Arr() AS ANY)
DECLARE SUB DoMpg (Gi AS ANY)
DATA 06/03/90, 235.4, 8.7, 9.25
DATA 06/04/90, 378.1, 11.2, 13.75
DATA 06/04/90, 177.5, 6.5, 7.50
DATA 06/05/90, 421.9, 13.8, 14.85
DATA 06/07/90, 315.2, 10.1, 10.30
TYPE GasInfo
    Date AS STRING * 20
    Miles AS SINGLE
    Gallons AS SINGLE
    Mpg AS SINGLE
    Cost AS SINGLE
END TYPE
DIM Trip(1 TO 5) AS GasInfo         ' Array of records
DIM TripCopy(1 TO 5) AS GasInfo
CLS
FOR Tank% = 1 TO 5
    READ Trip(Tank%).Date, Trip(Tank%).Miles
    READ Trip(Tank%).Gallons, Trip(Tank%).Cost
    CALL DoMpg(Trip(Tank%))         ' Argument is a record
    TripCopy(Tank%) = Trip(Tank%)   ' Copy record
NEXT Tank%
CALL SortMpg(TripCopy())            ' Sort copied records by Mpg
PRINT "Original Array of Records:"
CALL ShowRecs(Trip())               ' Display array by record element
PRINT "Sorted Array of Records:"
CALL ShowRecs(TripCopy())
END

' Calculate value for Mpg element of record
SUB DoMpg (Gi AS GasInfo)           ' Parameter is a record
    Gi.Mpg = Gi.Miles / Gi.Gallons
END SUB

' Display trip data
SUB ShowRecs (Arr() AS GasInfo)
    PRINT "Date"; TAB(21); "Miles"; TAB(30); "MPG"
    FOR Tank% = LBOUND(Arr) TO UBOUND(Arr)
        PRINT RTRIM$(Arr(Tank%).Date); TAB(21);
        PRINT USING "###.#"; Arr(Tank%).Miles;
        PRINT TAB(30);
        PRINT USING "##.#"; Arr(Tank%).Mpg
    NEXT Tank%
END SUB
```

Listing 10-8. *(continued)*

Listing 10-8. *continued*

```
' Sort array records by comparing Mpg elements
SUB SortMpg (Arr() AS GasInfo)
    Low% = LBOUND(Arr)
    High% = UBOUND(Arr)
    FOR Top% = Low% TO High% - 1
        FOR Comp% = Top% TO High%
            IF Arr(Comp%).Mpg < Arr(Top%).Mpg THEN
                SWAP Arr(Comp%), Arr(Top%)
        END IF
        NEXT Comp%
    NEXT Top%
END SUB
```

Here is the output:

```
Original Array of Records:
Date                Miles    MPG
06/03/90            235.4    27.1
06/04/90            378.1    33.8
06/04/90            177.5    27.3
06/05/90            421.9    30.6
06/07/90            315.2    31.2
Sorted Array of Records:
Date                Miles    MPG
06/03/90            235.4    27.1
06/04/90            177.5    27.3
06/05/90            421.9    30.6
06/07/90            315.2    31.2
06/04/90            378.1    33.8
```

The *SortMpg* subprogram resembles the *SortScores* subprogram in Listing 6-17. One minor but essential alteration changed the array type from STRING to *GasInfo*. The following lines are the most powerful part of the subprogram's code:

```
IF Arr(Comp%).Mpg < Arr(Top%).Mpg THEN
    SWAP Arr(Comp%), Arr(Top%)
```

Although the code compares record elements, it swaps entire records. That's one of the advantages of storing information in an array of records rather than in several arrays of fundamental types.

In general, as you've seen throughout this chapter, user-defined types are extremely useful for representing related data. By keeping related information in a single unit—the record—you can simplify the organizing and processing of data. Records are flexible: You can design them to meet specific needs, you can work with individual elements of a type, or you can treat the record as a whole. Simplicity, power, flexibility—all these make records and user-defined types valuable additions to the QuickBASIC repertoire.

Review Questions

1. Define a user type *FoodFact* to hold the name of a food and the number of calories per ounce for that food.
2. Define a variable and an array of the type defined in Review Question 1.
3. Define a *CarInfo* type that consists of two records: the first an *Automobile* type that holds a car's make, model, year, and body style; the second a *Location* type that holds a city name and a state name. (You must also define the component types.)
4. Define a variable of type *CarInfo* (Review Question 3), and set the value of the year element to 1968.
5. Write a procedure that prints each element of a record of type *FoodFact* (Review Question 2).
6. Write a procedure that prints, by each record element, the contents of an array of *FoodFact* records (Review Question 2).
7. Write a function that returns the total amount spent on gasoline for an array of *GasInfo* records as defined in Listings 10-4 through 10-8.

11

Files

CHDIR	**FILES**	**LOF**	**PRINT #**
CLOSE	**FREEFILE**	**LSET**	**PRINT # USING**
CVD	**GET**	**MKD$**	**PUT**
CVI	**INPUT #**	**MKI$**	**RESET**
CVL	**INPUT$**	**MKL$**	**RSET**
CVS	**KILL**	**MKS$**	**SEEK**
EOF	**LINE INPUT #**	**NAME**	**WRITE #**
FIELD	**LOC**	**OPEN**	

When you work with computers, you quickly learn the importance of files for holding or storing information. Applications such as QuickBASIC come in files; DOS comes in files. The programs you create, the novels you write, the spreadsheet and database data you compile—all are stored in files, typically on a hard disk or a floppy disk. QuickBASIC provides three models for files: *sequential* files, *random access* files, and *binary* files. We'll look at all three models in this chapter.

Sequential Files

Sequential files, which we've used in previous examples, are ASCII text files. The contents of a sequential file are stored in text form as a continuous sequence of characters. You can examine a sequential file with the DOS TYPE or DOS EDLIN commands, with word processors, or with the QuickBASIC editor. Sequential files, as the name implies, are usually processed from beginning to end in sequence rather than by moving around to various parts of the file. You can think of them as resembling cassette tapes. Sequential files are well suited for storing simple text—that is, text without boldface, italics, underlining, or complicated formatting. The README files that often come with new software, for instance, are typically sequential files.

Using a Sequential File

Open a sequential file with the OPEN statement, which connects the program to the file. You can open sequential files in one of three modes—OUTPUT, INPUT, or APPEND—that specify how the program is connected to the file.

Here is the syntax for the OPEN statement used with sequential files:

```
OPEN filename FOR mode AS [#]filenum [LEN = bufsize]
OPEN fmode, [#]filenum, filename[, bufsize]
```

The string *filename* is the name of the file to be opened. *mode* is one of the following:

- OUTPUT mode creates a file and opens it for sequential output from the program. If the file already exists, it is truncated to zero length—that is, its original contents are discarded.
- INPUT mode opens a file for sequential input to the program. If no file exists, an error message is generated.
- APPEND mode opens a file for sequential output from the program, letting the program add data to the end of the file. If no file exists, one is created.

Note that a sequential file cannot be open for reading and writing simultaneously.

In the second syntax version, *fmode* is O, I, or A (OUTPUT, INPUT, or APPEND). In both syntax versions, *filenum* is an integer in the range 1 through 255 that identifies the open file to other file operations. (If the file PIE is opened as 2, I/O statements use 2, not PIE, to describe the file.) INPUT mode allows you to reopen a file that is

Naming Files

QuickBASIC follows DOS conventions for naming files: Filenames can be as long as eight characters and can also include an extension with as many as three characters. Filenames in DOS are not case sensitive, so the following statements are equivalent:

```
OPEN "EXAMPLE.TXT" FOR OUTPUT AS #1
OPEN "example.txt" FOR OUTPUT AS #1
```

Files created or accessed with the OPEN statement are assumed to be in the current directory. If you want to open a file elsewhere, use the full pathname, again using the DOS conventions:

```
OPEN "c:\drudgery\letters\landlord.txt" FOR OUTPUT AS #2
```

already open, by using a different *filenum* value. OUTPUT and APPEND modes, however, allow only one *filenum* value at a time.

bufsize is the size of an intermediate I/O buffer. The default buffer size is 512 bytes. A larger buffer transfers information between a program and a file with greater speed but decreases the amount of memory available to the program.

Buffers

QuickBASIC file I/O functions use buffers to transfer data quickly from a file to a program. Reading single bytes directly from a file in a disk drive can be slow; reading large chunks of data is much faster. But programs often need to access data byte by byte. The solution is to copy a buffer-sized chunk of data from the file to a buffer (temporary space set aside in random access memory, or RAM). Because RAM can be read quickly byte by byte, the input function can read the data from the buffer efficiently (Figure 11-1). When each block of data has been read, the next chunk of the file is copied to the buffer. Output functions write to a buffer in a similar way. When the buffer is filled, the data is copied to the file.

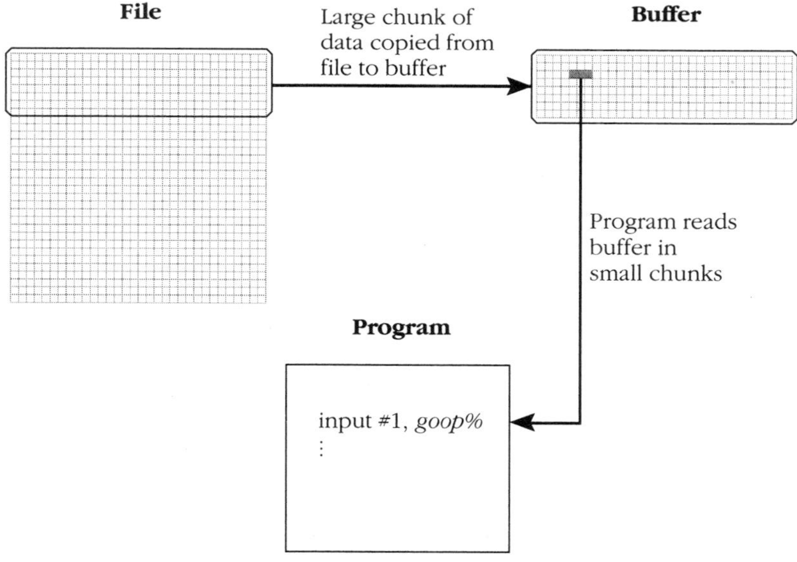

Figure 11-1.
An input buffer.

The OPEN statement has two additional modifiers (ACCESS and locking information) that apply to networking systems only. These modifiers control what happens when two or more users try to access the same file simultaneously.

When a file is open in INPUT mode, you can read from it using an INPUT #, LINE INPUT #, or INPUT$ statement. (The # symbol indicates file input rather than keyboard input.) An error will result if you try to read beyond the end of the file. You can avoid the error by using the EOF function (first discussed in Chapter 4) to test for the end of the file.

Here is the syntax for the EOF function:

```
EOF(filenum)
```

The EOF function returns –1, or true, if the end of the sequential file assigned the file number *filenum* has been reached.

When the file is open in APPEND or OUTPUT mode, you can write to it using a PRINT # or a WRITE # statement. (The # symbol indicates file output rather than screen output.)

We'll describe the I/O functions in more detail later in the chapter.

Use the CLOSE statement when you have finished reading from or writing to a file. This will send any data remaining in the output buffer to the file (if you have been writing to a file), close the file, and free the memory set aside for the buffer.

Here is the syntax for the CLOSE statement:

```
CLOSE [[#]filenum]
```

The CLOSE statement closes the file whose file number is *filenum*. If it is used without arguments, this statement closes all open files (as well as any devices a program has opened, such as a serial port).

To close all disk files without affecting devices, use QuickBASIC's RESET statement, which takes no arguments.

Let's review what we know about sequential files. The program in Listing 11-1 opens a file for output, reads keyboard input, and saves it in a file until you enter a blank line. Then the program closes the file for output and reopens it for input. Finally it opens the file, reads the contents line by line, displays them on the screen, and closes the file again.

```
CLS
OPEN "OurFile" FOR OUTPUT AS #1     ' Open file to receive data
PRINT "Enter text (blank line to quit):"
LINE INPUT "", In$                  ' Get first keyboard input
```

Listing 11-1. *(continued)*

Listing 11-1. *continued*

```
DO WHILE In$ <> ""                  ' Loop until blank line
    PRINT #1, In$                   ' Write line to file
    LINE INPUT "", In$              ' Get keyboard input
LOOP
CLOSE #1                            ' Close file
PRINT "OurFile contents:"
OPEN "OurFile" FOR INPUT AS #1      ' Open file to read data
DO UNTIL EOF(1)                     ' Loop until end of file
    LINE INPUT #1, OneLine$         ' Read line from file
    PRINT OneLine$
LOOP
CLOSE #1                            ' Close file
END
```

Here is a sample run:

```
Enter text (blank line to quit):
If you were to fill a table tennis ball with <Enter>
material from a neutron star, you would have <Enter>
a twenty-billion-ton ball to play with. <Enter>
<Enter>
OurFile contents:
If you were to fill a table tennis ball with
material from a neutron star, you would have
a twenty-billion-ton ball to play with.
```

We used PRINT # to write to the file and LINE INPUT # to read it. We'll discuss both these statements in the following sections.

Writing to Sequential Files

Both PRINT # and WRITE # can be used to write to sequential files. The PRINT # statement works like the screen-oriented PRINT statement, but it uses a file number to write to the selected file rather than writing to the screen. Similarly, PRINT # USING is the file version of PRINT USING.

Here is the syntax for PRINT # and PRINT # USING:

```
PRINT #filenum, [USING formatstring;] expressionlist[{,|;}]
```

filenum is the file number assigned in the OPEN statement when the file is opened. The optional *formatstring* specifies an output format that overrides the formatting specified by comma and semicolon separators, as it does for PRINT USING. *expressionlist* is a list of values separated by commas, semicolons, or both. When you use commas, each item is printed in a field 14 characters wide. When you use semicolons, items are printed consecutively; only numbers have a trailing space. PRINT # writes a blank line if *expressionlist* is omitted.

The WRITE # statement is simpler than PRINT # because it doesn't provide any formatting options. Values are separated by commas. String values are enclosed in double quotation marks, and numbers are printed without quotation marks.

Here is the WRITE # syntax:

```
WRITE #filenum, expressionlist
```

This statement writes to the file identified by *filenum*. *expressionlist* is a comma-separated list of values, written in the file as a single line.

Listing 11-2 shows an example of the WRITE # statement.

```
CLS
OPEN "OurFile" FOR OUTPUT AS #1
INPUT "Enter opera (blank line to quit): ", Opera$
DO WHILE Opera$ <> ""
    INPUT "Enter conductor: ", Leader$
    INPUT "Enter number of performances: ", Number%
    WRITE #1, Opera$, Leader$, Number%  ' Write values to file
    INPUT "Enter opera (blank line to quit): ", Opera$
LOOP
CLOSE #1
PRINT "OurFile contents:"
OPEN "OurFile" FOR INPUT AS #1
DO UNTIL EOF(1)
    LINE INPUT #1, OneLine$
    PRINT OneLine$
LOOP
CLOSE #1
END
```

Listing 11-2.

Here is a sample run:

```
Enter opera (blank line to quit): Aida
Enter conductor: De Bartini
Enter number of performances: 4
Enter opera (blank line to quit): Tosca
Enter conductor: Tortelli
Enter number of performances: 3
Enter opera (blank line to quit): <Enter>
OurFile contents:
"Aida","De Bartini",4
"Tosca","Tortelli",3
```

The WRITE # Statement and Records

The WRITE # statement organizes a file into a series of records, with each record consisting of a series of fields. In a QuickBASIC sequential file, each record corresponds to one line in the file. QuickBASIC follows the DOS convention of using the carriage-return/linefeed (CR-LF) combination to separate lines in a text file. This combination is called a *record separator*. Similarly, the comma serves as a *field separator*. The sample output from Listing 11-2, for example, shows a file consisting of two records, each containing three fields, as illustrated in Figure 11-2.

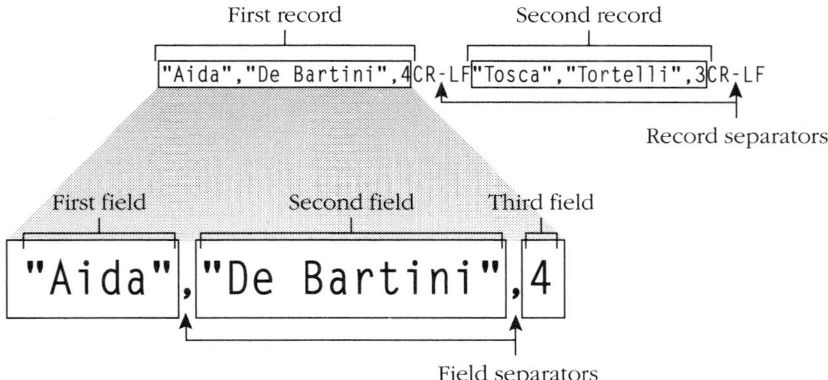

Figure 11-2.
Records and fields in a sequential file.

In Chapter 10 we used the term "record" to mean a user-defined type; here we use it to mean a component of a file. These different definitions both imply a unit of data containing subunits.

The inverse of the WRITE # statement is the INPUT # statement. The WRITE # statement sends data to a file formatted as fields and records, whereas the INPUT # statement reads data from a file as fields and records.

Reading from Sequential Files

You can use LINE INPUT #, INPUT #, or INPUT$ to read sequential files. Each reads a different unit of input:

- LINE INPUT # reads one record at a time as a string.
- INPUT # reads a field-sized block of data, which can be assigned to a string variable or to a numeric variable.
- INPUT$ reads as a string a block of data that consists of a specified number of characters.

The LINE INPUT # Statement

LINE INPUT # reads a line—a record—from the indicated file. Unlike LINE INPUT, it reads from a file rather than from the keyboard, and it does not use an optional prompt string.

Here is the syntax for the LINE INPUT # statement:

```
LINE INPUT #filenum, stringvariable
```

This statement reads one line from the file assigned the file number *filenum* and copies the line into *stringvariable*. Listings 11-1 and 11-2 illustrate the use of the LINE INPUT # statement.

The INPUT # Statement

The INPUT # statement works like the keyboard INPUT statement, but it reads from a file rather than from the keyboard, and it does not use a prompt string. INPUT # reads a file one field at a time, using commas to identify fields and assigning each field value to a variable.

Here is the INPUT # syntax:

```
INPUT #filenum, variablelist
```

The statement reads the file identified by *filenum*. *variablelist* is a comma-separated list of variables. Input values are separated by commas, with successive items (or fields) assigned to corresponding successive variables in *variablelist*.

When scanning a file for either a numeric value or a string, INPUT # ignores leading spaces, carriage returns, and linefeeds. For numbers, INPUT # assumes that the number begins with the first character other than a space, carriage return, or linefeed and that the number terminates with the first subsequent comma, space, carriage return, or linefeed. For strings, double quotation marks establish the limits of the string in the input file. If no double quotation marks are found, INPUT # assumes that the string begins with the first character other than a space, carriage return, or linefeed and that the string terminates with the first subsequent comma, carriage return, or linefeed.

Remember that numbers are stored as strings in text files. Whether a number string is read as a number or as a string depends on whether you assign the input to a numeric variable or to a string variable.

To see how INPUT # works, let's modify our preceding example. The new program is shown in Listing 11-3.

```
' Compare LINE INPUT # and INPUT # data retrieval
CLS
OPEN "OurFile" FOR OUTPUT AS #1
INPUT "Enter opera (blank line to quit): ", Opera$
DO WHILE Opera$ <> ""
    INPUT "Enter conductor: ", Leader$
    INPUT "Enter number of performances: ", Number%
    WRITE #1, Opera$, Leader$, Number%
    INPUT "Enter opera (blank line to quit): ", Opera$
LOOP
CLOSE #1
PRINT "OurFile contents (LINE INPUT #):"
OPEN "OurFile" FOR INPUT AS #1
DO UNTIL EOF(1)                          ' LINE INPUT # data retrieval
    LINE INPUT #1, OneLine$
    PRINT OneLine$
LOOP
CLOSE #1
PRINT "OurFile contents (INPUT #):"
OPEN "OurFile" FOR INPUT AS #1
DO UNTIL EOF(1)
    INPUT #1, Field1$, Field2$, Field3%  ' INPUT # data retrieval
    PRINT Field1$, Field2$, Field3%
LOOP
CLOSE #1
END
```

Listing 11-3.

Here is a sample run:

```
Enter opera (blank line to quit): Madame Butterfly
Enter conductor: MacTune
Enter number of performances: 3
Enter opera (blank line to quit): La Boheme
Enter conductor: Snurz
Enter number of performances: 4
Enter opera (blank line to quit): <Enter>
OurFile contents (LINE INPUT #):
"Madame Butterfly","MacTune",3
"La Boheme","Snurz",4
OurFile contents (INPUT #):
Madame Butterfly            MacTune        3
La Boheme     Snurz          4
```

The LINE INPUT # statement reads one entire record, including commas and double quotation marks, whereas the INPUT # statement reads individual fields in a record. The double quotation marks and commas are used as guides to identify strings and fields; they are not part of the fields and thus are not read into the variables.

The INPUT$ Function

The INPUT$ function reads a specified number of characters from a file. Unlike LINE INPUT # and INPUT #, which are used only with sequential files, INPUT$ can be used with all three file types (sequential, random access, and binary) as well as with keyboard input. Because INPUT$ is a function rather than a statement, it provides a string return value as input to the calling program.

Here is the syntax for the INPUT$ function:

```
INPUT$(n[, [#]filenum])
```

The INPUT$ function returns a string containing the next *n* characters (or bytes) from the file identified as *filenum*. If *filenum* is omitted, INPUT$ reads from standard input, which by default is the keyboard. (For stand-alone BASIC programs, DOS redirection (<) can make a file the standard input, and DOS piping (¦) can make the output of another program or of a DOS command the standard input.)

INPUT$ uses its first argument to determine how many bytes to read from the file. Because one character occupies 1 byte of storage, the byte count becomes a character count for text files. Numbers are read as strings, however, so 234 counts as three characters, or 3 bytes.

INPUT$ is convenient for examining individual characters in an input file. If, for example, you want to count the characters in a file, you can use the following program:

```
' Use INPUT$ to count characters in a file
CLS
OPEN "complit" FOR INPUT AS #1
DO UNTIL EOF(1)
    Ch$ = INPUT$(1, 1)
    CharCount% = CharCount% + 1
LOOP
CLOSE #1
PRINT CharCount%; "characters"
END
```

Try using the program for a text file named COMPLIT containing the following:

```
See the
nice cat!
```

How many characters do you count? Here's what the program counts:

```
 20 characters
```

The letters, spaces, and punctuation marks account for only 16 characters. To find the additional characters, we can modify the program to print all the characters it reads. Some might be control characters (those with ASCII codes less than 32), which are nonprinting. We'll give them special treatment—for example, printing Ctrl-M as *^M*. Adding 64 to the ASCII code for a control character produces the ASCII code for the corresponding uppercase character; for instance, the ASCII code for Ctrl-M is 13, and the ASCII code for M is 77. See Listing 11-4 for details.

```
CLS
OPEN "complit" FOR INPUT AS #1
DO UNTIL EOF(1)
    Ch$ = INPUT$(1, 1)
    CharCount% = CharCount% + 1
    IF ASC(Ch$) >= 32 THEN
        PRINT Ch$;                           ' Show regular characters
    ELSE
        PRINT "^" + CHR$(ASC(Ch$) + 64);     ' Show control characters
    END IF
LOOP
CLOSE #1
PRINT
PRINT CharCount%; "characters"
END
```

Listing 11-4.

Here is the new output:

```
See the^M^Jnice cat!^M^J
 20 characters
```

INPUT$ reads all the characters in a file, including the hidden ^M^J combinations. (DOS ASCII text files use CR-LF to mark line ends; the carriage-return character is ASCII 13, or ^M, and the linefeed character is ASCII 10, or ^J.)

Because LINE INPUT # reads a file one line at a time, it doesn't pass the ^M^J combination on to the program. INPUT # reads one field at a time, skipping double quotation marks, commas (unless they are within double quotation marks), and the ^M^J combination. But INPUT$ reads a fixed number of characters at one time and does not skip anything. Use INPUT$ when your program must read every character in a file. Figure 11-3 presents these three methods of reading a file.

LINE INPUT # reads a file:

"apples",78 CR-LF "pears",88 CR-LF "oranges",59 CR-LF

INPUT # reads a file:

"apples",78 CR-LF "pears",88 CR-LF "oranges",59 CR-LF

INPUT$ reads a file (assuming $n = 1$):

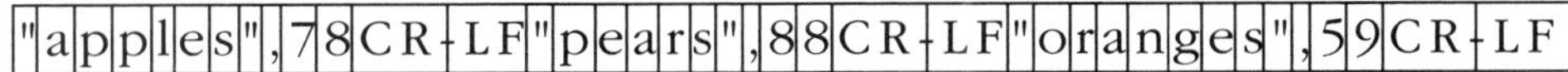

Figure 11-3.
Reading from a sequential file.

The LOF Function

If you want to know the size of a file, you don't need to count all the characters. Instead, you can use QuickBASIC's LOF (length-of-file) function to return the length of an open file.

Here is the syntax for the LOF function:

```
LOF(filenum)
```

LOF returns the length, in bytes, of the file opened with file number *filenum*.

The LOF function is a timesaver. But if you want to count particular characters—uppercase letters, for example—use INPUT$, which allows you to inspect each character as it is read.

Random Access Files

Random access files are more effective than sequential files for handling some forms of data—inventories, for example. Like the sequential model, the random access model views a file as consisting of a sequence of records and each record as a sequence of fields. But the two file models differ in several ways.

The sequential model uses the CR-LF combination to delimit records and the comma to mark fields, allowing files to contain records and fields of various lengths. The random access model, however, doesn't use special characters to mark limits; instead, each record in a random access file has the same user-specified length and contains the same number of fields, which are specified by length rather than by commas. Thus the file contains data only, with no field or record separators, as shown in Figure 11-4.

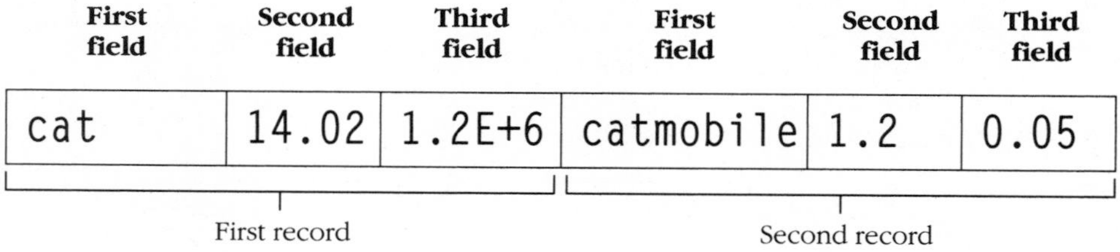

First field	Second field	Third field	First field	Second field	Third field
cat	14.02	1.2E+6	catmobile	1.2	0.05
First record			Second record		

Figure 11-4.
In a random access file, each record is the same length, and each field is the same length as the corresponding field in another record.

Numbers in sequential files are represented as text, allowing you to read these files with a text editor. For example, the number 28201 is represented by 5 characters (1 for each digit), and the number 6.31835E+12 is represented by 11 characters (1 for each digit, letter, and symbol). But random access files store numbers in the same binary format used internally by the computer: Integers are stored as 2-byte binary values, long integers are stored as 4-byte binary values, single-precision numbers are stored as 4-byte binary values, and double-precision numbers are stored as 8-byte binary values. For floating-point numbers, some bytes store a numeric value, and others store an exponent. In general, storing numbers in binary format requires less space than storing them in text format (Figure 11-5). Storing numbers in binary format is also more precise, because converting numbers from binary to text format and back can produce rounding errors.

Finally, random access files, unlike sequential files, can be opened in read/write mode, and records can be accessed in any order you choose (thus the name "random access"). If a sequential file is like a cassette tape, a random access file is more like a compact disc, which lets you jump to any selection.

6.31835E+12 stored as text

6	.	3	1	8	3	5	E	+	1	2

11 bytes (1 for each character)

6.31835E+12 stored as binary

6.31835E+12

4 bytes to represent single precision in binary form

2.1 stored as text

2	.	1

3 bytes (1 for each character)

2.1 stored as binary

2.1

4 bytes to represent single precision in binary form

Figure 11-5.
Text and binary storage of numbers.

Using a Random Access File

To use a random access file, you must first design the record format. Then use OPEN to open the file. To write to the file, use the PUT statement. To read the file, use the GET statement. (You can use INPUT$, but GET is designed to work with PUT.) Use CLOSE to close the file.

The best way to create a record format is with the TYPE statement. For example, the following statement creates a record template consisting of three fields:

```
TYPE DataType
    PartName AS STRING * 12     ' Fixed-length string
    PartNum AS INTEGER          ' 2-byte integer
    PartCost AS SINGLE          ' 4-byte floating point
END TYPE
```

The first field (*PartName*) is 12 bytes, the *PartNum* field is 2 bytes, and the *PartCost* field is 4 bytes. Altogether, the record is 18 bytes long.

After the record type is defined, you can create a variable of that type by using the DIM statement:

```
DIM Axle AS DataType
```

Use PUT to write the contents of the variable as a single unit to the file. Each record in the file then corresponds to a user-defined type.

Random access files are opened with the same OPEN statement used for sequential files; the mode, however, is set to RANDOM.

Here is the syntax for the OPEN statement used with random access files:

```
OPEN filename [FOR RANDOM] [ACCESS amode] AS [#]filenum [LEN = reclength]
OPEN R, [#]filenum, filename[, reclength]
```

The string *filename* is the name of the file to be opened. If the FOR RANDOM clause is omitted, the file will still be opened for random access, which is the default mode for the OPEN statement.

The ACCESS modifier can be used only with DOS versions that support networking (DOS versions 3 and later). The possible values for the *amode* parameter are READ (open the file for reading only), WRITE (open the file for writing only), and READ WRITE (open the file for reading and writing).

If the ACCESS clause is omitted, OPEN attempts to open the file in this sequence:

1. read/write
2. write only
3. read only

OPEN will make one attempt to open the file in each mode but quits after the first successful attempt.

In the second (older) syntax version, with file mode R, OPEN attempts to open the file in the random access read/write mode.

filenum is an integer in the range 1 through 255 used to identify the file to other file operations. RANDOM mode allows you to reopen a file that is already open, by using a different *filenum* value.

reclength sets the record length in bytes for a random access file. The default length is 128. The value of this argument must be at least as large as the record prototype used by the program. (If *reclength* is larger than the program record length, the file records are padded with extra bytes. For example, if you create a user-defined variable of 96 bytes and use the default *reclength* value, you'll have 32 unused bytes when you save the record to a file.)

Random Access Input/Output

With random access files, QuickBASIC's PUT statement writes an entire record to the file. The GET statement reads a random access file one record at a time.

Here is the syntax for GET and PUT used with random access files:

```
PUT [#]filenum[, [recnum][, variable]]
GET [#]filenum[, [recnum][, variable]]
```

filenum is the file number assigned to the file in the OPEN statement. *recnum* is the record number. The first record in the file is number 1, and the largest possible record number is 2147483647. For PUT, *variable* is the name of the variable to be copied to the file. For GET, *variable* is the name of the variable into which a record from the file will be copied. If the *recnum* argument is omitted, GET and PUT go to the next record in a file. When omitting *recnum*, retain commas in the statement:

```
PUT #1, , ThatStuff
```

If you omit the *variable* parameter, you must use the FIELD statement (discussed in the next section) to set up an alternative method for reading and writing records.

Let's bring these various concepts into focus with a program. In Chapter 4 (Listing 4-8), we presented a simple file program that saved names and phone numbers. A random access file can serve the same purpose. First let's create a suitable record template, as shown in the following:

```
TYPE NameType
    FirstName AS STRING * 15
    LastName AS STRING * 15
END TYPE
TYPE PhoneType                     ' Record template
    Who AS NameType
    PhoneNo AS STRING * 25
END TYPE
```

Using a string rather than a numeric type to hold the phone number allows *PhoneNo* to contain hyphens, parentheses, spacing, and so forth. User-defined types, which require fixed-length rather than variable-length strings, are well suited for random access files, which use fixed-length records. (Here the term "record" is used in both senses: as a file unit and as a user-defined template. The two concepts correspond because we copy information from a record variable to a file record and vice versa.)

Next we create a variable of this type:

```
DIM Client AS PhoneType
```

Then we open a file in RANDOM mode. Using a record notation such as *Client.PhoneNo* (discussed in Chapter 10), we can fill the elements of the record variable. PUT allows us to write the record as a unit to the file. After all the data has been entered, we can use GET to read the file, as shown in Listing 11-5.

```
' Random access database example, Version 1
TYPE NameType
    FirstName AS STRING * 15
    LastName AS STRING * 15
END TYPE
TYPE PhoneType                          ' Record template
    Who AS NameType
    PhoneNo AS STRING * 25
END TYPE
DIM Client AS PhoneType                 ' Record variable
File$ = "RANAMES"
CLS
' Copy keyboard input to file
OPEN File$ FOR RANDOM AS #1 LEN = LEN(Client)
PRINT "This program stores names and phone numbers. To quit,"
PRINT "press Enter without entering a name."
LINE INPUT "Enter first name: ", Client.Who.FirstName
DO WHILE LTRIM$(Client.Who.FirstName) <> ""
    LINE INPUT "Enter last name: ", Client.Who.LastName
    LINE INPUT "Enter phone number: "; Client.PhoneNo
    PUT #1, , Client
    LINE INPUT "Enter next first name: ", Client.Who.FirstName
LOOP
NumRecs% = LOF(1) / LEN(Client)         ' Find how many records
' Display the file contents
PRINT "Here are the current contents of the "; File$; " file:"
FOR Rec% = 1 TO NumRecs%                ' Start with first record
    GET #1, Rec%, Client
    PRINT Client.Who.LastName + ", ";
    PRINT Client.Who.FirstName + ": ";
    PRINT Client.PhoneNo
NEXT Rec%
CLOSE #1
PRINT "Bye."
END
```

Listing 11-5.

Here is a sample run:

```
This program stores names and phone numbers. To quit,
press Enter without entering a name.
Enter first name: Cynthia
Enter last name: Cilliguse
Enter phone number: 800-555-9281
Enter next first name: Baldar
Enter last name: Dash
Enter phone number: 800-555-8023
Enter next first name: <Enter>
Here are the current contents of the RANAMES file:
Cilliguse      , Cynthia        : 800-555-9281
Dash           , Baldar         : 800-555-8023
Bye.
```

The LEN term in the OPEN statement should be set to the record size being used. You can calculate the length yourself—the *PhoneType* record, for example, contains two 15-byte strings and one 25-byte string, for a total of 55 bytes—or you can let the computer calculate it. Because the LEN function, using a variable name like *Client* as an argument, returns the size of the variable, we set LEN equal to *LEN(Client).*

We want to terminate the program when the user enters an empty line. But record element strings such as *Client.Who.FirstName* are fixed-length and padded with spaces. Thus a fixed-length string cannot be equal to the null string. Using the LTRIM$ function to trim all the leading spaces makes the return value equal to the null string if the original string is all spaces, allowing the loop to terminate.

When each element of the *Client* record is filled, we write the record to the file:

```
PUT #1, , Client
```

When the second argument is omitted, PUT advances one record in the file each time it is used.

Because RANDOM mode is read/write by default, we don't need to close the file and reopen it before reading it, as we did with sequential files. But we must return to the beginning of the file to read it. The following statement takes the program to the first record in the file when *Rec%* equals 1 and copies it into the *Client* variable:

```
GET #1, Rec%, Client
```

We must also know when to stop reading the file. Because all records are the same length, we can calculate how many records the file contains by dividing the length of the file by the length of a record (in bytes), as shown here:

```
NumRecs% = LOF(1) / LEN(Client)    ' Find how many records
```

We then use a FOR loop with an index running from 1 through *NumRecs%* to read and display each record in turn. (Because this is a random access file, you could run the index from *NumRecs%* through 1 to print the records in reverse order.)

Let's run the program again and see what happens when we add new information. Here is the new output:

```
This program stores names and phone numbers. To quit,
press Enter without entering a name.
Enter first name: Cyril
Enter last name: Crassissimo
Enter phone number: 960-100-0000
Enter next first name: <Enter>
Here are the current contents of the RANAMES file:
Crassissimo    , Cyril          : 960-100-0000
Dash           , Baldar         : 800-555-8023
Bye.
```

The new entry has been written over the original first record (*Cynthia Cilliguse*). The following statement writes a new record immediately after the last record used:

```
PUT #1, , Client
```

But if the file has just been opened and no records have yet been used, this statement writes at the beginning of a file. (Because user-defined types use fixed-length strings, each record is the same length, which causes the new record to overwrite the original record exactly.)

To allow the program to append new records instead of writing over old ones, we must find out how many records the file contains when opened. Then we can use PUT's *recnum* argument to place new records at the end of the file. The following statement, which finds the number of records, must be moved near the beginning of the program:

```
NumRecs% = LOF(1) / LEN(Client)    ' Find how many records
```

Each time we read a new record from the keyboard, we can increase *NumRecs%* by 1 and use it as an argument to PUT. Listing 11-6 makes this modification.

```
' Random access database example, Version 2
TYPE NameType
    FirstName AS STRING * 15
    LastName AS STRING * 15
END TYPE
TYPE PhoneType                          ' Record template
    Who AS NameType
    PhoneNo AS STRING * 25
END TYPE
DIM Client AS PhoneType                 ' Record variable
File$ = "RANAMES"
CLS
' Copy keyboard input to file
OPEN File$ FOR RANDOM AS #1 LEN = LEN(Client)
NumRecs% = LOF(1) / LEN(Client)       ' Find how many records
PRINT "This program stores names and phone numbers. To quit,"
PRINT "press Enter without entering a name."
LINE INPUT "Enter first name: ", Client.Who.FirstName
DO WHILE LTRIM$(Client.Who.FirstName) <> ""
    NumRecs% = NumRecs% + 1           ' Add a new record
    LINE INPUT "Enter last name: ", Client.Who.LastName
    LINE INPUT "Enter phone number: "; Client.PhoneNo
    PUT #1, NumRecs%, Client
    LINE INPUT "Enter next first name: ", Client.Who.FirstName
LOOP
' Display the file contents
```

Listing 11-6. *(continued)*

Listing 11-6. *continued*

```
PRINT "Here are the current contents of the "; File$; " file:"
FOR Rec% = 1 TO NumRecs%                ' Start with first record
    GET #1, Rec%, Client
    PRINT Client.Who.LastName + ", ";
    PRINT Client.Who.FirstName + ": ";
    PRINT Client.PhoneNo
NEXT Rec%
CLOSE #1
PRINT "Bye."
END
```

Here is a sample run, with the new entries appended:

```
This program stores names and phone numbers. To quit,
press Enter without entering a name.
Enter first name: Cynthia
Enter last name: Cilliguse
Enter phone number: 800-555-9281
Enter next first name: Fergus
Enter last name: Flambeau
Enter phone number: 900-001-0001
Enter next first name: <Enter>
Here are the current contents of the RANAMES file:
Crassissimo     , Cyril          : 960-100-0000
Dash            , Baldar         : 800-555-8023
Cilliguse       , Cynthia        : 800-555-9281
Flambeau        , Fergus         : 900-001-0001
Bye.
```

The FIELD Statement

QuickBASIC also offers a second method, based on the FIELD statement, for creating and using records in random access files. This method is awkward and inconvenient compared to employing user-defined types, but it is sometimes used for compatibility with older versions of BASIC.

The first step in using the FIELD statement is to create a record template.

Here is the syntax for FIELD:

```
FIELD [#]filenum, fieldwidth AS stringvariable[, fieldwidth
 AS stringvariable,...]
```

This statement creates a buffer to be used with a random access file opened with file number *filenum*. The buffer consists of a series of string variables (*stringvariable*) of *fieldwidth* length. For instance, the following statement creates a buffer holding three strings that are 10, 2, and 4 bytes long:

```
FIELD #1, 10 AS Fish$, 2 AS Weight$, 4 AS Price$
```

Information is then placed into the buffer variables. Strings are loaded using the LSET or the RSET statement.

Here is the syntax for LSET and RSET:

```
LSET stringvariable = stringexpression
RSET stringvariable = stringexpression
```

Each statement loads *stringexpression* into the FIELD buffer variable *stringvariable*, as shown here:

```
LSET Fish$ = "Tuna"
```

The LSET statement left-justifies the string (puts it at the left end of the field), and the RSET statement right-justifies the string (puts it at the right end of the field). If *stringexpression* is longer than *stringvariable*, *stringexpression* is truncated to fit.

Numbers must be converted to strings using one of four special MK functions before they can be sent to the buffer with the LSET or the RSET statement.

Here is the syntax for the MK family of functions:

```
MKI$(integerexpression)
MKL$(longintegerexpression)
MKS$(numericexpression)
MKD$(numericexpression)
```

The MKI$ function converts its integer argument to a 2-byte string in which the characters represent the binary form of the number. The MKL$ function converts its long integer argument to a 4-byte string representing the binary form of the number. The MKS$ function converts its numeric argument to a 4-byte string representing the number in single-precision binary form. The MKD$ function converts its numeric argument to an 8-byte string representing the number in double-precision binary form. You must use LSET or RSET to load these strings into the field buffer, as shown in the following examples:

```
LSET Weight$ = MKI$(4)
LSET Price$ = MKS$(1.92)
```

When all the values are loaded into the buffer, use PUT without a variable name to write the information to a file:

```
PUT #1
```

To read a file, use GET without a variable name, which loads the next record into the FIELD buffer:

```
GET #1
```

You can then copy the results into regular variables. Data for string variables can be copied directly, but data for numeric variables must be converted by another set of functions, as shown in the following:

```
GET #1
MyFish$ = Fish$
ItsWeight% = CVI(Weight$)
ItsPrice! = CVI(Price$)
```

Here is the syntax for the CV family of conversion functions:

```
CVI(str2$)
CVL(str4$)
CVS(str4$)
CVD(str8$)
```

The CVI function converts a 2-byte string created by the MKI$ function to an integer and returns it. Similarly, CVL returns a long integer, CVS returns a single-precision value, and CVD returns a double-precision value; their arguments are the 4-byte and 8-byte strings created by MKL$, MKS$, and MKD$.

These elements are combined into the short program shown in Listing 11-7.

```
' Using the FIELD mechanism for random access files
DATA "Tuna", 68, 88.15
DATA "Cod", 40, 1.50
OPEN "FISH.DAT" FOR RANDOM AS #1 LEN = 16
FIELD #1, 10 AS Fish$, 2 AS Weight$, 4 AS Price$
CLS
FOR I% = 1 TO 2
    READ Fishy$, Wt%, Pr!
    LSET Fish$ = Fishy$         ' String -> buffer
    LSET Weight$ = MKI$(Wt%)    ' Convert integer then -> buffer
    LSET Price$ = MKS$(Pr!)     ' Convert single precision then -> buffer
    PUT #1                      ' Send buffer contents -> file
    PRINT Wt%; " is converted to "; MKI$(Wt%)
NEXT I%
PRINT "Species", "Weight", "Price"
FOR I% = 1 TO 2
    GET #1, I%
    PRINT Fish$, CVI(Weight$), CVS(Price$)
NEXT I%
END
```

Listing 11-7.

Here is the output:

```
 68  is converted to D
 40  is converted to (
Species       Weight        Price
Tuna           68            88.15
Cod            40            1.5
```

Note that 68 is converted to D. Because 68 is the ASCII code for D, the string *D* corresponds to the binary representation of the value. As you can see, user-defined types offer a simpler and more convenient way to handle random access file records.

Extending the Phone Database Program

We can illustrate the strengths of the random access approach by rewriting the database program from Listing 8-16 using a random access file. The entire program becomes smoother and better integrated. The original program failed if we tried to view a file that did not already exist, because we couldn't open a nonexistent file in INPUT mode. This problem is solved by opening the file in RANDOM mode. In this read/write mode, the program creates the file if the file does not already exist. See Listing 11-8 for the rewrite.

```
' Random access database example
DECLARE SUB FindString (File$)         ' Find specific string in file
DECLARE SUB SortArray (Arr() AS ANY)   ' Sort array contents
DECLARE SUB SortFile (File$)           ' Sort file contents
DECLARE FUNCTION MenuSelection$ ()     ' Show menu, return response
DECLARE SUB ShowFile (File$)           ' Display file contents
DECLARE SUB AddToFile (File$)          ' Append data to file
TYPE NameType
    FirstName AS STRING * 15
    LastName AS STRING * 15
END TYPE
TYPE PhoneType
    Who AS NameType
    PhoneNo AS STRING * 25
END TYPE
DIM Client AS PhoneType
DIM SHARED FileLen AS INTEGER
RecSize% = LEN(Client)                 ' Length of record
File$ = "RANAMES.DAT"
CONST msg$ = "The number of records in the file ="
CLS
OPEN File$ FOR RANDOM AS #1 LEN = RecSize%
FileLen = LOF(1) / RecSize%            ' Records in file
Response$ = MenuSelection$
DO WHILE Response$ <> "q" AND Response$ <> "Q"
    SELECT CASE Response$              ' Menu response chooses action
        CASE "D", "d": CALL ShowFile(File$)
        CASE "A", "a": CALL AddToFile(File$)
        CASE "C", "c": PRINT msg; FileLen
                       PRINT
        CASE "S", "s": CALL SortFile(File$)
        CASE "F", "f": CALL FindString(File$)
        CASE ELSE: PRINT "I don't understand that response."
    END SELECT
    Response$ = MenuSelection$
LOOP
PRINT "Farewell"
END
```

Listing 11-8. *(continued)*

Listing 11-8. *continued*

```
SUB AddToFile (File$)
    DIM Client AS PhoneType
    PRINT "Begin adding new names and phone numbers to the";
    PRINT "file. To quit, press Enter without entering a name."
    LINE INPUT "Enter first name: ", Client.Who.FirstName
    DO WHILE LTRIM$(Client.Who.FirstName) <> ""
        FileLen = FileLen + 1              ' Add a new record
        LINE INPUT "Enter last name: ", Client.Who.LastName
        LINE INPUT "Enter phone number: "; Client.PhoneNo
        PUT #1, FileLen, Client            ' Send data to file
        LINE INPUT "Enter next first name: ", Client.Who.FirstName
    LOOP
    PRINT "The new information has been added."
    LINE INPUT "Press Enter to continue.", Stuff$
    PRINT
END SUB

SUB FindString (File$)
    DIM Client AS PhoneType
    LINE INPUT "Enter the string you want to find: ", Thing$
    IF Thing$ = "" THEN
        PRINT "No string specified"
        PRINT
        EXIT SUB
    END IF
    FOR Rec% = 1 TO FileLen               ' Check each record
        GET #1, Rec%, Client
        IF INSTR(Client.Who.LastName, Thing$) THEN
            PRINT Client.Who.LastName
        END IF
    NEXT Rec%
    PRINT "End of search of the "; File$; "file."
    PRINT
END SUB

FUNCTION MenuSelection$
    PRINT "Enter the letter of your choice:"
    PRINT "D) Display file contents   A) Add to file"
    PRINT "C) Count records in file   S) Sort file by last name"
    PRINT "F) Find a last name        Q) Quit"
    LINE INPUT "> ", Ans$
    MenuSelection$ = LEFT$(Ans$, 1)
END FUNCTION

SUB ShowFile (File$)
    DIM Info AS PhoneType
    PRINT "Here are the contents of the "; File$; " file:"
    FOR Rec% = 1 TO FileLen
        GET #1, Rec%, Info                 ' Get each record
        PRINT Info.Who.LastName + ", ";
```

(continued)

Listing 11-8. *continued*

```
        PRINT Info.Who.FirstName + ": ";
        PRINT Info.PhoneNo
    NEXT Rec%
    LINE INPUT "Press Enter to continue.", Stuff$
    PRINT
END SUB

SUB SortArray (Arr() AS PhoneType)
    Low% = LBOUND(Arr)
    High% = UBOUND(Arr)
    FOR Top% = Low% TO High% - 1
        FOR Comp% = Top% TO High%
            IF Arr(Comp%).Who.LastName < Arr(Top%).Who.LastName THEN
                SWAP Arr(Comp%), Arr(Top%)
            END IF
        NEXT Comp%
    NEXT Top%
END SUB

SUB SortFile (File$)
    DIM Info(1 TO FileLen) AS PhoneType
    FOR Rec% = 1 TO FileLen                 ' Get each record
        GET #1, Rec%, Info(Rec%)
    NEXT Rec%
    CALL SortArray(Info())
    FOR Rec% = 1 TO FileLen
        PUT #1, Rec%, Info(Rec%)
    NEXT Rec%
    PRINT "File has been sorted."
END SUB
```

By using the size of the file as a shared variable and updating the value as needed, we make that information available to all parts of the program.

Here is a sample run:

```
Enter the letter of your choice:
D) Display file contents   A) Add to file
C) Count records in file   S) Sort file by last name
F) Find a last name        Q) Quit
> C
The number of records in the file = 0

Enter the letter of your choice:
D) Display file contents   A) Add to file
C) Count records in file   S) Sort file by last name
F) Find a last name        Q) Quit
> A
```

```
Begin adding new names and phone numbers to the
file. To quit, press Enter without entering a name.
Enter first name: Bigbee
Enter last name: Snuffers
Enter phone number: 800-555-2998
Enter next first name: Carolyn
Enter last name: Snacks
Enter phone number: 111-555-2022
Enter next first name: <Enter>
The new information has been added.
Press Enter to continue. <Enter>

Enter the letter of your choice:
D) Display file contents   A) Add to file
C) Count records in file   S) Sort file by last name
F) Find a last name        Q) Quit
> d
Here are the contents of the RANAMES.DAT file:
Snuffers        , Bigbee         : 800-555-2998
Snacks          , Carolyn        : 111-555-2022
Press Enter to continue. <Enter>

Enter the letter of your choice:
D) Display file contents   A) Add to file
C) Count records in file   S) Sort file by last name
F) Find a last name        Q) Quit
> s
File has been sorted.
Enter the letter of your choice:
D) Display file contents   A) Add to file
C) Count records in file   S) Sort file by last name
F) Find a last name        Q) Quit
> d
Here are the contents of the RANAMES.DAT file:
Snacks          , Carolyn        : 111-555-2022
Snuffers        , Bigbee         : 800-555-2998
Press Enter to continue. <Enter>

Enter the letter of your choice:
D) Display file contents   A) Add to file
C) Count records in file   S) Sort file by last name
F) Find a last name        Q) Quit
> q
Farewell
```

Binary Files

Binary files are files that contain both ASCII and nonprinting characters. Many data files, word processor document files, and even executable (EXE) files are binary files.

BINARY mode resembles RANDOM mode; the difference between them is how the data in the file is addressed. A file opened in BINARY mode is seen as a succession of bytes, whereas a file opened in RANDOM mode is seen as a succession of records. For instance, if the file GOOP has been opened in BINARY mode as #1, the following statement copies the variable *Poof%* to file GOOP beginning at byte 5, not at record 5:

```
PUT #1, 5, Poof%
```

Here is the syntax for the OPEN statement used with binary files:

```
OPEN filename FOR BINARY [ACCESS amode] AS [#]filenum
OPEN B, [#]filenum, filename
```

The string *filename* is the name of the file to be opened. The ACCESS modifier is the same as the ACCESS modifier in the RANDOM mode OPEN statement (page 290), opening the file in read only, write only, or read/write mode.

In the second syntax version, the file mode is B. In this case, OPEN attempts to open the file in the binary read/write mode.

filenum is an integer in the range 1 through 255 that is used to identify the file to other file operations. BINARY mode, like INPUT and RANDOM modes, allows you to reopen a file that is already open, by using a different *filenum* value.

BINARY mode ignores the LEN modifier used by the other modes.

When a file is opened in BINARY mode, you can access any byte by using the GET or the PUT statement.

Here is the syntax for GET and PUT used with binary files:

```
PUT [#]filenum, [bytenum], variable
GET [#]filenum, [bytenum], variable
```

filenum is the file number assigned to the file in the OPEN statement. *bytenum* is the byte number. The first byte in the file is number 1, and the largest possible byte number is 2147483647. For PUT, *variable* is the name of the variable to be copied to the file. For GET, *variable* is the name of the variable into which a record from the file will be copied. The GET statement reads a number of bytes equal to the size of *variable*. If *bytenum* is omitted, GET and PUT go to the byte following the last one read or written.

BINARY mode works well with nontext files that are not collections of records—EXE files, for example, or files created by WordPerfect or Microsoft Word.

The access to individual bytes in a binary file simplifies the code for programs that move through a file nonsequentially. The program in Listing 11-9, for example, prints the contents of a file in reverse order. It uses LOF to find the number of bytes and uses GET in a FOR loop to read the file from the last byte to the first.

```
' Use BINARY mode to display a file backward
DIM Character AS STRING * 1
CLS
INPUT "File to be examined: ", File$
OPEN File$ FOR BINARY AS #1
PRINT File$; " contains"; LOF(1); "bytes."
PRINT "Here they are in reverse order:"
FOR Byte% = LOF(1) TO 1 STEP -1        ' From end to beginning
    GET #1, Byte%, Character           ' Get 1 byte from file
    PRINT Character;
NEXT Byte%
PRINT
END
```

Listing 11-9.

If we make *Character* a string of length 1, the GET statement reads 1 byte at a time. Here is a sample run:

```
File to be examined: TRYME
TRYME contains 55 bytes.
Here they are in reverse order:

.dne na

ot emoc tsum sgniht doog

lla taht esoppus I
```

The TRYME file (a DOS text file) uses the carriage-return/linefeed combination to indicate the end of the line. Because both the carriage-return and the linefeed characters advance the screen output by one line when printed to the screen, the output is double spaced.

Other File Facilities

Let's take a brief look at some of QuickBASIC's additional file-related statements and functions. The QuickBASIC Help menu can supply more information and examples, especially if you use the Details and Example options.

The SEEK Function, the SEEK Statement, and the LOC Function

You can think of QuickBASIC as maintaining a pointer to the current position in a file. For files opened in RANDOM mode, the position is measured in record units; for files opened in all other modes, the position is measured in bytes. The first record or byte is 1. When a file is opened in any mode except APPEND, the current position is the beginning of the file. In APPEND mode, the current position is immediately after the last item in the file. Each subsequent read or write operation advances the current position to the next byte or record, where the next read or write action takes place.

The SEEK function returns the current file position, and the SEEK statement sets the current file position.

Here is the SEEK syntax:

```
SEEK(filenum)                  ' Function form
SEEK [#]filenum, position      ' Statement form
```

The function form returns the current file position for the file identified by *filenum*, and the statement form sets the current file position to *position* for the file identified by *filenum*. The current file position is where the next read or write operation will occur.

The LOC function also returns a file position. But rather than returning the current file position, LOC returns the position of the last item read or written.

Here is the LOC syntax:

```
LOC(filenum)
```

filenum is the file number used to open the file. For sequential files, LOC returns the current byte position divided by 128. For random access files, LOC returns the record number for the last record read. For binary files, LOC returns the byte number of the last byte read.

The FREEFILE Function: Selecting a File Number

If an application opens several files simultaneously, you must avoid using the same file number for different open files. This might be a problem if you don't know in advance which files will be opened or in what order. The FREEFILE function solves that problem by selecting a valid file number.

Here is the FREEFILE syntax:

```
FREEFILE
```

The FREEFILE function returns the next valid unused file number.

Suppose you want to write a function that takes the name of a sequential file as an argument and returns the number of records in the file. You don't want to build a file number into the function, because it might conflict with a file number already in use. Listing 11-10 shows how to use FREEFILE to select a valid file number.

Because sequential files don't have fixed-length records, the program can't calculate the number of records by dividing the file length by the record length. But it can count records by counting lines, because sequential files use one line per record.

```
' Use FREEFILE to generate a file number
DECLARE FUNCTION RecCount% (File$)
CLS
INPUT "Enter name of text file: ", TheFile$
Records% = RecCount%(TheFile$)
PRINT TheFile$; " contains"; Records%; "records."
END

FUNCTION RecCount% (File$)
    FileNo% = FREEFILE              ' Obtain next free file number
    OPEN File$ FOR INPUT AS FileNo%
    DO UNTIL EOF(1)
        LINE INPUT #FileNo%, Temp$  ' Count records
        Count% = Count% + 1
    LOOP
    RecCount% = Count%
END FUNCTION
```

Listing 11-10.

File Operations

QuickBASIC offers some statements that resemble DOS commands:

- The FILES statement lists files.
- The NAME statement renames a file.
- The KILL statement deletes a file.
- The CHDIR statement changes the current directory.

We'll summarize these statements and then use them in a short program.

Here is the syntax for the FILES statement:

```
FILES [filespec]
```

filespec is a string specifying a filename or directory. It can include the drive designation and the DOS wildcard characters ? and *. The FILES statement lists the specified files or directory much as the DOS DIR/W command does, prefacing the list with the pathname of the current directory. If no argument is given, FILES lists the current directory.

You can use the following statement, for example, to list all the BAS files in the c:\progs directory:

```
FILES "c:\progs\*.bas"
```

Here is the KILL syntax:

```
KILL filespec
```

This statement deletes the file indicated by *filespec*. This argument should be a filename, but it can include wildcard characters and path information.

The following statement deletes all files with the C extension from the OLDSTUFF subdirectory of the current directory:

```
KILL "oldstuff\*.c"
```

Here is the NAME syntax:

```
NAME filespec1 AS filespec2
```

filespec1 is the original name, and *filespec2* is the new name. The new name cannot be the name of a file that already exists. If the names are in different directories—that is, a path is included in the new name—the file is moved from one directory to another. Both directories must be on the same disk and in the same partition.

Here are some examples:

```
NAME "Sam" AS "Sally"      ' Change filename from Sam to Sally
NAME "Ed" AS "Old\OldEd"   ' Move Ed to Old subdirectory and
                           '  rename file OldEd
```

Here is the syntax for CHDIR:

```
CHDIR pathspec
```

This statement changes the current default directory to the one specified by the string *pathspec*. This variable has the following form:

```
[drive:][\]directory[\directory]...
```

Here are some examples:

```
CHDIR "ponk"     ' Change to ponk subdirectory of current directory
CHDIR "\zonk"    ' Change to zonk subdirectory of root
CHDIR "b:\conk"  ' Change to conk subdirectory of B drive
```

Changing the directory of a drive other than the default drive (as in the third example) does not cause your program to switch to a different default drive.

We use these QuickBASIC file statements in Listing 11-11 to produce a simple file-management program. Note that we use temporary files in a TEMP directory. If you erase files with this program, they are permanently lost.

```
' This program lists, renames, and deletes files
DECLARE SUB SetDir ()               ' Change default directory
DECLARE SUB RenameFile ()           ' Rename file
DECLARE SUB DeleteFile ()           ' Delete file
DECLARE FUNCTION GetMenu$ ()        ' Produce menu for choosing action
CLS
Choice$ = GetMenu$
```

Listing 11-11. *(continued)*

Listing 11-11. *continued*

```
DO UNTIL Choice$ = "Q"             ' Select action from menu selection
    SELECT CASE Choice$
    CASE "L"
        FILES
    CASE "R"
        CALL RenameFile
    CASE "D"
        CALL DeleteFile
    CASE "S"
        CALL SetDir
    END SELECT
    Choice$ = GetMenu$
LOOP
PRINT "Bye"
END

SUB DeleteFile
    INPUT "Enter name of file to be deleted: ", File$
    KILL File$
END SUB

FUNCTION GetMenu$
    PRINT "Pick a letter:"
    PRINT "L  List files            R  Rename a file"
    PRINT "D  Delete a file         S  Set Directory"
    PRINT "Q  Quit "
    INPUT "> ", Ans$
    Ans$ = UCASE$(Ans$)
    DO WHILE INSTR("LDRSQ", Ans$) = 0
        INPUT "Please enter L, D, R, S, or Q: ", Ans$
        Ans$ = UCASE$(Ans$)
    LOOP
    GetMenu$ = Ans$
END FUNCTION

SUB RenameFile
    INPUT "Enter name of file to be renamed: ", File1$
    INPUT "Enter new filename: ", File2$
    NAME File1$ AS File2$
END SUB

SUB SetDir
    INPUT "Set to which directory? ", Dir$
    CHDIR Dir$
END SUB
```

Here is a sample run:

```
Pick a letter:
L  List files          R  Rename a file
D  Delete a file       S  Set Directory
Q Quit
> s
Set to which directory? c:\temp
Pick a letter:
L  List files          R  Rename a file
D  Delete a file       S  Set Directory
Q  Quit
> l
C:\TEMP
        .  <DIR>          .. <DIR>  TRYME             OURFILE
JUNK               FILEF            COMPLIT           RANAMES
NAMES   .DAT       NAMES4   .DAT    RANAMES .DAT      FISH
.DAT

 27500544 Bytes free
Pick a letter:
L  List files          R  Rename a file
D  Delete a file       S  Set Directory
Q  Quit
> r
Enter name of file to be renamed: filef
Enter new file name: flash
Pick a letter:
L  List files          R  Rename a file
D  Delete a file       S  Set Directory
Q  Quit
> l
C:\TEMP
        .  <DIR>          .. <DIR>  TRYME             OURFILE
JUNK               FLASH            COMPLIT           RANAMES
NAMES   .DAT       NAMES4   .DAT    RANAMES .DAT      FISH
.DAT

 27500544 Bytes free
Pick a letter:
L  List files          R  Rename a file
D  Delete a file       S  Set Directory
Q  Quit
> q
Bye
```

Selecting a File Type

The type of file you select depends on the application you have in mind. Sequential files are well suited to text. For straight text—a form letter, for instance—you can use PRINT # and LINE INPUT # to write text one line at a time. In a program that analyzes a file of straight text (counting lines and words, for example), INPUT$ can read the file one character at a time. To create a database, you can use WRITE # and INPUT # to write and read one file at a time. Because sequential files use record separators (CR-LF) and field separators (commas), the lengths of records and fields need not be fixed and can expand and contract to match the data.

But sequential files have drawbacks, too. They don't store numeric data efficiently or accurately. To access data at the end of a file, you must read the entire file. A file opened for reading must be closed and reopened for writing if you want to add information. Also, opening a nontext file in the sequential mode can create problems. In particular, sequential input recognizes Ctrl-Z in the text as marking the end of the file. Nontext files, however, can contain binary code equivalent to the ASCII code for Ctrl-Z anywhere in a file, which can halt input long before the end of a file.

With random access files, you can move to various records in a file easily, and it's convenient to open a file in read/write mode. The fixed lengths of the fields and records are both a strength and a weakness. Finding information in a file is simplified, but storing text can waste memory because fixed-length strings can include a lot of empty spaces. Storing numeric values in binary form, however, is more efficient and more accurate than storing numeric data in text form, making random access files useful for databases of numeric values.

The binary file, which gives you random access to every byte in a file, is the most powerful and versatile approach, although its lack of structure (no records, for example) can require more programming. Binary files are the best choice for word processing and graphics files.

Review Questions

1. How does OUTPUT mode differ from APPEND mode?

2. How do sequential file records and random access file records differ?

3. What are the similarities and differences between BINARY mode and RANDOM mode?

4. Write a program that displays 20 lines of a sequential file at one time. Each time you press a key, the program should display another 20 lines.

5. Write a program that opens a random access file using the *PhoneType* record from this chapter. The program should count the records in the file and let you choose a record number to view that record. Put the record-viewing part of the program in a loop that terminates when an invalid record number is entered.

6. Write a program that asks you for a filename and a character and counts how often that character appears in the file. Have the program print an interim value each time the count is a multiple of 100.

PART IV

Multimedia

12

Screen Control and Graphics

CIRCLE	GET	PMAP	SCREEN
CLS	LINE	POS	VIEW
COLOR	PAINT	PRESET	VIEW PRINT
CSRLIN	PALETTE	PSET	WIDTH
DRAW	PALETTE USING	PUT	WINDOW

When you first learn to program, the screen is simply the place your program output appears. As you become more proficient, the screen becomes part of the programming process itself. You begin to be concerned about the screen's appearance. Perhaps you want to duplicate the slick look of professional programs and to display graphics as well as text.

In this chapter we'll discuss controlling the screen. You'll see how to select colors for the background and the text and how to use the arrow keys to select elements on the screen. Then we'll move from text to graphics. You'll learn how to choose a graphics mode, use and modify the graphics color palette, position output on the screen, use viewports, and draw shapes. You'll even learn a little about animation.

On-Screen Text Processing

Up to this point, we've generally used the simplest method for screen output. Typically, we use CLS to clear the screen and PRINT to write to the screen. The first line of output appears at the top of the screen, and each subsequent line appears one line lower. When the screen is full, additional lines cause the text to scroll upward to make room for the new material. The text itself is monochrome, white letters on a black background. (Although some screens display green or amber on black, we'll refer to monochrome as white on black for the sake of simplicity.)

But QuickBASIC allows you to do much more. With QuickBASIC, you can put a bit more zip into the output—and you can make input more sophisticated, too. Let's look at some examples.

Improving Your Menus

We'll start by creating a menu in the middle of the screen, one that doesn't scroll off. Instead of labeling the menu choices with letters, we'll use a movable highlight bar to identify a selection.

We've already used some text manipulation tools sparingly. The LOCATE statement (introduced in Chapter 3) lets you position the cursor, control its visibility, and govern its appearance. LOCATE's first argument is the line number (with the top line as line 1), and its second argument is the column number (with the first column as column 1). Its third argument sets visibility, with 0 indicating invisible and nonzero visible. The fourth and fifth arguments control the cursor shape. Arguments can be omitted; LOCATE retains the current column or row, for instance, if the argument specifying the column or row is omitted. Here are some examples:

```
LOCATE 2, 10            ' Move to row 2, column 10
LOCATE 5                ' Move to row 5, same column
LOCATE , , 0            ' Make cursor invisible
```

In this chapter we'll use the LOCATE statement to position menu choices and other text on the screen.

The INKEY$ function (discussed in Chapter 4) returns a string indicating the last key or key combination pressed. For instance, if you press Shift-A, the function returns the string *A*. INKEY$ provides *unbuffered, unechoed* input—that is, the keystroke is immediately transmitted to the program (without requiring you to press the Enter key), and the character is not shown on the screen.

Unlike other text input functions, INKEY$ does not cause the program to pause and wait for input. If no key has been pressed, INKEY$ returns the null string, and the program continues to the next line. To make INKEY$ wait for input, you must use a loop, as shown in the following example:

```
DO
    Key$ = INKEY$
LOOP UNTIL Key$ <> ""
```

You can use the following version if the program simply needs to know that any key was pressed:

```
DO
LOOP UNTIL INKEY$ <> ""
```

Either loop continues to check for input until a key is pressed. At that point, INKEY$ returns a value other than the null string, and the loop terminates. We'll use a similar loop in our menu. Because this input is unbuffered, we can let the user select a menu item by typing a letter, without pressing the Enter key. Because INKEY$ doesn't echo, this user response won't alter the screen display.

We'll also introduce two new functions, CSRLIN and POS, and the COLOR statement. The CSRLIN function returns the line number for the current cursor position, and the POS function returns the column number for the current cursor position.

Here is the syntax for the CSRLIN and POS functions:

```
CSRLIN
POS(n)
```

The integer *n* is a dummy argument for the column value and can be any integer; 0 is as good a value as any to use. Lines and columns are counted from the upper left corner; the numbering starts with 1.

The COLOR statement in text mode lets you set the foreground and background colors for text characters on the screen. Changing the background to white and the foreground to black, for example, gives you inverse video, which can be used for highlighting text. And, if you have a color monitor, you can choose from a variety of colors for the background and the text.

Here is the syntax for the COLOR statement used in standard text mode:

```
COLOR [foreground][, [background][, border]]
```

foreground specifies the foreground color used to form text characters; it must be in the range 0 through 31. These numbers represent eight colors in two intensity levels and two states (blinking or nonblinking). (These colors are described later in the chapter; see Figure 12-3, page 323.) *background* specifies the background color for text; it must be in the range 0 through 7. *border* determines the border color; it must be in the range 0 through 15. (The EGA, VGA, and MCGA systems, discussed later in this chapter, do not support a *border* argument.)

Listing 12-1 presents a menu combining the various elements we've just discussed.

```
' This program features a menu with a highlight bar. Pressing the key
'  corresponding to the initial letter of a menu choice highlights
'  that choice, and pressing the Enter key selects that choice.
DECLARE SUB ShowMenu ()
DECLARE FUNCTION GetChoice% ()
DATA Word Processor, Spreadsheet, Database
DATA Communications, Graphics, Quit
DIM SHARED Menu$(1 TO 6)
FOR I% = 1 TO 6                       ' Store menu strings in array
    READ Menu$(I%)
NEXT I%
COLOR 7, 0                            ' White-on-black text
LOCATE , , 0                          ' Hide cursor
```

Listing 12-1. *(continued)*

Listing 12-1. *continued*

```
CLS
MenuLine% = 1                      ' Highlighted menu choice
DO
    CALL ShowMenu
    MenuLine% = GetChoice%         ' Menu item chosen
    LOCATE 19, 1
    PRINT SPACE$(LastPos%)         ' Clear last message
    LOCATE 19, 10
    ' Dummy responses to show menu is working
    SELECT CASE MenuLine%
        CASE 1
            PRINT "WonderWord not yet functional";
        CASE 2
            PRINT "MightyCalc is out to lunch";
        CASE 3
            PRINT "DeBase: access denied";
        CASE 4
            PRINT "Try using the telephone";
        CASE 5
            PRINT "Graffo! finds your system inadequate";
    END SELECT
    LastPos% = POS(0)              ' End column of message
    PRINT
LOOP UNTIL MenuLine% = 6
PRINT "MicroPromise wishes you a happy day!"
END

' Responds only to key presses corresponding to valid
'  menu choices: W, S, D, C, G, and Q
FUNCTION GetChoice%
    SHARED MenuLine%
    Lb% = LBOUND(Menu$)
    Ub% = UBOUND(Menu$)
    DO
        DO
            Key$ = INKEY$          ' Get unbuffered, unechoed key input
        LOOP UNTIL Key$ <> ""
        Response$ = UCASE$(Key$)
        Index% = INSTR("WSDCGQ", Response$)
        IF Index% > 0 THEN         ' Valid response
            MenuLine% = Index%     ' Set highlight position
            ShowMenu               ' Show revised menu
        END IF
    LOOP UNTIL Key$ = CHR$(13)     ' Enter key ends loop
    GetChoice% = MenuLine%         ' Return current selection
END FUNCTION
```

(continued)

Listing 12-1. *continued*

```
' Shows menu with choice number MenuLine% highlighted
SUB ShowMenu
    SHARED MenuLine%
    Initial% = 6 + MenuLine%
    FOR I% = LBOUND(Menu$) TO UBOUND(Menu$)
        LOCATE 6 + I%, 30
        IF I% = MenuLine% THEN COLOR 0, 7  ' Inverse on
        PRINT Menu$(I%)
        IF I% = MenuLine% THEN COLOR 7, 0  ' Inverse off
    NEXT I%
    LOCATE CSRLIN + 2, 20                  ' Advance two lines
    PRINT "Type first letter of choice."
    PRINT TAB(20); "Use the Enter key to accept choice."
    LOCATE Initial%, 30                    ' Put cursor on highlighted line
END SUB
```

The colors black and white are represented by 0 and 7. Thus, *COLOR 7, 0* produces the standard white-on-black display, and *COLOR 0, 7* produces black-on-white (inverse video). The program begins by displaying a menu whose first line is highlighted in inverse video. Typing the initial letter of a menu choice moves the highlight bar to that line, and pressing Enter accepts the selected line and initiates the action described in the menu choice. Figure 12-1 shows the menu. (Note that the colors in Figure 12-1 are reversed—black letters on a white background—for readability on the printed page.)

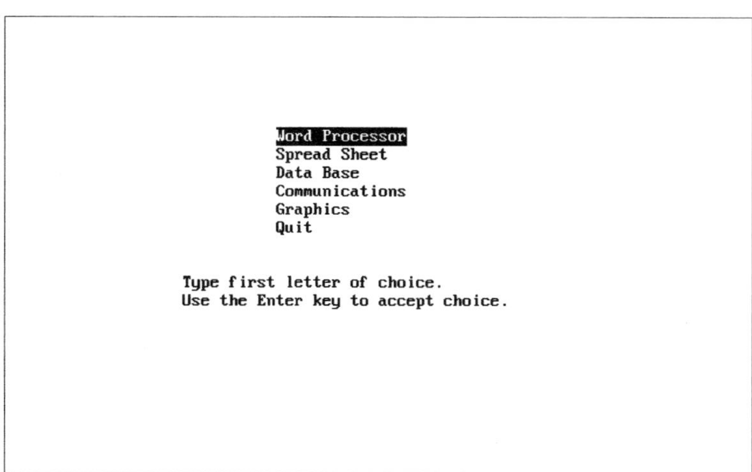

Figure 12-1.
Menu with highlight bar.

Examining Some Details

In the preceding program, the SHARED attribute makes the *Menu$* array available to all the subprograms. Because the various sections also need to know which menu item the user selects, we use the SHARED statement in the procedures, making *MenuLine%* in the procedures refer to *MenuLine%* in the module-level code.

The Module-Level Code

The module-level code creates the six-element *Menu$* array and initializes it. It also sets the monochrome color, turns off the cursor, and sets *MenuLine%* (the number of the menu item to be highlighted) to 1. Then the program sets up a loop that displays a menu, accepts the user's choice, and selects an action based on that choice.

Most of this code is similar to code in other menus we've created. This time, however, we use LOCATE to create a message line: Each message appears on line 19. Because a short message will overwrite only part of a longer one, leaving the rest of the older message on the screen, we use POS to save the position of the last character printed. At the next loop cycle, the program prints that number of spaces to clear the line. The following program fragment shows this technique:

```
LOCATE 19, 1
PRINT SPACE$(LastPos%)
```

The *ShowMenu* Subprogram

The *ShowMenu* subprogram prints the strings stored in the *Menu$* array. It uses the *MenuLine%* value to determine when to turn highlighting on and off, as shown in the following:

```
IF I% = MenuLine% THEN COLOR 0, 7   ' Inverse on
PRINT Menu$(I%)
IF I% = MenuLine% THEN COLOR 7, 0   ' Inverse off
```

The subprogram also uses the array subscript to position each string on screen:

```
LOCATE 6 + I%, 30
```

After the menu is printed, the subprogram uses CSRLIN to advance the cursor two lines beyond the previous location:

```
LOCATE CSRLIN + 2, 20
```

The *GetChoice%* Function

The *GetChoice%* function is the most complex part of Listing 12-1. It uses keystrokes to alter *MenuLine%*, and it returns the current *MenuLine%* value when the Enter key is pressed.

The function begins by setting *Lb%* and *Ub%* to the array limits. Then it initiates a loop that lets the user move the highlight bar. Within this loop, an INKEY$ loop obtains a value for *Key$*. The function converts the input to uppercase and checks to see if it matches the initial letter of a menu item. Using INSTR tells us if there is a match and where the matched menu item is located in the array. If a valid letter is found, the program resets *MenuLine%* to the corresponding position and recalls the *ShowMenu* subprogram. This works only if the letters in the string *WSDCGQ* are in the same order as corresponding menu items—that is, if you enter *D*, INSTR returns 3, the position of *D* in the array. Because 3 is also the array subscript for the *Database* string, setting *MenuLine%* to 3 highlights that line when *ShowMenu* is called, as shown in the following:

```
Response$ = UCASE$(Key$)
Index% = INSTR("WSDCGQ", Response$)
IF Index% > 0 THEN
    MenuLine% = Index%
    ShowMenu
END IF
```

This process of highlighting choices continues until you press Enter, which terminates the outer loop by generating a character whose ASCII code is 13. The function then returns the array subscript for the currently selected line, and the main program uses that value for its SELECT CASE statement.

Adding Arrow Key Control

You can also use the arrow keys to move the highlight bar. To do so, however, you need a more complete understanding of how INKEY$ works.

Ordinarily, INKEY$ returns a 1-byte string containing the ASCII character corresponding to the keystroke or keystroke combination. But some keys, such as the arrow keys and the function keys, don't correspond to ASCII characters. For these keys, INKEY$ returns a 2-byte string.

The first byte is a null string—that is, the character represented by "" and having ASCII code 0; this alerts you that a special key has been pressed. The second byte represents the *scan code,* which identifies the special key. Each entry from the keyboard generates a scan code: Pressing the F9 key, for instance, generates the scan code 67. Because INKEY$ returns a string, the number 67 is represented by the string *"C"*. (The character C has ASCII code 67.) Thus, the complete return value for the F9 key is the two-character string *"" + "C"*.

After you detect a non-ASCII key by finding a 2-byte INKEY$ return value, you must check the value of the second byte to identify the specific key. If *Key$* holds the response, you can use *RIGHT$(Key$, 1)* to isolate the rightmost character. Because the code is stored as a string, you must also use the ASC function to find the numeric equivalent. For instance, if a program has determined that the first byte is the null string, you can use the following code to detect the F9 key:

```
IF ASC(RIGHT$(Key$, 1)) = 67 THEN PRINT "F9 key!"
```

Or you can compare the scan code to the corresponding string:

```
IF RIGHT$(Key$, 1) = CHR$(67) THEN PRINT "F9 key!"
```

You can even use the entire return value, as shown in the following:

```
IF Key$ = "" + CHR$(67) THEN PRINT "F9 key!"    ' Compare 2 bytes
```

Figure 12-2 lists scan codes for some common non-ASCII keys, including Shift, Ctrl, and Alt combinations. (Not every combination has a scan code.) See Appendix F for a detailed list of DOS keyboard scan codes.

Key	Scan Code	Shift Scan Code	Ctrl Scan Code	Alt Scan Code
F1	59	84	94	104
F2	60	85	95	105
F3	61	86	96	106
F4	62	87	97	107
F5	63	88	98	108
F6	64	89	99	109
F7	65	90	100	110
F8	66	91	101	111
F9	67	92	102	112
F10	68	93	103	113
Up Arrow	72	56		
Left Arrow	75	52	115	
Right Arrow	77	54	116	
Down Arrow	80	50		

Figure 12-2.
Common scan codes.

Now you can modify Listing 12-1 to have the arrow keys move the highlight bar. Here is the additional code you need:

```
CONST uparrow% = 72                    ' Scan code for Up Arrow key
CONST downarrow% = 80                  ' Scan code for Down Arrow key

IF LEN(Key$) = 2 THEN                  ' Non-ASCII key
    SELECT CASE ASC(RIGHT$(Key$, 1))   ' Use scan code
        CASE downarrow%
            MenuLine% = MenuLine% + 1
            IF MenuLine% > Ub% THEN MenuLine% = Lb%
            CALL ShowMenu
        CASE uparrow%
            MenuLine% = MenuLine% - 1
            IF MenuLine% < Lb% THEN MenuLine% = Ub%
            CALL ShowMenu
    END SELECT
ELSE                                   ' Code for ASCII keys to follow
```

The program first checks *Key$* to see if INKEY$'s return value is 2 bytes. If it is, the program checks the numeric value of the second byte. If it is 80, the program increases *MenuLine%* by 1 and calls *ShowMenu* again. If *MenuLine%* already corresponds to the last menu item, *MenuLine%* is set to the first line, allowing the highlight bar to return to the top of the menu after it reaches the bottom. The scan code for the Up Arrow key is handled similarly. Listing 12-2 shows the complete program.

```
' This program adds menu choice by arrow key to
'  the features of Listing 12-1
DECLARE SUB ShowMenu ()
DECLARE FUNCTION GetChoice% ()
DATA Word Processor, Spreadsheet, Database
DATA Communications, Graphics, Quit
DIM SHARED Menu$(1 TO 6)
CONST uparrow% = 72                               ' Scan code for Up Arrow key
CONST downarrow% = 80                             ' Scan code for Down Arrow key
FOR I% = 1 TO 6
    READ Menu$(I%)
NEXT I%
COLOR 7, 0
LOCATE , , 0
CLS
MenuLine% = 1
DO
    CALL ShowMenu
    MenuLine% = GetChoice%
    LOCATE 19, 1
    PRINT SPACE$(LastPos%)
    LOCATE 19, 10
    SELECT CASE MenuLine%
        CASE 1
            PRINT "WonderWord not yet functional";
        CASE 2
            PRINT "MightyCalc is out to lunch";
        CASE 3
            PRINT "DeBase: access denied";
        CASE 4
            PRINT "Try using the telephone";
        CASE 5
            PRINT "Graffo! finds your system inadequate";
    END SELECT
    LastPos% = POS(0)
    PRINT
LOOP UNTIL MenuLine% = 6
PRINT "MicroPromise wishes you a happy day!"
END
```

Listing 12-2. *(continued)*

Listing 12-2. *continued*

```
' Allows user to highlight menu by pressing initial letter of menu item
'  or by using Up Arrow and Down Arrow keys to move the highlight
FUNCTION GetChoice%
    SHARED MenuLine%
    Lb% = LBOUND(Menu$)
    Ub% = UBOUND(Menu$)
    DO
        DO
            Key$ = INKEY$
        LOOP UNTIL Key$ <> ""
        IF LEN(Key$) = 2 THEN                  ' Non-ASCII key
            SELECT CASE ASC(RIGHT$(Key$, 1)) ' Use scan code
                CASE downarrow%
                    MenuLine% = MenuLine% + 1
                    IF MenuLine% > Ub% THEN MenuLine% = Lb%
                    CALL ShowMenu
                CASE uparrow%
                    MenuLine% = MenuLine% - 1
                    IF MenuLine% < Lb% THEN MenuLine% = Ub%
                    CALL ShowMenu
            END SELECT
        ELSE                                   ' 1-byte response, ASCII key
            Response$ = UCASE$(Key$)
            Index% = INSTR("WSDCGQ", Response$)
            IF Index% > 0 THEN
                MenuLine% = Index%
                ShowMenu
            END IF
        END IF
    LOOP UNTIL Key$ = CHR$(13)
    GetChoice% = MenuLine%
END FUNCTION

SUB ShowMenu
    SHARED MenuLine%
    Initial% = 6 + MenuLine%
    FOR I% = LBOUND(Menu$) TO UBOUND(Menu$)
        LOCATE 6 + I%, 30
        IF I% = MenuLine% THEN COLOR 0, 7
        PRINT Menu$(I%)
        IF I% = MenuLine% THEN COLOR 7, 0
    NEXT I%
    LOCATE CSRLIN + 2, 20
    PRINT "Use arrow keys to select choice"
    PRINT TAB(20); "or else type first letter of choice."
    PRINT TAB(20); "Use the Enter key to accept choice."
    LOCATE Initial%, 30
END SUB
```

Setting Text Color

Let's examine the color options for text. Figure 12-3 lists the colors available through the COLOR statement. The light colors are sometimes called *intensified* because they are formed by combining the base color with white to produce a lighter color. The visual difference between regular and light colors can depend on the contrast and brightness settings of your monitor.

Color Number	Color	Color Number	Color
0	Black	8	Grey
1	Blue	9	Light blue
2	Green	10	Light green
3	Cyan	11	Light cyan
4	Red	12	Light red
5	Magenta	13	Light magenta
6	Brown	14	Yellow
7	White	15	Bright white

Figure 12-3.
Text colors.

> **NOTE:** *Only colors 0 through 7 can be used for background. For foreground colors, the sum of 16 plus the color number produces a blinking variant of the same color.*

The program in Listing 12-3 shows you some possible color combinations. It also illustrates the use of the VIEW PRINT statement, which restricts the number of screen lines available for text and is thus often used to isolate text from graphics on the screen in a *text viewport.*

Here is the VIEW PRINT syntax:

```
VIEW PRINT [topline TO bottomline]
```

This statement creates a text viewport limited to the lines *topline* through *bottomline.* Subsequent text output is confined to the text viewport. When the port is filled, using PRINT to print additional lines causes text to scroll inside the viewport. The statement *CLS 2* clears only the screen within the viewport. A LOCATE statement used after a text viewport has been defined can reference only the line numbers contained in the viewport.

```
' Presents varied colors in text and background in a text
'  window, or viewport
DIM Message AS STRING * 80
M1$ = "HAPPY BIRTHDAY TO YOU!"
```

Listing 12-3. *(continued)*

Listing 12-3. *continued*

```
M2$ = SPACE$(40 - LEN(M1$) / 2)
Message = M2$ + M1$                ' Centered in 80-character line
COLOR 14, 1                        ' Yellow on blue
Fore% = 7
Back% = 0
CLS                                ' Set entire screen to current background
PRINT "This program demonstrates colors and the viewport."
PRINT "Type q to quit, c to clear, any other key to continue:"
VIEW PRINT 16 TO 20
DO
    DO
        Key$ = INKEY$
    LOOP UNTIL Key$ <> ""
    IF UCASE$(Key$) = "C" THEN
        CLS 2                      ' Clear text viewport
    ELSE
        COLOR Fore%, Back%         ' Reset colors
        PRINT Message
        Fore% = (Fore% + 1) MOD 32
        Back% = (Back% + 1) MOD 8
    END IF
LOOP UNTIL UCASE$(Key$) = "Q"      ' Type Q to quit
COLOR 7, 0                         ' Restore normal settings
PRINT "Bye"
END
```

Figure 12-4 is a black-and-white representation of the screen display. (Again, dark and light colors are reversed on the printed page for readability. Most displays in this chapter are presented in this fashion.)

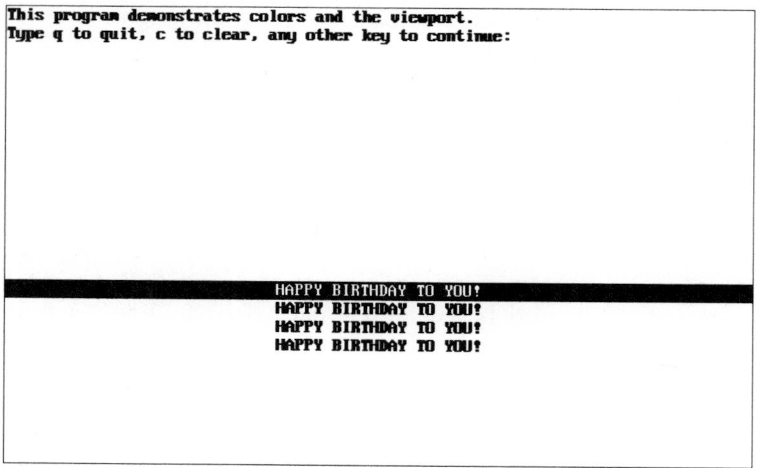

Figure 12-4.
Output of Listing 12-3.

When the CLS statement clears the screen, it sets the background for the entire screen to the current background color. In Listing 12-3, the screen is set to blue. Similarly, the statement *CLS 2* clears only the text viewport, setting its background to the current background color set in the DO/UNTIL loop. The background outside the text viewport remains blue, its original color. (Using CLS with no argument after the viewport is set clears the text viewport and the bottom line of the screen.)

The program creates a message line 80 characters wide to match the standard screen width. Thus, when the program prints a new line, the entire line shows the selected foreground and background colors. When the viewport is filled, the lines, including the foreground and background text, begin to scroll. In other words, the foreground and background colors are attached to the text, not to a particular screen position.

You can try adding color to the menu in Listing 12-2. For example, you might use 6 for the foreground and 1 for the background, reversing them for highlighting. For brighter text, use 14 for the foreground. Note that colors are set in two places: the main module and the *ShowMenu* subprogram.

Using the WIDTH Statement: Text and Display Types

IBM PCs and compatibles come with a variety of display types: monochrome, CGA (Color Graphics Adapter), HGC (Hercules Graphics Card), EGA (Enhanced Graphics Adapter), VGA (Video Graphics Array), and others. For graphics, the differences among these types are important; we'll describe them later in the chapter. For text, however, the differences are minor, at least from the programming standpoint. Each type displays, by default, 25 lines of 80 characters, for a total of 2000 characters. The degree of detail in the display might vary from one type to another, but that difference stems from the hardware, not from programming. In the default mode, the most important distinction is whether or not color is available.

Some displays do provide the option of using different line widths and numbers of lines, however. These choices are controlled by the WIDTH statement.

Here is the syntax for the WIDTH statement as it applies to a monitor display:

```
WIDTH [columns][, lines]
```

This statement sets the screen width to *columns* characters and sets the number of lines displayed to the value of *lines*. The value of *columns* must be either 40 or 80; it is 80 by default. (The Monochrome Display Adapter, or MDA, can be set only to 80.) *lines* can be set to the following values for various display types:

Display Type	***Possible Line Settings***
CGA, MDA	25
EGA	25, 43
VGA	25, 43, 50

The default value is the value in effect when the program begins.

For example, if you have an EGA display, the following statement sets the monitor to 43 lines per screen:

```
WIDTH , 43
```

And this statement sets the monitor to 40 columns per screen:

```
WIDTH 40
```

Graphics Modes

All our previous programs have operated in standard text mode, in which the screen is compartmentalized into character cells. In graphics modes, the screen is divided into hundreds of thousands of dots, each of which can be independently set to a color. Graphics modes are more complicated than text modes. You have many more options for action: coloring individual dots, drawing lines, drawing circles, filling enclosed figures with patterns, and so on. You also have several graphics modes from which to choose, depending on the combination of hardware display you use—in particular, the monitor and the video adapter card controlling the monitor.

In the early days of the PC, IBM offered a limited selection. You could buy a PC with the monochrome display connected to an MDA, which provided high-resolution text and no graphics capability. Or you could equip your PC with a color graphics adapter (the CGA) connected to either a black-and-white or a color monitor. This choice provided medium-resolution text and medium-resolution graphics. The CGA supports two graphics modes: a color mode that divides the screen into 320 columns and 200 rows of dots (a resolution of 320 × 200 *pixels*) and displays as many as four colors simultaneously, and a black-and-white mode with 640 columns and 200 rows.

But most users were dissatisfied with the CGA's text quality and the MDA's lack of graphics. Hercules introduced a graphics card (the HGC) that provided high-resolution monochrome graphics with the monochrome display. Then IBM introduced the Enhanced Graphics Adapter, which was designed to work with a new, higher-resolution color monitor, the enhanced color display. This combination provided better-looking text and several more graphics modes, including a 640 × 350 mode that displayed as many as 16 colors simultaneously. The EGA also offered graphics for the monochrome display.

IBM next introduced the Video Graphics Array video controller, which worked with yet another kind of monitor (a VGA monitor). This new combination emulated most of the older graphics modes and added some new ones, including a 640 × 480 mode with 16 colors and a 320 × 200 mode with 256 colors. IBM has also developed several other standards, such as the Professional Graphics Adapter (PGA), the Multicolor Graphics Array (MCGA), and the 8514; and independent video card producers have begun to promote some of their own, such as Super VGA. (Incidentally, the popular multisync monitors can operate with several adapters, not just one.) Figure 12-5 summarizes the modes currently available with QuickBASIC. (We'll explain the unfamiliar terms later in the chapter.)

In this book we'll concentrate on one display mode in order to focus our discussion. After you've had a chance to become familiar with the general principles involved in this mode, we'll summarize some of the features of other modes.

QB Mode	Adapters	Displays	Resolution	Colors per Palette	Palettes	Total Colors
0	All	All	80 × 25 text			16
1	CGA, EGA, VGA, MCGA	CD, MD ED, VD	320 × 200	4	2	16
2	CGA, EGA, VGA, MCGA	CD, MD ED, VD	640 × 200	2	1	2
3	HGC	MD	720 × 348	2	1	2
4	Olivetti	Olivetti	640 × 400	2	1	16
7	EGA, VGA	CD, ED, VD	320 × 200	16	User definable	16
8	EGA, VGA	ED, VD	640 × 200	16	User definable	16
9	EGA, VGA	ED, VD	640 × 350	4/16	User definable	16/64
10	EGA, VGA	MD	640 × 350	4	1	9
11	VGA, MCGA	VD	640 × 480	2	User definable	262,144
12	VGA	VD	640 × 480	16	User definable	262,144
13	VGA, MCGA	VD	320 × 200	256	User definable	262,144

Abbreviations:

MD	Monochrome Display
CD	Color Display
ED	Enhanced Display
VD	VGA Display
MDA	Monochrome Display Adapter
CGA	Color Graphics Adapter
HGC	Hercules Graphics Card
EGA	Enhanced Graphics Adapter
VGA	Video Graphics Array
MCGA	Multicolor Graphics Array

Notes: For mode 0, the character resolution depends on the hardware; a VGA character is more finely formed than a CGA character. Other text formats are also possible—for instance, EGA permits an 80 × 43 character display, and VGA allows 80 × 50.

Mode 3 requires that you first run the MS-HERC.COM driver, which comes with QuickBASIC.

For mode 9, the number of colors available to the EGA depends on the size of EGA memory. With 64 KB of EGA memory, 4 colors from a palette of 16 can be used; with 128 KB or more of EGA memory, 16 colors from a palette of 64 can be used.

Figure 12-5.
Video modes.

Selecting a Mode

The CGA 320 × 200 color mode is the most widely available, and it is also supported by both EGA and VGA. But it is somewhat antiquated. Its resolution is low by modern standards, and its color selection is limited.

We've instead chosen to base our examples on one of the EGA modes, mode 9. Mode 9 looks better, and it's more fun to use. Its resolution is fairly high: 640 × 350 pixels. And as many as 16 colors can be displayed simultaneously, selected from a list of 64.

To use this mode, you need an EGA or VGA video controller and an ED, VGA, or multisync color monitor. An EGA system is probably the minimum requirement for producing graphics that meet today's standards.

Using the SCREEN Statement

Use the SCREEN statement to select the mode. For example, the following statement selects mode 9:

```
SCREEN 9
```

Here is the syntax for the SCREEN statement:

```
SCREEN [mode][, [colorswitch][, [apage][, [vpage]]]
```

The statement sets the computer system to the specified display mode. *mode* must be an integer (or an expression that evaluates to an integer) from the list in Figure 12-5. The default value is mode 0. *colorswitch* turns color on and off for composite monitors (a low-quality option for CGA). The *colorswitch* argument applies only to modes 0 and 1; it must be in the range 0 through 255. A 0 value turns color off in mode 0 and on in mode 1. Nonzero values have the opposite effect.

One *page* is the amount of video memory needed to hold the image of one screen. Some modes permit more than one page of screen contents. The *apage* argument identifies the page to be written to, and the *vpage* argument identifies the page to be viewed. The values are integers whose range depends on the mode and the amount of memory installed in the adapter.

We'll use the page options later; for now, we'll simply use SCREEN to set the mode.

Graphics Skills and Color

Setting a graphics mode is simple. But you also need to manage colors, to control where things happen on the screen, to use various drawing tools, and to manage line and fill patterns—in short, you need the coloring, positioning, and drawing skills that are introduced in the remainder of this chapter.

Managing Color

Like text mode, graphics modes have a foreground color (white by default) and a background color (black by default). In text mode, the COLOR statement is used to reset the foreground and background colors; for instance, the following statement sets the foreground color to 14 (yellow) and the background color to 1 (blue):

```
COLOR 14, 1
```

In graphics mode 9, the following statements put the display into mode 9 and set the foreground color to yellow and the background color to blue:

```
SCREEN 9
COLOR 14, 1
```

There are three key differences in how text mode and graphics mode 9 use colors:

- The application of background color
- The range of background colors
- The significance of the foreground number

In text mode, the background color is associated with a specific character, allowing each character to have its own background color. In Listing 12-3, for instance, individual lines had different background colors. In graphics modes, however, the background applies to the entire screen. If you use COLOR to change the background in mode 9, you change it everywhere on the screen.

In text mode, the background color range is 0 through 7; in mode 9, the range is 0 through 63. Obviously, mode 9 greatly expands your display choices.

In both modes, the background value is a *color number*. In text mode, the foreground value is also a color number, but the foreground value in mode 9 is an *attribute number*. In mode 9, the color numbers range from 0 through 63, with each number representing one of the 64 available colors. The 16 colors that can be displayed simultaneously constitute a *palette,* and the attribute numbers are palette labels in the range 0 through 15. Each attribute can be assigned any one of the 64 color values. In general, the palette can be set to any 16 of these colors, allowing you to use all 16 for graphics. Selecting a foreground value of attribute 14, for example, means using the color value of the 14th position in the palette. By default, that color is light yellow (color value 62). Figure 12-6 illustrates the default palette.

We'll examine color numbers and palettes in more detail later in the chapter, but first let's use Listing 12-4 to see what a graphics mode looks like. The program selects mode 9 and sets the background to blue and the foreground to yellow. In the yellow foreground color, it prints the string *SCREEN MODE 9*, the background color number, and the foreground attribute number. Then it lets you use the arrow keys to change the color setting. Most of the code is devoted to handling the arrow keys; the only graphics statements are SCREEN and COLOR.

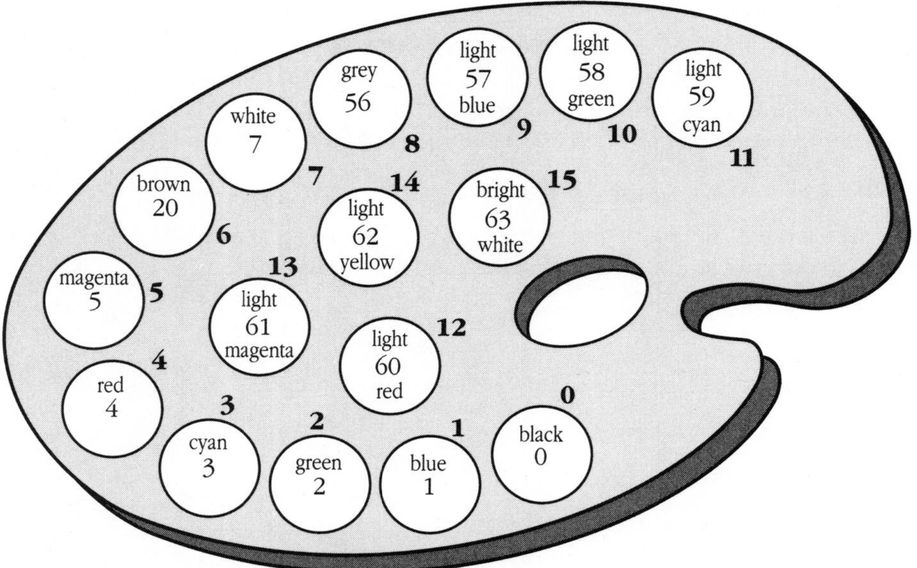

Figure 12-6.
The default palette.

The displayed numbers change as you change the colors in Listing 12-4. Note the following as you run the program:

- When you use numbers outside the usual range of 0 through 7 for background colors, you'll see colors on the screen that might be new to you.
- When you change the background color, the entire screen changes.
- When you change the foreground color, only text written after the change is affected. The *SCREEN MODE 9* message remains its original yellow because that message is not rewritten.
- When you use foreground color attribute 0, you can't read the text. This value always corresponds to the current background color. It makes the text the same color as the background and therefore impossible to read.

```
' This program displays background and foreground colors
'  for mode 9. The Left Arrow and Right Arrow keys decrease and
'  increase the foreground color attribute, and the Up Arrow
'  and Down Arrow keys increase and decrease the background
'  color number. Any character key terminates the program.
```

Listing 12-4. *(continued)*

Listing 12-4. *continued*

```
DECLARE SUB KeyColor (Key$)
CONST uparrow% = 72
CONST downarrow% = 80
CONST leftarrow% = 75
CONST rightarrow% = 77
Fore% = 14                      ' Yellow
Back% = 1                       ' Blue
SCREEN 9
COLOR Fore%, Back%
LOCATE 2, 34
PRINT "SCREEN MODE 9"
DO                              ' Loop changes color settings via arrow keys
    LOCATE 12, 18
    PRINT "Background color ="; Back%;
    PRINT "   Foreground color ="; Fore%
    DO
        Key$ = INKEY$
    LOOP UNTIL Key$ <> ""
    IF LEN(Key$) = 2 THEN
        KeyColor Key$           ' Change Fore% or Back%
        COLOR Fore%, Back%      ' Reset color assignments
    END IF
LOOP UNTIL LEN(Key$) = 1        ' Any ASCII key to quit
SCREEN 0                        ' Reset to text mode
END

' Arrow keys change Fore%, Back%
SUB KeyColor (Key$)
SHARED Back%, Fore%
    SELECT CASE ASC(RIGHT$(Key$, 1))
        CASE uparrow%
            Back% = (Back% + 1) MOD 64  ' Back% is 0 to 63
        CASE downarrow%
            IF Back% > 0 THEN
                Back% = Back% - 1
            ELSE
                Back% = 63
            END IF
        CASE leftarrow%
            IF Fore% > 0 THEN
                Fore% = Fore% - 1
            ELSE
                Fore% = 15
            END IF
        CASE rightarrow%
            Fore% = (Fore% + 1) MOD 16  ' Fore% is 0 to 15
    END SELECT
END SUB
```

EGA Color Numbers

The numbering scheme used to represent colors in mode 9 is based on the concept of mixing primary colors. For mixing light, which is what we do with a display screen, the three primary colors are blue, green, and red. Each pixel on the color display screen contains phosphors of these three colors. Other colors are produced by mixing the primary colors—yellow consists of equal levels of red and green, for example, and white consists of equal levels of all three primary colors.

The EGA monitor can display each primary color at four intensity levels: off, low, medium, and high. With four possible settings for each of the three colors, we have $4 \times 4 \times 4$, or 64, color combinations. EGA uses the codes shown in Figure 12-7 for the various intensities of the primary colors. (Off is 0 for all three.)

Color	Low Intensity	Medium Intensity	High Intensity
Blue	8	1	9
Green	16	2	18
Red	32	4	36

Figure 12-7.
Color numbers for primary colors.

The medium-intensity values 1, 2, and 4 are the same numbers that represent blue, green, and red in text mode. To calculate the low-intensity color values, multiply the medium-intensity values by 8. To calculate the high-intensity values, add the low-intensity and medium-intensity values.

All the other numbers through 63 can be represented as combinations of the values listed in Figure 12-7. Adding the numbers corresponds to adding the colors. For example, 1 + 2 is 3, the color number for medium cyan, which is equal levels of blue and green. And the number 62 is 32 + 16 + 8 + 4 + 2. The first three numbers represent low-intensity red, low-intensity green, and low-intensity blue, which together equal low-intensity white. The last two numbers represent medium-intensity red and medium-intensity green, which equal yellow. The result is low-intensity white plus yellow—the light yellow we saw earlier in text mode.

The COLOR statement uses these color numbers to set the background number. From the 64 colors, 16 constitute the default palette (Figure 12-6). Figure 12-8 describes the color values for the default palette in more detail.

With the default palette, attributes 0 through 15 produce the same colors that color numbers 0 through 15 produce in text mode. Note that attribute 6 is set to color number 20, not to 6 (red + green), to provide a better representation of brown. (CGA systems use the equivalent of color number 6 in text mode.) Attribute 0 always corresponds to the background color. Changing the background color with a COLOR statement actually changes the color value associated with attribute 0 to the background color value.

Attribute Number	Color Number	Description
0	0	Black
1	1	Blue
2	2	Green
3	3	Cyan (blue + green)
4	4	Red
5	5	Magenta (red + blue)
6	20	Brown (red + low-intensity green)
7	7	White (blue + green + red)
8	56	Low-intensity white, or grey (low-intensity red, low-intensity green, low-intensity blue)
9	57	Light blue (blue + low-intensity white)
10	58	Light green (green + low-intensity white)
11	59	Light cyan (cyan + low-intensity white)
12	60	Light red (red + low-intensity white)
13	61	Light magenta (magenta + low-intensity white)
14	62	Light yellow (yellow + low-intensity white)
15	63	Bright white (white + low-intensity white)

Figure 12-8.
Color values for the default palette.

You can reset the palette assignments, changing the 16 colors your program uses. But before we discuss changing the palette, let's take a brief detour. It would be interesting to color something besides text, so let's learn to draw a circle.

Drawing a Circle: Coordinates and Coloring

Drawing a circle requires superimposing the mathematical equation of a circle onto the screen and coloring the pixels that lie on the curve. Fortunately, the QuickBASIC CIRCLE statement does most of the work. But you must specify the center and the radius of the circle. To do that, you need to understand graphics coordinate systems.

QuickBASIC measures graphics locations in pixel units. The horizontal position, called the *x-coordinate,* is measured from the left. The vertical position, called the *y-coordinate,* is measured from the top. The upper left corner is the origin, whose coordinates are both 0. These are *physical* coordinates, but QuickBASIC also lets you use a system of *logical* coordinates in which you can choose an origin and devise a measuring unit other than 1 pixel. The default system corresponds to the physical coordinates.

The range of physical coordinates depends on the graphics mode. Because mode 9 features 640 pixels horizontally and 350 pixels vertically, the *x*-coordinate can vary from 0 through 639, and the *y*-coordinate can vary from 0 through 349 (Figure 12-9).

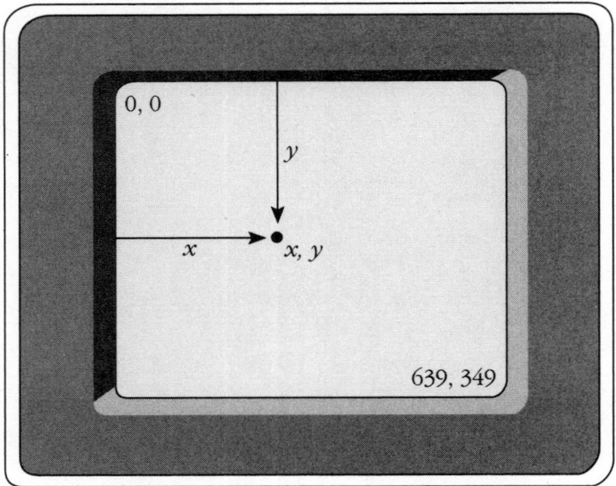

Figure 12-9.
Physical coordinates in mode 9.

In its simplest form, the CIRCLE statement looks like this:

```
CIRCLE (x, y), r
```

This statement produces a circle centered at the point whose *x*-coordinate is *x* and whose *y*-coordinate is *y*. The circle has a radius of *r* units. By default, CIRCLE uses the foreground color for drawing.

The CIRCLE statement produces only a circular outline. For a solid circle, use the PAINT statement to fill the circle with color. In its simplest form, the PAINT statement looks like this:

```
PAINT (x, y)
```

The region enclosing the point (*x*, *y*) is painted with the foreground color. The region is defined by a boundary in the foreground color. For example, if you paint a circle when (*x*, *y*) is inside the circle, the inside of the circle is painted. But if (*x*, *y*) is outside the circle, the outside is painted.

We've modified Listing 12-4 to draw two concentric circles and to fill the inner circle by using the PAINT statement. This new program (Listing 12-5) lets you control the colors with the arrow keys so that you can experiment with changing the foreground and background colors.

The location (320, 175) used in the CIRCLE statement is approximately the center of the screen for mode 9. When you run the program, the circle might look like an oval, depending on your monitor and how it is adjusted. QuickBASIC does its best to make the image circular, but you might need to adjust the shape, as we'll discuss when we examine the graphics commands.

```
' Demonstrates foreground and background colors as
'  well as drawing circles and painting
DECLARE SUB KeyColor (Key$)
CONST uparrow% = 72
CONST downarrow% = 80
CONST leftarrow% = 75
CONST rightarrow% = 77
Fore% = 14
Back% = 1
SCREEN 9
COLOR Fore%, Back%
CIRCLE (320, 175), 160          ' NEW! Draw a circle
DO
LOCATE 23, 18
    PRINT "Background color ="; Back%;
    PRINT "   Foreground color ="; Fore%
    CIRCLE (320, 175), 140      ' Draw a smaller circle
    PAINT (320, 175)            ' NEW! Fill it with color
    DO
        Key$ = INKEY$
    LOOP UNTIL Key$ <> ""
    IF LEN(Key$) = 2 THEN KeyColor Key$
    COLOR Fore%, Back%
LOOP UNTIL LEN(Key$) = 1
SCREEN 0                        ' Reset screen to text mode
END

SUB KeyColor (Key$)
SHARED Back%, Fore%
    SELECT CASE ASC(RIGHT$(Key$, 1))
        CASE uparrow%
            Back% = (Back% + 1) MOD 64
        CASE downarrow%
            IF Back% > 0 THEN
                Back% = Back% - 1
            ELSE
                Back% = 63
            END IF
        CASE leftarrow%
            IF Fore% > 0 THEN
                Fore% = Fore% - 1
            ELSE
                Fore% = 15
            END IF
        CASE rightarrow%
            Fore% = (Fore% + 1) MOD 16
    END SELECT
END SUB
```

Listing 12-5.

Changing the Palette

Now that you can draw a circle and paint its interior, let's use the PALETTE statement to select the 16 EGA colors for your display. This statement can be used in three ways.

First, it can change individual palette settings. For instance, the following statement sets palette attribute number 3 to the color value 28 rather than to the default color value 3:

```
PALETTE 3, 28
```

Thus, when the statement *COLOR 3* sets the foreground color to attribute number 3, color number 28, a salmon color, is displayed.

Because attribute 0 represents the background color, the statement

```
PALETTE 0, 1
```

sets the background to color value 1, as the following statement does:

```
COLOR , 1
```

You can use either *COLOR , n* or *PALETTE 0, n* to set the background color in mode 9. However, because only the PALETTE approach works with VGA modes (modes 11 through 13), we'll use that method in the rest of our examples.

Second, using the PALETTE statement with no arguments resets the palette to the default color values.

Third, the PALETTE USING statement can reset all 16 palette values at once. For example, the following statement resets the palette to the color values held in the 16-element array *ColorArray&*:

```
PALETTE USING ColorArray&
```

You can also use an element of the array as an argument, as shown in this statement, which specifies starting at element 0 of the array:

```
PALETTE USING ColorArray&(0)
```

You can, for instance, store four palette settings in a 64-element array, specifying *ColorArray&(16)* to use the second set of 16 values, *ColorArray&(32)* to use the third set, and *ColorArray&(48)* to use the fourth set.

For EGA mode 9, color values are regular integers, so the array can be of integer type. The VGA modes 11, 12, and 13, however, require an array of long integers. We'll use arrays of long integers so that you can more easily modify our programs later if you want to experiment with these other modes. Arrays of long integers work with regular integer values, too, so they can be used with both EGA and VGA modes.

Here is the syntax for PALETTE and PALETTE USING:

```
PALETTE [attribute, color]
PALETTE USING arrayname[(index)]
```

In the PALETTE statement, *attribute, color* sets the indicated attribute to the corresponding color. *color* is an integer color value for EGA modes and a long integer color value for VGA modes. In the PALETTE USING statement, *arrayname* sets the palette attributes to the color values stored in *arrayname*. Because all attributes are set, the array must be large enough to hold a complete palette setting. If the optional array subscript is provided, color assignment begins with the indicated array element.

We incorporate all three uses of the PALETTE statement in Listing 12-6. This program draws 16 circles using the foreground color and paints them in the 16 colors from the palette. The arrow keys let you manipulate the palette.

```
' This program illustrates palette shifting. The Left Arrow and Right
'  Arrow keys decrease and increase the background color number. The
'  Down Arrow key changes the palette assignments by shifting the color
'  values by 1. The Up Arrow key turns on continuous palette shifting.
'  If continuous palette shifting is taking place, pressing a key,
'  including any character key, stops the loop. Pressing any character
'  key terminates the program.

DECLARE SUB ShiftPal (PA&())
DECLARE SUB SetPalette (Key$, PA&())
CONST uparrow% = 72
CONST downarrow% = 80
CONST leftarrow% = 75
CONST rightarrow% = 77
DIM PalArray&(0 TO 15)
FOR I% = 0 TO 7                      ' Set array to default palette
    PalArray&(I%) = I%
    PalArray&(I% + 8) = 56 + I%
NEXT I%
PalArray&(6) = 20                    ' Default value
PalArray&(0) = 40                    ' Change background value
PalArray&(14) = 46                   ' Change color for attribute 14
Fore% = 14
SCREEN 9
PALETTE USING PalArray&(0)           ' Set altered palette
COLOR Fore%
Colr% = 0
FOR Y% = 40 TO 280 STEP 80
    FOR X% = 80 TO 560 STEP 160
        CIRCLE (X%, Y%), 50
        PAINT (X%, Y%), Colr%, Fore%
        Colr% = Colr% + 1
    NEXT X%
NEXT Y%
```

Listing 12-6. *(continued)*

Listing 12-6. *continued*

```
DO
    DO
        Key$ = INKEY$
    LOOP UNTIL Key$ <> ""
    IF LEN(Key$) = 2 THEN SetPalette Key$, PalArray&()
LOOP UNTIL LEN(Key$) = 1
PALETTE
SCREEN 0
END

SUB SetPalette (Key$, PA&())
    SELECT CASE ASC(RIGHT$(Key$, 1))
        CASE uparrow%
            DO
                ShiftPal PA&()
                Ky$ = INKEY$
            LOOP UNTIL Ky$ <> ""
        CASE downarrow%
            ShiftPal PA&()
        CASE leftarrow%
            IF PA&(0) = 0 THEN
                PA&(0) = 63
            ELSE
                PA&(0) = PA&(0) - 1
            END IF
            PALETTE 0, PA&(0)          ' Change attribute 0
        CASE rightarrow%
            PA&(0) = (PA&(0) + 1) MOD 64
            PALETTE 0, PA&(0)
    END SELECT
END SUB

SUB ShiftPal (PA&())
    FOR I% = 0 TO 15
        PA&(I%) = (PA&(I%) + 1) MOD 64
    NEXT I%
    PALETTE USING PA&(0)               ' Set palette to new values
END SUB
```

The module-level code sets the array *PalArray&* to the color values of the default palette. But it then sets *PalArray&(0)* to color value 40 (dark purple) and *PalArray&(14)* to color value 46, a shade of red. The following call makes this set of choices the palette:

```
PALETTE USING PalArray&(0)
```

The circles are drawn in red against a purple background. After a circle is drawn, it is painted with one of the palette colors, as shown here:

```
CIRCLE (X%, Y%), 50
PAINT (X%, Y%), Colr%, Fore%
```

Note that we used two additional arguments with PAINT. This simple statement uses the foreground color for painting:

```
PAINT (X%, Y%)
```

A third argument would specify using that attribute number instead. In our program, *Colr%* begins as 0, and its value increases by 1 each time a new circle is drawn. Thus, the program uses all 16 palette colors, one for each circle. The fourth paint argument (*Fore%*, in this case) specifies the color of the boundary. PAINT will paint pixels until it hits a pixel of the boundary color. Because each circle is drawn in the foreground color, painting stops at this boundary.

The Left Arrow and Right Arrow keys shift the background up or down one color value. Previously we changed the background by using the COLOR statement. This time we use the PALETTE statement to assign a new color value to attribute 0, as shown in the following:

```
PA&(0) = (PA&(0) + 1) MOD 64
PALETTE 0, PA&(0)
```

The Up Arrow and Down Arrow keys shift the entire palette, increasing or decreasing the number value assigned to each attribute by 1. The Up Arrow key initiates a cycle of palette shifting that continues until another key is pressed.

Shifting the Palette vs. Redrawing the Screen

To change the colors on the screen, you can either redraw the screen using new colors or simply remap the palette to the new colors. Shifting the palette is usually much faster than redrawing the screen. To understand why, you need to know how an EGA or VGA controller works.

Video controllers are equipped with a large chunk of memory to represent the screen. The memory stores an attribute number for each screen pixel. Because mode 9 has 640 × 350, or 224,000, pixels, describing the screen means assigning 224,000 attribute values to the appropriate locations in video memory. The video controller then reads each of these values and colors the corresponding pixels accordingly. To determine which color to use for a given attribute, the controller maintains a reference table describing the color matched to each attribute. If a program redraws the entire screen, it must reset 224,000 attribute values in video memory. If a program remaps the palette, it resets only the 16 colors in the reference table, an operation that is nearly instantaneous.

Listing 12-7 lets you compare redrawing the screen with remapping the palette. The first part of the program draws concentric circles in different colors and then redraws them, changing the colors. When you press a key, the program moves to the second part, in which it remaps the palette. If you have a very fast processor and a slow video card, you might not notice much difference between the two approaches. In that case, try running your computer at a slower clock rate temporarily, which will slow the redrawing but should not noticeably affect remapping.

```
' This program draws concentric circles and then uses
'  PAINT to redraw the screen in different colors.
' Press any key, and the program uses palette remapping
'  instead to change the colors. Press any key again to end.
DIM PalArray&(0 TO 15)
FOR I% = 0 TO 7                        ' Set array to default palette
    PalArray&(I%) = I%
    PalArray&(I% + 8) = 56 + I%
NEXT I%
PalArray&(6) = 20                      ' Default value
PalArray&(0) = 49                      ' Slate blue background
SCREEN 9
PALETTE USING PalArray&
DO                                     ' Redraw circles each cycle
    FOR I% = 1 TO 15
        Colr% = (I% + J%) MOD 16
        COLOR Colr%
        Radius% = 250 - 16 * I%
        CIRCLE (320, 175), Radius%
        PAINT (320 - Radius% + 8, 175)
    NEXT I%
    J% = J% + 1
LOOP UNTIL INKEY$ <> ""
DO                                     ' Remap palette each cycle
    FOR I% = 15 TO 2 STEP -1
        PalArray&(I%) = PalArray&(I% - 1)
    NEXT I%
    PalArray&(1) = PalArray&(15)
PALETTE USING PalArray&(0)
LOOP UNTIL INKEY$ <> ""
PALETTE
SCREEN 0
END
```

Listing 12-7.

We used the following statement to paint the circles:

```
PAINT (320 - Radius% + 8, 175)
```

Recall that these arguments must be a point inside the circle; we used the center earlier. In this program, however, because of the many concentric rings, the boundary color can be encountered before reaching the edge. To ensure that at least the outer ring of the current circle is painted, we chose an *x*-coordinate just inside the edge of the circle.

Other Modes

Much of the preceding information applies, in general, to modes other than graphics mode 9. But modes differ in resolution, in the number of colors available, in how the COLOR and PALETTE statements are used, and so forth. Although we cannot fully describe all the modes here, the following sections summarize certain features of the more important modes. If your system can use any of the modes we describe, you can try altering the preceding programs to work with these modes.

Mode 1

Mode 1 is the original CGA graphics mode. It has lower resolution (320 × 200) than mode 9, and it handles color differently. The color palette contains only four colors. Attribute 0, the background color, can be assigned any of the 16 color numbers from Figure 12-3 (page 323). The other attributes cannot be changed individually. Instead, you can choose one of the two prepackaged palettes shown in Figure 12-10.

Instead of setting the foreground and background colors, as it does in mode 9, the COLOR statement in mode 1 sets the background and the palette:

```
COLOR background, palette
```

background is a color value in the range 0 through 15, with the colors corresponding to the values in Figure 12-3. *palette* must be an integer in the range 0 through 255. If it is 0 or an even number, palette 0 is selected; otherwise, palette 1 is selected.

If you emulate the CGA mode with an EGA or VGA color system, you can use the PALETTE statement to set the four palette attributes to any of the available color values. But an actual CGA system limits you to the two palettes shown in Figure 12-10 and ignores the PALETTE statement.

Attribute Number	***Palette 0***	***Palette 1***
0	Background	Background
1	Green	Cyan
2	Red	Magenta
3	Yellow	White

Figure 12-10.
Mode 1 palette choices.

VGA Mode 12

VGA mode 12 provides higher resolution (640 × 480 pixels) and a greater color choice than mode 9. Mode 12, like mode 9, uses a palette of 16 attributes, but it offers 262,144 colors instead of 64.

The COLOR statement takes only one argument, the attribute number of the desired foreground color. To change the background in mode 12, use PALETTE to assign a new color value to attribute 0.

The PALETTE statement in mode 12 works much as it does in mode 9, but it requires a different numbering scheme for the color numbers. Whereas EGA provides 4 intensities (including off) for the three primary colors, VGA provides 64 intensities (0 through 63) for each primary color. To get a color value, you must combine the primary colors using the following formula:

colorvalue = *red* + 256 × *green* + 65536 × *blue*

colorvalue is a long integer. *blue*, *green*, and *red* are the intensities (numbers in the range 0 through 63) for the three primary colors. An intensity of 23 corresponds to the EGA low intensity, 46 to the EGA medium intensity, and 63 to the EGA high intensity. Depending on the brightness level of your monitor, some of the lowest-intensity levels, such as 5, can be difficult to see.

The color values produced by this scheme are not contiguous. For example, the lowest-intensity blue has the color number 65536, whereas bright yellow—the highest-intensity green and red—has the color number 16191. The numbers 16192 through 65535 don't correspond to any combination of blue, red, and green and are not valid color numbers.

VGA and MCGA Mode 13

Both VGA and MCGA support mode 13. Mode 13 resembles mode 12 but differs in three ways:

- Mode 13's resolution is 320 × 200 instead of 640 × 480.
- Mode 13's graphics text is 40 columns × 25 lines instead of 80 columns × 30 lines.
- Mode 13's palette consists of 256 attributes instead of 16. This expanded palette lets you display as many as 256 colors simultaneously, allowing a more natural rendering of coloring. The gradual shading tends to smooth over the rather coarse resolution.

Screen Positioning

As you've seen, a display is positioned on the screen using horizontal and vertical coordinates to specify locations. By default, QuickBASIC uses physical coordinates, with *x* measured from the left of the screen, *y* measured from the top, and the ranges for *x* and *y* depending on the mode. But there's more:

- You can create a graphics viewport that restricts graphics to a particular portion of the screen.
- You can establish a logical coordinate system that uses the origin and the units of your choice.
- Instead of using *absolute coordinates* (positions relative to the origin), you can use *relative coordinates,* which are positions relative to the most recently referenced screen location.

Graphics Viewports

Earlier we used the VIEW PRINT statement to create a text viewport in text mode, which confined text to a specified area on the screen. The VIEW PRINT statement also works in graphics modes. In addition, the VIEW statement lets you create a graphics viewport. You can even use both statements simultaneously to create separate windows for graphics and text.

Here is the syntax for the VIEW statement:

```
VIEW [[SCREEN] (x1, y1)-(x2, y2)[, [color][, border]]]
```

VIEW establishes a graphics viewport. Subsequent graphics commands affect points within that viewport only. The coordinates (*x1*, *y1*) and (*x2*, *y2*) specify the two diagonally opposite corners of the viewport. *color* is an attribute number indicating the color used to fill the viewport; if this argument is omitted, the viewport is not filled. *border* is a color attribute specifying the color used to draw a line border around the viewport; if this argument is omitted, the border is not drawn. VIEW used without arguments defines the entire screen as the viewport.

By default, graphics coordinates used after the VIEW statement has been executed are measured relative to the upper left corner of the viewport. Using the SCREEN argument causes the program to use coordinates relative to the entire screen rather than to the viewport (Figures 12-11 and 12-12).

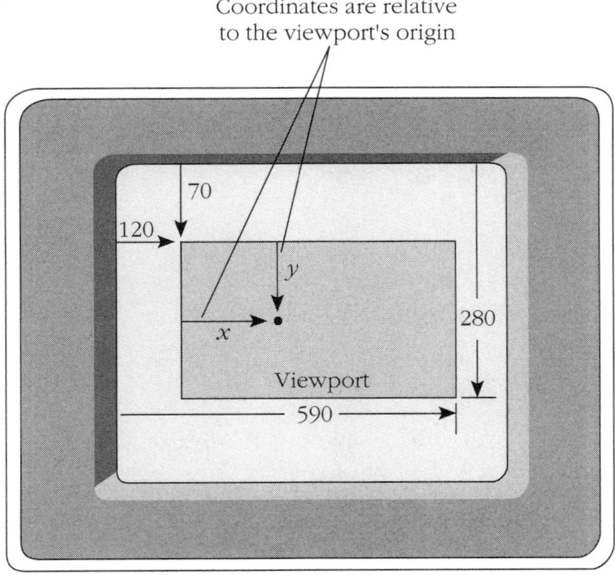


```
VIEW (120, 70)-(590, 280)
```

Figure 12-11.
Coordinates after a VIEW statement is executed.

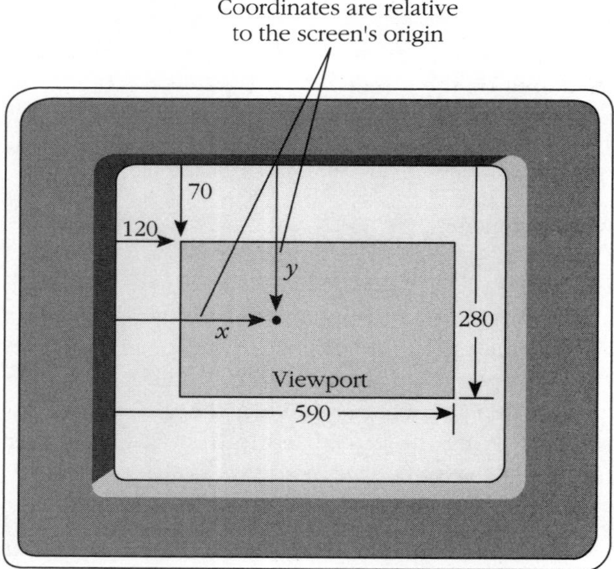


```
VIEW SCREEN (120, 70)-(590, 280)
```

Figure 12-12.
Coordinates after a VIEW SCREEN statement is executed.

Using viewports lets you control which parts of the screen are active. If you need both graphics and text, you can keep them separated.

CLS can be used to clear the entire screen or to clear individual viewports.

Here is the syntax for the CLS statement:

```
CLS [n]
```

The value of *n* specifies what is to be cleared:

- If *n* is 0, the statement clears the entire screen.
- If *n* is 1, the statement clears the active graphics viewport. If no graphics viewport exists, the entire screen is cleared.
- If *n* is 2, the statement clears the active text viewport. If no text viewport exists, the entire screen is cleared, except the bottom line of the screen, which is unchanged.
- If *n* is omitted, the statement clears the currently active viewport, including the bottom line of the screen.

The CLS statement also places the cursor in the upper left corner of the screen.

The program in Listing 12-8 establishes viewports and illustrates some of the uses of CLS. It also introduces LINE, a statement that causes a line to be drawn between two specified points. By default, LINE uses the foreground color, making the line the same color as the text.

```
' This program illustrates graphics and text viewports
DECLARE SUB Center (Words$)               ' Print text centered on screen
SCREEN 9
COLOR 6, 3
Center "This is printed before the viewports are created."
VIEW PRINT 20 TO 25                       ' Create text viewport
Center "SCREEN MODE 9"
Center "This is the text viewport."
Center "Above is the graphics viewport."
VIEW (30, 30)-(610, 260), 8, 14           ' Create graphics viewport
LINE (10, 10)-(570, 10)                   ' Draw a horizontal line
CIRCLE (290, 115), 100                    ' Draw a circle
PAINT (290, 115), 1, 6                    ' Paint the circle
Center "Press any key to clear the text window"
DO
LOOP UNTIL INKEY$ <> ""

CLS 2                                     ' Clear text viewport only
Center "Now press any key to clear the graphics window"
DO
LOOP UNTIL INKEY$ <> ""

CLS 1                                     ' Clear graphics viewport only
Center "Now press any key for a new graphics display"
DO
LOOP UNTIL INKEY$ <> ""
VIEW SCREEN (80, 80)-(560, 210), 10, 14   ' Smaller viewport
LINE (10, 10)-(570, 10)
CIRCLE (290, 115), 100
PAINT (290, 115), 1, 6

CLS 2                                     ' Clear text viewport
Center "Press any key to clear all"
DO
LOOP UNTIL INKEY$ <> ""
CLS 0                                     ' Clear entire screen
END

SUB Center (Words$)
    L% = LEN(Words$)
    IF L% < 80 THEN
        PRINT TAB(40 - L% / 2); Words$
    ELSE
        PRINT Words$
    END IF
END SUB
```

Listing 12-8.

Using the *Center* subprogram to print text without first using LOCATE or VIEW PRINT causes the display to start printing at the top of the screen, where our first message appears. When you use VIEW PRINT, however, the first subsequent PRINT statement appears at the top of the text viewport unless you use LOCATE to put it elsewhere in that viewport.

The following statement from Listing 12-8 creates a graphics viewport whose upper left corner is at the point (30, 30) and whose lower right corner is at the point (610, 260):

```
VIEW (30, 30)-(610, 260), 8, 14
```

The viewport is painted using color attribute 8 (grey by default) and is outlined with color attribute 14 (yellow by default).

Then the following statement draws a line from (10, 10) to (570, 10):

```
LINE (10, 10)-(570, 10)
```

Because this part of the program uses VIEW and not VIEW SCREEN, these coordinates (like those of the first CIRCLE statement) are relative to the upper left corner of the viewport. Thus, the *y* value 10 locates the line 10 pixels below the top of the viewport, not 10 pixels below the top of the screen. The *x* value 10 begins the line 10 pixels from the left border of the viewport. Some calculations are necessary to determine the end of the line. The VIEW statement sets the viewport from 30 to 610 on the *y*-axis, using screen coordinates. We must subtract 30 from each value to find the viewport range 0 through 580. To end the line 10 units before the right-hand border, we subtract 10 and get 570.

Later in the program, this statement is used to establish a smaller graphics viewport:

```
VIEW SCREEN (80, 80)-(560, 210), 10, 14
```

This time, the VIEW SCREEN statement makes the subsequent coordinates relative to the screen corner, not the viewport corner. Although the statement

```
LINE (10, 10)-(570, 10)
```

is the same one used earlier, it now specifies a line outside the graphics viewport, and the line is therefore not drawn.

Similarly, the part of the circle outside the graphics viewport is not drawn. Although the CIRCLE statement specifies points outside the graphics viewport, the statement is not invalidated. QuickBASIC draws all the points that lie within the viewport and ignores the others, a process called *clipping*.

Logical Coordinates

The default system of physical coordinates has its drawbacks. Using pixels as the unit of measurement can make it difficult to calculate positions if, for example, you want to draw a centered rectangle that occupies 80 percent of the screen. Having the origin in the upper left corner can also be inconvenient in certain situations. And coordinates that work for mode 9 might be offscreen for mode 1.

One solution to these problems is to use QuickBASIC's WINDOW statement to specify your choice of logical coordinates—that is, to specify your own values for the *xy*-coordinates of the borders of the current graphics viewport. The physical size of the viewport remains the same; QuickBASIC stretches or shrinks the coordinate system scale to fit the values you choose.

Suppose you're using the full screen (640 × 350 pixels) and you give the following command:

```
WINDOW (-100, -50)-(100, 50)
```

This statement sets the *x* values to run from –100 through 100 rather than from 0 through 639 and the *y* values to run from –50 through 50 rather than from 0 through 349. The origin (0, 0) is located in the center of the screen. The coordinates created by the WINDOW statement resemble traditional mathematical coordinates, with *y* increasing as it moves upward, in contrast to physical coordinates, in which *y* increases as it moves downward. You can, however, use the SCREEN modifier with logical coordinates to make *y* increase as it moves down.

Logical coordinates, unlike physical coordinates, do not always have a one-to-one relationship with pixels. In the preceding example, for instance, the range from –100 through 100 contains 201 units. If you are using the entire screen in mode 9, 640 pixels are contained in the 201 *x* units, making each *x* unit roughly 3.184 pixels. Similarly, each *y* unit is about 3.465 pixels (350 pixels divided by 101 units). Logical coordinates can be floating-point values—for example, a logical *x*-coordinate can be set to 23.4567.

Here is the syntax for the WINDOW statement:

```
WINDOW [[SCREEN] (x1, y1)-(x2, y2)]
```

This statement defines the logical coordinates of the left and right borders of the graphics viewport (which can be the entire screen) as *x1* and *x2*, with the left border set to the smaller value. If SCREEN is used, the coordinates of the top and bottom borders are defined as *y1* and *y2*, with the top border set to the smaller value. If SCREEN is omitted, the top border is set to the larger *y* value. Using WINDOW with no arguments disables logical coordinates.

Thus, the following two statements have the same effect because the lower values (–100 and –50) are assigned to the left and bottom borders:

```
WINDOW (-100, -50)-(100, 50)
WINDOW (100, 50)-(-100, -50)
```

This statement, however, reverses the *y* assignment:

```
WINDOW SCREEN (-100, -50)-(100, 50)
```

Figures 12-13 and 12-14 illustrate the contrast.

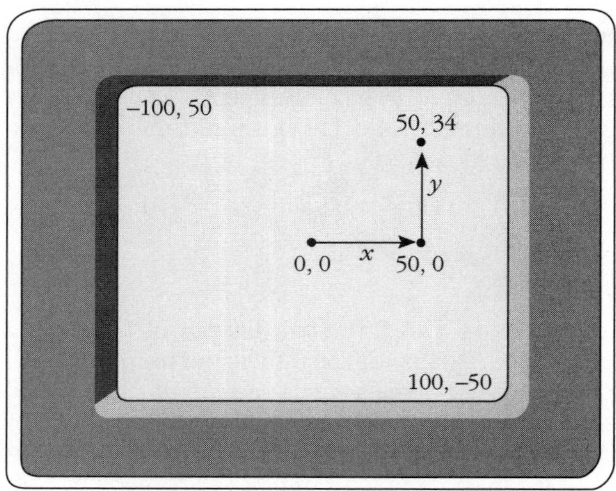


```
WINDOW (-100, -50)-(100, 50)
```

Figure 12-13.
Logical coordinates after a WINDOW statement is executed.

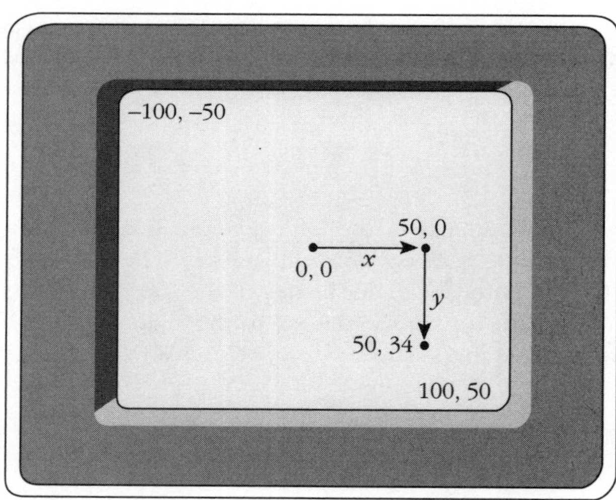


```
WINDOW SCREEN (-100, -50)-(100, 50)
```

Figure 12-14.
Logical coordinates after a WINDOW SCREEN statement is executed.

Using WINDOW can make a program less dependent on a particular mode. For instance, if you use the statement

```
WINDOW (100, 50)-(-100, -50)
```

to define coordinates for the entire screen, the point (0, 0) is the center of the screen regardless of the mode's resolution, and the point (100, 50) is the upper right corner.

Listing 12-9 shows how the WINDOW statement works. In the first part of the program, the logical coordinates apply to the entire screen. Thus, the following statement draws a line from the upper left corner of the screen to the lower right corner:

```
LINE (-100, 100)-(100, -100)
```

The CIRCLE statement draws a circle centered on screen center and tangent to the left and right borders. (Because the CIRCLE statement measures vertical and horizontal distances differently, a radius of 100 doesn't make the circle tangent to the top and bottom borders. We'll discuss CIRCLE in greater detail soon.) Then the program draws a smaller circle and paints the ring bounded by the two circles.

The program also uses VIEW to change the physical size of the graphics viewport twice, once radically altering the proportions. With WINDOW, however, the same logical coordinates apply to the new viewports, and the identical LINE and CIRCLE statements draw corner-to-corner lines and circles tangent to the left and right borders of the new viewports. This feature lets you easily "shrink" a window along with its contents (Figure 12-15).

```
' This program illustrates using logical coordinates
'  and rescaling a window and its contents
SCREEN 9
COLOR 6
PALETTE 0, 3
WINDOW (-100, -100)-(100, 100)     ' x and y range is -100 through 100
CIRCLE (0, 0), 100                 ' (0, 0) is screen center
CIRCLE (0, 0), 50
PAINT (70, 0), 12, 6
LINE (-100, -100)-(100, 100)       ' Corner-to-corner line
LINE (-100, 100)-(100, -100)
DO
LOOP UNTIL INKEY$ <> ""

CLS 1
VIEW (120, 60)-(500, 290), 10      ' Use smaller viewport
CIRCLE (0, 0), 100                 ' Draw circle with same coordinates
CIRCLE (0, 0), 50
PAINT (70, 0), 13, 6
LINE (-100, -100)-(100, 100)
LINE (-100, 100)-(100, -100)
DO
LOOP UNTIL INKEY$ <> ""
```

Listing 12-9. *(continued)*

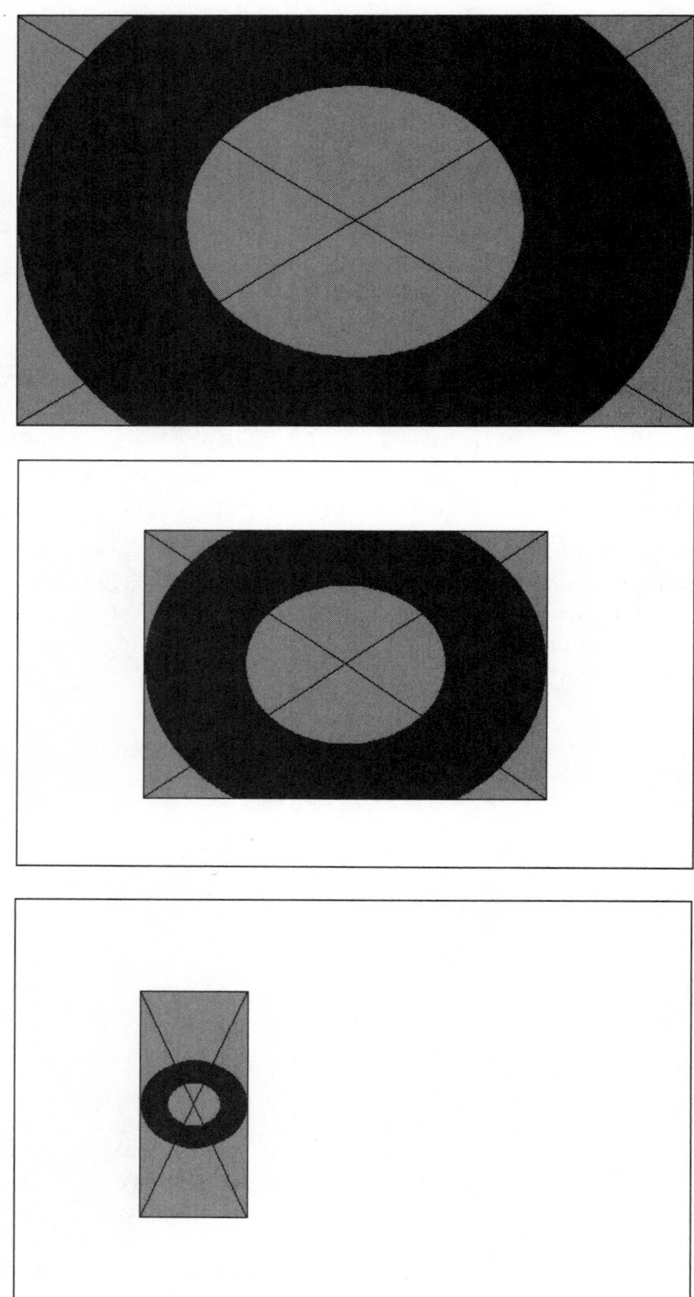

Figure 12-15.
Output of Listing 12-9.

Listing 12-9. *continued*

```
CLS 1
VIEW (420, 80)-(520, 270), 10       ' Change shape, position
CIRCLE (0, 0), 100
CIRCLE (0, 0), 50
PAINT (70, 0), 14, 6
LINE (-100, -100)-(100, 100)
LINE (-100, 100)-(100, -100)
DO
LOOP UNTIL INKEY$ <> ""
SCREEN 0
END
```

The ability to use the same logical coordinate system with viewports of different sizes provides a technique for rescaling, or *zooming,* a picture: Simply change the viewport size and redraw the picture using the same drawing statements. Another technique, illustrated in Listing 12-10, is to use the same size viewport and the same drawing statements but to change the logical coordinates. If the logical *x*-coordinate ranges from –100 through 100, for example, a circle of radius 20 is fairly small. But if we change the range for the *x*-coordinate to –25 through 25, a circle of radius 20 fills most of the viewport.

```
' This program enlarges an image by rescaling the logical coordinates
SCREEN 9
COLOR 6
PALETTE 0, 1
VIEW PRINT 24 TO 25                 ' Text viewport
PRINT "Press any key to continue"
VIEW (64, 35)-(576, 315), , 14
FOR X% = 100 TO 30 STEP -10
    WINDOW (-X%, -X%)-(X%, X%)      ' Rescale coordinates
    CIRCLE (0, 0), 20, 8
    PAINT (0, 0), 4, 8
    DO
    LOOP UNTIL INKEY$ <> ""
    CLS 1                           ' Clear graphics viewport
NEXT X%
PRINT "Done--press another key"
DO
LOOP UNTIL INKEY$ <> ""
END
SCREEN 0
```

Listing 12-10.

Coordinate Value Types

Coordinates, whether physical or logical, can be any of the four numeric types: integer, long integer, single precision, or double precision. Because you can't have a fractional pixel, integer values are the most sensible choice for physical coordinates. (QuickBASIC reduces fractional values to integers, but it's faster to simply start with integers.)

With logical coordinates, however, you might need to use single-precision values. For instance, as we noted earlier, setting *x* to run from –100 through 100 in mode 9 makes each *x* unit a little more than 3.18 pixels. To specify adjacent pixels in this case, you'd need to use fractional values for *x*.

The PMAP Function: Converting Coordinates

Occasionally, you need to know the physical coordinates that correspond to certain logical coordinates, or vice versa. For example, you might be using logical coordinates but find you need physical coordinates for the VIEW statement. QuickBASIC's PMAP function makes these conversions.

Here is the syntax for PMAP:

```
PMAP(coordinate, conversion)
```

coordinate is an expression that reduces to the value of the coordinate you want to convert. The *conversion* argument, with values 0 through 3, indicates the type of conversion:

- A value of 0 converts a logical *x*-coordinate to a physical coordinate.
- A value of 1 converts a logical *y*-coordinate to a physical coordinate.
- A value of 2 converts a physical *x*-coordinate to a logical coordinate.
- A value of 3 converts a physical *y*-coordinate to a logical coordinate.

Here are some examples:

```
Xb = PMAP(100, 0)   ' Set Xb to physical coordinate corresponding
                    '  to logical x = 100

Yb = PMAP(100, 1)   ' Set Yb to physical coordinate corresponding
                    '  to logical y = 100

Xe = PMAP(638, 2)   ' Set Xe to logical coordinate corresponding
                    '  to physical x = 638
```

Suppose you set up logical coordinates but then want to open a viewport half the width and height of the full screen. Because the VIEW command requires physical coordinates, you must check the number of pixels horizontally and vertically and calculate the required coordinates. With PMAP, you can simplify the process, as Listing 12-11 shows.

```
' Convert logical to physical coordinates with PMAP
SCREEN 9
PALETTE 0, 2
WINDOW (-100, 100)-(100, -100)
CIRCLE (0, 0), 70, 5
PAINT (0, 0), 6, 5
Xul = PMAP(-50, 0)                    ' Find physical coordinates
Yul = PMAP(50, 1)
Xlr = PMAP(50, 0)
Ylr = PMAP(-50, 1)
VIEW (Xul, Yul)-(Xlr, Ylr), 1, 15    ' Set graphics viewport
CIRCLE (0, 0), 70, 5
PAINT (0, 0), 4, 5
DO
LOOP UNTIL INKEY$ <> ""
SCREEN 0
END
```

Listing 12-11.

The program first sets up logical coordinates and draws a large circle. Because the logical coordinates run from –100 through 100, logical coordinates running from –50 through 50 define the half-size screen. The program uses PMAP to find the corresponding physical coordinates to be used with VIEW. It opens a new viewport inside the large circle and uses the same CIRCLE parameters to draw a new, smaller circle.

This program is not dependent on a particular mode. In mode 1 or mode 12, the program still draws a large circle, opens a viewport inside it, and draws a small circle. You can run the same program on your old CGA system at work and on your new VGA system at home because QuickBASIC does all the calculations for you.

Relative Coordinates

Absolute coordinates are measured from a shared, fixed origin: Physical coordinates are measured from the upper left corner, and logical coordinates are measured from the origin defined by a WINDOW statement. Relative coordinates, however, are measured from the most recently selected position, also called the *LPR* (last point referenced) or the *current graphics cursor location*.

Many QuickBASIC graphics statements let you use the STEP modifier to create relative coordinates. For example, suppose you use the following two statements in succession:

```
CIRCLE (100, 100), 50
CIRCLE STEP(20, 10), 20
```

The first CIRCLE statement tells the computer to draw a circle centered on the point (100, 100). The second statement tells it to *step* 20 units in the *x* direction, 10 units in the *y* direction, and draw a circle centered on that point—that is, to center the circle at (120, 110).

The STEP modifier always refers to the most recently specified location. Consider the following sequence:

```
CIRCLE (100, 100), 50
LINE (20, 30)-(80, 60)
CIRCLE STEP(20, 10), 20
```

The last point referenced before STEP is (80, 60). Adding 20 to the *x*-coordinate and 10 to the *y*-coordinate means that the second circle is centered on (100, 70), which now becomes the LPR.

Listing 12-12 uses the STEP modifier to draw a series of circles ascending from the lower left of the screen to the upper right. It uses the CIRCLE statement to specify absolute coordinates for the first circle and uses STEP for the remaining circles. Note the following lines in the loop:

```
CIRCLE STEP(5, 5), 10, I% - 1
PAINT STEP(0, 0), I% MOD 15 + 1, I% - 1
```

Using the STEP modifier with CIRCLE moves the center of the circle up and over 5 units at each loop cycle. Using *STEP(0, 0)* with PAINT tells the computer to use the same location just used for CIRCLE.

```
' Use relative coordinates to draw a series of circles
SCREEN 9
WINDOW (0, 0)-(100, 100)
CIRCLE (20, 20), 10, 1
PAINT (20, 20), 3, 1
FOR I% = 3 TO 15
    CIRCLE STEP(5, 5), 10, I% - 1
    PAINT STEP(0, 0), I% MOD 15 + 1, I% - 1
NEXT I%
DO
LOOP UNTIL INKEY$ <> ""
SCREEN 0
END
```

Listing 12-12.

Drawing

Now that we've examined colors and screen positioning, let's look at some of the drawing statements in more detail.

The CIRCLE Statement

We've already discussed the CIRCLE statement briefly, but it has a few more twists worth investigating. Among other things, you can use it to draw arcs and wedges and to produce noncircular ellipses.

Here is the full syntax for the CIRCLE statement:

```
CIRCLE [STEP](x, y), radius[, [color][, [start][, [end][, aspect]]]]
```

This statement draws a circle or other ellipse centered on the point (*x*, *y*) and with a radius of *radius* units. If the aspect ratio (discussed later in this section) is less than 1, the radius is measured in *x* units; otherwise, it is measured in *y* units. If STEP is used, the *xy*-coordinates are relative to the LPR; otherwise, CIRCLE uses absolute coordinates. The figure is drawn using the color specified by the attribute number *color*. If *color* is omitted, the current foreground color is used.

start and *end* specify the starting angle and the ending angle for drawing an arc (a part of a circle or other ellipse). Angles are measured in radians clockwise from the *x*-axis. The possible values range from -2π radians (–360 degrees) to 2π radians (360 degrees). A negative value specifies using the positive angle but drawing a radius line to that end of the arc.

The *aspect* argument specifies the ratio of the *y*-radius to the *x*-radius, thus affecting shape. The default value, which is intended to produce perfect circles on screen, is the following:

$$4 \times (ypixels/xpixels)/3$$

ypixels and *xpixels* are the screen resolution figures for the current mode. For example, the aspect ratio for graphics mode 9 is $4 \times (350/640)$ divided by 3, or 0.73. Actual monitor settings, however, might make the calculated value of the aspect ratio incorrect for drawing a perfect circle.

Let's look at some of these features in more detail.

Arcs and Wedges

To draw an arc, you must supply its starting and ending angles. For example, the following statement draws an arc of radius 60 running from an angle of 0 to an angle of π (180 degrees):

```
CIRCLE (200, 150), 60, 13, 0, 3.14159
```

This statement draws an arc of radius 60 from $\pi/2$ (90 degrees) to π (180 degrees):

```
CIRCLE (200, 150), 60, 13, -3.14159 / 2, -3.14159
```

Because we use negative values in the second statement, it also draws a radius line to each end of the arc, producing a large wedge.

The program in Listing 12-13 first sets up logical coordinates centered on the screen. Next it draws a semicircle and a wedge. Then, after you press a key, the program draws a circle divided into 12 equal wedges, or slices.

```
CONST pi! = 3.14159
SCREEN 9
PALETTE 0, 33
WINDOW (-100, -100)-(100, 100)
CIRCLE (0, 0), 60, 13, 0, pi!          ' Draw an arc
CIRCLE (0, 0), 50, 12, -pi! / 2, -pi!  ' Draw a wedge
DO
LOOP UNTIL INKEY$ <> ""
CLS 1
FOR I% = 0 TO 11                        ' Slice a pie
    CIRCLE (0, 0), 60, 12, -I% * pi! / 6, -(I% + 1) * pi! / 6
NEXT I%
DO
LOOP UNTIL INKEY$ <> ""
SCREEN 0
END
```

Listing 12-13.

Figure 12-16 shows the output of the second part of the program.

If you want to draw a radius line at an angle of 0, using a start or end value of −0 doesn't work. But you can use a very small negative value, such as −0.0001. Or you can use the method shown in Listing 12-13, in which the final loop uses an end value of -2π. Because 360 degrees is the same as 0, a line is drawn along the *x*-axis.

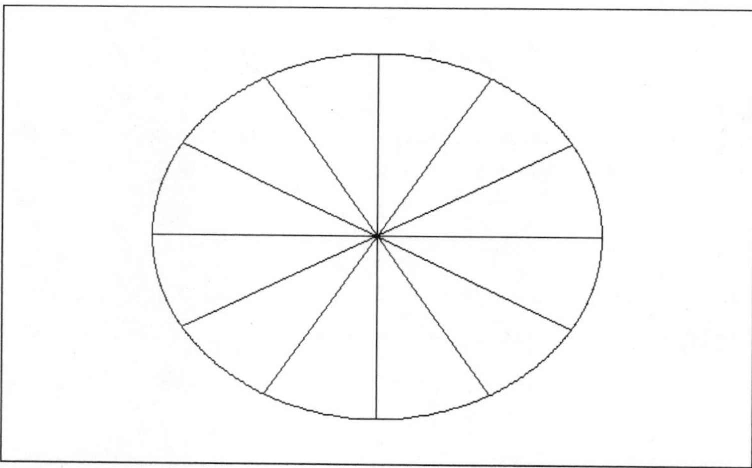

Figure 12-16.
A sliced pie.

The Aspect Ratio

The CIRCLE statement can be used to draw other ellipses besides circles. Indeed, on some systems, the circles our programs produce might look like other types of ellipses. Because 50 pixels vertically on a screen is not necessarily the same distance as 50 pixels horizontally, the QuickBASIC CIRCLE statement tries to compensate by adjusting the vertical scale of a circle. But if this adjustment does not exactly match your particular combination of video controller, monitor, and monitor settings, your circle will look somewhat less than circular.

You can use CIRCLE's *aspect* argument to control the shape of a circle—to generate various ellipses or to make circles on your system appear more circular. In mode 9, using physical coordinates with an aspect ratio of 1 and a radius of 50, CIRCLE draws an elliptical shape 100 pixels wide and 100 pixels high. If you change the aspect ratio to 0.8, the circle is 100 pixels wide and 80 pixels high. And an aspect ratio of 0.1 produces a circle 100 pixels wide and 10 pixels high—a very flat ellipse. Because the aspect ratio is less than 1 in these examples, only the y-radius is adjusted; hence only the height is affected.

Using an aspect ratio greater than 1, however, adjusts the horizontal dimensions and leaves the vertical unchanged. Thus, a radius of 50 and an aspect ratio of 4 produces an ellipse 100 pixels high and 25 pixels wide. Because the aspect ratio is defined as the ratio of y-pixels to x-pixels, not in terms of physical dimensions on the screen, an aspect ratio of 1 doesn't correspond to a circle.

The program in Listing 12-14 draws ellipses with various aspect ratios. On a color monitor, those ellipses with ratios of 1 or less than 1 (horizontally oriented) appear in green, and those with ratios of 1 or greater than 1 (vertically oriented) appear in red.

```
' This program draws ellipses of various shapes by
'  using different aspect ratios
SCREEN 9
WINDOW (-100, -100)-(100, 100)
FOR Aspect! = 1 TO .1 STEP -.1
    CIRCLE (0, 0), 50, 2, , , Aspect!    ' Green ellipses for aspect <= 1
NEXT Aspect!

FOR Aspect! = 1 TO 10
    CIRCLE (0, 0), 51, 4, , , Aspect!    ' Red ellipses for aspect >= 1
NEXT Aspect!

DO
LOOP UNTIL INKEY$ <> ""
SCREEN 0
END
```

Listing 12-14.

Figure 12-17 shows the output of this program.

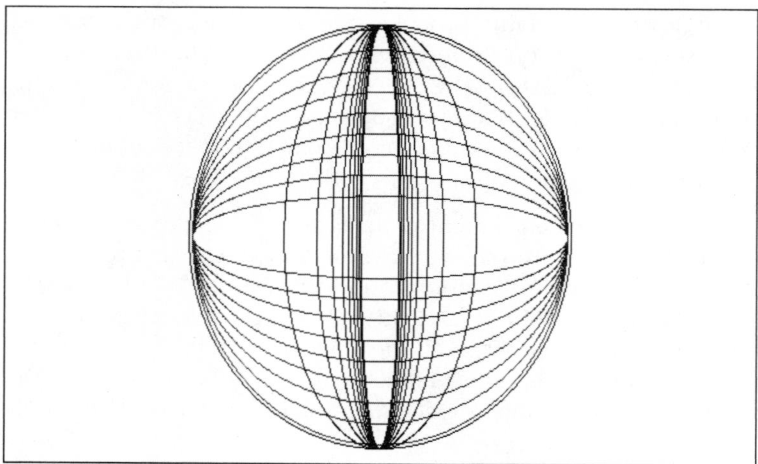

Figure 12-17.
Output of Listing 12-14.

Using logical coordinates doesn't affect the shape of the ellipses, even if you greatly distort the vertical scale. For example, replacing the WINDOW statement in Listing 12-14 with the following has no effect on the size or shape of the ellipses:

```
WINDOW (-100, -10)-(100, 10)
```

The Varied LINE Statement

In addition to drawing lines, the LINE statement also draws outline rectangles and filled rectangles and lets you specify a line style.

Here is the syntax for the LINE statement:

```
LINE [[STEP](x1, y1)]-[STEP](x2, y2)[, [color][, [B | BF]][, style]]]
```

The coordinates (*x1*, *y1*) and (*x2*, *y2*) specify the endpoints of the line. If the first coordinate pair is omitted, LINE uses the LPR. The STEP modifier makes the coordinates relative to the LPR. You can use absolute coordinates for one endpoint and relative coordinates for the other. The line is drawn using the attribute number *color*; if *color* is omitted, the current foreground color is used. The B option draws a box in outline with the given coordinates as opposite corners. The BF option draws a filled box.

style is a 16-bit integer. The LINE statement interprets the number as a binary bit pattern, with each bit representing a pixel on the line. If the bit is 0, the pixel is unaltered; if the bit is 1, the pixel is drawn.

Drawing Lines

Listing 12-15 uses several of the many options available for specifying line endpoints.

```
' Using LINE to draw lines and steps
' Press any key to advance the program to the next stage
SCREEN 9
PALETTE 0, 1
COLOR 12
WINDOW (-100, -100)-(100, 100)
LINE (0, 0)-(50, 50)
LINE -(50, 10)                      ' Start at (50, 50), end at (50, 10)
LINE STEP(-120, 20)-STEP(30, -20)   ' Start at (-70, 30), end at (-40, 10)
LINE (-80, 80)-STEP(60, -60)        ' End at (-20, 20)
DO
LOOP UNTIL INKEY$ <> ""

CLS                                 ' Make stairs
LINE (-100, -100)-STEP(0, 10)
FOR I% = 1 TO 20                    ' Loop for 20 stairs
    LINE -STEP(10, 0)               ' Up 10
    LINE -STEP(0, 10)               ' 10 to the right
NEXT I%
LINE -STEP(10, 0)
DO
LOOP UNTIL INKEY$ <> ""
SCREEN 0
END
```

Listing 12-15.

You should note several points about this program. First, the following statement draws a line from the LPR to the location (50, 10):

```
LINE -(50, 10)
```

The most recently specified point was (50, 50), and the line starts there.

Next, the statement

```
LINE STEP(-120, 20)-STEP(30, -20)
```

moves the starting point left 120 units and up 20 units. The end of the line is then established 30 units to the right and 20 units down.

Finally, the following sequence lets you draw a line 10 units up from the current point and a line 10 units to the right:

```
LINE -STEP(10, 0)
LINE -STEP(0, 10)
```

By putting this in a loop, you can draw a set of stairs.

Drawing Boxes

The LINE statement's B option draws boxes in outline, and the BF option draws filled boxes. Both use the LINE coordinates to define diagonally opposite corners. For instance, in graphics mode 9, the statements shown in Figure 12-18 first draw a red line from (20, 10) to (500, 280) and then draw a box with that line as a diagonal.

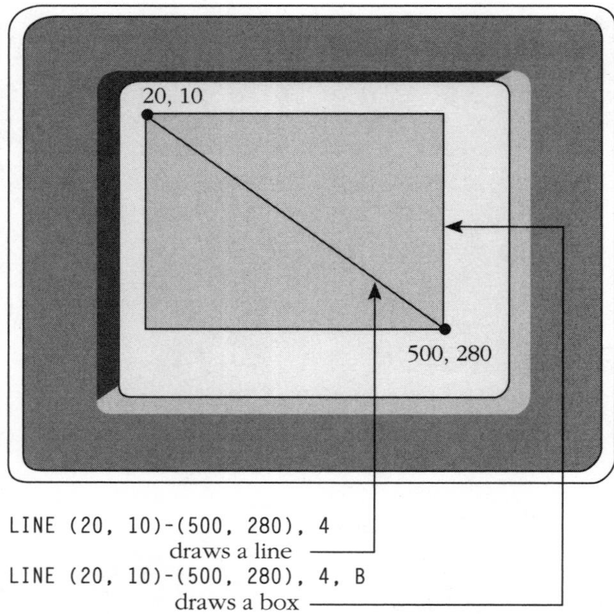
20, 10
500, 280
LINE (20, 10)-(500, 280), 4
draws a line
LINE (20, 10)-(500, 280), 4, B
draws a box

Figure 12-18.
Drawing a box and a line with the LINE statement.

The program in Listing 12-16 draws both outlined boxes and filled boxes; Figure 12-19 shows the output. Note that filled boxes are opaque, covering anything that lies beneath them.

```
SCREEN 9
PALETTE 0, 1
WINDOW (-100, -100)-(100, 100)
FOR Box% = 0 TO 40 STEP 10          ' Draw box outlines
    Colr% = Box% / 10 + 2
    LINE (Box%, Box%)-(100 - Box%, 100 - Box%), Colr%, B
NEXT Box%
```

Listing 12-16. *(continued)*

Listing 12-16. *continued*

```
FOR Box% = 0 TO 40 STEP 10          ' Draw filled boxes
    Colr% = Box% / 10 + 2
    LINE (-Box%, -Box%)-(-100 + Box%, -100 + Box%), Colr%, BF
NEXT Box%
DO
LOOP UNTIL INKEY$ <> ""
SCREEN 0
END
```

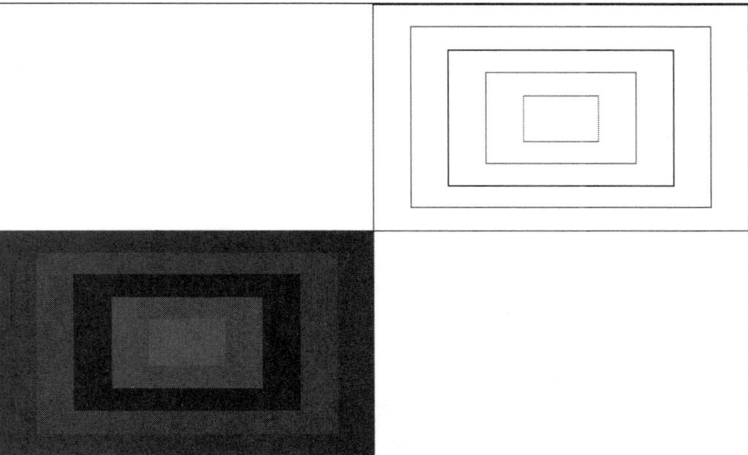

Figure 12-19.
Output of Listing 12-16.

Styling Lines

The LINE statement's *style* argument is used to create a line pattern—that is, to style a line. By default, all points along a line are plotted, producing a solid line. But with line styling you can be more selective.

The *style* argument defines a 16-bit *mask*. Each line is then drawn in units of 16 points in length. Points corresponding to on bits are drawn, whereas points corresponding to off bits are unaltered. To see how this works, let's go through an example step by step.

To produce a dashed line style of 4 points on, 4 points off, draw a row of 16 boxes on paper, as shown in Figure 12-20. Then shade 4 boxes, skip 4, shade the next 4, and so on. Write 1's under the shaded boxes and 0's under the empty boxes, producing the binary number 1111000011110000.

Convert this binary number to hexadecimal form by breaking up the binary number into groups of four bits, each corresponding to a hexadecimal digit: 1111 0000 1111 0000. The number 1111 corresponds to F and 0000 corresponds to 0, making the final value &HF0F0. (See Appendix B.) Now use this as a style value in the LINE statement. (You could also convert this binary number to decimal form, but the conversion from binary to hexadecimal is simpler.)

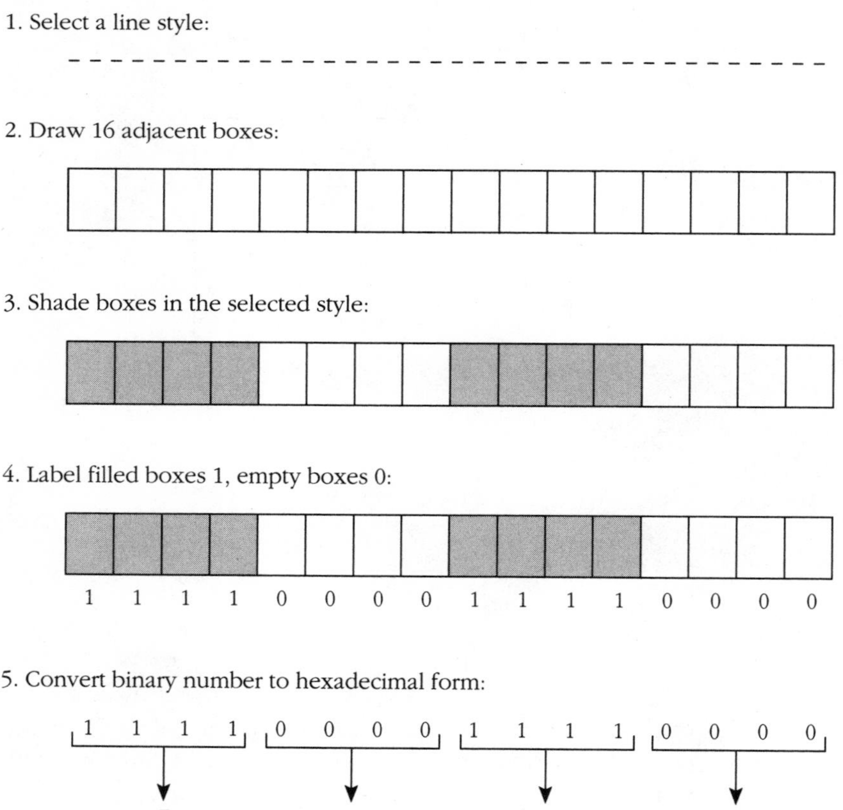
1. Select a line style:
2. Draw 16 adjacent boxes:
3. Shade boxes in the selected style:
4. Label filled boxes 1, empty boxes 0:
1 1 1 1 0 0 0 0 1 1 1 1 0 0 0 0
5. Convert binary number to hexadecimal form:
1 1 1 1 0 0 0 0 1 1 1 1 0 0 0 0
F 0 F 0
6. You now have a line style: &HF0F0

Figure 12-20.
Creating a line style.

Listing 12-17 uses 10 different styles to draw 10 boxes; Figure 12-21 shows the output of this program.

```
' This program demonstrates several line styles. The DATA
'  statements hold the hexadecimal values defining the values.
DATA &HFFFF, &HF0F0, &HFF00, &HFFF0, &HBBBB, &HB0B0
DATA &HBFBF, &HBFFB, &HF0B0, &HFFB0
SCREEN 9
WINDOW (-100, -100)-(100, 100)
FOR Box% = 10 TO 100 STEP 10
    Colr% = Box% / 10 + 2
    READ Style%
    LINE (Box%, Box%)-(-Box%, -Box%), Colr%, B, Style%
NEXT Box%
DO
LOOP UNTIL INKEY$ <> ""
SCREEN 0
END
```

Listing 12-17.

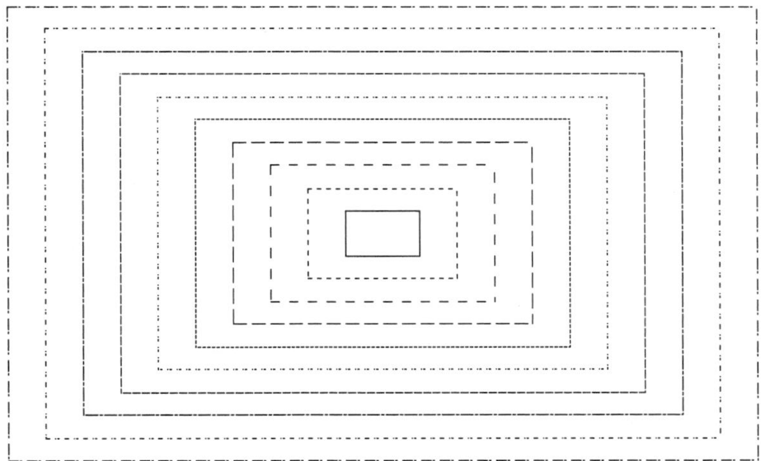

Figure 12-21.
Output of Listing 12-17.

If you first draw a line as a solid line in one color and then draw over it in another color using a style with gaps, the underlying color shows through the gaps, giving you a two-toned line. If you want a thicker line, draw two adjacent lines. (Lines are only one pixel thick.) Physical coordinates are easier to use for drawing adjacent lines; with logical coordinates, you must compute how many logical units correspond to one pixel, perhaps by using PMAP. The program in Listing 12-18 shows both these operations using physical coordinates.

```
SCREEN 9
' A two-tone line
LINE (20, 10)-(620, 340), 14, B
LINE (20, 10)-(620, 340), 12, B, &HF0F0
' A line of double thickness
LINE (40, 30)-(600, 320), 14, B
LINE (41, 31)-(601, 321), 14, B
DO
LOOP UNTIL INKEY$ <> ""
SCREEN 0
END
```

Listing 12-18.

Making Points with the PSET and PRESET Statements

Some programming situations require point-by-point plotting. QuickBASIC offers two related statements for drawing points: PSET and PRESET.

Here is the syntax for PSET and PRESET:

```
PSET [STEP](x, y)[, color]
PRESET [STEP](x, y)[, color]
```

These statements paint the point (*x*, *y*) using the attribute number *color*. When STEP is used, these statements use relative coordinates; otherwise, they use absolute coordinates. If the *color* argument is omitted, PSET uses the foreground color, and PRESET uses the background color.

Point plotting lets you draw curves of many sorts. Listing 12-19, for example, uses SIN and PSET to draw a sine curve, first in white (the default foreground color) and then in several colors by using the *color* argument. When the program uses PRESET to draw the curve, no color value is given. PRESET therefore uses the default background color, in effect erasing the curve, whose points can no longer be distinguished from the surroundings.

```
' Drawing sine curves point by point
CONST pi = 3.14159
SCREEN 9
WINDOW (-2 * pi, -1)-(2 * pi, 1)
I% = 0
FOR X! = -2 * pi TO 2 * pi STEP pi / 100
    PSET (X!, SIN(X!))              ' Plot point using foreground color
    I% = I% + 1
NEXT X!
```

Listing 12-19. *(continued)*

Listing 12-19. *continued*

```
LOCATE 24, 1
PRINT "Press any key to continue";
DO
LOOP UNTIL INKEY$ <> ""
FOR X! = -2 * pi TO 2 * pi STEP pi / 100
    Colr% = (I% / 20) MOD 7 + 9
    PSET (X!, SIN(X!)), Colr%        ' Plot point using Colr%
    I% = I% + 1
NEXT X!

DO
LOOP UNTIL INKEY$ <> ""
FOR X! = -2 * pi TO 2 * pi STEP pi / 100
    PRESET (X!, SIN(X!))             ' Plot point using background color
    I% = I% + 1
NEXT X!

DO
LOOP UNTIL INKEY$ <> ""
SCREEN 0
END
```

A Brief Fractal Excursion

Point-by-point plotting is essential for many applications. Perhaps you've seen some of the colorful plots produced by the mathematics of fractals and of chaos. (See, for example, James Gleick's book *Chaos: Making a New Science* [New York: Viking, 1987].) Listing 12-20 presents an interesting example, based on the following algorithm for selecting points:

1. Select coordinates for the three corners (vertices) of a triangle.
2. Pick a nearby point at random.
3. Select a vertex at random, and draw a point halfway between the first point and the vertex.
4. Select another vertex at random, and draw a point halfway between that vertex and the last point drawn.
5. Continue selecting and drawing points in this random manner.

You might expect to generate a random pattern of points; instead, you get a pretty pattern, as shown in Figure 12-22.

```
' Generating a fractal pattern using PSET
DECLARE SUB Twinkle (PA&())
' x, y coordinates for three vertices of a triangle
DATA 0, 1, .9, -.9, -.9, -.9
TYPE PlotPoint
    X AS SINGLE
    Y AS SINGLE
END TYPE
DIM Tri(1 TO 3) AS PlotPoint
FOR I% = 1 TO 3
    READ Tri(I%).X, Tri(I%).Y          ' Three vertices of triangle
NEXT I%
DIM PalArray&(0 TO 15)
FOR I% = 0 TO 7                        ' Set array to default palette
    PalArray&(I%) = I%
    PalArray&(I% + 8) = 56 + I%
NEXT I%
PalArray&(6) = 20                      ' Default value
PalArray&(0) = 8                       ' Background value is dark blue
SCREEN 9
PALETTE USING PalArray&(0)
COLOR 14
WINDOW (-1, -1)-(1, 1)
RANDOMIZE TIMER

FOR I% = 1 TO 3                        ' Draw vertices
    PSET (Tri(I%).X, Tri(I%).Y)
NEXT I%

Px! = 3 * RND - 1.5                    ' Pick x point at random
Py! = 3 * RND - 1.5                    ' Pick y point at random

FOR J% = 1 TO 15000
    PSET (Px!, Py!), J% MOD 15 + 1     ' Draw point
    Vertex% = INT(3 * RND) + 1         ' Pick vertex
    Px! = (Tri(Vertex%).X - Px!) / 2   ' Find new point halfway
    Py! = (Tri(Vertex%).Y - Py!) / 2   '  between old point and vertex
NEXT J%

DO
    CALL Twinkle(PalArray&())
LOOP UNTIL INKEY$ <> ""
END

SUB Twinkle (PA&())
    FOR I% = 1 TO 15
        PA&(I%) = PA&((I% MOD 15) + 1)
    NEXT I%
    PALETTE USING PA&(0)               ' Set palette to new values
END SUB
```

Listing 12-20.

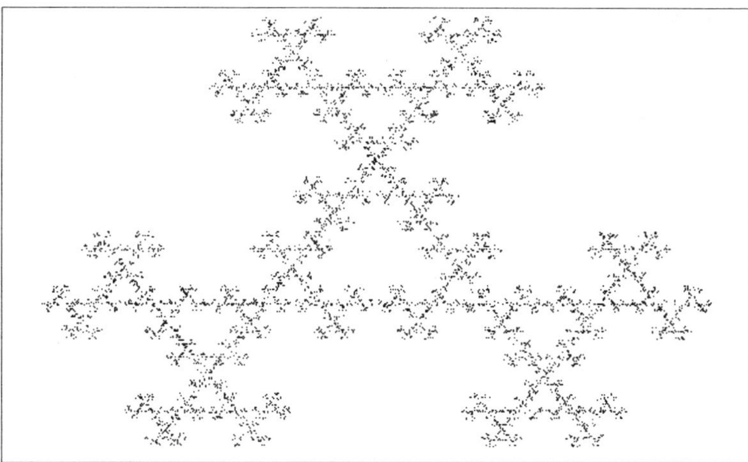

Figure 12-22.
Output of Listing 12-20.

This program illustrates a characteristic fractal property: When you magnify a small part of a fractal, it looks the same as it did on the previous scale. You can check this by, for example, increasing the window from (–0.10, 0.20) to (0.10, 0.40). (You must also increase the number of repetitions.)

You can also use fractions other than one-half to generate the new points. If you divide by 1.1 instead of 2, for instance, the points are spread quite randomly. But as you use divisors closer to 2, the pattern appears more and more organized.

Painting Patterns

The PAINT statement, which we introduced earlier, lets you paint with patterns as well as with solid colors. Painting with patterns—or *tiling*—requires a string rather than a color attribute number in the argument list.

Here is the complete syntax for PAINT:

```
PAINT [STEP](x, y)[, [paint][, [border][, background]]]
```

The coordinates (*x*, *y*) specify where painting is to begin. If the STEP modifier is used, the coordinates are relative to the last point referenced; otherwise, they are absolute coordinates.

If *paint* is a numeric expression, it is interpreted as the attribute number for the color used to paint the area. If *paint* is a string, it is interpreted as a description of the pattern used for painting.

border is the attribute number of the border of the painted area. The PAINT statement terminates painting on a line when it encounters a pixel of the border color. If *border* is omitted, the *paint* argument is used to define the border color.

background is a string used when *paint* is a tiling string. The *background* string describes a *background tile slice* that PAINT can skip when tiling an area. The default value is *CHR$(0)*.

Creating a Pattern

Creating a tiling pattern for PAINT is similar to creating a line style for LINE, although tiling is more complex. A tile pattern is two-dimensional rather than one-dimensional. A tile pattern also specifies the color attribute for each pixel, whereas a line style merely specifies whether a pixel is on or off.

The algorithm for defining a tile pattern depends on the mode chosen and its particular attribute ranges. We'll describe tiling for mode 9, in which you must be able to assign an attribute value in the range 0 through 15 to each pixel in the pattern. You could simply define a two-dimensional array of integers, with each element representing a pixel. But this approach wastes memory—only 4 bits are required to store a number in the range 0 through 15, leaving the other 12 bits of an integer empty. Instead, QuickBASIC uses a string. Because each character in a string is 8 bits long, it can hold information for 2 pixels.

As you did for line styles, you'll need to draw a pattern and translate it to a binary number. Each 4-bit group in the binary number is converted to a hexadecimal digit, and each pair of hexadecimal digits is combined into a two-digit ASCII code. Then the corresponding ASCII characters are strung together to form the paint string that describes the pattern. With this approach, all the information describing the pattern is packed into a string with no wasted memory.

In mode 9, the first 4 characters of the string describe the first line of 8 pixels in the pattern, the next 4 characters describe the next line, and so on. The entire string can be as long as 64 characters. With 4 characters per line of pixels, the tiling pattern can be as large as 8 pixels wide and 16 pixels high. The width is constant, but the height depends on the number of characters in the string.

Let's start by creating a tile pattern that, when repeated, produces a brick pattern. First draw an 8 × 8 grid and indicate the proposed colors and attribute numbers for each pixel in the pattern (Figure 12-23).

Next you must generate the binary code corresponding to the top row of the pattern. The method reflects the EGA hardware design for storing attributes. With 16 attributes, you can think of the 4 bits of memory it takes for each pixel as being numbered 0 through 3. The EGA represents the graphics screen with four *bit planes.* Each bit for a pixel attribute value is stored in a separate bit plane. Bit plane 0 stores the bit 0 value for all the pixels, bit plane 1 stores the bit 1 values, and so on. If a pixel is set to attribute 8 (binary 1000), the corresponding bit in bit plane 3 is set to 1, and the corresponding bits in planes 2, 1, and 0 are set to 0, as illustrated in Figure 12-24.

grey 8	grey 8	grey 8	grey 8	grey 8	grey 8	grey 8	grey 8
grey 8	red 4	red 4	red 4	red 4	red 4	red 4	red 4
grey 8	red 4	red 4	red 4	red 4	red 4	red 4	red 4
grey 8	red 4	red 4	red 4	red 4	red 4	red 4	red 4
grey 8	grey 8	grey 8	grey 8	grey 8	grey 8	grey 8	grey 8
red 4	red 4	red 4	red 4	grey 8	red 4	red 4	red 4
red 4	red 4	red 4	red 4	grey 8	red 4	red 4	red 4
red 4	red 4	red 4	red 4	grey 8	red 4	red 4	red 4

Figure 12-23.
The brick pattern.

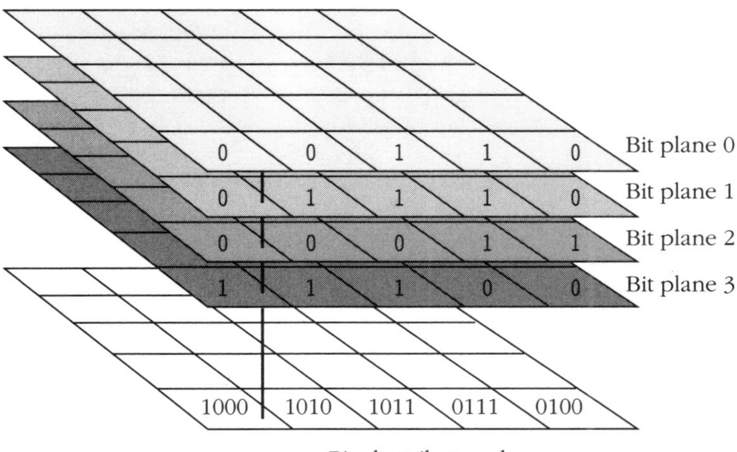

Figure 12-24.
Pixels and bit planes.

The QuickBASIC representation for tile patterns is based on this bit plane representation. To represent the top row of the pattern, draw a grid with four rows of eight cells (Figure 12-25). Each column represents one pixel from the row, and each row represents one bit plane. Write the eight binary numbers representing the color under the corresponding columns, and then copy each number into the column above it, with the first bit going into the bottom row, the next bit into the next row, and so on. For our pattern, the binary value for grey is 1000.

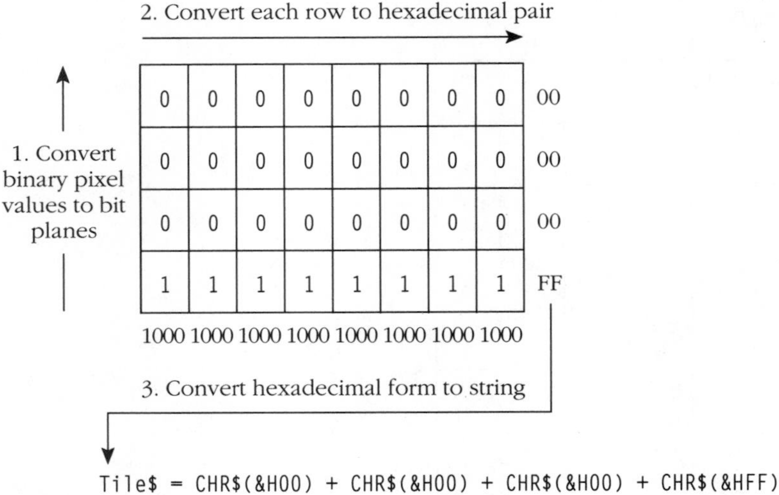

Figure 12-25.
Converting pixel values to hexadecimal form and then to a string.

Next convert each row to two hexadecimal digits by dividing the 8 bits into two groups of 4 and converting each group to the corresponding hexadecimal digits. For our example, the top three rows are 00 in hex, and the bottom row is FF. Finally, use CHR$ and string addition to form the string that represents the pixel pattern. If you call the string *Tile$*, the example of all grey pixels produces the following string, which represents the top row in the brick pattern in Figure 12-23:

```
TILE$ = CHR$(&H00) + CHR$(&H00) + CHR$(&H00) + CHR$(&HFF)
```

The next step is to find the four characters representing the second row of the brick pattern. These are added to the end of *Tile$*, as are the codes for subsequent rows. The process moves along quickly, despite its complexity.

Listing 12-21 presents the complete string information for the brick pattern and uses the pattern to paint a brick wall. The *RowGrey$* string represents the all-grey row. The *RowGreyRed$* string is the code for a row with one grey pixel followed by seven red pixels. The *RowRedGreyRed$* string represents a row with four red, one grey, and three red pixels. Because several of the rows are repeated, you can use these strings more than once to construct the *Tile$* string.

The program begins by painting the entire screen blue and then drawing and painting a yellow sun. When you press a key, the program draws a brown wall and a boundary around it. (The new drawing covers up the old.) When you press another key, the program tiles the wall using the brick pattern. Note that the final argument to PAINT is 0, the attribute used to draw a boundary around the wall. This information tells the program where to stop tiling. If it is omitted, the entire screen is tiled.

```
' Laying bricks with PAINT tiling
' Press a key to advance program
' Define the strings that are used for the row patterns
RowGrey$ = CHR$(0) + CHR$(0) + CHR$(0) + CHR$(&HFF)
RowGreyRed$ = CHR$(0) + CHR$(0) + CHR$(&H7F) + CHR$(&H80)
RowRedGreyRed$ = CHR$(0) + CHR$(0) + CHR$(&HF7) + CHR$(&H8)
Tile$ = RowGrey$ + RowGreyRed$ + RowGreyRed$ + RowGreyRed$
Tile$ = Tile$ + RowGrey$
Tile$ = Tile$ + RowRedGreyRed$ + RowRedGreyRed$ + RowRedGreyRed$
SCREEN 9
WINDOW (-100, -100)-(100, 100)
PALETTE 0, 1
PAINT (0, 0), 9                       ' Paint in the sky
CIRCLE (0, 20), 20, 14                ' Draw the sun
PAINT (0, 20), 14, 14                 ' Paint the sun
LOCATE 1, 30
PRINT "Press any key to continue";
DO
LOOP UNTIL INKEY$ <> ""
LINE (-100, 20)-(100, -100), 6, BF    ' Establish the wall
LINE (-100, 20)-(100, -100), 0, B     ' Draw boundary around wall
DO
LOOP UNTIL INKEY$ <> ""
PAINT (0, 0), Tile$, 0                ' Tile to boundary
DO
LOOP UNTIL INKEY$ <> ""
SCREEN 0
END
```

Listing 12-21.

Stopping the Tiling

The algorithm for tiling stops if it encounters the boundary color or if it encounters a line of pixels matching its own pattern. For instance, brick tiling stops when it encounters more brick tiling or part of the tiling pattern or when it runs into a horizontal grey line (that matches one of the tile lines).

The optional *background* argument can allow you to override the second barrier, depending on the complexity of the tile pattern. This argument can specify as many as two lines that can be skipped. In our example, an argument *RowGrey$* could be used to let tiling pass over a barrier of grey. Listing 12-22 modifies Listing 12-21 to create a grey wall. When the program attempts to paint the wall with the brick pattern, it succeeds only in painting a single row of bricks because the grey wall is equivalent to the *RowGrey$* pattern. When you press a key, the program tries again, this time using the *background* argument, and paints the whole wall. Note, however, that the program must paint twice, once starting below the layer of brick and once starting above, because PAINT won't cross the existing brick pattern.

```
' This program crosses boundaries with tiling
' Define the strings for the row patterns
RowGrey$ = CHR$(0) + CHR$(0) + CHR$(0) + CHR$(&HFF)
RowGreyRed$ = CHR$(0) + CHR$(0) + CHR$(&H7F) + CHR$(&H80)
RowRedGreyRed$ = CHR$(0) + CHR$(0) + CHR$(&HF7) + CHR$(&H8)
Tile$ = RowGrey$ + RowGreyRed$ + RowGreyRed$ + RowGreyRed$
Tile$ = Tile$ + RowGrey$
Tile$ = Tile$ + RowRedGreyRed$ + RowRedGreyRed$ + RowRedGreyRed$
SCREEN 9
WINDOW (-100, -100)-(100, 100)
PALETTE 0, 1
PAINT (0, 0), 9
CIRCLE (0, 20), 20, 14
PAINT (0, 20), 14, 14
LOCATE 1, 30
PRINT "Press any key to continue";
DO
LOOP UNTIL INKEY$ <> ""
LINE (-100, 20)-(100, -100), 8, BF  ' Grey wall
LINE (-100, 20)-(100, -100), 0, B   ' Draw boundary
DO
LOOP UNTIL INKEY$ <> ""
PAINT (0, 0), Tile$, 0              ' Tile to grey boundary
DO
LOOP UNTIL INKEY$ <> ""
PAINT (0, -5), Tile$, 0, RowGrey$   ' Tile with background argument
PAINT (0, 10), Tile$, 0, RowGrey$
DO
LOOP UNTIL INKEY$ <> ""
SCREEN 0
END
```

Listing 12-22.

The DRAW Statement

The DRAW statement is used primarily for drawing lines, although it also lets you paint (but not tile) enclosed areas. DRAW takes a string as an argument, which consists of a series of DRAW "language" instructions. *U50*, for instance, means draw a line 50 units upward, and *R100* means draw a line 100 units to the right. The following statement draws a rectangle:

```
DRAW "U60 R80 D60 L80"
```

As you might expect, *D60* means draw a line downward 60 units, and *L80* means draw a line 80 units to the left.

DRAW starts with the graphics cursor at the center of the screen. The direction considered "up" is, initially, straight upward. The A and TA arguments can alter this direction, however, providing a convenient way to change the orientation of a figure when it is redrawn. For instance, the following statement turns the orientation 30 degrees, defining "up" as 30 degrees to the left of the vertical:

```
DRAW "TA 30 U60 R80 D60 L80"
```

This has the effect of rotating the rectangle 30 degrees.

Here is the syntax for DRAW:

```
DRAW stringexpression
```

stringexpression consists of one or more DRAW commands (*macros*) that describe the graphics actions to be taken. These macros, summarized in Figure 12-26, can be grouped into movement commands, modifier commands, and a substring command.

For movement macros, physical coordinates are used for movement unless a V modifier command is used. By default, moving the graphics cursor draws a line. If the *n* parameter is omitted, the value 1 is used. The prefixes B (move without drawing) and N (return to starting point after completing movement) are optional for each movement macro.

Movement Macro	***Description***
U[*n*]	Moves up *n* units.
D[*n*]	Moves down *n* units.
L[*n*]	Moves left *n* units.
R[*n*]	Moves right *n* units.
E[*n*]	Moves diagonally up *n* units and right *n* units.
F[*n*]	Moves diagonally down *n* units and right *n* units.
G[*n*]	Moves diagonally down *n* units and left *n* units.
H[*n*]	Moves diagonally up *n* units and left *n* units.
M *x*, *y*	Moves to location (*x*, *y*). If *x* is preceded by a plus or a minus sign, movement is relative to the LPR. Otherwise, movement is to the point with absolute coordinates (*x*, *y*).

Figure 12-26. *(continued)*
Macros used with the DRAW statement.

Figure 12-26. *continued*

Modifier Macro	***Description***
A *n*	Sets the angle used as "up" by the movement macros. The parameter *n* can have values 0 through 3. A value of 0 defines up as 0 degrees from the vertical. Values of 1, 2, and 3 denote angles of 90, 180, and 270 degrees counterclockwise from the vertical. Figures rotated 90 or 270 degrees have the size scale adjusted to match the standard aspect ratio.
TA *n*	Sets the angle used as "up" by the movement macros. The parameter *n* is an angle in the range –360 through 360 degrees. Rotation is counterclockwise for positive angles. Unlike the A macro, TA doesn't adjust the scale as the angle changes.
C *n*	Sets the color to attribute number *n*.
S *n*	Sets the scale factor to *n*, an integer in the range 1 through 255. The scale factor is multiplied by the distances in the movement macros to yield the actual distance moved. This macro lets you rescale drawings.
P *paint,border*	Paints using attribute number *paint* up to border of attribute color *border*.
V	Uses logical rather than physical coordinates.

Substring Macro	***Description***
X + VARPTR$(*stringvariable*)	Executes the command described by the value of *stringvariable*.

The following program lets you experiment with DRAW commands. It uses a text viewport at the bottom of the screen to let you enter commands such as *C10 U50 R30* and see the result. Enter *Q* to quit.

```
SCREEN 9
VIEW PRINT 24 TO 25
LINE INPUT "Command: ", Cmd$
DO UNTIL UCASE$(Cmd$) = "Q"
    DRAW Cmd$
    LINE INPUT "Command: ", Cmd$
LOOP
END
```

If you want a more foolproof program, you can use INKEY$ or the SELECT CASE statement to associate particular commands with particular keys.

What about using variables as arguments? Suppose you store the distance traveled in a variable because the program needs to calculate it, as in the following example:

```
Up% = INT(30 * LOG (D%))
```

The STR$ function lets you convert the number to a string that DRAW can use:

```
DRAW "U" + STR$(Up%)
```

You can even do the following:

```
DRAW "U" + STR$(INT(30 * LOG (D%)))
```

Alternatively, you could use the VARPTR$ function. It takes a variable as an argument and returns the address of the variable. This approach also requires putting an equal sign after the macro letter, as shown here:

```
DRAW "U=" + VARPTR$(Up%)
```

The argument in this case must be a variable. You can't use a longer expression, as we did with STR$.

If you are familiar with the DRAW statement from using BASICA, you should note some differences. BASICA allows the following two forms:

```
DRAW "TA = Angle%"      ' OK in BASICA, not in QuickBASIC
DRAW "X String$"        ' OK in BASICA, not in QuickBASIC
```

In QuickBASIC, use the following statements instead:

```
DRAW "TA=" + VARPTR$(Angle%)    ' Equal sign
DRAW "X" + VARPTR$(String$)     ' No equal sign
```

Paging

The memory in the video card (or the built-in controller, for PS/2 systems) holds the information describing the screen. Statements such as CIRCLE and PAINT change the video memory contents, and the video controller then sets the display according to the stored information. In some cases, video memory is large enough to hold more than one screen's worth of data, allowing memory to be divided into separate pages, each large enough to describe one complete screen display.

QuickBASIC lets you use multiple pages, a handy feature for changing the screen quickly and for animation. With SCREEN, you can, for example, designate one page as the *display page* and another as the *active page*. The display page appears on the screen, but graphics commands such as CIRCLE and LINE are executed on the invisible active page.

The number of pages available depends on the amount of video memory available and on the mode. Mode 1 has one page, for instance, whereas EGA mode 9 (16 colors) has one page per 128 KB of video memory. (EGA cards come with 64 KB, 128 KB, or 256 KB; VGA cards come with 256 or 512 KB.) Our examples assume that you have at least two pages of memory.

So far, our programs have set both the display page and the active page to page 0 (the default setting), which has allowed you to watch the graphics commands as they are executed. But it is also common to display one page while working on another. When the program finishes working on the active page, that page becomes the display page, showing the final product. Meanwhile, the former display page becomes the active page, and the program prepares the next image there.

When you use four arguments with SCREEN, the third argument is the active page number, and the fourth argument is the display page number. Numbering starts with page 0, the default value for these two variables. For instance, the following statement sets the mode to 9 and makes page 1 the active page while page 0 is displayed:

```
SCREEN 9, , 1, 0
```

Listing 12-23 shows a common use for paging: setting the two pages, drawing something, and then swapping page settings. We use DRAW to create a multicolored spiral pattern on the active screen. When the pattern is completed, the program displays it while drawing the same pattern rotated 10 degrees in the new active window. This continues until you press a key. Because you see only the rotated finished products and not the drawing process, you get the visual impression of a rotating pattern.

```
' This program demonstrates animation by paging. While
'  one page shows the finished image, the concealed page is
'  used to construct the next image.
DIM Col%(1 TO 4)                     ' Colors to be used
Col%(1) = 9                          ' Light blue
Col%(2) = 10                         ' Light green
Col%(3) = 12                         ' Light red
Col%(4) = 14                         ' Yellow
PageA% = 1
PageV% = 0
Angle% = 360
SCREEN 9
WINDOW (-1, -1)-(1, 1)
CIRCLE (0, 0), .6, 14
PAINT (0, 0), 12, 14
LOCATE 13, 25
PRINT " Working on a pretty spiral...";
DO
    SCREEN 9, , PageA%, PageV%       ' Active and visual pages different
    CLS 1
    CI% = 1
    Clr% = Clr% MOD 7 + 1            ' Message color
    COLOR Clr%
    LOCATE 24, 1
    PRINT "Press any key to halt";
```

Listing 12-23. *(continued)*

Listing 12-23. *continued*

```
    FOR D% = 1 TO 360 STEP 6          ' Draw spiral to active page
        Ang% = D% - Angle%
        Cmd$ = "TA" + STR$(Ang%) + "NU"
        Cmd$ = Cmd$ + STR$(INT(30 * LOG(D%)))
        Cmd$ = Cmd$ + "C" + STR$(Col%(CI%))
        DRAW Cmd$
        CI% = CI% MOD 4 + 1
        IF INKEY$ <> "" THEN EXIT DO
    NEXT D%
    IF Angle% > 10 THEN
        Angle% = Angle% - 10
    ELSE
        Angle% = 360
    END IF
    SWAP PageA%, PageV%               ' Switch active and visual pages
LOOP UNTIL INKEY$ <> ""
SCREEN 0
END
```

Animation: The GET and PUT Statements

QuickBASIC supports animation—programming moving images—both with paging and with the GET and PUT graphics statements. The GET statement lets you copy a specified rectangle from the screen to an array in memory, and the PUT statement lets you copy the saved image to a specified location on screen. PUT also offers several ways to combine the copied image with its background.

These names might seem familiar to you, for QuickBASIC also uses GET and PUT statements to read from and write to files (Chapter 11). QuickBASIC distinguishes the various GET and PUT statements by their syntax.

The graphics GET statement has the following syntax:

```
GET [STEP](x1, y1)-[STEP](x2, y2), arrayname[(index)]
```

The GET statement copies to memory the rectangle whose diagonally opposite corners are the coordinates (*x1*, *y1*) and (*x2*, *y2*). If a coordinate pair is prefaced with STEP, the coordinates are relative to the last point referenced; otherwise, the coordinates are absolute.

arrayname is the name of the array into which the image is copied. By default, storage starts at the beginning of the array, but you can use *index* to indicate a different starting point in the array. For example, an argument of *StoreIt%(400)* starts storage at subscript 400 in the array, and an argument of *Picture%(50, 100)* starts at element 50, 100 of a two-dimensional array.

The array must be large enough to hold the entire rectangle. The size of the array depends on the size of the rectangle and on the mode. Here's the formula for calculating the minimum size, in bytes:

$$4 + \text{INT}((x2-x1+1) \times (Bpppp + 7)/8) \times planes \times (y2-y1 + 1)$$

The coordinates in this formula are physical, not logical, coordinates. *planes* is the number of planes, and *Bpppp* is the number of bits per pixel per plane. Figure 12-27 lists the values of *planes* and *Bpppp* for various modes.

Mode	Bpppp	Planes	Mode	Bpppp	Planes
1	2	1	9 (>64KB)	1	4
2	1	1	10	1	2
7	1	4	11	1	1
8	1	4	12	1	4
9 (64KB)	1	2	13	8	1

Figure 12-27.
Bits per pixel per plane and number of planes.

The array can be of any numeric type, although an integer array is usually the simplest. An integer type contains 2 bytes per element, a long integer type 4 bytes per element, a single-precision type 4 bytes, and a double-precision type 8 bytes. For example, if an image requires 124 bytes, you can store it in an integer array of 62 elements.

Physical coordinates are needed to calculate the amount of memory because they have a one-to-one correspondence to pixels. For instance, a rectangle 10 units high and 20 units wide, measured in physical coordinates, contains 10 × 20, or 200, pixels; this isn't necessarily true when logical coordinates are used. You can use GET with logical coordinates, however—simply use PMAP to convert the logical coordinates describing the rectangle to physical coordinates.

After you've copied an image to memory, you can use PUT to copy the image back to the screen.

Here is the syntax for the graphics PUT statement:

```
PUT [STEP](x, y), arrayname[(index)][, actionverb]
```

The PUT statement copies the image stored in the array *arrayname* to the screen. The coordinates (*x*, *y*) mark the upper left corner of the image's location. The subscripts (*index*), if any, indicate the array element from which copying begins; by default, copying starts at the beginning of the array.

actionverb specifies how the image interacts with its background; XOR is the default. The following list summarizes the choices for this argument:

Action Verb	*Description*
PSET	Copies the image as stored, replacing the underlying background.
PRESET	Copies the image as stored, replacing the underlying background. The colors of the image are reversed from the original. To determine the reversed color, write the attribute number as a binary number, and change each 1 to 0 and each 0 to 1. For instance, green is 2, or 0010; the reverse is 1101, or 13, light magenta.
AND	Determines the color of each pixel by applying the logical AND operator to the image color and to the existing screen color. Write each color in binary form and compare corresponding bits. The corresponding bit for the resulting color is 1 only if both contributing bits are 1. For instance, if the image is brown (0110) and the screen is magenta (0101), the resulting color is 0100 (red).
OR	Determines the color of each pixel by applying the logical OR operator to the image color and to the existing screen color. Write each color in binary form and compare corresponding bits. The corresponding bit for the resulting color is 1 if either contributing bit is 1 or if both are 1. For instance, if the image is brown (0110) and the screen is magenta (0101), the resulting color is 0111 (white).
XOR	Determines the color of each pixel by applying the logical XOR operator to the image color and to the existing screen color. Write each color in binary form and compare corresponding bits. The corresponding bit for the resulting color is 1 if either contributing bit is 1 but not if both are 1. For instance, if the image is brown (0110) and the screen is magenta (0101), the resulting color is 0011 (cyan).

Although other QuickBASIC drawing statements such as LINE and CIRCLE truncate, or clip, any part of the drawing outside the current graphics viewport, the PUT statement does not do this. If you attempt to place even part of an image outside the current graphics viewport, you'll get a runtime error message.

Action Verbs in Action

Listing 12-24 provides a visual display of how the action verbs work. The program creates and stores the image of a magenta circle in a red box, saves the image with GET, and copies the image to the screen using each of the action verbs. The program uses each verb twice: once to copy the image onto a background of horizontal stripes, and once to copy the image onto a blank background.

With the action verbs PSET and PRESET, the image simply clobbers (completely covers) whatever is underneath it. With PRESET, the color reversal turns red (0100) to light cyan (1011), and magenta (0101) to light green (1010).

When AND is used, magenta superimposes on each horizontal bar. Magenta (0101) and blue (0001) produce blue; magenta and red (0100) produce red; magenta and green (0010) produce black (0000), which is also the default background color. Note that the image is invisible on a blank background because using AND to compare 0 (the binary code for the background) and any bit value yields 0.

```
' This program uses the graphics GET and PUT statements
'  to copy an image over different backgrounds to illustrate
'  how PUT's action verbs work
' Create a barred backdrop tiling pattern
RowBlue$ = CHR$(&HFF) + CHR$(0) + CHR$(0) + CHR$(0)
RowRed$ = CHR$(0) + CHR$(0) + CHR$(&HFF) + CHR$(0)
RowGreen$ = CHR$(0) + CHR$(&HFF) + CHR$(0) + CHR$(0)
Tile2$ = RowBlue$ + RowBlue$ + RowBlue$ + RowBlue$ + RowBlue$
Tile2$ = Tile2$ + RowBlue$ + RowRed$ + RowRed$ + RowRed$
Tile2$ = Tile2$ + RowRed$ + RowRed$ + RowRed$ + RowGreen$
Tile2$ = Tile2$ + RowGreen$ + RowGreen$ + RowGreen$ + RowGreen$
' Set the image size
X1% = 290
X2% = 350
Xc% = (X1% + X2%) / 2
Y1% = 10
Y2% = 60
Yc% = (Y1% + Y2%) / 2
' Calculate the storage requirements using an integer array
Bytes% = 4 + INT(((X2% - X1% + 1) + 7) / 8) * 4 * (Y2% - Y1% + 1)
REDIM Store%(1 TO Bytes% / 2)
SCREEN 9
' Construct the initial image
LINE (X1%, Y1%)-(X2%, Y2%), 2, B
PAINT (Xc%, Yc%), 4, 2
CIRCLE (Xc%, Yc%), 24, 15, , , 1     ' Aspect ratio equals 1
PAINT (Xc%, Yc%), 5, 15
' Make the barred backdrop
LINE (40, 80)-(600, 182), 11, B
PAINT (320, 81), Tile2$, 11
' Save the image
GET (X1%, Y1%)-(X2%, Y2%), Store%(1)
' Copy stored image onto backdrop and onto blank background
FOR I% = 0 TO 1
PUT (65, 100 + 100 * I%), Store%(1)
PUT STEP(90, 0), Store%(1), PSET
PUT STEP(90, 0), Store%(1), PRESET
    PUT STEP(90, 0), Store%(1), AND
    PUT STEP(90, 0), Store%(1), OR
    PUT STEP(90, 0), Store%(1), XOR
NEXT I%
LOCATE 21, 9
PRINT "Default"; SPC(6); "PSET"; SPC(6); "PRESET"; SPC(7);
PRINT "AND"; SPC(9); "OR"; SPC(9); "XOR"
DO
LOOP UNTIL INKEY$ <> ""
SCREEN 0
END
```

Listing 12-24.

An XOR image, however, is visible against any background. When XOR is used, the resulting color always differs from both the image color and the underlying color unless either of those colors is black.

Simple Animation

If you use XOR first to put an image on screen and then to overlay it with the same image, the new image exactly cancels the old one, restoring the original background. In effect, it lets you erase an image without affecting the background.

The program in Listing 12-25 illustrates this property by appearing to move an image across the screen.

```
' Using GET and PUT to animate a moving square
' Define brick wall tiling patterns
RowGrey$ = CHR$(0) + CHR$(0) + CHR$(0) + CHR$(&HFF)
RowGreyRed$ = CHR$(0) + CHR$(0) + CHR$(&H7F) + CHR$(&H80)
RowRedGreyRed$ = CHR$(0) + CHR$(0) + CHR$(&HF7) + CHR$(&H8)
Tile1$ = RowGrey$ + RowGreyRed$ + RowGreyRed$ + RowGreyRed$
Tile1$ = Tile1$ + RowGrey$ + RowRedGreyRed$
Tile1$ = Tile1$ + RowRedGreyRed$ + RowRedGreyRed$
X1% = 20                                    ' Set image size
X2% = 80
Xc% = (X1% + X2%) / 2
Y1% = 50
Y2% = 100
Yc% = (Y1% + Y2%) / 2
Bytes% = 4 + INT(((X2% - X1% + 1) + 7) / 8) * 4 * (Y2% - Y1% + 1)
REDIM Store%(1 TO Bytes%)                   ' Create storage array
SCREEN 9
LINE (X1%, Y1%)-(X2%, Y2%), 2, B            ' Create moving square
PAINT (Xc%, Yc%), Tile1$, 2
CIRCLE (Xc%, Yc%), 24, 15, , , 1
PAINT (Xc%, Yc%), "Santa Claus ", 15        ' Use string to tile
GET (X1%, Y1%)-(X2%, Y2%), Store%(1)        ' Store square image
LINE (130, 0)-(289, 200), 2, BF             ' Create varied backgrounds
LINE (290, 0)-(449, 200), 2, B
PAINT (321, 1), Tile1$, 2
LINE (450, 0)-(609, 200), 2, B
PAINT (481, 1), "STEPHEN W. PRATA", 2       ' Prove author repeats himself
DO
    FOR I% = 0 TO 420 STEP 80
        SLEEP 1
        PUT (X1% + I%, Y1%), Store%(1), XOR
        PUT STEP(80, 0), Store%(1), XOR
        IF INKEY$ <> "" THEN EXIT DO
```

Listing 12-25. *(continued)*

Listing 12-25. *continued*

```
    NEXT I%
    SLEEP 1
    PUT STEP(0, 0), Store%(1), XOR
    PUT (X1%, Y1%), Store%(1), XOR
LOOP UNTIL INKEY$ <> ""
DO
LOOP UNTIL INKEY$ <> ""
SCREEN 0
END
```

Here is the key section of the code:

```
FOR I% = 0 TO 420 STEP 80
    SLEEP 1
    PUT (X1% + I%, Y1%), Store%(1), XOR
    PUT STEP(80, 0), Store%(1), XOR
    IF INKEY$ <> "" THEN EXIT DO
NEXT I%
```

XOR is used to place an image atop a previous version of the same image, canceling it. It then puts another copy of the image 80 units to the right, making the image appear to move across the screen. Because the SLEEP 1 command causes the computer to pause for 1 second, each move takes 1 second. Note that the image stays visible, though altered in appearance, as it moves across the backgrounds.

Review Questions

1. How do you produce inverse video in text mode?
2. How do the text background and the graphics background differ?
3. How can you use INKEY$ to tell if an arrow key or a function key has been pressed?
4. What is the difference between a color number and an attribute number?
5. If EGA systems recognize 64 colors, why do they display only 16 at a time?
6. In mode 9, what would the following statements produce?

```
CIRCLE (100, 100), 20, 4
PAINT STEP(0, 0), 1,4
PAINT (0, 0), 2, 4
```

7. How do physical coordinates and logical coordinates differ?
8. What is the difference between VIEW and WINDOW?

9. What will the program in Listing 12-Q9 do?

```
SCREEN 9
WINDOW (-100, -100)-(100, 100)
Dx% = 10
Dy% = 10
LINE (0, 0)-STEP(Dx%, 0)
FOR I% = 1 TO 30
    LINE -STEP(0, Dy%)
    Dx% = -1.1 * Dx%
    Dy% = -1.1 * Dy%
    LINE -STEP(Dx%, 0)
NEXT I%
DO
LOOP UNTIL INKEY$ <> ""
SCREEN 0
END
```

Listing 12-Q9.

10. The LINE statement uses either logical or physical coordinates, whichever are currently active. Is this true of VIEW?
11. Define a line style of 12 pixels on, 4 pixels off.
12. Suppose you've executed the following statements:

    ```
    SCREEN 9
    ' Using physical coordinates
    LINE (10, 10)-(310, 310), , B
    CIRCLE (160, 160), 150
    ```

    To which two sides of the box will the circle be tangent? How can you change the CIRCLE statement to make the resulting ellipse tangent to all four sides?
13. Create a tiling pattern matching the following description: The top two rows of the pattern consist of the pixel pattern magenta, magenta, yellow, yellow, yellow, yellow, magenta, magenta. The next two rows are the same, but with yellow and magenta reversed in position.
14. Find the tiling pattern your name makes as a string. Pad the name with spaces or punctuation if necessary to make its length a multiple of four characters.

13

Sound

BEEP	**PLAY**	**SOUND**
ON PLAY	**PLAY ON**	

You can incorporate sounds and music into your programs with the programming tools provided by QuickBASIC. QuickBASIC lets you use far more than a simple beep—it allows you to add sound play to backgrounds and to use musical sequences with various tempos, accents, and ranges to enhance your programs.

QuickBASIC's sound capabilities do have some limitations, reflecting the limitations of the IBM PC computer design. The PC was not developed as a game machine or a music machine. It has one small speaker, one tonal quality and volume level, a single voice, and little built-in programming support for sound. Although sound enhancement boards are available, the stock PC is not the way to go if you want to synthesize your voice or create a computerized musical accompaniment to a videotape. But if you simply want to make your programs livelier and more interesting, adding even a limited range of sounds or music can do the trick.

QuickBASIC has three sound-producing statements:

- The BEEP statement causes the speaker to beep. (It is equivalent to using the statement *PRINT CHR$(7)*, the ASCII control code for a bell or a beep.)
- The SOUND statement lets you select the frequency and duration of a sound.
- The PLAY statement can play a sequence of musical notes.

We'll focus on SOUND and PLAY in this chapter.

The SOUND Statement

The SOUND statement, as its name implies, generates sounds. You simply specify the frequency and duration, and SOUND plays the corresponding tone.

Here is the syntax for the SOUND statement:

```
SOUND frequency, duration
```

This statement sounds the speaker at a pitch of *frequency,* in hertz (Hz; cycles per second), for *duration* clock ticks. One second is approximately 18.2 clock ticks. *frequency* must be an expression that reduces to an integer in the range 37 through 32767. *duration* must be an expression that reduces to an integer in the range 0 through 65535. A duration of 0 turns off the sound currently being generated.

The following simple program uses the SOUND statement to play a note with a frequency of 300 Hz for 18 ticks (about 1 second):

```
' Use SOUND to play a 300-Hz tone
CLS
PRINT "Coming next..."
SOUND 300, 18                 ' 300 Hz for 18 ticks
PRINT "AURAL EXCELLENCE!"
END
```

Understanding the Properties of SOUND

Your computer's speaker is controlled not by the CPU but by programmable chips that set the frequency and turn the speaker on and off. The SOUND statement sends its instructions to these chips, and the QuickBASIC program continues with its next statement, without waiting for the sound to finish. (That's why the preceding program displays the second printed message while the sound is still playing.)

SOUND sends instructions for only one note at a time, however, and consecutive SOUND statements do wait for each previous sound to finish. Thus, you can't expect the default version of SOUND to play an entire tune while other actions take place on screen.

The timer chip that controls the speaker also keeps track of the system time. It is not the same as the CPU clock, which governs how fast the CPU executes instructions and which varies from system to system. All IBM PC and compatible systems use the same clock speed for the system time and the speaker. The clock speed used by SOUND, as we mentioned before, is about 18.2 ticks per second for these systems.

NOTE: *Frequent use of SOUND or PLAY can cause the computer to occasionally miss updating the system clock, making the system clock lose time.*

Average human hearing can detect sounds in the frequency range 20 through 20,000 Hz. Low-pitched sounds have low frequencies, and high-pitched sounds have high frequencies. The PC's sound output can be set to frequencies in the range 37 through 32,767 Hz, although the speaker cannot reproduce all those frequencies faithfully. If you play lower frequencies such as 50 Hz, the sound has more of a buzz than the bass sound you'd get from a large high-fidelity speaker playing the same frequency.

What can you do with SOUND? You can work with musical sounds, and you can make noise.

Making Music

The SOUND statement can produce a wide range of frequencies, but music—traditional tonal music, at least—uses only the frequencies that correspond to the keys on a piano. To play music, you need to know which frequencies correspond to musical notes. Musical scales are defined in several ways; Figure 13-1 lists frequencies for three octaves of a chromatic scale. We've numbered the octaves with the numbering scheme used by the PLAY statement.

Note	*Frequency for Octave 1*	*Frequency for Octave 2*	*Frequency for Octave 3*
C	130.81	261.63	523.25
C#	138.59	277.14	554.37
D	146.83	293.66	587.33
D#	155.56	311.13	622.25
E	164.81	329.63	659.26
F	174.61	349.23	698.46
F#	185.00	369.99	739.99
G	196.00	392.00	783.99
G#	207.65	415.30	830.61
A	220.00	**440.00**	880.00
A#	233.08	466.16	932.33
B	246.94	493.88	987.77

Figure 13-1.
Frequencies of musical notes (American Standard pitch).

As you can see, American Standard pitch sets the note A in the second octave to 440 Hz. The frequency of a note in one octave is roughly twice its frequency in the next lower octave. Adjacent notes differ by a factor of the 12th root of 2 (approximately 1.059463). For instance, A# is 440 times the 12th root of 2, and G# is 440 divided by the 12th root of 2.

To play a tune with SOUND, you don't need to enter frequencies for every note. Instead, you can store the frequencies in an array. In Listing 13-1 we store one octave and one additional note in an array, which allows the program to identify a note by its array subscript. We use a second array to store the subscripts for the notes to be played—the sequence *12 3,* for instance, plays the 12th note and then the 3rd note from the musical scale. A third array stores note durations. The result is a program that plays the first line of a familiar Christmas carol. (LBOUND and UBOUND in the FOR loop will make it easier for you to add more notes to the tune later.)

```
' QuickBASIC Christmas Card
' American Standard pitch, rounded to nearest integer
'     C    C#   D    D#   E    F    F#   G    G#   A    A#   B    C
DATA 262, 277, 294, 311, 330, 349, 370, 392, 415, 440, 466, 494, 523
'     C   B   A   G  F  E  D  C        First eight notes of tune
DATA 13, 12, 10, 8, 6, 5, 3, 1
DATA 12, 9, 3, 15, 6, 12, 12, 18: ' Length of first eight notes
DIM Notes%(1 TO 13)               ' Array stores notes
DIM Tune%(1 TO 8)                 ' Array stores tune to be played
DIM Timing%(1 TO 8)               ' Array stores duration of notes
FOR I% = 1 TO 13
    READ Notes%(I%)
NEXT I%
FOR I% = 1 TO 8
    READ Tune%(I%)
NEXT I%
FOR I% = 1 TO 8
    READ Timing%(I%)
NEXT I%

CLS
PRINT "Joy to the World!"
FOR I% = LBOUND(Tune%) TO UBOUND(Tune%)
    SOUND Notes%(Tune%(I%)), Timing%(I%)
NEXT I%
END
```

Listing 13-1.

Making Noise

Because SOUND can produce any frequency in its range—not only frequencies from the musical scale—you can use it to create many interesting, if nonmusical, effects. Listing 13-2 presents a few of these.

Try experimenting with SOUND to hear the various kinds of noise you can make. You might find a sound that could draw a user's attention to some feature or action in your other programs.

```
CLS
PRINT "Press any key to go on to next sound"
DO                                     ' Rising sound
    SOUND 400 + 3 * I%, 1
    I% = (I% + 1) MOD 300
LOOP UNTIL INKEY$ <> ""
DO                                     ' Buzz
    SOUND 50, 1
    SOUND 70, 1
LOOP UNTIL INKEY$ <> ""
DO                                     ' Noise
    SOUND 500, 1
    SOUND 700, 1
LOOP UNTIL INKEY$ <> ""
DO                                     ' Random sounds
    SOUND 300 + 200 * RND, 1 + RND
LOOP UNTIL INKEY$ <> ""
END
```

Listing 13-2.

The PLAY Statement

PLAY is a versatile statement with its own "language," much like the DRAW statement. PLAY is less powerful than SOUND in some ways and more powerful in others. It plays only frequencies from the musical scale. But it uses durations based on musical notation, offers two modes of operation, and recognizes a great variety of commands.

Here is the syntax for the PLAY statement:

```
PLAY commandstring
```

The PLAY statement follows the instructions, or macros, in the command string. These macros control the octave, the notes played, the duration of the notes, the tempo, and the mode of operation. Some of the macros accept a suffix, and one executes a substring. Figure 13-2 presents the complete list.

Octave Macro	***Action***
o *n*	Sets the current octave to octave *n*. The range for *n* is 0 through 6; the default octave is 4. Octaves start on the note C; the lowest C has a frequency of about 65 Hz.
>	Increases the current octave by 1. If the current octave is 6, it is not changed.
<	Decreases the current octave by 1. If the current octave is 0, it is not changed.

Figure 13-2. *(continued)*
Macros used with the PLAY statement.

Figure 13-2. *continued*

Tone Macro	***Action***
A–G [*n*]	Plays the musical note in the range A through G. Uses the plus sign or the pound sign as a suffix (as in F#) to indicate a sharp, and uses the minus sign (as in B–) to indicate a flat. The note is selected from the currently active octave. Notes can be followed by a number *n* to indicate duration. The range for *n* is 1 through 64; the value 1 is a whole note, 2 is a half note, 4 is a quarter note, and so on. If *n* is not used, the default value is 4 unless a different value has been set with L.
N *n*	Plays note number *n*. The range for *n* is 0 through 84; 0 is a rest, and 1 is the lowest note (C) in octave 0. Because each octave contains 12 notes, note 13 is the first note in the second octave.

Duration Macro	***Action***
L [*n*]	Sets the default note duration. The range for *n* is 1 through 64; 1 is a whole note, 2 is a half note, 4 is a quarter note, and so on. If L is not used, the default value is 4.
MN	Sets *music normal.* Each note plays for seven-eighths of its allotted time. This is the default setting.
ML	Sets *music legato.* Each note plays for its entire allotted time.
MS	Sets *music staccato.* Each note plays for three-fourths of its allotted time.

Tempo Macro	***Action***
P *n*	Pauses, or rests, for the duration *n*. The *n* parameter behaves as it does for the L macro and has the range 1 through 64.
T *n*	Sets the tempo (the rate of playing) to *n* quarter notes (L4) per minute. The range is 32 through 255, and the default value is 120.

Operation Macro	***Action***
MF	Sets both PLAY and SOUND to run in the foreground. Each subsequent PLAY or SOUND statement begins only when the previous note or sound has finished. This is the default mode.
MB	Sets both PLAY and SOUND to run in the background. Each note or sound is placed in a buffer, allowing the QuickBASIC program to continue executing while the sounds play. As many as 32 notes can be stored in the buffer at one time. This option is typically used with PLAY ON event trapping.

(continued)

Figure 13-2. *continued*

Suffix	***Action***
# or +	Follows a note (A through G), making it sharp.
–	Follows a note (A through G), making it flat.
.	Follows a note, changing its duration. A single dot extends a note's duration by 50 percent; a second dot extends the duration by 50 percent of the first dot (an additional 25 percent of the note's duration). Thus, the notes A4. and A4.. have durations 1.50 times and 1.75 times that of a regular quarter note. Dots can also be used with the L and the P macros.

Substring Macro	***Action***
"X" + VARPTR$(*string*)	Executes the macro commands in the string variable *string*.

Playing with PLAY

To see how the various macros work, let's look at—and listen to—some examples. Try entering each example in the Immediate window and listening to the results. We'll start by playing the notes E, C, and E:

```
PLAY "ECE"
```

The second note has a lower pitch than the other two—within a given octave, C is the lowest, or beginning, note.

In our first example, PLAY uses the default octave (4), the default note duration (4, or a quarter note), and the default tempo (120 quarter notes per minute). Now let's change the tempo and octave defaults:

```
PLAY "L8 T240 o2"
```

The preceding statement plays no notes. Instead, it makes notes eighth notes by default (L8), increases the tempo to 240 (T240), and changes the default octave to octave 2 (o2). (Note that spaces in the settings are optional.) These settings will hold until we change them. Now repeat the original statement:

```
PLAY "ECE"
```

This time the sounds are lower in pitch and faster. Next let's set the pattern several notes lower:

```
PLAY "CAC"
```

The second note is now higher than the other two. Within one octave, A is higher than C, as shown in Figure 13-3.

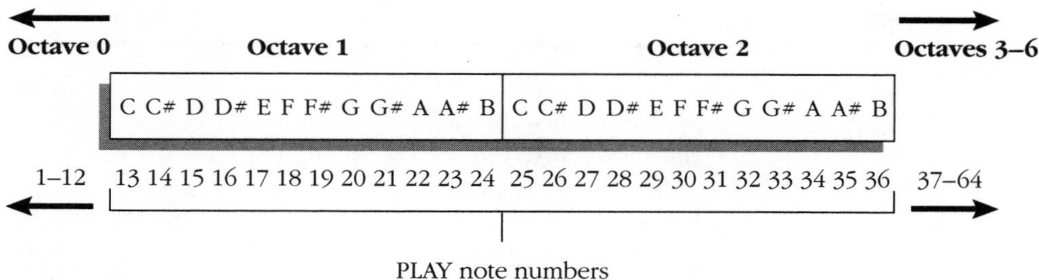

Figure 13-3.
Notes in two octaves.

To play an A that is lower than the C, we can use octave shift macros, as shown in the following example:

```
PLAY "C<A>C"
```

The < symbol lowers the current octave from octave 2 to octave 1, placing the following A in the octave below the initial C. The > symbol raises the octave, allowing us to play the original C again.

We can achieve the same result by using the o macro to select octaves by number, as in the following statement:

```
PLAY "C o1 A o2 C"
```

Another approach is to use note numbers instead of A and C. Note 1 is C in octave 0. Each octave has 12 notes, making C in octave 1 note 13, and C in octave 2 note 25. The A below the C in octave 2 is note 22 (Figure 13-3). The previous example can therefore be replaced with the following:

```
PLAY "N25 N22 N25"
```

Note that the N notation does not use the suffixes for sharps and flats, because sharps and flats are built into the numbering scheme. (Figure 13-1 does not list flats as such; A-sharp is considered the same as B-flat in this scale.)

Now let's listen to the effects the staccato and legato settings have on the sound. Staccato notes are played crisply, with a well-defined break between adjacent notes; legato, in contrast, calls for a smoother sound. Both settings are included in the following example:

```
PLAY "T120 MN CEEC P4 MS CEEC P4 ML CEEC"
```

The example begins by restoring the regular tempo setting and playing a four-note sequence in the default (MN) mode. After a short pause, the same sequence is played staccato, and you can hear that the notes are more distinctly separated. After another pause, the same sequence is played legato, and the two E notes blend into a single note with no break.

Now let's try some different durations, as shown here:

```
PLAY "o3 L4 MN C4 F8. F16 F"
```

Four notes are played in the default (MN) mode and with the default note duration (L4): a quarter note, a dotted eighth note, a sixteenth note, and a quarter note. Because the quarter note is the default, you could omit the 4 after the C as well as after the final F.

> **NOTE:** *If you run these programs in a multitasking environment such as DesQview, the tempo can become distorted. Because a multitasking environment allocates "time slices" among several programs, the ticks are not counted properly within any one program.*

Playing "Greensleeves"

Now we can try to play something more ambitious: the beginning of the song "Greensleeves." The notes in Listing 13-3 were transcribed from a musical score using the A–G notation, which is simpler than using the N macros.

Note that we don't need to add spaces between the macros. Adding spaces makes the string easier to read, but it also makes the string longer.

For changing octaves within a melody, we use octave shifts (< and >) rather than o macros. The o macros are placed in front of a complete string when we want to shift the entire melody higher or lower.

The note durations are set according to the note types shown in Figure 13-4 (quarter note, eighth note, and so on). When a note is dotted in the musical notation, the dot suffix is also used in the corresponding macro—a dotted quarter note, for instance, becomes *E4.* in the command string.

```
' Applying PLAY to a song
CLS
' Beginning of Greensleeves
Part1$ = "E8G4A8MLB8.>C16.MN<B8A4F#8MLD8.E16.MNF#8G4E8"
Part2$ = "MLE8.D#16.MNE8F#4.<B4>E8G4A8MLB8.>C16.MN<B8A4F#8"
Part3$ = "MLD8.E16.MNF#8MLG8.F#16.MNE8MLD#8.C#16.MND#8E4.E4."
Green$ = Part1$ + Part2$ + Part3$
PRINT "Playing Greensleeves"
PRINT "Briskly"
PLAY "o4 T240" + Green$
PRINT "Slower and lower"
PLAY "o2 T100" + Green$
END
```

Listing 13-3.

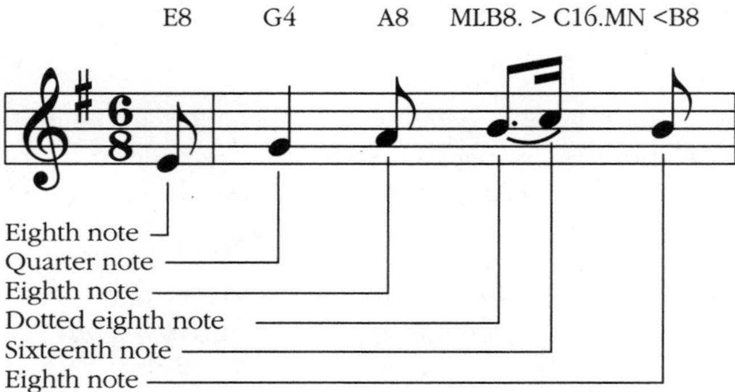

Figure 13-4.
Musical notation and PLAY notation for "Greensleeves" fragment.

Also note that in Figure 13-4 the musical score shows two notes (B and C) tied together. To represent this, we use the legato macro (ML) to tie the notes and MN to restore the normal setting afterward.

Using Foreground and Background Modes

The preceding program plays "Greensleeves" in the default foreground mode. In this mode, PLAY sends a note to be played, waits for the note to finish, and then sends the next note. When the final note is sent, the program moves on to the following statement, which can be completed before the note finishes. When you run the program, notice that the *Slower and lower* message is displayed while the final note of the first PLAY statement continues to sound.

In background mode, PLAY doesn't wait for each note to finish before sending the next note. Instead, it sends the notes to a buffer. The next statement in the program is then executed in the foreground while the notes in the buffer are played in the background until the buffer is empty.

We'll use part of our "Greensleeves" tune to demonstrate background mode. (Remember that the buffer holds only 32 notes.) Listing 13-4 plays a bit of "Greensleeves" twice, first in foreground mode and then in background mode. In each case, the PLAY statement precedes a loop that prints a few lyrics. In foreground mode, the lyrics don't appear until the tune is nearly finished, whereas in background mode they appear immediately after the tune starts.

The *PLAY "MB"* statement also turns on background mode for SOUND. Thus, you could replace the PLAY statement in this program with a series of SOUND statements that cause the specified sounds to play in the background.

```
' Foreground and background modes for PLAY
CLS
' Beginning of Greensleeves
Part1$ = "E8G4A8MLB8.>C16.MN<B8A4F#8MLD8.E16.MNF#8G4E8"
Part2$ = "MLE8.D#16.MNE8F#4.<B4>"
Green$ = Part1$ + Part2$
PRINT "Playing Greensleeves"
PLAY "MF o4 T240" + Green$          ' Play in foreground
DO WHILE INKEY$ = ""                ' Print lyrics
    PRINT TAB(I%); "Tra la, la la, lala la la la"
    I% = (I% + 10) MOD 40
    IF I% = 0 THEN
        PRINT "Press a key to stop"
        PRINT
    END IF
    StartTimer! = TIMER             ' Pause between loops
    DO WHILE NowTimer! - StartTimer! < .15
        NowTimer! = TIMER
    LOOP
LOOP
PRINT
PRINT "Press a key to continue!"
DO WHILE INKEY$ = ""
LOOP
PLAY "MB o4 T240" + Green$          ' Play in background
I% = 0
DO WHILE INKEY$ = ""                ' Print lyrics
    PRINT TAB(I%); "Tra la, la la, lala la la la"
    I% = (I% + 10) MOD 40
    IF I% = 0 THEN
        PRINT "Press a key to stop"
        PRINT
    END IF
    StartTimer! = TIMER             ' Pause between loops
    DO WHILE NowTimer! - StartTimer! < .15
        NowTimer! = TIMER
    LOOP
LOOP
END
```

Listing 13-4.

ON PLAY and Event Trapping

In the program shown in Listing 13-4, the music stops after the background tune plays once. To keep the background music going, you need a way to tell when the tune is complete so that it can be played again. QuickBASIC uses a method called *event trapping* to accomplish this.

Suppose you want a program to keep running until a particular event takes place. You could do this with a method called *polling,* in which the program checks, or polls, periodically to see whether the event has occurred. For instance, in Listing 13-4 we used the following code to see whether a key had been pressed:

```
DO WHILE INKEY$ = ""
LOOP
```

Event trapping works differently, however. The program is set to watch for a particular event. When the event occurs, the event-trapping mechanism sends a signal to the program, and the program then executes a specified subroutine.

When PLAY is used in background mode, QuickBASIC can detect the point at which the number of notes left in the buffer falls below a given value. To get continuous background music, you can run PLAY every time the buffer is nearly empty, using the following steps:

1. Tell the program what to watch for. The general form is the following:

   ```
   ON PLAY(n) GOSUB label
   ```

   n is the trigger count for the input queue of notes to be played. Event trapping is triggered when the number drops from *n* to $n-1$. At that time, program execution passes to the subroutine *label.* The *label* parameter can be a line number or a line label.

2. Tell the program to pay attention if the event occurs. Do this with the following statement:

   ```
   PLAY ON
   ```

   (You can use PLAY OFF to disable event trapping temporarily.)

3. Write a subroutine telling the program what to do when the event is trapped. Label the subroutine with *label* from the ON PLAY statement.

The program in Listing 13-5 plays the "Greensleeves" fragment continuously in the background.

```
CLS
ON PLAY(3) GOSUB Green
PLAY ON
Part1$ = "E8G4A8MLB8.>C16.MN<B8A4F#8MLD8.E16.MNF#8G4E8"
Part2$ = "MLE8.D#16.MNE8F#4.<B4>"
Green$ = "T240 o2" + Part1$ + Part2$
PLAY "MB" + Green$                    ' Start tune in background
I% = 0
DO WHILE INKEY$ = ""                  ' Print lyrics
    PRINT TAB(I%); "Tra la, la la, lala la la la"
    I% = (I% + 10) MOD 40
```

Listing 13-5. *(continued)*

Listing 13-5. *continued*

```
    IF I% = 0 THEN
        PRINT "Press a key to stop"
        PRINT
    END IF
    StartTimer! = TIMER             ' Pause between loops
    DO WHILE NowTimer! - StartTimer! < .15
        NowTimer! = TIMER
    LOOP
LOOP
END
Green:
        PLAY Green$
RETURN
```

The program sets up event trapping, starts the tune in background mode, and then proceeds to the other statements in the program. When the number of notes in the PLAY queue drops from 3 to 2, the program stops what it is doing, executes the *Green* subroutine, and resumes where it left off.

The program in Listing 13-6 follows this outline. For the overall program, we use the spiral-drawing program from Listing 12-23.

```
' Sound and light show
ON PLAY(3) GOSUB Green                 ' Event trapping to subroutine
PLAY ON                                ' Enable event trapping
Part1$ = "E8G4A8MLB8.>C16.MN<B8A4F#8MLD8.E16.MNF#8G4E8"
Part2$ = "MLE8.D#16.MNE8F#4.<B4>"
Green$ = "T240 o2" + Part1$ + Part2$
PLAY "MB" + Green$
DIM Col%(1 TO 4)                       ' Colors to be used
Col%(1) = 9                            ' Light blue
Col%(2) = 10                           ' Light green
Col%(3) = 12                           ' Light red
Col%(4) = 14                           ' Yellow
PageA% = 1
PageV% = 0
Angle% = 360
SCREEN 9
WINDOW (-1, -1)-(1, 1)
CIRCLE (0, 0), .6, 14                  ' Create opening image
PAINT (0, 0), 12, 14
LOCATE 13, 25
PRINT " Working on a pretty spiral...";
DO
    SCREEN 9, , PageA%, PageV%
    CLS 1
    CI% = 1
```

Listing 13-6. *(continued)*

Listing 13-6. *continued*

```
    Clr% = Clr% MOD 7 + 1           ' Message color
    COLOR Clr%
    LOCATE 24, 1
    PRINT "Press any key to halt";
    FOR D% = 1 TO 360 STEP 6        ' Draw the spiral
        Ang% = D% - Angle%
        Cmd$ = "TA" + STR$(Ang%) + "NU"
        Cmd$ = Cmd$ + STR$(INT(30 * LOG(D%)))
        Cmd$ = Cmd$ + "C" + STR$(Col%(CI%))
        DRAW Cmd$
        CI% = CI% MOD 4 + 1
        IF INKEY$ <> "" THEN EXIT DO
    NEXT D%
    IF Angle% > 10 THEN
        Angle% = Angle% - 10
    ELSE
        Angle% = 360
    END IF
    SWAP PageA%, PageV%             ' Switch active/display pages
LOOP UNTIL INKEY$ <> ""
SOUND 300, 0                        ' Turn off PLAY sequence
SCREEN 0
END

Green:                              ' Event trapping branches to subroutine
    PLAY Green$
RETURN
```

Note the following line in the program:

```
SOUND 300, 0
```

The program executes this line when it terminates. The SOUND statement used with a duration of 0 ticks terminates sound, even if PLAY originated the sounds. This statement is useful when PLAY or SOUND is being used in background mode, which allows the buffer to be partially full. If the statement is omitted and the program ends while PLAY is in the middle of its tune, the melody continues to play until the buffer is empty, even when you return to the QuickBASIC editor. *SOUND 300, 0* terminates the playing immediately, however.

Using Variables as Arguments

String variables or variables that can be converted to strings can be incorporated into PLAY statements. For instance, if you want to hear all 84 notes of the PLAY repertoire, you can use the N macro with a variable specifying the note number. Simply convert the variable to a string, as shown in the following example:

```
CLS
PLAY "MF L32"
FOR Note% = 1 TO 84
    PLAY "N" + STR$(Note%)    ' Integer converted to string
NEXT Note%
END
```

VARPTR$ can also be used with PLAY, as it is with DRAW, to convert numbers to strings. You must use the equal sign as part of the macro in this form, as shown here:

```
CLS
PLAY "MF L8"
FOR Octave% = 0 TO 6
    PLAY "o=" + VARPTR$(Octave%) + "GGG E-2 P4"
NEXT Octave%
END
```

VARPTR$ requires a variable as an argument, whereas STR$ can use any numeric expression, as the following example demonstrates:

```
Note% = 27
PLAY "N" + STR$(Note%)          ' Play note 27
PLAY "N" + STR$(Note% + 1)      ' Play note 28
PLAY "N=" + VARPTR$(Note%)      ' Play note 27
PLAY "N=" + VARPTR$(Note% + 1)  ' Invalid statement
```

Review Questions

1. What statement will cause a note of frequency 1000 Hz to play for approximately 4 seconds?
2. What can the SOUND statement do that the PLAY statement cannot?
3. The note A in octave 3 has a frequency of 880 Hz. What is the frequency of A in octave 4? In octaves 5 and 6?
4. A standard G scale consists of the following notes: G, A, B, C, D, E, F-sharp. Write a program that plays a G scale of three octaves both ascending and descending, with both sequences ending on G. Then have the program repeat the scale twice, once legato and once staccato. Use sixteenth notes, and remember to include octave shifts.
5. What is the difference between ON PLAY and PLAY ON?

PART V

Pokes, Peeks, Ins, and Outs

14

Memory and Ports

DEF SEG	**OUT**	**POKE**
INP	**PEEK**	**WAIT**

Thus far, you haven't had to worry about exactly where QuickBASIC puts data in memory. For example, when you define the string *Hello*, QuickBASIC stores the individual characters in successive locations, or *addresses*, in memory. To retrieve the contents of such a string variable in a program, you simply use its name in a statement; QuickBASIC takes care of the details of finding the data.

But not all of memory is used to store QuickBASIC variables and statements. DOS, for instance, uses certain memory locations to store information about the status of the system. As we'll demonstrate in this chapter, QuickBASIC provides statements and functions that enable you to access any portion of memory.

In this chapter we'll also look at *ports*, memory locations that are the IBM PC's means of communicating with devices such as modems, printers, and video display adapters. Unlike other memory locations, ports are connected directly to hardware devices. QuickBASIC lets you read information about the status of a device from a port, and it also lets you send information to a port to change how a device operates.

Finding Out What's Stored Where

The IBM PC and IBM PS/2 can have as much as 1024 KB (1 MB) of memory that can be accessed by QuickBASIC. Your programs can directly read from or write to any location in the available memory. For example, by reading values from the memory locations that store information about the system, a program can determine how many disk drives are available, whether your computer is equipped with a math coprocessor chip, and other details about the system's hardware. By writing a value to a certain memory location, your program can change the way a device operates. For instance, you can store a value that turns on the Num Lock key, allowing the user to enter numbers easily from the numeric keypad.

Of course, you must be able to determine which memory location you want to read from or write to. The IBM PC and compatibles organize memory in a particular order. This order, shown in the memory map in Figure 14-1, helps you find the memory location you want to access. QuickBASIC allows you to access bytes only within a 64-KB section of memory called a *segment.* To access memory locations outside the current segment, you must change segments. By default, your program accesses the DGROUP segment, the QuickBASIC default data segment that contains most of a program's variables and strings.

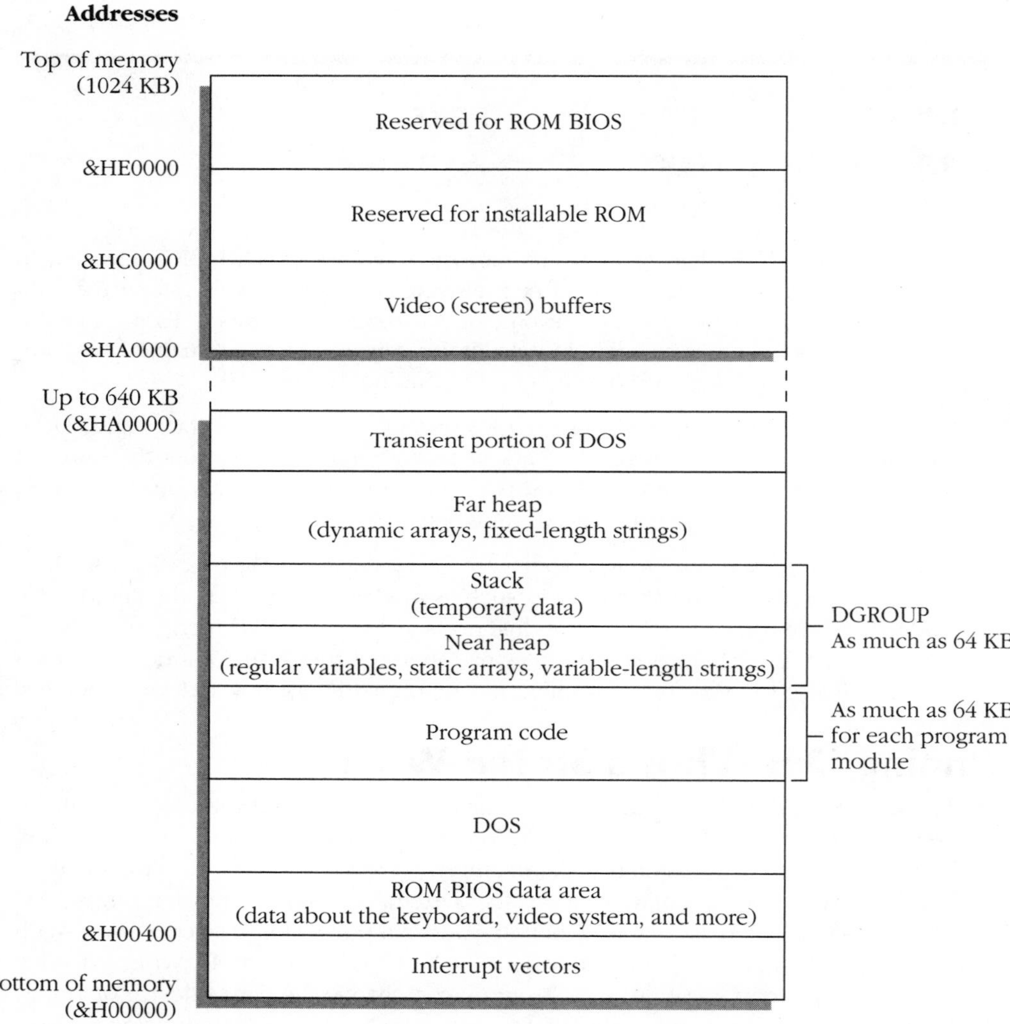

Figure 14-1.
A memory map.

As shown in Figure 14-1, you can also access the segment that contains the characters on the video screen, the segment that contains information about the keyboard and the video system, and any other segment that contains data you need.

Reading a Value in Memory: The PEEK Function

The PEEK function returns the value stored in a specified memory location in the current segment. For example, *PEEK(1000)* returns the value stored at location 1000. Because each memory location contains an 8-bit byte, the value returned is in the range 0 through 255, the range of possible values for a byte. (Because 0 and 1 are the only bit values, a byte has 2^8, or 256, possible values.)

Here is the syntax for the PEEK function:

```
PEEK(location)
```

location can be a number, a numeric expression, or a numeric variable in the range 0 through 65535. If the value is single precision or double precision and less than 32767, PEEK converts it to an integer. If the value is in the range 32768 through 65535, the value must be a long integer rather than an integer because the value of an integer is limited to the range −32768 through 32767.

The following example uses a loop to read the values stored in memory locations 1 through 10:

```
FOR Location% = 1 TO 10
    PRINT PEEK(Location%); " ";
NEXT Location%
```

The values stored in these locations vary according to your machine's configuration, the memory-resident programs you have loaded, the contents of the currently running program, and whether you are running QuickBASIC from the interactive environment or running the command-line compiler (BC). But the displayed values should look something like the following:

```
 51  255  255  255  255  255  255  110  60  30
```

Storing a Value in Memory: The POKE Statement

The counterpart to the PEEK function is the POKE statement, which stores, or writes, a specified byte value in a specified location in memory.

Here is the syntax for the POKE statement:

```
POKE location, value
```

location can be a number, a numeric expression, or a numeric variable in the range 0 through 65535. *value* is a number, a numeric expression, or a numeric variable in the range 0 through 255.

The following example combines POKE and PEEK to let you see how a value can be stored in memory and retrieved directly from memory:

```
POKE 1000, 10
PRINT PEEK(1000)
```

POKE stores the value 10 at the memory location 1000. PEEK then looks at memory location 1000 and returns the value 10.

Using Segments and Offsets

PEEK and POKE can access locations only within a particular segment of memory. But how can you access the complete range of memory locations?

Your computer's CPU uses pairs of 8-bit registers (internal storage locations in the CPU) to access memory locations. Because these paired *index registers* contain 16 bits, they can address 65,536 (2^{16}) locations, or 64 KB of memory. PCs, however, are capable of addressing as much as 1024 KB of memory (or more, depending on the processor and mode of operation). They do so by using a special 20-bit addressing system, which can address 1,048,576 (2^{20}) locations. These 20-bit addresses, however, must be adapted to work with the 8-bit registers.

This problem is solved in the PC by dividing memory into 64-KB segments. Any memory location can be accessed by using a *segmented address* that consists of the number of a segment and an *offset.* The offset is a number specifying the position of a memory location within a segment. For example, the offset of the location 80 bytes from the beginning of a segment is 80.

Each segment's starting *absolute address* (its 20-bit address) must be evenly divisible by 16—that is, a new segment begins every 16 bytes. Because a segment contains 65,536 bytes, the segments overlap each other. Thus a single memory location can be accessed by more than one segmented address.

Memory and port addresses are often referred to in hexadecimal (base 16) notation (discussed in detail in Appendix B). Two hexadecimal digits can represent eight binary digits—the contents of 1 byte of memory. A word of memory (16 bits, or 2 bytes) can thus be represented as four hexadecimal digits.

Segmented addresses are often written in the form *segment:offset,* using four hexadecimal digits for each part, with leading zeros if necessary—B800:0008, for example. (You might have seen the segment number B800 before; the video memory for some modes of the PC's color graphics system begins in this segment.)

Accessing Memory in Segments: The DEF SEG Statement

You can use the DEF SEG statement to specify which segment will be used by PEEK, POKE, and other memory-related statements and functions. Until you enter a different DEF SEG statement, all locations specified by PEEK or POKE will be offsets from the address specified in the most recent DEF SEG statement.

Here is the syntax for DEF SEG:

```
DEF SEG  [= segmentnumber]
```

segmentnumber, which is the number of the segment, can be a number, a numeric variable, or a numeric expression in the range 0 through 65535. You can specify a hexadecimal value for *segmentnumber* by adding the &H prefix to the value.

The DEF SEG statement used without *segmentnumber* sets the current segment to the QuickBASIC default data segment, DGROUP. DGROUP is also used if a program contains no DEF SEG statement. (We used this segment earlier, in our examples of PEEK and POKE.)

DEF SEG enables you to change from one segment to another anywhere in the 1 megabyte of standard addressable memory. You might find it necessary, for instance, to look at the memory containing the characters currently displayed on the video screen. On a color display in text mode, this memory starts at segment &HB800. (Monochrome display adapters start at segment &HB000.) If you have a color adapter (CGA, EGA, or VGA), you can use the following program to peek into the screen memory and display what is stored there:

```
VideoString$ = "This goes on the top line of the screen"
CLS
PRINT VideoString$;
DEF SEG = &HB800 ' Set segment to beginning of screen memory
LOCATE 2, 1
FOR CharPos = 0 TO (LEN(VideoString$) - 1) * 2 STEP 2
    PRINT CHR$(PEEK(CharPos));
NEXT CharPos
END
```

The program begins by displaying a string on the first line. After setting the segment to the start of screen memory, the LOCATE statement places the cursor at the beginning of the next line. A FOR loop then uses PEEK to read every second memory location in screen memory until it reads the number of bytes equal to the length of the string displayed. (The screen data is arranged so that the first byte contains the ASCII code for the first character, the second byte contains bits specifying that character's attributes or colors, the third byte contains the ASCII value for the second character, and so on.)

With POKE, you can put characters directly on the screen by writing them to screen memory, as shown in the following program:

```
CONST videoSeg& = &HB800
DEF SEG = videoSeg&
CLS
INPUT "Enter some text"; Text$
FOR CharPos = 1 TO (LEN(Text$))
    POKE (1600 + (CharPos - 1) * 2), ASC(MID$(Text$, CharPos, 1))
NEXT CharPos
END
```

Because each screen line uses 160 (80 × 2) bytes of memory, using POKE with an offset of 1600 in the video display segment displays the text at the start of line 11. The ASC function is used to obtain the ASCII code for each character of text.

DOS stores many pieces of information about your system in specific memory locations. Try using Listing 14-1 to find out what model your computer is.

```
DEF SEG = &HF000                ' Define the segment
EquipByte = PEEK(&HFFFE)        ' Use offset for location
CLS
SELECT CASE EquipByte           ' Value at address indicates equipment
    CASE 255:
        PRINT "An old-fashioned IBM PC"
    CASE 254:
        PRINT "A PC/XT or a portable PC"
    CASE 253:
        PRINT "A PCjr"
    CASE 252:
        PRINT "A PC/AT or a PS/2 Model 30-286, 50, or 60"
    CASE 250:
        PRINT "A PS/2 Model 25 or an old Model 30"
    CASE 248:
        PRINT "A PS/2 Model 70 or 80"
    CASE ELSE:
        PRINT "I don't know what you've got!"
END SELECT
END
```

Listing 14-1.

Working with Individual Bits

On any computer, the smallest unit of information you can work with is an individual bit, which can be on (1) or off (0). Bit manipulation is useful for storing many pieces of information, each of which can have only one small value. For example, using one element in an integer array to represent the status of each pixel on a video screen would be extremely inefficient—indeed, with a high-resolution screen, you'd run out of memory. Instead, you can use 1 bit to represent the on/off status of an individual pixel on a monochrome screen and a small number of bits to represent a pixel on a color screen (4 bits representing the binary values 0000 through 1111, for example, which allows each pixel to have 1 of 16 colors). You can then perform bit manipulation to examine and change the individual bits.

Some of the bytes that hold information in memory about the status of devices (as well as the port bytes that we will discuss later) assign separate meanings to their 8 bits of true/false (on/off) information. To examine or set these individual bits, QuickBASIC provides the arithmetic operators AND, OR, XOR, and NOT for bit manipulation. These operators are *bitwise*—that is, they compare corresponding bits in two numeric values and produce a resulting byte that reflects the operation.

These operators are the same as the logical operators discussed in Chapter 4. We are now using them with numeric operands (bytes) instead of Boolean expressions.

Let's look at a practical demonstration of bit manipulation. DOS uses a byte in segment 0, offset &H417, to hold a set of flags (individual bytes) indicating which of several special keys (called *shift keys*) are on. Listing 14-2 first turns on the Num Lock key and then, by using a DO loop, displays the current status of the shift keys. (For the Scroll Lock, Num Lock, Caps Lock, or Ins key, simply press the key to turn it on or off; for the Right Shift, Left Shift, Ctrl, or Alt key, hold down the key until the program registers its changed status.) In this program, we use a FOR loop inside the DO loop to slow down the display.

```
DECLARE SUB SetBit (Addr&, BitPos%)           ' Set bit to 1
DECLARE SUB CheckKey (KeyFlag%)               ' Get key status
DECLARE FUNCTION GetBit% (Byte&, Bit%)        ' Return bit value

DEF SEG = 0
CONST keyStatus& = &H417                      ' Location of key status bits
' Bit positions for key status
CONST rtShift% = 0
CONST lftShift% = 1
CONST ctrl% = 2
CONST alt% = 3
CONST scrlLock% = 4
CONST numLock% = 5
CONST capsLock% = 6
CONST insMode% = 7

IF NOT GetBit%(PEEK(keyStatus&), 5) THEN     ' Check whether Num Lock is on
    SetBit keyStatus&, 5                      ' If necessary, turn Num Lock on
END IF

DO
    CLS
    PRINT "Press Esc to end program."
    PRINT
    PRINT "Right Shift:  "; : CheckKey (rtShift%)
    PRINT "Left Shift :  "; : CheckKey (lftShift%)
    PRINT "Ctrl       :  "; : CheckKey (ctrl%)
    PRINT "Alt        :  "; : CheckKey (alt%)
    PRINT "Scroll Lock:  "; : CheckKey (scrlLock%)
    PRINT "Num Lock   :  "; : CheckKey (numLock%)
    PRINT "Caps Lock  :  "; : CheckKey (capsLock%)
    PRINT "Insert Mode:  "; : CheckKey (insMode%)
    ' Delay loop to slow down display
    FOR n = 1 TO 2000
    NEXT n
    KeyPress$ = INKEY$                        ' Get a key
LOOP UNTIL KeyPress$ = CHR$(27)               ' Loop until user presses Esc
END
```

Listing 14-2. *(continued)*

Listing 14-2. *continued*

```
SUB CheckKey (KeyFlag%)
    IF GetBit%(PEEK(keyStatus&), KeyFlag%) THEN
        PRINT ("ON")
    ELSE
        PRINT ("OFF")
    END IF
END SUB

FUNCTION GetBit% (Byte&, Bit%)
    GetBit% = -SGN(Byte& AND 2 ^ Bit%)
END FUNCTION

SUB SetBit (Addr&, BitPos%)
    POKE Addr&, PEEK(Addr&) OR 2 ^ BitPos%
END SUB
```

The program first uses the *GetBit%* function to determine whether the Num Lock key is turned on. This function returns the status of a bit by using the AND operator combined with the SGN function. The AND operator compares the values of corresponding bits in the operands. If the bits in both operands are turned on, the corresponding bit in the resulting byte is turned on. Suppose that the value of *Byte&* passed to the *GetBit%* function is 11100000, indicating that the Num Lock, Caps Lock, and Ins keys are on. To check the status of the Num Lock bit, *GetBit%* first performs an AND operation with *Byte&* and 2^5, or 00100000 (Figure 14-2).

```
     11100000 ┐
AND  00100000 ┘─ Operands
     00100000 ── Resulting value
```

Figure 14-2.
The AND operation used in GetBit%.

Because bit 5 in both operands is on, bit 5 of the resulting value is also on. (Note that bit 5 occupies the sixth bit position; bit 0 occupies the first bit position.) You can see that the resulting value is greater than 0 only when bit 5 in *Byte&*, the first operand, is turned on. *GetBit%* then negates the value returned by the SGN function. The result of this process is that *GetBit%* returns –1 if bit 5 is on or 0 if bit 5 is off:

```
GetBit% = -SGN(Byte& AND 2 ^ Bit%)
```

In Listing 14-2, if the Num Lock bit is not on, the program calls the *SetBit* subprogram to turn it on. *SetBit* uses the OR operator to turn on the Num Lock bit before using the POKE statement to write the changed key status byte to memory. Like the AND operator, the OR operator compares the values of corresponding bits in the operands. If the bit in one or both of the operands is turned on, then the corresponding bit in the resulting byte is turned on. Suppose that the value of *Addr&* passed to the *SetBit* subprogram is 11000000, which indicates that the Caps Lock and Ins keys are on and that the Num Lock key is off. To set the Num Lock key, *SetBit* performs an OR operation with *Addr&* and 2^5, or 00100000 (Figure 14-3).

```
    11000000 ]
OR  00100000 ]- Operands
    --------
    11100000 --- Resulting value
```

Figure 14-3.
The OR operation used in SetBit.

Because bits 5, 6, and 7 in one or both operands are on, bits 5, 6, and 7 of the resulting value are also on. Notice that the resulting value in the OR operation is equal to *Addr&*, the first operand, except that bit 5 in the resulting value is set.

The program then reports the status of each key by calling the *CheckKey* subprogram, which calls the *GetBit%* function.

Let's look at another example. If your computer has a math coprocessor, you might be able to use a greater range of routines to perform extensive calculations in a program. To find out whether your computer has a coprocessor installed, use PEEK to read the byte in segment &H40 in memory, offset &H10. The second bit is 1 if a coprocessor is installed and 0 otherwise. Listing 14-3 performs this check.

```
DECLARE FUNCTION GetBit% (Addr&, Bit%)
DEF SEG = 0
CONST equipLow& = &H410
CLS
IF GetBit%(equipLow&, 1) = 1 THEN
    PRINT "Math coprocessor installed"
ELSE
    PRINT "No coprocessor installed"
END IF
END

FUNCTION GetBit% (Addr&, Bit%)
    GetBit% = -SGN(Addr& AND 2 ^ Bit%)
END FUNCTION
```

Listing 14-3.

Many books on BASIC offer lists of addresses that you can read from by using PEEK or write to by using POKE. Much useful information on screen settings and text position, the current print position, and so on is stored in DGROUP. But these values can vary with the version of QuickBASIC, BASICA, or other language being used. Using an appropriate QuickBASIC statement or function to obtain the desired information is more reliable than using PEEK or POKE.

Values stored by DOS in segment 0 and in ROM (usually in segment &HF000) are also fairly reliable, but even these can change with a particular version of DOS. The best way to get system information is to call the appropriate BIOS service. (The BIOS is the Basic Input/Output Service of DOS. You can call a BIOS service to set the cursor size, scroll the screen, initialize the ports, and more. See Chapter 17 for a discussion of CALL INTERRUPT, which can be used to call a BIOS service.)

With that caution, here are the descriptions of the contents of some interesting memory locations and the statements used to access them:

- Location of the first of seven ports associated with COM*n* (*n* being 1, 2, or 3)

  ```
  DEF SEG = 0
  PRINT PEEK(&H3FE + 2 * n) + 256 * PEEK(&H3FF + 2 * n)
  ```

  If the result is 0, no serial ports are available.

- Location of the first of seven ports associated with parallel port LPT*n* (*n* being 1, 2, or 3)

  ```
  DEF SEG = 0
  PRINT PEEK(&H406 + 2 * n) + 256 * PEEK(&H407 + 2 * n)
  ```

- Number of floppy disk drives available

  ```
  DEF SEG = 0
  PRINT (PEEK(&H410) AND 1) * (1 + PEEK(&H410) \ 64)
  ```

- Amount of installed RAM in KB (up to the 640 KB used by DOS)

  ```
  DEF SEG = 0
  PRINT PEEK(&H413) + 256 * PEEK(&H414)
  ```

  A 640-KB total is actually reported as 639 KB.

- Date of your machine's BIOS chip

  ```
  DEF SEG = &HF000
  FOR J% = &HFFF5 TO &HFFFC
      PRINT CHR$(PEEK(J%));
  NEXT J%
  ```

- Equipment byte (the computer being used)

  ```
  DEF SEG = &HF000
  PRINT PEEK(&HFFFE)
  ```

Ports and Devices

Regular memory (RAM) locations have no direct connection to devices such as printers, modems, or video adapters, although program code stored in RAM can communicate with and control devices. Direct access to the hardware is provided through special memory locations called ports. In theory, as many as 256 ports can exist; in reality, only a few dozen are commonly used. As you write more advanced programs, you'll sometimes need to work directly with ports, especially when using printers and serial communications (Chapter 15).

Port addresses are not part of the system of memory addresses. The two sets of addresses deal with different places in the computer. Memory location &H3FC and port location &H3FC, for example, are not the same.

When you write a value into a memory location by using POKE, the value remains until another statement changes it. Writing to a port location, however, sends instructions or data to the device connected to that port. What happens to the instructions or data depends on the device.

Many devices have several port addresses—read-only, write-only, or read/write ports. Printer ports, for instance, have one location for sending data to be printed and another from which you can read the device's current status (ready, busy, out of paper, and so on). Figure 14-4 lists some commonly used port addresses and the devices that can be accessed through the ports.

Port Addresses (in Hex)	***Device***
060 through 06F	8255A Programmable peripheral interface keyboard controller
0C0 through 0CF	Complex sound generator (PCjr and Tandy 1000 only)
0F0 through 0FF	Math coprocessor (8087, 80287, or 80387)
1F0 through 1F8	Hard-disk controller (PC/AT and PS/2)
200 through 207	Game controller (joystick)
278 through 27F	Third parallel port (LPT3)
2F8 through 2FF	Second serial port (COM2)
320 through 32F	Hard-disk controller (PC/XT and PS/2 Model 30 only; not PS/2 Model 30–286)
378 through 37F	Second parallel printer
3B0 through 3BB	MDA, as well as EGA and VGA in monochrome video modes
3BC through 3BF	First parallel port (LPT1 or PRN)
3C0 through 3CF	EGA and VGA
3D0 through 3DF	CGA and MCGA, as well as EGA and VGA in color video modes
3F0 through 3F7	Floppy-disk controller
3F8 through 3FF	First serial port (COM1)

Figure 14-4.
Commonly used port addresses.

Because ports aren't part of regular memory, you can't use PEEK or POKE to access them. Instead, QuickBASIC provides the INP function and the OUT statement.

Here is the syntax for INP and OUT:

```
INP(portnumber)
OUT portnumber, bytevalue
```

INP reads and returns a byte from the specified port number, and OUT writes a byte (*bytevalue*) to the specified port number. *portnumber* can range from 0 through 65535. *bytevalue* is a value in the range 0 through 255.

Controlling the Speaker

Listing 14-4 demonstrates controlling a port directly—in this case, the speaker port. (Because the speaker is a separate hardware device, the PC can communicate with it only through a port.) We use defined constants for the speaker's port address and the value of the bit pattern that turns the speaker on.

```
CONST speakerPort% = &H61
CONST speakerOn% = &H3                        ' Bits that turn speaker on
CLS
INPUT "Sound for how many seconds? ", Seconds%
Start& = TIMER                                ' Get time that speaker begins
                                              '  to sound
OldPortVal% = INP(speakerPort%)               ' Save current port value

OUT speakerPort%, OldPortVal% OR speakerOn%   ' Turn speaker on

DO
LOOP UNTIL TIMER > Start& + Seconds%          ' Check how much time elapsed
OUT speakerPort%, OldPortVal%                 ' Restore original port value
END
```

Listing 14-4.

We begin by saving the current speaker port value (off). Next a new bit pattern is set by using the OR operator to turn on the bits in the port value that switch on the speaker. Using the current TIMER value plus the number of seconds entered by the user, the program sets up a loop. The OUT statement sends the new bit pattern to the speaker, which starts to sound a constant tone (using the default frequency).

Unlike the short beep produced by the BEEP statement, this sound continues in the background until the speaker is turned off. By including additional statements between turning the speaker on and turning it off, you can let the sound run while your program flashes a warning on the screen or performs other actions. You can also directly control the frequency of the sound (as you can, indirectly, with the PLAY and SOUND statements) by writing to other speaker port locations.

The program in Listing 14-4 continues to sound the speaker until the port receives the off value again. Another OUT statement is used to send the variable in which this value is stored.

Controlling a Video Adapter

Listing 14-5 shows you how to control another important device, the video adapter, by directly accessing its port addresses. As demonstrated in this program, you can access the video adapter ports to create special effects not easily provided by QuickBASIC statements. (To run this program, you must have an EGA or a VGA display adapter and a color monitor.)

```
CONST maxY% = 350
CONST maxX% = 640
CONST bytesPerRow% = maxX% / 8
CONST egaPort1% = &H3C4
CONST egaPort2% = &H3C5

SCREEN 9                      ' Initialize screen mode 9

DEF SEG = &HA000              ' Start of EGA memory in graphics mode

FOR Row% = 0 TO maxY% - 1
    Colr% = (Row% / 12) AND &HF
    OUT egaPort1%, 2          ' Prepare egaPort2% to accept color
    OUT egaPort2%, Colr%      ' Specify a color
    FOR Col% = 0 TO bytesPerRow% - 1
        POKE (Row% * bytesPerRow% + Col%), &HFF
    NEXT Col%
NEXT Row%
END
```

Listing 14-5.

The program first sets the beginning of the current segment to the start of EGA memory with a DEF SEG statement. The outer loop then draws horizontal lines of various colors on the screen. To draw these lines, the program first sends the value 2 to the EGA port address &H3C4. This value tells the video adapter to treat the value going into the EGA port address &H3C5 as a value for the color of the screen. The inner loop then calculates the 80 addresses in regular memory for the bytes containing the pixels for that row, and it writes a value to each byte that turns on all the bits in each byte, thus drawing a block of color on the screen.

Controlling the Printer

Suppose you want to design a program that can be used to check whether the printer is turned on and is in the online mode. A printer can be attached to a parallel port, which sends data to the printer 8 bits (1 byte) at a time, or to a serial port, which sends data 1 bit at a time. The printer attached to parallel port 1 (LPT1) reports its status through the port at address &H3BD. When bit 5 of the value at this port is off, the printer is online. Your program must check the status of this bit. If bit 5 isn't off, the program should first tell the user to get the printer ready and should then wait until the printer comes online and the bit is turned off before proceeding.

The QuickBASIC WAIT statement repeatedly checks a specified port for a specific bit pattern. WAIT performs an AND operation (and, optionally, an XOR operation) with the value read from the port. If this operation yields the result 0, the port is checked again and again until a nonzero result occurs, after which the program continues executing. The AND operator, as you have seen, can be used to check that a specific bit is on. The AND operation combined with the XOR operation can be used to check that a specific bit is off. Depending on the port, a bit can also convey other important information about the device, such as whether the device wants to send data, is waiting for data, or is busy.

Here is the syntax for the WAIT statement:

```
WAIT portnumber, ANDvalue[, XORvalue]
```

portnumber is a number in the range 0 through 255. It must specify an active port. *ANDvalue* is an 8-bit value in the range 0 through 255 that is compared with the value at the port, using the AND operator. *XORvalue* is an optional 8-bit value in the range 0 through 255; if it is omitted, the default is 0. If XOR is included, WAIT performs an XOR operation with the value at the port and then performs an AND operation with the result and *ANDvalue*.

For example, to make your program wait until bit 5 in the byte read from a port is off, have WAIT perform both an XOR operation and an AND operation with the value 32 (2^5), which is 00100000 in binary:

```
WAIT port%, 32, 32
```

Suppose that the value read from the port is 151, which is 10010111 in binary. Then WAIT performs the XOR and AND operations shown in Figure 14-5. Because the final result does not equal 0, you know that bit 5 in the byte read from the port is off. WAIT no longer must check the port for a byte with bit 5 turned off, and the program continues.

```
    10010111   = 151
XOR 00100000   =  32
    --------
    10110111   = 183


    10110111   = 183
AND 00100000   =  32
    --------
    00100000   =  32
```

Figure 14-5.
Using XOR and AND with WAIT.

Note that the XOR operator compares corresponding bits of its operands. If one of the bits is on (but not both bits), the resulting value's bit is on.

The following program uses the WAIT statement to check the printer's status:

```
CONST lpt1Status% = &H3BD
CLS
IF (INP(lpt1Status%) AND 32) <> 0 THEN    ' Check whether printer is online
    PRINT "Please turn on the printer and put it online."
    WAIT lpt1Status%, 32, 32              ' Pause until printer is online
END IF
PRINT "Printer is now online."
END
```

The program checks the value at the LPT1 status port (usually &H3BD), using AND to see whether bit 5 is on. If it is, the program asks the user to turn on the printer and put it online. The WAIT statement continues to check the port repeatedly for a byte in which bit 5 is off. (Note that if you specify the wrong port or a bit pattern that can never be true, the program will lock up, and you will need to reboot your system.)

This chapter has presented only an introduction to working with ports from QuickBASIC. For more information about the many ports available in your computer, see, for example, *The New Peter Norton Programmer's Guide to the IBM PC & PS/2* (Redmond, Wash.: Microsoft Press, 1988).

Review Questions

1. As you have seen, PEEK and POKE deal with 1 byte at a time. Sometimes, however, you must read or write 2 bytes (16 bits) at a time. Write a function that will read 16 bits from a memory location and a subprogram that will write 16 bits to a memory location.
2. Are programs that use DEF SEG, PEEK, and POKE likely to work under other versions of BASIC? Are they likely to work on machines other than IBM PCs or compatibles?
3. Write a subprogram that will display a message on a specified row of the screen by writing the message directly to video memory. Remember that video text memory on a color adapter starts at segment &HB800, with 80 characters per line and 2 bytes per character.
4. How do INP and OUT resemble PEEK and POKE? How do they differ?

15

Printers and Communications

COM ON	**LPRINT**	**OPEN COM**
$INCLUDE	**LPRINT USING**	**WIDTH**
LPOS	**ON COM**	**WIDTH LPRINT**

This chapter focuses on program output as it appears on the printed page—and on the process that gets it there. This process often involves utilizing a variety of typestyles, fonts, and special formatting, which can give your work a distinctive and professional look.

In this chapter we'll discuss sending data to the printer with the LPRINT and LPRINT USING statements as well as sending control commands that allow you to use the various features of your printer. Our examples are based on the two dominant printer standards in the PC world, the Hewlett-Packard LaserJet and the Epson dot-matrix printer, but the techniques are applicable to almost any printer.

QuickBASIC's printer-oriented statements send output by default to your computer's parallel printer port. Some printers, however, are connected to a serial port instead, so we'll explain how to configure and use such a port. You can also hook up a modem to a serial port and write programs that communicate with a remote system such as an online information service or a bulletin board system (BBS). You can even use the serial port to exchange files with other computers.

Throughout this chapter we assume that you have a printer connected to your computer, using either a parallel or a serial interface. It can be a daisy-wheel, dot-matrix, inkjet, or laser printer. We'll identify those examples that require an HP LaserJet or an Epson-compatible printer.

Understanding Printer Basics

As you know, the character set on your IBM PC or compatible computer consists of the ASCII character set (codes 0 through 127) and the IBM extended character set (codes 128 through 255). (See Chapter 7 and Appendix C.) The IBM extended character set is used to create simple character graphics (lines and boxes), to display math or currency symbols, and to print certain foreign-language characters. You must be aware, however, that your printer might assign a different set of characters to the codes 128 through 255.

Many printers can be directed to use either the IBM extended character set or another built-in set of special characters. On Epson and other dot-matrix printers, you can control this setting with a DIP (dual in-line package) switch. On an HP LaserJet, use the front panel controls to choose the IBM-US symbol set, which contains the symbols used by IBM PCs.

Although printers can vary considerably, nearly all of them have certain features in common. One such feature is the printer buffer, an area of memory that holds data waiting to be printed. In most printers, this memory is physically installed in the printer itself. The buffer size can vary from a few kilobytes in dot-matrix printers to a megabyte or more in many laser printers.

A computer can send data much faster than even a laser printer can print it. Printing would be a very slow process if a printer accepted data from the computer only as fast as it could print the data. To solve this problem, the printer buffer quickly accepts all the data to be printed and then parcels it out to the printer in manageable chunks. The computer is thereby freed to perform other tasks.

Another common feature of most printers (except daisy-wheel) is that they can operate in both text mode and graphics mode. In text mode, the printer interprets each byte of data as a code from a character set. The printer finds the corresponding character in its internal table and performs the actions needed to print that character. Because these character patterns are already stored, printing in text mode is typically fast.

In graphics mode, each byte of data is interpreted not as a code in a character set but as a pattern of eight individual dots—one dot for each bit. Graphics mode provides great flexibility, for you are not limited to the stored character patterns. Because it deals with bit patterns directly, however, printing in graphics mode is usually much slower than printing in text mode. A printed page of graphics also requires much more memory than a printed page of text. (Many laser printers can print 300 dots per inch; a laser printer normally needs a megabyte of memory to hold a full page at that resolution.)

Parallel and Serial Connections

Your printer is connected to your PC through either a parallel or a serial interface. A *parallel connection,* usually made with the port LPT1, simultaneously sends to the printer all 8 bits that make up each value. A *serial connection,* usually made with the COM1 or COM2 port, sends the data for each value 1 bit at a time, in a series.

Line Printers and Page Printers

Every printer, whether connected at a parallel interface or a serial interface, is either a *line printer* or a *page printer.* Most dot-matrix and daisy-wheel printers print one line at a time (a string of text terminated by a carriage-return/linefeed, or CR-LF, combination). Laser printers, in contrast, print an entire page at one time; the end of a page is indicated by a formfeed character (which has an ASCII value of 12). Thus, dot-matrix printers start printing as soon as QuickBASIC sends them characters, whereas laser printers store characters in a buffer and do not print until a full page accumulates (and the formfeed has been sent) or until the program prints a formfeed character. With a page printer, your program should print a formfeed before the program terminates, in order to print any partial page that might be left in the buffer. You can print a formfeed by using the statement *LPRINT CHR$(12).*

Printer Command Languages

Nearly all printers accept special commands to set margins, change fonts and typestyles, and so on. In most cases, you must begin a printer command with *CHR$(27),* which generates the escape character, to let the printer know that what follows is a command rather than text to be printed.

The two most widely used printer command languages are the HP LaserJet standard (called PCL, for Printer Control Language) and the Epson standard. (A third, PostScript, which is a complete typesetting and page layout language, is not covered here.) Most dot-matrix printers can be set either to an Epson emulation mode or to their own proprietary mode. The mode determines the set of commands that the printer recognizes. (We will identify commands in our examples as Epson or HPLJ.) In general, it's preferable to set most printers to Epson mode when working with QuickBASIC, because many BASIC programs are written to use these printer codes. Sometimes, however, your printer's proprietary mode might be the best choice for a program that will be used only with your printer.

Using a Serial Printer

QuickBASIC statements and functions for printing are designed to work with a printer connected to the parallel port LPT1. But they will also work with a printer connected to a serial port if you use the DOS command MODE. For example, if your printer is connected to the serial port COM1, you can enter the following on the DOS command line:

```
MODE LPT1 = COM1
```

This command redirects to COM1 any output sent to LPT1, making it possible to use the QuickBASIC printer statements and functions.

You can also print to a printer with a serial connection by opening the serial port as a device and then writing to it with the PRINT # statement. We will examine this more complex method when we discuss the OPEN COM statement.

Checking Your Printer from Within QuickBASIC

Before you begin testing a program that performs printing, you should check to be sure that the printer cable is physically connected to the computer and that the printer is turned on and is online. To test the printer, simply enter the following statement in the Immediate window:

```
LPRINT "This is a test"
```

The printer should print the line of text. (If you are using a page printer, follow this statement with a formfeed.) If the printer isn't properly connected or is not turned on, you'll receive the error message *Device not ready* or *Device timeout*.

Changing the Default Parallel Port

Although by default the QuickBASIC LPRINT and LPRINT USING statements send output to the parallel port LPT1 only, it's possible to use a different parallel port. To send output to LPT2, for example, use the following statement to open LPT2 as a file:

```
OPEN "LPT2:" FOR RANDOM AS #1
```

Then use PRINT #1 or PRINT #1 USING, rather than LPRINT or LPRINT USING, to print.

Sending Characters to the Printer

When your printer is properly set up, you can begin to experiment with printing. Let's begin by looking at the LPRINT statement, which sends data to a printer by specifying the items to be printed.

Here is the LPRINT syntax:

```
LPRINT valuelist [{,|;}]
```

valuelist consists of the values to be printed. They can be literals, constants, variables, or, more generally, expressions with a value. When the arguments in *valuelist* are separated by commas, each argument is printed in a field 14 characters wide. When semicolons are used as separators, the arguments are printed without any space between them.

If an LPRINT statement does not end in a comma or a semicolon, the output of the statement is followed by a CR-LF combination, which advances the printer to the next line. If the statement ends in a comma, the next LPRINT statement will begin printing in the next print field on the same line. If it ends in a semicolon, the next LPRINT statement will begin printing immediately after the last character printed.

For instance, you could use the following statements to print today's date and time on one line and then print headers for a report about your softball league:

```
LPRINT "Date: "; DATE$,
LPRINT "Time: "; TIME$
LPRINT
LPRINT "Team", "Won", "Lost", "Average"
```

Here is a sample run:

```
Date: 09-07-1990            Time: 13:35:41

Team            Won             Lost            Average
```

Now try the following program, which sends all the printable ASCII characters and IBM extended characters to the printer, to verify that your printer is configured for the character set used in the IBM PC:

```
FOR Char = 32 TO 254                           ' Printable characters
    LPRINT CHR$(Char);                         ' Print the character
    IF (Char - 32) MOD 50 = 0 THEN LPRINT      ' Print 50 characters per
                                               '  line
NEXT Char
END
```

With a page printer, you must add *LPRINT CHR$(12)* following the loop to issue a formfeed character and print the page. The output is shown in Figure 15-1.

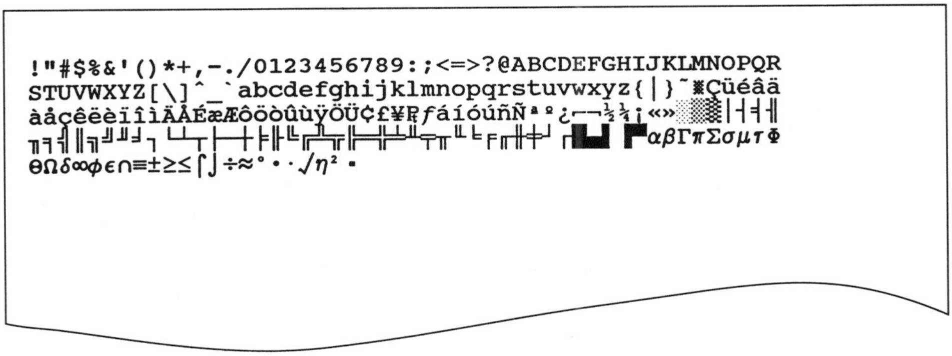

```
 !"#$%&'()*+,-./0123456789:;<=>?@ABCDEFGHIJKLMNOPQR
STUVWXYZ[\]^_`abcdefghijklmnopqrstuvwxyz{|}~⌂Çüéâä
àåçêëèïîìÄÅÉæÆôöòûùÿÖÜ¢£¥₧ƒáíóúñÑªº¿⌐¬½¼¡«»░▒▓│┤╡╢
╖╕╣║╗╝╜╛┐└┴┬├─┼╞╟╚╔╩╦╠═╬╧╨╤╥╙╘╒╓╫╪┘┌█▄▌▐▀αßΓπΣσµτΦ
ΘΩδ∞φε∩≡±≥≤⌠⌡÷≈°∙·√η² ■
```

Figure 15-1.
Printable ASCII and IBM extended character sets.

Printing Graphics Characters

The IBM extended character set includes several graphics characters (shown in Figure 15-1) that you can use to draw lines and boxes. You can generate these characters with the CHR$ function. The program in Listing 15-1 constructs a grid of rectangular cells. It prompts you to specify how many spaces wide the cells will be and how many lines high.

```
CONST charsAcross% = 72 ' Good for HPLJ; you can use 80 for Epson
CONST charsDown% = 52   ' Good for HPLJ; you can use 60 for Epson
CLS
INPUT "Cells how many characters wide? ", CellWidth%
INPUT "Cells how many characters high? ", CellHeight%
CellsAcross% = charsAcross% \ CellWidth%   ' Integer division
CellsDown% = charsDown% \ CellHeight%

FOR Down% = 1 TO CellsDown%

    ' Print top of cells in one row
    FOR Across% = 1 TO CellsAcross%
        LPRINT CHR$(201);                   ' Print left corner
        FOR Char% = 1 TO CellWidth% - 2
            LPRINT CHR$(205);               ' Print top
        NEXT Char%
        LPRINT CHR$(187);                   ' Print right corner
    NEXT Across%
    LPRINT

    ' Print inside part of cells in one row
    FOR LineDown% = 1 TO CellHeight% - 2
        FOR Across% = 1 TO CellsAcross%
            LPRINT CHR$(186);               ' Print left side
            FOR Char% = 1 TO CellWidth% - 2
                LPRINT " ";
            NEXT Char%
            LPRINT CHR$(186);               ' Print right side
        NEXT Across%
        LPRINT
    NEXT LineDown%

    ' Print bottom of cells in one row
    FOR Across% = 1 TO CellsAcross%
        LPRINT CHR$(200);                   ' Print left corner
        FOR Char% = 1 TO CellWidth% - 2
            LPRINT CHR$(205);               ' Print bottom
        NEXT Char%
        LPRINT CHR$(188);                   ' Print right corner
    NEXT Across%
    LPRINT
NEXT Down%
END
```

Listing 15-1.

Figure 15-2 shows the output based on a cell width of eight characters and a cell height of four lines. You could use the grid to sketch how your company will be organized when you become CEO or to map the latest convoluted adventure game.

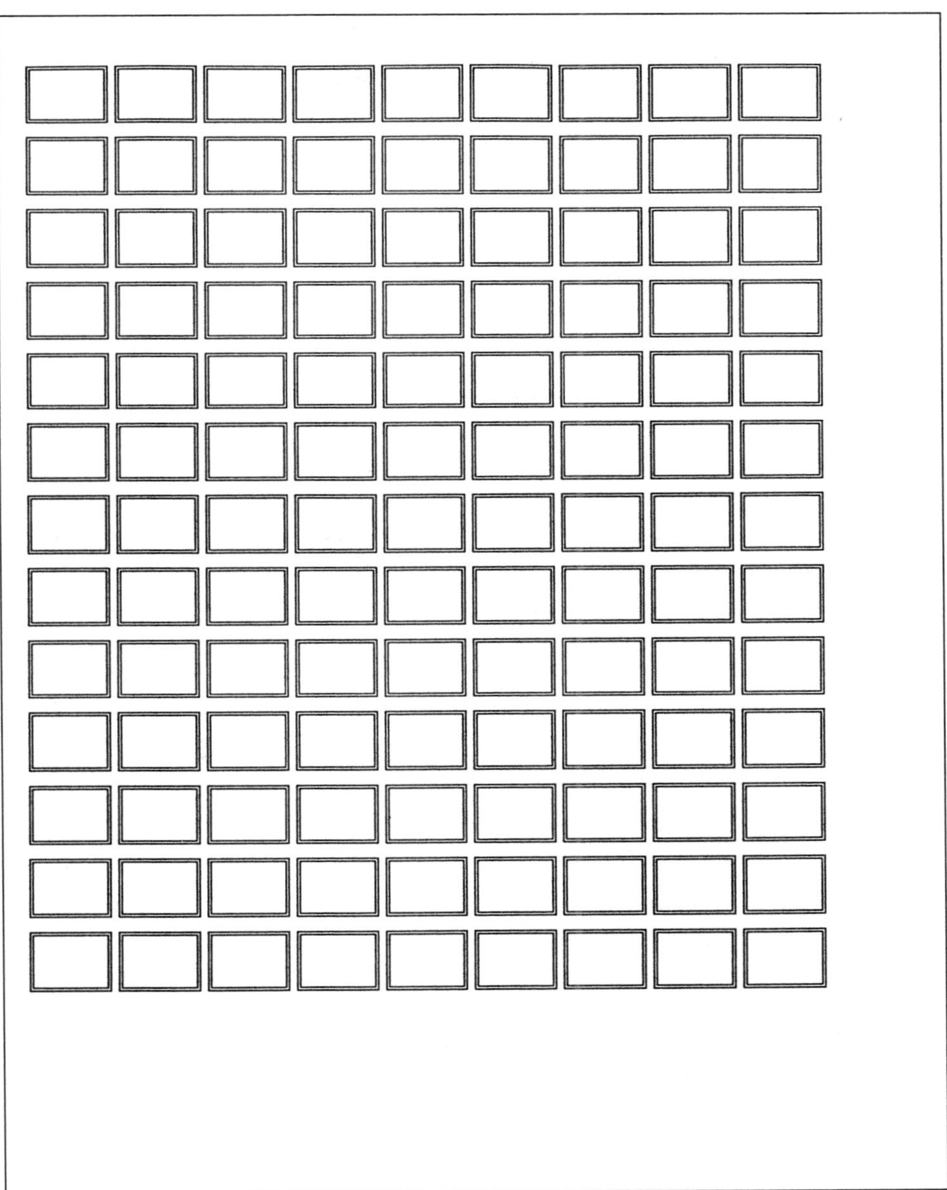

Figure 15-2.
Output of Listing 15-1 (HP LaserJet II).

Using Special Printer Control Characters

Certain nonprinting ASCII characters control the operation of the printer. Figure 15-3 lists those most commonly used; Appendix C contains the complete list.

Control Character	ASCII Value		Purpose
	Dec	Hex	
Beep or Bell (BEL)	7	07	Sounds beep or buzzer
Backspace (BS)	8	08	Moves left one space (not applicable to some older printers)
Horizontal tab (HT)	9	09	Moves to next tab stop
Linefeed (LF)	10	0A	Goes to next line (same column)
Formfeed (FF)	12	0C	Goes to start of next page
Carriage return (CR)	13	0D	Goes to start of next line
Escape (ESC)	27	1B	Starts a printer command (not applicable to some printers)

Figure 15-3.
Common printer control characters.

The following program fragment uses some of these characters to prepare for printing a report that requires special paper:

```
CONST alert = 7
CONST formfeed = 12
PRINT CHR$(alert)        ' Sound the computer's bell
PRINT "Change paper now" ' Show message on screen
LPRINT CHR$(formfeed)    ' Start a new page
' Now do report
END
```

This example uses the CONST keyword to make the ASCII values constants and to give them names that are easy to remember. Because some printers, such as the HP LaserJet, have no built-in speaker and cannot sound a beep, the program also uses a PRINT statement to sound the computer's built-in speaker.

Let's look at another example that demonstrates printer control characters. Printing a character followed by the backspace character and an underscore is a generic method of underlining that doesn't depend on particular printer commands. Listing 15-2 defines a function that prepares a string for underlined printing using this technique.

```
DECLARE FUNCTION Underline$ (AString$)
COMMON SHARED backspace$, under$
backspace$ = CHR$(8)          ' Backspace
under$ = CHR$(95)             ' Underscore

Title$ = "A Tale of Two Cities"
LPRINT "I'm reading "; Underline$(Title$); "."

FUNCTION Underline$ (AString$)
Temp$ = ""
FOR Char = 1 TO LEN(AString$)    ' Add underscore one character at a time
    Temp$ = Temp$ + MID$(AString$, Char, 1) + backspace$ + under$
NEXT Char
Underline$ = Temp$
END FUNCTION
```

Listing 15-2.

Here is the output:

```
I'm reading A Tale of Two Cities.
```

Sending Commands to the Printer

Most printers support a versatile set of commands that control special settings for margins, font, pitch, superscripts or subscripts, and style of characters. The escape character, accessed by the function call *CHR$(27)*, usually introduces a printer command. When the printer receives this character, it switches internally to a mode in which it interprets subsequent characters in that statement as commands rather than as values of characters to be printed. (The printer returns to regular printing mode after it receives a complete command.) For instance, the following statement turns on double-width characters on an Epson-compatible printer:

```
LPRINT CHR$(27); "W"; CHR$(1)
```

This statement restores normal character size:

```
LPRINT CHR$(27); "W"; CHR$(0)
```

Printer commands also offer an alternative method of underlining text. This program, designed to work with the HP LaserJet, defines a function that uses printer commands to turn underlining on, print a string, and then turn underlining off:

```
DECLARE FUNCTION Underline$ (AString$)
LPRINT "You can turn underlining "; Underline$("on"); " or off."
LPRINT CHR$(12)    ' Print the formfeed character

FUNCTION Underline$ (AString$)
' Make a string with the underline-on command, text, and
'  the underline-off command
Temp$ = CHR$(27) + "&dD" + AString$ + CHR$(27) + "&d@"
Underline$ = Temp$
END FUNCTION
```

To use the preceding program with an Epson-compatible dot-matrix printer, change the assignment to *Temp$* as shown here:

```
Temp$ = CHR$(27) + "-" + CHR$(1) + AString$ + CHR$(27) + "-" + CHR$(0)
```

You can also create a file of printer commands for each printer you use, with each printer command in a string variable. Give each function the same name regardless of the printer. For example, you could establish an Epson file called EPSON.BI that includes the following:

```
UlOn$ = CHR$(27) + "-" + CHR$(1)
UlOff$ = CHR$(27) + "-" + CHR$(0)
```

Your HP LaserJet file (HPLJ.BI) might include these command definitions:

```
UlOn$ = CHR$(27) + "&dD"
UlOff$ = CHR$(27) + "&d@"
```

After you've prepared files for each printer, you can use the $INCLUDE metacommand in your program to load the file for a particular printer:

```
REM x$INCLUDE: 'EPSON.BI'
REM x$INCLUDE: 'HPLJ.BI'
```

The *x* suppresses execution of the metacommand. When you're ready to run the program, simply delete the *x* for the printer you want to use, and the appropriate file of printer command definitions will be loaded and compiled with your program. In effect, you've created your own printer drivers for use with QuickBASIC.

The $INCLUDE Metacommand

With the $INCLUDE metacommand, you can direct QuickBASIC to insert statements from a file into a program. Here is the syntax for this metacommand:

```
{REM | '} $INCLUDE: 'filename'
```

filename is the name of the file to be included in the program. If you want to include a file that is not in the current directory, specify the full pathname. The file that is inserted can contain only module-level code; it cannot contain any subprograms or function procedures.

Suppose you want to include a file called SUBS.BI that contains the DECLARE statements for all the subprograms in your program. If the file is found in the PROGRAM subdirectory on the C drive, use $INCLUDE as follows:

```
' $INCLUDE: 'C:\PROGRAM\SUBS.BI'
```

When you create and name a file to be included, it's a good idea to use BI (which stands for BASIC include) as the filename extension.

Figure 15-4 and Figure 15-5 list some of the most useful commands for Epson-compatible and HP LaserJet printers. Note that you can separate parts of a command string with either a plus sign or a semicolon in LPRINT statements. Remember to include a semicolon (or comma) at the end of any LPRINT statement unless you want the output of the next LPRINT statement to start on a new line.

Command String for Epson-compatible Printers	***Meaning***
"-"; CHR$(1);	Turns on underlining
"-"; CHR$(0);	Turns off underlining
"3"; CHR$(*n*);	Sets line spacing to *n*/216 inch
"4";	Turns on italics
"5";	Turns off italics
"C"; CHR$(*n*);	Specifies *n* lines per page
"E";	Turns on emphasized mode
"F";	Turns off emphasized mode
"G";	Turns on double-strike mode
"H";	Turns off double-strike mode
"M";	Turns on elite mode (12 characters per inch)
"P";	Turns off elite mode
"Q"; CHR$(*n*);	Sets right margin to *n* characters
"S"; CHR$(1);	Turns on subscript
"S"; CHR$(0);	Turns on superscript
"T";	Turns off subscript or superscript
"W"; CHR$(1);	Turns on double-width mode
"W"; CHR$(0);	Turns off double-width mode
"p"; CHR$(1);	Turns on proportional spacing
"p"; CHR$(0);	Turns off proportional spacing

Note: All commands listed here begin with the escape character.

Figure 15-4.
Common commands for Epson-compatible printers.

Command String for HP LaserJet Printers	Meaning
"&l*n*C";	Sets line spacing to *n*/48 inch
"&l*n*D";	Sets line spacing to *n* lines per inch
"&l3D";	Sets double spacing (3 lines per inch)
"&l*n*P";	Sets page length to *n* lines
"&l*n*E";	Sets top margin to *n* lines
"&l*n*F";	Sets text length to *n* lines per page
"&a*n*L";	Sets left margin to *n*
"&a*n*M";	Sets right margin to *n*
"&l0O";	Sets portrait orientation
"&l1O";	Sets landscape orientation
"(10U";	Selects IBM PC symbol set
"(0U";	Selects ANSI ASCII symbol set
"(s0P";	Sets fixed spacing
"(s1P";	Sets proportional spacing
"(s*n*H";	Selects pitch of *n* characters per inch
"(s*n*V";	Selects height of *n* points
"(s1S";	Sets italics
"(s0S";	Sets regular (upright) characters
"(s3B";	Sets boldface
"(s0B";	Sets normal (medium) weight
"(s-3B";	Sets light characters
"(s*n*T";	Sets typeface to HP typeface number *n*
"&dD";	Turns on underlining
"&d@";	Turns off underlining

Note: All commands listed here begin with the escape character.
Some font-related commands such as height are not available for all fonts.

Figure 15-5.
Common commands for HP LaserJet printers.

Formatted Printing

Chapter 3 introduced you to the PRINT USING statement, which uses a special format string to specify how numbers or strings will be displayed on the screen. LPRINT USING provides the same service for formatting string output to the printer. (In fact, you might want to test your formats on the screen with PRINT USING statements and then change to LPRINT USING for sending output to the printer.)

Here is the syntax for LPRINT USING:

```
LPRINT USING formatstring; valuelist [{,|;}]
```

formatstring contains the printing instructions; it can be a string literal or a string variable. QuickBASIC provides several special symbols that can be used in this string. Note that *formatstring* must be followed by a semicolon. *valuelist* is a list of arguments. It resembles the *valuelist* used in the LPRINT statement except that commas and semicolons are interchangeable as separators in an LPRINT USING statement because *formatstring* dictates the spacing.

LPRINT USING uses the same set of formatting instructions that PRINT USING does. See Appendix E for a complete description of these formatting instructions.

Listing 15-3 uses LPRINT and LPRINT USING to format the names and amounts for a check. Because the format character for leading asterisks works only with numbers, we use the QuickBASIC STRING$ function to generate asterisks before and after *Amt$* and to generate top and bottom lines as borders.

```
INPUT "Check number: ", CheckNo%
INPUT "Pay to: ", Payee$
INPUT "Amount in words: ", Amt$
INPUT "Amount in figures: ", Amt#
INPUT "Your name: ", YourName$

LPRINT STRING$(75, "_")
LPRINT "No. "; CheckNo%
LPRINT SPC(60); "Date: "; DATE$
LPRINT
LPRINT "Pay to: "; Payee$
LPRINT
LPRINT "Amount: ";
FillerLen = LEN(Amt$) / 5
LPRINT STRING$(FillerLen, "*");
LPRINT Amt$;
LPRINT STRING$(FillerLen, "*");
LPRINT USING "*$###.##"; Amt#     ' Print a formatted string
LPRINT : LPRINT
LPRINT SPC(60); YourName$
LPRINT
LPRINT STRING$(75, "_")
END
```

Listing 15-3.

Figure 15-6 shows the output of the following sample run:

```
Check number: 11
Pay to: Serendip Software
Amount in words: Three Hundred Thirty-five Dollars
Amount in figures: 335.00
Your name: Bill Fenster
```

```
No.  11
                                                    Date: 09-10-1990

Pay to: Serendip Software

Amount: *******Three Hundred Thirty-five Dollars********$335.00

                                                    Bill Fenster
```

Figure 15-6.
Output of Listing 15-3 (HP LaserJet II).

Setting Margins and Checking Print Position

The easiest way to set page length as well as top, bottom, left, and right margins with QuickBASIC is simply to use LPRINT to send the printer command that sets the margin. But not all printers support commands that set these margins. For example, with the HP DeskJet and Epson-compatible printers, the bottom margin is established by setting the top margin and the text length.

You can set a right margin on any printer by using the WIDTH LPRINT statement to specify the column at which the printer moves to the start of the next line.

Here is the syntax for WIDTH LPRINT:

```
WIDTH LPRINT columns
```

columns is a number in the range 1 through 255 that specifies the number of characters per line. If your program reads lines from a file that uses carriage returns at the ends of paragraphs only (rather than at the ends of lines), you can write a program that sets the width of the printed page to 80 characters, thus breaking up the long lines in the printout.

Using WIDTH LPRINT with a value of 255 suppresses the carriage return that is normally sent when a line extends past the right margin. The printer moves to the next line only when the program calls another LPRINT statement. Neither printer commands nor QuickBASIC itself offers wordwrap as such. If the printer reaches the right margin in the middle of a word, it prints the remaining letters of the word on the next line without wordwrapping and without adding a hyphen. If you are concerned about words being broken between lines, use the LPOS function. LPOS returns the column at which the next character will be printed.

The syntax for LPOS is the following:

```
LPOS(portnumber)
```

portnumber is 1, 2, or 3, corresponding to the parallel ports LPT1, LPT2, and LPT3. Thus, if your program is printing a string one word at a time, it can use LPOS to check that enough space remains on the current line for the next word. This test is demonstrated in the following statements:

```
IF LPOS(1) + LEN(NextWord$) > RightMargin% THEN
    LPRINT
END IF
```

Using WIDTH LPRINT with Various Fonts

You can also use the WIDTH LPRINT statement to keep the right margin constant even when you change fonts. Listing 15-4 prints two fonts (Courier and Lineprinter) on an HP LaserJet.

```
' Test string to show text alignment in printout
Tst1$ = "12345678901234567890123456789012345678901234567890123456789O"
Tst$ = Tst1$ + "1234567890"

' Send command to set Courier typeface, 12 pitch, 10 points
LPRINT CHR$(27); "(8U"; CHR$(27); "(s0p12h10v0s0b3T";

WIDTH LPRINT 48          ' Set printing width to 48 characters
LPRINT Tst$

' Send command to set Lineprinter typeface, 16.66 pitch, 8.5 points
LPRINT CHR$(27); "(8U"; CHR$(27); "(s0p16.66h8.5v0s0b0T";

WIDTH LPRINT 67          ' Set printing width to 67 characters
LPRINT Tst$

LPRINT CHR$(12)          ' Send formfeed to print page
END
```

Listing 15-4.

The 12-pitch Courier font prints 12 characters per inch, whereas the 16.66-pitch Lineprinter font prints slightly more than 16 characters per inch. Thus, 48 12-pitch characters and 67 16.66-pitch characters are needed to print a 4-inch line. The program uses WIDTH LPRINT to control the number of characters printed. As you can see in the output (Figure 15-7), the output of the two fonts lines up at the right margin.

```
123456789012345678901234567890123456789012345678
90123456789012345678 90

1234567890123456789012345678901234567890123456789012345678901234567
890
```

Figure 15-7.
Output of Listing 15-4.

Controlling the Print Position

Creating forms with a page printer is simple. The LOCATE statement lets you position items to be displayed on the screen at a specified row and column. Similarly, with a page printer such as the HP LaserJet, you can use printer commands to position items to be printed to any location on the page.

The program in Listing 15-5 accepts data for as many as 10 transactions and both prints a form and displays the form on the screen. Two subprograms, *PrintStr* and *PrintNum*, each use a LOCATE statement to position items on the screen and a PRINT or PRINT USING statement to display the items. For the printer form, the subprograms use the HP cursor positioning command to position the output. (Separate subprograms for printing strings and numbers allow us to take advantage of PRINT USING and LPRINT USING formatting for numbers.)

```
DECLARE SUB PrintStr (LineNum%, Col%, AString$)    ' Print a string
DECLARE SUB PrintNum (LineNum%, Col%, ANum!)       ' Print a number

' Print a form on both screen and printer
OPTION BASE 1
DIM Items$(10)                   ' Array to hold items purchased
DIM Prices!(10)                  ' Array to hold prices of items
CLS
' Prompt for as many as 10 items and prices, and store in arrays
PRINT "Enter up to 10 items. Press Enter to exit."
FOR Item = 1 TO 10
    INPUT "Name of item: ", Items$(Item)
    IF Items$(Item) = "" THEN EXIT FOR
    INPUT "Price: ", Prices!(Item)
NEXT Item
```

Listing 15-5. *(continued)*

Listing 15-5. *continued*

```
CLS                                  ' Clear screen

' Print headings
PrintStr 1, 50, "Date:"
PrintStr 1, 56, DATE$
PrintStr 2, 50, "Time:"
PrintStr 2, 56, TIME$
PrintStr 4, 25, "Marty's Market"
PrintStr 5, 25, "Transaction Record"
PrintStr 8, 15, "Item"
PrintStr 8, 50, "Price"

Total! = 0
Item = 1
LineNum% = 10

' Print items and prices
DO WHILE Items$(Item) <> ""
    PrintStr LineNum%, 15, Items$(Item)
    PrintStr LineNum%, 50, "$"
    PrintNum LineNum%, 51, Prices!(Item)
    Total! = Total! + Prices!(Item)
    LineNum% = LineNum% + 1
    Item = Item + 1
LOOP

' Print total
PrintStr LineNum% + 5, 43, "Total: "
PrintStr LineNum% + 5, 50, "$"
PrintNum LineNum% + 5, 51, Total!
LPRINT CHR$(12)                      ' Print formfeed to print page
END

SUB PrintNum (LineNum%, Col%, ANum!)
    LOCATE LineNum%, Col%
    PRINT USING "###.##"; ANum!      ' Display number on screen
    ' Send command to position cursor at line, column
    LPRINT CHR$(27); "&a"; LineNum%; "R"; CHR$(27); "&a"; Col%; "C";
    LPRINT USING "###.##"; ANum!     ' Print number
END SUB

SUB PrintStr (LineNum%, Col%, AString$)
    LOCATE LineNum%, Col%
    PRINT AString$                   ' Display string on screen
    ' Send command to position cursor at line, column
    LPRINT CHR$(27); "&a"; LineNum%; "R"; CHR$(27); "&a"; Col%; "C";
    LPRINT AString$                  ' Print string
END SUB
```

Figure 15-8 presents a sample of the program's output.

```
                                                   Date: 09-10-1990
                                                   Time: 17:24:08

                      Marty's Market
                      Transaction Record

           Item                                    Price

           Cabbage                                 $  0.59
           Rice                                    $  0.75
           Beans                                   $  1.12
           Bread                                   $  1.39
           Milk                                    $  1.05
           Coffee                                  $  4.59



                                            Total: $  9.49
```

Figure 15-8.
Output of Listing 15-5.

Positioning items with a line printer can be more difficult. Although you can use horizontal and vertical tabs, you often can't move back to a previous line. To solve this problem, you could put all the row and column positions for the items you want to print in an array, with the positions for items to be printed at the top of the page preceding the positions for the lower ones. Your positioning routine could then use vertical tabs to set the row positions and use spaces or horizontal tabs to set the column positions on each line.

Using Graphics Mode

Most dot-matrix and laser printers have graphics capabilities, allowing the printer to print individual dots instead of text on the page. The simplest way to print graphics is to perform a graphics screen dump of your program's output. DOS allows you to output a text screen to your printer simply by pressing Shift-Prt Scr. To output a graphics screen from a QuickBASIC program, however, you must run the DOS utility GRAPHICS.COM before you start QuickBASIC. In early versions of DOS, GRAPHICS.COM supports only IBM dot-matrix printers; later versions support other IBM and compatible printers.

Early versions of GRAPHICS.COM support only CGA graphics modes; but starting with DOS version 4, GRAPHICS.COM supports EGA and VGA graphics modes as well. Check your DOS manual to see whether graphics screens can be output to your printer using GRAPHICS.COM.

The GRAPHICS.COM utility resides in memory and monitors the keyboard until Shift-Prt Scr is pressed. It then sends the currently displayed graphics to the printer. (With a page printer, you might need to send a formfeed character to the printer to print the image.)

The GRAPHICS.COM utility actually responds to the hardware interrupt 5 used by IBM PCs and compatible computers. This means that your program can output its own graphics by using a CALL INTERRUPT statement to call interrupt 5. (CALL INTERRUPT is discussed in Chapter 17. Interrupt 5 doesn't require you to set register values, although you must declare the register data types.)

Controlling Bit-Mapped Graphics from QuickBASIC

In addition to outputting screen images to the printer, your program can also generate images directly on most dot-matrix or laser printers. The commands and methods vary with the printer type and model. Although the examples in this section demonstrate techniques designed for Epson-compatible dot-matrix printers, an understanding of the concepts will help you work with any printer.

A graphics image can be written as a series of bits with values of either 1 or 0; 1 represents a dot on the page, and 0 represents an empty space. An image defined by 0's and 1's—called a *bit-mapped* image—is most often stored as a series of bytes, with 8 bits per byte. To generate a bit-mapped image on a dot-matrix printer, send the bits of the image to the printer 1 byte at a time. Each pin in the print head (which presses against a ribbon and the paper to create a dot on the paper) corresponds to a bit position in the byte of data, as shown in Figure 15-9. Dot-matrix printers that have 9 pins typically use only 8 (or occasionally 7) for graphics output; printers with 24 pins use more complex arrangements.

Pin	Bit value	Output
⑧	0	
⑦	1	●
⑥	0	
⑤	1	●
④	0	
③	1	●
②	0	
①	0	

Byte value = 01010100 (binary) = 84 (decimal)

Figure 15-9.
Correspondence between print head pins and byte values.

Here are the basic steps to follow to print graphics on a dot-matrix printer:

1. Use the statement *WIDTH LPRINT 255* to prevent the printer from issuing a carriage return (and therefore breaking the graphics image) if the image extends past the right margin.

2. Define the bytes of a line of the bit-mapped image. A line consists of columns of eight dots that are each represented by 1 byte. A one-line, 8 × 8 bit checkerboard pattern can be represented in 8 bytes. You can use graph paper to plot the dot positions and convert them to byte values. (See Figure 15-10.)

Bit position								
8	X	X			X	X		
7	X	X			X	X		
6			X	X			X	X
5			X	X			X	X
4	X	X			X	X		
3	X	X			X	X		
2			X	X			X	X
1			X	X			X	X
Byte value	204	204	51	51	204	204	51	51

Figure 15-10.
The plot for a one-line, 8 × 8 graphic.

3. Determine the width of the line. For example, if a line in the graphic is 480 dots across, its width is 480.

4. Issue the printer command that turns on the printer's bit-mapped graphics mode. For the Epson printer, this command is the following:

```
LPRINT CHR$(27); "K"; CHR$(Low); CHR$(High)
```

Here *Low* represents the low byte (the first byte) of the number that indicates the width of the line to be printed, and *High* represents the high byte (the second byte) of the number. The printer uses both *Low* and *High* because the CHR$ function accepts only numbers in the range 0 through 255 (a 1-byte number), and the width of a printed page is usually 480, a number that requires 2 bytes. A program can use *Low* and *High* to specify a 2-byte number so that a line can have a width greater than 255 dots. For example, the high byte of the width 480 is 1, and the low byte is 224. To calculate the high byte, divide the width by 256. To calculate the low byte, use the MOD operator to find the remainder of the width divided by 256. An easy way to calculate the values of the high and low bytes is to use the Immediate window. Enter these statements:

```
PRINT 480 \ 256      ' Prints 1 for the high byte
PRINT 480 MOD 256    ' Prints 224 for the low byte
```

5. Send each byte of the line of the bit-mapped image to the printer by using LPRINT and CHR$. You will probably want to read the bytes from a file or from DATA statements.

6. Send an LPRINT command to move the printer to the next line.

7. Perform steps 2 through 5 for the next line of the graphics image.

8. Reset the printer.

The following program sends the one-line checkerboard shown in Figure 15-10 to an Epson or a compatible dot-matrix printer:

```
WIDTH LPRINT 255                              ' Suppress carriage returns
LPRINT CHR$(27); "K"; CHR$(8); CHR$(0)        ' Start bit graphics; set
FOR Column% = 1 TO 8                          '  width to 8
    READ Byte%
    LPRINT CHR$(Byte%);
NEXT Column%
DATA 204, 204, 51, 51, 204, 204, 51, 51
LPRINT CHR$(27); "@"                          ' Reset the printer
```

Configuring the Serial Port for Communications

Let's look more closely at the serial port and at the QuickBASIC statements that work specifically with such ports.

As we mentioned earlier, printers can be attached to either a parallel port or a serial port. Other devices, such as modems, joysticks, and fax machines, can be attached to a serial port. Serial devices are more complicated than parallel devices. Parallel devices can receive an entire byte of data at one time, whereas serial devices can receive only 1 bit of data at a time. The serial device must determine when it has received enough bits for one character (usually 8 bits, although some devices use 7). *Data bits* are the bits that make up each value sent to the serial device. *Stop bits* serve as separators between the groups of data bits. (*Start bits,* which usually don't need to be configured, can be used to indicate the beginning of the data bits.)

Many serial connections add *parity bits* to check for errors in the communications. A parity bit is set to either 1 or 0 to make the total number of 1 bits in the value an even number if the even parity setting is used or an odd number if the odd parity setting is used. (Alternatively, a no parity setting could be specified.) If, for example, a value arrives with an odd number of 1 bits when an even parity setting has been used—indicating that some of the data bits might have been inadvertently changed during transmission—a message is sent to the sending device asking it to try the transmission again.

Figure 15-11 shows how a character is sent along a serial connection.

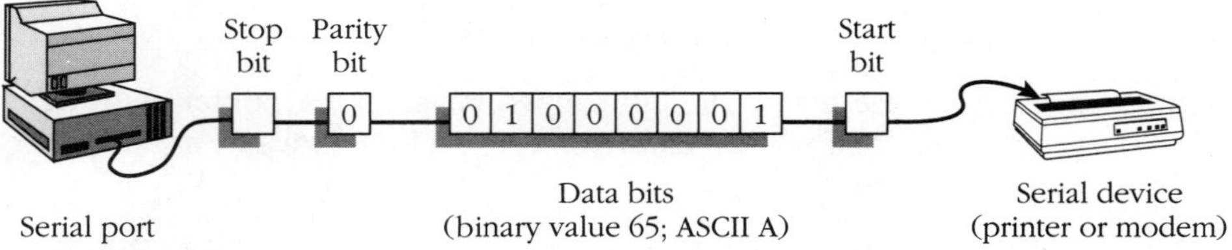

Figure 15-11.
Serial data transmission.

A serial connection's data transmission speed is measured in signals per second, called *baud.* Most modems run at 1200 baud or 2400 baud (roughly 150 or 300 characters per second). Printers operate reliably at higher speeds, such as 9600 baud.

The settings on the serial port and the settings on the serial device (a printer or another device) must correspond. Be sure you know how to set the receiving control data bits, stop bits, parity, and baud rate.

To configure a serial device to be used by a QuickBASIC program, use the OPEN COM statement, and specify the various settings.

Here is the syntax for the OPEN COM statement:

```
OPEN "COMportnum:optionlist" [FOR mode AS [#]filenum] [LEN = reclen]
```

portnum is either 1 or 2, indicating COM1 or COM2, the two DOS serial ports. (QuickBASIC doesn't support COM3 and COM4, which can be added to some machines.) *portnum* and *optionlist* are enclosed in double quotation marks. *optionlist* is a list containing any of the options listed in Figure 15-12. The first four settings must be specified in order—speed, parity, data bits, and stop bits—with a comma replacing any option skipped. The remaining options can be specified in any order.

mode can be INPUT, OUTPUT, or RANDOM. RANDOM, the default mode, is often used for serial printers and modems because it allows both input and output. *filenum* is an integer that identifies the device being opened. The LEN parameter is used only with RANDOM mode; it specifies the length of the device's input buffer.

Parameter	***Meaning***	***Comments***
Speed	Baud rate (signals per second)	Use 75, 110, 150, 300, 600, 1200, 1800, 2400, or 9600. Most dial-up connections are 1200 or 2400. If you use a modem, it must be capable of the speed you specify.
Parity	Type of parity checking used for error detection	Use the letter N (none), E (even), O (odd), S (space), or M (mark).

Figure 15-12. *(continued)*
Parameters used with the OPEN COM statement.

Figure 15-12. *continued*

Parameter	***Meaning***	***Comments***
Data bits	Number of bits that make up each value	Use 5, 6, 7, or 8. Use 8 only if parity checking is not performed; use 7 if it is.
Stop bits	Number of bits used to mark the end of each value	Use 1, 1.5, or 2. The appropriate setting is usually 1. Use 2 for slow transmission rates, and use 1.5 only if the number of data bits is 5.
ASC	Treats characters as ASCII; expands tabs; forces a carriage return at the end of each line; considers Ctrl-Z the end-of-file marker	This is the standard setting for sending and receiving ASCII text files.
BIN	Performs none of the actions specified by ASC	This is the default setting. Use either ASC or BIN but not both.
CD*ms*	Specifies the milliseconds to wait for the timeout on the Data Carrier Detect (DCD) line	*ms* must be a number in the range 0 through 65535. A value of 0 disables the timeout. The default is 0.
CS*ms*	Specifies the milliseconds to wait for the timeout on the Clear to Send (CTS) line	*ms* must be a number in the range 0 through 65535. The default is 1000 (1 second).
DS*ms*	Specifies the milliseconds to wait for the timeout on the Data Set Ready (DSR) line	*ms* must be a number of milliseconds in the range 0 through 65535. The default is 1000 (1 second).
LF	Adds a linefeed to each carriage return	This setting is used for printing with serial printers.
OP*ms*	Specifies the milliseconds to wait for the OPEN COM statement to be successful	*ms* must be a number in the range 0 through 65535. The default is 1000 (10 seconds). If this parameter is omitted, OPEN COM waits for 10 times the larger of any values used with CD or DS.
RB*bytes*	Allocates a number of bytes to the receive buffer (input buffer)	*bytes* must be a number in the range 0 through 32767. The default is 512.
TB*bytes*	Allocates a number of bytes to the transmit buffer (output buffer)	*bytes* must be a number in the range 0 through 32767. The default is 512.
RS	Suppresses detection of the Request to Send (RTS) signal	

If your serial printer is connected to COM1 and is set to 9600 baud, 8 data bits, 1 stop bit, and no parity, you can open communications with the printer by using the following statement:

```
OPEN "COM1:9600,N,8,1" FOR RANDOM AS #1
```

Then, to send output to the printer, use the PRINT # or PRINT # USING statement. You could test your serial printer by entering the following statement:

```
PRINT #1, "This is a test."
```

If the printer does not print, check the physical connection. If characters are garbled or misplaced on the page, be sure that the baud rate, data bits, stop bits, and parity settings on the printer match the values used in the OPEN COM statement.

Speed and Parity for Modems

Most modems operate at 1200 or 2400 baud, a slower rate than that used by most serial printers. Phone lines can contain a great deal of "noise," or interference, and increasing the speed of transmission tends to increase the error rate. Using parity checks to detect errors is important with modems. When the parity set by your program and the parity used by the remote service match, your program can transmit or receive ordinary text with reasonable reliability, although exact transmission cannot be guaranteed without the use of a special error-correcting protocol.

Some remote services require specific serial port settings. These are the most common: 8 data bits, no parity, 1 stop bit; and 7 data bits, even parity, 1 stop bit.

Timeouts

A program can't anticipate exactly how long it will take for a remote system to answer the phone or how much time will elapse between a transmission and its acknowledgment. QuickBASIC, however, provides default timeout values that work well in most cases. After the communications device waits the amount of time specified by the timeout value, it stops waiting and returns a *Device timeout* error message to the program. If you get device errors or if the connection is not completed, you might need to adjust the values for the CD, CS, DS, or OP timeout parameters described in Figure 15-12. These timeout values are specified in milliseconds, with a value of 0 specifying that the device will wait forever for the signal in question.

Data Buffers

If a program had to stop what it was doing every time a character arrived at the serial port from a remote system or had to send each bit out the port individually, execution would slow to a crawl. Instead, QuickBASIC sets up two buffers for the serial device—an input buffer and an output buffer. If you find that you are losing incoming characters, the input buffer might be overflowing before your program's communications routines can service it. In that case, try increasing the value of the RB (receive buffer) parameter in the OPEN COM statement. If your program slows down while sending data out the port to another system, try increasing the value of TB (transmit buffer) so that more data will be accumulated before it is sent out the port to the device. Remember, though, that communicating is a cooperative activity between two systems; if the device at the other end, such as a printer, can't process data quickly, you won't be able to send data quickly, because your system won't get the go-ahead.

Sending and Receiving Data with a Cable

Let's consider two computers whose serial ports are connected by a *null modem cable.* This cable connects pin 2 of the cable at one end with pin 3 at the other end, and vice versa. Thus each computer receives the other's output and sends to the other's input.

If you have two computers available and can connect them with a null modem cable, you can try to run the following program, which simply opens the serial port and uses a loop to send data continuously out the serial port:

```
' Open the port to send data
OPEN "COM1:1200,N,8,1,CD0,CS0,DS0,OP0,RS" FOR OUTPUT AS #1
DO
    PRINT #1, "This is a test..."
LOOP WHILE INKEY$ = ""
CLOSE     ' Close the port
END
```

As data comes into the serial port from the computer that runs the preceding program, the data is inserted in the input buffer. Because QuickBASIC treats the serial port like a file, you can use the EOF function to check the contents. If EOF returns a value of true, no characters are waiting.

If characters are found, you can read them with input statements. The INPUT$ statement is the best choice because it reads all the available characters. (The INPUT # and LINE INPUT # statements, in contrast, might read only part of the data because they stop reading at specified points—the end of a line or the first comma or space, for instance.) How do you know how many characters are waiting? You can use the LOC function, which tells you how many characters remain to be read in a file.

The following program uses these statements and functions to receive the data sent by the preceding program:

```
OPEN "COM1:1200,N,8,1,CD0,CS0,DS0,OP0,RS" FOR INPUT AS #1
DO WHILE NOT EOF(1)
    PRINT INPUT$(LOC(1), #1); ' Display the data
LOOP
CLOSE                         ' Close the port
END
```

The WIDTH Statement

Earlier in this chapter we used the WIDTH LPRINT statement to set the right margin on a printer. You can use the WIDTH statement to set the line width of a sequential file or a device. Here is the syntax for WIDTH used with a file:

```
WIDTH #filenum, columns
```

filenum is the identifying number of an open sequential file. *columns* is the maximum number of characters in one line.

Here is the syntax for WIDTH used with a device:

```
WIDTH "devicename", columns
```

devicename is the name of a device, such as COM1:, LPT1:, KYBD:, SCRN:, or CONS:. *columns* is the maximum number of characters in one line.

Using WIDTH with a file number allows you to change the line width of a file (or a device opened as a file) after it has been opened. Using WIDTH with a device name lets you set the line width of a device that will be opened later in the program. For example, if you have opened a serial port as file #1 with an OPEN COM statement, you can use the following statement to set the line width to 128 characters, for a serial printer connected to this port:

```
WIDTH #1, 128
```

Alternatively, you can use the WIDTH statement with a device name to specify the line width for a serial printer before you use OPEN COM to open it:

```
WIDTH "COM1:", 128
OPEN "COM1:9600,N,8,1" FOR RANDOM AS #1
```

Event Trapping

In Chapter 13 we demonstrated event trapping using the ON PLAY statement—that is, we set up a subroutine to be executed whenever a particular event occurred (in that case, when the number of notes in the buffer fell below a given value). You can also use event trapping to monitor the arrival of data at the serial port.

Begin by using an ON COM statement with the name of the subroutine that will handle communications with the serial port. Here is the syntax:

```
ON COM(portnumber) GOSUB subroutine
```

portnumber is 1 or 2, and *subroutine* is the name of the subroutine (which must be a GOSUB-type subroutine, not a subprogram).

Next use the COM ON statement to turn on event trapping, which tells the program to watch for the occurrence of an event.

The syntax for this statement is the following:

```
COM(portnumber) ON
```

portnumber must be 1 or 2 (referring to COM1 or COM2). It is also used with the COM OFF statement, which disables event trapping temporarily.

Listing 15-6 uses communications event trapping in a revised version of the preceding program.

```
OPEN "COM1:1200,N,8,1,CD0,CS0,DS0,OP0,RS" FOR INPUT AS #1   ' Open port

ON COM(1) GOSUB WatchPort          ' Specify the subroutine
COM(1) ON                          ' Start trapping
CLS
DO
    LOCATE 1, 1
    PRINT "Waiting for data at COM1: "
    PRINT "Press any key to end program "
    IF INKEY$ <> "" THEN EXIT DO
LOOP
CLOSE                              ' Close the port
END

WatchPort:
    DO WHILE NOT EOF(1)
        PRINT INPUT$(LOC(1), #1);  ' Display the data
    LOOP
RETURN
```

Listing 15-6.

The PRINT statements inside the DO loop are executed repeatedly until the user presses a key. When data arrives at the serial port, however, the COM ON statement sends control to *WatchPort*, the subroutine specified in the ON COM GOSUB statement, which prints characters from the buffer until the buffer is empty.

Dialing Remote Systems

To participate in bulletin board services or to access the wide range of knowledge and features available through online information services, you can simply dial a phone number with the modem and then communicate with the remote system that manages the BBS or contains the information you need. The program in Listing 15-7 represents a bare-bones approach that should establish a connection with a remote system through a modem.

```
OPEN "COM1:1200,E,7,1" FOR RANDOM AS #1    ' Settings to match remote system

Quit$ = "@"
PRINT "Type the symbol @ to quit"
INPUT "Number to dial: ", Dial$
Dial$ = "ATDT" + Dial$

PRINT #1, Dial$              ' Dial the number
```

Listing 15-7. *(continued)*

Listing 15-7. *continued*

```
DO                                          ' Main communications loop
    Send$ = INKEY$                          ' Get character from keyboard
    IF (LEFT$(Send$, 1)) = Quit$ THEN       ' Exit loop if @ pressed
        EXIT DO
    END IF

    IF Send$ <> "" THEN                     ' Send user's input to modem
        PRINT #1, Send$;
    END IF

    IF NOT EOF(1) THEN                      ' Incoming characters waiting
        Received$ = INPUT$(LOC(1), #1)
        PRINT Received$;                    ' Display characters
    END IF
LOOP
PRINT #1, "+++ATH0"                         ' Hang up
CLOSE                                       ' Close port
END
```

The OPEN COM statement in Listing 15-7 sets the speed, parity, data bits, and stop bits. If the service you dial requires different settings (for example, no parity, 8 data bits, 1 stop bit), change the statement accordingly.

If a connection is made, the DO loop sends the lines typed by the user to the remote system and exits if the user enters the @ character. The program checks for EOF in communications files to see if any data has been sent from the remote system, and it prints any data that it finds. (If the remote system accepts terminal settings, you must specify *none* or *dumb terminal,* because this program does not respond properly to terminal control codes.)

If you have trouble making reliable connections, try using a value of 0 in your OPEN COM statement for the four timeout parameters (CD, CS, DS, and OP).

You can also extend the program to store a series of settings for various remote systems and to include a dialing directory.

This program assumes that your modem (like most of those sold for use with IBM PCs) uses the Hayes command set. Figure 15-13 lists some common commands for Hayes-compatible modems.

Command	***Meaning***
AT	Gets the modem's attention for subsequent commands. Any string of commands must end with a carriage return.
DP	Dials a number using pulse dialing.

Figure 15-13.
Common commands for Hayes-compatible modems.

(continued)

Figure 15-13. *continued*

Command	Meaning
DT	Dials a number using tone dialing.
E*n*	*n* must be 0 or 1. Echoes (E1) or doesn't echo (E0) to the screen characters entered by the user and sent through the modem.
F*n*	*n* must be 0 or 1. Establishes duplex setting. In full-duplex (F1), the two systems can communicate at the same time, so the remote system echoes characters back to the user; in half-duplex (F0), only one system can communicate at a time, so the local system echoes the characters.
H0	Hangs up the line.
L	Tests the modem (echoes characters from the keyboard back to the screen).
S0 = *rings*	*rings* must be a number in the range 0 through 255. Sets the number of rings before an incoming call will be answered.
S7 = *seconds*	*seconds* must be a number in the range 0 through 255. Waits the specified number of seconds for a carrier signal (response from the remote system).
V*n*	*n* must be 0 or 1. Sets the modem to return response codes as numbers (V0) or strings (V1) that describe the progress of the call.
X*n*	*n* must be 0 or 1. Displays a limited range (X0) or a full range (X1) of response codes.
, (comma)	Causes phone dialing to pause for two seconds; sometimes needed when dialing 9 to get an outside line, for example.
+++	Hangs up the modem and returns to command mode.

Review Questions

1. In what two ways can you enable a QuickBASIC program to output text to a serial printer?
2. How can you make special characters or printer commands more understandable in your programs?
3. Write a function that accepts a string as a parameter and returns it with the codes that direct your printer to print the string in italics.
4. Why do many programs that communicate through the serial port use event trapping? What statements are used to set up event trapping for a serial port?
5. Your communications program appears to be losing some of the incoming text. What might be the problem, and what should you do?

PART VI

Development

16

Errors and Error Trapping

ERDEV	**ERR**	**ON ERROR GOTO**	**RESUME NEXT**
ERDEV$	**ERROR**	**RESUME**	

By simplifying the process of finding and correcting errors, QuickBASIC's combination of helpful error messages and built-in debugging tools can make your programs more reliable and easier to use. The QuickBASIC editor, for example, checks each statement for correct syntax as soon as you press the Enter key. Compile-time errors such as duplicate definitions, erroneous data types, or incorrect subprogram or function calls are pointed out in error messages that appear in dialog boxes. QuickBASIC also intercepts, or "traps," runtime errors such as division by 0 or numeric overflow. In addition, you can access online help that explains the probable cause of an error and often offers suggestions for correcting it.

Of course, even a program that runs without obvious glitches can contain errors in loop logic or incorrectly initialized variables. As you've seen in earlier chapters, you can use QuickBASIC's Watch window to examine various test conditions, expressions, and variables. You can set breakpoints and then step through a loop to find out where things went wrong.

Programmers must also anticipate user-caused runtime errors and include a way for the program to handle such problems. This chapter shows you how to construct routines that both intercept runtime errors and provide information to get the user and the program back on track. For example, if the user has neglected to turn the printer on before the program tries to print, you can trap the error, tell the user what happened and what to do about it, and resume execution of the program.

Runtime Errors and Error Messages

Let's review what happens when a runtime error occurs. Consider, for example, this one-line program:

```
FILES "A:"     ' List the files on drive A
```

This program uses the FILES statement to list the files in the current directory on drive A. When the compiled code for the FILES statement is executed, it calls a DOS service that tries to read the disk in that drive. If no disk has been loaded, the drive runs for a moment, and DOS generates a critical error interrupt, indicating a hardware problem. If you were running DOS directly (using the DIR A: command), you would receive the following message:

```
Not ready reading drive A
Abort, Retry, Fail?
```

QuickBASIC, however, intercepts the critical error interrupt and presents a dialog box containing the message shown in Figure 16-1.

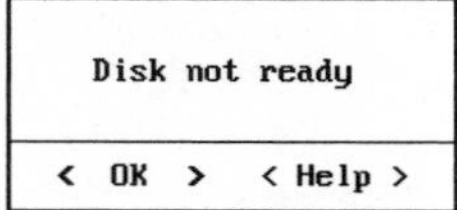

Figure 16-1.
Dialog box with error message.

Selecting Help provides the explanation shown in Figure 16-2, which points out two likely causes of the problem.

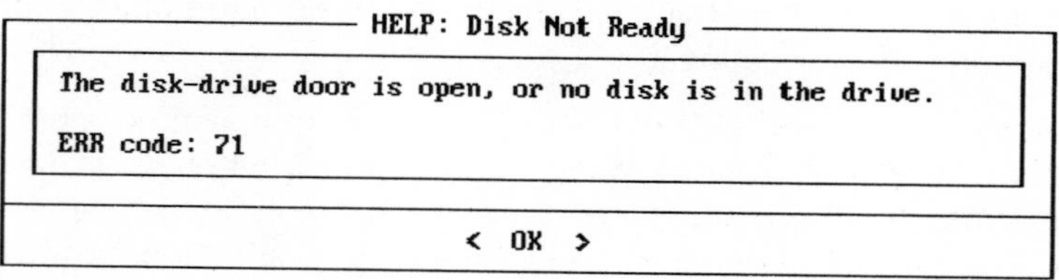

Figure 16-2.
Dialog box with Help information.

Knowing the error code will help you find additional information in the manual *Programming in BASIC.*

Setting Up Error Trapping

If you compile the preceding program to an EXE file, the user who forgets to load the disk is offered only a *Disk not ready* message and the option of exiting to the operating system and beginning again. QuickBASIC, however, allows you to add your own error-handling code. By using the ON ERROR GOTO statement, you can specify a section of code to be executed if QuickBASIC detects a runtime error.

Here is the syntax for ON ERROR GOTO:

```
ON ERROR GOTO location
```

location is the line number or label of the first line of the block of error-handling code that will be executed if an error occurs. If *location* is 0, error trapping is disabled. As GOTO implies, the ON ERROR statement causes the program to jump directly to the specified label or line number when the error is found. (Although you can't jump to a subroutine or subprogram, you can call it from the labeled code.)

A label used in a GOTO statement must start with an alphabetic character and can contain as many as 40 characters. Case is not significant. The label does not end in a colon within the statement itself, but a colon is used with the label at the start of the program section, as shown here:

```
ErrorHandler:
    ' Statements to be executed if a runtime error occurs
    :
END
```

Listing 16-1 demonstrates a simple error trap that handles the problem of the missing disk in drive A.

```
ON ERROR GOTO DiskErr
CLS
FILES "A:"                          ' List the files on drive A
END                                 ' Prevent execution from falling into the
                                    '  error-handling routine
DiskErr:
    PRINT "Please put a disk in drive A."
    PRINT "Then press a key to continue."
    Resp$ = INPUT$(1)
    RESUME
END
```

Listing 16-1.

The ON ERROR GOTO statement specifies that the code labeled *DiskErr* will be executed if a runtime error occurs. Now compile this program to an EXE file, and run.it from DOS with drive A empty. The drive will run for a moment before giving you this message:

```
Please put a disk in drive A.
Then press a key to continue.
```

If you press a key without putting a disk in the drive, the FILES statement generates the same error again, and the message reappears, giving you another chance to correct the problem.

When you load the disk and press a key, the RESUME statement sends control back to the line that caused the error—the FILES statement. This time, a list of the files from the disk in drive A is displayed. Figure 16-3 shows the flow of execution for this program. Note that the END statement preceding *DiskErr* prevents the program from running the error-trapping code inadvertently.

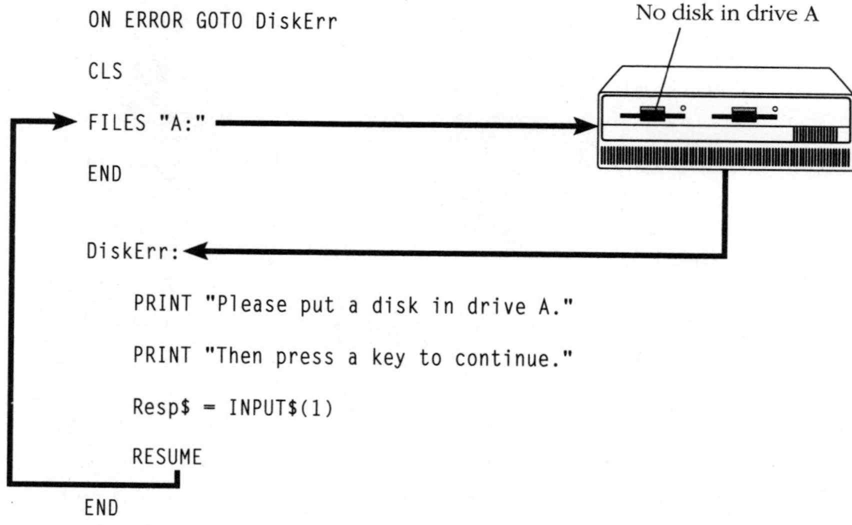
ON ERROR GOTO DiskErr
CLS
FILES "A:"
END
DiskErr:
PRINT "Please put a disk in drive A."
PRINT "Then press a key to continue."
Resp$ = INPUT$(1)
RESUME
END
No disk in drive A

Figure 16-3.
Operation of the ON ERROR GOTO and RESUME statements.

Controlling Execution After an Error

The RESUME statement allows you to choose where your program will resume execution after an error has been corrected. Here is the syntax for RESUME:

```
RESUME [location]
RESUME NEXT
```

location is the line number or label at which execution is to continue. RESUME *location* sends execution to the specified line—that is, it performs a GOTO operation to that location. If *location* is omitted, RESUME sends execution back to the statement that caused the error. RESUME NEXT sends execution back to the statement following the one that caused the error.

Resuming at a Specified Location

Resuming at a specified location in the program can be useful. The code at that location can, for example, decide whether to write data from the file buffers on disk or to clear the buffers, close files, or otherwise minimize the damage an error can cause.

Listing 16-2 provides a menu of directory-related operations and illustrates how an error-handling routine can make file-handling programs friendlier. (The CHDIR, MKDIR, and RMDIR statements are the QuickBASIC equivalents of the DOS CHDIR, MKDIR, and RMDIR commands; they are discussed in Chapters 11 and 17.)

```
ON ERROR GOTO DiskErr
DO
Redo:              ' Jump to here to run loop over again
    CLS
    PRINT "     L)ist Files in Current Directory"
    PRINT "     C)hange Current Directory"
    PRINT "     M)ake a Directory"
    PRINT "     R)emove a Directory"
    PRINT "     E)xit the Program"
    PRINT "Enter first letter of your choice: ";
    Choice$ = UCASE$(INPUT$(1))
    PRINT
    SELECT CASE Choice$
        CASE "L"
            INPUT "List what directory? ", Path$
            FILES Path$
            PRINT
            PRINT "Press any key to continue:"
            Resp$ = INPUT$(1)
        CASE "C"
            INPUT "Change to what directory? ", Path$
            CHDIR Path$
        CASE "M"
            INPUT "Make what directory? ", Path$
            MKDIR Path$
        CASE "R"
            INPUT "Remove what directory? ", Path$
            RMDIR Path$
        CASE "E"
            EXIT DO
    END SELECT
LOOP
END

DiskErr:                                ' Error-handling routine
    PRINT "*********"; CHR$(7)          ' Sound a beep
    PRINT "An error has occurred--please be sure there"
    PRINT "is a disk in the drive and the door is closed."
    PRINT "Press Enter to abort or any other key to continue:"
    Choice$ = INPUT$(1)
    IF ASC(Choice$) = 13 THEN           ' CR entered
        RESUME Redo                     ' Redo menu
    ELSE
        RESUME                          ' Try operation again
    END IF
END
```

Listing 16-2.

To test this program, be sure drive A is the current drive. (Select DOS Shell from the File menu, and enter *A:* at the DOS prompt if you need to change the drive.) First try the List Files option with a disk in A, and then remove the disk and try it again to see how the error handler works.

The error-handling routine *DiskErr* sounds a beep and asks you to be sure that a disk is in the current drive and that the door is shut. If you press Enter to abort the operation, the *RESUME Redo* statement sends control to the *Redo* label, which appears at the start of the DO loop, so that the menu can run again. If you press another key instead of Enter, the RESUME statement sends execution back to the statement that caused the error, and the operation is tried again.

Resuming at the Next Statement

The RESUME NEXT statement resumes execution after the statement that caused the error. You might use RESUME NEXT to ignore an activity that is impossible to execute at the moment or to continue execution after the error-handling code has performed an alternative activity. Or you can use RESUME NEXT to get out of the program.

The program in Listing 16-1 continues to try the disk and run the error-handling code until you put a disk in the drive or until you press Ctrl-Break to exit the program. If your program disables the Ctrl-Break interrupt to prevent uncontrolled exits, you will be forced to either insert a disk or reboot the system.

To avoid this, you can have the program shut down after an error. Listing 16-3 aborts the program if no disk is in the drive.

```
ON ERROR GOTO DiskErr
CLS
FILES "A:"
END                         ' RESUME NEXT brings us here, and the program ends

DiskErr:
    PRINT "There's no disk in drive A."
    PRINT "Program aborted--Restart to run again"
    PRINT "after fixing problem."
    RESUME NEXT
END
```

Listing 16-3.

Note that RESUME NEXT sends control to the statement following the FILES statement. Because that statement is END, the program shuts down. An abrupt exit like this usually isn't appropriate for programs run interactively from the keyboard, because it forces you to start over. But for utility programs designed to be run from the command line (perhaps from batch files), a routine like this is sometimes the only way to prevent a program from getting "stuck" when the hardware isn't ready.

Using Debug to Check Error Trapping

The QuickBASIC Debug menu has a Break on Errors command, which lets you treat an error as a breakpoint. (Breakpoints are discussed in Chapter 6.) To use Break on Errors, first be sure to select Full Menus from the Options menu. Next select History On from the Debug menu, which makes QuickBASIC keep track of the last 20 statements executed in the current program. Then select Break on Errors from the Debug menu.

Now try running Listing 16-3. After the drive runs for a moment, the View window returns with the first statement in the *DiskErr* block highlighted. If you press Shift-F8 (History Back), the cursor moves back to *FILES "A:"*, the statement that caused the error (Figure 16-4).

You can now step backward through the program by continuing to press Shift-F8 or step forward through the error-handling code by using F8. If you step forward to RESUME NEXT, execution jumps to the END statement.

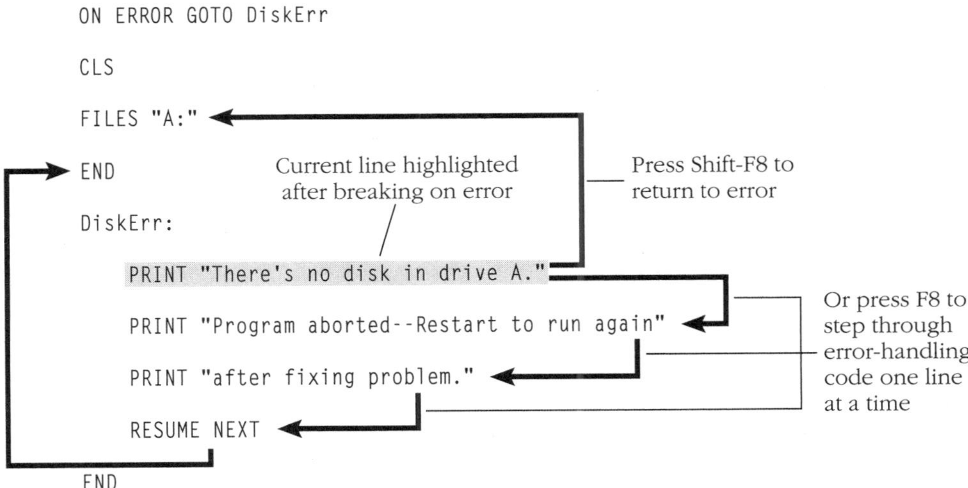

Figure 16-4.
Tracing with Break on Errors.

Turning Off Error Trapping

You might want to use error trapping in only one part of a program, particularly if the complete program is large and if you aren't sure what errors might occur throughout its execution. A special form of the ON ERROR GOTO statement, using 0 for the line number in the *location* argument, can turn off error trapping. QuickBASIC's default error messages are then used, and program execution is terminated whenever a runtime error is encountered.

You can also use this form of the ON ERROR GOTO statement to exit the program after an error has been trapped, by turning off error trapping within the error-handling routine itself. When an error is encountered in the following program, the error-handling routine displays information, and the program terminates. QuickBASIC's default error message is also displayed.

```
ON ERROR GOTO DiskErr
CLS
FILES "A:"
END

DiskErr:    ' Error-handling routine
    PRINT "An unrecoverable error has occurred!"
    ON ERROR GOTO 0
END
```

This technique can be useful when you don't want to retry the statement that caused the error (perhaps because the program is running unattended) or when you don't want to execute the next statement (if, for example, that statement tries to open a file on a disk that hasn't been loaded).

Errors in Error-Handling Routines

What happens if another runtime error occurs while an error-handling routine is being executed? Such an error can't be trapped, because it would cause the error-handling routine to be called from within itself, probably resulting in another error, which would result in another call, and so on until QuickBASIC ran out of stack space. To avoid such recursive error handling, QuickBASIC does not trap errors while running an error-handling routine. If an error occurs in the error-handling routine, QuickBASIC displays a default error message and terminates program execution.

Getting Information About Errors

Determining which errors might occur in a program is often difficult. Directory or disk-related errors, for example, have many causes: using an incorrect path, naming a nonexistent file, or trying to delete a directory that contains files, to name a few. Each runtime error has a code number (Figure 16-5), which your program can use to identify a particular error.

Code	Description	Code	Description
1*	NEXT without FOR	38*	Array not defined
2*	Syntax error	39	CASE ELSE expected
3	RETURN without GOSUB	40	Variable required
4	Out of data	50	Field overflow
5	Illegal function call	51	Internal error
6	Overflow	52	Bad filename or number
7	Out of memory	53	File not found
8*	Label not defined	54	Bad file mode
9	Subscript out of range	55	File already open
10	Duplicate definition	56	FIELD statement active
11	Division by 0	57	Device I/O error
12*	Illegal in direct mode	58	File already exists
13*	Type mismatch	59	Bad record length
14	Out of string space	61	Disk full
16*	String formula too complex	62	Input past end of file
17*	Cannot continue	63	Bad record number
18*	Function not defined	64	Bad filename
19	No RESUME	67	Too many files
20	RESUME without error	68	Device unavailable
24	Device timeout	69	Communications-buffer overflow
25	Device fault	70	Permission denied
26*	FOR without NEXT	71	Disk not ready
27	Out of paper	72	Disk-media error
29*	WHILE without WEND	73	Advanced feature unavailable
30*	WEND without WHILE	74	Rename across disks
33*	Duplicate label	75	Path/File access error
35*	Subprogram not defined	76	Path not found
37*	Argument-count mismatch		

*Errors that usually occur at compile time but can occur at runtime under special circumstances

Figure 16-5.
QuickBASIC runtime error codes.

The ERR function is used to find the error code for the most recent error occurring in a program.

The syntax for ERR is simply the following:

```
ERR
```

ERR returns a number in the range 1 through 255, although the number is usually one of the error codes listed in Figure 16-5. Typically, an error-handling routine assigns the value of ERR to a variable. Because the variable value identifies which error has occurred, the appropriate action for that error can be chosen.

Listing 16-4 reads and displays the first 10 lines of a text file. As a first step toward providing error handling for specific problems that might arise in this program, we have the error handler print the value of ERR.

First run the program with a valid file on the disk (to see how the program should work). Next try to run it using a path on drive A without a disk in the drive. Also try it with the name of a nonexistent file, with an incorrect path (an intermediate directory that doesn't exist), or with the name of a directory instead of a file. Try introducing other errors, too.

```
ON ERROR GOTO ErrorHandler
CLS
Redo:                                   ' Start over if error
INPUT "What file do you want to see"; FileName$
OPEN FileName$ FOR INPUT AS #1
LineNum% = 1
WHILE (NOT EOF(1)) AND (LineNum% < 11)  ' Print up to 10 lines
    LINE INPUT #1, Temp$                ' Get next line
    PRINT Temp$                         '  and display it
    LineNum% = LineNum% + 1
WEND
CLOSE                                   ' Close the file
END

ErrorHandler:
    PRINT "*********"; CHR$(7)          ' Sound a beep
    PRINT "Error number "; ERR; " has occurred!"
    PRINT "Press Enter to abort or any other key to continue:"
    Choice$ = INPUT$(1)
    IF ASC(Choice$) = 13 THEN           ' CR entered
        ON ERROR GOTO 0                 ' Abort program
    ELSE
        RESUME Redo                     ' Get filename again
     END IF
END
```

Listing 16-4.

When you look at the error values printed by the program, your collection of errors might include the following:

```
53   File not found
71   Disk not ready
75   Path/File access error
76   Path not found
```

Listing 16-5 uses a SELECT CASE statement in the error handler to deal with each of these errors appropriately. Note that we include a CASE ELSE statement, which simply aborts the program, in case our user discovers a new way to create an error.

```
ON ERROR GOTO ErrorHandler
CLS
Redo:                                   ' Start over if error
INPUT "Enter filename, or press Enter to quit: ", FileName$
IF FileName$ = "" THEN END
OPEN FileName$ FOR INPUT AS #1          ' Open the file
LineNum% = 1

WHILE (NOT EOF(1)) AND (LineNum% < 11)  ' Print up to 10 lines
    LINE INPUT #1, Temp$                ' Get next line
    PRINT Temp$                         '  and display it
    LineNum% = LineNum% + 1
WEND
CLOSE                                   ' Close the file
END

ErrorHandler:
    PRINT "*********"; CHR$(7)          ' Sound a beep
    ErrCode% = ERR                      ' Get number of error
    SELECT CASE ErrCode%
        CASE 53                         ' File not found
            PRINT "File not found "
            RESUME Redo
        CASE 71                         ' Disk not ready
            PRINT "Please put a disk in the drive and press a key, or"
            PRINT "press Enter to abort:"
            Choice$ = INPUT$(1)
            IF ASC(Choice$) = 13 THEN
                END                     ' Terminate program
            ELSE
                RESUME                  ' Try to read disk again
            END IF
        CASE 75
            PRINT "You tried to read a directory instead of a file"
            RESUME Redo
        CASE 76
            PRINT "The path you specified is invalid"
            RESUME Redo
        CASE ELSE                       ' Can't handle this one
            PRINT "Error number "; ErrCode%; " has occurred"
            ON ERROR GOTO 0             ' So terminate program
    END SELECT
END
```

Listing 16-5.

Calling Subprograms from the Error Handler

A complex program might need a dozen or more error-handling cases to handle file, disk, printer, or other errors. To avoid a long and unwieldy SELECT CASE statement, you can have the error handler call an appropriate subprogram to handle each error. Using subprograms in this way can help you organize and maintain code. Listing 16-6 implements this strategy.

```
DECLARE SUB DirRead ()
DECLARE SUB IOerror ()
DECLARE SUB NoDisk ()
DECLARE SUB NotFound ()
DECLARE SUB OtherErr ()
ON ERROR GOTO ErrorHandler
CLS
Redo:                                     ' Start over if error
INPUT "Enter filename, or press Enter to quit: ", FileName$
IF FileName$ = "" THEN END
OPEN FileName$ FOR INPUT AS #1            ' Open the file
LineNum% = 1
WHILE (NOT EOF(1)) AND (LineNum% < 11)    ' Print up to 10 lines
    LINE INPUT #1, Temp$                  ' Get next line
    PRINT Temp$                           '  and display it
    LineNum% = LineNum% + 1
WEND
CLOSE                                     ' Close the file
END

ErrorHandler:
    PRINT "*********"; CHR$(7)            ' Sound a beep
    ErrCode% = ERR                        ' Get number of error
    SELECT CASE ErrCode%                  ' Execute appropriate subprogram
        CASE 53
            NotFound
        CASE 57
            IOerror
        CASE 71
            NoDisk
        CASE 75
            DirRead
        CASE ELSE
            OtherErr
    END SELECT
    PRINT "Press Enter to abort or any other key to continue:"
    Choice$ = INPUT$(1)
    IF ASC(Choice$) = 13 THEN
        END
    ELSE
        RESUME Redo
    END IF
END
```

Listing 16-6. *(continued)*

Listing 16-6. *continued*

```
SUB DirRead
    PRINT "You tried to read a directory instead of a file"
END SUB

SUB IOerror
    PRINT "Disk I/O error--possibly a bad disk"
END SUB

SUB NoDisk
    PRINT "Please put a disk in the drive and close the door"
END SUB

SUB NotFound
    PRINT "File not found"
END SUB

SUB OtherErr
    PRINT "An unrecoverable error has occurred"
    ON ERROR GOTO 0
END SUB
```

After the appropriate subprogram is called, program execution continues past the SELECT CASE block to the PRINT statement, which lets you choose whether to abort the current operation or try it again.

Determining Which Device Caused the Error

A disk error can involve any drive in the system, a communications error can involve either port COM1 or COM2, and so on. You can use the ERDEV function to determine which device caused an error and the ERDEV$ function to identify the device that reported the error.

The syntax for these two functions is the following:

```
ERDEV
ERDEV$
```

ERDEV returns a 2-byte integer. This value is obtained directly from DOS's critical error handler (interrupt &H24) and uses each byte separately to provide coded information about the error. The low byte (the first 8 bits from the right) contains the error code. The high byte (the last 8 bits) contains the device status information. When a critical error occurs, the low byte always has a value, but the high byte has a value only if the error involves a block device. (A *block device,* such as a disk drive, deals with information as chunks of data; a *character device,* such as a printer, deals with information as a stream of characters.)

Because the value returned by ERDEV comes directly from DOS, these codes (listed in Figure 16-6) are not the same as the QuickBASIC error codes listed earlier in Figure 16-5. For additional information on these codes, see the *Microsoft MS-DOS Programmer's Reference.*

Error Code in Low Byte of ERDEV Value

Code	Description
0	Write-protect error
1	Unknown unit
2	Drive not ready
3	Unknown command
4	Date error (CRC)
5	Bad request structure length
6	Seek error
7	Unknown media type
8	Sector not found
9	Printer out of paper
10	Write fault
11	Read fault
12	General failure
13	Reserved
14	Reserved
15	Invalid disk change (DOS versions 3.0 and later)

Block Device Status Information in High Byte of ERDEV Value

Bit Position	Significance
8	0 if block device
7	1 if IOCTL read and write supported
6	1 if BIOS parameter block in boot sector should be used to determine media characteristics; 0 if media ID byte should be used
5	Always 0 (not used)
4	1 if current CLOCK device
3	1 if current NUL device
2	1 if driver supports 32-bit sector addressing (DOS version 4); prior to version 4, 1 if current standard output device (stdout)
1	1 if current standard input device (stdin)

Figure 16-6.
ERDEV codes and device status values.

Because ERDEV returns 2 bytes, its return value is usually split into two integer variables, as shown in Listing 16-7. Run this program with your printer offline. If you are using a serial printer, substitute the following lines for the LPRINT statement:

```
OPEN "COM1:1200,N,8,1" FOR RANDOM AS #1
PRINT #1, "Test"
```

(You might need to use different settings for COM1 or use a different serial port; see Chapter 15 for details.)

```
CLS
ON ERROR GOTO Handler
LPRINT "Test"
END

Handler:
    DevName$ = ERDEV$
    ErrCode% = VAL("&H" + LEFT$(HEX$(ERDEV), 2))      ' Low byte
    DevStatus% = VAL("&H" + RIGHT$(HEX$(ERDEV), 2))   ' High byte
    PRINT ErrCode%, DevStatus%, DevName$
END
```

Listing 16-7.

> **NOTE:** *Converting ERDEV to a hexadecimal string value and then converting this value to a numeric value eliminates negative numbers whose sign bit would cause the wrong values to be generated.*

If your parallel printer is connected to port LPT1 but turned off, the program pauses for the device timeout to be completed and then prints the following:

```
128        10         LPT1
```

The value 128 (10000000 in binary) in the high byte of the ERDEV value tells you that only the bit in the eighth position is on. As the device status information in Figure 16-6 indicates, this value means that the printer is not a block device. The value 10 in the low byte is the error code for a Write fault—a failed attempt to write to a device (the printer, in this case). The name of the device, LPT1, refers to the first parallel port. (If you used a serial printer, the device might be COM1.)

Testing and Simulating Errors

ERROR is another useful QuickBASIC error-handling statement. This statement tells QuickBASIC to simulate a specified error, and it also allows you to define your own error codes.

The syntax for ERROR is the following:

```
ERROR errornumber
```

errornumber is a number in the range 1 through 255. When this statement is executed, QuickBASIC acts as if the specified error had occurred, and any error trapping you have set up is performed.

ERROR allows you to define additional errors by assigning your own code numbers to them. QuickBASIC's current error codes extend only through 88, so you can use numbers in the range 89 through 255. (Code numbers 200 through 255 are most commonly used because future QuickBASIC releases might use error code numbers greater than 88.)

A user-defined error is defined in the error-handling routine. By incorporating code within the error definition, you can have that code executed from any point in your program simply by executing an ERROR statement with the appropriate error code. The program in Listing 16-8 demonstrates how user-defined errors can help you handle invalid runtime input.

```
ON ERROR GOTO ErrorHandler
CLS
Redo:                                   ' Start over if error
INPUT "Enter filename, or press Enter to quit: ", FileName$
IF FileName$ = "" THEN END              ' End if Enter pressed
FirstChar$ = UCASE$(LEFT$(FileName$, 1))
IF FirstChar$ < "A" OR FirstChar$ > "Z" THEN ERROR 250
' First character not a letter

' Break filename into name and extension and check length of name
DotPos% = INSTR(FileName$, ".")
IF DotPos% > 0 THEN
    FirstPart$ = LEFT$(FileName$, DotPos% - 1)
ELSE
    FirstPart$ = FileName$
END IF
IF LEN(FirstPart$) > 8 THEN ERROR 251  ' Name too long
OPEN FileName$ FOR INPUT AS #1         ' Open the file
LineNum% = 1
WHILE (NOT EOF(1)) AND (LineNum% < 11) ' Print up to 10 lines
    LINE INPUT #1, Temp$               ' Get next line
    PRINT Temp$                        '  and display it
    LineNum% = LineNum% + 1
WEND
```

Listing 16-8. *(continued)*

Listing 16-8. *continued*

```
CLOSE                                   ' Close the file
END

ErrorHandler:
    PRINT "*********"; CHR$(7)          ' Sound a beep
    ErrCode% = ERR                      ' Get number of error
    SELECT CASE ErrCode%
        CASE 53                          ' File not found
            PRINT "File not found "
            RESUME Redo
        CASE 57                          ' Device I/O error
            PRINT "Disk I/O error: possibly bad disk media"
            RESUME Redo
        CASE 71                          ' Disk not ready
            PRINT "Please put a disk in the drive and press a key, or"
            PRINT "press Enter to abort:"
            Choice$ = INPUT$(1)
            IF ASC(Choice$) = 13 THEN
                END
            ELSE
                RESUME NEXT
            END IF
        CASE 75
            PRINT "You tried to read a directory"
            RESUME Redo
        CASE 250
            PRINT "Filename must begin with a letter"
            RESUME Redo
        CASE 251
            PRINT "Filename can't exceed eight letters"
            PRINT "plus a three-character extension"
            RESUME Redo
        CASE ELSE
            PRINT "Error "; ErrCode%; " has occurred"
            RESUME Redo
     END SELECT
END
```

In Listing 16-8, we define error 250 to handle a filename that starts with a nonalphabetic character and error 251 to deal with a filename that is too long. (Paths are not allowed in this program.) The program tests the user's input and uses ERROR statements to trigger the errors if appropriate. Although you could accomplish the same purpose with subroutine calls, using the error mechanism can help keep all your error-handling routines in one section of the code.

> **Using ERROR to Get Help**
>
> You can use the ERROR statement to locate information about an error code from QuickBASIC's online help. Simply enter an ERROR statement with the specified code in the Immediate window, and a dialog box with the appropriate error message appears. For example, entering the statement *ERROR 53* in the Immediate window (or running it from the View window) produces the dialog box for error 53 (File not found). Choose Help, and detailed information about the error will be displayed.

Error Handling, Modules, and Subprograms

Code for error handling must always be part of the module-level code (Figure 16-7). As long as error trapping is active, any error that occurs during execution of a particular module will cause the error-handling code at the module level to be executed. You might expect this to make it difficult to execute various error handlers under differing circumstances, but QuickBASIC provides a solution to this problem.

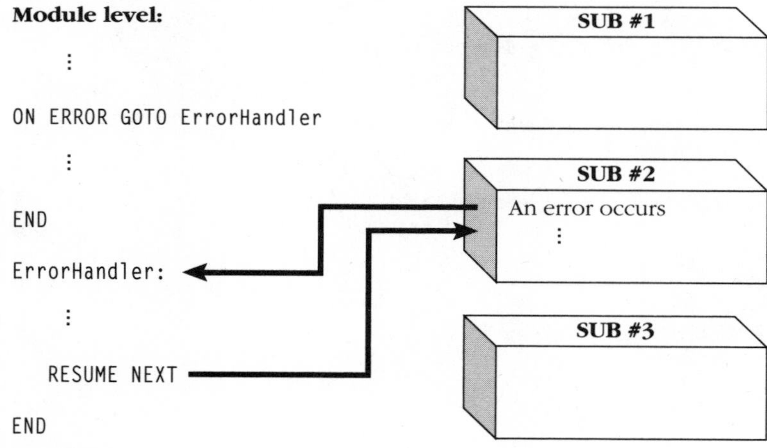

Figure 16-7.
Error handler at the module level.

Error Handling Within Subprograms

Although a subprogram can't contain error-handling code, it can include an ON ERROR GOTO statement that will jump to specified code at the module level. You can include more than one error handler at the module level, and each subprogram can choose which handler to use, as illustrated in Figure 16-8. The program in Listing 16-9 provides an example.

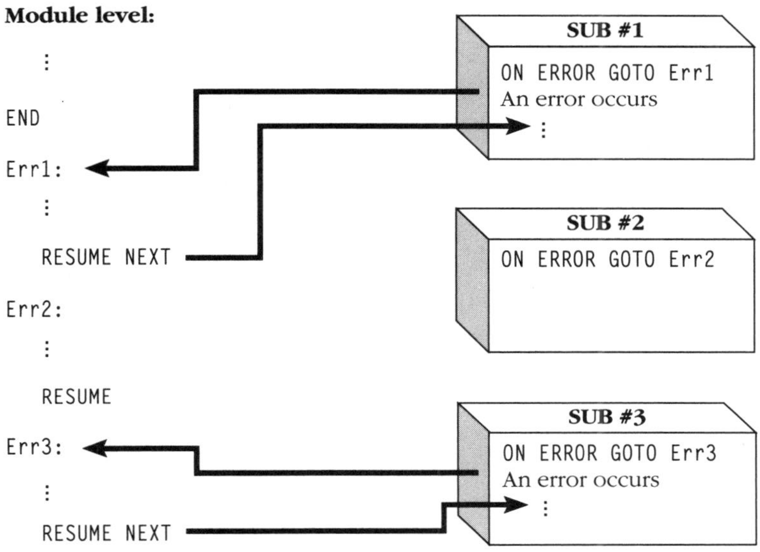

Figure 16-8.
Multiple error handlers at the module level.

```
DECLARE SUB PrintDir (Directory$)
DECLARE SUB ViewDir (Directory$)
CLS
' Call subprogram to view disk directory
Redo:                               ' To restart after directory error
VDir$ = "C:\TEST"                   ' For testing, this directory
ViewDir (VDir$)                     '  shouldn't exist
' Now call subprogram to print disk directory
Redo2:                              ' To restart after printer error
PDir$ = "C:\TEST"
PrintDir (PDir$)
END

DirError:                           ' Error handling for ViewDir subprogram
    PRINT "*********"; CHR$(7)      ' Sound a beep
    ErrCode% = ERR                  ' Get number of error
    PRINT "Error number:"; ErrCode%; "in subprogram ViewDir"
    SELECT CASE ErrCode%
        CASE 53
            PRINT "Directory not found"
            RESUME NEXT
```

Listing 16-9. *(continued)*

Listing 16-9. *continued*

```
        CASE 57                     ' Device I/O error
            PRINT "Disk I/O error: possibly bad disk media"
            RESUME Redo
        CASE 71                     ' Disk not ready
            PRINT "Please put a disk in the drive and press a key, or"
            PRINT "press Enter to abort:"
            Choice$ = INPUT$(1)
            IF ASC(Choice$) = 13 THEN
                END
            ELSE
                RESUME
            END IF
        CASE 75                     ' Path/File error
            PRINT "You probably specified a file instead of a directory"
            RESUME Redo
        CASE 76                     ' Path not found
            PRINT "Invalid path"
            RESUME Redo
        CASE ELSE                   ' Some other error
            PRINT "Unrecoverable error"
            ON ERROR GOTO 0         ' Exit to system
     END SELECT
END

PrinterErr:                         ' Error handling for PrintDir subprogram
    PRINT "*********"; CHR$(7)    ' Sound a beep
    ErrCode% = ERR                  ' Get number of error
    PRINT "Error number:"; ErrCode%; "in subprogram PrintDir"
    SELECT CASE ErrCode%
        CASE 25                     ' Device fault
            PRINT "Please turn on the printer"
            RESUME Redo2
        CASE 27                     ' Printer out of paper
            PRINT "Please put paper in the printer"
            RESUME NEXT
        CASE ELSE                   ' Some other error
            PRINT "Unrecoverable error"
            ON ERROR GOTO 0         ' Exit to system
    END SELECT
END

SUB PrintDir (Directory$)           ' Print contents of directory
    ON ERROR GOTO PrinterErr
    ERROR 27                        ' Simulate "out of paper" error
END SUB

SUB ViewDir (Directory$)
    ON ERROR GOTO DirError
    ERROR 53                       ' Simulate "file not found" error
END SUB
```

In this program, *DirError* and *PrinterErr* are error handlers at the module level. The *ViewDir* and *PrintDir* subprograms each have an ON ERROR GOTO statement specifying the appropriate error handler in the module-level code. To test error handling, each subprogram simulates an error.

Here is the output:

```
*********
Error number: 53 in subprogram ViewDir
Directory not found
*********
Error number: 27 in subprogram PrintDir
Please put paper in the printer
```

Using multiple error handlers makes it easier to manage complicated programs, which can have several kinds of errors, perhaps involving the disk, the printer, or the communications port. You can, for example, have an error handler for each device, and each subprogram can execute an ON ERROR GOTO statement specifying the handler it needs.

Error Handling in Multimodule Programs

QuickBASIC's error handling in multimodule programs has improved over the years. Before QuickBASIC version 4, errors could not be trapped in a module without an active error handler in that module's code—that is, an error handler at the module level, activated by an ON ERROR GOTO statement somewhere in the module. Thus, if module A (containing an error handler) called module B, and an error occurred in module B, the error was not trapped unless B itself contained an active error handler.

Starting with version 4, however, QuickBASIC uses *global error handling*. If module A calls module B, which in turn calls module C, and if an ON ERROR GOTO statement has been executed, error trapping can be activated for all three modules. If an error occurs while module C is running, QuickBASIC searches for an error handler first in module C, then in B, and finally in A. The first active error handler QuickBASIC finds is executed, and the search stops, as shown in Figure 16-9. If no error handler is found anywhere along the chain of calls, the default error message is displayed, and the program terminates.

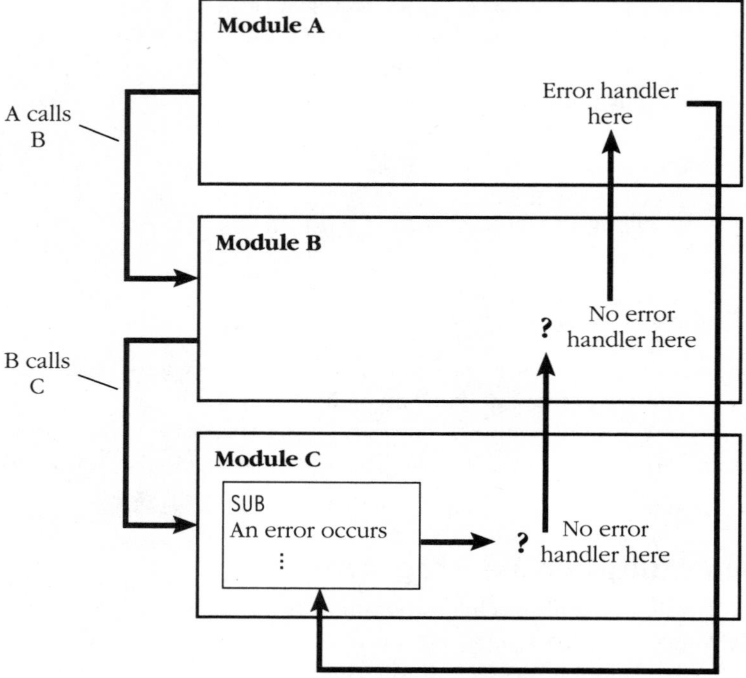

Figure 16-9.
Global error handling across modules.

Review Questions

1. Why do even bug-free programs need error handling?
2. How do the RESUME and RESUME NEXT statements differ?
3. Write a program that tries to print a sentence and that traps the two most common errors involving the printer.
4. Rewrite the program in Listing 16-5 so that it tells the user which disk drive has caused error 71 (Disk not ready).
5. What is global error handling?

17

DOS and Program Management

CALL INTERRUPT	**COMMAND$**	**ENVIRON$**	**RUN**
CALL INTERRUPTX	**COMMON**	**MKDIR**	**SHELL**
CHAIN	**ENVIRON**	**RMDIR**	

Although QuickBASIC supplies you with an extremely diverse assortment of statements and functions, some of your programs will also require DOS commands. The QuickBASIC SHELL statement lets your programs run the DOS command processor, COMMAND.COM, even if the user hasn't mastered DOS command syntax. Thus, users benefit from menu-driven operation, and programmers benefit from already-existing code that helps to manage files.

In addition to its command-level operations, DOS has many internal services that can be called through software interrupts by using the QuickBASIC CALL INTERRUPT and CALL INTERRUPTX statements. For example, you can use one service to set the number of lines to appear on the screen when using an EGA or a VGA adapter and another to read the mouse position.

DOS can also provide information from the command line to a QuickBASIC program. The QuickBASIC COMMAND$ function lets a program access the commands that were used to start it, commands that often contain information such as option switches and filenames.

Another source of information for a QuickBASIC program is the DOS environment, a series of strings DOS provides when a program is first run. Reading these strings can tell you the location of a directory or the name of a database file to be loaded.

Besides examining these topics, this chapter also focuses on program management—what to do when available memory isn't sufficient to handle all the code and data of a complex QuickBASIC program. We'll show you how to break your programs into separate sections and how to chain programs together.

The QB File Manager

Let's begin with a simple menu-driven program that allows you to select a directory and to list, delete, or rename files. With QuickBASIC's ability to run DOS commands, this program (adapted from Listing 11-11) can be expanded for more versatile and extensive file management. This file management package can be linked to your program as a module and called from your program's main menu.

Here is the main menu for the file management package:

```
*** QB File Manager ***
D)irectory Management
F)ile Management
R)un a DOS Command
Q)uit
```

The Directory Management menu offers the following options:

```
Work with directories:
C)hange Current Directory
S)elect Default Drive
M)ake a New Directory
R)emove a Directory
V)iew a Directory
B)ack to Main Menu
Q)uit the Program
```

The File Management menu lists these choices:

```
Work with files:
C)opy a File
D)elete a File
F)ind a File
P)rint a File
R)ename a File
V)iew a File
B)ack to Main Menu
Q)uit the Program
```

The third choice on the main menu, Run a DOS Command, simply uses the SHELL statement, which we'll describe later, to execute a DOS command.

Writing the Stub Program

Our QB File Manager program requires several subprograms: The main menu, each option on the main menu, and each option on the Directory Management and File Management menus are all implemented as subprograms. Like a writer who prepares an outline of a proposed paper and fills in the details later, you can write an outline of the program you are designing by using stubs as placeholders for various procedures. Listing 17-1 is a stub outline for the QB File Manager.

```
DECLARE SUB Pause ()
DECLARE SUB SelectDrive ()
DECLARE SUB MakeDir ()
DECLARE SUB RemoveDir ()
DECLARE SUB ViewDir ()
DECLARE SUB ChangeDir ()
DECLARE SUB CopyFile ()
DECLARE SUB DeleteFile ()
DECLARE SUB FindFile ()
DECLARE SUB PrintFile ()
DECLARE SUB RenameFile ()
DECLARE SUB ViewFile ()
DECLARE SUB MainMenu ()
DECLARE SUB DirMan ()
DECLARE SUB FileMan ()
DECLARE SUB RunDOS ()

' Main menu loop
DO
    MainMenu
LOOP

SUB ChangeDir
    PRINT "Change current directory:"
    Pause
END SUB

SUB CopyFile
    PRINT "Copy a file:"
    Pause
END SUB

SUB DeleteFile
    PRINT "Delete a file:"
    Pause
END SUB

SUB DirMan
    DO
        CLS
        PRINT "Work with directories:"
        PRINT "C)hange Current Directory"
        PRINT "S)elect Default Drive"
        PRINT "M)ake a New Directory"
        PRINT "R)emove a Directory"
        PRINT "V)iew a Directory"
        PRINT "B)ack to Main Menu"
        PRINT "Q)uit the Program"
```

Listing 17-1. *(continued)*

Listing 17-1. *continued*

```
        Cmd$ = UCASE$(INPUT$(1))
        IF Cmd$ = "Q" THEN END
        SELECT CASE Cmd$
            CASE "C": ChangeDir
            CASE "S": SelectDrive
            CASE "M": MakeDir
            CASE "R": RemoveDir
            CASE "V": ViewDir
            CASE "B": EXIT SUB
            CASE ELSE: BEEP
        END SELECT
    LOOP
END SUB

SUB FileMan
    DO
        CLS
        PRINT "Work with files:"
        PRINT "C)opy a File"
        PRINT "D)elete a File"
        PRINT "F)ind a File"
        PRINT "P)rint a File"
        PRINT "R)ename a File"
        PRINT "V)iew a File"
        PRINT "B)ack to Main Menu"
        PRINT "Q)uit the Program"

        Cmd$ = UCASE$(INPUT$(1))
        IF Cmd$ = "Q" THEN END
        SELECT CASE Cmd$
            CASE "C": CopyFile
            CASE "D": DeleteFile
            CASE "F": FindFile
            CASE "P": PrintFile
            CASE "R": RenameFile
            CASE "V": ViewFile
            CASE "B": EXIT SUB
            CASE ELSE: BEEP
        END SELECT
    LOOP
END SUB

SUB FindFile
    PRINT "Find a file:"
    Pause
END SUB

SUB MainMenu
    DO
        CLS
        PRINT "*** QB File Manager ***"
        PRINT "D)irectory Management"
```

(continued)

Listing 17-1. *continued*

```
        PRINT "F)ile Management"
        PRINT "R)un a DOS Command"
        PRINT "Q)uit"

        Cmd$ = UCASE$(INPUT$(1))
        IF Cmd$ = "Q" THEN END
        SELECT CASE Cmd$
            CASE "D": DirMan
            CASE "F": FileMan
            CASE "R": RunDOS
            CASE ELSE: BEEP
        END SELECT
    LOOP
END SUB

SUB MakeDir
    PRINT "Make a new directory:"
    Pause
END SUB

SUB Pause
    PRINT "Press any key to continue:"
    Temp$ = INPUT$(1)
END SUB

SUB PrintFile
    PRINT "Print a file:"
    Pause
END SUB

SUB RemoveDir
    PRINT "Remove a directory:"
    Pause
END SUB

SUB RenameFile
    PRINT "Rename a file:"
    Pause
END SUB

SUB RunDOS
    PRINT "Run a DOS command:"
    Pause
END SUB

SUB SelectDrive
    PRINT "Change the current drive:"
    Pause
END SUB
```

(continued)

Listing 17-1. *continued*

```
SUB ViewDir
    PRINT "View a directory:"
    Pause
END SUB

SUB ViewFile
    PRINT "View a file:"
    Pause
END SUB
```

The main menu, the Directory Management menu, and the File Management menu call the appropriate stub subprograms. Each subprogram prints a brief description of what it does and then calls the *Pause* subprogram, which waits for you to press a key. This use of stubs allows you to examine and verify the overall structure of your program.

Using the Calls Menu

The QB File Manager has several levels of execution, which are diagramed in Figure 17-1. The first level, as in all programs, is the module-level code, which contains global declarations and an error-handling routine, as well as a loop that keeps the program running until you decide to exit. In our example, a DO loop repeatedly executes *MainMenu*.

The second level is the *MainMenu* subprogram, which presents the main menu. The third level contains the submenu subprograms *DirMan* and *FileMan*, which are called when you choose Directory Management or File Management from the main menu. (The Run a DOS Command option on the main menu performs its task directly rather than requiring a submenu.) The fourth level contains subprograms that perform the tasks listed in the submenus. Finally, these subprograms call the *Pause* subprogram, which is at the fifth level.

Consider the steps involved in making a new directory. First the program shows you the main menu, from which you select the Directory Management option. This in turn displays the directory operations submenu by calling *DirMan*. From this menu, you select Make a New Directory, and the subprogram *MakeDir* is called. When *MakeDir* runs, it in turn calls *Pause*. The shaded portions of Figure 17-1 illustrate this path of execution.

QuickBASIC provides the Calls menu to help you keep track of the levels of procedure calls in your program. To see how this menu works, load Listing 17-1. Select the *Pause* subprogram, either by pressing F2 and selecting the subprogram from the list QuickBASIC presents or by pressing Shift-F2 until *Pause* appears in the active window. Put the cursor on the line *Temp$ = INPUT$(1)*, and press F9 to set a breakpoint.

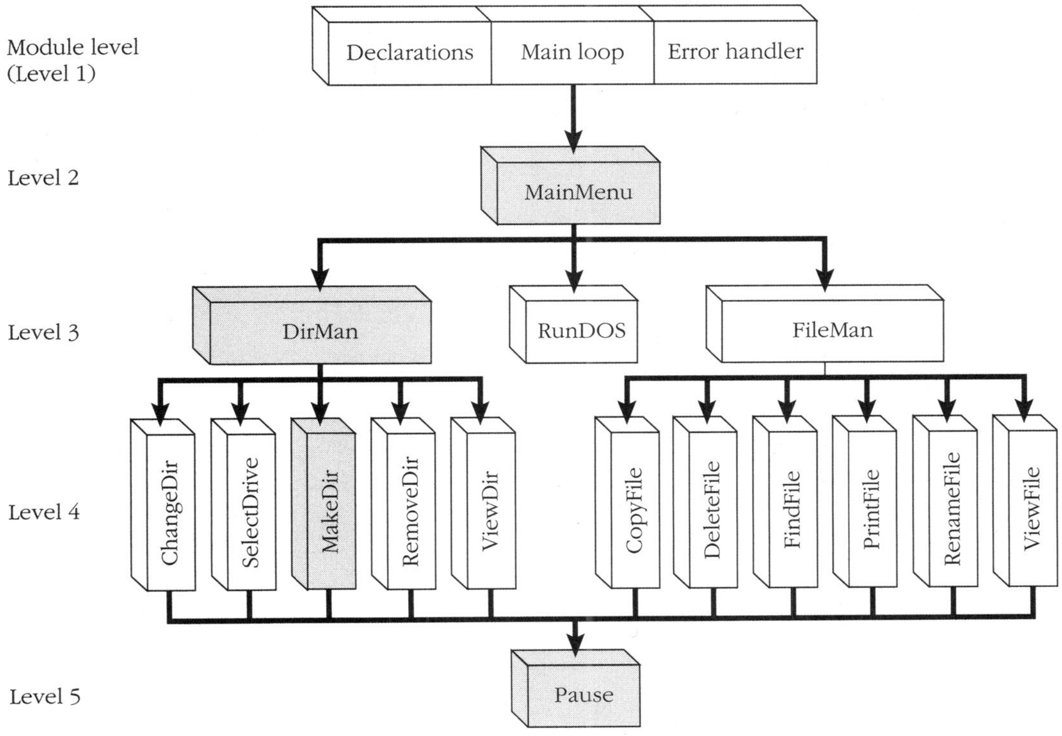

Figure 17-1.
Levels called in QB File Manager (Listing 17-1).

When you run the program and choose Directory Management from the main menu and Make a New Directory from the submenu, the program stops at the breakpoint. Open the Calls menu, and you will see the following list:

```
Pause
MakeDir
DirMan
MainMenu
LIST-01.BAS
```

When QuickBASIC calls a procedure, it sets a pointer to the program line that will be executed when the program returns from the called procedure. QuickBASIC must often keep track of pointers on several levels until all the called procedures have been run. The Calls menu shows you the *procedure stack*—the list of procedures waiting to be completed, with the last one called listed first. The Calls menu in our example shows you that the program module LIST-01.BAS called the *MainMenu* subprogram, which called the *DirMan* subprogram. *DirMan* in turn called the *MakeDir* subprogram, which called the *Pause* subprogram—where execution halted at the breakpoint.

If you select one of these procedures, it is displayed in the active window with the cursor at the statement following the statement that called the next procedure. For example, if you select *DirMan*, the cursor appears on the line *CASE "R": RenameDir* because the preceding line, *CASE "M": MakeDir*, called the *MakeDir* procedure. By looking at each procedure on the Calls menu and noting the cursor position, you can see where each call was made, all the way up to the module level.

When you select a procedure from the Calls menu and press F7, QuickBASIC executes the program up to and including that procedure. If you choose *DirMan* and press F7, the program completes the *Pause* subprogram, returns to *MakeDir*, and then returns to *DirMan* and executes it. The submenu waits there for your next command.

Creating and Removing Directories

Now that the stub program works, you must write and test the code for each subprogram. As you saw in Chapter 11, you can use the CHDIR statement to change the current directory. Here you'll need additional directory-related QuickBASIC statements: MKDIR and RMDIR. These statements, which make and remove directories, resemble the DOS commands of the same name.

Here is the syntax for MKDIR:

```
MKDIR directoryname
```

The syntax for RMDIR is the following:

```
RMDIR directoryname
```

For both statements, *directoryname* is a string expression specifying the directory to be created or removed. If the directory is not a subdirectory of the current directory, *directoryname* must include a path, such as "C:\QB\TEST." (If *directoryname* is a string literal, it must be enclosed in double quotation marks.)

A program could, for example, ask you for the name of the directory to create:

```
INPUT "Make what directory? ";NewDir$
MKDIR NewDir$
```

You cannot use RMDIR to remove a directory unless the directory is empty. To remove a directory with files in it, use the following two steps:

```
KILL "C:\TEMP\*.*"          ' Remove the files
RMDIR "C:\TEMP"             ' Remove the directory
```

Although you can abbreviate the MKDIR and RMDIR statements as MD and RD in DOS, you cannot use these abbreviations in QuickBASIC.

Executing DOS Commands

The QB File Manager program should be able to show the current directory to the user. However, although the DOS version of CHDIR (or CD) displays the current directory when no directory is specified, QuickBASIC's CHDIR displays an error message. Our program also needs a way to change the current drive, but QuickBASIC has no statement that changes the drive.

To solve these problems, you must harness the power of DOS from QuickBASIC by using the SHELL statement. This statement creates a *shell* (a copy of the DOS command processor, COMMAND.COM) that executes whatever DOS commands it is given. It also runs programs and batch files—in fact, anything that can be typed at the command-line prompt. (Note, however, that when you run a program from the QuickBASIC environment on a 640-KB system, you have only about 200 KB of available memory; somewhat more is available in stand-alone EXE programs.)

Here is the syntax for the SHELL statement:

```
SHELL [DOScommand]
```

DOScommand is a string expression that specifies the DOS command to be executed. When used without *DOScommand*, SHELL lets you leave the running program temporarily. A DOS message and the DOS prompt are displayed, as shown in the following:

```
Type EXIT to return to QuickBASIC

IBM DOS Version 4.00
        (C)Copyright International Business Machines Corp 1981, 1988
        (C)Copyright Microsoft Corp 1981-1986

C:\QB45>
```

DOS commands can now be entered. The DOS EXIT command allows you to return to the QuickBASIC programming that executed the SHELL statement.

When it is used with *DOScommand*, the SHELL statement sends the DOS command to COMMAND.COM to be executed and then returns immediately to QuickBASIC. For example, the following first executes the DOS CD command, which lists the current directory because no directory is specified:

```
SHELL "CD"
Cmd$ = "DIR /P"
SHELL Cmd$
```

The second SHELL statement executes the DIR /P command stored in the string *Cmd$*, which prints a full directory listing, pausing after each screen of information. The ability to store a DOS command in a variable allows user input to be translated into valid DOS commands.

With SHELL, all the Directory Management menu options in the QB File Manager can be implemented, as shown in Listing 17-2. Error handling has also been added.

(In this and subsequent listings for this program, only the sections that have been added to the stub program are shown.)

```
' Main menu loop
ON ERROR GOTO ErrorHandler      ' Set up error trapping
ShowMain:                       ' Label for resuming after error
DO
    MainMenu
LOOP

ErrorHandler:
    PRINT "*********"; CHR$(7)  ' Sound a beep
    ErrCode% = ERR              ' Get error code number
    SELECT CASE ErrCode%
        CASE 25
            PRINT "Printer not ready"
            PRINT "Be sure it is turned on and online"
        CASE 53                 ' File not found
            PRINT "File not found "
        CASE 57                 ' Device I/O error
            PRINT "Disk I/O error: possibly bad disk media"
        CASE 70                 ' Protected disk or file
            PRINT "Permission denied"
            PRINT "Disk might be write-protected, or"
            PRINT "file might be locked"
            PRINT "Check write-protect tab or slide on disk"
        CASE 71                 ' Disk not ready
            PRINT "Please put a disk in drive "; ERDEV$;
            PRINT "and press a key, or"
            PRINT "press Enter to abort:"
            Choice$ = INPUT$(1)
            IF ASC(Choice$) = 13 THEN
                END
            ELSE
                RESUME
            END IF
        CASE 75
            PRINT "File access error: File might be read-only,"
            PRINT "you might have tried to read a directory,"
            PRINT "or you might have tried to delete a directory"
            PRINT "that was not empty"
        CASE 76
            PRINT "Path not found"
        CASE ELSE
            PRINT "Error "; ErrCode%; " has occurred"
    END SELECT
    PRINT "Press any key to continue:"
    Temp$ = INPUT$(1)
    RESUME ShowMain             ' Show main menu again
END
```

Listing 17-2. *(continued)*

Listing 17-2. *continued*

```
SUB ChangeDir
    PRINT "Change the current directory:"
    PRINT "Current directory is: "
    SHELL "CD"
    INPUT "Change to what directory"; NewDir$
    CHDIR NewDir$
    PRINT "Directory changed to: "; NewDir$
    Pause
END SUB

SUB MakeDir
    PRINT "Make a new directory:"
    INPUT "Make what directory"; NewDir$
    MKDIR NewDir$
    PRINT "Directory "; NewDir$; " has been made"
    Pause
END SUB

SUB RemoveDir
    PRINT "Remove a directory:"
    INPUT "Remove which directory"; RmDir$
    RMDIR RmDir$
    PRINT "Directory: "; RmDir$; " has been removed"
    Pause
END SUB

SUB SelectDrive
    PRINT "Select the default drive: "
    INPUT "Change to what drive"; Drive$
    Drive$ = UCASE$(Drive$)
    ChgDrive$ = LEFT$(Drive$, 1) + ":"
    SHELL ChgDrive$
    PRINT "Current drive changed to "; ChgDrive$
    Pause
END SUB

SUB ViewDir
    PRINT "View a directory:"
    INPUT "View what directory"; Dir$
    Cmd$ = "DIR " + Dir$ + " /p"
    SHELL Cmd$
    Pause
END SUB
```

Note that when the SHELL statement is used, DOS is in complete control. If an error occurs during the execution of a DOS command, a DOS message appears; the error cannot be trapped by the QuickBASIC error-handling routine.

The File Management options require no new QuickBASIC statements. The Find a File option, which lets you find all copies of a specified file on a specified disk, involves the most complicated SHELL statement, as shown here:

```
FileName$ = CHR$(34) + UCASE$(File$) + CHR$(34)
Cmd$ = "CHKDSK " + Drive$ + " /V ¦ FIND " + FileName$
```

In addition to listing the full path to every file on the specified disk (given here in *Drive$*), the DOS CHKDSK command with the /V switch also checks your hard disk for errors. (Note that if your hard disk contains errors, the program won't continue until you press Ctrl-C.) The broken pipe (¦) symbol in the preceding program fragment "pipes," or redirects, the output of this command to the DOS FIND command. The FIND command needs the filename of the specified file, typed in uppercase letters and enclosed in double quotation marks supplied by using *CHR$(34)*. The FIND command searches the list of files provided by the CHKDSK command and lists all pathnames containing the specified file.

Listing 17-3 contains the rest of the subprograms.

```
SUB CopyFile
    CLS
    PRINT "Copy a file:"
    INPUT "Copy what file"; File$
    INPUT "Copy to what destination"; Dest$
    Cmd$ = "COPY " + File$ + " " + Dest$
    SHELL Cmd$
    Pause
END SUB

SUB DeleteFile
    PRINT "Delete a file:"
    INPUT "Name of file to delete"; File$
    KILL File$
    PRINT "File "; File$; " has been removed"
    Pause
END SUB

SUB FindFile
    PRINT "Find a file:"
    INPUT "Find what file (filename only)"; File$
    INPUT "Look on what drive (Enter for current drive)"; Drive$
    IF LEN(Drive$) <> 0 THEN Drive$ = LEFT$(Drive$, 1) + ":"
    FileName$ = CHR$(34) + UCASE$(File$) + CHR$(34)
    Cmd$ = "CHKDSK " + Drive$ + " /V ¦ FIND " + FileName$
    SHELL Cmd$
    Pause
END SUB
```

Listing 17-3.

(continued)

Listing 17-3. *continued*

```
SUB PrintFile
    PRINT "Print a file:"
    INPUT "Print what file"; File$
    Cmd$ = "PRINT " + File$      ' Assumes DOS PRINT is in PATH
    SHELL Cmd$
    Pause
END SUB

SUB RenameFile
    PRINT "Rename a file:"
    INPUT "Old name"; Old$
    INPUT "New name"; New$
    NAME Old$ AS New$
    PRINT Old$; " is now "; New$
    Pause
END SUB

SUB RunDOS
    PRINT "Run a DOS command:"
    PRINT "Type your command: ";
    LINE INPUT Cmd$
    SHELL Cmd$
    Pause
END SUB

SUB ViewFile
    CLS
    PRINT "View a file:"
    INPUT "View which file"; File$
    Cmd$ = "more <" + File$
    SHELL (Cmd$)
    Pause
END SUB
```

Calling DOS Services (Interrupts)

Although DOS can perform many tasks at the command-line level, other services are available only in the DOS internal code as *system services*. DOS provides access to these services through *software interrupts*. A hardware interrupt is a signal to DOS that a problem has occurred with a physical device or that DOS should process information about the status of the device—the printer is not turned on, the disk drive is empty, and so forth. A software interrupt is a signal to DOS that a program needs to execute a routine in the internal code—that is, to access a system service.

When a subprogram is called, it often receives information through the parameter list. The subprogram can in turn change the value of one or more of these variables, thus communicating the results of its execution back to the calling program. CALL INTERRUPT is conceptually similar. However, instead of using variables to pass information to and from the called routine, the program must specify the contents of certain CPU registers, which represent storage locations within the CPU itself.

You can use the CALL INTERRUPT statement (or its variant CALL INTERRUPTX) in QuickBASIC versions 4 and later to call a DOS system service. (Earlier versions of QuickBASIC used CALL INT86 and CALL INT86X, which were more cumbersome techniques. These procedures can be used in later versions of QuickBASIC with the CALL INT86OLD and CALL INT86XOLD statements.) Note that calling interrupts isn't supported in OS/2 protected mode, although most interrupts work in OS/2 DOS compatibility ("real") mode. (Most of the same services are provided by calls to OS/2 functions using a C-like syntax.)

Here is the syntax for the CALL INTERRUPT statement:

```
CALL INTERRUPT (interruptnumber, inregs, outregs)
```

interruptnumber is a number in the range 0 through 255 that corresponds to the DOS system service. It is usually in hexadecimal form. *inregs* and *outregs* are variables of the user-defined type *RegType*. The following statement, for example, calls interrupt &H21:

```
CALL INTERRUPT (&H21, InRegs, OutRegs)
```

The syntax for CALL INTERRUPTX is identical to that for CALL INTERRUPT; its user-defined type is *RegTypeX*.

Preparing to Use Interrupts

Just as a call to a subprogram requires code in the subprogram, the CALL INTERRUPT statement requires additional code. This code is supplied by QuickBASIC in its Quick library (QB.QLB) and stand-alone library (QB.LIB) files. The Quick library (discussed in detail in Chapter 18) is useful when you are working within the QuickBASIC environment. The stand-alone library must be used whenever the program is made into an EXE file either from the command line or from within the environment.

The Quick library is loaded when QuickBASIC is first started, by using the /L option switch on the command line as shown here:

```
C:\QB> QB /L
```

The default Quick library QB.QLB is loaded unless another Quick library filename is used after the /L switch.

After you've loaded QB.QLB (or linked with QB.LIB), you must incorporate the contents of the library file QB.BI into your program code. You can include this file in the program by using the $INCLUDE metacommand:

```
REM $INCLUDE:'QB.BI'
```

This file contains definitions of the user-defined types that hold the data passed in the registers when the interrupt is called. These types are defined as follows:

```
TYPE RegType
    Ax AS INTEGER
    Bx AS INTEGER
    Cx AS INTEGER
    Dx AS INTEGER
    Bp AS INTEGER
    Si AS INTEGER
    Di AS INTEGER
    Flags AS INTEGER
END TYPE

TYPE RegTypeX
    Ax AS INTEGER
    Bx AS INTEGER
    Cx AS INTEGER
    Dx AS INTEGER
    Bp AS INTEGER
    Si AS INTEGER
    Di AS INTEGER
    Flags AS INTEGER
    Ds AS INTEGER
    Es AS INTEGER
END TYPE
```

RegTypeX is used with CALL INTERRUPTX for those few interrupts that require use of the DS and ES registers—mainly interrupts that work with video data or other data not in the current segment.

Next declare two variables of the appropriate type: one to hold the register values that will be sent to the called routine, and the other to hold the values returned after the interrupt has been processed. Use the DIM statement as shown here:

```
DIM InRegs AS RegType, OutRegs AS RegType
```

Substitute *RegTypeX* for *RegType* if you are using the DS or ES registers.

Loading Register Values

Before calling an interrupt, you must assign an appropriate value to one or more registers. For example, when a function under interrupt &H21 is called, the function number must be assigned to the high byte of the AX register.

Registers whose names end in X are actually pairs of 1-byte registers: AX consists of AH and AL (high byte and low byte). To assign a value to AH, *Ax* is assigned a hexadecimal number whose first two (high) digits are the desired value and whose lower digits are 0. The following statement assigns the value &H30 to AH and 0 to AL:

```
InRegs.Ax = &H3000
```

To assign a value to the low byte only, assign 0 to the high byte, as shown here:

```
InRegs.Bx = &H0021
```

After you've supplied the register values, you can call the system service.

Getting Return Register Values

Depending on the interrupt call, one or more changed register values are passed back in the variable you specify for the return registers (*OutRegs* in our examples). These values can be stored in appropriate QuickBASIC variables and then used or checked to determine the status of specified bits. To split a return register value into two integer values representing the high and low bytes of the register pair, use statements such as the following:

```
Al% = OutRegs.Ax MOD 256    ' AL register
Ah% = OutRegs.Ax \ 256      ' AH register
```

The MOD statement returns the low byte of the register pair, and integer division (\) returns the high byte.

Listing 17-4, which returns the version of DOS you are using, demonstrates how all this fits together.

```
' Start QB with the QB.QLB Quick library or link with QB.LIB
REM $INCLUDE: '\QB45\QB.BI'
' Modify path if file is in different directory
DIM InRegs AS RegType, OutRegs AS RegType
' Load register
InRegs.Ax = &H3000           ' Function number in high byte (AH)
' Call the interrupt
CALL INTERRUPT(&H21, InRegs, OutRegs)
' Get returned register values
Al% = OutRegs.Ax MOD 256     ' AL register has major version number
Ah% = OutRegs.Ax \ 256       ' AH register has minor version number
PRINT "MS-DOS Version is: "; Al%; "."; Ah%
```

Listing 17-4.

Listing 17-5 uses several CALL INTERRUPT statements to determine the mouse position and button status. (The Microsoft Mouse driver is designed to interface with programs through the functions of interrupt &H33.) The program first calls interrupt &H33, function 0, to see whether mouse support is available. If it is, the mouse is initialized. The program next calls interrupt &H33, function 1, to display the mouse pointer. The driver then draws and redraws the pointer as you move the mouse. The program also calls interrupt &H33, function 3, to find the pointer's coordinate position and the mouse button status. Because the interrupt is repeatedly called in a DO loop, the changing values are displayed on the screen as you move the mouse. The right button is also checked; when it is pushed, the program is terminated. Note that individual bits are checked to determine the button values.

```
DECLARE FUNCTION GetBit% (Byte%, Bit%)
REM $INCLUDE: '\QB45\QB.BI'
' Your path might be different
DIM InRegs AS RegType, OutRegs AS RegType
SCREEN 1                      ' CGA screen
InRegs.Ax = &H0               ' Function number 0 of INT &H33 checks for
                              '  mouse support and initializes
CALL INTERRUPT(&H33, InRegs, OutRegs)
MouseAvail% = OutRegs.Ax      ' -1 if mouse support available
IF NOT MouseAvail% THEN
    PRINT "No mouse support"
    END                       ' Exit the program
END IF

' Now show mouse pointer
InRegs.Ax = &H1               ' Function number 1 shows mouse pointer
CALL INTERRUPT(&H33, InRegs, OutRegs)

' Show mouse position until button is pressed
LOCATE 20, 20
PRINT "Left Button is: ";
DO
    InRegs.Ax = &H3           ' Function number 3 gets mouse status
    CALL INTERRUPT(&H33, InRegs, OutRegs)
    MouseStatLow% = OutRegs.Bx MOD 256      ' Get low register (BL)

    LOCATE 21, 20: PRINT "X = "; OutRegs.Cx;
    LOCATE 21, 30: PRINT "Y = "; OutRegs.Dx;

    IF GetBit%(MouseStatLow%, 0) THEN       ' 1 if pressed
        LOCATE 20, 35
        PRINT "down";
    ELSE
        LOCATE 20, 35
        PRINT "up  ";
    END IF

    ' Now check right button
    IF GetBit%(MouseStatLow%, 1) THEN END   ' Exit if down
LOOP

FUNCTION GetBit% (Byte%, Bit%)
    GetBit% = -SGN(Byte% AND 2 ^ Bit%)
END FUNCTION
```

Listing 17-5.

For more details on using DOS interrupts, see the following books: *Advanced MS-DOS Programming,* 2nd ed., by Ray Duncan (Redmond, Wash.: Microsoft Press, 1988); *Advanced C Primer Plus ++,* by Stephen Prata/The Waite Group (Indianapolis, Ind.: Howard W. Sams, 1986); and *MS-DOS Developer's Guide,* 2nd ed., by The Waite Group (Indianapolis, Ind.: Howard W. Sams, 1989).

Reading the Command Line

The command line is another useful information source for many programs. When you run a DOS command or other utility or application program from the DOS command prompt, you often include information such as an option switch and a filename or pathname. For example, the DOS command CHKDSK A: /V tells DOS to run the CHKDSK program, to check the disk in drive A, and to list all paths found on the disk. Although command-line programs aren't as friendly as menu-driven programs, they have two advantages: They are faster, and they can be run in batch files without having the user enter menu responses.

When DOS runs a program, the program can access whatever was entered on the command line when the program was started. All QuickBASIC programs can access the command line through the COMMAND$ function. This function returns the contents of the command line as a string.

The syntax for COMMAND$ is simply the following:

```
COMMAND$
```

COMMAND$ always returns the command line in uppercase letters, allowing you to check command-line elements against uppercase strings without using UCASE$. The name of the program itself is not included in the accessible command line.

The command line can be assigned to a string variable for later processing:

```
CmdLine$ = COMMAND$
```

Information in the command line must usually be broken into individual elements such as option switches (specified by a slash) and filenames or pathnames. Listing 17-6 includes a subprogram, *Parse*, that breaks a command line into individual elements (words) and stores them in an array. Using this subprogram, the program prints the elements of its command line.

You can test this program in either of two ways. From the QuickBASIC environment, choose Modify COMMAND$ from the Run menu, and enter a command line (for example, */a /b /c somefile.txt*). QuickBASIC then supplies this command line to any program you run from the environment. Alternatively, you can compile the program to an EXE file (such as COMLINE.EXE) and run it from the DOS command prompt, supplying the command line directly, as shown here:

```
C:\QB45>comline /a /b /c somefile.txt
```

```
DECLARE SUB Parse (AString$, Words$(), MaxWords%, WordsFound%, Sep$)
CLS
Cmd$ = COMMAND$
DIM ParmsFound$(10)
Parse Cmd$, ParmsFound$(), 10, Found%, " "
PRINT "Parameters found:"; Found%
```

Listing 17-6. *(continued)*

Listing 17-6. *continued*

```
FOR Parm% = 1 TO Found%
    PRINT ParmsFound$(Parm%)
NEXT Parm%

SUB Parse (AString$, Words$(), MaxWords%, WordsFound%, Sep$) STATIC
' AString$ is string to be parsed
' Words$() is string array to hold words found
' MaxWords% is largest number of words to be accommodated
' WordsFound% is number of words found
' Sep$ is character to be treated as word separator
CONST true = -1, false = 0
WordsFound% = 0                        ' Count words found
In = false                             ' Flag if inside a word
StrLen% = LEN(AString$)
' Go through string one character at a time
FOR Char = 1 TO StrLen%
    Char$ = MID$(AString$, Char, 1) ' Get next character
    ' Test for character being a separator
    IF Char$ <> Sep$ THEN              ' Not a separator
        ' Test to see if already inside a word
        IF NOT In THEN
            ' Found the start of a new word
            ' Test for too many words
            IF WordsFound% = MaxWords% THEN EXIT FOR
            WordsFound% = WordsFound% + 1
            In = true
            END IF
        ' Add the character to the current word
        Words$(WordsFound%) = Words$(WordsFound%) + Char$
    ELSE
        ' Found a separator
        ' Set "Not in a word" flag to false
        In = false
    END IF
NEXT Char
END SUB
```

Here is the output:

```
Parameters found: 4
/A
/B
/C
SOMEFILE.TXT
```

Listing 17-7 modifies the program from Listing 16-5, which prompted for a filename and then displayed the first 10 lines of the file. The new program expects to find the filename and, optionally, the number of lines to print on the command line. When this program is compiled to the EXE file HEAD.EXE, the syntax is the following:

head *filename* [*lines*]

Thus, *head textfile* prints the first 10 lines of TEXTFILE, and *head letter 20* prints the first 20 lines of LETTER. (The code for the error handler and for the *Parse* subprogram is omitted here.)

Note that the program checks the number of commands returned from the *Parse* subprogram and exits with an error message if fewer than one or more than two parameters are specified on the command line. The error handler from Listing 16-5 should also be modified to exit the program if an incorrect filename is used; this is accomplished by deleting the *RESUME Redo* statements.

```
' Merge the Parse subprogram from Listing 17-6
' Add error-handling routine from Listing 16-5
DECLARE SUB Parse (AString$, Words$(), MaxWords%, WordsFound%, Sep$)
ON ERROR GOTO ErrorHandler
CmdLine$ = COMMAND$
DIM Parms$(10)
Parse CmdLine$, Parms$(), 10, NumCmds%, " "
IF NumCmds% < 1 OR NumCmds% > 2 THEN         ' Wrong number of parameters
    PRINT "Syntax: head <filename> OR"
    PRINT "        head <filename> NumberOfLines"
    END
END IF

FileName$ = Parms$(1)                        ' Get filename
IF NumCmds% = 2 THEN                         ' Number of lines specified
    Lines% = VAL(Parms$(2))
ELSE
    Lines% = 10                              ' Default as many as 10 lines
END IF
OPEN FileName$ FOR INPUT AS #1               ' Open the file
LineNum% = 1
WHILE (NOT EOF(1)) AND (LineNum% <= Lines%) ' Print up to 10 lines
    LINE INPUT #1, Temp$                     ' Get next line
    PRINT Temp$                              '  and display it
    LineNum% = LineNum% + 1
WEND
CLOSE                                        ' Close the file
END
```

Listing 17-7.

Using the DOS Environment

Another potentially important source of information for QuickBASIC programs is the DOS environment, a series of strings (or *environmental variables*) maintained in memory that specify such items as the directory search path, the location of the command processor COMMAND.COM, and the current DOS command prompt. Choose DOS Shell from the QuickBASIC File menu, and enter the DOS SET command to see what is in the current environment on your machine. The display should look something like the following:

```
C:\QB45>set
MEMO_DIR=c:\memo
MEMO_FILE=daybook
COMSPEC=C:\DOS\COMMAND.COM
PATH=C:\WORD;C:\DOS;C:\MEMO;C:\QB45;C:\BATCH;C:\UTILS
PROMPT=$P$G
```

MEMO_DIR and *MEMO_FILE* in the preceding example are additional variables that tell a database program where to find its data directory and which database to use.

Whenever a program (including QuickBASIC itself) is run, DOS provides it with a copy of the environment list. QuickBASIC programs can use this information to find directories or to specify other conditions. The QuickBASIC ENVIRON$ function returns the names and values of environmental variables.

Here is the syntax for the ENVIRON$ function:

```
ENVIRON$ (variablenumber)
ENVIRON$ (variablename)
```

When used with *variablenumber*, ENVIRON$ returns the complete name and value of the variable in the specified position in the environment list. For instance, *ENVIRON$(1)* returns *MEMO_DIR=c:\memo* in our example. When used with *variablename*, ENVIRON$ searches the environment list for the specified name. Thus, *ENVIRON$("PATH")* returns *PATH=C:\WORD;C:\DOS;C:\MEMO;C:\QB45;C:\BATCH;C:\UTILS*. Because DOS variables are case sensitive, *variablename* must be entered in uppercase characters. If the specified name or position doesn't exist, ENVIRON$ returns the null string.

Listing 17-8 demonstrates both variants of ENVIRON$, first listing all variables in the environment and then letting you retrieve values by name.

```
Var = 1                                         ' Display the environment
WHILE (ENVIRON$(Var) <> "")                     '  as a numbered list
    PRINT Var; ": "; ENVIRON$(Var)
    Var = Var + 1
WEND

DO                                              ' Display the requested variable
    PRINT "Type 'q' to quit or "                '  and value
    INPUT "name of variable to examine: "; VarName$
    VarName$ = UCASE$(VarName$)
    IF (VarName$) = "Q" THEN END
    PRINT VarName$; " ";
    IF ENVIRON$(VarName$) = "" THEN
        PRINT "is not defined"
    ELSE
        PRINT "is "; ENVIRON$(VarName$)
    END IF
LOOP
END
```

Listing 17-8.

Here is a sample run:

```
 1 : MEMO_DIR=c:\memo
 2 : MEMO_FILE=daybook
 3 : COMSPEC=C:\DOS\COMMAND.COM
 4 : PATH=C:\WORD;C:\DOS;C:\MEMO;C:\QB45;C:\BATCH;C:\UTILS
 5 : PROMPT=$P$G
Type 'q' to quit or
name of variable to examine: ? PATH
PATH is PATH=C:\WORD;C:\DOS;C:\MEMO;C:\QB45;C:\BATCH;C:\UTILS
Type 'q' to quit or
name of variable to examine: ? PROMPT
PROMPT is $P$G
Type 'q' to quit or
name of variable to examine: ? q
```

Changing the Environment

The ENVIRON statement lets you change a variable in your program's copy of the current environment (though not in the original environment). These changes are in turn reflected in the copy received by programs run from your program by a SHELL, RUN, or CHAIN statement.

Here is the syntax for the ENVIRON statement:

```
ENVIRON variablestring
```

variablestring is in the form *variablename* = *valuestring* where *variablename* is the name of the variable you want to change or add. *valuestring* is the actual pathname or other value to be given to this variable.

If ENVIRON finds the variable in the list, it changes the original value to the specified value. If it doesn't find the variable, it adds the variable's name and value to the end of the list.

Very little memory is available for new variables in QuickBASIC's copy of the environment. Thus, it's a good idea to execute a statement such as the following in DOS before running QuickBASIC:

```
C:\QB45>SET JUNK=abcdefghijklmnopqrstuvwxyz
```

Because QuickBASIC gives a copy of the original environment to the programs it runs, this statement ensures that the environmental variable *JUNK* will pass to the copy additional bytes that can be used for more productive purposes later.

A QuickBASIC program can then execute the following statement:

```
ENVIRON "JUNK="
```

Specifying a variable name without assigning a value removes that variable and its value from the current environment, freeing its space to be used for other variables.

Listing 17-9 shows the current environment, frees some space, and changes the value of the *PROMPT* variable. This change is reflected in the new prompt displayed when the SHELL statement is executed.

```
CLS
' Be sure you use SET JUNK = abcdefghijklmnopqrstuvwxyz
'  before starting QuickBASIC
PRINT "Current environment is: "
SHELL "set"                        ' Show the current DOS environment
ENVIRON "JUNK ="                   ' Free some environment space

PRINT
PRINT "Changing the prompt: "
ENVIRON "PROMPT=Type 'exit' to return to BASIC ==>"
PRINT "Prompt is now "; ENVIRON$("PROMPT")

PRINT "Now running a new shell"
SHELL                              ' Run COMMAND.COM with the new prompt

PRINT
PRINT "This is now QB's copy of the original environment: "
SHELL "set"                        ' Show the environment
END
```

Listing 17-9.

Here is a sample run:

```
Current environment is:
MEMO_DIR=c:\memo
MEMO_FILE=daybook
COMSPEC=C:\DOS\COMMAND.COM
PATH=C:\WORD;C:\DOS;C:\MEMO;C:\QB45;C:\BATCH;C:\UTILS
PROMPT=$P$G
JUNK=abcdefghijklmnopqrstuvwxyz

Changing the prompt:
Prompt is now Type 'exit' to return to BASIC ==>
Now running a new shell


IBM DOS Version 4.00
          (C)Copyright International Business Machines Corp 1981, 1988
          (C)Copyright Microsoft Corp 1981-1986

Type 'exit' to return to BASIC ==> exit

This is now QB's copy of the original environment:
MEMO_DIR=c:\memo
MEMO_FILE=daybook
COMSPEC=C:\DOS\COMMAND.COM
PATH=C:\WORD;C:\DOS;C:\MEMO;C:\QB45;C:\BATCH;C:\UTILS
PROMPT=Type 'exit' to return to BASIC ==>
```

The copy of the environment being used by QuickBASIC has been changed, and the new prompt will be passed on to other programs run during the current session in the QuickBASIC environment.

Listing 17-10 demonstrates how a QuickBASIC program can access the current *PATH* variable. The program uses the *Parse* subprogram from Listing 17-6 to break the path into its component directories and then reports all EXE and COM files currently executable from your DOS path. (The code for the *Parse* subprogram is omitted here.)

```
' Merge the Parse subprogram from Listing 17-6
DECLARE SUB Parse (AString$, Words$(), MaxWords%, WordsFound%, Sep$)
CLS
ON ERROR GOTO ErrorHandler

Path$ = ENVIRON$("PATH")
PRINT Path$
DIM Dirs$(15)    ' Hold directories found in path

' Tell Parse to separate items between semicolons
Parse Path$, Dirs$(), 15, DirsFound%, ";"
FOR D = 1 TO DirsFound%
    CLS
    PRINT "Directory: "; Dirs$(D)
    PRINT ".EXE files: "
    FILES Dirs$(D) + "\*.EXE"

    PRINT
    PRINT ".COM files: "
    FILES Dirs$(D) + "\*.COM"
    PRINT
    PRINT "Press any key to continue: "
    Temp$ = INPUT$(1)
NEXT D
END

ErrorHandler:
    PRINT "No files found "
    RESUME NEXT
END
```

Listing 17-10.

Note that the FILES statement displays the current directory before listing the specified files. Here is a sample run:

```
Directory: C:\DOS
.EXE files:
C:\QB45\CHAP17
XCOPY   .EXE      FASTOPEN.EXE      APPEND  .EXE      ATTRIB  .EXE
FIND    .EXE      JOIN    .EXE      MEM     .EXE      REPLACE .EXE
SORT    .EXE      SUBST   .EXE
 1490944 Bytes free
```

```
.COM files:
C:\QB45\CHAP17
COMMAND .COM       FORMAT  .COM       MORE    .COM       GRAPHICS.COM
CHKDSK  .COM       BACKUP  .COM       DISKCOPY.COM       LABEL   .COM
MODE    .COM       SYS     .COM       FDISK   .COM       KEYB    .COM
ASSIGN  .COM       COMP    .COM       DEBUG   .COM       DISKCOMP.COM
GRAFTABL.COM       PRINT   .COM       RECOVER .COM       RESTORE .COM
TREE    .COM
 1490944 Bytes free

Press any key to continue:
```

Using DOS commands and interrupts, the command line, and the environment, your program can be in touch with almost everything going on in the computer. Next let's look at some of the ways you can manage your programs so that they don't run out of memory.

Program Management

If you find that available memory can't hold all the code modules and data structures you need, you have two choices. You can try using smaller data structures, which might force your program to write data continually to and from disk. Alternatively, you can break your program into separate programs and run only one at a time, freeing memory for more efficient handling of data.

Running Another Program

The RUN statement runs the current program, a certain part of the current program, or another program.

Here is the syntax for RUN:

```
RUN [linenumber]
RUN [programname]
```

Using RUN without arguments runs the current program from the beginning. (This is a handy way to restart a simple game program.) *linenumber* specifies the line number in the current program at which execution should begin. *programname* specifies the name (or full pathname) of a program to be loaded and run, replacing the current program.

If the current program is run from within the QuickBASIC environment, the program to be run must be a BASIC source file, with a BAS extension. If the current program is run as an EXE file, the program to be run must be another EXE or COM program. In both cases, the extensions are assumed and need not be specified.

Because this structure does not allow you to pass information in variables to the other program being run, RUN is used infrequently in modern BASIC programming. Suppose, however, that you have a utility EXE or COM file on disk that lacks documentation, as many programs distributed on bulletin boards do. You can compile a

QuickBASIC program to provide instructions and run the cryptic program on request, as shown in the following:

```
PRINT                   ' Add instructions for using program
INPUT "Do you want to run this program (Y/N)?", Ans$

IF UCASE$(Ans$) = "Y" THEN
    RUN "C:\UTILS\DRAW" ' Substitute correct path and filename
ELSE
    PRINT "Returning to system..."
END IF
END
```

Chaining Programs

Unlike RUN, the CHAIN statement lets you pass variables to other QuickBASIC programs by using the COMMON statement. Using CHAIN is probably the best solution if available memory is not adequate for your program.

Here is the syntax for the CHAIN statement:

```
CHAIN programname
```

programname is the name or path of the program to which control is passed. Like RUN, CHAIN expects a BASIC source file when run inside the QuickBASIC environment and an EXE or COM file when run outside the QuickBASIC environment.

When several programs are chained, they often need access to the same variable or the same group of variables. For example, one program might open and process a file and put the name of the file in a string variable. The next program in the chain could use the value of that string variable to find the name of the file being processed. The COMMON statement lets you specify which variables are to be used in common by the chained programs. (COMMON is also used to share variables in multimodule programs; see Chapter 8 for discussion.)

Here is the syntax for using COMMON with chained programs:

```
COMMON variablelist
```

variablelist consists of one or more variable names (and, optionally, type declarations) separated by commas. The COMMON statement must appear at the beginning of each program that uses the specified variables. (Although COMMON must precede any executable statements, it can follow declaration statements such as DIM.)

For example, to make the variables *LeftMargin!*, *RightMargin!*, *Header$*, and *Footer$* accessible to the programs STYLE.BAS, FORMAT.BAS, and PRINTOUT.BAS, each program must include the following statement:

```
COMMON LeftMargin!, RightMargin!, Header$, Footer$
```

Whenever the value of one of these variables changes in one program, the other programs also use the new value.

The variables must appear in the same order and the variable types must be the same in all the COMMON statements because QuickBASIC matches the lists of variables in the order specified if the variable types match. Suppose you added the chained program PREVIEW.BAS containing the following statement:

```
COMMON RightMargin!, LeftMargin!, Header$, Footer$
```

A change in *LeftMargin!* in one of the other programs (where it is the first variable listed) would cause a change in the first variable listed in PREVIEW.BAS, which is *RightMargin!*; the names needn't correspond.

Listing 17-11 demonstrates using CHAIN to break a large program into manageable pieces to be run from a main menu. Each part of the program becomes a separate QuickBASIC program—for example, the Display File Contents option becomes SHOWFILE.BAS. Note that we declare one common variable, *File$*, whose value is available to all the chained programs.

```
' DBMS.BAS, the master program for chained DBMS system
COMMON File$                  ' Filename to be shared with chained programs

CLS : PRINT "Enter the letter of your choice:"
DO                            ' Show the menu and wait for valid response
    PRINT "Current file is: "; File$
    PRINT
    PRINT "D) Display File Contents      A) Add to File"
    PRINT "C) Count Records in File      S) Sort File by Last Name"
    PRINT "F) Find a Last Name           N) Set New File"
    PRINT "Q) Quit"
    Ans$ = INPUT$(1)
    Choice$ = UCASE$(Ans$)
LOOP UNTIL (INSTR("DACSFNQ", Choice$))

SELECT CASE Choice$           ' Chain to appropriate program
    CASE "D"
        CHAIN "SHOWFILE"
    CASE "A"
        CHAIN "APPEND"
    CASE "C"
        CHAIN "COUNTREC"
    CASE "S"
        CHAIN "SORTRECS"
    CASE "F"
        CHAIN "FINDNAME"
    CASE "N"
        CHAIN "SETFILE"
    CASE "Q"
        SYSTEM
END SELECT
END
```

Listing 17-11.

The chained programs (stubs) are shown in Listing 17-12. Each one declares the common variable *File$*, which contains the name of the database file in use.

```
' SHOWFILE.BAS
COMMON File$
CLS
PRINT "Current file is: "; File$
PRINT "Show contents of a file:"
PRINT "Press any key to continue: "
Temp$ = INPUT$(1)
CHAIN "DBMS"
END

' APPEND.BAS
COMMON File$
CLS
PRINT "Current file is: "; File$
PRINT "Append records to a file:"
PRINT "Press any key to continue: "
Temp$ = INPUT$(1)
CHAIN "DBMS"
END

' COUNTREC.BAS
COMMON File$
CLS
PRINT "Current file is: "; File$
PRINT "Count records in a file:"
PRINT "Press any key to continue: "
Temp$ = INPUT$(1)
CHAIN "DBMS"
END

' SORTRECS.BAS
COMMON File$
CLS
PRINT "Current file is: "; File$
PRINT "Sort records in a file:"
PRINT "Press any key to continue: "
Temp$ = INPUT$(1)
CHAIN "DBMS"
END

' FINDNAME.BAS
COMMON File$
CLS
PRINT "Current file is: "; File$
PRINT "Find names in a file:"
PRINT "Press any key to continue: "
```

Listing 17-12. *(continued)*

Listing 17-12. *continued*

```
Temp$ = INPUT$(1)
CHAIN "DBMS"
END

' SETFILE.BAS
COMMON File$
CLS
PRINT "Current file is: "; File$
INPUT "Change current file to:"; NewFile$
File$ = NewFile$
PRINT "Press any key to continue: "
Temp$ = INPUT$(1)
CHAIN "DBMS"
END
```

After running Listing 17-11, choose Set New File from the menu. Then, if you run any of the other options, the current file is displayed as the name you set, showing that the chained program has been run and that the value of *File$* is common to the entire chained system of programs.

Review Questions

1. How are the SHELL and RUN statements similar? How do they differ?
2. Name two ways that your program can get configuration information before it begins processing.
3. DOS interrupt &H12 returns the amount of DOS-accessible memory installed in the system. This interrupt requires no input register values and returns the total memory in the AX register. Write a program that calls this interrupt and displays the amount of installed memory.
4. The regular DOS DELETE command can remove only one file (or set of files specified with wildcards) at a time. Write a program that will delete all files or sets of files specified on the command line. (Hint: Use the *Parse* subprogram from Listing 17-6 to access the command line. Test the program in a temporary directory containing junk files, in case a programming error causes the wrong files to be deleted.)
5. When should you consider using the CHAIN statement? How do CHAIN and RUN differ?

18

Using Mixed Languages

ANY	**CALL**	**CDECL**	**SEG**
BYVAL	**CALLS**	**DECLARE**	

Some programmers are fanatically dedicated to or opposed to certain languages. Those with a more balanced view, however, regard all languages as programming tools and the programmer's job as deciding which tool best suits a particular task.

Mixed-language programming—combining more than one computer language into a single program—reflects this balanced view. Mixed-language programming with QuickBASIC as the core lets you tap the strengths of other languages by incorporating procedures that are written in other Microsoft programming languages: Pascal, FORTRAN, C, and Macro Assembler (MASM). Using more than one language is also convenient, for it allows you to add existing routines in other languages to your programs without having to rewrite the routines in QuickBASIC.

In this chapter we'll examine how you can use non-BASIC procedures in your QuickBASIC programs. We'll begin by giving you some background, and then we'll move on to some examples.

Background

The key to mixed-language programming is translating everything to a common language. The natural choice is machine language, the language native to the CPU. Compilers and assemblers in fact do such translation. When you create an EXE or a COM file from a program in any language, you create a file of machine language instructions and data. Because all PC compilers produce a final product in the same machine language, it's not surprising that you can mix the resulting code from various languages. But high-level languages do differ in important ways, and mixing them is not completely straightforward. To see what is involved, we'll review a typical compilation process.

Stand-alone Executable Programs

Let's follow the steps needed to create a stand-alone executable program. For simplicity, we assume that you're using a command-line compiler such as the BASIC compiler (BC) that comes with QuickBASIC.

1. Write a program in the language of your choice. This program is called the *source code*. The file holding the source code has a filename extension indicating the language: BAS for BASIC, C for C, ASM for assembly, and so on.
2. Use either a compiler or (for assembly language) an assembler to convert the source code to machine language. This process is called *compiling* or *assembling*. The result is called the *object code,* which is stored in a file with the filename extension OBJ.
3. Use a linker to combine the object-code file with additional object code from libraries and with object code that lets the operating system run the program. This process is called *linking*. The result is an executable file with the filename extension EXE or COM.

Figure 18-1 summarizes these steps.

Suppose you want to combine QuickBASIC code with C code. You can use the BASIC compiler to produce object code for the BASIC part and use a C compiler, such as Microsoft's QuickC, to produce object code for the C part. Then you can use Microsoft's linker, called LINK, to link the parts and produce the final code. (LINK comes with DOS as well as with QuickBASIC and other Microsoft languages. You might have more than one version on your system; here you should use the one that comes with QuickBASIC.)

When you work in the QuickBASIC integrated environment, the steps followed are somewhat different. The fundamental concept, however, is the same: Convert the foreign-language procedure to object code, and combine the object code with the BASIC program.

All Microsoft languages use the same object-file format. This makes the object-code files compatible, allowing them to work with the same LINK program. Nevertheless, differences can exist between object files in various languages. For instance, some languages offer several memory models, with the object files for one model differing from the object files for another. Also, languages differ in how they pass arguments to procedures. We'll elaborate on these topics later in the chapter.

Libraries

You can use command-line compilers, object-code files, and LINK to create mixed-language programs. When you use QuickBASIC, however, you must also create libraries of your mixed-language procedures.

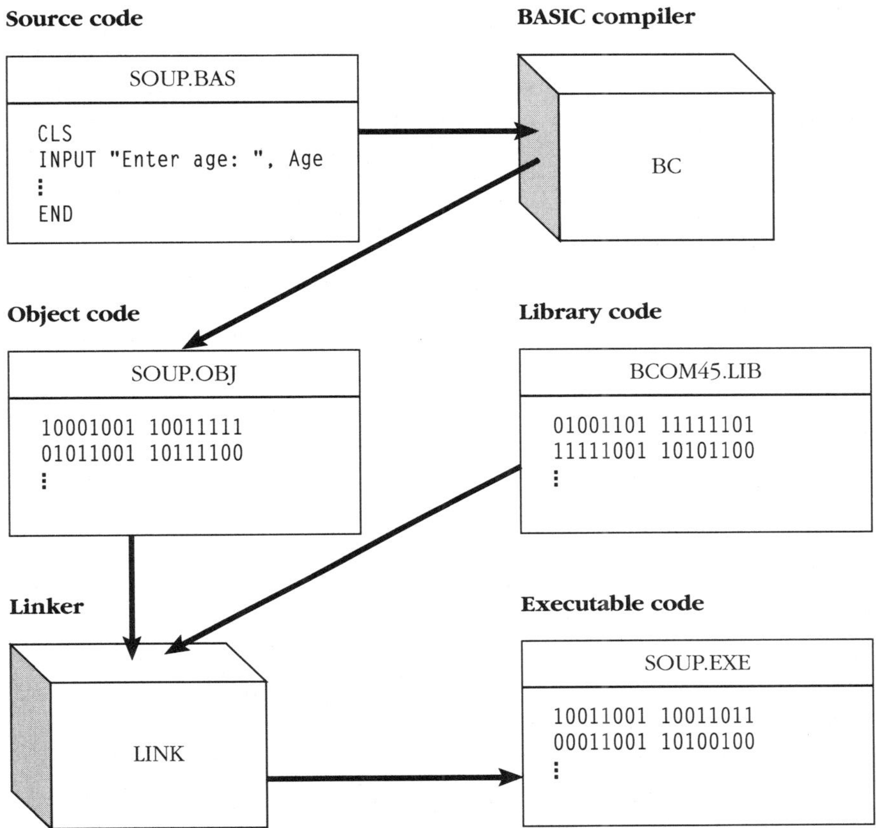

Figure 18-1.
Creating an executable program.

A *library* is a file containing object code for one or more procedures. Although a single library can hold code for dozens of procedures, LINK and QuickBASIC are designed to extract from the library only those procedures needed for a particular program. QuickBASIC uses two kinds of libraries: the Quick library and the stand-alone library. Quick libraries have a QLB extension. They are used for standard, in-memory program compilation in the QuickBASIC integrated environment. To create a stand-alone executable program, however, QuickBASIC uses the second kind of library, which has a LIB extension. The stand-alone library, unlike the Quick library, can be linked to programs written in any Microsoft programming language, not only QuickBASIC. The LINK program, which QuickBASIC uses when it creates stand-alone programs, recognizes only stand-alone libraries. Thus, as you build a set of mixed-language procedures, you must develop two parallel library files: the Quick library (QLB) for in-memory compilation, and the stand-alone (LIB) library for stand-alone compilation.

Language Differences

The high-level languages QuickBASIC, Pascal, FORTRAN, and C are roughly comparable in many ways. For instance, each language uses loops, IF/THEN statements, and a variety of data types. Each can create programming units that correspond to QuickBASIC's subprogram and function procedures. But for now, let's focus on some of the differences between these languages.

Naming Conventions

Different Microsoft languages have different naming conventions for procedures. For example, C allows an underscore but not a period as part of a name, whereas QuickBASIC allows a period but no underscore. To produce mutually acceptable names, therefore, it's best to simply use letters and numbers.

You can use % and the other special suffixes in a QuickBASIC program to indicate type, but you must omit the suffix in the corresponding non-BASIC procedure. *Num%* in QuickBASIC thus corresponds to the integer variable *Num* in Pascal or C.

You must also limit the number of characters in a name. In a Pascal or a C module, use no more than eight characters; in a FORTRAN module, use no more than six. The special QuickBASIC type suffixes aren't part of the character count—that is, the name *BookMark%* contains eight characters.

When the Microsoft C compiler or the QuickC compiler creates object code, it adds an underscore as a prefix to function names. Thus, a C function called *city* becomes *_city* in the object code. For compatibility, use the QuickBASIC keyword CDECL when declaring the *city* procedure in a QuickBASIC module; CDECL will make the name in the QuickBASIC object code match the name in the C code.

Unlike some other languages, C distinguishes between uppercase and lowercase characters in names. The Microsoft C compiler and QuickC typically invoke the linker using the /NOIGNORE (or /NOI) option, which means "don't ignore case." When conjoining QuickBASIC and C, however, you need to link without using this option. To eliminate worries about case, use QuickBASIC, which does not invoke the /NOI option, to manage linking.

Memory Models

The IBM PC and PS/2 families of computers use a CPU family (the 80x86 processors such as 8086, 80286, and 80386) with two ways of accessing memory. One method uses a 16-bit address, called a *near pointer;* the other uses a 32-bit address, called a *far pointer.* (A *pointer* is an address or a variable holding an address as its value.) Accessing memory by using near pointers is faster than using far pointers, but it lets you access only 64 KB of memory. Using far pointers allows you to access up to 1024 KB of memory. Typically, a program loaded in memory has two parts: a *code segment,* which holds the program code; and a *data segment,* which holds the data for a program. Each segment can use either near pointers or far pointers. The various combinations of choices for pointers used in these segments are called *memory models.*

	Code Pointers	Data Pointers
Language		
QuickBASIC	Far	Near
Pascal	Far	Near, far
FORTRAN	Far	Near (as of version 4), far
C	Near, far	Near, far
Assembly	Near, far	Near, far
Memory model name		
Small	Near	Near
Compact	Near	Far
Medium	Far	Near
Large	Far	Far
Huge	Far	Far

Figure 18-2.
Available memory models for Microsoft languages.

Figure 18-2 describes memory models used by various languages. QuickBASIC uses the medium memory model, with far pointers as code pointers that allow access to more than 64 KB of code in a program; its data pointers, however, are near pointers that limit QuickBASIC to 64 KB of data. (Although the descriptions of the large and huge memory models are similar, the large model restricts any one data object such as an array to a size smaller than 64 KB.)

When you combine object files, the code in the files must use the same type of code pointers. Otherwise, the object modules are incompatible and cannot be linked. QuickBASIC, Pascal, and FORTRAN use far pointers for code by default, so they pose no problem. But when you work with C and assembly language, you must be sure to specify a memory model with far code pointers.

Terminology

You can create equivalent modules of procedures in several languages, although the terminology for the procedures differs, as summarized in Figure 18-3.

Language	No Return Value	Return Value
QuickBASIC	Subprogram	Function procedure
Pascal	Procedure	Function
FORTRAN	Subroutine	Function
C	(void) Function	Function
Assembly	Procedure	Procedure

Figure 18-3.
Procedure terms.

Parameter Passing

Languages differ in how they pass arguments to procedures—that is, they differ in their *parameter-passing requirements.* (Passing arguments in QuickBASIC is discussed in more detail in Chapters 5 and 8.) Microsoft languages use three methods: passing by value, passing by near reference, and passing by far reference. When a variable is passed by value, the receiving procedure assigns the value to a new, independent variable. When a variable is passed by reference, the procedure receiving the variable uses the original variable.

The internal mechanism for passing by reference is to pass the address of the variable. Passing by near reference passes a near pointer, and passing by far reference passes a far pointer. Figure 18-4 summarizes the methods various languages use to pass procedure parameters.

Language	***Passing by Value***	***Passing by Near Reference***	***Passing by Far Reference***
QuickBASIC		Used exclusively	
Pascal	Default	Possible (VAR, CONST)	Possible (VARS, CONSTS)
FORTRAN	Possible (PASCAL or C attribute)	Possible (NEAR)	Default
C	Default	Possible (near *)	Possible (far *)
Assembly	Possible	Possible	Possible

Figure 18-4.
Methods of passing parameters.

A QuickBASIC program and a mixed-language procedure must agree on the convention for passing variables. In general, either you can write the procedure to match QuickBASIC's convention or you can write the QuickBASIC portion of the program to match the convention used by the other language.

When declaring procedures to match the argument-passing method of other languages, use the QuickBASIC keyword BYVAL to indicate an argument passed by value and the keyword SEG to indicate an argument passed by far reference. (Passing by near reference is the default and thus needs no keyword.) These keywords are used in DECLARE statements as well as in procedure calls; the keyword precedes the name of the variable it modifies. For example, if *Bell* is a QuickBASIC procedure that must pass *Ding%* by value and *Dong%* by far reference, it can be declared as shown here:

```
DECLARE SUB Bell (BYVAL Ding%, SEG Dong%)
```

Figure 18-5 lists the options for matching QuickBASIC procedure calls to procedures written in other languages.

Language	***When Adapting to Match QuickBASIC***	***When Adapting QuickBASIC***
Pascal	Use VAR and CONST parameters as variable form	Use QuickBASIC keywords BYVAL for default, SEG for VARS and CONSTS parameters
FORTRAN	Use NEAR parameters as variable form	Use QuickBASIC keywords SEG for default mode, BYVAL for C and PASCAL modes
C	Use near pointer formal arguments as variable form	Use QuickBASIC keywords BYVAL for default, SEG for far pointers

Figure 18-5.
Matching the argument-passing methods of QuickBASIC and other languages.

Calling Conventions

The *calling convention* for a language is the order in which it passes arguments to a procedure. C passes arguments in an order opposite that of most other languages. For example, the QuickBASIC subprogram call

```
CALL Book(X, Y, Z)
```

passes its arguments in the order X, Y, Z, whereas the C function call

```
book(x, y, z);
```

passes its arguments in the order z, y, x—that is, it passes the last argument first.

Fortunately, using the QuickBASIC keyword CDECL in the declaration can reconcile this difference. For instance, if *Vroom* is the name of a C function you're calling from QuickBASIC, you can declare it this way:

```
DECLARE SUB Vroom CDECL (BYVAL Ooh%, BYVAL Aah%)
```

QuickBASIC then passes the values in the order in which the C function expects them. Using CDECL also causes QuickBASIC to generate the object-code name *_vroom* for the procedure, as required for the C interface.

Types

When you pass an argument from a QuickBASIC program to a procedure in another module, the argument types in the two modules must match. For example, if a procedure expects an integer, you must pass it an integer. Likewise, if you define a function with a return value, the two modules must agree on the type for the return value. Mixed-language programming complicates this requirement because languages use different names for equivalent types. In addition, identical types are not available in every language.

Integers and real numbers are the easiest to pass from one language to another. Figure 18-6 summarizes types corresponding to QuickBASIC's fundamental types. (Some languages have additional integer types that have no QuickBASIC equivalent; these are not listed.)

QuickBASIC	*Pascal*	*FORTRAN*	*C*
INTEGER	INTEGER2, INTEGER	INTEGER*2	int, short
LONG	INTEGER4	INTEGER*4, INTEGER	long
SINGLE	REAL4, REAL	REAL, REAL*4	float
DOUBLE	REAL8	REAL*8, DOUBLE PRECISION	double

Figure 18-6.
Equivalent data types.

Strings and arrays are more problematic. To pass these elements as arguments, you must understand in detail how each language handles them. We won't venture that far into mixed-language programming in this book; you can consult the *Microsoft Mixed-Language Guide,* which is packaged with Microsoft C and with Microsoft Macro Assembler (MASM), for more information.

Using C with QuickBASIC

Now that we've reviewed some of the considerations that are involved in mixed-language programming, we can demonstrate a few examples. We'll first use a simple C module containing a function with one argument (QuickBASIC-style, passing by reference) and no return value. This simplicity will let us concentrate on the steps needed to create a mixed-language program.

Example 1: Passing by Reference

We'll start by writing a QuickBASIC program calling a C function that doubles the value of its argument. Next we'll write the C function, compile it, and then place the resulting object code in a Quick library. Finally we'll use QuickBASIC to bring the whole program together.

Writing the QuickBASIC Program

Listing 18-1 presents our QuickBASIC program.

```
' Step 1: Declare the C function
DECLARE SUB CTwice CDECL (N%)  ' Pass by reference QuickBASIC-style
CLS
X% = 10
PRINT "X% has the value"; X%
PRINT "This program now will call a C function to double X%!"
' Step 2: Call the C function
CALL CTwice(X%)
PRINT "Now X% has the value"; X%
END
```

Listing 18-1.

To use a C function (or any other procedure in another language), use DECLARE to declare the procedure and CALL to call it.

Here is the syntax for the DECLARE statement when using a procedure module written in another language:

```
DECLARE SUB name [CDECL] [ALIAS "aliasname"] [([parameterlist])
DECLARE FUNCTION name [CDECL] [ALIAS "aliasname"][([parameterlist])
```

name is the name of the non-BASIC procedure. For functions, use a QuickBASIC type suffix to indicate the function's return type. The CDECL option causes the C calling convention (passing parameters from the parameter list in right-to-left order) to be used. Using CDECL also ensures that QuickBASIC will generate an internal name for the subprogram consistent with C practice. The ALIAS option establishes *aliasname* as the name to be used in the object-code file, thus allowing you to use one name (*name*) in the QuickBASIC program and a second name (*aliasname*) in the non-BASIC program.

parameterlist is a comma-separated list of variables. Each element of the list has the following syntax:

```
[{BYVAL | SEG}] variablename [AS type]
```

BYVAL indicates that the parameter is to be passed by value. This keyword can be used only with INTEGER, LONG, SINGLE, and DOUBLE parameters. Expressions used as arguments when the subprogram is called are converted to values of the corresponding type.

SEG indicates that the value is passed by far reference—that is, a 32-bit address (a far pointer) is passed.

When AS *type* is used, *type* can be INTEGER, LONG, SINGLE, DOUBLE, STRING, ANY, or a user-defined type. (When a subprogram is called, QuickBASIC normally checks to see that the number of arguments and the types are correct; using ANY overrides this type checking.)

If the subprogram uses no arguments, you can declare it either without parentheses or with empty parentheses. If you use parentheses, QuickBASIC checks to see that no arguments are used. If you omit the parentheses, QuickBASIC doesn't check.

Our QuickBASIC declaration, then, looks like this:

```
DECLARE SUB CTwice CDECL (N%)
```

This tells us that the program will use a subprogram called *CTwice*, which uses the C calling and naming conventions. The subprogram has one argument, which will be passed in the standard QuickBASIC method of passing by reference.

> **NOTE:** *QuickBASIC generates DECLARE statements when you place the code for a QuickBASIC procedure in the main module. But when you create a procedure in another language and another file, you must generate the DECLARE statement yourself.*

The QuickBASIC CALL statement for non-BASIC procedures has nearly the same syntax as CALL for BASIC procedures, except that BYVAL and SEG are used as qualifiers in the argument list. A CALLS variant also exists for non-BASIC procedures.

Here is the syntax for CALL and CALLS:

```
CALL name [(argumentlist)]
name [argumentlist]
CALLS name [(callsargumentlist)]
```

name is the name of the procedure being called. *argumentlist* is a list of arguments separated by commas. Each element of the list has the following syntax:

```
[{BYVAL | SEG}] argument
```

BYVAL or SEG can be omitted from the call if they have been used in the corresponding declaration. The CALLS variant, in effect, precedes all its arguments with SEG; hence *callsargumentlist* is a comma-separated list of arguments that do not use BYVAL or SEG modifiers.

Note that you can omit the keyword CALL, as you can for regular QuickBASIC procedures, if you also omit the parentheses enclosing the argument list. For instance, we could have used the following in Listing 18-1:

```
CTwice X%
```

Writing the C Function

Next we must write the C function, matching its properties to the QuickBASIC declaration. Because the QuickBASIC procedure is a subprogram and not a function, it has no return value. That means that the C function must be type *void*. Also, the C function must have only one argument, which must be the address of an integer variable because the program uses the QuickBASIC convention of passing by reference. The C type that represents the address of an integer is pointer-to-integer (*int **). Listing 18-2 shows the function definition.

```
/* ctwice() is a C function */
void ctwice (int *pn)   /*  pn is address of a variable  */
{
    *pn = 2 * (*pn);    /*  *pn is value at that address */
}
```

Listing 18-2.

Here the C variable *pn* is assigned the address of the passed variable. The expression **pn* represents the value stored at the passed address. The *ctwice()* function doubles that value by multiplying **pn* by 2. Because the function uses the address of the passed variable, the new value is stored in that variable. We'll store the code in a file called CTWICE.C.

Creating the Object Code

Next we must compile the C code using the medium memory model. In Microsoft C, we use the /AM option to override the default (the small model) and the /c option to compile the program without linking it:

```
CL /AM /c CTWICE.C
```

If you are using QuickC version 2 or later, open the Options menu and select Make. Then select Compiler Flags from the dialog box. A new dialog box appears, from which you can select the medium memory model. Then choose Compile File from the Make menu to compile CTWICE.C. Either compiler produces the object file, which is called CTWICE.OBJ. The object file is created in the directory from which you invoked CL or started QuickC.

Creating the Quick Library

Because we want to produce a program that runs in the QuickBASIC environment, the next step is creating the Quick library. We'll need three files:

- The LINK.EXE file is the linker.
- The BQLB45.LIB library file contains information used to build Quick libraries.
- The CTWICE.OBJ file contains the machine code for the C function we wrote.

QuickBASIC comes with LINK.EXE and BQLB45.LIB; by default, the QuickBASIC installation program places them in the QB45 directory. To use the LINK.EXE that comes with QuickBASIC, we'll copy CTWICE.OBJ to the QuickBASIC directory and then execute the following command in that directory:

```
LINK /Q CTWICE.OBJ,CLIB.QLB,,BQLB45.LIB
```

The /Q option instructs the linker to create a Quick library, constructed from the BQLB45.LIB stand-alone library and the CTWICE.OBJ file, to be named CLIB.QLB. (You can choose any name with a QLB extension.) Note the use of single and double commas in the command; LINK requires that they be used exactly as shown here.

Figure 18-7 summarizes the creation of a Quick library and the incorporation of a C procedure into it.

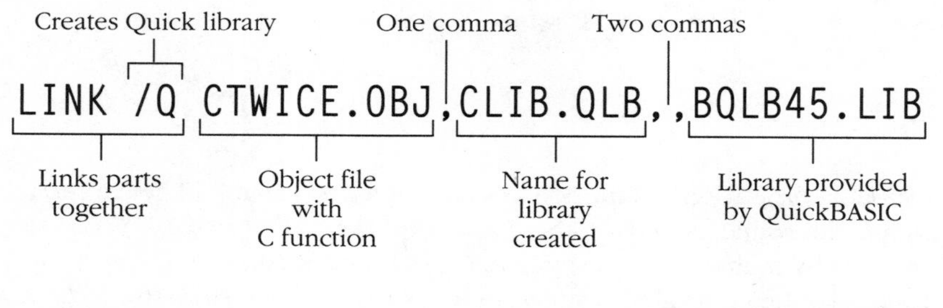

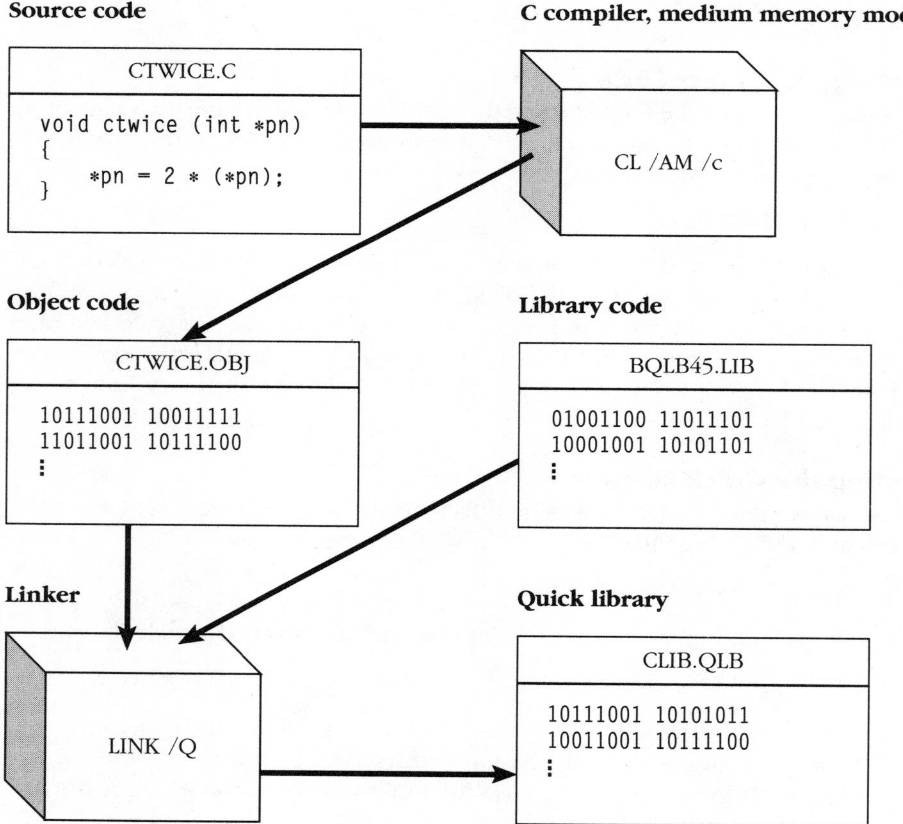

Figure 18-7.
Creating a Quick library.

Using the Quick Library

To use the Quick library CLIB.QLB that we just created, we must load the Quick library when we start QuickBASIC by using the /L (library) option:

```
QB /L CLIB.QLB
```

QuickBASIC now can access all the routines in the Quick library. When we open the file containing Listing 18-1 and try to run the program, we get the following output:

```
X% has the value 10
This program now will call a C function to double X%!
Now X% has the value 20
```

QuickBASIC uses the C function in the CLIB.QLB Quick library when it executes the *CTwice* subprogram.

> **NOTE:** *You can load a Quick library only when you start QuickBASIC. If you create a Quick library in a multitasking environment that is already running QuickBASIC or create it from a QuickBASIC DOS shell, you must exit QuickBASIC and then restart it with the /L option.*

Creating a Stand-alone Program

The method we've outlined creates a program that runs only in the QuickBASIC environment. Creating a stand-alone program requires further work. In particular, we must create the second form of library file, the CLIB.LIB file. (If we merely select Make EXE File from the Run menu, an error message will eventually inform us that the program can't find the CLIB.LIB file.)

The tool for creating this library file is LIB.EXE, another program that comes with QuickBASIC. With CTWICE.OBJ in the QuickBASIC directory, we use the following command:

```
LIB CLIB.LIB+CTWICE.OBJ;
```

The first argument (*CLIB.LIB*) is the name selected for the library. The expression *+CTWICE.OBJ* adds that code to the library. The closing semicolon prevents LIB from prompting us for more information and causes default values to be used.

After we've completed this step, we can load the Quick library CLIB.QLB when starting QuickBASIC and open the file containing Listing 18-1. Now we can use Make EXE File from the QuickBASIC Run menu. We can create either a complete stand-alone program or one that requires the runtime module BRUN45.EXE (discussed in Chapter 1).

Example 2: Passing by Value and Return Values

Let's be a bit bolder and try passing arguments by value. Let's also create a procedure with a return value. This time, we'll write a function that reports the value of a particular bit in a 16-bit integer. C is especially well suited for this task because it has several bitwise operators (operators designed to work with individual bits). Listing 18-3 presents the QuickBASIC part of the program.

```
DECLARE FUNCTION BitVal% CDECL (BYVAL Num%, BYVAL Bit%)
CLS
INPUT "Enter number to be checked: ", N%
DO WHILE N% > 0
    INPUT "Enter bit to be checked (0-15): ", B%
    Ans% = BitVal%(N%, B%)
    IF Ans% < 0 THEN
        PRINT B%; "is not a valid bit value"
    ELSE
        PRINT "Bit"; B%; "of"; N%; "is"; Ans%
    END IF
    INPUT "Next number (<=0 to quit): ", N%
LOOP
END
```

Listing 18-3.

In this program, which declares a QuickBASIC function rather than a subprogram, we must indicate the type for the return value. The name *BitVal%* tells us that the return value is an integer. Because we plan to use the C method of passing arguments by value, we use the BYVAL modifier in front of each variable in the declaration of the function. Using BYVAL in the declaration makes it possible to specify parameters in the function call without preceding them with BYVAL.

The first argument used by *BitVal%* is the integer to be examined. The second argument is the bit number to be checked. The function returns the value (0 or 1) of that bit in the number. For instance, *BitVal%(255, 4)* returns 1, the value of bit number 4 in the number 255. The bit number must be in the range 0 through 15 for an integer. The function returns –1 if an invalid bit value is provided.

Writing the C Function

Let's proceed to the C portion of the program. We want to write a C function with an integer return value and two integer arguments. The corresponding ANSI C declaration of the function is the following:

```
int bitval (int num, int bit)
```

Note that the % suffix is not used for the C name. In QuickBASIC, % serves to indicate the type; in C, *int* serves the same purpose. Because we are passing arguments by value, the C function uses ordinary integer variables rather than pointers.

Listing 18-4 presents the complete C function. It begins by checking to be sure that the *bit* argument is in the proper range (using the `||` operator, the OR operator in C). If it is, the function uses the following expression to evaluate the bit:

```
(num >> bit) & 1
```

To see how this works, try to visualize the number *num* written in binary form. The expression *num* >> *bit* shifts the digits *bit* bits to the right. If *bit* is 3, for example, bit 3 winds up in the bit 0 position. In this context, & is not the address operator but the bitwise logical AND operator. In effect, it sets all the bits to 0 except the 0 bit, which is unaltered. As a result, the entire expression has the same value as the 0 bit, which equals the original value of bit number *bit*. In C, the keyword *return* identifies the value returned by a function, as shown in Listing 18-4.

```
int bitval (int num, int bit)
{
     if ( bit >= 8 * sizeof (int) || bit < 0)
          return -1;                /* bit value out of range */
     else
          return (num >> bit) & 1;
}
```

Listing 18-4.

We'll store the source code in a file called BITVAL.C. Once again, we'll use the medium memory model option in C or in QuickC to produce an object file.

Making Libraries

The next step is to produce libraries QuickBASIC can use: a stand-alone library for stand-alone programs, and a Quick library for the integrated environment. These two forms differ in some important practical ways. For instance, you can load only one Quick library when you start QuickBASIC, but you can use more than one stand-alone library if you go through the linking process. In addition, you can use LIB to add or subtract object-code modules from stand-alone libraries, but LINK won't do the same for Quick libraries. These differences affect how the *bitval* function is added to the QuickBASIC repertoire.

For the LIB library, we'll simply add the new object code to our CLIB.LIB library. Assuming that we have all our files in the same directory, we can give the following command from DOS:

```
LIB CLIB.LIB+BITVAL.OBJ;
```

Now CLIB.LIB contains both BITVAL.OBJ and CTWICE.OBJ. We can also add more than one object file at a time by repeating the + operation:

```
LIB CLIB.LIB+MOD1.OBJ+MOD2.OBJ+MOD3.OBJ;
```

For the Quick library, we must decide whether we want our two procedures in separate libraries or in the same library. For separate libraries, we proceed as before, using a different Quick library name:

```
LINK /Q BITVAL.OBJ,CLIB1.QLB,,BQLB45.LIB
```

With this approach, we can load one or the other Quick library—but not both.

To place both procedures into one Quick library, we must add them both at the same time, as shown here:

```
LINK /Q CTWICE.OBJ BITVAL.OBJ,CLIB.QLB,,BQLB45.LIB
```

We'll use this approach. (Notice that commas are not used between the two object-code file names.)

> **NOTE:** *You can easily create or add to a Quick library when QuickBASIC is running; load the modules to be placed in the Quick library and then choose the Make Library command from the Run menu.*

Now that we have both a stand-alone and a Quick library for our C routines, we can produce either a stand-alone program or one that runs in the QuickBASIC environment. The second approach is simpler and faster, so we'll use it to check the program's operation.

Running the Example

Once again, start QuickBASIC and load the library:

```
QB /L CLIB.QLB
```

Then load the file containing Listing 18-3, and begin running the program. Here is a sample run:

```
Enter number to be checked: 255
Enter bit to be checked (0-15): 3
Bit 3 of 255 is 1
Next number (<=0 to quit): 12
Enter bit to be checked (0-15): 5
Bit 5 of 12 is 0
Next number (<=0 to quit): 0
```

Using BC

Another approach to mixed-language programming involves the command-line compiler (BC) and the linker (LINK) that come with QuickBASIC. Using this approach, you can produce a file from object-code files without creating libraries. For example, you could follow these steps to produce a stand-alone version of Listings 18-3 and 18-4:

1. Use QuickBASIC to write the BASIC source code in Listing 18-3. Save it in a file we'll call TESTBIT.BAS.

2. Use BC with the /O option to create the object code. The /O option produces code for a stand-alone program; if you omit this option, you'll need the BRUN45.EXE file available at runtime. The following command produces an object-code file called TESTBIT.OBJ:

   ```
   BC /O TESTBIT.BAS;
   ```

3. Use C or QuickC to produce the BITVAL.OBJ file as before.
4. Use LINK to create the executable file. If all the relevant files are in the QuickBASIC directory, you can use this command, which produces an executable file named TESTBIT.EXE:

```
LINK TESTBIT.OBJ BITVAL.OBJ;
```

In some ways, using BC is simpler than using the QuickBASIC integrated environment. If you are developing the BASIC program and need to make changes, however, using BC can be awkward; each time you change the BASIC source code, you must recompile it and repeat the linking process.

Accessing Functions in the C Library

Both Microsoft C and QuickC come with an extensive library of functions. To include one of these functions in a QuickBASIC program, use BC to create the object code for the BASIC part, and then use LINK to combine your code with code from the library.

Let's look at an example. The C library contains a function called *clock()* that resembles the QuickBASIC TIMER except that it returns the time in milliseconds instead of seconds, allowing you to measure shorter times. The *clock()* function is based on the system clock, which ticks 18.2 times a second. Although *clock()* reports time in milliseconds, each tick advances the time by about 55 milliseconds, or 0.055 seconds, which is called the clock resolution.

The *clock()* function takes no arguments, and it returns a type LONG value, as declared in Listing 18-5. This QuickBASIC program uses the C *clock()* function to time a FOR loop that carries out some simple addition.

```
' QuickBASIC program that calls the C library clock() function
DECLARE FUNCTION Clock& CDECL ()
INPUT "Enter loop limit: ", Limit&
Time1& = Clock&                       ' Starting time
FOR I& = 1 TO Limit&
    Sum& = Sum& + 1
NEXT I&
Time2& = Clock&                       ' Stopping time
Elapsed! = (Time2& - Time1&) / 1000   ' Convert to seconds
PRINT "Sum ="; Sum&
PRINT USING "##### cycles took ###.## seconds"; Limit&; Elapsed!
END
```

Listing 18-5.

Now save the QuickBASIC source code in a file called CLOCK.BAS, and use BC to create an object-code file called CLOCK.OBJ, as shown here:

```
BC /O CLOCK.BAS;
```

Next use LINK to create the final stand-alone program, called CLOCK.EXE:

```
LINK CLOCK.OBJ,,,BCOM45+MLIBCE /NOE;
```

The argument *BCOM45+MLIBCE* means that the BCOM45.LIB and the MLIBCE.LIB libraries will be used. The /NOE option means that duplicate definitions should be ignored (necessary here because some procedures are defined in both the C and the QuickBASIC libraries).

The LINK program will find the libraries if they are in the current directory or in a directory specified by the *LIB* DOS environmental variable. We'll assume that you have the C library MLIBCE.LIB. The M indicates that this is a medium memory model library, the C that it is a C library, and the E that it is a floating-point emulation library. Because our function doesn't use floating-point values, our primary concern is using a medium memory model.

Here is a sample run for CLOCK.EXE:

```
Enter loop limit: 10000
Sum = 10000
10000 loops took    .33 seconds
```

Using Assembly Language with QuickBASIC

Using assembly language with QuickBASIC requires more technical knowledge than using a high-level language such as C or Pascal, but it allows greater speed and more compact programs. You will need an assembler, such as Microsoft MASM 5.0 or QuickAssembler (available with QuickC), that produces object code compatible with QuickBASIC.

QuickBASIC Conventions

QuickBASIC observes certain conventions for producing object code. You should observe the same conventions when creating an assembly procedure. The following list summarizes these rules:

- The names of QuickBASIC procedures are converted to uppercase when object code is generated, and type suffixes are dropped. For instance, if you declare a procedure with the name *SetBit%* in QuickBASIC, the corresponding assembly procedure name is *SETBIT*. (If you omit the /NOI option, however, the linker will ignore case differences.)
- QuickBASIC always uses 32-bit addresses for code. An assembly procedure should therefore be type FAR. You can set the code pointers to be far pointers with MASM 5.0 by using the .MODEL MEDIUM directive.
- QuickBASIC assumes that procedure calls preserve the values of the CPU's BP, SI, DI, SS, SP, and DS registers. A procedure that uses any of these registers—and at least one, BP, is always used—should save the registers' values at the beginning of the procedure and restore them at the end. You can use the

assembly *push* command to save a register value on the stack and the *pop* command to restore the value. (The SP register is handled differently; see the final point in this list.)

- QuickBASIC arguments are placed on the stack in the order in which they appear in the argument list. The stack grows downward in memory, with the first argument at the highest memory location. Arguments can be passed by reference (the default) or by value (with BYVAL).
- QuickBASIC expects to find integer return values in the AX register.
- Upon exit, a QuickBASIC procedure resets the SP (stack pointer) register to the value it held before parameters were placed on the stack. In assembly language, this is done with the *ret size* instruction, where *size* is the number of bytes used to hold the arguments.

The following assembly procedure template is based on these conventions. Note that the semicolon is used to mark program comments in assembly language.

```
.MODEL MEDIUM                     ; Medium memory model
.CODE                             ; Code segment
         PUBLIC NAME              ; NAME can be used by other modules
NAME     PROC                     ; NAME is a procedure
         push      bp             ; Save old BP register value
         mov       bp, sp         ; Set BP to point at stack

         push      regs           ; Save other registers if required
         mov       ...            ; Load arguments into registers
         :                        ;  or use as needed
         :                        ; Perform tasks
         mov       ax, ...        ; Place return value in AX

         pop       regs           ; Restore other registers
         pop       bp             ; Restore BP
         ret       size           ; Reset SP and return
NAME     ENDP                     ; End of procedure
         END                      ; End of module
```

Stacks and Registers

Don't confuse stacks with registers. Registers are work spaces built into the microprocessor. They are used to store information temporarily, to keep track of addresses, and to perform arithmetic and logical calculations. They are identified by name (AX, BX, and so forth). A register usually holds 16 bits (2 bytes), although some can be divided into two 8-bit registers. For instance, AL is the low byte and AH the high byte of the AX register. (Registers are discussed in Chapters 14 and 17.) A stack is a block of memory allocated from the general system memory. The CPU manages the stack, keeping track of its location and its size. Typically, a stack is used for temporary storage and for passing arguments between procedures.

Example 1: Passing Arguments by Value to Assembly

To use assembly language with QuickBASIC, we must enable the assembly routine to access arguments correctly. If we use BYVAL on the QuickBASIC side to pass arguments by value, the assembly programming is simpler. The QuickBASIC program in Listing 18-6 calls a procedure named *OffBit%*, which turns off the specified bit of an integer (sets it to 0). *OffBit%* takes two integer arguments: The first is the value to be modified, and the second is the number of the bit (0 through 15) to be turned off, with the rightmost bit called bit 0.

```
DECLARE FUNCTION OffBit% (BYVAL Num%, BYVAL Bit%)
CLS
INPUT "Enter number to be adjusted: ", N%
DO WHILE N% >= 0
    INPUT "Enter bit to be turned off (0-15): ", B%
    Ans% = OffBit%(N%, B%)
    PRINT "Result =", Ans%
    INPUT "Next number (<0 to quit): ", N%
LOOP
END
```

Listing 18-6.

Next we'll create the assembly code in Listing 18-7 and save it using a filename with the ASM extension (OFFBIT.ASM, for example).

```
.MODEL MEDIUM
.CODE
        PUBLIC OFFBIT
OFFBIT  PROC
        push    bp
        mov     bp, sp
                                    ; bp+8 points to Num%
                                    ; bp+6 points to Bit%
        mov     dx, [bp+8]          ; Num% into DX
        mov     cl, BYTE PTR [bp+6] ; Bit% into CL
        mov     ax, 1               ; Set AX to 1
        shl     ax, cl              ; Shift left Bit% bits
        not     ax                  ; Toggle 1's and 0's
        and     ax, dx              ; AND AX with DX
        pop     bp
        ret     4                   ; 2 integers = 4 bytes
OFFBIT  ENDP
        END
```

Listing 18-7.

Now we'll use MASM or QuickAssembler to create an object-code file and then proceed as we did with C, either creating a Quick library to use with QuickBASIC or using BC and LINK to create an executable file. Here is a sample run:

```
Enter number to be adjusted: 15
Enter bit to be turned off (0-15): 1
Result =        13
Next number (<0 to quit): -3
```

Explaining the Assembly Procedure

Let's take a look at the assembly procedure code—in particular, at how the procedure accesses the arguments passed by QuickBASIC. When QuickBASIC calls a procedure, it passes information by placing it on a stack, in which each new item is added (pushed) on top of the preceding item, and items are removed (popped) in the opposite order (Figure 18-8).

Using *push* to add values to a stack

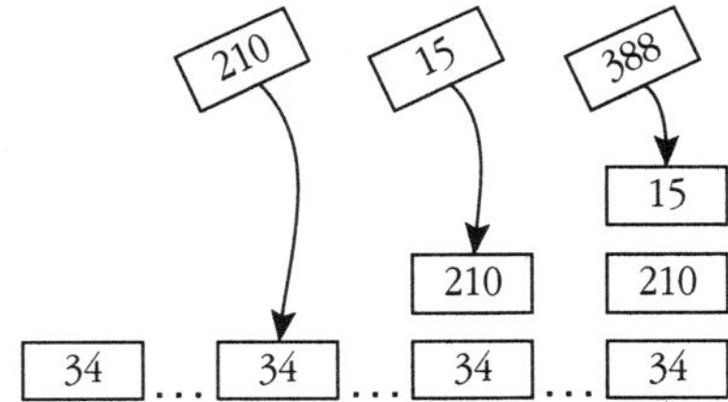

Using *pop* to remove values from a stack

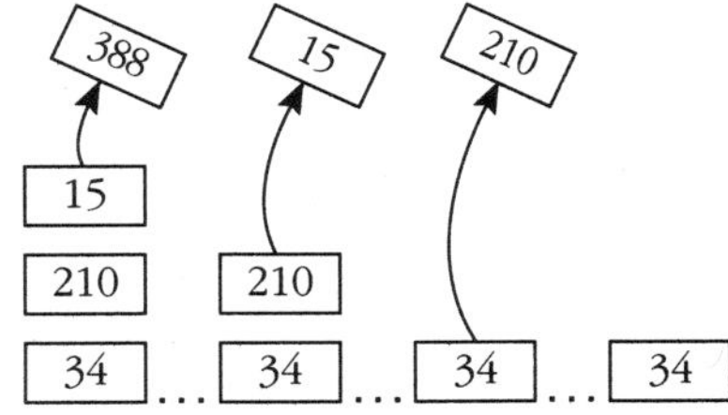

Figure 18-8.
Adding data to and removing data from a stack.

In assembly language, the instruction *push* places a value on the stack, and *pop* removes it. For example, if a procedure needs to save the SI and DI registers, you could do the following:

```
push si         ; Save value of SI register
push di         ; Save value of DI register
 ⋮              ; Main body of procedure
pop di          ; Restore DI
pop si          ; Restore SI
```

Note that in the example the order used to pop values is the opposite of the order used to push them.

When QuickBASIC calls a procedure, it will push the first argument and then the second argument, and so on. If you are passing by reference, each argument is a 2-byte address. If you are passing integer types by value, each argument is a 2-byte integer. (Passing a long integer by value uses 4 bytes.) Next the program will push the address of the code to which the procedure should return when finished. For the medium memory model, this address is a 4-byte quantity. Finally the called procedure will push the value of the BP register onto the stack and then set BP to the address of the top of the stack. Figure 18-9 shows what the stack looks like after we start our program. Note that the stack is implemented "upside down," giving the most recently pushed item a lower address than items pushed earlier.

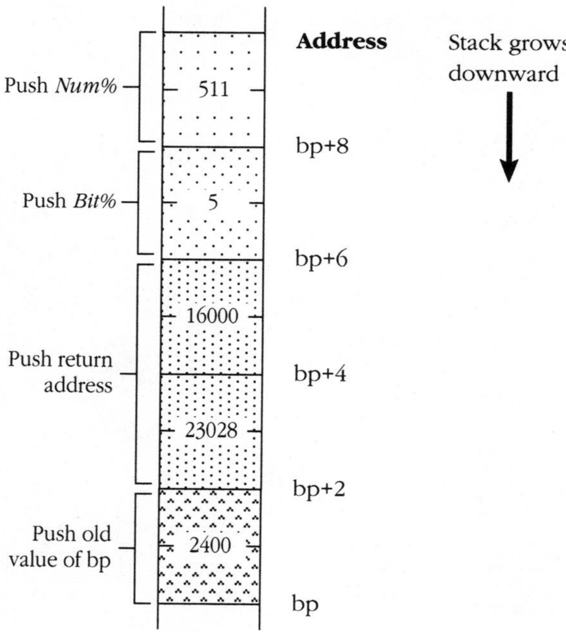

Figure 18-9.
The OFFBIT *stack.*

The microprocessor does most of its calculations using the AX, BX, CX, and DX registers, so we must copy data to these registers. In our example, the value of *Num%* is stored at a location whose address is *bp+8*. The assembly language notation *[bp+8]* indicates the value stored at address *bp+8*. Thus, the program uses the following code to copy the value of *Num%* to the DX register:

```
mov   dx, [bp+8]
```

Similarly, this instruction copies *Bit%* to the CL register:

```
mov   cl, BYTE PTR [bp+6]
```

The CL register is the low byte of the 2-byte CX register, and the BYTE PTR modifier indicates that *bp+6* is the address of a single byte rather than the default 2 bytes. Although we declared *Bit%* to be type INTEGER (2 bytes), the shift-left instruction (SHL) requires a 1-byte value, so this *mov* instruction trims the original value to 1 byte. Because the value should be in the range 0 through 15, and 1 byte can hold numbers in the range 0 through 255, this is no problem.

We do not need to move the final answer to the AX register, because the following instruction leaves the result of the operation in the AX register:

```
and  ax, dx
```

The QuickBASIC program passes two integers as arguments. Because they occupy 4 bytes on the stack, we use 4 as the argument for the *ret* command, which resets the SP register.

Example 2: Passing Arguments by Reference to Assembly

The QuickBASIC program in Listing 18-8 calls a procedure named *SetBit*, which takes two variables as arguments. Because we do not use the BYVAL qualifier, they are passed by reference rather than by value. We'll use the fact that *Num%* is passed by reference to have the procedure alter *Num%* directly instead of using a return value. Also, unlike the *OFFBIT* procedure in Listing 18-7, the *SETBIT* procedure in Listing 18-9 turns a bit on (sets it to 1) instead of turning it off.

```
DECLARE SUB SetBit (Num%, Bit%)
CLS
INPUT "Enter number to be set: ", N%
DO WHILE N% >= 0
    INPUT "Enter bit to be set (0-15): ", B%
    CALL SetBit(N%, B%)
    PRINT "Result ="; N%
    INPUT "Next number (<0 to quit): ", N%
LOOP
END
```

Listing 18-8.

Listing 18-9 shows the corresponding assembly procedure. Note how arguments passed by reference are handled.

```
.MODEL MEDIUM
.CODE
        PUBLIC SETBIT
SETBIT  PROC
        push    bp
        mov     bp, sp
                                ; bp+8 is address of Num%'s address
                                ; bp+6 is address of Bit%'s address
        mov     bx, [bp+6]      ; Copy Bit%'s address to BX
        mov     cl, BYTE PTR [bx]       ; Copy Bit%'s value to CL
        mov     bx, [bp+8]      ; Copy Num%'s address to BX
        mov     dx, [bx]        ; Copy value of Num% to DX
        mov     ax, 1           ; Set AX to 1
        shl     ax, cl          ; Shift 1 to bit position Bit%
        or      ax, dx          ; OR result with Num%, store in AX
        mov     [bx], ax        ; Copy answer to Num%'s address
        pop     bp
        ret     4               ; 2 addresses = 4 bytes
SETBIT  ENDP
        END
```

Listing 18-9.

The value of *Num%* is assigned to the DX register in two steps. QuickBASIC passes the address of *Num%*, making the address of *Num%* the value on the stack at the address *bp+8*. *[bp+8]* is used to access the address of *Num%* itself and is assigned to the BX register. Because *bx* then contains the address of *Num%*, *[bx]* is used to access the value of *Num%* and is assigned to the DX register. Similarly, it takes two steps to assign the value of *Bit%* to *cl*. Of the arithmetic registers (AX, BX, CX, and DX), only the BX register can be used with the [ ] operator.

The procedure is intended to change the value of *Num%*, and we must write code to accomplish that. The *or* instruction leaves the desired result in the AX register. Because the BX register contains the address of *Num%*, we copied *Num%* to a register after copying *Bit%*; this order of actions left BX containing the address of *Num%* rather than the address of *Bit%*. The following command would copy the answer to the BX register:

```
mov bx, ax          ; Wrong way
```

But this command copies the answer to the address held in BX:

```
mov [bx], ax        ; Right way
```

Because *[bx]* is the address of *Num%*, the answer is placed in the *Num%* variable.

Review Questions

1. What is a mixed-language program?
2. What common ground makes mixed-language programming possible?
3. How does the calling convention used in C differ from the calling conventions of other high-level languages?
4. Suppose a C function takes three arguments: an integer, a 16-bit address of an integer, and a 32-bit address of an integer. The function returns a long integer. The function heading looks like this:

   ```
   int toad(int x, int *py, int far *pz)
   ```

   How could you declare this procedure in a QuickBASIC program?
5. How do stand-alone libraries and Quick libraries differ?
6. Consider the following QuickBASIC declaration:

   ```
   DECLARE FUNCTION Tick%(Tock%)
   ```

   If the code for *Tick%* is written in assembly language, what assembly instructions are needed to place the value of *Tock%* into the AX register?

Appendixes

Appendix A

QuickBASIC Statements, Functions, and Reserved Words

The following is a complete list of QuickBASIC statements, functions, and reserved words; most are described in the text.

ABS function
ACCESS
ALIAS
AND operator
ANY type
APPEND
AS
ASC function
ATN function

BASE
BEEP statement
BINARY
BLOAD statement
BSAVE statement
BYVAL

CALL statement
CALL ABSOLUTE statement
CALL INT86OLD statement
CALL INT86XOLD statement
CALL INTERRUPT statement
CALL INTERRUPTX statement
CALLS statement
CASE
CDBL function
CDECL
CHAIN statement
CHDIR statement
CHR$ function
CINT function
CIRCLE statement
CLEAR statement
CLNG function
CLOSE statement

CLS statement
COLOR statement
COM OFF statement
COM ON statement
COM STOP statement
COMMAND$ function
COMMON statement
CONST statement
COS function
CSNG function
CSRLIN function
CVD function
CVDMBF function
CVI function
CVL function
CVS function
CVSMBF function

DATA statement
DATE$ function
DATE$ statement
DECLARE statement
DEF
DEFDBL statement
DEF FN statement
DEFINT statement
DEFLNG statement
DEF SEG statement
DEFSNG statement
DEFSTR statement
DIM statement
DO/LOOP statement
DOUBLE type
DRAW statement
$DYNAMIC metacommand

ELSE
ELSEIF
END statement
END IF
ENVIRON statement
ENVIRON$ function
EOF function
EQV operator
ERASE statement
ERDEV function
ERDEV$ function
ERL function
ERR function
ERROR statement
EXIT DEF statement
EXIT DO statement
EXIT FOR statement
EXIT FUNCTION statement
EXIT SUB statement
EXP function

FIELD statement
FILEATTR function
FILES statement
FIX function
FOR/NEXT statement
FRE function
FREEFILE function
FUNCTION statement

GET (file I/O) statement
GET (graphics) statement
GOSUB/RETURN statement
GOTO statement

HEX$ function

IF/THEN/ELSE statement
IMP operator
$INCLUDE metacommand
INKEY$ function
INP function
INPUT$ function
INPUT statement
INPUT # statement
INSTR function
INT function
INTEGER type
IOCTL statement
IOCTL$ function
IS

KEY LIST statement
KEY OFF statement
KEY ON statement
KEY (*n*) OFF statement
KEY (*n*) ON statement
KEY (*n*) STOP statement
KILL statement

LBOUND function
LCASE$ function

LEFT$ function
LEN function
LET statement
LINE (graphics) statement
LINE INPUT statement
LINE INPUT # statement
LIST
LOC function
LOCAL
LOCATE statement
LOCK/UNLOCK statements
LOF function
LOG function
LONG type
LOOP
LPOS function
LPRINT statement
LPRINT USING statement
LSET statement
LTRIM$ function

MID$ function
MID$ statement
MKD$ function
MKDIR statement
MKDMBF$ function
MKI$ function
MKL$ function
MKS$ function
MKSMBF$ function
MOD operator

NAME statement
NEXT
NOT operator

OCT$ function
OFF
ON
ON COM statement
ON ERROR GOTO statement
ON/GOSUB statement
ON/GOTO statement
ON KEY (*n*) statement
ON PEN statement
ON PLAY statement
ON STRIG statement
ON TIMER statement
ON UEVENT statement
OPEN (file I/O) statement
OPEN COM statement
OPTION BASE statement
OR operator
OUT statement
OUTPUT

PAINT statement
PALETTE statement
PALETTE USING statement
PCOPY statement
PEEK function
PEN function
PEN statement
PEN OFF statement
PEN ON statement
PEN STOP statement
PLAY function
PLAY (music) statement
PLAY OFF statement
PLAY ON statement
PLAY STOP statement
PMAP function
POINT function
POKE statement
POS function
PRESET statement
PRINT statement
PRINT # statement
PRINT USING statement
PRINT # USING statement
PSET statement
PUT (file I/O) statement
PUT (graphics) statement

RANDOM
RANDOMIZE statement
READ statement
REDIM statement
REM statement
RESET statement
RESTORE statement
RESUME statement
RESUME NEXT statement
RETURN statement
RIGHT$ function
RMDIR statement
RND function
RSET statement

RTRIM$ function
RUN statement

SADD function
SCREEN function
SCREEN statement
SEEK function
SEEK statement
SEG
SELECT CASE statement
SETMEM function
SGN function
SHARED statement
SHELL statement
SIGNAL
SIN function
SINGLE type
SLEEP statement
SOUND statement
SPACE$ function
SPC function
SQR function
$STATIC metacommand
STATIC statement
STEP
STICK function
STOP statement
STR$ function
STRIG function
STRIG OFF statement
STRIG ON statement
STRIG STOP statement
STRING type
STRING$ function
SUB statement
SWAP statement
SYSTEM statement

TAB function
TAN function
THEN
TIME$ function
TIME$ statement
TIMER function
TIMER OFF statement
TIMER ON statement
TIMER STOP statement
TO
TROFF statement
TRON statement
TYPE statement

UBOUND function
UCASE$ function
UEVENT OFF statement
UEVENT ON statement
UEVENT STOP statement
UNLOCK
UNTIL
USING

VAL function
VARPTR function
VARPTR$ function
VARSEG function
VIEW (graphics) statement
VIEW PRINT statement

WAIT statement
WEND
WHILE/WEND statement
WIDTH statements
WIDTH LPRINT statement
WINDOW statement
WRITE statement
WRITE # statement

XOR operator

Appendix B

Binary, Octal, and Hexadecimal Number Systems

The decimal, or base 10, number system represents a number as a combination of powers of 10. For instance, consider the number 4152, which means 4 thousands, 1 hundred, 5 tens, and 1 one. You can write the number this way:

4×10^3 (or $10 \times 10 \times 10$) $+ 1 \times 10^2 + 5 \times 10^1 + 2 \times 10^0$

This general method of representing numbers can also be used with bases other than 10. Binary numbers, for example, are based on powers of 2, octal numbers on powers of 8, and hexadecimal numbers on powers of 16.

Binary Numbers

Computers store integers as binary numbers. The most elementary unit of computer memory, the bit, has only two possible settings, and binary numbers use only two numerals, 0 and 1, making computer memory and binary numbers a good match.

A binary number consists of a series of 0's and 1's. Just as a decimal number represents a sum of various powers of 10, a binary number is the sum of various powers of 2. For example, the binary notation 1101 means the following:

$1 \times 2^3 + 1 \times 2^2 + 0 \times 2^1 + 1 \times 2^0$

You can find the decimal equivalent of this number by calculating the powers of 2 and performing the indicated multiplication and addition:

$1 \times 8 + 1 \times 4 + 0 \times 2 + 1 \times 1 = 8 + 4 + 1 = 13$

A byte contains 8 bits. Because each bit can be set to 1 or 0, a byte corresponds to an eight-digit binary number, with each bit corresponding to a particular power of 2. The bits in a byte are numbered according to the power of 2 they represent; the rightmost bit, for example, is bit 0 (2^0). Figure B-1 shows the bit numbering scheme in a byte, the value each bit would represent if it were set to 1, and a sample value.

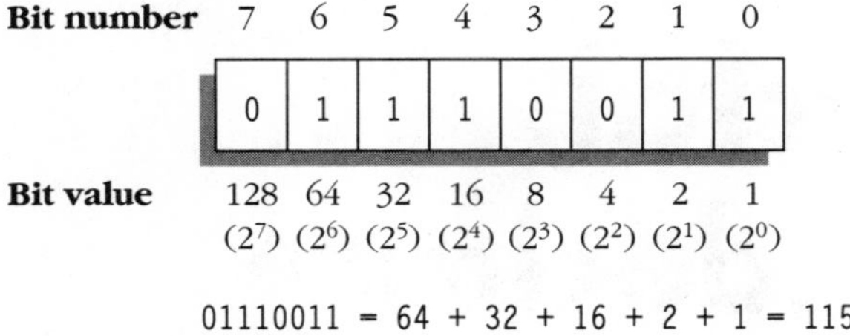

Figure B-1.
Bits in a byte and a sample value.

In the example shown in the figure, bits 6, 5, 4, 1, and 0 are *set*—that is, these bits have the value 1. To find the decimal equivalent of the binary number 01110011, simply add the corresponding bit values.

The QuickBASIC integer type represents a 2-byte, or 16-bit, integer. Each bit except bit 15 (the leftmost bit) represents a power of 2. Bit 15 is 0 for positive integers. Thus, the largest possible positive integer has the other 15 bits set to 1, with a value of 1 + 2 + 4 + 8 + 16 + 32 + 64 + 128 + 256 + 512 + 1024 + 2048 + 4096 + 8192 + 16384, or 32767 (Figure B-2).

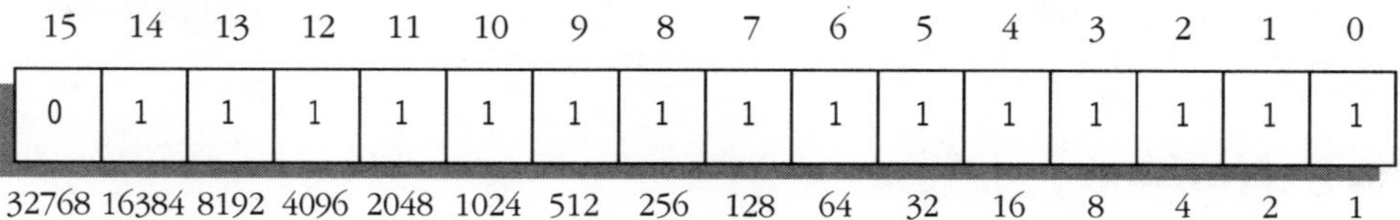

Figure B-2.
The largest QuickBASIC integer, 32767.

To represent negative integers, QuickBASIC uses the *two's complement* method. To represent a 2-byte negative number, add 2^{16}, or 65536, to the number. For instance, –1 is 65536 + (–1), or 65535 (the binary number 1111111111111111). This system is able to represent negative numbers in the range –32768 (binary 1000000000000000) through –1. Bit 15 is always set to 1 for negative integers (Figure B-3).

Bit number

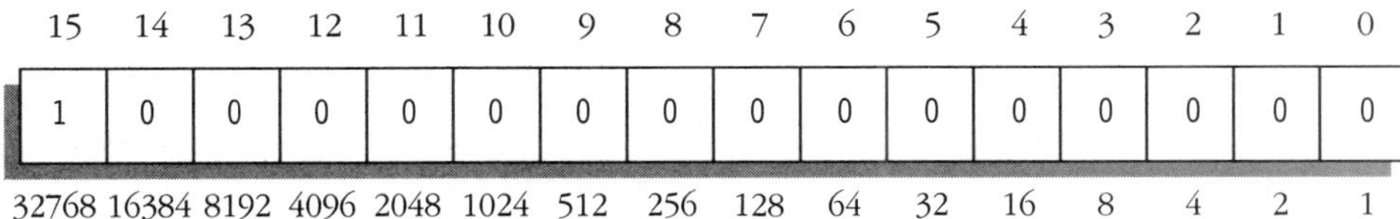

Bit value

Figure B-3.
The smallest QuickBASIC integer, −32768.

The long integer type resembles the regular integer, but it uses 32 bits (4 bytes). The leftmost bit (bit 31) is 0 for positive numbers and 1 for negative numbers. A negative number is represented by adding 2^{32}, or 4294967296, to the number.

QuickBASIC uses a different technique to represent floating-point values. The binary system in this case must also be able to represent fractions and exponents. Consider the decimal fraction 0.1426. It represents 1 tenth, 4 hundredths, 2 thousandths, and 6 ten-thousandths. Again, each position represents a power of 10:

$$0.1426 = 1 \times 10^{-1} + 4 \times 10^{-2} + 2 \times 10^{-3} + 6 \times 10^{-4}$$

Here 10^{-1} is $1/10^1$, or 1 tenth; 10^{-2} is $1/10^2$, or 1 hundredth; and so on. A binary fraction is expressed as a sum of powers of 2. The binary fraction 0.1011, for example, means the following:

$$1 \times 2^{-1} + 0 \times 0^{-2} + 1 \times 2^{-3} + 1 \times 2^{-4}$$

This evaluates to $1/2 + 0/4 + 1/8 + 1/16$, or a total of $11/16$ (0.6875 in decimal).

QuickBASIC represents single-precision numbers in the following general form:

Number = (sign) exponent of 2 × binary fraction

The exponent of 2 is stored—that is, if the term is 2^5, the 5 is stored. The binary fraction is referred to as the *mantissa*.

The single-precision type uses 4 bytes, or 32 bits. Bit 31 is set to 0 for a positive number and 1 for a negative number. Bits 30 through 23 are used to represent, as a binary integer, the power of 2 to be multiplied by the fraction. The remaining 23 bits are used to represent a binary fraction (Figure B-4).

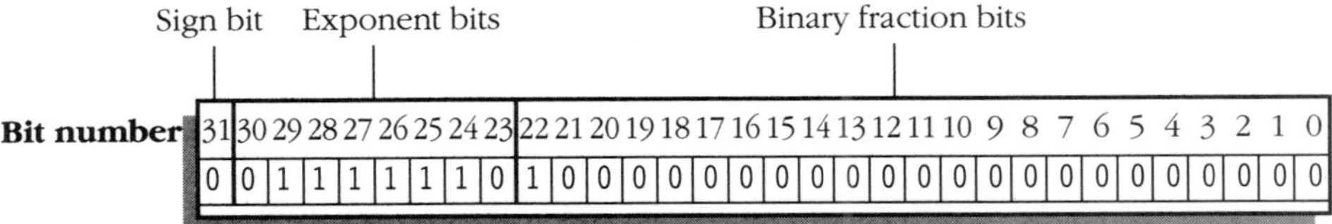

Figure B-4.
The fraction 3/8 in binary single-precision form.

Suppose you want to store the fraction 3/8 (which is 1/4 + 1/8, or 0.011 in binary). You could use 0 as the power of 2 (2^0 is 1) and 0.011 as the binary fraction. The computer, however, always normalizes the fractional part to appear in the form 1.*bbbb*... (where *b* is a binary digit—that is, 1 or 0) so that the first digit is always 1. That corresponds to storing the value 3/8 as $2^{-2} \times 1.100$. (The binary fraction is increased by a factor of 4, and the exponent of 2 is decreased by the same factor.)

Because the first digit is always adjusted to 1, the computer doesn't need to store the 1. Instead, it can assume the 1 is present, leaving an additional bit free to store the rest of the number. For the number 3/8, the fractional part stored is .10000000000000000000000, which is understood to be 1.10000000000000000000000.

The exponent bits hold the value of the exponent plus 128, not the actual exponent. For the fraction 1/4, which is represented as $2^{-2} \times 1.000$, the −2 exponent is stored as 126. This allows the 8-bit range 0 through 255 to represent exponents in the range −128 through +127. In binary notation, 126 is 01111110. Thus, the final representation of the fraction 3/8 has the sign bit set to 0, the exponent bits set to 0111110, and the binary fraction bits set to 10000000000000000000000. This evaluates to 1/4 × 3/2, which is 3/8.

The double-precision type uses 64 bits. One bit is used for the sign, 11 bits are used for the exponent, and the remaining 52 bits are used for the binary fraction.

Octal Numbers

Octal numbers are based on powers of 8. In QuickBASIC, octal numbers are written with an & prefix. The octal value &4152, for instance, means the following:

$$4 \times 8^3 + 1 \times 8^2 + 5 \times 8^1 + 2 \times 8^0$$

This is the decimal equivalent:

$$4 \times 512 + 1 \times 64 + 5 \times 8 + 2 = 2154$$

Just as decimal numbers use 10 numerals and binary numbers use 2 numerals, octal numbers use 8 numerals: 0, 1, 2, 3, 4, 5, 6, and 7.

Hexadecimal Numbers

Hexadecimal (base 16) numbers are the simplest and most convenient form for expressing the line style and the tiling patterns used in QuickBASIC graphics programs (discussed in Chapter 12). Each hexadecimal (or hex) digit position represents a power of 16. The &H (or &h) prefix identifies hex values. For instance, &H4152 means the following:

$$4 \times 16^3 + 1 \times 16^2 + 5 \times 16^1 + 2 \times 16^0$$

or

$$4 \times 4096 + 1 \times 256 + 5 \times 16 + 2 = 16384 + 256 + 80 + 2 = 16722$$

Base 16 notation uses 16 numerals, which are listed in Figure B-5, along with decimal and binary equivalents. Note that alphabetic characters function as numerals. Thus, the hex number &H12AF (or &h12af) means the following:

$$1 \times 4096 + 2 \times 256 + 10 \times 16 + 15 \times 1 = 4783$$

Converting a binary number to hexadecimal form is simple. Each hexadecimal digit corresponds to a particular four-digit binary group, and vice versa, as shown in Figure B-5. For example, the 16-bit binary number 0011110010100101 can be broken into four groups of four digits:

0011   1100   1010   0101

When each group is replaced by the corresponding hexadecimal digit (3, C, A, and 5), the resulting hexadecimal number is &H3CA5.

Hexadecimal Digit	***Decimal Equivalent***	***Binary Equivalent***
0	0	0000
1	1	0001
2	2	0010
3	3	0011
4	4	0100
5	5	0101
6	6	0110
7	7	0111
8	8	1000
9	9	1001
A or a	10	1010
B or b	11	1011
C or c	12	1100
D or d	13	1101
E or e	14	1110
F or f	15	1111

Figure B-5.
Hexadecimal digits and equivalents.

Appendix C

ASCII Character Set and IBM Extended Character Set

Char	Number Dec	Number Hex	Ctrl-Key	Control Code	Char	Number Dec	Number Hex
	0	00	^@	NUL (Null)	<space>	32	20
☺	1	01	^A	SOH (Start of heading)	!	33	21
☻	2	02	^B	STX (Start of text)	"	34	22
♥	3	03	^C	ETX (End of text)	#	35	23
♦	4	04	^D	EOT (End of transmission)	$	36	24
♣	5	05	^E	ENQ (Enquiry)	%	37	25
♠	6	06	^F	ACK (Acknowledge)	&	38	26
•	7	07	^G	BEL (Bell)	'	39	27
◘	8	08	^H	BS (Backspace)	(	40	28
○	9	09	^I	HT (Horizontal tab)	)	41	29
◙	10	0A	^J	LF (Linefeed)	*	42	2A
♂	11	0B	^K	VT (Vertical tab)	+	43	2B
♀	12	0C	^L	FF (Formfeed)	,	44	2C
♪	13	0D	^M	CR (Carriage return)	-	45	2D
♫	14	0E	^N	SO (Shift out)	.	46	2E
☼	15	0F	^O	SI (Shift in)	/	47	2F
►	16	10	^P	DLE (Data link escape)	0	48	30
◄	17	11	^Q	DC1 (Device control 1)	1	49	31
↕	18	12	^R	DC2 (Device control 2)	2	50	32
‼	19	13	^S	DC3 (Device control 3)	3	51	33
¶	20	14	^T	DC4 (Device control 4)	4	52	34
§	21	15	^U	NAK (Negative acknowledge)	5	53	35
▬	22	16	^V	SYN (Synchronous idle)	6	54	36
↨	23	17	^W	ETB (End transmission block)	7	55	37
↑	24	18	^X	CAN (Cancel)	8	56	38
↓	25	19	^Y	EM (End of medium)	9	57	39
→	26	1A	^Z	SUB (Substitute)	:	58	3A
←	27	1B	^[	ESC (Escape)	;	59	3B
∟	28	1C	^\	FS (File separator)	<	60	3C
↔	29	1D	^]	GS (Group separator)	=	61	3D
▲	30	1E	^^	RS (Record separator)	>	62	3E
▼	31	1F	^_	US (Unit separator)	?	63	3F

(continued)

continued

Char	Number Dec	Number Hex	Char	Number Dec	Number Hex	Char	Number Dec	Number Hex
@	64	40	`	96	60	Ç	128	80
A	65	41	a	97	61	ü	129	81
B	66	42	b	98	62	é	130	82
C	67	43	c	99	63	â	131	83
D	68	44	d	100	64	ä	132	84
E	69	45	e	101	65	à	133	85
F	70	46	f	102	66	å	134	86
G	71	47	g	103	67	ç	135	87
H	72	48	h	104	68	ê	136	88
I	73	49	i	105	69	ë	137	89
J	74	4A	j	106	6A	è	138	8A
K	75	4B	k	107	6B	ï	139	8B
L	76	4C	l	108	6C	î	140	8C
M	77	4D	m	109	6D	ì	141	8D
N	78	4E	n	110	6E	Ä	142	8E
O	79	4F	o	111	6F	Å	143	8F
P	80	50	p	112	70	É	144	90
Q	81	51	q	113	71	æ	145	91
R	82	52	r	114	72	Æ	146	92
S	83	53	s	115	73	ô	147	93
T	84	54	t	116	74	ö	148	94
U	85	55	u	117	75	ò	149	95
V	86	56	v	118	76	û	150	96
W	87	57	w	119	77	ù	151	97
X	88	58	x	120	78	ÿ	152	98
Y	89	59	y	121	79	Ö	153	99
Z	90	5A	z	122	7A	Ü	154	9A
[	91	5B	{	123	7B	¢	155	9B
\	92	5C	¦	124	7C	£	156	9C
]	93	5D	}	125	7D	¥	157	9D
^	94	5E	~	126	7E	₧	158	9E
_	95	5F	△	127†	7F	ƒ	159	9F

† ASCII code 127 has the code DEL. Under DOS, this code has the same effect as ASCII 8 (BS). The DEL code can be generated by the Ctrl-Backspace key combination.

continued

	Number			Number			Number	
Char	**Dec**	**Hex**	**Char**	**Dec**	**Hex**	**Char**	**Dec**	**Hex**
á	160	A0	└	192	C0	α	224	E0
í	161	A1	┴	193	C1	β	225	E1
ó	162	A2	┬	194	C2	Γ	226	E2
ú	163	A3	├	195	C3	π	227	E3
ñ	164	A4	─	196	C4	Σ	228	E4
Ñ	165	A5	┼	197	C5	σ	229	E5
ª	166	A6	╞	198	C6	μ	230	E6
º	167	A7	╟	199	C7	τ	231	E7
¿	168	A8	╚	200	C8	Φ	232	E8
⌐	169	A9	╔	201	C9	Θ	233	E9
¬	170	AA	╩	202	CA	Ω	234	EA
½	171	AB	╦	203	CB	δ	235	EB
¼	172	AC	╠	204	CC	∞	236	EC
¡	173	AD	═	205	CD	∅	237	ED
«	174	AE	╬	206	CE	ε	238	EE
»	175	AF	╧	207	CF	∩	239	EF
░	176	B0	╨	208	D0	≡	240	F0
▒	177	B1	╤	209	D1	±	241	F1
▓	178	B2	╥	210	D2	≥	242	F2
│	179	B3	╙	211	D3	≤	243	F3
┤	180	B4	╘	212	D4	⌠	244	F4
╡	181	B5	╒	213	D5	⌡	245	F5
╢	182	B6	╓	214	D6	÷	246	F6
╖	183	B7	╫	215	D7	≈	247	F7
╕	184	B8	╪	216	D8	°	248	F8
╣	185	B9	┘	217	D9	•	249	F9
║	186	BA	┌	218	DA	·	250	FA
╗	187	BB	█	219	DB	√	251	FB
╝	188	BC	▄	220	DC	η	252	FC
╜	189	BD	▌	221	DD	²	253	FD
╛	190	BE	▐	222	DE	■	254	FE
┐	191	BF	▀	223	DF		255	FF

Appendix D

QuickBASIC and BASICA

Programs written in BASICA (and GW-BASIC) can be run in the QuickBASIC environment but must sometimes be modified first. Differences in file format and in statements and functions can cause problems.

File Format

QuickBASIC can read source files (whose code is written in BASIC) that are either in the standard ASCII text format or in the QuickBASIC format. BASICA can save files in the standard ASCII text format or, by default, in a compressed format that QuickBASIC cannot read. Therefore, to use a BASICA source file, you must save in the ASCII format, which requires using the ,A option. For instance, to save a BASICA file called BIGTHOT.BAS in ASCII format, use the following BASICA command:

```
SAVE "BIGTHOT.BAS",A
```

Statements and Functions

The following BASICA statements and functions cannot be used in QuickBASIC:

AUTO	LOAD
CONT	MERGE
DEF USR	MOTOR
DELETE	NEW
EDIT	RENUM
LIST	SAVE
LLIST	USR

Some BASICA statements and functions must be modified to work under Quick-BASIC. The following list summarizes the differences and possible modifications:

BASICA Statement or Function	***Modification or Difference in QuickBASIC***
BLOAD/BSAVE	Memory locations can differ.
CALL	The argument must be the name of the SUB procedure called.
CHAIN	The ALL, MERGE, DELETE, and *linenumber* options are not supported. (See also RUN, below.)
COMMON	COMMON statements must appear before any executable statements.
DEF*type*	DEF*type* statements must appear at the beginning of the source file.
DIM	DIM statements declaring static arrays must appear at the beginning of the program.
DRAW, PLAY	The VARPTR$ function must be used with embedded variables.
RESUME	When an error occurs in a single-line function, QuickBASIC tries to resume program execution at the line containing the function.
RUN	For QuickBASIC executable files, a RUN or a CHAIN statement object must be an executable file, not a BAS file. QuickBASIC does not support the R option. Within the QuickBASIC environment, a RUN or a CHAIN command still uses a BAS file as the object.

Appendix E

The PRINT USING Statement

The PRINT USING statement, its syntax, and its three string format characters are discussed in Chapter 3; the formatters for numbers are also introduced there. The following list summarizes all 10 of the numeric formatters you can use with PRINT USING. (Examples from the Immediate window are included.) In general, use the # symbol to specify digit positions and the other formatters to modify a # formation.

Numeric Formatter	Description

#	Represents a digit. For instance, ### displays a value in a field three digits wide. Numbers are right justified. A value that exceeds the field width is printed with a % prefix. Digits to the right of a decimal point are not displayed (that is, floating-point values are converted to integers) unless # is used in conjunction with a decimal point. Numbers are rounded as necessary. Here is an example:
	`PRINT USING "##"; 2; 20.3; 50000`
	`   2  20%50000`

.	Represents the decimal point. For instance, ###.## displays a number with two decimal places using a field width of three for the integer part of the number. Values are rounded as necessary. Here is an example:
	`PRINT USING "###.##"; 13; 43.3224`
	` 13.00 45.32`

(continued)

continued

Numeric Formatter	Description

+	Causes the sign (plus or minus) of a value to be displayed. The sign precedes the number if + precedes the rest of the format string, as in +###. The sign follows the number if + follows the rest of the format string, as in ###+. Here are two examples:
	`PRINT USING "+###"; 16; -5`
	` +16  -5`
	
	`PRINT USING "###+"; 16; -5`
	` 16+  5-`

−	Displays a trailing minus sign for negative numbers; used only after a # sequence. Here is an example:
	`PRINT USING "##-"; 16; -5`
	`16  5-`

**	Fills the field with leading asterisks if the number is smaller than the field width. Using this formatter adds two more positions to the field width. Here is an example:
	`PRINT USING "**###.##"; 18.86`
	`***18.86`

$$	Displays a dollar sign to the immediate left of the formatted number. It adds two more digit positions to the field width, one of which is used for the printed dollar sign. Here is an example:
	`PRINT USING "$$###.##"; 2.34; 34.00; 129`
	`   $2.34  $34.00 $129.00`

**$	Displays a dollar sign to the immediate left of the formatted number and fills leading spaces in the field with asterisks. This formatter adds three positions to the field width. Negative amounts show the minus sign to the left of the dollar sign. Here is an example:
	`PRINT USING "**$###.##"; 2.34; -34.00; 129`
	`****$2.34**-$34.00**$129.00`

,	Adds commas to divide the integer part of a number into groups of three digits if it appears to the left of the decimal point in a format string. The comma can appear anywhere between the first # and the decimal point. Neither the position nor the number of commas in the format string affects the placement of commas in the display, but the field width is increased by one position for each comma used. Here are some examples:
	`PRINT USING "#########,.##"; 1056; 1300100`
	`     1,056.00 1,300,100.00`
	
	`PRINT USING "###,###,###.##"; 1056; 1300100`
	`     1,056.00  1,300,100.00`

(continued)

continued

Numeric Formatter	Description

^^^^	Causes output to appear in exponential format (in the form E+xx) when it appears to the immediate right of a # sequence. It adds four positions to the field width. Using five carets (^^^^^) provides a three-digit exponent and adds five positions to the field width. Significant digits are left justified in the field and include a leading space for positive numbers. (The + and – formatters override the leading space.) Here are some examples:
	`PRINT USING "##.##^^^^"; 1056; 0.000246`
	` 1.06E+03 2.46E-04`
	
	`PRINT USING "####.##^^^^"; 1056; 0.000246`
	` 105.60E+01 246.00E-06`

_ (underscore)	Displays the next character literally. For instance, _# causes # to be displayed literally rather than being interpreted as a digit position, and _! displays an exclamation mark instead of interpreting ! as a string formatter. Use _ _ to print an underscore. Here is an example:
	`PRINT USING "That's a _## pencil_!"; 2`
	`That's a #2 pencil!`

Multiple Formats

You can combine more than one formatting symbol to create a format description. For instance, $$##,###.## displays values using the dollar sign and commas. You can also have several formats in one format string, with each format applying to a different variable. And you can intermingle ordinary text with the formatting characters. The PRINT USING statement is especially useful for producing tables of formatted information, as the program in Listing E-1 demonstrates.

```
DATA Mercury,0.38,4878,Venus,0.91,12104,Earth,1.00,12756
DATA Mars,0.38,6794,Jupiter,2.53,142796,Saturn,1.07,12000
DATA Uranus,0.92,50800,Neptune,1.18,50450,Pluto,.03,2290
DIM Pnames$(1 TO 9), Pgees(1 TO 9), Pdiams(1 TO 9)
FOR P% = 1 TO 9
    READ Pnames$(P%), Pgees(P%), Pdiams(P%)
NEXT P%
Format$ = "\          \   #.##    ##.##^^^^"
CLS
PRINT "PLANET"; TAB(13); "GRAVITY"; TAB(23); "DIAMETER"
PRINT TAB(12); "Earth =1"; TAB(24); "in kms"
FOR P% = 1 TO 9
    PRINT USING Format$; Pnames$(P%); Pgees(P%); Pdiams(P%)
NEXT P%
END
```

Listing E-1.

Here is the output:

```
PLANET       GRAVITY    DIAMETER
            Earth = 1    in Kms
Mercury        0.38     4.88E+03
Venus          0.91     1.21E+04
Earth          1.00     1.28E+04
Mars           0.38     6.79E+03
Jupiter        2.53     1.43E+05
Saturn         1.07     1.20E+04
Uranus         0.92     5.08E+04
Neptune        1.18     5.05E+04
Pluto          0.03     2.29E+03
```

Appendix F

Keyboard Scan Codes

This table lists the DOS keyboard scan codes. These codes are returned by the INKEY$ function.

Key combinations with NUL in the Char column return 2 bytes—a null byte (&H00) followed by the value listed in the Dec and Hex columns. For example, pressing Alt-F1 returns a null byte followed by a byte containing 104 (&H68).

	Scan Code		**ASCII or Extended†**			**ASCII or Extended† with Shift**			**ASCII or Extended† with Ctrl**			**ASCII or Extended† with Alt**		
Key	**Dec**	**Hex**	**Dec**	**Hex**	**Char**	**Dec**	**Hex**	**Char**	**Dec**	**Hex**	**Char**	**Dec**	**Hex**	**Char**
Esc	1	01	27	1B		27	1B		27	1B				
1 or !	2	02	49	31	1	33	21	!				120	78	NUL
2 or @	3	03	50	32	2	64	40	@	3	03	NUL	121	79	NUL
3 or #	4	04	51	33	3	35	23	#				122	7A	NUL
4 or $	5	05	52	34	4	36	24	$				123	7B	NUL
5 or %	6	06	53	35	5	37	25	%				124	7C	NUL
6 or ^	7	07	54	36	6	94	5E	^	30	1E		125	7D	NUL
7 or &	8	08	55	37	7	38	26	&				126	7E	NUL
8 or *	9	09	56	38	8	42	2A	*				127	7F	NUL
9 or (	10	0A	57	39	9	40	28	(				128	80	NUL
0 or)	11	0B	48	30	0	41	29	)				129	81	NUL
- or _	12	0C	45	2D	-	95	5F	-	31	1F		130	82	NUL
= or +	13	0D	61	3D	=	43	2B	+				131	83	NUL
Backspace	14	0E	8	08		8	08		127	7F				

(continued)

continued

	Scan Code		ASCII or Extended†			ASCII or Extended† with Shift			ASCII or Extended† with Ctrl			ASCII or Extended† with Alt		
Key	**Dec**	**Hex**	**Dec**	**Hex**	**Char**	**Dec**	**Hex**	**Char**	**Dec**	**Hex**	**Char**	**Dec**	**Hex**	**Char**
Tab	15	0F	9	09		15	0F	NUL						
Q	16	10	113	71	q	81	51	Q	17	11		16	10	NUL
W	17	11	119	77	w	87	57	W	23	17		17	11	NUL
E	18	12	101	65	e	69	45	E	5	05		18	12	NUL
R	19	13	114	72	r	82	52	R	18	12		19	13	NUL
T	20	14	116	74	t	84	54	T	20	14		20	14	NUL
Y	21	15	121	79	y	89	59	Y	25	19		21	15	NUL
U	22	16	117	75	u	85	55	U	21	15		22	16	NUL
I	23	17	105	69	i	73	49	I	9	09		23	17	NUL
O	24	18	111	6F	o	79	4F	O	15	0F		24	18	NUL
P	25	19	112	70	p	80	50	P	16	10		25	19	NUL
[or {	26	1A	91	5B	[	123	7B	{	27	1B				
] or }	27	1B	93	5D	]	125	7D	}	29	1D				
Enter	28	1C	13	0D	CR	13	0D	CR	10	0A	LF			
Ctrl	29	1D												
A	30	1E	97	61	a	65	41	A	1	01		30	1E	NUL
S	31	1F	115	73	s	83	53	S	19	13		31	1F	NUL
D	32	20	100	64	d	68	44	D	4	04		32	20	NUL
F	33	21	102	66	f	70	46	F	6	06		33	21	NUL
G	34	22	103	67	g	71	47	G	7	07		34	22	NUL
H	35	23	104	68	h	72	48	H	8	08		35	23	NUL
J	36	24	106	6A	j	74	4A	J	10	0A		36	24	NUL
K	37	25	107	6B	k	75	4B	K	11	0B		37	25	NUL
L	38	26	108	6C	l	76	4C	L	12	0C		38	26	NUL
; or :	39	27	59	3B	;	58	3A	:						
' or "	40	28	39	27	'	34	22	"						
` or ~	41	29	96	60	`	126	7E	~						
Left Shift	42	2A												
\ or ¦	43	2B	92	5C	\	124	7C	¦	28	1C				
Z	44	2C	122	7A	z	90	5A	Z	26	1A		44	2C	NUL
X	45	2D	120	78	x	88	58	X	24	18		45	2D	NUL
C	46	2E	99	63	c	67	43	C	3	03		46	2E	NUL
V	47	2F	118	76	v	86	56	V	22	16		47	2F	NUL
B	48	30	98	62	b	66	42	B	2	02		48	30	NUL
N	49	31	110	6E	n	78	4E	N	14	0E		49	31	NUL
M	50	32	109	6D	m	77	4D	M	13	0D		50	32	NUL
, or <	51	33	44	2C	,	60	3C	<						
. or >	52	34	46	2E	.	62	3E	>						

(continued)

continued

Key	Scan Code		ASCII or Extended†			ASCII or Extended† with Shift			ASCII or Extended† with Ctrl			ASCII or Extended† with Alt		
	Dec	Hex	Dec	Hex	Char	Dec	Hex	Char	Dec	Hex	Char	Dec	Hex	Char
/ or ?	53	35	47	2F	/	63	3F	?						
Right Shift	54	36												
* or Prt Scr	55	37	42	2A	*		INT 5††		16	10				
Alt	56	38												
Spacebar	57	39	32	20	SPC	32	20	SPC	32	20	SPC	32	20	SPC
Caps Lock	58	3A												
F1	59	3B	59	3B	NUL	84	54	NUL	94	5E	NUL	104	68	NUL
F2	60	3C	60	3C	NUL	85	55	NUL	95	5F	NUL	105	69	NUL
F3	61	3D	61	3D	NUL	86	56	NUL	96	60	NUL	106	6A	NUL
F4	62	3E	62	3E	NUL	87	57	NUL	97	61	NUL	107	6B	NUL
F5	63	3F	63	3F	NUL	88	58	NUL	98	62	NUL	108	6C	NUL
F6	64	40	64	40	NUL	89	59	NUL	99	63	NUL	109	6D	NUL
F7	65	41	65	41	NUL	90	5A	NUL	100	64	NUL	110	6E	NUL
F8	66	42	66	46	NUL	91	5B	NUL	101	65	NUL	111	6F	NUL
F9	67	43	67	43	NUL	92	5C	NUL	102	66	NUL	112	70	NUL
F10	68	44	68	44	NUL	93	5D	NUL	103	67	NUL	113	71	NUL
Num Lock	69	45												
Scroll Lock	70	46												
Home or 7	71	47	71	47	NUL	55	37	7	119	77	NUL			
Up Arrow or 8	72	48	72	48	NUL	56	38	8						
PgUp or 9	73	49	73	49	NUL	57	39	9	132	84	NUL			
– (keypad)	74	4A	45	2D	-	45	2D	-						
Left Arrow or 4	75	4B	75	4B	NUL	52	34	4	115	73	NUL			
5 (keypad)	76	4C				53	35	5						
Right Arrow or 6	77	4D	77	4D	NUL	54	36	6	116	74	NUL			
+ (keypad)	78	4E	43	2B	+	43	2B	+						
End or 1	79	4F	79	4F	NUL	49	31	1	117	75	NUL			
Down Arrow or 2	80	50	80	50	NUL	50	32	2						
PgDn or 3	81	51	81	51	NUL	51	33	3	118	76	NUL			
Ins or 0	82	52	82	52	NUL	48	30	0						
Del or .	83	53	83	53	NUL	46	2E	.						

† Extended codes return NUL (ASCII 0) as the initial character. This is a signal that a second (extended) code is available in the keystroke buffer.

†† Under DOS, Shift-Prt Scr invokes interrupt 5, which prints the screen unless an interrupt handler has been defined to replace the default interrupt 5 handler.

Appendix G

Answers to Review Questions

Chapter 1

1. The QuickBASIC compiler uses an integrated editor. It is also interactive, and it gets programs running quickly.
2. The QuickBASIC compiler can create a stand-alone program. It can also create programs that run much faster than those created by an interpreter.
3. Here is an example:

```
CLS
PRINT "Beau Dudley"
```

4. Select Start from the Run menu, or press Shift-F5.
5. Select Make EXE File from the Run menu, accept the proposed filename (or choose a new one), choose the Stand-Alone option, and select the Make EXE command button. To run the program, go to DOS, and enter the filename. (You can omit the period and the EXE extension.) If you compile the program with the BRUN45.EXE option selected, the BRUN45.EXE runtime module must be available to run the compiled program.

Chapter 2

1. a. Integer
   b. String
   c. Integer (in hexadecimal form)
   d. Single precision
   e. Double precision
   f. Long integer

2. a. Single precision
   b. Integer
   c. Long integer
   d. Single precision
   e. Double precision
   f. String

3. The computer handles the integer type most efficiently, but some numbers can't be represented by this type. Long integers allow a bigger range in values but slow down computations. Similarly, single precision and double precision increase the range further and allow fractional values but slow the system even more. QuickBASIC lets you choose the type that best fits your needs.

4. a. Integer is fine, provided you have fewer than 32,768 disks.
   b. Integer is probably too small, so use long integer.
   c. Use single precision because the result might have a fractional part.
   d. Use string for representing text.
   e. Use double precision for accuracy.

5. a. 11.5
   b. 11
   c. 4
   d. 176
   e. 500000
   f. 154000
   g. 8.812E+21

6. Here is the program:

```
CLS
INPUT "Enter a number: ", Num!
PRINT Num! ^ 3
END
```

Chapter 3

1. (The underscore indicates the cursor position.)
   a. `? _`
   b. `Your age _`
   c. `Your age? _`

2. Here is the output:

```
 2.000000030094932D+30       2E+30         0
 63700          The one and only            Earth
Circumference is              400238.6
 2.000000030094932D+30  2E+30  0
 63700 The one and onlyEarth
Circumference is 400238.6
```

Note that 2E+30 is single precision. When we assign that value to the double-precision variable *Mass#*, errors occur in the low end of the number. Assigning 2D+30 instead of 2E+30 would avoid that problem.

3. a. With INPUT, the string *Donkey Hotey* is assigned to *Name$*. The LINE INPUT statement produces the same result.

   b. If you use INPUT, you receive a *Redo from start* error message—the comma signifies two input items, but the statement contains only one variable. With LINE INPUT, the string *Hotey, Donkey* is assigned to *Name$*.

   c. With INPUT, the string *Hotey, Donkey* is assigned to *Name$*. With LINE INPUT, the string *"Hotey, Donkey"* (including double quotation marks) is assigned to *Name$*.

4. Here is the output:

```
IowaW
IowaWIowa
Iowa Washington
Iow Washi
```

5. The program prints the following:

```
3%-1235   3
 3 1235    3
 3.00 1234.57    3.00
 $3.00 $1234.57    $3.00
```

6. The PRINT statement prints items either in fields that are 14 characters wide or in adjacent fields, depending on whether you use commas or semicolons to separate items. The WRITE statement separates items by commas when displaying them. PRINT displays positive numbers with a leading space; WRITE does not. WRITE encloses strings in double quotation marks; PRINT does not.

7. Here are three possibilities:

```
PRINT TAB(10); "Hello"

PRINT SPC(9); "Hello"

LOCATE , 10
PRINT "Hello"
```

8. The statement opens a file called PAYROLL, creating the file if it does not already exist or deleting the original contents if the file does already exist. It sets up the program and the file so that the program can write information in the file. It establishes the number 2 as the file identifier, which will be used in subsequent program statements.

9. Change OUTPUT to INPUT.

Chapter 4

1. a.
```
1  2  3  4  5
6
```
   b.
```
1  3  5
7
```
   c.
```
1  4
7
```

2. Here is the output:

```
Hello! Hello! Hello! Hello!
Hello! Hello! Hello!
Hello! Hello!
Hello!
```

3. a. First, the relational expression contains a type mismatch. The variable should be *X$* (a string). Second, the keyword THEN, which has been omitted before the PRINT statement, should be added.

   b. An END IF line should follow the second PRINT statement.

4. Here is the loop:

```
FOR N% = -3 TO 3
    IF N% <> 0 THEN PRINT N%;
NEXT N%
```

5. a, b, and c are true. Note that because d uses integer division, *X% \ 2* evaluates to 2.

6. a.
```
IF Age% < 25
    PRINT "RAD"
ELSE
    PRINT "VERY NICE"
END IF
```
   b.
```
IF Age% < 25
    PRINT "RAD"
ELSEIF Age% <= 45
    PRINT "GROOVY"
ELSE
    PRINT "NEAT"
END IF
```

7. a.
```
Loop #1 prints 1
Loop #1 prints 2
Loop #1 prints 3
Loop #2 prints 1
Loop #2 prints 2
Loop #2 prints 3
```
   b.
```
Loop #2 prints 5
```

8. The WHILE forms loop as long as the test condition is true, and the UNTIL forms loop as long as the test condition is false.

9. Example b is suitable. Example a contains an incorrect test. The text is correct in example c, but a comma is missing after *#1*. Example d will work unless the file is empty. (It tests after trying to read the file.)

10. a. `IF Age > 40 AND Age < 60 THEN PRINT "Hi!"`

    b. `IF Age < 40 OR Age > 60 THEN PRINT "Hi!"`

    c. `IF NOT (Age < 70) THEN PRINT "Hi!"`

    or

    `IF Age >= 70 THEN PRINT "Hi!"`

    d. `IF Height > 60 XOR Weight > 150 THEN PRINT "Hi!"`

    e. `IF Age <> 35 AND (Weight > 200 OR Height > 72) THEN PRINT "Hi!"`

11. *Syntax errors:*

    - *Choice$* is a string, and the CASE labels are numeric; change *Choice$* to *Choice%* throughout.
    - ELSE should be CASE ELSE.
    - The first END should be END SELECT.
    - *CASE 2 - 4* should be *CASE 2 TO 4*. *CASE 2 - 4* is not a true syntax error, but QuickBASIC will interpret the hyphen as a minus sign, reducing the line to *CASE –2*.

    Design error:

    - *CASE 2 * 3* is never reached because 2 × 3 is 6, which is matched by the preceding CASE.

Chapter 5

1. The two parts are the module-level code and the procedures section. The procedures section contains subprograms and function procedures. All other code is module-level code.

2. The program won't print anything. The *X%* in *Vapid* is a local variable, unrelated to the *X%* in the module-level code. New variables are set to 0 by default, and the loop is not executed.

3. Use an argument, as shown here:

```
DECLARE SUB Vapid (X%)
X% = 4
CALL Vapid(X%)
END

SUB Vapid (X%)
    FOR I% = 1 TO X%
        PRINT "Have a nice day!"
    NEXT I%
END SUB
```

4. Listing 5-A4 presents one possibility.

```
DECLARE SUB Greetings ()
DECLARE SUB LastName (Name$)
DECLARE SUB ShowName (First$, Last$)
CLS
REM The following subprogram prints a greeting
CALL Greetings
REM The following subroutine asks your first name and
REM  places your response in the variable NameF$
GOSUB FirstName
REM The following subprogram asks your last name and
REM  places your response in the variable NameL$
CALL LastName(NameL$)
REM The following subprogram prints your name in the
REM  form last name, first name
CALL ShowName(NameF$, NameL$)
END

FirstName:
    INPUT "Enter your first name, please >> ", NameF$
RETURN

SUB Greetings
    PRINT "Salutations, most valued user!"
END SUB

SUB LastName (Name$)
    INPUT "Enter your last name >> ", Name$
END SUB

SUB ShowName (First$, Last$)
    PRINT USING "&, &"; Last$; First$
END SUB
```

Listing 5-A4.

5. Omit CALL and any parentheses around the argument list:

```
ShowMotto
FineDay X%
Retrofit N%, M%
```

6. Subprograms can use arguments and local variables, whereas subroutines cannot. Subprograms can be used by other modules, whereas subroutines cannot.

7. *Problems with the* Explain *subprogram:*

- *CALL Explain()* is invalid syntax. Parentheses should either contain an argument or be omitted.
- *Limit%* is 0 because it is local to the subprogram and is not assigned a value.

To correct this subprogram, you could delete the parentheses from the CALL statement and make *Limit%* a shared value. Or you could pass *Limit%* as an argument. The latter approach is better; see the code in Listing 5-A7.

Problems with the Multiply *subprogram:*

- Because *Product!* is not assigned an initial value, it starts with the value 0 and yields 0 as a result regardless of the numbers entered.
- The UNTIL test uses *Count* = *N%* instead of *Count%* = *N%*. Because *Count* is 0 by default, the test is always false.
- Because the program fails to increment *Count%* in each loop, *Count%* never reaches *N%*.
- *Num$* is a string and therefore can't be used for arithmetic.
- The END IF statement is missing.

To correct this subprogram, initialize *Product!* to 1; change *Count* to *Count%*, and add 1 to *Count%* in each loop; convert the string *Num$* into a number by using VAL; and insert the missing END IF statement. Correcting these problems produces the program shown in Listing 5-A7.

```
DECLARE SUB Explain (N%)
DECLARE SUB Multiply (N%)
CLS
Limit% = 5
CALL Explain(Limit%)
CALL Multiply(Limit%)
END

SUB Explain (N%)
    PRINT "This program calculates the product of all"
    PRINT "the numbers you enter. It accepts numbers"
    PRINT "until you enter an empty line or reach"; N%
    PRINT "numbers, whichever comes first."
END SUB

SUB Multiply (N%)
    Product! = 1
    Count% = 0
    INPUT "Enter a number >> ", Num$
    DO UNTIL Num$ = "" OR Count% = N%
        Num! = VAL(Num$)
        Count% = Count% + 1
        Product! = Product! * Num!
        IF Count% < N% THEN
            INPUT "Next value >> ", Num$
        END IF
    LOOP
    PRINT "Product = "; Product!
END SUB
```

Listing 5-A7.

8. Here is the revised program:

```
DECLARE SUB Pigs (Times%, Pignumber%)
CLS
CALL Pigs(2, 3)
CALL Pigs(4, 8)
CALL Pigs(3, 5)
END

SUB Pigs (Times%, Pignumber%)
    FOR I% = 1 TO Times%
        PRINT Pignumber%; "little piggies!"
    NEXT I%
END SUB
```

Chapter 6

1. By default, the statement

   ```
   DIM Grub(19)
   ```

   creates an array of 20 elements, with subscripts from 0 through 19. Or you can create an array with 20 elements indexed from 1 through 20, as shown here:

   ```
   OPTION BASE 1
   DIM Grub(20)
   ```

   The following statement will accomplish the same thing:

   ```
   DIM Grub(1 TO 20)
   ```

2. An element of an array can be treated like an ordinary variable of the same type. For instance, if a subprogram requires an integer as an argument, you can use an element of an array of integers.

3. Here is the program:

   ```
   CLS
   DIM Series%(1 TO 20)
   Series%(1) = 0
   Series%(2) = 1
   FOR I% = 3 TO 20
       Series%(I%) = Series%(I% - 1) + Series%(I% - 2)
   NEXT I%
   FOR I% = 1 TO 20
       PRINT USING "##:  ####"; I%; Series%(I%)
   NEXT I%
   END
   ```

4. Use one or more DATA statements to store the values in the program code, and use the READ statement to assign the values to the array elements.

5. You could declare the array in either of the following ways, depending on whether you want rows to represent districts or months:

```
DIM Sales1!(1 TO 12, 1 TO 5)
DIM Sales2!(1 TO 5, 1 TO 12)
```

6. When you define the subprogram, the corresponding parameter should be followed by empty parentheses to indicate an array. For instance, if the subprogram *Blip* is to be passed an array of integers, use the following statement:

```
SUB Blip(Arr%())
```

7. Passing by reference allows the procedure to operate on the original array. (See Review Question 8.)

8. This subprogram will work:

```
SUB ScaleArray (Arr!(), Factor!)
FOR I% = LBOUND(Arr!) TO UBOUND(Arr!)
    Arr!(I%) = Factor! * Arr!(I%)
NEXT I%
END SUB
```

9. One advantage of using a shared array is that you don't need to pass the array as an argument. One disadvantage is that you can use the subprogram only for the particular array that is shared.

10. Here is one version:

```
SUB SumCols (Arr!(), Sums!())
    FOR Row% = LBOUND(Arr!, 1) TO UBOUND(Arr!, 1)
        Sums!(Row%) = 0
        FOR Col% = LBOUND(Arr!, 2) TO UBOUND(Arr!, 2)
            Sums!(Row%) = Sums!(Row%) + Arr!(Row%, Col%)
        NEXT Col%
    NEXT Row%
END SUB
```

Chapter 7

1. Arrays and strings both consist of a series of like elements stored sequentially.

2. Here are two ways to create the string variable:

```
DEFSTR J
Job = "Truffle taster"

DIM Job AS STRING
```

3. Use the DIM statement as follows:

```
DIM Dinner AS STRING * 12
```

A fixed-length string of 12 characters is always 12 characters long, regardless of the length of the string assigned to it. If you assign *Chicken* to *Dinner*, *Chicken* is padded with five spaces. If you assign *Beef Wellington* to *Dinner*, only the first 12 characters are used.

4. Here is the output:

```
The Resplendent Programmer
 26
 84
T
The Res
grammer
splendent Programmer
The
```

5. Here is one version:

```
CLS
LINE INPUT "Enter line: ", Line$
PRINT UCASE$(Line$)
END
```

6. Listing 7-A6 demonstrates an approach you could take.

```
CLS
LINE INPUT "Enter line: ", Line$
FOR I% = 1 TO LEN(Line$)
    Char$ = MID$(Line$, I%, 1)
    IF Char$ <> " " THEN           ' Capitalize up to first space
        PRINT UCASE$(Char$);
    ELSE
        EXIT FOR
    END IF
NEXT I%
PRINT MID$(Line$, I%)              ' Print rest of line
END
```

Listing 7-A6.

7. Listing 7-A7 offers one solution.

```
CLS
Old$ = "rat"                          ' Define string variables
New$ = "dog"
LINE INPUT "Enter a string: "; Line$
I% = INSTR(Line$, Old$)
DO WHILE I% <> 0
    MID$(Line$, I%, 3) = New$
    I% = INSTR(I% + 1, Line$, Old$) ' Set start position after
                                    '  last find
LOOP
PRINT Line$
END
```

Listing 7-A7.

8. Listing 7-A8 illustrates one method.

```
CLS
LINE INPUT "Enter a string: "; Line$
FOR I% = 1 TO LEN(Line$)
    Char$ = MID$(Line$, I%, 1)        ' One character at a time
    SELECT CASE Char$
        CASE "a" TO "x", "A" TO "X"
            PRINT CHR$(ASC(Char$) + 2);
        CASE "Y", "Z", "y", "z"
            PRINT CHR$(ASC(Char$) - 24);
        CASE ELSE
            PRINT Char$;
    END SELECT
NEXT I%
PRINT
END
```

Listing 7-A8.

Chapter 8

1. Among the features common to subprograms and function procedures are the following:

   - Both are procedures and are found in the procedures section of a module.
   - Both can take an argument list.
   - Both pass variables by reference.
   - Both use local, automatic variables.
   - Both can use the STATIC attribute to make local variables static instead of automatic.

   The main distinction is that the function has a return value, whereas the subprogram does not.

2. Listing 8-A2 offers one possibility.

```
DECLARE FUNCTION DollarToGlox! (Cash!)
DECLARE FUNCTION FirstName$ ()
DECLARE SUB Greetings ()
CLS
REM The following subprogram prints a greeting
CALL Greetings
REM The FirstName$ function asks your first name and
REM  returns your response
NameF$ = FirstName$
```

Listing 8-A2. *(continued)*

Listing 8-A2. *continued*

```
PRINT "Vile "; NameF$;
INPUT ", enter your dollar value!: ", Dollars!
REM The DollarToGlox! function converts dollars to glox,
REM  with 1 dollar equal to 0.83 glox
Glox! = DollarToGlox!(Dollars!)
PRINT "That's"; Glox!; "glox in real money."
END

FUNCTION DollarToGlox! (Cash!)
    DollarToGlox! = .83 * Cash!
END FUNCTION

FUNCTION FirstName$
    INPUT "Divulge your first name! ", Name$
    FirstName$ = Name$
END FUNCTION

SUB Greetings
    PRINT "Greetings, Earthlings!"
END SUB
```

3. Function procedures pass arguments by reference, whereas DEF FN functions pass them by value.

4. The SHARED statement is used at the beginning of a procedure. It lists those variables that are shared with the module-level code. The SHARED attribute is a modifier of a DIM, a REDIM, or a COMMON statement in module-level code. It identifies variables that are shared among the module-level code and all the procedures in the same module.

5. Making a procedure variable static means that its value is maintained between calls to that procedure.

6. Here is one solution:

```
FUNCTION OnlyIn$ (S$)
    INPUT "", In$
    In$ = LEFT$(LTRIM$(In$), 1)
    DO UNTIL INSTR(S$, In$) <> 0
        PRINT "Response must be one of the following letters: ";
        PRINT S$
        INPUT "", In$
        In$ = LEFT$(LTRIM$(In$), 1)
    LOOP
    OnlyIn$ = In$
END FUNCTION
```

7. This function returns the sum of the elements of an array:

```
FUNCTION SumArray! (Arr!())
    FOR I% = LBOUND(Arr!) TO UBOUND(Arr!)
        Sum! = Sum! + Arr!(I%)
    NEXT I%
    SumArray! = Sum!
END FUNCTION
```

8. Here is one version of the function *Sum!*:

```
FUNCTION Sum! (N!)
    STATIC Total!
    Total! = Total! + N!
    Sum! = Total!
END FUNCTION
```

9. The following program contains a recursive subprogram:

```
DECLARE SUB GetAndShow ()
CLS
CALL GetAndShow
END

SUB GetAndShow
    INPUT "Enter a number (0 to end): ", Num%
    IF Num% <> 0 THEN CALL GetAndShow
    PRINT Num%
END SUB
```

10. To combine separate modules into one program, use the Load File option of the File menu to add program files to your program.

Chapter 9

1. The TIME$ function returns the current time; the TIME$ statement lets you set the time.

2. The TIMER function returns the time elapsed, in seconds, since midnight. To get the loop time, find the time before and the time after the loop, and subtract one from the other.

3. a. 5

   b. 4

   c. 5

   d. −1

   e. 0

4. This function rounds its argument up:

```
FUNCTION RndUp% (N!)
    M% = INT(N!)
    IF N! > M% THEN
        RndUp% = M% + 1
    ELSE
        RndUp% = M%        ' N! was already a whole number
    END IF
END FUNCTION
```

5. Here is an example:

```
FUNCTION RadiusOf! (Area!)
    RadiusOf! = SQR(Area! / 3.141592654#)
END FUNCTION
```

6. Here is a version using radians for angles:

```
FUNCTION ThirdSide! (X!, Y!, A!)
    ThirdSide! = SQR(X! * X! + Y! * Y! - 2 * X! * Y! * COS(A!))
END FUNCTION
```

7. This function could be used to calculate the results of exponential decay:

```
FUNCTION Remains! (Time!, Halflife!)
    Remains! = EXP(-Time! * LOG(2) / Halflife)
END FUNCTION
```

8. The program in Listing 9-A8 simulates the card selection.

```
DECLARE FUNCTION ChooseCard$ ()
DATA ace, two, three, four, five, six, seven, eight
DATA nine, ten, jack, queen, king
DATA clubs, diamonds, hearts, spades
DIM SHARED CardValue$(1 TO 13)  ' Store card values ace through king
DIM SHARED Suits$(1 TO 4)       ' Store card suits
FOR I% = 1 TO 13
    READ CardValue$(I%)
NEXT I%
FOR I% = 1 TO 4
    READ Suits$(I%)
NEXT I%
RANDOMIZE TIMER                 ' Use timer for setting seed
CLS
PRINT "I choose the " + ChooseCard$
END

FUNCTION ChooseCard$
    Pips% = INT(13 * RND) + 1   ' Random selection of card value
    Suit% = INT(4 * RND) + 1    ' Random selection of card suit
    ChooseCard$ = CardValue$(Pips%) + " of " + Suits$(Suit%)
END FUNCTION
```

Listing 9-A8.

Chapter 10

1. The following statements define the user type:

```
TYPE FoodFact
    FoodName AS STRING * 15
    Calories AS SINGLE
END TYPE
```

2. The variable and the array can be defined as follows:

```
DIM Squid AS FoodFact
DIM Veggies(1 TO 20) AS FoodFact
```

3. Here is one version:

```
TYPE Automobile
    Make AS STRING * 12
    Model AS STRING * 12
    Year AS INTEGER
    BodyStyle AS STRING * 12
END TYPE
TYPE Location
    City AS STRING * 20
    State AS STRING * 15
END TYPE
TYPE CarInfo
    Car AS Automobile
    Place AS Location
END TYPE
```

4. Here is the variable:

```
DIM Igor AS CarInfo
Igor.Car.Year = 1968
```

5. This procedure will work:

```
SUB ShowFacts (Ff AS FoodFact)
    PRINT Ff.FoodName; Ff.Calories
END SUB
```

6. The following subprogram prints the contents of the array:

```
SUB ShowAllFacts (Ff() AS FoodFact)
    FOR I% = LBOUND(Ff) TO UBOUND(Ff)
        PRINT Ff(I%).FoodName; Ff(I%).Calories
    NEXT I%
END SUB
```

7. This function returns the total amount spent on gasoline:

```
FUNCTION Cost! (Arr() AS GasInfo)
    FOR I% = LBOUND(Arr) TO UBOUND(Arr)
        Temp! = Temp! + Arr(I%).Cost
    NEXT I%
    Cost! = Temp!
END FUNCTION
```

Chapter 11

1. Both modes open a sequential file for output, but OUTPUT causes any data in the file to be discarded, whereas APPEND causes new output to be appended to the existing contents.

2. All the records in a random access file are identical in length and in field structure. Records in a sequential file can vary in length and in the number and sizes of fields. Random access files use size to determine field and record limits. Sequential files use special characters to delimit fields and records.

3. Both modes open files in the read/write mode and allow random access to the elements of a file. RANDOM mode views a file as a succession of records. For instance, GET reads a RANDOM file one record at a time and measures file position by records. But BINARY mode views a file as a succession of bytes; in this mode, GET measures file position by bytes.

4. Listing 11-A4 demonstrates one approach.

```
CLS
INPUT "Name of file to be viewed: ", File$
OPEN File$ FOR INPUT AS #1
DO UNTIL EOF(1)                      ' Loop until reaching end of file
    LineCount% = LineCount% + 1      ' Count lines
    LINE INPUT #1, Text$             ' Get one line of text
    PRINT Text$
    IF LineCount% MOD 20 = 0 THEN
        DO
        LOOP WHILE INKEY$ = ""       ' Loop until any key is pressed
    END IF
LOOP
CLOSE #1
END
```

Listing 11-A4.

5. Listing 11-A5 offers a solution.

```
TYPE NameType
    FirstName AS STRING * 15
    LastName AS STRING * 15
END TYPE
TYPE PhoneType                         ' Record template
    Who AS NameType
    PhoneNo AS STRING * 25
END TYPE
DIM Client AS PhoneType                ' Record variable
File$ = "RANAMES"
CLS
```

Listing 11-A5.

(continued)

Listing 11-A5. *continued*

```
OPEN File$ FOR RANDOM AS #1 LEN = LEN(Client)
NumRecs% = LOF(1) / LEN(Client)    ' Find how many records
PRINT File$; " contains"; NumRecs%; "records."
INPUT "Enter the record number to be viewed: ", Num%
DO WHILE (Num% >= 1) AND (Num% <= NumRecs%)
    GET #1, Num%, Client
    PRINT Client.Who.LastName + ", ";
    PRINT Client.Who.FirstName + ": ";
    PRINT Client.PhoneNo
    INPUT "Enter next record number to be viewed: ", Num%
LOOP
CLOSE #1
PRINT "Bye."
END
```

6. Listing 11-A6 presents the character-counting program.

```
DIM Byte AS STRING * 1
CLS
INPUT "Enter the name of the file to be opened: ", File$
LINE INPUT "Enter the character to be counted: ", Char$
OPEN File$ FOR BINARY AS #1
Size# = LOF(1)                        ' Find number of bytes in file
PRINT Size#; "characters to be examined"
FOR ByteNo# = 1 TO LOF(1)             ' Loop through file byte by byte
    GET #1, ByteNo#, Byte
    IF Byte = Char$ THEN
        CharCount# = CharCount# + 1
        IF CharCount# MOD 100 = 0 THEN
            PRINT CharCount#; "..."    ' Print interim values
        END IF
    END IF
NEXT ByteNo#
PRINT File$; " contains"; CharCount#; Char$; " characters"
END
```

Listing 11-A6.

Opening the file in INPUT mode would be faster but would limit the program to text files. Using LINE INPUT instead of INPUT for reading *Char$* allows the user to enter characters such as the space character and the comma in addition to alphabetic characters.

Chapter 12

1. Use the *COLOR 0, 7* statement to make the foreground black (0) and the background white (7).

2. The graphics background applies to the entire graphics display, whereas the text background applies to a particular character; adjacent characters can have different text backgrounds. Also, the text background is a color value in the range 0 through 7, whereas the range for the graphics background depends on the video adapter.

3. If an arrow key or a function key has been pressed, INKEY$ returns a 2-byte string. The first byte is the null string, and the second byte is the ASCII character corresponding to the scan code for that key.

4. A color number identifies a specific color, whereas an attribute number identifies a specific location in the color palette. For EGA and VGA systems, the PALETTE statement lets you choose which color number is assigned to each palette location. Selecting the corresponding attribute number then selects the color assigned to that location.

5. The EGA uses bit planes to specify the color for each pixel. Four bit planes mean that 2^4, or 16, possible combinations exist. To provide 64 colors, you need 6 bits per pixel.

6. The statements produce a red circle with a blue interior; the rest of the screen is green.

7. Physical coordinates measure locations in pixels from the upper left corner of the screen or from the upper left corner of the current graphics viewport. For logical coordinates, the user determines both the size of the measuring units and the location of the origin.

8. VIEW defines the physical region used for graphics on the screen. WINDOW defines the coordinates that describe the current graphics viewport.

9. The program produces a graphics image of a series of connected horizontal and vertical lines, in which each horizontal line is longer than the previous horizontal line and each vertical line is longer than the previous vertical line.

10. No. You must use physical coordinates with VIEW.

11. A line style of 12 pixels on and 4 pixels off is represented in binary as 1111 1111 1111 0000, which, in hexadecimal, is &HFFF0.

12. The circle is tangent to the left and right sides. Change the CIRCLE statement to the following:

    ```
    CIRCLE (160, 160), 150, , , , 1
    ```

The aspect ratio 1 causes both horizontal and vertical distances to be measured in pixels, making the ellipse 300 pixels wide and 300 pixels high.

13. Here is the tiling pattern:

```
RowA$ = CHR$(&HC3) + CHR$(&H3C) + CHR$(&HFF) + CHR$(&H3C)
RowB$ = CHR$(&H3C) + CHR$(&HC3) + CHR$(&HFF) + CHR$(&HC3)
Tile$ = RowA$ + RowA$ + RowB$ + RowB$
```

14. You could define the string variable *YourName$* with your name and then fill the screen with your tiling:

```
Paint (100, 100), YourName$
```

Chapter 13

1. You can use the following command:

```
SOUND 1000, 73
```

2. The SOUND statement can produce any integer frequency in the system's range, whereas the PLAY statement can produce frequencies from the musical scale only.

3. The frequency of a note in a given octave is double the frequency of that note in the preceding octave. The frequencies for the note A are 1760 Hz, 3520 Hz, and 7040 Hz.

4. The program in Listing 13-A4 plays the G scale.

```
DIM Mstyle$(1 TO 3)
Mstyle$(1) = "MN"
Mstyle$(2) = "ML"
Mstyle$(3) = "MS"
Octave1$ = "GAB>CDEF#"              ' Need > so that C is higher than B
Octave2$ = "F#EDC<BAG"              ' Need < so that B is lower than C
PLAY "L16"
FOR I% = 1 TO 3                     ' Loop for three note lengths
    FOR O% = 2 TO 4                 ' Loop for three octaves (rising)
        PLAY Mstyle$(I%) + "o" + STR$(O%) + Octave1$
    NEXT O%
    PLAY "o5Gp16G"
    FOR O% = 5 TO 3 STEP -1         ' Loop for three octaves (falling)
        PLAY Mstyle$(I%) + "o" + STR$(O%) + Octave2$
    NEXT O%
NEXT I%
END
```

Listing 13-A4.

5. ON PLAY installs the event-trapping mechanism and tells the program what to do if the event is detected. PLAY ON activates this feature.

Chapter 14

1. The following function reads a 16-bit value, and the test program calls the function:

```
DECLARE FUNCTION Peek2! (Addr&)
A% = 1000
PRINT Peek2!(VARPTR(A%))

FUNCTION Peek2! (Addr&)
    Peek2! = PEEK(Addr&) + (PEEK(Addr& + 1) * 256)
END FUNCTION
```

   Here is a subprogram that writes a 2-byte value into 16 bits, starting at a specified address:

```
DECLARE SUB Poke2 (Addr&, Value&)
IntVar% = 10
Poke2 VARPTR(IntVar%), 1000
PRINT IntVar%

SUB Poke2 (Addr&, Value&)
    POKE Addr&, Value& MOD 256
    POKE Addr& + 1, INT(Value& / 256)
END SUB
```

2. Programs that use PEEK or POKE with the default segment (DGROUP) might not be reliable because various versions of BASIC store system values in different locations. None of the programs that use these statements are portable to other machine architectures. Programs that use DEF SEG and PEEK or POKE to work with segment 0 or with the ROM BIOS are more likely to be reliable across DOS versions and PC-compatible systems that use a similar BIOS.

3. Listing 14-A3 presents one solution, with a main program to test it. Note that this version starts numbering rows and columns with 0.

```
DECLARE SUB ScreenString (Row%, Col%, AString$)
CLS
ScreenString 10, 20, "Here I am!"

SUB ScreenString (Row%, Col%, AString$)
CONST videoSeg& = &HB800
CONST charsPerLine% = 80

DEF SEG = videoSeg&

FOR CharPos = 1 TO (LEN(AString$))
    ByteLoc% = (Row% * charsPerLine% + Col% + CharPos - 1) * 2
    POKE ByteLoc%, ASC(MID$(AString$, CharPos, 1))
NEXT CharPos
END SUB
```

Listing 14-A3.

4. The syntax for INP and OUT resembles that of PEEK and POKE, but INP and OUT refer to port addresses, whereas PEEK and POKE refer to locations in RAM.

Chapter 15

1. You can use the DOS MODE command to redirect output from the parallel port to the serial port and then use the LPRINT statement to output data to the serial printer. You can also open communications with the serial printer by using the OPEN COM statement and then output data to the printer by using the PRINT # statement.

2. You can define a string variable that contains the code of the special character or printer command, as shown here:

```
formfeed$ = CHR$(12)          ' Assign formfeed to formfeed$
:
LPRINT formfeed$              ' Print a formfeed
```

   You can also use a constant for the code of the special character and then use the constant with the CHR$ function in an LPRINT statement, as shown here:

```
CONST formfeed = 12
:
LPRINT CHR$(formfeed)    ' Print a formfeed
```

3. The codes for italics vary with the printer. The following example is for an Epson-compatible printer:

```
FUNCTION Ital$ (AString$)
Temp$ = CHR$(27) + "4" + AString$ + CHR$(27) + "5"
Ital$ = Temp$
END FUNCTION
```

   For readability, you could define the strings *ItalOn$* and *ItalOff$* by using the statements *ItalOn$ = CHR$(27) + "4"* and *ItalOff$ = CHR$(27) + "5"*. Then you could change the second line of the function to the following:

```
Temp$ = ItalOn$ + AString$ + ItalOff$
```

4. Event trapping allows the program to perform other tasks while monitoring the serial port and responding appropriately when data is received. An ON COM GOSUB statement specifies the subroutine that will be executed when input arrives at the specified serial port, and a COM ON statement activates serial event trapping.

5. Data is probably coming in so quickly that the serial port's input buffer is overflowing before your program can read the input. You can increase the size of the input buffer by specifying a value for the parameter RB in your OPEN COM statement; a value of 2048 or more might be helpful.

Chapter 16

1. Even if a program is free of coding errors, error handling is needed to correct for user interactions. For example, the user might reply inappropriately to an input statement, or a disk drive might be empty.

2. The RESUME statement with no arguments causes the program to resume execution with the statement that triggered the error; RESUME *location* resumes execution at the specified location. RESUME NEXT resumes execution with the statement following the one that triggered the error.

3. Listing 16-A3 offers an example.

```
ON ERROR GOTO ErrorHandler
CLS
LPRINT "This should be printed on the printer"
END

ErrorHandler:
    PRINT "*********"; CHR$(7)  ' Sound a beep
    ErrCode% = ERR             ' Get number of error
    SELECT CASE ErrCode%
        CASE 25:
            PRINT "Please turn on the printer"
            PRINT "and be sure it is online"
        CASE 27:
            PRINT "Please put some paper in the printer"
        CASE ELSE:
            PRINT "Error "; ErrCode%; " has occurred"
    END SELECT
        PRINT "Press Enter to abort,"
        PRINT "or press any other key to continue:"
        Choice$ = INPUT$(1)
        IF ASC(Choice$) = 13 THEN
            ON ERROR GOTO 0
        ELSE
            RESUME
        END IF
END
```

Listing 16-A3.

4. Modify the section of the program that deals with error 71 as follows:

```
CASE 71                     ' Disk not ready
    PRINT "Please put a disk in drive "; ERDEV$
    PRINT "and press a key, or";
    PRINT "press Enter to abort:"
    Choice$ = INPUT$(1)
    IF ASC(Choice$) = 13 THEN
        END                 ' Terminate program
    ELSE
        RESUME              ' Try to read disk again
    END IF
```

5. Global error handling was introduced with QuickBASIC version 4. If the module that triggers an error doesn't contain its own error handler, QuickBASIC searches the module that called the current module and so on, back to the original caller. The search stops when QuickBASIC either finds and executes an error handler or runs out of modules to search.

Chapter 17

1. Both the SHELL and RUN statements run programs from a QuickBASIC program. The SHELL statement runs DOS commands, batch files, or other programs through the DOS command processor. When a command specified in a SHELL statement is executed, control returns to the QuickBASIC program at the statement that follows the SHELL statement. RUN can run all (or part) of the current program, but it can also load a program from disk and run it. Unlike SHELL, RUN does not automatically return control to the QuickBASIC program.

2. Programs are able to receive configuration instructions from the command line (using option switches and filenames). Programs can also search the environment for configuration information such as pathnames and filenames.

3. Here is one solution:

```
REM $INCLUDE: '\QB45\QB.BI' ' Your path might be different
                            ' Remember to have Quick library loaded
DIM InRegs AS RegType, OutRegs AS RegType
CALL INTERRUPT(&H12, InRegs, OutRegs)
Ax& = OutRegs.Ax            ' AX register gives size of installed
                            '  memory
PRINT "Installed memory is: "; Ax&; "KB."
END
```

   Although you do not need to supply register values before the call to this interrupt, you must declare an *InRegs* variable and use it in the CALL INTERRUPT statement.

4. Listing 17-A4 presents one solution.

```
DECLARE SUB Parse (AString$, Words$(), MaxWords%, WordsFound%, Sep$)
CmdLine$ = COMMAND$
DIM Parms$(10)

CLS
Parse CmdLine$, Parms$(), 10, NumCmds%, " "
IF NumCmds% < 1 THEN          ' Not enough parameters
    PRINT "You must specify at least one file"
    PRINT "Syntax: kill filespec(s)"
    END
END IF
```

Listing 17-A4. *(continued)*

Listing 17-A4. *continued*

```
FOR File = 1 TO NumCmds%            ' For each filespec on command line
    KILL Parms$(File)               ' Delete files specified
NEXT File
END

SUB Parse (AString$, Words$(), MaxWords%, WordsFound%, Sep$) STATIC
' AString$ is string to be parsed
' Words$() is string array to hold words found
' MaxWords% is largest number of words to be accommodated
' WordsFound% is number of words found
' Sep$ is character to be treated as word separator
CONST true = -1, false = 0
WordsFound% = 0                        ' Count words found
In = false                             ' Flag if inside a word
StrLen% = LEN(AString$)
' Go through string one character at a time
FOR Char = 1 TO StrLen%
    Char$ = MID$(AString$, Char, 1)   ' Get next character
    ' Test for character being a separator
    IF Char$ <> Sep$ THEN              ' Not a separator
        ' Test to see if already inside a word
        IF NOT In THEN                 ' Found the start of a new word
            ' Test for too many words
            IF WordsFound% = MaxWords% THEN EXIT FOR
            WordsFound% = WordsFound% + 1
            In = true
            END IF
        ' Add the character to the current word
        Words$(WordsFound%) = Words$(WordsFound%) + Char$
    ELSE
        ' Found a separator
        ' Set "Not in a word" flag to false
        In = false
    END IF
NEXT Char
END SUB
```

5. Consider using the CHAIN statement if your program requires additional memory. CHAIN lets you load one part of the program at a time into memory, freeing more memory for data. CHAIN lets you pass common variables to another program, but RUN does not.

Chapter 18

1. A mixed-language program uses elements from more than one programming language.

2. First, compilers and assemblers convert the source code of various languages to the same final form—machine language. Second, Microsoft has designed its languages to share the same object-code format and to work with the LINK program.

3. C passes arguments from an argument list in right-to-left order, whereas the other languages pass them in left-to-right order.

4. Declare the procedure this way:

   ```
   DECLARE FUNCTION Toad% CDECL(BYVAL X%, Y%, SEG Z%)
   ```

   Note the % suffix used with *Toad%*; it declares that the return value is an integer.

5. Stand-alone libraries with the LIB extension are accessed by the LINK program. Because all Microsoft languages use LINK to create EXE files, all of these languages can use stand-alone libraries. Quick libraries, however, are used within the QuickBASIC environment for in-memory compilation.

6. You must first copy the address of *Tock%* to the BX register and then use that address to place a value in AX, as shown here:

   ```
   mov bx, [bp+6]
   mov ax,
   ```

Index

Note: Italicized page numbers refer to figures or tables.

Special Characters

A

B

C

H

I

K

L

M

S

W

X

Z

Stephen Prata, Ph.D., is Professor of Physics and Astronomy at the College of Marin in Kentfield, California, where he teaches C and UNIX. Dr. Prata is coauthor of several Waite Group books, including *Microsoft QuickC Programming*, published by Microsoft Press, and the *New C Primer Plus*, *C: Step by Step*, *UNIX Primer Plus*, *UNIX System V Primer*, and *The Waite Group's HyperTalk Bible*, all published by Howard W. Sams.

Harry Henderson is a freelance technical writer and editor. He has written documentation for a major software manufacturer as well as educational material. He is a coauthor of many Waite Group books, including *The Waite Group's Microsoft QuickBASIC Bible*, published by Microsoft Press, and *Understanding MS-DOS*, 2nd ed., *The Waite Group's Using PC-DOS*, and *UNIX Communications*, published by Howard W. Sams.

The Waite Group can be reached at 100 Shoreline Highway, Building A, Suite 285, Mill Valley, California 94941.

The manuscript for this book was prepared and submitted to Microsoft Press in electronic form. Text files were processed and formatted using Microsoft Word.

Principal word processors: Debbie Kem and Judith Bloch
Principal proofreader: Cynthia Riskin
Principal typographer: Ruth Pettis
Interior text designer: Darcie S. Furlan
Principal illustrators: Rebecca Geisler-Johnson and Kim Eggleston
Cover designer: Thomas A. Draper
Cover color separator: Rainier Color Corporation

Text composition by Microsoft Press in Garamond with display type in Futura Bold, using the Magna composition system and the Linotronic 300 laser imagesetter.

Printed on recycled paper stock.